# PROMOTION

# PROMOTION:
## *Analysis, Creativity, and Strategy*

WILLIAM P. DOMMERMUTH

University of Southern Illinois, Carbondale

KENT PUBLISHING COMPANY

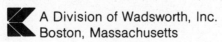

A Division of Wadsworth, Inc.
Boston, Massachusetts

**Editor:** David V. Anthony
**Production Editor:** Nancy J. Crow
**Interior Design:** Anna Post
**Cover Art:** © 1981, design and concept/Images, Julius Friedman
**Cover Design:** Nancy Lindgren
**Production Coordinator:** Linda Siegrist

Kent Publishing Company
A Division of Wadsworth, Inc.

Printed in the United States of America
3  4  5  6  7  8  9—88  87  86

**Library of Congress Cataloging in Publication Data**
Dommermuth, William P.
    Promotion: analysis, creativity and strategy.

    Includes bibliographies and index.
    1. Marketing.   2. Consumers.   3. Sales promotion.
4. Advertising.   I. Title.
HF5415.D64        658.8′2        84-970
ISBN 0-534-03106-4

For Joan, Karin, Peggy, and Jean

# *Preface*

I am enthusiastic about promotion. Not only does it fulfill a highly important function in making our economic system vibrant and strong, but it is also fascinating because of its intricate and dynamic nature. This book is written with the hope that it will encourage you to share my enthusiasm.

The text is professional and managerial in orientation. It is aimed at readers preparing for careers in marketing management and intended mainly for courses which introduce the field of promotional strategy. Typically, such courses center around four major promotional elements—advertising, personal selling, sales promotion, and publicity. Twelve of the book's twenty-two chapters concentrate directly on these four topics. Chapter Three introduces all of the elements, compares them and outlines approaches toward optimizing relationships between them. Chapters Ten through Eighteen focus on specific promotional elements, covering each in a comprehensive fashion. Chapter Nineteen illustrates their applications in selling to and through wholesalers and retailers. Chapter Twenty discusses alternative techniques for allocating budgets to advertising, personal selling, sales promotion, and publicity.

The remaining chapters cover procedures for collecting facts and figures needed to build a total integrated strategy, blending individual promotional elements into a cohesive mix, monitoring results to obtain guidance through market feedback and operating within acceptable social and legal bounds.

A theme recurrently stressed and illustrated throughout the book is that individual promotional elements work best when they are carefully planned to work together. Although most readers will probably find that their entry level jobs, or their current positions, tend to be highly specialized in one area such as personal selling or advertising, the text consistently emphasizes the need for *all* professional promotional strategists to understand both the nature of all promotional elements and the nature of interactions among them. There are two reasons for this emphasis: 1. Even in a specialized capacity, for example as an advertising copywriter or a sales representative, a professional performs best when she or he understands how that specialized area of promotion fits into a full, interactive process. 2. As a career-oriented professional, he or she should be aiming at a higher level position, which will require broader promotional knowledge and an ability to play a role in shaping all aspects of the full marketing program.

Promotion is an exciting, complex field. To help readers sense its exciting nature and understand how practitioners cope with its complexities, you will find many examples of actual promotional problems and strategies presented throughout the book. It is also important to recognize that the construction of successful strategies must be based on a solid understanding of corporate objectives, competitive activities and, *very importantly*, the buying habits, attitudes, needs, and lifestyle outlooks of your customers. For this reason, the scope of the book includes coverage of each of these topics.

The two opening chapters relate promotional strategy to its location in the corporate decision-making process and introduce views of how competitive behavior can affect promotional planning. They also explore interdependencies among all components in the marketing mix—including product, price, and place—as well as the major elements of promotion. Chapter Five presents an overview of methods for acquiring and using basic research data concerning current consumer responses in the marketplace—such as total demand for your product category, market share figures, seasonal purchase patterns and sales by outlet types—to assist you in developing your promotional strategy. Its later counterpart is Chapter Twenty-One, which summarizes methods of acquiring and using research data to evaluate consumer response to your promotional strategy, *after* that strategy has been developed.

Chapter Four proposes a framework for analyzing promotional strategy and viewing it in the context of the full environment which shapes its design and affects its outcome.

Chapters Six through Nine draw heavily on examples of consumer behavior concepts and communication theory, to demonstrate how you can secure and use information about the more deep-seated forces which underlie consumer responses to your promotional efforts. This section aims at equipping you with insights about such matters as the attitudes, needs, lifestyle goals and information-processing patterns of your target prospects. Readers who have previously completed a course in consumer behavior may find that much of this material is familiar. However, when compared with consumer behavior texts, both the goals and style of the presentation are quite different. Operational in nature, these chapters demonstrate how behavioral concepts and information can be applied in everyday practice. Methods of putting such concepts to use in business strategy are illustrated with specific, "real-world" examples and suggestions for incorporating them into your decision-making process.

The book closes with an appraisal of legal and social constraints which must be considered in implementing promotional strategy. The enforcement of legal restrictions may sometimes prove to be cumbersome or even questionable in terms of results attained. The views of social critics of promotion may often appear to be overdrawn and sharply one-sided. Nonetheless, the point of view taken in the concluding chapter is that neither government regulation nor social criticism should be automatically treated as a threat or viewed with disdain. The laws affecting promotion are intended to protect the competitive system in which business operates, as well as to protect the consumers who are served by business. While some of the most severe critics of promotional practices may be unduly harsh in their interpretations, this does not imply their opinions should be totally ignored or rejected without examination. The philosophy of the entire book is that a promotional practitioner should be regarded as a professional and behave as a professional. Given that philosophy, it follows that promotional strategists should conduct themselves with the same level of ethics expected of any other professional, such as medical or legal practitioners. When viewed from a positive perspective, recognition of the law and alertness to social criticisms can aid you in adopting and maintaining an ethical, socially responsible, and genuinely professional posture.

Many people have given me much valuable assistance in preparing this book. They include colleagues, students, business executives, and very patient and understanding secretaries. While it is impossible to acknowledge all of them by name, I do want to express my sincere gratitude to each of them. In particular, I want to acknowledge the aid I received from the reviewers who provided me with critiques that were both pertinent and constructive. And special thanks to: Professors Sharon E. Beatty of the University of Oregon, Robert R. Harmon of Portland State University, William J. Lundstrom of Old Dominion University, Malcolm L. Morris of the University of Oklahoma, and Dan Sarel of the University of Miami at Coral Gables. Their valuable help enabled me to improve and strengthen every part of the book. If errors or shortcomings remain, the fault is mine.

William P. Dommermuth
*January, 1984*

# Contents

**PART FOUR      ADVERTISING    399**

### Chapter 13    Advertising Objectives, Decision Areas, and Organizations    401

### Chapter 14    Developing Advertising Creative Strategy    435

### Chapter 15    Appraising Advertising Media    482

# PART ONE

# The Promotional Mix and the Marketing Program

# CHAPTER ONE

# Business Goals and Promotional Strategies

## FOCUS OF THE CHAPTER

This book is written for promotional strategists and for those planning to become promotional strategists. In the broad sense, this includes anyone who can influence any significant part of a firm's promotional mix. In particular, it includes top-level marketing and other corporate officials, various levels of sales management executives, advertising managers and agency account representatives, persons involved in publicity and public relations activities, sales promotion specialists, advertising copywriters and media planners, product and package designers, and all types of salespeople.

No matter what specific role you play in working with promotional strategy, you will find yourself involved in one of the most exciting and fast-paced areas of business activity. A firm's promotional program operates in a highly dynamic climate. Not only is that climate likely to include ever-changing competitive assaults, but it is dominated by the needs, goals, hopes, and whims of potential customers; moreover, each of those four customer characteristics can change rapidly and unpredictably. To play your role effectively in this setting, you must be prepared to search, study, and sometimes sense the complexities of the marketplace. Then you must make decisions on how to best pursue your course of action. The purpose of this book is to help you improve your abilities to accomplish these objectives.

# PROMOTION—A DEFINITION AND OVERVIEW

In any situation involving a promotional decision the most basic question you will face is, "How can I best communicate with prospective customers and persuade them to buy my product?" The two key words in this question are *communicate* and *persuade*; the following definition of promotion from which we shall work is built around them: *Promotion involves any technique, under the control of a seller, that can communicate favorable, persuasive information about that seller's product to potential buyers, either directly or through others who can influence purchase decisions.*

***Explicit Promotion and Implicit Promotion***

The major thrust of promotional strategy is generally thought of in terms of four explicit promotional elements—advertising, personal selling, sales promotion, and publicity. However, it is important to emphasize at the outset that these four explicit elements work in conjunction with other components to form a total marketing mix. The other components in the mix—product, price, and place—not only influence the manner in which you must handle the explicit promotional elements, but can also convey a type of communication impact of their own. In keeping with the definition of promotion we are using, this means that because they can transmit communication, certain aspects of these other marketing components can be viewed as implicit promotion.

# PROMOTION IN THE MARKETING MIX

A widely used approach to describing the marketing mix is illustrated in Figure 1.1. Dividing the mix into four major components of product, price, promotion, and place (or channels of distribution) makes it possible to discuss the fundamentals of marketing strategy in a more orderly fashion. This conventional four-way division highlights the fact that four very broad and distinct decision areas must be considered in developing your total marketing plan. At the same time, it is important to emphasize that decisions made in

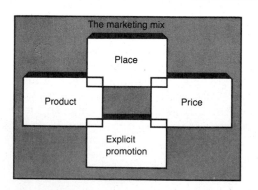

**FIGURE 1.1 The marketing mix**

each of the four areas must blend with decisions made in the others to form a coordinated composite. Furthermore, as mentioned above, the product itself, its price, and the types of outlets through which it is sold can also communicate information to consumers. For that reason, product, price, and place can have "implicit" promotional aspects. To distinguish between the persuasive communication that can flow from these three components of the mix and the more commonly recognized promotional communication achieved through advertising, personal selling, sales promotion, or publicity, the following two definitions are used.

*Implicit promotion is persuasive communication that is inherent in the product itself, its price, or the places through which it is sold.*

*Explicit promotion is persuasive communication about the product, transmitted by advertising, personal selling, sales promotion, publicity, or some combination of these elements.*

## THE NATURE OF IMPLICIT PROMOTION

Most of the emphasis in this book is on explicit promotion. However, because the term "implicit promotion" is also used at many points, we shall begin with a brief look at how this form of persuasive communication can operate.

*Promotional Implications of the Place Component*

As a first illustration, consider the place component in terms of the retail outlets through which your brand is sold. In some cases, the image of a particular store that handles your brand can communicate a message about that brand. For example, it is likely that most makers of high-fashion, expensive watches or jewelry would be reluctant to have their lines sold through mass-market discount chains such as K-Mart. One of the problems that could be created through such distribution stems from customers' likely perceptions of inconsistency between brand image and store image. Most consumers do not expect to find high-style, up-scale merchandise in mass-market discount stores. If such retailers display and feature your brand, your target consumers may conclude it is less exclusive than pictured through other promotional techniques such as advertising. This is one factor that prompts some manufacturers to limit distribution, making their brands available only through selected outlets whose reputations add luster to the brand name rather than possibly diminish its reputation.

*The Contac Example.* A more specific illustration of the connotations that can be imputed to a brand by virtue of the place component is provided by the introduction of Contac cold capsules. Contac is now sold through a wide variety of outlet types including supermarkets and discount stores. When it was first introduced, however, retail distribution was carefully limited to drugstores. The makers of Contac reasoned that they should convey a clearly pharmaceutical image to their brand to position it as a superior drug for relief of symptoms associated with colds. Restricting distribution to pharmacies, which are associated with the dispensing of ethical or prescription drugs, was consistent with this initial marketing objective. Only after the brand had begun to establish itself more firmly in the market was distribution extended to other outlet types.

*The Ethan Allen Example.*   Using somewhat similar reasoning, though in a much different product category, the Ethan Allen line of furniture is sold through independently owned stores which, while they also carry other brands, closely identify themselves with Ethan Allen through both their store designs and their own explicit promotional programs. Their building exteriors usually have a distinctly colonial motif and include prominent display of the Ethan Allen name. The selling atmosphere presented by these selected retailers is consistent with the image the firm creates through its own product designs and advertising themes—namely, quality furniture for consumers who prefer colonial styling.

*Reseller Promotional Support.*   Resellers who carry your brand can also play an important role in your promotional planning through their own promotional activities such as advertising and personal selling. The role they can play in these respects is so important that a full chapter will be devoted to the subject of working with resellers to obtain their support (see Chapter 19).

*Promotional Implications of Price and Product*

Like place, price and product can also have promotional implications because they can communicate messages to consumers. Chapter 2 will discuss ways in which a low price can sometimes retard consumer demand whereas a high price can have a positive effect, which is a seeming contradiction of standard economic theory. It will also look at ways in which completely incidental physical product characteristics—which have no direct relationship to how the product performs—can nonetheless influence consumers' evaluations of your brand's performance. When this occurs, such product characteristics are properly considered as promotional components because they contribute to the total persuasive communication package you deliver.

*Reasons for Stressing the Role of Implicit Promotion*

Again, the term "promotion" as used in this book is somewhat broader than conventional usage. While most of our attention will be concerned with the explicit promotional elements of advertising, personal selling, sales promotion, and publicity, the degree of stress placed on implicit promotion will be somewhat heavier than that customarily found in books on promotional strategy. There are three reasons for this higher degree of emphasis. First, in some cases, implicit promotion may be the major or even the only type of information flow aimed at consumers. In other words, some marketing mixes include very little in the way of explicit promotion. Second, in the more typical case in which explicit promotion is also used, implicit promotion is the base on which it must be built. To begin evaluating your total communication package, it is necessary that you understand what the product, its price, and sometimes its place of distribution are "saying." Third, all parts of the promotional mix—both implicit and explicit—interact in their impact on consumers' attitudes.

On this basis, each component should be designed to blend with and to reinforce the others for maximum persuasive effectiveness. There is no absolute rule to the order in which the designing and blending must occur. For example, though a tool such as advertising is usually shaped to fit the product, sometimes the reverse is desirable; the product may be shaped to fit the advertising. Chapters 2 and 3 will illustrate in greater detail these three reasons for giving careful attention to the implicit elements in your promotional mix.

## ANTECEDENT INFLUENCES IN PLANNING THE MARKETING MIX

Marketing normally exists as a major functional area within a business firm or similar organization. It works with other functional areas such as production and finance to fulfill organizational aims. For this reason, the design of your marketing mix—including both implicit and explicit promotional elements— must start with consideration of overall organizational objectives. Along with those objectives, there are two factors in the external environment that you must consider at the outset. The first of these is composed of existing legal and social constraints that set restrictions on your alternatives. The second is the competitive setting in which you operate, including the current and potential market actions and promotional strategies of all firms whose products compete with your brand.

Although it is not the purpose of this book to delve deeply into general business management or even general marketing management, the climate that prevails in these areas can have a critical impact on your promotional planning. In other words, promotional strategy does not exist in a vacuum. It develops in an atmosphere circumscribed by preexisting conditions both within and outside your own organization. Figure 1.2 summarizes these

**FIGURE 1.2 Major antecedent influences affecting the planning of the marketing mix**

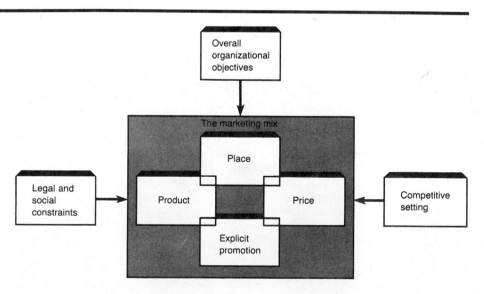

preexisting conditions—or antecedents of the marketing mix—by adding them to our previous diagram of the marketing mix.

## ORGANIZATIONAL OBJECTIVES

Because marketing is one major arm of a company's operations, it must work in conjunction with the other basic business areas. Like those other areas, it has to perform a role consistent with the overall business objectives set by top management. These objectives will be affected by the resources available to the business entity, executives' perceptions of particular strengths and weaknesses peculiar to the organization, management's interpretation of the general economic climate, and finally, the philosophy of top management regarding the broad directions in which the business should move.

*Present Position versus Desired Position*

Figure 1.3 shows, in schematic form, one consultant's view of how executive perceptions and judgments can combine to produce an overall company strategy. Basic corporate goals are evaluated in terms of anticipated and ongoing environmental forces to produce a perspective regarding the company's desired position at some future time. For example, a general desired position might be "raising net income by fifty percent over the next five years by both improving production efficiency and expanding our product lines to include new items related to those we now sell." This desired position would then be assessed relative to the company's present position, including its own strengths and weaknesses along with those of competition.

*Inside-Out versus Outside-In Assessments*

There are two basic approaches that can be used to initiate the assessment. The first begins with consideration of the company's strengths and weaknesses, then works outward to environmental forces. This has been dubbed the

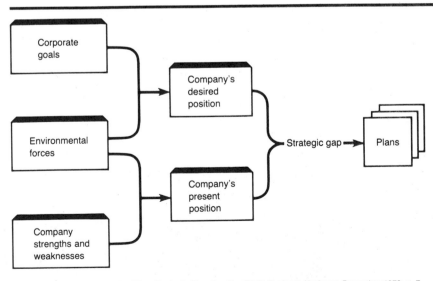

**FIGURE 1.3 Translating corporate goals into strategic plans**

*Source:* Gerstner, Louis V. Jr., "Can Strategic Planning Pay Off?" *Business Horizons,* December 1972, p. 7.

**FIGURE 1.4**
**Corporate planning approaches: inside–out versus outside–in**

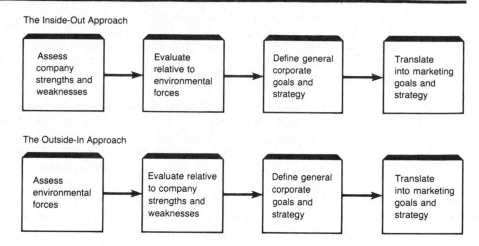

The Inside-Out Approach

Assess company strengths and weaknesses → Evaluate relative to environmental forces → Define general corporate goals and strategy → Translate into marketing goals and strategy

The Outside-In Approach

Assess environmental forces → Evaluate relative to company strengths and weaknesses → Define general corporate goals and strategy → Translate into marketing goals and strategy

"inside-out" approach. The second begins with analysis of forces in the outside environment, singles out such forces as may be considered especially pertinent, and then works with them in terms of the company's strengths and weaknesses. This has been dubbed the "outside-in" approach (see Figure 1.4). One writer has described and illustrated these alternative assessment routes in the following way:

> The inside-out approach begins with a self-appraisal which delineates the company's strengths and weaknesses. Then, with the company's strengths in mind, the planners look outside the company for feasible exploitation opportunities. For example, one obvious strength of the Procter and Gamble Company is its distribution network. To make the most of this strength, the company seriously considers only products with a great potential which is realizable through strong distribution. . . . The outside-in approach can be considered analogous to a marketing orientation in the sense that everything is based on the market and its environment. For example, the manufacturer of water systems might discover that direct selling through company-owned stores is becoming exceedingly popular and will in future years count as an important competitive strategy. As a result of this finding, the company will give serious consideration to opening company-owned stores in various parts of the nation in order to strengthen its position. [1]

Whether it follows an inside-out approach, an outside-in approach, or some combination of the two, this initial assessment produces an analysis of the "strategic gap" between present and desired positions. Based on that analysis, specific plans must be developed to close the strategic gap. An example of how the process operates is provided by the following description of the development of a breakfast menu by McDonald's hamburger chain.

> McDonald's . . . has among its corporate objectives the goal of increasing the productivity of its operating units. Given a high proportion of costs in fixed facilities, it was decided to increase facility utilization during off-peak hours, particularly during the morning hours. The program developed to accomplish

these goals was the Egg McMuffin followed by a breakfast menu consistent with the limited product line strategy of McDonald's regular fare. In this example, the corporate strategy of increased productivity of assets led to the marketing strategy of the breakfast fare [desired position] built upon realization of variation and store utilization throughout the day [present position] and favorable customer attitudes toward the chain [present position]. [2]

*Managerial Philosophies*

Even with similar assessments of environmental forces and company strengths and weaknesses, competing firms can decide to follow quite dissimilar paths because of variations in the philosophies of their top executives. In turn, these overall corporate paths will affect all aspects of the marketing mix including those directly concerned with implicit and explicit promotional planning.

*Corporate Decisions and Promotional Resources*

Figure 1.5 illustrates the potential impact of such variations in corporate philosophies on marketing decision making. The illustration assumes we are looking at one division of a multiproduct business. Top corporate management personnel have determined which units of the enterprise should be marked for growth and given the resources to move toward such growth. When management concludes that a particular division deserves heavy growth emphasis, promotional strategies are designed to outdistance competitors. In contrast, when management treats the unit as an "earnings–oriented" division, promotional strategists will most likely be held back in their efforts because of limited availability of resources. Their strategic approach might be to aim at responding to competition rather than leading it.

**FIGURE 1.5**
**Relationships between corporate strategy and marketing mix strategy**

| Marketing Decision Area | Strategy Adopted for Division or Product Line | | |
| --- | --- | --- | --- |
| | Invest for Future Growth | Manage for Earnings | Manage for Immediate Cash |
| Market share | Aggressively build across all segments | Target efforts to high-return/high-growth segments<br>Protect current franchises | Forego share development for improved profits |
| Pricing | Lower to build share | Stabilize for maximum profit contribution | Raise, even at expense of volume |
| Explicit promotion | Invest heavily to build share | Invest as market dictates | Avoid |
| Existing product line | Expand volume<br>Add line extensions to fill out product categories | Shift mix to higher profit product categories | Eliminate low contribution products/varieties |
| New products | Expand product line by acquisition, self-manufacture, or joint venture | Add products selectively and in controlled stages of commitment | Add only sure winners |

*Source:* Adapted from Gerstner, Louis V. Jr., "Can Strategic Planning Pay Off?" *Business Horizons,* December 1972, p. 15.

*Business Goals and Promotional Strategies*

Even the details of promotional execution can be affected by the downward force of higher-level decisions. Consider the question of whether greater emphasis should be placed on advertising or personal selling in your explicit promotional mix. An example of how a major corporate strategy decision can ultimately determine the division of budget and effort allocated to these two explicit elements can be drawn from the American brewing industry. In the mid 1970s, the Adolph Coors and G. Heileman Brewing Companies were both "second-tier" regional producers of beer. Coors' strength was in the Rocky Mountain region and other western states. Heileman's main strength was in the midwest. The top management of both firms opted for geographic expansion programs but chose quite different routes to achieve expansion. Coors determined to grow by entering new market areas with their existing brand. Heileman executives chose to grow by acquiring other regional breweries, and maintaining the brand names of the acquired firms. Heileman bought out such established brands as Blatz, Rainier, and Carling Black Label.

Promoting their brand in new territories required Coors to seek rapid consumer recognition and interest in order to break established buying habits. In consequence, Coors' overall expansion approach led to a promotional strategy mix that leaned heavily on advertising. Between 1976 and 1981 Coors advertising budget reportedly jumped from $7 million to $90 million, a rise of almost 1,200 percent. In contrast, because they were dealing with preestablished brands, Heileman's promotional strategists started with a stronger base of existing consumer recognition and brand preference. Their position required relatively less emphasis on advertising but more on personal selling to maintain distribution and gain greater retailer support in order to capitalize on consumers' familiarity with their brands' images. Heileman's budgeted much less for advertising but relatively more on sales force effort.

*Promotional
Strategy Influences
on Overall
Corporate Planning*

Although Figure 1.5 suggests that the flow of influence runs from top management decisions to marketing management decisions, it is also true that influence can flow in the opposite direction. Opportunity appraisals by marketing planners, including promotional strategists, can help frame overall company goal orientation. In other words, some higher-level planning can actually develop as an outgrowth of proposals generated by the marketing division. One study suggested that the impact on general strategy that is exerted by different functional areas of the firm varies from company to company and is directly related to each department's ability to cope with the most pressing environmental uncertainties facing corporate decision makers.[3] For example, if a firm is selling in a product category where intense price competition dominates the business climate, production executives may exert a high degree of relative power. This is because determination of optimal pricing policies can be heavily dependent on superiority in production technology and manufacturing efficiencies. However, in instances where some aspect of explicit promotion is vital in coping with the competitive environment, marketing personnel who are specialists in that area tend to acquire increased power in shaping overall corporate strategy. The analysts who conducted this study offered the following example of such a circumstance, "As for the case of

Clorox, notice the high power scored by the sales group. Based on the debriefing, a major source of uncertainty is the problem of getting shelf space in supermarkets. This would explain why the sales group is perceived as having a degree of power second only to that of the marketing group."[4]

In summary, design of the marketing mix starts from corporate objectives as determined by a firm's top executives. Through their knowledge of both the internal and external environments and their power to cope with them, promotional strategists may influence the shaping of those objectives. However, once the corporate objectives have been set, the marketing mix—including its implicit and explicit promotional elements—must be geared toward fulfilling those objectives and its details must be implemented to work in conjunction with the total pattern of all other functional activities undertaken by the firm.

## LEGAL AND SOCIAL CONSTRAINTS

Extended discussion of legal and social constraints will be deferred until the final chapter. At this point, some preliminary comments concerning these constraints are in order. *Legal and social constraints are formal or informal rules created by government or imposed by cultural convention that restrict the content and style of promotional messages.*

Sellers of alcoholic beverages do not openly advertise the fact that their products can provide users with a temporary and chemically induced relief from worries over the woes of one's world, even though their products are frequently used with that goal in mind. Although the dramatic portions of television shows may include profanity, the commercials rarely if ever do so, at least up to the time of this writing. You cannot give one reseller a promotional allowance to attain cooperation and support unless you make the same allowance available to others. Rules like these restrict promotional strategy. They may be imposed by government, by corporate policy, or by competitive convention. Whatever their origins, you must be aware of the nature of the limitations prescribed by such constraints and design your program to fit within the boundaries they define.

## THE COMPETITIVE SETTING

In a free-enterprise economy, virtually every business entity and every marketing program operates in an atmosphere of constant competition. Determination of the stance your firm should take in relationship to competitors plays an important role in shaping your marketing mix and the promotional strategies you adopt within that mix. One business analyst has pictured this aspect of the economic scene as follows:

The cornerstone of business strategy is the concept which has been referred to as "niche." Except in the case of total monopoly, each company in an industry seeks to find a place for itself among its competitors. A niche may be a small nook or cranny in the marketplace where the winds of competition blow with somewhat less force, or it may be the top of the mountain which is occupied by a company with a commanding market share, while the storms of competition range below. But even staying on the mountain top, or finding a larger and somewhat more comfortable cave higher up the slope, requires a clear understanding of a relationship between a company and its competitors who are seeking to serve the same set of customers. [5]

**Brand Positioning**

In promotional practice, the process of placing your brand in its proper niche is commonly referred to as market positioning. Positioning has two major stages. The first stage involves determination of the generic product category in which your brand belongs. The second stage involves determination of where it should be placed within that product category relative to competing brands.

*First-Stage Positioning.* For example, if you are given full responsibility for promoting a new low-calorie, vitamin-enriched chocolate bar, you have at least two options from which to choose in the first stage of positioning. The bar could be presented to customers as a candy item or as a food to be used as part of a weight-control program. The choice you make determines the generic product category and the general nature of the other brands against which you will compete.

*Second-Stage Positioning.* In the second stage you must determine how you will compete against those other brands in the category. If you choose to position the bar as a weight-control food item in stage one you might decide in stage two to aim it primarily at persons with serious weight problems. Alternatively, you might choose to aim it primarily at young, active consumers interested in maintaining their current weight rather than overcoming a serious, existing problem. This second positioning stage calls for selection of a market segmentation and/or product differentiation approach. A more complete discussion of this second stage of positioning will be deferred until Chapter 5, by which time the groundwork for that discussion will have been covered more completely. However, some further discussion of the first stage of positioning is appropriate at this point because your choice of the basic, generic product category in which to fit your brand is fundamental to everything that follows in terms of your competitive posture.

**Illustrations of First-Stage Positioning**

On initial consideration, it might seem that the intrinsic makeup of a product or service determines its product category status in an almost automatic fashion. As suggested by the hypothetical chocolate bar described above, this is not necessarily true. Rather than relying on a hypothetical example, the point can be demonstrated more effectively by drawing on two classic cases.

When first placed on the market, Kleenex was positioned as a facial tissue. After market research using an advertising copy test, Kleenex was repositioned primarily as a disposable handkerchief. While Kleenex had been a solid market success as a facial tissue, its repositioning into an essentially new product category turned it into a much greater success. Coca-Cola was originally marketed as a headache remedy. Several years after its introduction, it was repositioned as a soft drink. In this different product category, with its customer appeal changed from relief of pain to refreshment, Coca-Cola went on to become the profitable and internationally known brand it is today.

The point to be drawn from these examples is that, though the basic physical or structural character of your market offering will certainly play a substantial role in determining your product category, the truly critical role is that played by the benefits your market offering can deliver to its users. When you are working with a brand that has a variety of potential benefits for consumers, you may have a high degree of flexibility in the first stage of the positioning process. Admittedly, this is not likely to hold true in the majority of marketing situations. Often your product category placement is well defined and ill suited to change. In that circumstance, you will move directly to the second stage of positioning. However, at least at the outset of your decision making, the range of primary consumer benefits offered by your brand should be carefully considered to determine if alternative product category positionings might be feasible. When you do have alternatives, each should be studied in terms of its market advantages and disadvantages. These include both the size of potential consumer demand for the generic product category involved and your brand's likely strength within that product category vis-à-vis competitive brands in the same category.

## Challenges to Market Position

No matter how distinctively and successfully you position your brand, you will still face a market in which you are continually challenged by explicit promotional strategies of competitors. It is unlikely that there is any such thing as a truly safe niche or market position. Especially when implementing such aspects of your program as advertising campaigns and personal selling efforts, you can expect to find yourself in an ongoing type of adversary relationship with other brands or even with other product categories. When your promotional strategies prove successful, one or more competitors may change their strategies to challenge your improved status. As positioning schemes taken by competitors change, your own promotional strategies may require modification. As a result, constant analysis of what rival business firms are doing and achieving is a vital ingredient in the formulation of your planning.

## Types of Competitive Interplays

The interplay between your marketing efforts and those of your competitors can have diverse and complex implications for strategy planning. In general, you will want to maintain perpetual surveillance of competitors and stand ready to interpret three broad types of conditions that may arise. The first involves actions by one or more competitors that can actually create an improved business climate for your own firm. When this happens, you may wish to increase your promotional efforts to exploit your enhanced opportunity. The second and more common condition stems from aggressive competitive behavior that threatens your market position. Cases in this category usually call for rapid but carefully conceived countermeasures to stave off the attack. The third condition is one in which the market offers an enticing promotional opportunity that is potentially precarious because it can place you in an unfavorable position from which to defend against a subsequent assault by competitors. Each of these three conditions merits further illustration.

***Competitive Behavior That Improves Your Business Climate.*** There are cases in which heightened promotional efforts by another firm can actually represent a benign type of competition that increases your own promotional opportunities. Most commonly this occurs because the other firm's marketing strategy has the effect of raising sales for the entire generic product category. As a result, even less active participants may profit by sharing in a larger total volume for the product class.

A case in point involves Evian and Perrier.[6] Both are French mineral waters that have been imported and sold in the United States at premium prices for many years. With sales slackening in its home market in France, Perrier management decided to initiate an aggressive attempt to capture a much larger volume in the United States. Beginning in the late 1970s Perrier completely revised its American marketing strategy. Distribution, which had been limited largely to gourmet food shops, was expanded to achieve widespread availability through virtually all types of appropriate retail outlets such as supermarkets and liquor stores. The price was lowered and a very active personal selling plan was put into operation. An advertising program was developed that repositioned the brand as an adult soft drink rather than as merely a mineral water. To carry its advertising theme, Perrier increased its budget from virtually nothing to about $2 million annually. In short, Perrier moved to a completely new marketing approach that included a total change in its use of implicit and explicit promotion. Perrier's efforts were extremely successful. Within a two-year period the brand's sales increased dramatically. Annual volume reportedly jumped from $1 million to $30 million during that time span.

Meanwhile Evian, which in a sense had been a major competitor to Perrier, decided to do virtually nothing in response to Perrier's shift in marketing strategy. Evian maintained its higher price, used almost no advertising, and continued to pursue a rather limited distribution policy. Despite the firm's passivity, Evian's sales increased by 300 percent. Evian executives credited much of their gain to Perrier's intensified marketing efforts. By focusing greater consumer attention on French mineral waters, Perrier had increased sales not only for itself but also for a competitor.

Although Evian's reaction was both passive and profitable, the wisdom of opting for such a passive reaction is open to question. As suggested above, you would be well advised at least to consider an expansion of promotional activity if confronted with a similar situation. The issue involved is "opportunity loss." If sales rise 300 percent with almost no additional promotional effort, it might be reasonable to speculate that the rise would have been even higher had greater promotional pressure been exerted. Quite probably, Evian unknowingly lost potentially greater profits by failing to press an unexpected advantage.

***Competitive Behavior That Threatens Your Position.*** The type of benign competitive effect described above tends to be the exception rather than the rule. Generally, a successful marketing thrust by a competitor is likely to put you at a disadvantage and force you to retaliate with some type of counterthrust. A classic illustration of this more common situation is provided by the "pizza battle" that took place between Pillsbury Company and Jeno's, Incorporated during the early 1980s.[7]

The frozen pizza market in the United States is estimated as generating a total volume of $600 million annually. It is a field in which there are many competitors both large and small, national and local. The competition among brands is fast paced. In the late 1970s Jeno's achieved the top market share position in this market. Jeno's explicit promotional program was intense and centered around a heavily budgeted advertising campaign featuring a humorous theme. Its number one position was then challenged by Pillsbury, which introduced a new entry under the name Totino's. Like Jeno's, it was aggressively promoted with a heavy investment in advertising, personal selling, and sales promotion. The product feature—or implicit promotional element—highlighted by Totino's was a "revolutionary crisp crust." Some competitors felt that Totino's advertising strategy was too aggressive. Among other things, it reportedly used a comparative theme that implied that other frozen pizza brands had crusts that "taste like cardboard." It was not just this charge that disturbed competitors such as Jeno's. They were disturbed even more by the success of Totino's campaign and the inroads it made on their sales. In particular, Jeno's lost its number one position as Totino's took over a twenty-six percent share of the market.

Jeno's counterthrust was a product modification dubbed "revolutionary crisp and tasty crust pizza." To be certain its revised product would be perceived by consumers as clearly different from and superior to Totino's, Jeno's also developed new topping ingredients and introduced a "flavor shaker" packet of herbs with which consumers could season the pizza to suit their tastes. Then Jeno's launched a heavy national advertising campaign coupled with intensified personal selling efforts to convince retailers it had a product that would displace Totino's and regain the number one position for Jeno's.

***Enticing Competitive Positionings with Dangerous Long-Term Possibilities.*** Laker Airlines represents a case that falls into the third category listed above. The same promotional strategy that assisted Laker to its success helped lay the groundwork for its ultimate bankruptcy. In the late 1970s, Freddie Laker offered transatlantic air travelers a new way to fly at remarkably low fares. Laker dubbed his airline "Skytrain" and characterized it as "no frills" service. Beyond emphasis on low price and the no-frills promotional theme, Laker chose one other unusual course in building his promotional mix. In place of the heavy reliance on advertising favored by most international airlines, Laker did very little advertising. Instead, he relied on publicity to carry promotional messages to the public.

At its inception, Laker Airlines enjoyed huge success. It not only earned significant profits but also earned knighthood for its founder who became "Sir

Freddie." In 1982, Laker Airlines was forced into bankruptcy and suspended operations. In commenting on the postmortem that followed Laker's demise, one publication made the following points regarding Laker's promotional strategy, the pattern of competitive response to that strategy, and the company's ultimate failure:

> Insiders report that the words Freddie Laker most regretted uttering were "no frills"—his description of the original Skytrain service.
> "There was effectively no real marketing at Laker," says one airline expert. "It was a seat-of-the-pants operation. There was no awareness of the need for long-term planning and thinking. And, in absolute terms, Laker probably never spent enough on advertising. He sees advertising as a necessary evil but spends as much as possible looking for free advertising and publicity."
> While traffic across the Atlantic was buoyant, the scheduled airlines were prepared to let him take the cheap-fare passengers. Indeed, for a time they concentrated on the up-market where the takings per seat are higher and the load factors (percentage of the plane filled) not so crucial.
> Ironically, the early success of Skytrain—and of Sir Freddie's drive for free publicity ended up by damaging him when he had to compete head-on with the scheduled carriers. . . . When times got hard . . . Mister Laker was attacked on his home ground of price and had no strong consumer image with which to attract the businessmen and the higher-fare paying passengers who could make up for the lower-priced passengers he was losing. [8]

In summary, competition is a force with which you must constantly reckon and take into consideration in your promotional planning. In most cases you will be likely to view that force as a threat to your position, though in some cases competitors' efforts may actually improve your own status. When responding to competitive activities or when initiating new programs of your own, you will be well advised to consider the type of reaction your strategy is likely to prompt from rival firms. Importantly, this last aspect must be assessed in terms of long-term possibilities as well as its immediate effects.

## ILLUSTRATIONS OF PROMOTIONAL MIX DECISION MAKING

Having outlined the corporate, socio-legal, and competitive settings in which your promotional mix is built, a few in-depth illustrations of selected promotional programs are in order. We will look at ways in which broad-scale organizational strategies are carried forward to develop marketing plans and how elements of the promotional mix—both implicit and explicit—blend together to form a total and persuasive communications package. The three programs to be discussed will also demonstrate the diversity of settings in which promotional strategy is formed. The first case describes a promotional approach aimed at industrial buyers, who purchase goods and services to be used in operating a business or institution. That will be followed by two cases discussing programs targeted toward ultimate consumers, who buy products either for their own personal use or for the personal use of some other individual. The three products involved range from a rather low-priced grocery item, to a rather high-priced piece of machinery, to a third situation in which the offering has no clear "price" in the usual sense. Two of the organizations involved in our examples operate as typical profit-oriented enterprises. The third is a nonprofit organization and its product is not a tangible commodity but a specialized type of service. Although the nature of the organizations, the price ranges, the product types, and the markets involved portray a wide range of situations, you will see that there are also common denominators of promotional logic that pervade all three cases.

Beyond the diversity of situations in which promotion operates, the cases demonstrate some of the major decision alternatives a promotional strategist confronts. At points in each case you will be given a set of such alternatives from which you can choose. At the end of each case, you will see which were chosen by the promotional strategists who bore responsibility for them and what the market results of those choices were. It is important that you recognize at the outset that there are no absolutely right or wrong answers among the alternatives you will consider. In actuality, each decision was made on the basis of both information available to the marketing executives concerned with it and on the basis of their particular philosophies and experience. Different decision makers may have opted for other strategies—perhaps with less success, perhaps with more. The rationale behind having you consider alternatives at this early stage in the text rests on two premises. First, it should assist you in developing your ability to view promotional decision making in the context of organizational goals. Second, it will help reinforce the concept of interaction between promotional components. As you will see, decisions made in one promotional area, such as advertising, are interrelated with those made in other areas such as personal selling. To produce maximum effectiveness, all elements within the promotional mix must be both consistent and cross-reinforcing.

*Case One: Your Product Duplicates an Original*[9]

**Your Situation.**    Your company is a relatively small producer of office copying machines, small at least when compared to such large and well-established competitors as Xerox, Addressograph-Multigraph, IBM, and Eastman Kodak.

Plain paper copiers—those that do not require a special type of paper for duplication—are big ticket items. Depending on the size of the machine and such features as color reproduction capability and speed, the price ranges from about $7,000 to $85,000 per unit. Xerox is generally recognized as being the pioneer in the plain paper copier field. At the time you are planning your marketing strategy there are a total of 250,000 plain paper copiers in use in the United States. Approximately seventy-five percent of those are Xerox units.

Your company has achieved a technological breakthrough. After five years of research and development at a cost of $13 million, your technical team has perfected a "liquid-toner" transfer method. In the past, the liquid-toner approach has been avoided by industry leaders because of uneven copy quality. Not only have your engineers overcome the problems previously experienced with liquid toners, but their research has led to a machine that is much less expensive to manufacture and service. Your first model will be priced at less than $5,000. This puts it some fifty percent below the price of a closely comparable Xerox copier. Because your equipment promises to have advantages in reliability and more economical servicing, company officials feel they can offer a service contract at less than half the price of a similar Xerox contract.

The custom in the industry has been for producers to rent machines rather than sell them. Another practice common among your competitors has been to contact customers via company salespeople rather than via independent office equipment dealers. There are several reasons for this last approach. One involves the degree of service and follow-up often required by customers. Presumably, company-trained and company-directed sales personnel are better able to handle these jobs. Another reason sometimes cited has to do with the matter of "loyalty." The last twenty years have seen a rash of technological breakthroughs in office machinery and an influx of new firms. In a market like this, it is not surprising that independent dealers are quick to look for and concentrate their selling efforts on the newest items with the greatest potential. As one observer put it, ". . . dealers have the reputation of being quick to shift loyalty to the vendor with the newest 'hot box'."[10]

One way to classify customer groups is on the basis of their experience with plain paper copiers. Such a scheme would picture the potential market in three parts:

**1.** The replacement market, made up of firms that now own, or more probably lease, plain paper copiers. Such a customer would be looking for new machines to replace those currently in use, either because the new equipment is better or because the existing equipment is worn out.

**2.** The expanded use market, made up of firms that now use copiers but can be sold additional machines on the appeal of greater convenience and efficiency. "Distributed copying" is gaining widespread demand. Essentially this means that companies want to decentralize their reproduction facilities and install additional units at different locations to save employee time.

**3.** The undeveloped market, made up of firms that have a clear need for copiers but that have not yet installed such machines.

Although personal selling is the backbone of most marketing efforts in the office equipment field, the very large companies—especially IBM and Xerox—have been spending an increasingly large number of dollars on advertising. This includes television advertising, which at first glance seems a little unusual. TV is almost certain to involve much "waste circulation." The proportion of viewers who would be active prospects for copying equipment is low, compared to the proportions who are potential buyers for most TV promoted products, such as cold remedies, soup mixes, or automobiles. However, TV is an excellent way of impressing prospects with the company's name as well as giving a quick visual demonstration of relatively complex products. Xerox apparently feels such advertising is worth the cost. It is currently spending $10 million on advertising, with $5 million going to television.

Now it is time for your decisions.

*Your Options.*   As the person charged with the responsibility for developing promotional strategy for this company, how would you choose among the following alternatives?

With respect to general target market selected, would you

**a.** Aim heavily at the existing user groups—replacements and expanded usage? Most of these firms would now have Xerox equipment in place. You might want to do this on the theory that they are presold on the generic product category and would be easier to reach on the appeal of an improved piece of equipment.

**b.** Aim at the "undeveloped" part of the market, potential users who don't yet have any plain paper copiers installed? You might want to do this on the theory that they could be especially open to a lower price appeal and are not yet wedded to one of the major firms such as IBM or Xerox. Therefore, you would not have any brand loyalty habits to break.

**c.** Not try to target toward any special group at all on the theory that it is best to get your business wherever you can find it?

With respect to advertising strategy, would you

**a.** Decide to follow the general media mix pattern of the industry leaders, using business-oriented magazines such as the *Wall Street Journal* and *U.S. News and World Report* but also including a sizable dosage of television advertising?

**b.** Decide that the media mix that might be correct for Xerox would be all wrong for your firm, because your advertising budget is much more limited? Therefore, you will use business journals but avoid television. You will back up the business publication campaign with a heavy direct mail effort. Your direct mail campaign will be designed to include specialty advertising items, such as desk calendars and pens imprinted with your company name. It is meant to both impress your name on prospects via reminder advertising, and to generate leads for your sales personnel.

**c.** Decide to use only the direct mail and specialty advertising approach? You will schedule your mailings carefully to precede the visit of one of your sales representatives. In other words, your technique is to pave the way for the sales rep's visit, perhaps with a sequence of mailing pieces, carefully timed to reach the prospect just before the representative calls.

With respect to personal selling strategy, you start with one hard fact. You have only 275 sales representatives spread among forty sales branches located throughout the United States. Xerox has 3,000 sales representatives. Would you

**a.** Cut the number of your sales branches to concentrate your company representatives in fewer areas? Assign the remaining territory to independent dealers even though this would leave you with questions of control and loyalty?

**b.** Launch the introduction of your new machine using your present sales force but draw up a plan for phased expansion? This would call for the number of your branches to increase to 150 within a three-year period with a parallel expansion of sales personnel to 1,200. While this might slow your initial growth rate it would also bring you advantages in control, as well as providing more incentive for your existing sales force by giving them opportunities for promotion to branch management posts.

**c.** Expand the number of branches and size of the sales force as rapidly as possible? Recruit heavily from the existing sales forces of your competitors?

*The Actual Decisions and Results.* If you chose the first answer—**a**—in all three of the above decision situations, you picked almost exactly the same strategy pattern used by Savin Business Machines. With a unique product advantage, but not much image or stature in the market, Savin broke with some promotional traditions of the industry but adapted itself to others. The company actually cut the number of its sales branches from forty to nineteen and raised the number of franchised dealers from 190 to 550. With its own offices covering prime territories, and independent dealers covering the remaining areas, Savin was able to get almost immediate national impact through a total selling force of 1,900 representatives, although only 275 of those were the company's own people. Savin broke with another tradition when it decided to aim at selling machines outright, rather than leasing them as Xerox and IBM had done.

In terms of general market positioning, Savin took the view that, because it believed it had a better machine than Xerox, it should compete with that company head-on, going after its existing customers and openly comparing itself to Xerox in advertising. Print ads featured headlines such as, "We owe our success to Xerox (In fact, one out of every two copiers we place—replaces a Xerox)" and "Xerox is going to make you an offer you should refuse." Speaking about the general philosophy behind Savin's approach, its executive vice-president is quoted as saying, "We were unknown to would-be buyers, so we tried to create the illusion of two giants fighting each other so that we could move from cold canvassing to working with leads."[11]

Even though its total advertising budget was much smaller than that of Xerox (only 1.5 million dollars in its first full year), the company included spot television advertising in nineteen top markets. Print advertising was designed mainly to generate leads for sales representatives, and included "information please" coupons. Television advertising was aimed mainly at reputation building. Again, in the words of the executive vice-president, "TV [gave] us tremendous awareness and made it easier for our salespeople to close the sale."[12]

Savin is one of the most interesting promotional success stories of recent vintage. In only one year it went from being a very small, unknown company to achieving the top spot in new installations of plain paper copiers in the United States. Its total placements during that year were estimated at fifteen thousand units domestically, versus thirteen thousand for Xerox, which had dominated the field up to that point.

*Case Two: Your Product Is a Piece of Cake*[13]

***Your Situation.*** This time your product is not radically new but really an extension of an existing successful product. You are in charge of promotional strategy for a large bakery goods producer. Your firm sells a high-quality line, mainly cakes, in both the retail and institutional markets. Your institutional sales division has introduced an upgraded—and much higher priced—extension of the line. The four cakes in this line extension have met with excellent acceptance in top hotels and first-rate restaurants. Your company is considering introducing the same items in retail supermarkets. The specific products involved are French Cheesecake, Strawberry French Cheesecake, Chocolate Bavarian cake, and Lemon Bavarian cake. They are much lighter and creamier than any comparable products now in supermarket freezer bins, including your own cheesecakes.

Although they have achieved solid success in the institutional market, you know there is going to be resistance from retailers. The big problem is price. Your new cheesecakes will have to be priced at about a dollar above your other retail items. This means a relatively big price jump, from slightly over a dollar for the existing cheesecakes, to something over two dollars for each of the four new flavors. The two-dollar price level has been considered the price ceiling for this product. Not only are supermarket operators likely to resist a higher cost, but the current mood of consumers may not be right for a higher-priced bakery product. The country is in a recession. The economic downturn has been accompanied by ongoing inflation and price increases are especially heavy in the grocery field. As a result, frozen baked goods have been hit by a five percent drop in sales. The total retail market for frozen baked sweet goods is estimated at around $450 million per year.

Another possibility causing you some second thoughts is the chance that the new cakes will simply "cannibalize" your existing line by taking sales from your other cakes. Your current market share is very high. Would the additional varieties add to your share or simply carve into it?

***Your Options.*** Your possible promotional strategies are as follows:

a. Continue product development and market research on the new line but don't attempt to introduce it right now. Wait until the economic climate improves, on the theory that you can then get a better reception from both retailers and consumers. You have the top line in the field, so why not just ride with it for a while?

**b.** Work on reducing the size of the cakes and perhaps make some minor compromises on quality. Try to develop a product variation that gets your price at least slightly under two dollars. Then introduce the new flavors as trade-up variations within your recognized and established line.

**c.** Treat these four products as an entirely new line. Promote them under your general brand name but distinguish them with some secondary branding strategy. Clearly differentiate the line through advertising and packaging. Hold the product quality as is, even though this will require customers to jump about one dollar and break a recognized price barrier.

**d.** Follow about the same plan as option **c**, but price them so that they will retail at under two dollars—say at about $1.89. Although this will produce little or no profit for you at the beginning (perhaps you'll have to take a loss), your long-term goal will be to raise the price gradually after you have achieved consumer acceptance of the new product variation.

What is your choice?

*The Actual Decision and Results.* The product line involved was Sara Lee International Desserts. The company chose option **c** after some careful market investigation and preliminary test marketing. By testing the new cheesecakes at various price levels above and below two dollars, Sara Lee learned that consumers were willing to go above two dollars for a high-quality, well-promoted product. The price was set at $2.19.

The company recognized it was aiming at a very specific market segment—primarily families with incomes over $25,000 per year and living in or near large urban areas. Both the test marketing and the final product introduction were planned with that segment in mind. For example, in addition to television and print ads, the company directed an intensive direct mail effort to residents of upper income urban neighborhoods and suburbs, which included "cents-off" coupons and took place prior to the use of TV and magazine campaigns.

Personal selling efforts to secure distribution and support from grocers concentrated on supermarkets in the same neighborhoods and suburbs. To overcome initial retailer resistance the company offered stores an attractive introductory price discount. What about retailers' reluctance to take on a frozen baked good above the two-dollar price point? The company's sales representatives sold the higher price as an advantage to the store, because it results in a higher profit per item. Then they provided stores with point-of-purchase materials to get consumer attention and help the product move. When television advertising was begun, programs, stations, and times were methodically chosen on the basis of how well they would reach the more affluent income groups.

Sara Lee's director of marketing reported the International line as an outstanding success. An executive of a major food chain in the New York area commented that, far from cannibalizing the original line, the International line actually increased volume on Sara Lee's lower-priced cakes by creating excitement for the entire product category.

## Case Three: Your Product Needs Help[14]

**Your Situation.** In the first two cases, your goal was increasing profits. Would the same kind of techniques work for a nonprofit organization? You are in charge of developing a promotional program for an animal shelter. Because it is privately operated, it is always in need of contributions. Moreover, it faces a problem that is somewhat unique. Although the great majority of animal shelters destroy an estimated eighty-five percent of the cats and dogs they receive, yours has a firm policy that no animal may be destroyed. Of course, this creates some difficulties. Your kennel area is only 700 square feet in size, making it impossible to handle more than about thirty-nine dogs, cats, puppies, and kittens at any one time. Unless you can achieve a high adoption rate with few returns, you are going to be very limited as to the number of animals you can accept. Last year you were able to place only 127 animals for adoption. Your return rate ran at about twenty-five percent.

Your shelter has only one full-time employee. It is open five days a week for two hours a day and depends for its financial existence on ninety people who contribute money for its support. Persons adopting animals are normally asked for a contribution that is appropriate to the size and quality of the dog or cat. Although this isn't exactly a required fee, it is possible that it could be hindering adoptions to some extent. Some of the animals you take in are handicapped—a three-legged cat, a cat with a hairless tail, dogs and cats that are blind or deaf. These are the types of animals for whom it is especially hard to find homes.

Because this is a nonprofit organization, the results of your promotional efforts will not be measured in the usual return-on-investment terms. Instead, its effectiveness will be judged on the basis of how well you can achieve three major objectives: (1) to raise money so that the shelter's activities can be expanded, (2) to find suitable homes for more animals, including those who have physical disabilities, and (3) to reduce the rate of animals returned.

Now for your decisions.

**Your Options.** With respect to fund raising would you recommend:

**a.** A television campaign using twenty-second spot commercials in the low-priced, late evening viewing hours? These commercials would feature animals received at the shelter, especially puppies and kittens. Contributors would be offered attractive bumper stickers recognizing their humanitarian effort. The bumper stickers should not only increase contributions by giving donors something they can use as a sort of status symbol to demonstrate their social consciousness, but will also help to further advertise your shelter.

**b.** Conducting a direct mail solicitation campaign. Start with a list of known charitable contributors and dog owners in the area. Use a celebrity testimonial to endorse the shelter and ask each person to send one dollar to save the lives of a puppy and a kitten pictured on your direct mail piece.

**c.** Locating professional salespeople living in your area and asking them to volunteer as fund raisers. Provide them with "sales materials" that they can show when they call at homes of potential contributors. Conduct small-scale sales training programs so they will understand what the product is all about and the types of appeals effective in reaching contributors.

**d.** Not doing any of these things because they are not proper techniques in a nonprofit situation.

With respect to the problem of getting more adoptions would you recommend:

**a.** Concentrating on generating more traffic at the shelter. Start with better business hours. Rather than being open two hours a day for five days a week, open the shelter on Saturday and Sunday afternoons only, times when families go shopping or are out driving. Sponsor a weekly "name the kitten or puppy" contest, offering pet grooming kits as prizes. Raise the requested contributions by enough to cover the cost of generating the additional traffic.

**b.** Remaining open more during every day of the week and using point-of-purchase sales material on the animal cages. Let this material tell prospects something about each animal and build selling appeal into the messages. Also, use some small-space newspaper ads. Where you have a handicapped animal, try to make the defect into a selling feature that will appeal to at least some of your customers.

**c.** Keeping your current hours but also staying open all day Sunday. Buy billboard space in your market area. Feature a "pet of the week" on the billboards, picking the most attractive dog or cat currently in residence at the shelter.

**d.** Not doing any of these things because they are not proper techniques in a nonprofit situation.

*The Actual Decisions and Results.* If you picked option **b** in both of the above lists, you chose the same general route very successfully followed by the

North Shore Animal League on Long Island. One of the more interesting things about this situation is that the approach was developed by a retired marketing executive, who had once been dubbed one of "America's twelve master salesmen." His philosophy, on accepting the assignment, was that the same principles used in selling vacuum cleaners or headache remedies or printing presses can be applied in nonprofit situations.

After he implemented the new promotional approach for the North Shore Animal League, the number of contributors rose from ninety to 100,000. The number of animals placed increased from 127 per year to over 3,700. Even the return rate improved by going down from twenty-five percent to a fifteen or twenty percent level. The League now finds it easier to place animals with physical problems by taking the view that, regardless of the pet's handicap, somewhere there is a person who wants exactly that kind of animal. In other words, match the "product" with the right kind of consumer segment; design the message for the market.

As an illustration, a three-legged cat was advertised the following way: "Big, beautiful, gentle American short-hair gray and white cat with a head like a lion. But Ahab has only three paws. You wouldn't notice it unless we told you. He gets around just fine."

Five and a half years after the new promotional program began, the North Shore Animal League was a high-volume "business" with a staff of twenty-five employees. It was still not making any money because that was never one of the objectives.

## GENERALIZING FROM THE CASES

While Savin, Sara Lee, and North Shore operated from quite different organizational objectives and competitive settings, as a promotional planner for any one of these organizations you would be facing the same question posed at the beginning of this chapter: "How can I best communicate with prospective customers and persuade them to buy my product?" Taken together, the cases provide specific illustrations that reiterate three vital points. First, promotional planning calls for decisions in a variety of diverse areas, each concerned with a specific technique for conveying persuasive communication. Second, these techniques interact with each other to form a composite mix. Third, although there is no general formula for building your mix and strategists may differ in terms of the precise promotional formats they choose in a particular marketing situation, there are general principles that you can use to guide your own decision making.

*The Diversity of Promotional Decision Areas*

Each of the strategy options you confronted involved making decisions about communication techniques intended to persuade prospective customers. Some posed alternatives about the market at which you should aim, which is the same as asking, "To whom should we communicate? Who is most likely to be persuaded?'' Other options involved such general problems of persuasive communication as the following:

- What types of promotional elements (for example, advertising or personal selling) shall we emphasize to carry our communications?
- What decisions should we make about the specific channels through which the communications will be sent (principally choices among advertising media and ways of organizing or training the sales force)?
- What should the communications themselves be like in terms of general appeals and message content?
- Because the product, its price, and perhaps its place of sale will also be communicating a type of message, is there anything we should do to change them?

*The Interactive Nature of the Mix*

Ideally, all promotional elements blend to work with a maximum synergistic thrust. In considering the cases, you saw some of this blending clearly emphasized. Savin's executive vice-president was telling you something about the intent behind that company's mix of promotional elements when he said that print advertising generated leads for sales representatives whereas television advertising helped them close the sale. Advertising's job, in the total mix, was to support the salespeople in two very specific and different ways. Sara Lee's "cents-off" coupons helped circumvent probable customer resistance to a higher price, but the sales force first had to get the product into supermarkets to make the coupons and the television advertising work. In a sense, the task of the sales force was to "pave the way" for a successful outcome to communications initiated through advertising and sales promotion. To increase its adoption rate, the North Shore Animal League used small-space newspaper ads, which both helped locate adopters for hard-to-place animals and drew more "customers" to the shelter. Once inside, potential adopters found point-of-purchase material on the cages, which helped "sell" the individual animals.

Because a promotional plan will work best when it is well blended, that is, when the various techniques reinforce each other, a thorough study of all elements of promotion and their interrelations should serve you well whether your goal is to be a top-level, general marketing executive or to specialize in one of the technique areas. As a top-level decision maker, understanding as much as possible about the total mix is essential to you. As a specialist, such understanding will help you plan your own function much more effectively by giving you a better grasp of how it fits into the overall pattern and what help you should try to get from or give to the people in the other technique areas.

*Variations in Decisions Based on Common General Principles*

In each of the cases above, you were given several decisions to consider. If you happened to pick the options that were successfully used in each case, congratulations. If you did not, don't worry about it. The experts who made those decisions had much more information than you did and more time to consider the possibilities. Moreover, even if you had the same amount of time and information—and the same amount of promotional expertise—you might have decided on a different approach and achieved excellent results.

Experts often disagree among themselves as to which is the best approach. This makes promotion an especially competitive, interesting, and exciting field in which to work. It also means that it is impossible to lay out a precise or absolute formula that a promotional strategist must follow. One way to illustrate the implications of this fact is to compare the promotional strategist to two other types of professionals—the architect and the construction contractor.

Ten competent contractors, each assigned to put up a high-rise building and working from the same blueprints, should come up with ten virtually identical structures. Ten top-flight architects, each commissioned to design a high-rise building for the same purpose and the same location, could very easily come up with ten very different structures—and each of them could be an excellent design. Developing promotional strategy is much more like being an architect than like being a construction contractor. All the architects would be working from the same general information base—engineering principles, types of building materials, knowledge of architectural styles, and so on. However, each might have an entirely unique and creative approach as to how these factors should be combined to best get the job done. The work of a promotional strategist is much the same. He or she does not start with an exact blueprint. The idea is to develop a "blueprint," to set up a strategy based on a thorough analysis of the situation, followed by a creative approach toward a solution.

Like the architect, the promotional strategist also starts with an information base. Its major components revolve around issues such as the following:

- What forces in the marketplace should be examined and considered to find "open" segments of buyers and develop basic promotional appeals?
- How can information and theories about human behavior in general be used to explore promotional possibilities and suggest improved approaches?
- What techniques are available to reach prospective buyers?
- What basic facts should be known about each of these techniques and alternative ways of handling them?
- In what ways can they be fused into a coordinated mix?
- How can promotional programs be "monitored" or evaluated to determine which parts are weak and which are strong, so they can be improved or changed over time?

These are issues we will be discussing in the following chapters.

Mark Twain once wrote, "It [is] not best that we should all think alike; it is difference of opinion that makes horse races." If every promotional strategist made exactly the same set of decisions there would be no "horse race" and no winners. For example, if there are six brands in a product category, and you introduce a seventh that customers think is just like all the others, why should they buy your brand? Generally, a promotional decision maker aims at producing a strategy deliberately different from competitors, because success usually depends on convincing people that you have a differential advantage.

# SUMMARY

Promotional strategy centers around making decisions about persuasive communications to potential buyers. A variety of elements can send such communications—advertising, personal selling, sales promotion, and publicity, along with certain aspects of the product itself, its price, and its place of distribution, although the last three elements belong in a separate category from the others. Taken together, the combination of elements you use should form a well-integrated promotional mix.

Promotion is one aspect of a firm's total marketing mix that, in turn, is one part of the total functional activities of the firm. All of these activities, including promotion, are derived from and directed toward specified organizational objectives, keeping in mind the effects of competitive strategies and the constraints imposed by social custom or law.

Anyone who has some degree of control over planning the mix or any one of its parts can be considered a promotional strategist. Although expert strategists may arrive at quite different solutions to the same promotional problems and though there is no rigid formula that all must use, there is a general base of knowledge and techniques that can help a strategist analyze market opportunities, stimulate the development of creative approaches, and lead to effective strategy decisions.

## DISCUSSION QUESTIONS

1. Discuss the dynamic climate in which promotional programs operate, framing your discussion in terms of current circumstances affecting the sales in a particular product category.
2. Discuss the difference between a marketing mix and a promotional mix.
3. How do marketing mix components interact with explicit promotion? Explain and give examples.
4. How do an organization's internal subjective factors relate to marketing activities?
5. What is a strategic gap and how does it originate?
6. To what extent can marketing considerations influence the firm's overall objectives?
7. Define the term "market positioning," and give an example of its use.
8. Discuss alternative ways in which competitors' strategies can affect your market results.
9. Give several examples of competitive positioning opportunities and their potentially dangerous long-term consequences.
10. What is the difference between an "inside-out" and an "outside-in" assessment approach?
11. Choose a local nonprofit organization and discuss ways in which it might use promotional techniques.
12. What two general steps should be followed when you are beginning to develop your promotional mix?

# REFERENCES

1. Subhash C. Jain, *Marketing Planning and Strategy* (Cincinnati, OH: Southwestern Publishing Company, 1981), p. 25.
2. *Ibid.*, p. 11.
3. I. Nonoka and F. N. Nicosia, "Marketing Management, Its Environment, and Information Processing: A Problem of Organizational Design," *Journal of Business Research*, December 1979, pp. 277–300.
4. *Loc. cit.*, p. 295.
5. Richard F. Vancil, "Strategy Formulation in Complex Organizations," *Sloan Management Review*, Winter 1976, pp. 27–42.
6. Nancy Giges, "Evian's Sales Pitch: Let 'em drink pure water," *Advertising Age*, 22 May 1978, p. 26.
7. "Jeno's has the crust to battle Pillsbury," *Advertising Age*, 12 May 1980, p. 4.
8. Howard Sharman, "Laker got caught in no-frills trap," *Advertising Age*, 15 February 1982, p. 3.
9. The Savin case description is based mainly on the following articles: "Savin Expanding Anti-Xerox Effort," *Advertising Age*, 13 December 1976, p. 4.
Thayer C. Taylor, "Savin's Savvy Sell," *Sales and Marketing Management*, 10 October 1977, p. 34.
Robert Levy, "The Big Battle in Copiers," *Dun's Review*, May 1977, p. 97.
10. Taylor, "Savin's Savvy Sell," p. 38.
11. *Ibid.*, p. 39.
12. *Ibid.*
13. The Sara Lee International Desserts case is based mainly on the following article:
Kevin V. Brown, "Sara Lee Beats the Recession with Costly Cakes," *Product Marketing*, April 1977, p. 21.
14. The North Shore Animal League case is based mainly on the following article:
William Mathewson, "With Right Tactics, It's Easy to Market a Three-Legged Cat," *The Wall Street Journal*, 6 March 1975, p. 203.

# CHAPTER TWO

# *Product and Price as Implicit Promotion*

## FOCUS OF THE CHAPTER

A team of production specialists has suggested that "the objective of a business is to make a product which costs a dime, sells for a dollar and is habit forming."[1] Although our field of interest is promotion rather than production, this bit of hyperbole serves as a useful backdrop for explaining why we will begin with a quick overview of product and price before surveying the explicit promotional elements of advertising, personal selling, sales promotion, and publicity. Product and price—along with place—form the bases on which your explicit mix must be built. As the above quote suggests, the ideal situation from the perspective of a product's seller would be one in which customers felt an almost irresistible compulsion to purchase the brand at a price that both appealed to target prospects and generated a very high profit. Although it is most unlikely that fate will place you in such an ideal position, the fact remains that the innate attractiveness of your product and its price will be important forces in determining the promotional success you achieve. Furthermore, those forces will interact with your explicit promotional efforts to produce a total persuasive communications effect. Therefore, to appreciate fully the workings of explicit promotion, you must first have some appreciation of the basic promotional impact conveyed by your product and its price.

At the same time it is important to reemphasize that the product and price components of your marketing mix have many aspects that go beyond the realm of promotion. For example, in making decisions in these areas, marketing management must cope with such nonpromotional issues as production capabilities and cost and revenue analysis. Our interest in discussing product and price does not extend to any of these nonpromotional issues. It is limited to those aspects of these marketing components that can convey persuasive information to consumers or can intermingle with and affect the handling of your explicit promotion.

## THE DISTINCT PARTS OF PRODUCT AND PRICE

Figure 2.1 depicts one way to portray product and price in the context of the total marketing mix. It indicates that each can be separated into two distinct parts. In the case of product, these parts are *functional features* and *surrogate cues*. In the case of price they are a *transactional dimension* and an *informational dimension*. The figure further suggests that product and price not only affect the explicit promotional elements of advertising, personal selling, sales promotion, and publicity but can also have a direct communication impact of their own because they can provide a type of information flow to customers. This chapter will build from the basic relationships outlined in Figure 2.1 and use them to discuss ways in which you can work with product and price to strengthen your overall promotional mix.

## FUNCTIONAL PRODUCT FEATURES

*Functional product features are product qualities that provide benefits in use, that are generally measurable, and that relate directly to the purposes and reasons the consumer has in mind when making the purchase.*

Consumers buy products to receive benefits. They will rate your brand on the basis of what they believe about how well it delivers the benefits they

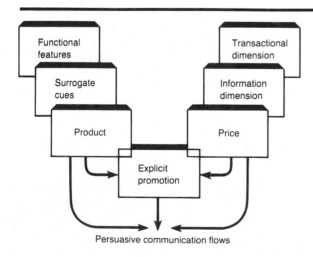

**FIGURE 2.1 Product and price in the total promotional mix**

*Product and Price as Implicit Promotion*

want. Actual brand performance depends on its functional features—its ingredients, components, design, construction, and so on. Your customer may or may not be interested in the technical details. He or she will certainly be interested in how well its features deliver the desired benefits. The best way for a customer to make this kind of judgment is by using the product to see what happens. In this situation, your brand communicates about itself; to the extent that it communicates favorably and persuasively it "promotes" itself.

The board chairman of the Procter and Gamble Company has said, "While advertising and selling are terribly important, we have never been able to build a successful brand through those skills alone. . . . If [consumers] do not perceive any real performance benefits in the brand, then no amount of ingenious advertising and selling can save the brand. This is the way it has been in our business since our company was founded in 1837."[2]

**An Ideal Brand**

To set the stage for the discussion of functional product features and their role in the promotional mix, we shall first consider what an ideal brand would be like from your standpoint as a seller. Then, because your brand will almost certainly not be ideal, we can talk about how you can better analyze your non-ideal situation. From your view as a seller, an ideal brand would have the following qualities:

1. Its functional features and the benefits they deliver would be self-evident to consumers. Once a person saw or used your brand, those features would be apparent.
2. Its functional product features would be exclusive and far better than those offered by competitors. No other seller could duplicate them or even come close.
3. Its functional product features would provide benefits that relate to very strong lifestyle goals of the consumer.
4. Every consumer in the marketplace would rate those benefits as being highly important.

If your product were as good as all this, you would have a virtual monopoly. Building the rest of your promotional strategy mix would be simple. Your main concern would be getting people to try your brand—just once. Very occasionally, a person or group has achieved this ideal by securing exclusive rights to sell some vital commodity such as salt. But the world you face as a promotional strategist is likely to be much different. At times a firm can come close to matching some of these conditions for a while, and it is informative to see what happens to the rest of the promotional mix when it does. It is equally informative to see what happens when competitors respond.

**The Tylenol Example**

The Tylenol story provides a good illustration of a nearly ideal brand. Tylenol was introduced to the pain reliever market in 1961. Its main functional product feature is chemical—the use of acetaminophen to replace aspirin. The major benefit in use is the same as that of aspirin—relief of pain, but it also provides a second benefit—the absence of undesirable side effects, usually related to stomach disorders, which can trouble many people when they take aspirin.

The story of the relationship between implicit promotion and explicit promotion in the marketing of Tylenol can be viewed as unfolding in three distinct phases over a twenty-three-year period.

*Phase One: Implicit Promotion Dominates the Persuasive Communications Mix.*   For more than a decade Tylenol had no serious competitor. In short, the brand had three of the four ideal qualities. The major product feature was virtually "self-demonstrating"; it was nearly exclusive; it matched a criterion of extremely high importance to many consumers—relief of pain without causing stomach upset. The criterion was not of high importance to every consumer, but appealed to a sizable segment of the market.

Even with these advantages, Tylenol needed some explicit promotion, but not very much. Implicit promotion did most of the work. For over a decade, Johnson & Johnson, the company that makes Tylenol, was able to sell the product with no consumer advertising and very little personal selling effort. During that time, Tylenol was able to attain an estimated twelve percent of the analgesic market, even while competing against such heavily promoted brands as Bayer, Bufferin, Excedrin, and Anacin. A small amount of explicit promotion was aimed at getting support from physicians who could recommend it to their patients. Supermarkets and drugstores gave it shelf space, not because of strong personal selling effort by the company, but because of strong consumer demand. With Tylenol, Johnson & Johnson had a brand that was almost promoting itself. More accurately, its functional feature provided such strong implicit promotion, that not much explicit promotion was needed to generate favorable consumer purchase behavior.

*Phase Two: Explicit Promotion to the Support of Implicit Promotion.*   In 1974 Datril, a product generally equivalent to Tylenol, invaded the market with the same key functional feature plus a sales force, heavy advertising, and well-tested promotion techniques. Tylenol was forced to abandon its placid approach to explicit promotion.[3] In the ensuing years, Tylenol marketing executives proved themselves highly adept at responding to competitive pressure. Accelerated personal selling efforts were directed not only at physicians but also at retailers. A variety of sales promotion activities were introduced and a heavy investment made in consumer advertising. By 1980, the advertising budget was reported to be more than $33 million, spread over an expanded Tylenol product line including such variations as Extra-Strength Tylenol and Children's Tylenol in both liquid and tablet forms. The results were described as "seemingly unstoppable growth," for by 1981 the market share was up to an amazing thirty-one percent.[4] Not only had Tylenol withstood the challenge of Datril, it was now outpacing such long-established competitors as Anacin, Bayer, Bufferin, and Excedrin. In short, a brand that had done extremely well on product features alone, with little explicit promotion, turned into a market giant when the implicit promotion was exploited by an intensive explicit promotional mix.

*Phase Three: Explicit Promotion to the Rescue of Implicit Promotion.*[5]   You are probably aware of the tragedy that occurred at this point. In September of

1982, seven deaths resulted from poisonings caused by cyanide having been injected into Extra-Strength Tylenol capsules. This was not due to any dereliction on the part of the company; it resulted from an outside criminal act. Johnson & Johnson withdrew Tylenol capsules from retailers' shelves and suspended its advertising program. Moreover, sales of those versions of the product that remained available for purchase (Tylenol liquid and tablets) plunged to a 6.5% market share. In the opinion of many marketing and advertising experts, Tylenol's consumer acceptance appeared to have been permanently destroyed. A common recommendation was that the Tylenol brand be abandoned and the product reintroduced under a new name. One leading advertising personality announced publicly that anyone who could revive the Tylenol name would also be capable of turning water into wine.

Despite such gloomy predictions, Johnson & Johnson's management had faith in both their product and its essential reputation. A new, tamper-resistant package was designed to hold Tylenol capsules. Aside from that, no major change was made in implicit promotional aspects. Based on its prior success with explicit promotion, the company relied on that component of the marketing mix to restore the brand's market acceptance. They backed their decision with an estimated $100 million commitment for advertising, personal selling, sales promotion, and publicity. Explicit efforts took a variety of forms: the sales force was enlarged; newspaper advertising carried coupons offering a savings of $2.50 on the purchase of Tylenol; the company's chairman made publicity appearances on such television programs as "Sixty Minutes" and the "Phil Donahue Show"; finally, at the beginning of 1983, a new, low-key television advertising campaign began emphasizing the long-standing and well-placed trust of consumers in the Tylenol brand. As a result of all these efforts, it was reported that Tylenol had regained virtually all of the market share position it enjoyed prior to the tragedy.

In short, a brand that at first had eschewed explicit promotion learned to use it with expertise because of competitive pressure. Armed with that expertise, it was able to perform a remarkable feat of trade name revival when the reputation of its implicit promotional content was threatened.

## The More Typical Promotional Situation

The Tylenol example is unusual not only because of its ending but also because of its beginning. Relying so heavily on implicit promotion to carry the message for a new product entry is the exception rather than the rule among most large firms. More typically, market-oriented companies are likely to search for functional feature improvements of high importance to a consumer segment, and when they find them, initiate a full-scale promotional mix, even though the features may be "self-promoting" and "exclusive." For example, Ralston Purina spent four years developing a cat food that would stay moist without refrigeration and also not smell like the typical cat food. When they finally succeeded, they named it Tender Vittles. Then they made sure the world knew about it through advertising, personal selling, and sales promotion. The television commercial was able to say, "He'll love the taste; you'll love the smell." In other words, they made certain that the benefits of that feature, which was of high importance to many customers, was reinforced through explicit promotion. In a highly competitive world, the promotional mix is likely to be built around functional features, but it is not likely to rely too heavily on those features by letting them do the job all by themselves.

***Decisions at the Product Planning Level.*** Your exact role in working with functional features will depend on the position you occupy in your firm's marketing organization. As a product planner or a top-level marketing strategist, you may be working with the development of a new brand or the redesign of an existing brand. In that case, your best starting point is a search for benefits of high importance to a large group of consumers. Once these are discovered, the next step is developing a brand with functional features that deliver those benefits. Ideally, such features will be exclusive to your brand, or at least your brand will be able to demonstrate superiority with respect to one or more of them.

In a position such as salesperson, advertising planner, or sales promotion specialist, you will probably be working with a brand that is "in place," in other words, already designed. In this case, much of your task will be concerned with relating existing product features to the lifestyle goals of your customers. You will still have some alternatives to consider concerning the handling of functional features; for example, which features should you emphasize and which should you let "speak for themselves," or, when a given feature can be related to more than one benefit, which benefit or combination of benefits should you stress. (Chapter 6 will go into much more detail about ways to analyze functional features for their potential appeal to consumers.)

***Prestudying the Promotional Implications of Technical Product Development.*** Only rarely will any given feature appeal to all consumers in your market. For that reason, when functional features are in the technical research and development stages, their promotional potential should be prestudied in terms of the specific market segments at which they could be aimed.

Since implicit promotion, especially the functional feature aspect, is the core around which the rest of your program must be built, it makes sense to look ahead to see what kinds of problems or opportunities a potential functional feature is likely to bring to the rest of your mix. Not only must a functional feature provide a benefit but that benefit ideally should be of significant importance—one that will be easy to promote to a reasonably large market segment through your advertising, personal selling, and other explicit elements. Where you see difficulties ahead, you may wish to re-route the product research effort.

Consider the following example of an industrial marketing situation; in the words of a professional consultant:

> One of our clients had a problem designing an electric pavement breaker. He was trying to design the electric breaker to plug into a standard wall socket but still be able to perform like a pneumatic breaker. . . . To obtain such performance with an electric tool was virtually impossible, according to the engineers, but the marketing people felt that unless the electric tool could show such performance, there would be no market for it. We were called in to try to resolve the dilemma. . . . After talking to a good cross section of paving-breaker users, we

found that users of pneumatic breakers would not use electric breakers under any circumstances, no matter what their performance. [6]

It could be argued that, with enough effort, such a product could be sold to an initially reluctant group of customers, but even then you would be left with some questions. Are your available promotional resources strong enough to carry that much effort? Would it be worth it if you were successful or do you have better alternatives for your investment?

In this case, it was found that a lighter and more easily engineered breaker had a strong market appeal. It would not be a substitute for a pneumatic breaker but for a sledge hammer. Its logical market segment was not the pneumatic breaker users but smaller-scale contractors who were now relying on hand tools. The result was abandonment of a hard-to-engineer—and hard-to-promote—functional product feature. Instead, the company aimed its effort toward a different functional approach and successfully promoted it to a more easily persuaded customer group.

## SURROGATE CUES

*Surrogate cues are product features that provide no direct benefits in use but serve as subsidiary aspects that have the power to convey a message about functional features.*

In a literal sense, a surrogate cue serves as a *substitute* measure that aids a consumer in forming a judgment about a functional, benefit-delivering feature, even though the product feature connected with the surrogate cue does not deliver any desired benefit in and of itself. The line that separates a surrogate cue from a functional feature can be very thin. In the end, it is your customers' perceptions that make the difference. When consumers feel a particular feature delivers a clear benefit, it is a functional feature. When consumers do not see a feature as being of any direct benefit, but still use it as a substitute or surrogate means of judging a product's ability to deliver a functional benefit, it is a surrogate cue.

For example, suppose you are promoting a mouthwash that stresses its ability to "make your mouth come alive with a fresh, tingly taste." To achieve that "fresh, tingly taste" your brand includes an ingredient such as oil of cloves. This is a functional feature. It delivers a benefit that you believe a segment of purchasers will rate very highly. When designing your brand of mouthwash, you would probably want to put in some kind of coloring agent to improve its appearance. It might make sense to use a deep red color. This could help reinforce and communicate about the spicy, clovelike taste of your product. Probably, you would not find many purchasers who rate the color as being a benefit in and of itself. However, if you ran an experimental study you would be likely to find that the red color helped convince people that your product was spicy and refreshing. As a practical matter, your mouthwash would have exactly the same taste and tingle whether it was red, white, brown, or perfectly clear. The red color simply helps convey meaning that strengthens users' impressions of spiciness. Therefore, it serves as a surrogate cue.

Because the line between functional features and surrogate cues can be very thin, there is an important point to consider. Just because customers say a feature is of little or no importance to them does not always mean you should eliminate that feature from your product design or your explicit promotional considerations. When the feature provides no direct benefit to them, customers will probably rate it as not being important. In one sense, they are right. It is not important in terms of relating directly to a benefit that helps them achieve some lifestyle goal. In another sense they may be wrong. It is possible that the feature serves as an important surrogate cue because it helps communicate about a functional feature of your brand that does relate to an important benefit.

In a published survey on mouthwash brands, color actually was ranked as being of low importance by consumers.[7] When they compared brands such as Micrin, Cepacol, Listerine, and Lavoris, they rated features such as "kills germs," "effectiveness," and "flavor" as being very important. Color came in last, suggesting it had little meaning to them. However, you might ask yourself whether Listerine would "speak" as forcefully about its germ killing ability, if it were milk white, or if Lavoris would do as good a job of telling you about its taste if it were light blue.

To determine the effects of surrogate cues, you will often have to do more than ask customers how important those features are. As suggested above, you may want to do some experimentation, for example, test to see how people change their ratings on functional features when you change the way you are handling surrogate cues.

Anything about a brand that helps suggest something positive and persuasive, without directly delivering a functional benefit to the user, can be treated as a surrogate cue. The major types of surrogate cues deserving your special consideration fall into three categories: (1) brand names, (2) package designs, and (3) incidental physical characteristics.

## Brand Name as a Surrogate Cue

When Henry Ford needed a brand name for his automobile, he did not have to look far to find one. Neither did W. K. Kellogg do much research to name his corn flakes. In both cases, the producer's own last name did the job very well. A German shoe manufacturer went to just slightly greater effort when he had to reach a decision on a name for a high-quality line of athletic shoes. He decided to combine part of his first name with part of his last name; his full name was Adolf Dassler, and the brand name became Adidas. If these well-known and highly accepted brands were named this easily, perhaps there is not much point in spending time worrying about your brand name. Of course, it is also possible that these names turned out to have consumer appeal just by coincidence. Consider what might have happened if Henry Ford's name had been Adolf Dassler and Adolf Dassler's name had been Henry Ford!

**The Brand Name as a Promotional Mechanism.** It is not easy to determine precisely how important a brand name is in promoting a product. Although your brand name can help promote the image of quality for your product, the quality of your product probably does even more to promote the image of your brand name. This suggests that the name by itself may be most important when your brand is new and struggling to gain a foothold in the market. An effective name is more likely to help persuade consumers to try the product. After they do, their experience with the brand should start to influence the way they view your name. Given this situation, some observers feel that the brand name assigned to a new product can account for as much as forty percent of its success or failure.[8]

One illustration of how this can work involves a food product. A convenience-type packaged mix of ingredients was designed to be used with meat in preparing a low-cost main course for a meal. According to a published report, it was consumer tested for taste, convenience, and price with very positive test results. Then it was sent to market in a well-designed package and backed by an excellent ad campaign with a $5.5 million budget. Its name was "Pennsylvania Dutch Casserole," and it failed. After the market failure, research reportedly showed the name was largely responsible for killing a very good product. In the view of a marketing consultant, "the name Pennsylvania Dutch didn't mean anything to anybody outside of the general area of Lancaster, Pennsylvania. And the word 'casserole' was a negative indicating a second class meal."[9]

A few years later, a very similar product was introduced under the name "Hamburger Helper." It became one of the most successful new food products of the decade.

The Campbell Soup Company experienced a very similar chain of events when it introduced a new spaghetti sauce.[10] Acting on the assumption that the Campbell name had a high degree of consumer acceptance, the firm test-marketed the sauce under the name "Campbell's Very Own Special Sauce." The product failed its market test. Follow-up study showed that consumers felt the name described a sauce that was soupy or watery. The same sauce reintroduced under the name "Prego" became a market success.

***Choosing a Brand Name.*** Selection of a name is one of the most permanent promotional decisions you can make. Advertising, prices, personal selling strategies, and even functional features may change over time, but your brand name usually stays with your product as long as it is on the market. Because of its importance and permanence, it is a good idea to test the name for consumer response before making your final decision.

A very effective way to test consumer response is through a market survey in which consumers evaluate a name by itself, unaware of any details about the special features of the brand. For example, if you were planning to introduce a new dog food and thinking of naming it "Wag," you could ask a sample of users to tell you what kind of dog food that name would suggest. By separating the name from all other promotional elements, you can begin to get a reading on what that name by itself brings into your planned promotional mix or takes away from it. Is the name compatible with the rest of your message or is there something about it that interferes with your total strategy?

Before obtaining consumer reactions, of course, you must have some way of developing a list of names that might be suitable.[11] There is no rigid format for doing this but there are some sensible points you should consider.

**1.** At the very least, your brand name should be "open," that is, able to take on the kind of meaning the rest of your promotion will give it. Above all, it should not have any potentially negative implications. It should not cause customers to misinterpret your functional product features. Although Dr. Pepper is a very successful soft drink, its name can cause it to be misunderstood. For instance, some consumers may incorrectly perceive it as having an extremely sharp taste or being medicinal in nature. It is possible that Dr. Pepper would have been even more successful—or easier to promote on an explicit basis—with a different name.

**2.** It is a clear asset if the name contributes its own positive impact, suggesting to customers in an appealing way what the product is and does. Its message can be subtle and indirect. For example, "Tide" is an excellent name for a laundry detergent. Although the word was not originally connected with washing clothes, it suggests the power and force of water in motion. Indirectly, it hints that Tide gives you powerful help in doing your laundry.

**3.** The name should be distinctive. In part, there is a legal aspect to this. You do not want to risk a lawsuit charging infringement of an existing name. Beyond this, you seek a distinctive name because you want your product to stand out from competitors' brands. You are searching for a unique market position and a unique name can help.

**4.** The name should be physically adaptable to all the ways in which it will appear. You will be using it on packaging, in advertising, and possibly with display materials. You will be showing it in a variety of sizes. The name and the trademark design in which it is presented should be able to fit all of these situations without losing its character or visibility.

*Package Design as a Surrogate Cue*

Essentially, a "package" is simply the container that holds your product. It might be a bag, a box, a can, a bottle, a tube, or any other container. A part of packaging strategy involves functional product features rather than surrogate cues. When there is something you can do to improve your packaging to deliver an additional benefit to your customers, you are dealing with a functional product feature. A notable example is the aerosol can. It not only holds such things as paint, hair sprays, and insecticides, but it makes them easier to apply. When a package feature is functional, you will want to consider all the points raised earlier in the discussion of such features. However, our concern here is with the purely surrogate cue effect of package design—features that communicate meaning about product benefits rather than delivering those benefits directly. The following are some examples of how packages can promote your brand through surrogate cue effects.

**The Influence of Package Material on Perceptions of Product Quality.** In one study, the same brand of potato chips was bagged in two different ways. Half the bags were made of wax-coated paper. The other half were made of polyvinyl. Consumers were then asked to open each bag, taste the chips, and rate them. The results were as follows: "Chips in the polyvinyl packages were viewed as both [significantly] crisper . . . and tastier . . . . Since the product was approximately a week old during the testing period, it was assumed that the perceived differences were psychological."[12]

**The Influences of Package Color and Design on Brand Image.**   Tab has been reported as the top-selling, low-calorie soft drink in the United States. When the Coca-Cola Company first introduced Tab, the market for low-calorie soft drinks was made up mainly of women interested in dieting. The original and highly successful Tab can was designed with this market in mind. The name "Tab" was printed in curving stylized letters. The background color of the can was pink.

However, an increasing number of men started switching to low-calorie drinks. Eventually, surveys began to show that one third of Tab drinkers were males. The great majority of them were not especially interested in dieting. They simply wanted a light, low-calorie drink for other reasons. Even though the basic product remained the same, consumers were shifting their reasons for buying Tab. To help fit the brand's image to suit its new market position, Coca-Cola made some changes in Tab's promotional mix. Among the promotional techniques used to give a slightly different meaning to the product was a revamped package approach. The new package is meant to be more "masculine." The letters that spell out the brand name are sharper and straighter. The background color has been switched from hot pink to dark red.

**The Promotional Role of Package Design in Self-Service Selling Situations.** In one study, a research team actually watched the way people shopped in supermarkets. They reported as follows: "Twenty-two percent—more than one in five—of the cereal shoppers and the detergent shoppers spent enough time inspecting the package to cause the observer to make note of the fact. The figure for candy was lower—sixteen percent. These figures suggest that it is worth paying close attention to what the package looks like, how it feels, and what it says since people look them over carefully."[13]

In self-service shopping, the package must be easy to find. If at all possible, it should be made to stand out from the crowd. The package design used to introduce the Reach toothbrush provides an excellent example of how this can affect your strategy. The Reach toothbrush has unique functional design features. Its entry was supported by heavy television advertising. As for the package design, an advertising agency executive described the thinking this way:

> At the drug store, all toothbrush packages look alike. Have you seen them? Most of them are white with messages all over them and are covered with cellophane so you can see part of the brush. I guess white is supposed to say clean. But everybody else is white. So I designed a pack with a photograph of the whole brush in all its gloriously innovative shape and color on a black field so people can *see* how different we are. The result makes the pack stick out on the shelf like a sore tooth. [14]

***Relating Package Design to Other Elements in Your Promotional Mix.***   In planning the Reach package, more than just shopping behavior was considered. A good package is also built with an eye toward making the rest of your promotional strategy easier to handle and more effective. The same advertising executive just quoted pointed out that television spot commercials for the Reach toothbrush were built around the product and package. Part of this was possible because the package was also designed with an eye to its advertising potential. As he explained it, "Television puts a whole new dimension into packaging, creating challenges in visual communication unknown to other media. The reader can stay with a print ad as long as he wants; in a commercial, the package has to register in seconds. Commercials typically end with a picture of the product."[15]

## *Incidental Physical Characteristics as Surrogate Cues*

For the most part, incidental physical characteristics involve situations in which you must make some decisions regarding product qualities that will not affect the functional delivery of customer benefits. The illustration involving mouthwash colors, which opened this section, is a good example. Such decisions are commonly required regarding product color, odor, and texture, when these are unrelated to the main or secondary benefits that consumers seek from your brand. Because your choices will not really change product performance, they might not seem critically important. However, because such surrogate cues can influence the way customers perceive performance, they can make all the difference in the world. The key question to ask yourself is, "What will be the effect of this characteristic in helping customers understand and appreciate my brand's functional features and benefits?" The following examples can give you a better feel for how this works in practice.

***Buttery-Colored Soap.***   A major benefit used in the promotion of Tone soap is its ability to moisturize the skin. The functional feature that provides this benefit is cocoa butter, which is talked about in Tone's advertising. The color of the soap is nonfunctional. The makers of Tone can choose any color they wish for the soap, but because the message they want to convey is "moisturizing with cocoa butter," their color choice is buttery yellow. This choice is not based on mere executive imagination. It is used because field studies reveal this is the color that reflects the consumer's image of cocoa butter. The surrogate cue of color is built to reinforce consumer perception of a major functional feature.[16]

***Yellow-Skinned Chickens.***   How can color help a customer decide whether a chicken will be succulent? In the northeastern part of the United States, many consumers do it by looking for a yellow-skinned chicken. In the New York City area, a producer named Frank Perdue is said to have increased his market share in the chicken business from one percent to almost twenty percent over a nine-year period.[17] Among other things, Perdue makes sure that his chickens have a golden yellow skin by using a heavy mixture of marigold petals and corn in their feed.

***Multicolored Toothpastes and Cold Remedies.***  A trade publication reported on the trend toward multicolored products by concluding, "Those stripes of color in new toothpastes are pretty. More importantly, they communicate the claim of 'new and improved.' . . . And would a cold remedy like Contac be as successful in promoting its time-release idea if the grains were all laboratory white, instead of varied colors?"[18]

***Soap Odors—From Carbolic Acid to Roses.***  Again using bar soap as an example, think of how odors—another feature not usually functional in this product category—can affect consumer perception of qualities. The following quote comes from a trade journal of the soap and cosmetics industry:

> The marketing people's responsibility is to coordinate the product, its advertising, its initial impression, its continuing impression and its actual and perceived performance. . . . While fragrance does not contribute to the cleansing ability of soap, it can prejudice a user to expect a certain performance quality. A strong, carbolic odor, as was featured in the old "Lifebuoy," gave the impression that the soap was "tough" against body odor and "was really strong." The same soap base today, with a rose or lilac fragrance, could, however, make the user perceive the product as a gentle, mild soap. "Dove," for example, which is considered a "gentle" soap, mild to the skin, has a soft rose scent which reinforces its "mildness" positioning. [19]

***Odor and the Perceived Quality of Facial Tissues.***  One consultant ran a consumer test with facial tissues. Using a standard brand, he scented one half with one fragrance, the other half with another fragrance. A consumer sample was then asked to rate and compare tissues from each of the two groups. Facial tissues scented one way were described as "elegant, expensive and high quality." The same tissues, carrying a different odor, scored low on the same qualities; they were seen as a product to be used mainly in the kitchen.[20]

***Hard-to-Pour Ketchup.***  Consider the texture of ketchup. Thickness might seem to be a functional disadvantage. Actually, market tests show buyers think of a good ketchup as one containing "many tomatoes"; and they judge the number of tomatoes in the ketchup on the basis of how it pours. The slower it goes, the more tomatoes it is perceived as containing. For this reason, Heinz ketchup built an advertising campaign around a "hard-to-pour" theme.[21]

***Lumpy Coffee.***  Texture can also influence consumers' acceptance of a product like freeze-dried coffee, and it may not necessarily do so in the way common sense might suggest. For example, at the time Maxim freeze-dried coffee was being developed by General Foods, the company found there were two ways of producing it. Under one method, the finished product would look very much like regular ground coffee. Under the other, it would have a lumpy or chunky appearance dissimilar from that which consumers associate with coffee. Common sense might suggest the first form would be preferred by consumers. However, consider the following report of the results of test marketing.

In consumer home-testing, the granules were greatly preferred. After all shouldn't a product which is meant to taste like ground coffee look like ground coffee? But the lumpy product gave better market test results and eventually a large market share to General Foods. Why? Consumers were more likely to accept Maxim as a new form of coffee—different from conventional instants—when it looked unlike anything else they had seen before. [22]

*Using Incidental Physical Characteristics in Your Promotional Mix*

After you have made sure your product has the functional features your consumers want, you often have some choices about seemingly nonfunctional features. On the surface they might appear unimportant; they are not really what the product is "all about." As a practical matter, however, because of their potential roles as surrogate cues, nonfunctional features may be critical to communicating the proper promotional messages that sell your functional product features. The examples above might suggest that incidental physical characteristics are the concern only of product designers and top-level promotional strategists—people who make the original decisions that influence everything else in the promotional mix. This is not necessarily true.

***Using Incidental Characteristics to Dramatize Important Benefits.*** As a salesperson, a publicist, a developer of sales promotion, or an advertising strategist, you can employ such characteristics to help you in building explicit messages. Indeed, very often you may find you have to use them. Especially in cases where a functional feature that relates to an important benefit is not readily self-evident to consumers through examination or use of the product, your most effective explicit approach may be to demonstrate that functional advantage by associating it with a self-evident surrogate cue. Consider such features as nutritional value in a food product, decay prevention ability in a dentifrice, or potency in a vitamin preparation. Although each of these is important to consumers, they are difficult for consumers to measure in any direct sense. In framing your explicit promotional messages, it is quite possible that portrayal of your product's differential advantages can be made both more vivid and more understandable by relating them to easily measured surrogate cues. This was the basic situation illustrated in the Heinz ketchup example above. Even when a desired benefit is rather readily measurable by consumers, some degree of emphasis on association with a surrogate cue may be desirable as a means of reinforcing consumer perceptions. The Tone soap example given earlier illustrates this second situation.

***A Suggested Three-Step Procedure.*** In summary, as a strategist working on an explicit promotional program for a predesigned brand, part of your job may frequently involve the following three-step procedure in dealing with incidental physical characteristics: (1) examine your brand to see what cues it possesses that can convey positive meaning, (2) study these characteristics to determine how they may influence the way customers interpret your brand's delivery of important functional features and their benefits, and (3) determine if and how you want to use such cues to help you build your explicit mix (e.g., emphasizing them in a way that clearly connects them with more or less hard-to-demonstrate functional features).

# PRICE AS AN IMPLICIT PROMOTIONAL ELEMENT

Marketing textbooks usually treat price and promotion as separate and different parts of the marketing mix and they do so with good reason. Viewed from one aspect, pricing decisions are separate and different from promotional decisions. It is this nonpromotional aspect of price that is most heavily covered in the literature of marketing and economics. A good deal of that coverage tells you how to analyze revenue curves and cost curves to find your most profitable price point. The assumption is that your other marketing variables—including promotion—have established a more or less fixed demand curve from which you are now working.

But there is another dimension to pricing decisions that is really promotional in nature. A writer who has studied the effects of price on consumer attitudes states that "the research findings indicate the importance of considering price as a communication technique similar to, for example, advertising."[23]

Because price can be viewed from at least two different perspectives, we have distinguished them as *the transactional dimension* and *the informational dimension*. In its transactional dimension, price is simply the amount of money (or its equivalent) for which a given quantity of product is bought, sold, or offered for sale. From this standpoint, you would usually assume that the lower your price the more attractive your product will be to consumers. For example, when airlines cut their fares in the late 1970s, traveling by air became more attractive because it was more economical. This is the most standard view of pricing in marketing and economics. However, in its informational dimension, price is a communication to prospective buyers that may have an opposite effect. Because buyers may use price to judge a brand's quality, the lower your price is, the less attractive your brand may be to consumers if the lower price suggests it is inferior in some respect. Two researchers in the field have concluded, "Higher prices have a denotative meaning and will have a tendency to repel persons with limited resources as well as to attract because of their apparent connotative or quality implications."[24]

Pricing, then, is part of your implicit promotional mix insofar as it influences the way a product offering is likely to be interpreted or judged, in other words, in its informational dimension only. Because the two dimensions of price decisions have the potential to work at cross purposes with each other, what can you do to handle the situation? How might this affect the rest of your promotional mix? To examine some suggested answers, we will start with a brief review of the traditional demand curve, or transactional dimension, and then consider the informational dimension of price.

## THE TRANSACTIONAL DIMENSION

You are probably familiar with the downsloping demand curve shown in Figure 2.2. It is at the heart of analyzing the effects of price on your sales and profit from a purely transactional point of view.

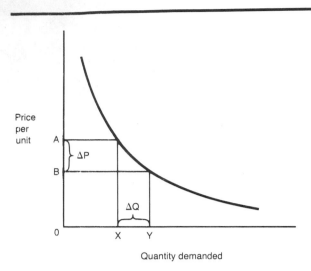

FIGURE 2.2 The price-quantity relationship

Price per unit

A

ΔP

B

ΔQ

0    X   Y

Quantity demanded

The figure illustrates the principle that the less you charge for your brand, the more of it you will be able to sell. For example, if you set your price high—say at point A—you will only be able to sell the amount indicated by letter X. If you lower your price to the point indicated by letter B, you will be able to increase unit sales to the amount shown by letter Y. Pricing viewed in this way—from a purely transactional standpoint—is an important part of your marketing mix. However, though it will interact with your promotional strategy, it is not really a direct part of your promotional strategy mix per se.

## THE INFORMATIONAL DIMENSION

The downsloping demand curve in Figure 2.2 is based on a number of assumptions. One of those assumptions is that the consumer has full information about your brand and all other brands. Furthermore, he or she secured that information without considering the price. In other words, the price does not tell your customer anything about the features or benefits of your brand. It simply tells how much she or he has to pay to obtain it. As suggested above, this assumption does not always seem to hold true. Sometimes, higher prices seem to increase demand. One often mentioned example concerns the introduction of home permanent kits. When these were first put on the market, they were offered at a very low price, but they did not sell well. When they were reintroduced at a substantially higher price, the home permanent kits were much more successful.

There are also more recent examples. Reportedly, a new brand of mustard was packaged in a crockery jar and put on the market at 49¢. At that price, the mustard did not find too many buyers. When the price was raised to $1.00, sales increased significantly.[25] Even in the industrial market, where buyers are supposed to be better informed and more "rational," they may use price as a

*Product and Price as Implicit Promotion*

guide to judging quality. One writer cites the example of a purchasing agent who apparently judged water pipes on the basis of their price. In his view the highest priced pipe was "the Cadillac" of the industry.[26]

Because cases like this keep cropping up, there is suspicion that the informational dimension of price can often overwhelm the transactional dimension. If this is true, the downsloping demand curve could be deceiving you. One alternative that has been suggested is the rather curious looking "backward bending" demand curve, shown in Figure 2.3. This seems to be saying that you will attain your highest volume by avoiding either a price that is too high or a price that is too low. However, it does not really help you analyze your exact situation very well. Nor does it say much about potential links with other promotional elements.

*Price as an Information Input*

The possibility that buyers may use price as an important source of information about a brand has been tested in a variety of studies. Generally, such studies seem to support the idea that customers may look at a higher-priced brand as being a "better brand." They also suggest that price, as an implicit promotional information input, may be especially important in situations such as the following:

1. When customers do not have enough information or experience to help them compare brands on relevant features, and are therefore forced to use price as a way to rate brands
2. When the product seems complex and there is high risk in making an incorrect choice
3. When there is a social prestige—or "snob appeal"—associated with owning certain brands; paying a high price may almost provide its own reward, since it tells people that you can afford the best
4. When the absolute difference between prices is rather small; in such cases, customers may choose the higher-priced brand because they feel they are

**FIGURE 2.3 The backward bending demand curve**

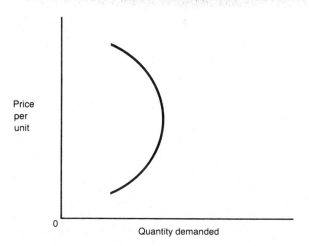

Price per unit

0

Quantity demanded

receiving a sense of assurance of higher product quality for "just a few pennies more."

All of this suggests that, in considering price as a promotional element, you should begin by trying to understand how people in your specific market segment use price to gauge brand value when shopping in your specific product category; its influence is likely to vary by both segments and product types.

*Handling Price as Part of the Promotional Mix*

It has been suggested that consumers use price as a source of information about a product by thinking in terms of a *reference price*.[27] When customers are familiar with a product category, they tend to have some idea of different reference prices connected with each quality level of brands in that category. For example, if you were shopping for tennis rackets, you might soon get the idea that low-priced rackets sell for around twenty dollars, middle-quality rackets sell for around fifty dollars, and high-quality rackets sell for around one hundred dollars.

You would probably then start to judge different brands on the basis of how close they came to one of those reference prices. If you were looking for a middle-quality racket, you would expect to pay about fifty dollars. Suppose that a clerk shows you a racket priced at thirty dollars. Based on the price information alone, you might write it off as being in the low-quality range. To convince you that it really is in the middle-quality range, the clerk—or more probably the manufacturer's advertising—would have to provide you with more information to explain why that price is so far below your reference price, even though the brand still has the functional features you want.

***Offsetting the Informational Aspect of a Lower Price.*** In the television advertisement shown in Figure 2.4, the J. C. Penney company wants to take advantage of the downsloping demand curve—the transactional dimension of price. To do this, they feature a low price. They are also aware of the informational dimension of price and the possibly negative effect it can have if it runs below a reference price. Therefore, they have structured their explicit promotional message to offset that effect. Their advertisement is telling you that you should not be misled by the informational dimension of their price. They provide a reason for that low and otherwise attractive price; it is due to giving up a nonessential product feature (some extra decorative stitching). Thus, explicit promotion explains the low price in terms of a product feature that is not important to many people. In that way, it seeks to reinstate high ratings on the features that are important.

***Using the Informational Aspect of a Higher Price to Reinforce the Rest of Your Promotion.*** Suppose you are in the reverse situation. Your price is higher than the reference price for competing brands. You might want to do just the opposite from the J. C. Penney example. You might actually feature your higher price as proof of an additional or better functional product feature. This is what the makers of L'Oreal Preference Hair Color do in the advertise-

**FIGURE 2.4 Offsetting the informational aspect of price through advertising strategy**

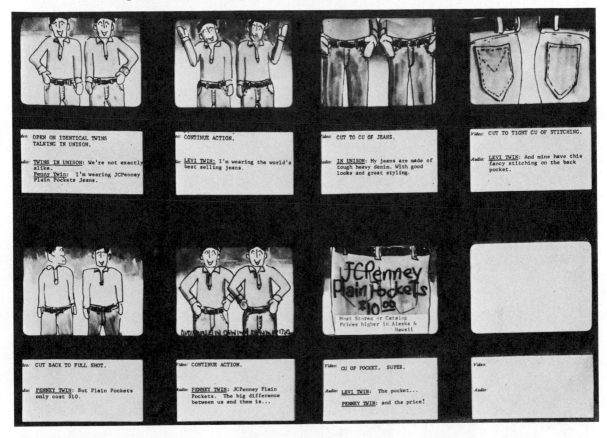

Courtesy of J.C. Penney.

ment you see in Figure 2.5. The informational dimension of a higher-than-reference price is explicitly promoted because it helps reinforce the appeal of superiority in functional features. It both supports and is supported by the total advertising appeal.

***Promoting Reduced Prices.*** Again, because of the informational dimension of price, it has been suggested that, "The perception of a sale price may depend on the position of the price in the range (relative to some reference price). . . . For example, buyers might react more favorably if a $600 television were on sale at $450 than if the set were advertised as being on sale at $299."[28]

To reap the benefit of increased sales from reduced prices, and still avoid the possibly negative informational effects, sellers often "dress up" temporary price cuts. Frequently, this involves the use of some sales promotion device, for example, a coupon or a factory rebate offer. A part of the rationale underlying such techniques is that the informational dimension of the higher regular price is retained, because the lower transactional price is made available only under certain restricted conditions.

*The Informational Dimension* 49

**FIGURE 2.5 How the informational aspect of price can reinforce an advertising appeal**

# L'OREAL PREFERENCE HAIR COLOR
## "YOU CAN SEE"

LENGTH: 30 SECONDS      COMM'L NO.: ZCJP 9301

MEREDITH: You can't touch my hair.

But you can see how luxurious my hair color makes it feel.

You can see how soft.

You can see why I color my hair with Preference by L'Oreal.

Rich color, soft hair.

It looks like it feels, like silk. See?

Preference by L'Oreal is the most expensive. But you can see, it's worth it.

And so am I.

Because you're worth it.

Preference. Because you're worth it.

Courtesy of Cosmair, Inc.

***Interactions of Price and Other Promotional Elements.*** The issue of price demonstrates the interdependence of promotional elements. When your price runs significantly below or above some competitive reference price it may take on a special promotional implication. Sometimes this may have to be offset by another promotional technique; sometimes it can be used to strengthen another promotional technique. In either case, it should be thought of as part of your total promotional strategy process and blended with the other elements.

# SUMMARY

Functional product features form the core around which the rest of the promotional mix must be built. To the extent that your brand has functional features that "speak for themselves," are exclusive, and are important to a large segment of consumers, the burden on the rest of the mix is lightened. Rarely, however, will you start with functional features so strong that they do an optimum job by themselves. Functional features generally must be "spoken for" through explicit promotion. Often they need reinforcement from other implicit elements.

Surrogate cues are nonfunctional product features and include your brand name, package design, and incidental physical characteristics. The brand name is probably most important when a product is new. An effective name can help secure consumer trial of the product and start it off with positive meaning to prospective buyers. Package designs and materials can influence the type of rating that customers give a product, even when the package itself is not making any real contribution to the delivery of the benefit. Packaging should also be considered in terms of how it can be used in the explicit promotional mix, for example how it can add to the power of television commercials or in-store displays.

Incidental physical characteristics include such things as odor, color, and texture, and can be important features even when they provide no functional benefit. Consumers will probably not rate them as having much meaning or importance when asked about them. To learn what their effect is may require market experimentation.

Price has two distinct dimensions—transactional and informational. Because the two can influence product demand in opposite ways, they often have to be balanced through some explicit promotional technique. For example, a low price tends to increase demand because of its transactional effect but may tend to decrease demand because of its informational effect. The solution may lie in using an explicit element, such as advertising, to explain away the negative informational effect while exploiting the positive transactional effect.

In looking at the implicit elements of promotion individually, it becomes apparent that a discussion of one element tends to lead almost automatically to consideration of other promotional elements—both implicit and explicit—because they generally interact with each other.

## DISCUSSION QUESTIONS

1. In developing a new product, why is it desirable for a firm to prestudy the explicit promotional implications of a highly innovative new feature?
2. ABC Cosmetics Company has just added a new ingredient to their skin care cream. It is highly effective in minimizing wrinkles caused by aging. This new ingredient is slow acting. The results are not noticeable until after at least six weeks of consistent use.
    a. Is the new ingredient functional or a surrogate cue?
    b. In terms of persuasive communication, what special problems does this feature present?
    c. Discuss alternative ways to deal with these problems.
    d. Traditionally, ABC has promoted this brand to women between 18 and 30 years of age. What problems might the firm encounter if they decided to sell the product to older women?
3. In the example above, ABC Cosmetics Company has decided to create another, entirely new brand that contains the new wrinkle-minimizing ingredient. In choosing the brand name, what are some of the more important points the firm should consider when generating a list of suitable names?
4. Working from the points you suggested in answering question 3, propose three different names for this new brand and explain your reasoning.
5. Several examples were cited regarding the transactional and informational dimensions of price. Define and distinguish between these two dimensions. Which is most likely to predominate in your consideration of a promotional strategy for a new product? Why?
6. What is meant by a "reference price"? If the new cosmetics product offered by ABC is priced substantially higher than competing products, how might the firm use the informational dimension of price to advantage when designing a promotional strategy?
7. Higher-priced brands may be regarded more favorably by consumers. Is this fact consistent with the transactional dimension of price? Cite additional situations in which the informational dimension may help consumers evaluate brands. Why might a company feel it has to justify reduced prices?
8. Choose three product categories and then compare the three best-selling brands within each in terms of how close they approach the "ideal brand" as described in the chapter.
9. Discuss surrogate cues that might be of special importance in the promotion of the following product categories: yogurt, breakfast cereal, cough syrup, home computers, skis.
10. Pick three popular brands of laundry detergent and analyze their package designs. What tentative changes would you suggest for each brand and why?

## REFERENCES

1. Richard B. Chase and Nicholas J. Aquilano, *Production and Operations Management,* 3rd ed. (Homewood, IL: Richard D. Irwin, Inc., 1981), p. 3.
2. Edward G. Harness, *Some Basic Beliefs About Marketing* (Cincinnati, OH: The Procter and Gamble Company, 1977), p. 13.
3. Bernard Wysocki, Jr., "Punching Is Furious in Tylenol-Datril Fight for Non-Aspirin Users," *Wall Street Journal,* 24 May 1976, p. 1.
4. "Marketing Profiles—Johnson & Johnson," *Advertising Age,* 10 September 1981, p. 100.
5. "A Death Blow for Tylenol?," *Business Week,* 18 October 1982, p. 151.
   Michael Waldholz, "Bold Bid to Return Tylenol to Homes Is Called Risky by Marketing Experts," *Wall Street Journal,* 15 November 1981, p. 12.
   "Burke Reflects on Tylenol Woes," *Advertising Age,* 22 November 1982, p. 50.
   Michael Waldholz, "Speedy Recovery," *Wall Street Journal,* 24 December 1982, pp. 1, 19.
6. Louis H. Goldish, "High Technology Market Re-

search Can Find Foibles That Affect Sales," *Marketing News,* 13 July 1979, p. 4.

7. James F. Engel, Wayne W. Talarzyk, and C. M. Larson, eds., *Cases in Promotional Strategy* (Homewood, IL: Richard D. Irwin, Inc., 1971), pp. 86–95.

8. Gerald Zaltman and Melanie Wallendorf, *Consumer Behavior: Basic Findings and Management Implications* (New York: John Wiley and Sons, 1979), p. 3.

9. Willard H. Doyle, "Brand Still Crucial, But Now It's 'manufactured,' not dreamed up," *Marketing News,* 10 February 1978, p. 12.

10. "Name Game," *Time,* 31 August 1981, p. 42.

11. James U. McNeal and Linda M. Zeren, "Brand Name Selection for Consumer Products," *Business Topics,* Spring 1981, pp. 35–39.

12. Carl McDaniel and R. C. Baker, "Convenience Food Packaging and the Perception of Product Quality," *Journal of Marketing*, October 1977, p. 58.

13. William D. Wells and Leonard A. Lo Sciuto, "Direct Observation of Purchasing Behavior," *Journal of Marketing Research,* August 1966, p. 232.

14. Herman Davis, "Harness That Marketing Knowledge, and Let the Package Reflect It," *Advertising Age,* 8 May 1978, p. 45. (Reprinted with the permission of Advertising Age.)

15. *Ibid.*

16. "Redesigned 'Tone' Package Boosts New Soap's Sales," *Soap/Cosmetics/Chemical Specialties,* October 1974, p. 41.

17. William Copulsky and Katherin Marton, "Sensory Cues; You've Got to Put Them Together," *Product Marketing,* January 1977, p. 31. .

18. *Ibid.*

19. "Creating Bar Soap Fragrances," *Soap/Cosmetics/Chemical Specialties,* November 1977, p. 31.

20. Copulsky and Marton, "Sensory Cues; You've Got to Put Them Together," p. 31.

21. *Ibid.,* p. 32.

22. *Loc. cit.,* p. 33.

23. Benson P. Shapiro, "Price Reliance: Existence and Sources," *Journal of Marketing Research,* August 1973, p. 293.

24. John J. Wheatley and John S. Y. Chiu, "The Effects of Price, Store Image, and Product and Respondent Characteristics on Perceptions of Quality," *Journal of Marketing Research,* May 1977, p. 185.

25. Kent B. Monroe, *Pricing: Making Profitable Decisions* (New York: McGraw-Hill, 1979), p. 38.

26. *Ibid.,* p. 45.

27. Fred E. Emory, "Some Psychological Aspects of Price," in Bernard Taylor and Gordon Wills (eds.), *Pricing Strategy* (Princeton, N.J.: Brandon/Systems, 1970), pp. 98–111.

28. Monroe, *Pricing: Making Profitable Decisions,* p. 45.

*Summary*

53

# CHAPTER THREE

# Explicit Promotion and Approaches to an Optimum Mix

## FOCUS OF THE CHAPTER

Functional features, surrogate cues, and pricing dimensions are all direct parts of your product offering. Explicit promotion is not. In one way or another, it communicates about your brand, often without the product's physical presence.

At this point we will examine the explicit elements and compare their strengths and limitations. We will then consider particular purposes that each element can serve in your total plan and conclude with a discussion of three approaches you can use to interrelate the explicit elements to build a coordinated strategy.

## THE POWER AND PURPOSES OF EXPLICIT PROMOTION

As you have just read, implicit promotion is highly important, but rarely can it do an adequate job by itself. It almost always needs the help that explicit promotion provides. With the explicit elements you can do the following:

1. Work to assure that your brand is widely available and easy to purchase
2. Urge prospects to try your brand and give it a chance to speak for itself

3. Encourage influential sources to speak favorably about your brand—to recommend, explain, endorse, or prescribe it
4. Dramatize features so that they are easier for customers to recognize and appreciate when they use your product
5. Extend the meaning of product features or price to inject greater force and enthusiasm into the buying situation
6. Remind customers of features and benefits they learned about from using your brand in the past but may have forgotten between usage situations
7. Provide your customers with vivid illustrations of how your product's features and benefits work to make their lives better and more enjoyable

With all these capabilities, it is no surprise that explicit promotion is such a vital force in our economy and such an exciting field in which to work. There are even people who argue that some kinds of explicit promotion can add genuine value to certain types of products. For example, in Chapter 1 a brief reference was made to the highly successful promotion of Perrier mineral water in the United States (see p. 15). As noted, Perrier increased its annual American sales from less than $1 million to over $30 million in the first two years of its program. To a large extent, the success of Perrier stemmed from the power of explicit promotion to enrich the benefits the brand was able to deliver to consumers.

Essentially, Perrier is simply carbonated water with some mineral content. Viewed in another way, it is an unflavored soft drink that is priced much higher than most flavored soft drinks. However, by means of its advertising and publicity programs, Perrier was endowed with a sophisticated character. Orson Welles extolled its merits in ponderous tones during television commercials. Through publicity efforts, Perrier was associated with such "in" sports as jogging and tennis. Expert observers have concluded that much of the brand's appeal is due to its ability to enhance the user's social position.[1] This ability, in turn, is largely the result of well-conceived advertising and publicity efforts. In part, many people may drink Perrier because their friends regard it as the "right thing" to drink. To the extent that advertising and publicity have led to that belief, it could be argued that they have added a type of value to the brand that actually exceeds the value of its basic ingredients.

## THE ELEMENTS OF EXPLICIT PROMOTION

This chapter introduces the explicit elements of advertising, personal selling, publicity, and sales promotion. Later chapters will expand on each of them in much greater detail. As depicted in Figure 3.1, they should be thought of as potential parts of a total system or mix of persuasive communication flows. At the end of the chapter, we will return to a consideration of the total promotional mix and suggest decision procedures that can help you in planning its general structure.

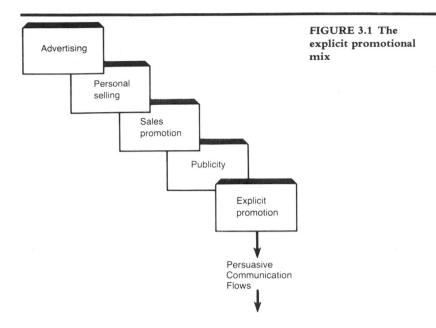

FIGURE 3.1 The
explicit promotional
mix

## ADVERTISING

**The Nature and
Impact of
Advertising**

*"Advertising is any paid form of non-personal presentation and promotion of ideas, goods, or services by an identified sponsor."*[2] Advertising is the most omnipresent of the explicit promotional elements. Most of us are surrounded by it almost every day of our lives. By one estimate, the average American consumer is exposed to over 2,100 advertisements and commercials during an average week.[3] Such a degree of exposure to advertising has two important implications. First, it is a very potent promotional technique. The fact that you see and hear so much advertising means a great many companies must be willing to invest in it very heavily. In turn, this implies they have good reason to believe that advertising achieves the results they seek. The stories of outstanding marketing successes in which advertising has played a major role support the strength of that belief. Second, advertising must operate in an extremely competitive environment. When you use it, you have to begin by realizing that your advertisement will be one of a multitude in which each is struggling with the others for the attention of buyers.

**Advertising
Expenditures and
Media Trends**

Figure 3.2 depicts a different impact of advertising. When advertising expenditures are traced over a period of time, you can see it is not only a big business in the United States but one that is still growing vigorously. During the twentieth century, total United States advertising budgets rose from a relatively modest $450 million in 1900, to over $53 billion in 1980. For the most part, these advertising dollars are spent in the "measured media"— newspapers, magazines, television, radio, business and farm publications, and

*Explicit Promotion and Approaches to an Optimum Mix*

outdoor advertising. Taken together, these account for roughly two-thirds of the total expenditure. The remainder goes to direct mail and to miscellaneous advertising forms including matchbooks, catalogues, programs, and circulars.

Figure 3.3 traces the changes in percentages of dollars going to major media types between 1950 and 1982. Not surprisingly, television has been the big gainer. Its percentage increase has come mainly at the expense of newspapers, magazines, and radio. Despite their drops in percentages, however, all of these latter media have still gained handsomely in actual dollars because of the fast rise in total advertising expenditures.

## The Comparative Advantages of Advertising

Each element of explicit promotion has certain fairly unique advantages. The strong points most widely discussed for advertising are low cost per contact, repetitive message potential, creative versatility, relaxed atmosphere of message presentation, and the impressiveness of the mass media.

*Low Cost per Contact.* The base price for a nationally run advertisement can be very high. However, because so many people see or hear that ad, the cost per person reached can be amazingly low. A thirty-second network television

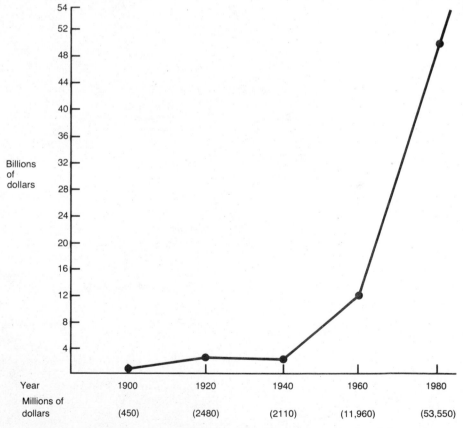

**FIGURE 3.2 Rise in United States advertising expenditures during the twentieth century**

| Year | 1900 | 1920 | 1940 | 1960 | 1980 |
|------|------|------|------|------|------|
| Millions of dollars | (450) | (2480) | (2110) | (11,960) | (53,550) |

Source: Prepared for *Advertising Age* by Robert J. Coen, McCann-Erickson, Inc.

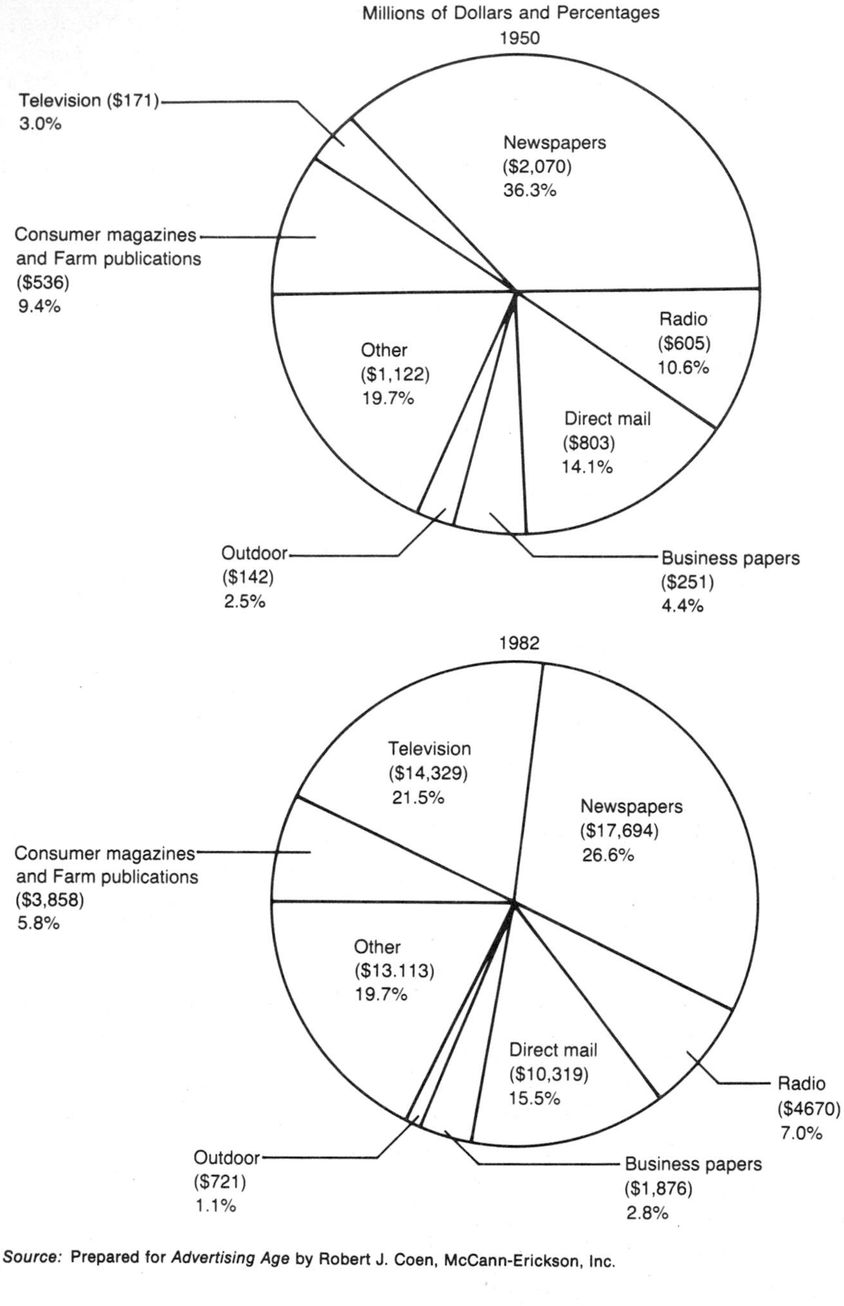

Millions of Dollars and Percentages

1950

Television ($171)
3.0%

Newspapers
($2,070)
36.3%

Consumer magazines
and Farm publications
($536)
9.4%

Radio
($605)
10.6%

Other
($1,122)
19.7%

Direct mail
($803)
14.1%

Outdoor
($142)
2.5%

Business papers
($251)
4.4%

1982

Television
($14,329)
21.5%

Newspapers
($17,694)
26.6%

Consumer magazines
and Farm publications
($3,858)
5.8%

Other
($13.113)
19.7%

Direct mail
($10,319)
15.5%

Radio
($4670)
7.0%

Outdoor
($721)
1.1%

Business papers
($1,876)
2.8%

FIGURE 3.3 Distribution of
estimated advertising
expenditures among media
in 1950 and 1982

*Source:* Prepared for *Advertising Age* by Robert J. Coen, McCann-Erickson, Inc.

*Explicit Promotion and Approaches to an Optimum Mix*

commercial shown on a weekday evening may cost you eighty or ninety thousand dollars. If it exposes your message to 15 million households, which would not be uncommon, it costs you roughly half a penny for each household that sees and hears your message. An executive of the Pepsi Cola company drew the following cost comparison:

> Of course, the basic reason why companies such as mine prefer media advertising to other more personal forms of selling are economy and efficiency. There is literally no way to count how many salesmen at the front door it would take to reach the number of people who see and hear a television commercial. But even if such a massive sales force could be assembled, the cost of their salaries or commissions would raise product prices astronomically. [4]

*Repetitive Message Potential.* As you will see later, repetition can be an important factor in some types of learning. In a sense, promotion "teaches" customers about things like brand names and product benefits. When frequent repetition is needed to get the teaching job done, advertising probably has more power than any other promotional element. Think of how many times you have been exposed to certain television commercials or print ads. If a salesperson tried to call on you five or ten or more times per week just to deliver the same short message, you would not put up with it. Yet a piece of advertising can do just that at a price that makes it affordable.

*Creative Versatility.* Advertisers can use fanciful artwork, flamboyant techniques, and even absurd situations to communicate. By contrast, the other forms of explicit promotion—especially publicity and personal selling—tend to be relatively straightforward and matter-of-fact in their presentations. When forcefully different creative methods are needed to attract attention or dramatize features and benefits, advertising often has a distinct edge.

*The Relaxed Atmosphere of a Nonpersonal Presentation.* When you deal with a salesperson, you may feel yourself under at least a slight amount of tension. It is a face-to-face encounter to which you must respond. You are probably going to be asked to make some kind of decision. When you hear or view or read an ad, you are under no pressure to make any kind of decision immediately. One result could be that you are less likely to "fight" the message. To the extent that you do not try to "defend" actively against advertisements—perhaps not even taking them seriously in many instances—it can be easier for advertisers to deliver a message without much resistance.

*The Impressiveness of the Mass Media.* There is a general feeling and some evidence that the mass media are viewed as having power and prestige simply because they are mass media. After all, we rely on sources such as television, newspapers, radio, and magazines both to entertain us and tell us about the world. They deal with and show important events and important people. It has been found that even a low-prestige magazine can upgrade the image of a product advertised in it.[5] Other research suggests that "a strong link between quality and national advertising exists in the minds of consumers."[6] The more national advertising people think a brand is receiving, the more likely it is that they will see the brand as being of high quality. Some of the prestige of the mass media seems to reflect on the products advertised in them.

**Limitations of Advertising**

If advertising has all of these advantages, why even bother with any other type of explicit promotion? The answer, of course, is that some of the advantages have corresponding disadvantages. These will be uncovered in our treatment of the other explicit elements, especially in the discussion on personal selling. Furthermore, we'll see there are things that advertising simply cannot do—or at least not do nearly as well as one or another of the other elements.

# PERSONAL SELLING

**The Nature and Importance of Personal Selling Activities**

*"Personal selling is oral presentation in a conversation with one or more prospective purchasers for the purpose of making a sale."*[7] Personal selling comes in many different forms: It is a sales clerk answering your questions when you are shopping for clothing; it is a person calling on a retailer and trying to get better shelf position for a particular brand; it is a technically trained sales representative demonstrating a complex piece of equipment to a manufacturing firm; it is an insurance agent working to convince you that you need a larger policy. Not everyone who is classed as a salesperson fits our definition of a promotional strategist. Our concern is really with those salespeople who actively engage in persuasive communication, in other words, those who really try to convince customers to buy, as opposed to those who merely fill orders.

Expenditures on personal selling are not as easy to document and analyze as are those for advertising. Because of its individualized or personal nature, personal selling is not as open to public view or easy measurement. However, it is generally estimated that the total budget for sales forces is much higher than that for advertising media. One estimate placed personal selling expenditures at roughly three times those for advertising.[8]

**Some Comparisons of Personal Selling and Advertising**

In some respects personal selling almost looks like the mirror image of advertising, with the strengths of one being the weaknesses of the other, and vice versa.

*Cost per Call.* The cost per person contacted is usually low for advertising, but high for personal selling. In 1981, the average sales call was estimated as costing $106.[9] Of course, that figure will vary greatly by length of call, kind of product, and kind of salesperson involved. In one sense, cost comparisons between advertising and personal selling have little meaning because the type and length of contact is so different. For example, how do you compare the promotional efficiency of a thirty-second television commercial with that of a thirty-minute sales call? However, the dollars-per-contact comparison does start to suggest that the relative cost feasibility of personal selling depends in part on the potential size of the sale.

*Prestige.*   A sales representative does not automatically command the type of prestige and influence that seems attached to the mass media. She or he is just one human being talking to another. Prestige and influence have to be earned on an individual basis. Often, firms use advertising to prepare the way for salespeople. In a sense, this approach tries to transfer some of the impressiveness and legitimacy of television, radio, or print publications to the personal-selling situation. You will recall from Chapter 1 that the sales chief of Savin Business Products thinks that television commercials help sales representatives "close the sale" (see p. 22), presumably because television conveys an image of importance and solid reputation to the company.

*Atmosphere of the Selling Situation.*   In contrast to advertising, the atmosphere of sales calls can present some special challenges. If, as pointed out above, the nonpersonal nature of advertising helps prospects receive messages in a relaxed and nondefensive mood, the interpersonal nature of selling can do just the opposite. It is not unreasonable to think there may be a fair amount of tension on both sides in many selling situations.

*The Comparative Advantages of Personal Selling*

The straightforward and clear advantages of personal selling are its individualized and customized nature, instant communication feedback, precision in customer targeting, and potential for immediate customer action.

*Individualized and Customized Presentation.*   Each sales call is one-to-one, person-to-person. The customer can ask questions and receive answers. It is possible in personal selling to involve the prospect actively in the presentation. Features and benefits can be put in the context of the exact needs and goals of the specific customer being visited. Objections can be answered directly. Customer interest can be observed and capitalized on at the very moment it occurs. If necessary, your product can often be physically demonstrated. Your customer can frequently be given a "hands on" experience—a trial before purchase that lets implicit promotion speak for itself. These advantages are not attainable through advertising.

*Instant Feedback and Two-Way Interaction.*   An advertising message continues to run its course even if it "loses" the prospect or does not deal with the issues of interest to that prospect. In personal selling, messages can be adjusted. By listening and watching for customer reaction you can make sure your message is getting through in the way you intend. If you are losing a prospect's attention, you can take steps to regain it. If your prospect does not understand what you are saying, you can stop and explain your meaning. If the benefits you are stressing are not striking a favorable response, you can shift your emphasis to a different set of benefits.

*More Precise Customer Targeting.*   Because it aims at audiences on a large-group basis, advertising almost always involves some waste circulation. Many of the advertising contacts for which you pay are lost on people who are not logical prospects for your brand. Because it approaches customers on a one-at-a–time basis, personal selling allows you to pinpoint logical prospects much more effectively. A salesperson can prescreen customers. Some potential buyers may be worth a great deal of effort, whereas some may be worth only a moderate amount. Others may present such a low probability for a possible sale that they are worth no effort at all. In any case, you can pick and choose.

***The Ability to Get Immediate Action.*** In some cases, such as mail-order selling, advertising can actually solicit and obtain an order directly. However, advertising's usual effect is to change people's attitudes so that it is more likely that they will buy your brand at some future time. Advertising generally depends on a delayed response. Of course, not every visit by a salesperson results in a sale. However, the potential to close the sale—write the order on the spot or secure a direct promise of action—is always present. While advertising tends to affect consumer purchase behavior in rather indirect ways, personal selling can in many cases change it directly and immediately.

*The Ideal Climate for Personal Selling*

Given these advantages, it follows that personal selling is especially workable and useful when one or more of the following situations exists: (1) the unit of sale is large enough to justify the cost of a sales call; (2) the product or offering is relatively complex so that detailed explanation and demonstration are needed to make things clear to your customer; and (3) benefits have to be tailored carefully to fit the individual case, especially when there is a need for someone with the training and skills required to study a prospect's problems and propose a solution.

# PUBLICITY

*The Nature of Publicity*

*"Publicity is nonpersonal stimulation of demand for a product, service, or idea by means of commercially significant news planted in the mass media and not paid for directly by a sponsor."*[10] If you could get as much of it as you wanted—and get the kind you wanted—publicity might be your most often used promotional element. It has been pointed out that there are many mountain peaks in Colorado that are higher than Pike's Peak. The reason that Pike's Peak is so much better known than the others is not that it has been advertised, or sold personally, or sales promoted; rather it has been well *publicized*.

*The Comparative Advantages of Publicity*

***Mass Media Prestige Coupled with an Implied Endorsement.*** Advertising acquires some added luster because it appears in the mass media. Publicity not only appears in those same media but also seems to have been initiated by them. For example, when a fashion editor tells you about a new line of clothing, it may impress you more than if the manufacturer had told you the same thing. After all, the manufacturer has a selfish motive. The fashion editor is an independent and acknowledged expert, free to say what he or she wishes. We are assuming, of course, that the publicity is good. Our definition of publicity included the phrase "stimulation of demand." Negative publicity about your product is hardly promotion. It is just bad news.

*Low Cost.*   Technically, the time or space you obtain to publicize your brand is not purchased. It is given to you at the discretion of those managing the media vehicle in which it appears. As a practical matter, however, a firm may invest a good deal of money to generate publicity. Professionally written press releases, specially staged demonstrations, and the background efforts to develop a story with news or entertainment significance can be expensive. Nonetheless, a well-designed publicity program can often get space or time that would cost a great deal more if it had to be purchased in a conventional manner.

*Some Limitations and Questions*

*Lack of Control.*   One of the problems associated with publicity is that it is not fully under your control. You do control the efforts to generate it; for instance, your publicity staff can send out press releases, contact reporters, and put on special events for the media people. However, the message your prospective customers finally receive may be changed, shortened, or slanted quite differently from the way you had planned—or the message may never appear.

*Lack of Continuity.*   Another problem connected with publicity is that it tends to be something you can secure occasionally, but not on a consistent, ongoing basis. To be successful, most promotion has to have a continuous effect. Advertising, personal selling, and sales promotion are much better suited to achieve that effect. Publicity can then supplement them with a periodic, temporary boost. Of course, if your product is short lived by nature and has inherent news appeal, publicity may become a major promotional factor. Motion pictures and some types of fashion clothing are good examples of such product categories. Their newsworthiness is strong. It is also temporary, but then so are their normal market lifespans.

Even if your product is not basically newsworthy, you can sometimes develop a publicity tie-in that adds strength to your total promotional strategy mix for a short period. However, achieving this may call for some high-level imagination on your part. Try to think of how you might get good press coverage to publicize a breakfast cereal or a chain saw, or to introduce a new chemical that retards the wetting of paper to make it stronger and less likely to break. In a later section of this book, we'll be coming back to this topic and you will see how companies obtained publicity for these very products. Furthermore, you will see how they managed to build publicity programs that were well integrated with the rest of their promotional mix and helped make all the elements work together.

# SALES PROMOTION

*The Nature of Sales Promotion*

*"Sales promotion involves marketing activities, other than personal selling, advertising, and publicity, that stimulate consumer purchasing and dealer effectiveness."*[11] American businesses invest heavily in sales promotion. One estimate places total expenditures as being in excess of \$40 billion annually.[12] As the definition above suggests, these dollars are allocated to a variety of quite different explicit

promotional techniques. In one sense, "if it isn't advertising or personal selling or publicity, then it must be sales promotion." This sometimes leads to thinking of sales promotion as a "grab-bag of odds and ends." To look at it in this way is a serious mistake, however. Sales promotion provides you with very powerful ways to tie the rest of your promotional campaign together, thus infusing it with added strength. It should be carefully conceived, considered, and coordinated as a vital part of your promotional mix.

*Types of Sales Promotion*

Sales promotion techniques fall into two broad categories, special communication methods and special offers.

***Special Communication Methods.*** Whereas advertising and publicity generally channel messages through the mass media and personal selling relies on face-to-face conversations, sales promotion offers still other routes with which to communicate with your target audience. The most commonly used special communication methods are the following:

- Advertising specialties
- Point-of-purchase promotional materials
- Point-of-purchase demonstrations
- Sampling
- Visual aid materials for salespeople
- Exhibits at trade and professional shows
- Training programs for resellers and industrial buyers

***Special Offers.*** Most special offers revolve around the issue of pricing. Earlier you read of the dilemma that can occur because of the different directions in which the transactional and informational dimensions of price can work. Some special offers address this problem directly. In others, there is at least a hint that the dilemma is part of the reason for relying on a sales promotion solution. Frequently used types of special offers include:

- Coupons
- Price-off deals and combination offers
- Money-refund offers or factory rebates
- Trade inducements and performance allowances
- Premiums
- Contests and sweepstakes
- Recognition programs

When special offers are made to consumers or resellers they can generate added attention and interest. They are also inducements to spur immediate action—to speed up the sale—because they are frequently tied to some sort of time limit.

| | |
|---|---|
| ***The Comparative Advantages of Sales Promotion*** | The exact advantages you can reap from sales promotion will depend on the specific type you are using. In very general terms, however, its advantages can be summarized in the following ways. |

***Increased Flexibility in Communication Approaches.*** Sales promotion gives you added avenues for reaching customers. The availability of these avenues means you are not limited to the television screen, the printed page, or the spoken word. You can expand your inventory of communication vehicles to include banners, moving displays, life-sized figures of celebrities, and a host of others. When these fit the special needs of your message or open up an opportunity to stand out from competitors, they can offer you unique advantages over more conventional communication carriers.

***Flexibility in Timing.*** Sales promotion is often described as involving "non-recurrent efforts," though perhaps "generally noncontinuous" would be more accurate. Whereas advertising and personal selling tend to be ongoing and more or less continuing activities, many sales promotion efforts are planned to be used only for short periods of time or on an intermittent basis. Sometimes sales promotion techniques are emergency measures. For example, if sales are declining or a competitor introduces a new brand, you may wish to counter with a special contest or coupon offer. To be prepared for situations like this, your annual sales promotion plan may call for holding such a technique in reserve to meet a promotional crisis.

***Potential for Added Excitement.*** When used with imagination and creativity, some sales promotion devices can help make your offer seem more attractive and somewhat out of the ordinary. As one writer puts it, "Nothing delights people more than to get more than they expect in a market transaction. This is as true for what they buy in stores as it is for unexpected gifts and unexpected raises. Sales promotion is a very effective tool for giving consumers more than they expect."[13]

***The Use of Sales Promotion***

Most of the detrimental things that are said about sales promotion concern ways in which it can be misused. It is not a substitute for a sound promotional plan. Rather, it can be an important part of such a plan. The excessive use of a device such as a coupon offer or a contest can wear out the efficacy of that device or make customers suspicious of the basic value of the brand. Sales promotion's noncontinuous nature should not mislead you into treating it as a quickly developed and almost unplanned mechanism. Like all other elements in your promotional mix, sales promotion should be built into a planning process that looks toward the future. Furthermore, that planning process should consider the role of sales promotion in conjunction with other explicit promotional elements. On this basis, it should be judged and used with consideration of how well it will interact with advertising, personal selling, and publicity.

# THE PROMOTIONAL MIX—APPROACHES TOWARD THE "OPTIMUM"

*Marketing Objectives and Promotional Tasks*

Developing your promotional program begins with information about your consumers and your target markets. You must also consider the nature of your competitors and their promotional efforts. With this in mind, you will attempt to set some general marketing objective, which is usually expressed as a targeted market share or dollar sales volume. Your promotional mix is then structured to perform the tasks needed to achieve that marketing objective. For example, if you aim at raising sales to a level that gives your brand a fifteen percent market share, you must plan a promotional mix that you believe will produce that kind of result. Although there is no simple or constant solution as to how your mix should be built, there are some straightforward questions to guide you in starting your approach. Some of the more pertinent questions are as follows:

1. What features do we have—or should we build into our brand—to both deliver benefits sought by our prospects and communicate those benefits as effectively as possible?
2. What pricing strategy will best communicate the quality of our product and also stimulate the sales volume at which we are aiming?
3. What problems or opportunities do our brand's features and price suggest in terms of developing our explicit promotional mix?
4. What goals should we set for each of the elements in the explicit promotional mix? In other words, exactly what are we trying to accomplish with our advertising, our personal selling, and so on?
5. How can the explicit elements be managed to best reinforce each other?
6. How can the promotional goals be achieved? What specific tasks are involved and how much will it cost to accomplish them?
7. Is our marketing objective worth that promotional expenditure? (If not, the objective may have to be revised.)
8. How can we measure our results? Specifically, how can we check to see that an individual element—such as personal selling—is accomplishing the objectives we set for it? Because all the promotional elements interact and work together, it is sometimes difficult to sort things out and determine where you are weak and where you are strong. Insofar as possible, however, you would like to do this so that you can make adjustments in the use of individual elements, as your promotional program moves forward.

*Basic Approaches to Building a Coordinated Mix*

With questions such as these in mind, you are ready to begin considering how to plan and blend your promotional mix. We will consider three possible approaches that can guide you in building your program and coordinating its individual promotional elements. These approaches are not mutually exclusive; indeed, they blend into each other. You can use all three to help build a single promotional program and to keep that program on course. To place them in perspective, each will first be described very briefly. Then, each will be given a more extended discussion with examples of how it can be applied in practice.

**The Lead Element Approach.**   Implicit promotion may be the core around which the total mix revolves. However, many companies feel that once such a core is in place, one or another of the explicit elements becomes the "lead element," which means that it is the most important and the one around which the other explicit elements are built. Because the same lead element is so often chosen by competing firms within the same general industry, this approach might be characterized very generally as saying, "Build your promotional mix and coordinate its individual elements by *studying your competition.*"

**The Customer Decision Stage Approach.**   Consumers can be viewed as decision makers using information to help them choose among alternative products and brands. Consumer decision making is often analyzed by stages, the series of mental steps that people go through to reach their purchase decisions. The various promotional elements—both implicit and explicit—may have different levels of importance as a consumer moves through such decision stages.

A number of different models have been suggested for analyzing decision stages and using them to guide the development of the promotional mix. As a general class, they are often referred to as "hierarchy of effects" models.[14] We will be looking at two such models: a short one called the Customer Flow Model, and a second one, which is slightly longer and more detailed, called the Adoption Process Model. In large measure, the adoption process model amounts to a more extended version of the customer flow model. Regardless of the particular model used, the customer decision stage approach might be characterized generally to be saying, "Build your promotional mix and coordinate its individual elements by *studying your customers*, especially the decision sequence they follow in judging a new brand."

**The Planning Sequence Approach.**   This approach is also concerned with decisions, but not with the decision-making sequence of your customers. Instead, it focuses on your organizational decision-making sequence. Promotional elements work together, therefore they should be planned together. However, you cannot do several different things at once. Very often, you must work with one element at a time, even though you know its effectiveness will depend on how the other elements are planned. Furthermore, such activities as advertising, personal selling, and product development are usually handled by different types of specialists housed in different units of your firm.

Given a timing problem and possibly an organizational communication problem, what kind of planning sequence can help you overcome both of these problems in working toward an optimum mix? Where should you start? What do you do next? How do you ensure coordination?

The planning sequence approach suggests a simple procedure to remind you of total mix considerations even as you work on individual elements. It might be characterized, again very generally, as one that says, "Build your promotional mix by constantly *studying and restudying the potential for interactions among its individual elements.*"

Now, we will take a more extensive look at each of these approaches.

# THE LEAD ELEMENT APPROACH

As noted earlier, many businesses seem to believe that one or another of the explicit promotional elements is the lead element—the prime mover in their explicit promotional mix. Usually, the lead element is either personal selling or advertising. Observation of business practice suggests that the degree of emphasis placed on one or the other of the promotional techniques tends to follow the general pattern illustrated in Figure 3.4.[15] Firms whose products are aimed mainly at industrial buyers usually place extremely heavy emphasis on personal selling. Companies that market durable goods intended chiefly for ultimate consumers (e.g., household appliances and furniture) may also treat personal selling as the lead element, though it is common for them to place a somewhat larger amount of emphasis on advertising than is found among the industrial goods producers. Firms marketing nondurables to ultimate consumers (e.g., drug, cosmetic, and grocery products) are most likely to place the greatest amount of emphasis on advertising. Regardless of the market at which the organization is aiming, in the majority of cases sales promotion and publicity are treated as supporting elements.

## *The Typical Lead Element in Industrial Markets*

If you think back to the types of situations in which personal selling was described as being especially well suited to do the job, you can easily see why it would be so important in many industrial sales situations. Generally speaking, industrial marketing tends to involve higher-value transactions, and requires more complex descriptions, more customizing, and more service. Its needs are often likely to demand face-to-face conversation. The dollar value of each sale is likely to justify the cost.

## *The Typical Lead Element in Marketing to Ultimate Consumers*

When you are selling goods to ultimate consumers, just the opposite is often true. Unit transactions tend to be rather small. The products are often much simpler and easier to understand. As the Pepsi Cola executive quoted earlier pointed out (see p. 59), it would be impossible to find enough salespeople to deliver personal messages repeatedly to soft drink users or the buyers of many

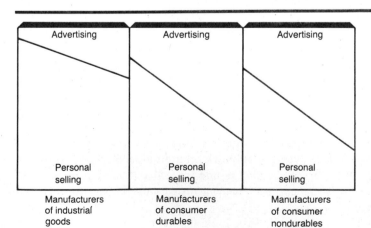

**FIGURE 3.4**
**Generalized relative ranges of emphasis on advertising versus personal selling among different categories of manufacturers**

similar products, even if you could afford it. Therefore, advertising may seem better suited to carry those messages. When advertising leads the mix, the sales force is assigned the task of gaining reseller support and rarely comes into direct contact with a consumer.

There are many exceptions to the above generalizations. Life insurance, for example, is mainly an ultimate consumer item. However, personal selling dominates the field because of both the nature and the size of the sale. Some companies in the industrial field, as we will see later, have dropped all or part of their personal selling effort, at least in the conventional sense, and substituted a different promotional approach.

## Choosing the Right Lead Element

*Variations Among Competing Firms.* The patterns of lead element stress represented in Figure 3.4 are generalizations. In many industries you are likely to find firms that opt to follow a much different course in designing their explicit mix than that used by the rival sellers in their particular product line. For example, at least some sellers of industrial goods might determine that they should pursue a course of investing most heavily in advertising, even though their direct competitors rely mainly on personal selling and devote a relatively small proportion of their total promotional budgets to advertising.

At least one study concentrated on this issue with the goal of assessing the wisdom associated with departing from the industry norm.[16] The product category investigated was peripheral data processing equipment, which is an industrial good. Not surprisingly, it was found that the typical firm in this field stressed personal selling as its lead element. On average, companies allocated almost two-thirds of their promotional expenditures to sales force activities. In contrast, the average maker of peripheral data processing equipment was found to spend only twenty percent on advertising. However, there were exceptions. A few sellers virtually reversed their promotional emphasis, putting two-thirds of their budgets into advertising and rather little into personal selling. Given a situation in which there appears to be an industry standard and where some firms depart drastically from that standard, the question to be asked is, "Does one or another of the promotional elements seem to work best in the lead role for this industry, and if so, is it also the same one being stressed by the majority of the firms?"

The answer has to be approached with some caution. The number of firms that were involved in this study was rather small. Additionally, the survey considered only the explicit portion of the mix. As a result, we know very little about differences between companies in terms of product features, prices, or channels of distribution. We also do not know how long they had been in business or how well they were handling each of the separate elements in the mix. Nonetheless, keeping these points in mind, the conclusion reached by the analyst who conducted the study is most interesting. He divided the firms into two groups and then compared market shares held by each group. Those in Group I all spent eighty percent or more of their promotional budgets on personal selling. Those in Group II all spent forty percent or less in that way. The study found that firms in Group I enjoyed a significant advantage in terms of market share. In consequence, the study concluded that personal selling may be the best choice as a lead element for all firms in the industry, with advertising, sales promotion, and publicity used in distinctly supporting roles.

> The strategy of Group I may be summed up. Personal selling is employed as the major promotional tactic [or lead element] with an allocation of 80% of the promotion budget. The sales force is organized along product lines so the salesmen may develop skills in selling a highly technical product. Advertising, trade shows, and publicity are used in minor supporting roles, probably with the objective of stimulating market awareness [17].

*Using Competitive Practice as an Initial Guide.*   An implication of the analysis above is that starting with a look at the lead element strategy of your competitors could make good sense regardless of your product category. In particular, you will be most interested in looking at the more successful competitors. You will then have to see if your total situation is sufficiently similar to warrant following their course of action. Having done these things, you will know where to start building your explicit mix. Because the lead element is so critical to your promotional enterprise, it is also the logical starting point in terms of defining goals, determining tasks, and considering budgets. The next step is to give careful consideration to the parts that must be played by the supporting promotional elements, especially in terms of the roles they should play in bolstering the lead element.

*Working with Supporting Elements in a Lead Element Approach*

Placing too much reliance on an inappropriate lead element could be an error. Failure to recognize the value and roles of supporting elements could be an equally serious mistake. In some situations, the roles of supporting elements may be somewhat hidden. For example, suppose that you are selling an industrial good or consumer product such as life insurance. Your lead element is personal selling. As one analyst points out, "The reputation of the company (developed through advertising, research and publicity) is very important in determining how the prospects react to the salesman and his presentation. Salesmen from companies with good reputations obtain better response to their efforts."[18]

*Setting Specific and Measurable Objectives.*   The effectiveness of the lead element may seem easy to measure in a situation such as the one above. Determining the influence that supporting elements may have had in building that effectiveness may seem rather difficult to measure. The real key to a useful measurement approach starts with the question, "What specific objectives should we set for each of the supporting elements as well as the lead element in our mix?" If clearly defined objectives have been set in advance, the contribution and effectiveness of each element is more easily measured after the fact. An example of how this can work in practice follows.

*The Northwestern Mutual Case.*[19]   As reported by one of its marketing executives, Northwestern Mutual Life Insurance Company had been spending around $800,000 a year on advertising. There was little evidence of positive results. Company management decided to drop its advertising. Advertising staff members switched most of their time over to developing sales promotion devices to be used by individual salespeople. As this executive pointed out, "[Our] marketing system depended on the person-to-person contact between agent and customer and turned in good results, even without ads."

When the firm decided to review its no-advertising decision, it began with recognition of advertising as a supporting element with a clearly specified mission. "Northwestern Mutual decided to advertise again, only because ads would improve the level of receptivity among prospective buyers and improve agents' and policy owners' morale . . . ."

The new advertising was meant to achieve specific tasks that could be measured for results. And measured they were. Consumer studies were first done to determine what kind of advertising approach would best do the desired job. Then surveys were planned to check on results after the advertising had been run. On the basis of those studies, Northwestern's management could clearly ascertain whether advertising was serving its intended purpose. Results could not be measured in terms of dollar sales but they could be analyzed in terms of customer and agent attitudes.

In reporting the final results, it was noted that "Morale went up among policyowners, as it had among agents. The number of policyowners who said they would be extremely likely to recommend the Northwestern to a friend climbed from a remarkably high level of 50.8% to 55.1%. The number who would buy new insurance from Northwestern increased from 64.3% to 66.4%."

## THE CUSTOMER DECISION STAGE APPROACH

The second way to look at your mix begins with your target consumer group rather than with competitors' practices. As mentioned earlier, we will look at two decision stage models: the customer flow model and the adoption process model. Both tend to speak in terms of innovations, or new products. In practice, you will often find yourself working with a well-established product that does not look much like an innovation upon first examination. However, you should consider the fact that a product can be innovative or new in a number of different ways.

*Types of Innovations*

1. *Totally new.* You may be promoting a completely new product or brand just entering the market. Home devices for videotaping from television sets were a totally new generic product category just a few years ago. A completely new brand of cake mix or fork lift truck could be introduced at any time.

2. *New in terms of improved features.* Your brand may have been on the market for some time but you may be changing it in some way. Very old brands are often repositioned. Some of their functional features and/or surrogate cues are altered and, as a consequence, this means there are new aspects about them that must be promoted as innovations. Cheer laundry detergent has been repositioned again and again. Each time this happens, it can be thought of as a new product, in the "improved feature" sense.

**3.** *New in terms of added uses.* You may be working with a long established brand that is now being promoted for new uses. For example, Arm & Hammer baking soda has been on the market for many decades. A few years back the company began advertising the product as a freshening agent in refrigerators. Still later it was promoted as a way to clean drain pipes, then as a powder for deodorizing carpets. For promotional purposes, every additional use makes it a new product, because each is aimed at satisfying a different set of customers' needs.

**4.** *New to a portion of your target market.* Your brand may be an old one but still be relatively unknown or unused by many consumers. As individuals mature they face new buying situations, and they enter different markets. The brands available in those markets are likely to be new to those consumers. From this standpoint, your brand is always likely to be a new product to a great many potential prospects. Depending on the market in which you are working, the number of target customers involved may range from thousands to millions each year.

***The Customer Flow Model***

As shown in Figure 3.5, the idea behind this model is fairly simple, straightforward, and direct. It has been reported to have "very much affected people's

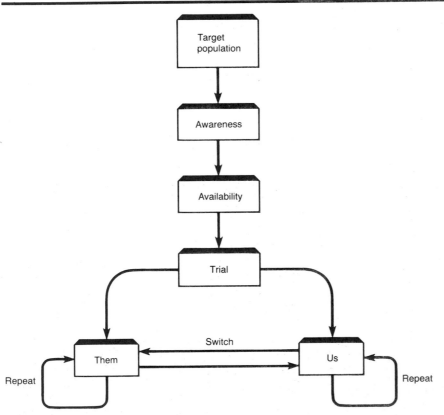

**FIGURE 3.5 A simple customer flow model**

*Source:* Little, John D. C., "Decision Support Systems for Marketing Managers," *Journal of Marketing,* Summer, 1979, p. 17.

thinking about new products in the past fifteen years."[20] The four main parts of the model are: target population, awareness, availability, and trial.

**Target Population.**   The model starts with the idea that any product must be aimed at some specific group of consumers, who form your target population. Suppose your product is an improved type of photographic film. Your basic target population is made up of photographers. However, you will want to refine this definition and determine exactly what types of photographers will want your film or be its heaviest buyers. Your explicit mix will be built to aim primarily at those specific prospects.

**Awareness.**   Once the people who form your target market have been defined as carefully as possible, they must then be encouraged to try your product. Before they can even think about trying it, however, they must be made aware that your brand exists. Generally, the most efficient way to do this is through the mass media (advertising and/or publicity), especially when selling to ultimate consumers.

**Availability.**   Simply making people aware that your new brand of film exists is usually not enough to ensure its trial. If they are to try it, they must have ready access to it. This translates to a need for easy availability. In some markets, you might handle the issue of availability through direct contact with consumers. For example, if your company sells insurance or heavy industrial equipment, your own sales force might take your product directly to consumers. In other markets, especially those in which the sale is made to an ultimate consumer, some kind of reseller or middleman is more typically involved. It is that reseller who provides easy availability. In the case of your improved film, for instance, it is very likely that you would need sales representatives to call on the trade to seek reseller support and availability.

**Trial.**   If you have been doing things properly, some reasonable proportion of those target consumers who have been made aware of your film and now find it readily available will buy a small quantity to try it. It is at the trial stage that your implicit promotion begins going to work with full force. Your functional features and possibly your surrogate cues now start speaking for themselves.

**"Them" or "Us."**   Assuming that people who try your film find that it serves their needs and goals better than competitive offerings you should be able to expect a fairly high probability of future purchase intentions. This is suggested by the arrow to "Us" in the customer flow model diagram. The notion is that your product will continue speaking for itself with each repurchase and use, though ongoing explicit promotion will most probably be required to maximize your established market advantage and maintain your acceptance level. On the other hand, if your brand does not live up to expectations, there will be a switch to "Them," your competitors.

*Some Implications.* The model helps demonstrate how different elements of promotion can affect different stages of consumer decision making, or "customer flow." Advertising, and possibly publicity, tend to be very important in creating awareness. Personal selling is important in creating availability. Implicit promotion is important in assuring favorable reaction to the trial so that the prospect makes a repeat purchase. The world is not quite so uncomplicated that this pattern will be absolutely true in every single product situation. But, the model is generally thought to be accurate in a high percentage of situations involving innovations. On this premise, the customer flow model can be a useful way to analyze the purposes for which each of your promotional elements is best suited.

*The Adoption Process Model*

In considering the customer flow model, you may have wondered if it might be "too simple." You may be asking yourself whether a large number of people will be persuaded to try your brand just because you have made them aware of it and made it available to them. After all, do you try everything you have heard about and seen on a retailer's shelf? Of course not! You must remember, however, that the customer flow model is a way of getting at the basic structure of new product purchase decisions. It is not meant to deal with all the details. In the words of the model's originator, "Once a person in the target market is aware of the product and has a place to buy it, the next question is will that person try the product, i.e. buy it once? Involved here is the success of advertising in communicating the product's attributes to the prospective customer [generating interest] and how the customer evaluates the desirability of those attributes."[21]

In other words, some other stages could be occurring between awareness and trial. Those additional in-between stages are included in the second model we will examine, the adoption process model. In Figure 3.6, the adoption process model is illustrated in a way that ties it into the simple customer flow model just discussed. The two additional stages were suggested by the above quote concerning how consumers progress from awareness to trial of a product.

The adoption process can be viewed as involving five stages. Although three of them have already been defined as part of the customer flow model, a more formal definition of each of the five is useful at this juncture. Then, research findings that suggest ties between each of these stages and the various promotional elements can be discussed.[22] The five stages are: awareness, interest, evaluation, trial, and adoption.

*Awareness.* At this point your prospect knows your brand exists but has little or no other information about it. Furthermore, he or she is not actively seeking any additional information.

*Interest.* At this stage, your prospect not only knows your brand exists but also knows at least some of the facts about it. Beyond this, she or he wishes to know more and may be actively searching for additional information, or at least be very open to receiving it.

**FIGURE 3.6 The adoption process model**

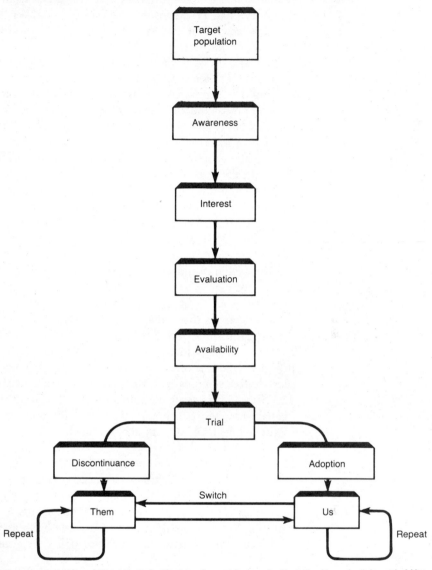

*Source:* Adapted from Little, John D. C., "Decision Support Systems for Marketing Managers," *Journal of Marketing,* Summer, 1979, p. 17.

*Evaluation.*    Now your prospect is seriously considering trying your brand. To put it more formally, "at the evaluation stage, the individual mentally applies the innovation to [his or her] present or anticipated future situations and then decides whether or not to try it."[23] It is generally agreed that the evaluation stage is the most difficult to measure. It is really sort of a bridge between being interested and actually trying the brand. As the originator of the adoption process model states, "The evaluation stage is probably least distinct of the five adoption stages and empirically one of the most difficult about which to question respondents. . . . The innovation carries a subjective risk to the individual. He is unsure of its results, and for this reason a reinforcement effect is needed at the evaluation stage to convince the individual that his thinking is on the right path."[24]

The amount of risk and therefore the need for serious evaluation are usually related to the nature of your product. If its price is high and/or if the results of making a bad purchase decision are potentially serious, the evaluation stage may be prolonged and important. If the price is low and/or if the results of a bad buy are rather trivial, it may be hard to find anything even resembling an evaluation stage when you survey consumers. For example, how long would you spend evaluating a new brand of candy bar before you bought one to try it for yourself? Probably not very long if it looked as though it might be good and you found it easily available. How long would you spend evaluating the purchase of a new type of electrically powered automobile that sold for $20,000? Most likely, you would want to do some serious thinking about it.

In the case of the battery-powered car, the intermediate stages might be critically important to move you from awareness to purchase. In the case of the candy bar, mild curiosity and ready availability might help bridge that same gap.

**Trial.**   During this stage, your customer uses your brand on a small scale or for a short time period. She or he then decides whether to adopt or discontinue any further use, which is the "Them" or "Us" decision. In actual promotional practice, trial can often be stimulated by a sales promotion technique. Examples are free samples, point-of-purchase promotional materials, coupon offers, and price-off deals or combination offers. These are possible supplements to availability. Most importantly, once you achieve trial your product should begin selling itself via implicit promotion.

**Adoption.**   If your customer adopts, it means that he or she plans to continue using your brand. This does not necessarily imply that no competitive brands will be used in the future. Often, you will simply be holding a share of future purchases. For example, someone who adopts Perrier water may continue drinking 7-Up, Coca-Cola, and Orange Crush as well. But some percentage of that person's soft drink purchases will start going to Perrier.

*Promotional Mix Implications from the Combined Models*

In introducing the concept of an adoption process, its originator commented, "A generalization, supported by many studies is that impersonal information sources are most important at the awareness stage, and personal forces are most important at the evaluation stage in the adoption process."[25]

Impersonal sources are usually interpreted as meaning mass media—television, magazines, and so on—that provide information either through advertising or publicity. Personal sources include salespersons as well as information sources in the form of peers and professional advisors. Views on the importance of different information sources at the other stages of customer decision making have also been discussed. Some are based on survey information, some on general observations of practice. Although there are differences in the findings, Table 3.1 summarizes what appear to be the most common conceptions of how various elements in the promotional mix might rate in importance at various customer information stages.

This table includes availability at the evaluation stage for two reasons. First, though some hierarchy-of-effects models do not openly mention availability, they all imply that the product is available. If it were not, there would be no way for the customer to reach the trial stage. Second, as mentioned earlier, the evaluation stage can be a somewhat elusive idea. At least in the case of very low-priced and low-risk products, it seems reasonable to assume that once customers are interested they may be willing to try a product without a great degree of evaluation provided it is easily available. In that sense, sheer availability might be considered as a substitute for evaluation at least for certain product categories.

*Using the Customer Decision Stage Approach to Help Plan Promotional Objectives*

The summaries in Table 3.1 are generalizations. They must be carefully considered and tailored to your individual situation. Nonetheless, they do provide you with starting points and ideas to develop your own thinking. Some examples follow.

***The Customer Decision Stage Approach with Personal Selling as the Lead Element.*** When you regard personal selling as your lead element, the customer decision stage approach calls attention to the potential status of advertising and publicity as supporting elements. One study of an industrial marketing situation concluded that advertising and publicity might be more effective than personal selling efforts in making industrial purchasers aware of and interested in the company and its product. However, personal selling might still be the lead or most important element in these situations because it dominates the highly critical evaluation stage.[26] In commenting on the study, one writer had the following to say:

> These findings have important practical implications. First, the company [selling in the industrial market] could effect promotional economies by cutting back on the involvement of salespeople in the early stages of the selling job so that they can concentrate on the vital phase: closing the sale. Second, when advertising is relied on to do more of the job, it should take different forms, some addressed to building product awareness and some to producing comprehension. [27]

In short, when personal selling is your lead element, the customer decision stage approach can help you determine both how to use it and what roles should be assigned to your supporting elements.

***The Customer Decision Stage Approach with Advertising as the Lead Element.*** In ultimate consumer goods markets, company salespeople usually do not come into direct contact with consumers. The company's explicit mix tends to lean heavily on advertising plus sales promotion, coupled with whatever publicity can be obtained. The danger is that the vital function of personal selling at the evaluation/availability stage could be short-changed. At least one marketing consultant thinks this is often the case, pointing out that ". . . over

**TABLE 3.1**

| Customer Decision Stage | Relative Importance of Individual Promotional Elements | | | | |
|---|---|---|---|---|---|
| | Advertising | Personal Selling | Sales Promotion | Publicity | Implicit Elements |
| Awareness | Likely to be highly important. Regarded as an effective and economical way to start consumers toward adoption and/or increase effectiveness of salespersons. | Usually an expensive way to start generating awareness without some market preparation via the mass media. | May present opportunities, e.g., trade show exhibits for industrial products, in-store demonstrations for ultimate consumer goods. | Highly important and economical if you can obtain it. | Important mainly in terms of providing a basis for building your explicit mix. |
| Interest | Usually regarded as highly important although personal selling may take over more of tasks where your salespeople have direct contact with consumers. | Usually seen as gaining somewhat in importance at this stage, although this may depend on the product category and be true mainly of industrial goods or higher-priced, durable goods for ultimate consumers. | Same as above. Advertising specialties and training programs may also be especially useful where applicable. | Importance probably drops but still useful if you can obtain it. | Same as above. |
| Evaluation and/or Availability | Generally thought to drop sharply in importance in most situations. | When salespeople are in active contact with consumers this is probably the most important element. When salespersons' contact with consumers is "passive" (e.g., self-service outlets), personal selling is often critical in getting availability, displays, etc. from resellers. | Often of strong importance as back-up techniques, e.g., visual aids for salespeople, point-of-purchase displays in retail outlets. | Importance drops further. | Functional features still important mainly as basis for building explicit mix. Price and surrogate cues, especially physical appearance, might logically be more important at this stage. |
| Trial and Adoption | Function generally changes to providing reassurance, reminders, or information on proper use. | Where continued customer contact and service are involved may be quite important. In other cases, main function may be in assuring continued availability to consumers. | May stimulate repeat purchases through reminders or special offers. | Importance drops sharply. | Critical in importance. |

*Explicit Promotion and Approaches to an Optimum Mix*

85 percent of all new product introductions that go into launch fail to become successful brands. In over 60 percent of these cases, the primary reason for failure is the lack of proper levels of distribution. All aspects of the promotional campaign may be strong; even the product is right; but when the advertising breaks, the product is not there for the consumer."[28]

In short, when advertising is your lead element, the customer decision stage approach again can help determine both how to use it and what roles should be assigned to your supporting elements.

**Guidelines for Planning and Coordination.** What has been said about the customer decision stage approach can be summarized by five suggestions for its implementation. First, you should begin by looking at the prospects in your target market. Where do they stand in terms of what they know about your brand and what are they doing about it?

Second, if research data or other observations tell you that consumers are either unaware that your brand exists or barely aware and not very interested, you should probably consider heavy use of the mass media for advertising and publicity. You should also think about whether there are any appropriate sales promotion techniques that can be used to reinforce the mass media emphasis. In doing these things, you are assuming that you have good reason to believe that the implicit elements of your promotional mix have genuine appeal to your target consumer group. Presumably, you have learned this through prior research and testing.

Third, if the people in your target market are aware of your brand and interested in it, but do not seem to be moving toward trial, your personal selling efforts may need some careful attention. If you are aiming your product at ultimate consumers, this often means that your sales force must work to secure cooperation from resellers. Emphasis on availability plus appropriate sales promotion support may be required to bridge the gap between interest and trial.

Fourth, if you are aiming your product at industrial consumers, your salespeople will often be reaching them directly. Their efforts in moving prospects through the evaluation stage by face-to-face sales presentations can be critical. The role of the mass media in this situation is largely one of preparing the ground for sales force efforts.

Fifth, when customers try the product, your implicit elements are critical, but explicit promotion is still needed to reinforce customer beliefs, assure availability and visibility, and provide information on use.

The customer decision stage approach is not meant to give you a finished promotional plan any more than the lead element approach did. However, when used in conjunction with the lead element approach, it can assist you in analyzing your position, especially when you are dealing with a brand that can be considered an innovation in any of the four ways cited earlier—totally new, new in terms of improved features, new in terms of additional uses, or new to a portion of your target market. Furthermore, taken together these two approaches can help you establish clear-cut objectives for individual promotional elements. Not only is this very useful at the strategy planning phase, but it can be extremely important to you when you want to measure the effectiveness of individual elements. We will later consider ways to monitor the performance of promotional programs and the separate elements in the mix. Setting clear-cut objectives in advance is necessary for such monitoring and analysis. With your objectives in mind, you can check market reaction to find your weak spots and your strong points. Then you can take corrective action to improve your promotional mix.

*Promotion in the Postadoption Period*

The typical presentation of the customer decision stage approach says virtually nothing about the need for or purpose of explicit promotion once your customer has tried your brand and decided to continue using it. In this sense it could be misleading. Through observation of business practice, it is readily apparent that brands that have established themselves and have attained widespread popularity are still advertised and otherwise heavily supported by explicit promotion. In some cases, this ongoing explicit effort may relate to new features, new uses, or new target market consumers but, in most cases, none of these innovative characteristics is the major factor.

Even though product features and other implicit elements are extremely important in the postadoption period, they are not normally adequate either to optimize your market potential or even to hold your current position without continued explicit promotional support. There are two reasons for this, and they must be understood if you are to develop and handle strategy successfully in the postadoption period. The reasons involve a *retentive objective* and an *exploitive objective*.

**The Retentive Objective.**    The first objective stems from the temporal nature of purchase and usage patterns for most products. Typically, your brand will be both purchased and used at intervals, not continuously. For example, if you were selling a brand of dry soup mix, it is not likely that customers would use such a product every day. It is more likely that it might be used once every two or three weeks. Explicit promotion, especially advertising and sales promotion, can be critical in retaining consumers' "share-of-mind" in the open periods during which the product is neither purchased nor used. It can do this (1) by reminding users of the brand's features and benefits when the brand cannot speak for itself because it is not being used, and (2) by acting to offset competitive claims of superiority for rival brands that might cause consumers to switch at least on a trial basis.[29]

**The Exploitive Objective.**    The second or exploitive objective stems from a point mentioned earlier in discussion of the adoption stage. You will recall that adoption does not necessarily mean that no competitive brands will be used. For example, if you were promoting that new brand of dry soup mix and a given consumer tried your brand and adopted it, adoption would usually imply that each time the customer was buying a dry soup mix product, your brand had some fairly good chance of being selected. However, that is merely a good chance or reasonable probability. It is far from a certainty. As later chapters will emphasize, various types of promotion are especially useful in converting such a probability of purchase into an actual sale. In particular, personal selling and sales promotion techniques are widely used as promotional mechanisms that exploit such opportunities for potential sales in the postadoption period.

# THE PLANNING SEQUENCE APPROACH

Using the lead element and customer decision stage approaches puts you on the way toward sizing up your situation. However, since you have a number of promotional elements to consider, usually you cannot make decisions about all of them at the same time. Therefore, regardless of what method you use to initiate your planning, it would also be helpful to have an overall framework for your actual decision-making process. It might make good sense to start by working on that element—either lead or supporting element—that appears to be most critically in need of revision, development, or assistance. Then, you can work with the other elements in a priority sequence determined by which is the next most critical, and so on.

*Assessing the Promotional Mix for Interaction Effects*

If the elements are to be coordinated for optimum results, you must also determine how a change in any one of them will affect the others. Again, you cannot do this all at once. Most often, you have to think of each element separately even while you are trying to combine them most effectively. Figure 3.7 pictures a way to go about doing this in an orderly fashion. You should remember that there is really no clear theory or set of rules that defines exactly how promotional elements interact. Each promotional situation is going to be at least slightly different. The planning sequence approach is designed to help you think your way through a total promotional situation. It is intended to be logical, not magical.

Primarily, a planning sequence constantly reminds you to consider the effects of interactions between elements. It is very possible that you could make a decision early in the sequence concerning one promotional element, and then want to change it later after you have made a decision regarding some other element.

For example, a certain strategy regarding surrogate cues might look good at the beginning of your planning. Later, when you are deciding on an advertising strategy, you may realize that those surrogate cues would prove more effective if changed to fit the advertising theme, which could call for still further changes in other parts of your mix. The following example demonstrates how the planning sequence approach can work. In particular, this case provides an excellent example of how elements in your planning sequence approach must be thought of in terms of their interactions.

*Johnson Car Polish*

S. C. Johnson and Sons developed a new car polish. Their product had what company officials considered to be the right blend of functional features and surrogate cues. It was to be price positioned at 69¢ a jar. The subsequent step was development of an advertising program, which was placed in the hands of

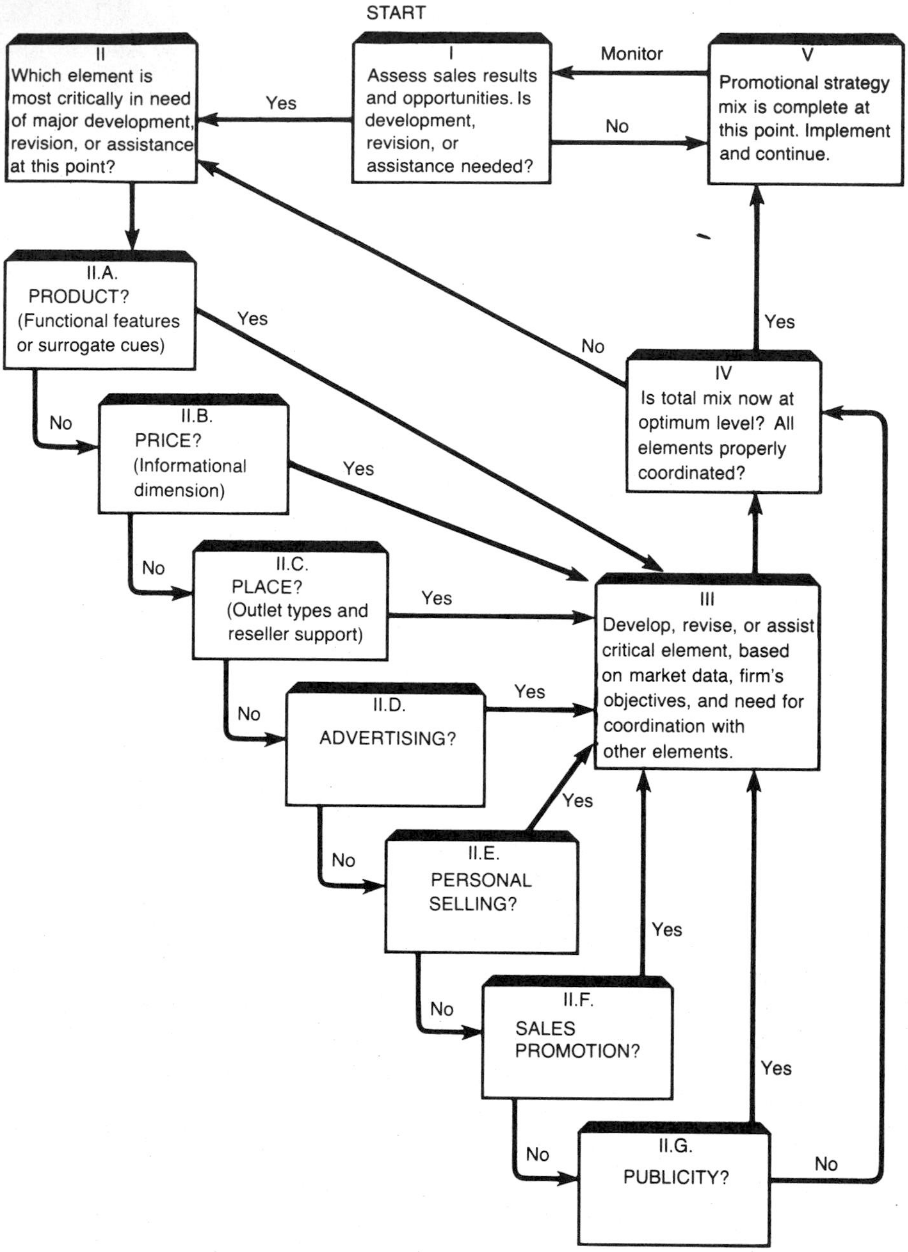

FIGURE 3.7 A planning sequence approach to promotional strategy

START

**I** Assess sales results and opportunities. Is development, revision, or assistance needed?

**II** Which element is most critically in need of major development, revision, or assistance at this point?

Yes

**II.A. PRODUCT?** (Functional features or surrogate cues)

**II.B. PRICE?** (Informational dimension)

**II.C. PLACE?** (Outlet types and reseller support)

**II.D. ADVERTISING?**

**II.E. PERSONAL SELLING?**

**II.F. SALES PROMOTION?**

**II.G. PUBLICITY?**

**III** Develop, revise, or assist critical element, based on market data, firm's objectives, and need for coordination with other elements.

**IV** Is total mix now at optimum level? All elements properly coordinated?

**V** Promotional strategy mix is complete at this point. Implement and continue.

Monitor

No

Yes

No

No

No

No

No

No

No

Yes

Yes

Yes

Yes

Yes

Yes

Yes

Yes

No

*Source:* Adapted from Dommermuth, William P., "Promoting Your Product: Managing the Mix," *Business*, July/August, 1980, p. 19.

*Explicit Promotion and Approaches to an Optimum Mix*

the company's advertising agency. To see what happened next, consider the following published statement on the sequence that evolved:

> Every once in awhile the copywriter's feelings for believability will force an odd change in a client marketing pattern. [The agency] worked up what it considered to be a particularly persuasive campaign on the excellence of Johnson Car Polish and what it could do for the finish of an automobile. But the creative staff felt that nobody would believe it of a wax selling for 69¢ a jar and that people would be wary about applying a cheap wax to the paint job of an expensive automobile. Tests were run at different prices, and the higher priced can sold better. Johnson added some new and expensive ingredients to the polish, upped the advertising budget, and priced the product at $1.69. [30]

In other words, after the advertising had been developed the answer to the question, "Is the total promotional mix now at an optimum level with all elements properly coordinated?" (see Figure 3.7) was "No." The promotional element most critically in need of revision was either the advertising or the price positioning. The price positioning was chosen for revision. In turn, that meant that the functional product features were then most critically in need of revision. They were no longer consistent with either the price or the advertising. Finally, after making all the changes in a sequenced procedure, the company felt it had a coordinated and optimum mix. They were right.

## SUMMING UP THE THREE APPROACHES

Despite widespread agreement that promotional elements should be coordinated, the exact path for achieving proper coordination remains somewhat uncharted. Neither the lead element approach, nor the customer decision stage approach, nor the planning sequence approach claims to give you a ready-made route. However, when combined, they can provide you with some very substantial help in charting your own course—developing your own set of rules—appropriate to your target market and your immediate situation.

It is true that all three approaches are framed in terms of top-level decision makers. If you are working at some lower level, such as a salesperson or an advertising copywriter, you are not going to be in charge of the overall design of the promotional mix. Nonetheless, you may be in a position to make recommendations concerning important parts of that design. Above all, you should be in a position to see where your promotional efforts fit into the total plan. You should also be ready to do whatever you can to contribute to better coordination of all elements. In these respects, all three approaches can help you see things more clearly, regardless of your level in the promotional organization.

Wherever possible, this book will continue to give examples of the coordination between elements. It will help you on those occasions to refer to these three approaches and Figure 3.7.

# SUMMARY

Although implicit promotion is the core around which the rest of your mix is built, the elements of explicit promotion allow you to extend the meaning of your implicit promotion and to work toward giving your brand a chance to communicate about itself. The four elements of explicit promotion are: advertising, personal selling, publicity, and sales promotion.

The comparative advantages of advertising are usually considered to be: low cost per contact, repetitive message potential, creative versatility, relaxed atmosphere of presentation, and impressiveness of the mass media. The major comparative advantages of personal selling are usually thought to be: individual and customized presentation, instant feedback and two-way interaction, precise customer targeting, and ability to spur immediate action. The advantages of publicity are mainly seen as being: mass media prestige coupled with an implied endorsement, and low cost (at least in the direct sense). The major comparative advantages of sales promotion are usually understood to be: increased diversity in communication approaches, flexibility in timing, and a potential for added excitement.

In a well-coordinated promotional mix, these elements are geared to work together, with each contributing special advantages and reinforcing the other elements. Although there is no formula for achieving this goal, three approaches can be very helpful to you when you are assigning objectives and budget resources to the various elements in your mix. These approaches are as follows:

**1.** *The Lead Element Approach*, which suggests you build your promotional mix and coordinate its individual elements by studying your competition. Essentially, this gives you an initial basis for judging your own situation in the light of what successful competitors are doing. Then you can assign "lead" and "supporting" roles to separate elements, with coordinated objectives clearly specified for each.

**2.** *The Customer Decision Stage Approach*, which suggests you build your promotional mix and coordinate its individual elements by studying your customers, especially by learning where they stand in relation to things like brand preference levels and purchase intentions for your brand. Two "hierarchy of effects" models, taken in combination, can guide you in doing this especially when you are dealing with innovations. Based on the available findings, there is reason to believe that the various elements have special and different roles to play as your consumers move through their decision stages.

**3.** *The Planning Sequence Approach*, which suggests you build your promotional mix by constantly studying and restudying the potential for interaction among its various elements. In essence, this approach is intended as a way of coping with the fact that the elements of your mix usually must be considered individually, even though you know they are going to blend together in the end. It is also a way of reminding yourself of potential interaction effects and of searching them out during the planning process.

Taken together, these three approaches will not chart your course for you, but they can help you get started in the right direction. However, before you can do that, you must define and study your market and the consumers who form that market. Finding methods to accomplish this will be the general topic of the next five chapters.

## DISCUSSION QUESTIONS

1. Usually, the explicit elements of promotion are not thought of as adding value to the brand. Perrier water was mentioned as a possible exception. Another example might be designer jeans. List and discuss five more examples in which the explicit elements of promotion enhance the value of the brand.

2. The owner of a firm that manufactures heavy mining equipment has decided to expand sales efforts from a regional to a nationwide basis. However, he is unable to decide whether to continue the present promotional policy of the firm—using personal sales calls exclusively. As a marketing manager, would you encourage the president to include national advertising in the promotional mix? Why or why not? What other strategies might you suggest?

3. A small chain of department stores recently opened a new store in an area in which it was totally unknown. The promotional mix consisted entirely of advertising that appeared in local newspapers. Even though the store was located in a heavy-traffic location (the area's only indoor mall) and the advertising was heavy, the targeted volume of sales was still not reached by one year after the store opened. Using the techniques described in this chapter, respond to the president's statement, "Let's keep the promotional mix the way it is. The only thing we need to do now is change advertising agencies."

4. In planning an optimum promotional mix, why is it essential for a firm to devise a general marketing objective before proceeding any further? What are some of the other considerations in building an optimum mix?

5. Why might a firm introducing a new line of home computers (one of the first firms to do so) prefer the customer decision stage approach instead of the lead element approach when devising a promotional mix? What are the two models used in the customer decision stage approach and what is the basic difference between each?

6. Explain the methods used in the planning sequence approach to developing an optimum promotional mix. Can this approach be used alone?

7. Discuss the Laker Airlines example (see Chapter One) in terms of the general promotional planning approaches presented in this chapter.

8 Life insurance was cited as an example of an ultimate consumer market category in which heavy emphasis is put on personal selling rather than advertising. What unique aspects of this field might contribute to this difference in emphasis?

9. Discuss the relative importance of retentive versus exploitive objectives in promoting the following brands: Coca-Cola, Campbell's Soups, Levis, Wrigley's Chewing Gum.

10. What basic questions should precede your development of a promotional plan?

## REFERENCES

1. "Perrier: The Astonishing Success of an Appeal to Affluent Adults," *Business Week*, 22 January 1979, p. 64.
2. Committee on Definitions, *Marketing Definitions,* *A Glossary of Marketing Terms* (Chicago: American Marketing Association, 1960).
3. Calvin L. Hodock, "Copy Testing and Strategic Positioning," *Journal of Advertising Research*, February 1980, p 37.
4. Donald M. Kendall, *Federal Trade Commission*

*Hearings on Modern Advertising Practices* (New York: American Association of Advertising Agencies, 1971), pp. C-10 to C-11.

5. Douglas A. Fuchs, "Two Source Effects in Magazine Advertising," *Journal of Marketing Research*, August 1964, p. 61.

6. Arch G. Woodside and James L. Taylor, "Consumer Purchase Intentions, Perceptions of Product Quality and National Advertising," *Journal of Advertising*, Winter 1978, pp. 48–51.

7. Committee on Definitions, *Marketing Definitions, A Glossary of Marketing Terms.*

8. Philip Kotler, *Marketing Management*, 4th ed. (Englewood Cliffs, N.J.: Prentice-Hall, Inc., 1980), p. 544.

9. "Average Sales Rep Pay Hits $30,444," *Marketing News*, 5 February 1982, p. 1.

10. Committee on Definitions, *Marketing Definitions, A Glossary of Marketing Terms.*

11. *Ibid.*

12. Louis J. Haugh, "Sales Promotion Grows to $40 Billion Status," *Advertising Age*, 30 April 1980, p. 20.

13. William G. Nickels, *Marketing Communications and Promotion,* 3rd ed. (Columbus, Ohio: Grid Publishing, Inc., 1984), p. 246.

14. Only two such models are discussed in this book. Other variations that you may wish to examine can be found in the following sources:
Gerald Zaltman and Melanie Wallendorf, *Consumer Behavior: Basic Findings and Management Implications,* 2nd ed. (New York: John Wiley and Sons, 1983), p. 562.
Robert Blattberg and John Golanty, "Tracker: An Early Test Market Forecasting and Diagnostic Model for New Product Planning," *Journal of Marketing Research*, May 1978, pp. 192–202.
William J. McGuire, "An Information Processing Model of Advertising Effectiveness," in David A. Aaker and John G. Myers, *Advertising Management* (Englewood Cliffs, N.J.: Prentice-Hall, Inc., 1975), p. 261.
Everett M. Rogers and F. Floyd Shoemaker, *Communication in Innovation* (New York: The Free Press, 1971), p. 102.
Russell H. Colley, *Defining Advertising Goals for Measured Advertising Results* (New York: Association of National Advertisers, 1961).
Robert J. Lavidge and Gary A. Steiner, "A Model for Predictive Measurements of Advertising Effectiveness," *Journal of Marketing,* October 1961, pp. 59–62.

15. Kotler, *Marketing Management*, pp. 491–492; and Jon G. Udell, *Successful Strategies in American Marketing* (Madison, WI: MIMIR Publications, Inc., 1972).

16. Martin R. Schlissel, "Promotional Strategy in a High Technology Industry," *Journal of Business and Economics*, Fall 1973, p. 71.

17. *Ibid.,* p. 72.

18. Frederick E. Webster, Jr., "Interpersonal Communication and Salesman Effectiveness," *Journal of Marketing,* July 1968, p. 13.

19. This case description, and the quotations within it, are based on the following article: "Olympics TV ads enable Northwestern Mutual Life to reach awareness goals," *Marketing News*, 24 March 1978, p. 9.

20. John D. C. Little, "Decision Support Systems for Marketing Managers," *Journal of Marketing*, Summer 1979, p. 17.

21. *Ibid.*, p. 18.

22. The descriptions and definitions presented to illustrate the adoption process model are based, in large measure, on ideas presented in Everett M. Rogers, *Diffusion of Innovations* (New York: Free Press, 1962).

23. Rogers, *Diffusion of Innovations*, p. 83.

24. *Ibid*, pp. 83–84.

25. *Ibid.*, p. 99.

26. Theodore Levitt, *Industrial Purchasing Behavior: A Study in Communications Effects* (Boston: Division of Research, Harvard Business School, 1965).

27. Kotler, *Marketing Management*, p. 494.

28. Stephen A. George, "Proper Distribution: Product Marketing Must," *Product Marketing*, December 1978, p. 3.

29. S. P. Raj, "The Effects of Advertising on High and Low Loyalty Consumer Segments," *Journal of Consumer Research*, June 1982, pp. 77–89.

30. Martin Mayer, *Madison Avenue, U.S.A.* (New York: Harper & Row, 1958), p. 128.

# PART TWO

# The Analysis of Promotional Opportunities

# CHAPTER FOUR

# A Framework for Analyzing Promotional Strategy

## FOCUS OF THE CHAPTER

Promotion is a decision-oriented and action-oriented topic. In keeping with this fact, most of the discussion in this book will aim at relating principles and general findings to their implications for your decision making and illustrating them with examples drawn from actual practice.

This chapter is an exception, however. Its main purpose is to describe a set of interconnected, basic terms that will be used throughout the rest of the book to achieve a broad view of our subject matter. The reason for placing this much emphasis on the terms to be presented stems from the complex nature of promotion as an area of business strategy.

## THE MULTIFACETED NATURE OF PROMOTION

As you have probably sensed from the illustrations presented thus far, promotion is a multifaceted field of activity. Not only can it utilize diverse communication modes such as advertising, personal selling, and publicity, but there are variations of forms within each mode. The diversity of issues involved in promotional strategy grows even wider when you consider the fact that, though all promotional activities seek to generate some type of favorable audience response, the exact type of response being sought can vary between different parts and stages of the promotional process. Thus, although the ultimate response that is typically sought is a sale or some other sort of positive action, there are usually intermediate responses to be considered as well, for example, creating brand awareness or producing a favorable change in consumer attitudes.

## AIMING AT A COHESIVE OUTLOOK

Because of the multifaceted nature of promotion, later chapters will consider such disparate questions as the following:

- What guidelines can prove helpful when a sales promotion technique, such as a contest, is being considered?

- In attempting to gain the attention of prospective customers, what techniques can be used and what are the dangers to be considered in using them?

- Is there any evidence to suggest that subliminal advertising could "work," and if so, how?

- What use can a marketing manager make of learning theory?

- What general principles should be followed in designing sales territories?

- How can you employ psychographic research to improve promotional effectiveness?

- What alternative approaches are available to you in determining the amount of money you should allocate to the various promotional elements?

While recognizing the heterogeneous nature of promotion, however, the need for a cohesive outlook in the shaping and execution of your program must also be emphasized. With this in mind, the interrelationships between the major subtopics with which promotion is concerned will be referred to throughout the book. In order to provide one means of unifying and bringing more order into coverage of the field, this chapter will describe a framework for analyzing promotion. The remaining chapters are built around this framework and will use the terms it introduces to suggest ways of studying markets, creating plans, and implementing promotional strategy.

## TARGET AUDIENCES

A market has been pictured as an arena for potential exchanges, each of which involves a buyer and a seller. Chapter 1 dealt with the origins of promotional strategies mainly in terms of their corporate and competitive antecedents. In a way, we were then looking at the market from the seller's vantage point. Because promotional strategy is designed to persuade potential buyers, either directly or through others who can influence their decisions, the development of a successful plan also rests heavily on analyzing the buyer's side of the

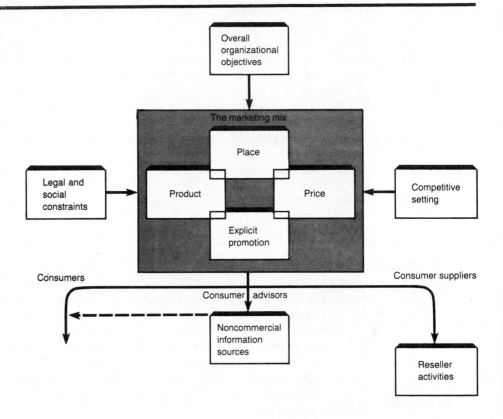

**FIGURE 4.1 The three broad audience categories to which promotion can be directed.**

market, the arena into which your promotional messages are transmitted. There are three distinct, broad categories of audiences involved on this side of the market. These are, (1) consumers, (2) consumer advisors, and (3) resellers who serve as consumer suppliers (see Figure 4.1). Each requires separate consideration because their information interests and their potential roles in your total promotional planning can be quite different.

*The Consumer Audience*

Essentially, the word "consumer" refers to anyone who buys a product for the purpose of consumption or use, rather than for resale. As noted in Chapter 1, there are two primary types of consumers—ultimate consumers and industrial buyers.

Ultimate consumers make decisions about the purchase of goods or services for personal use. This may be for strictly personal use, for example when someone buys a pair of skis that she or he alone will use. Alternatively, the purchase may be for personal group use, for instance when one family member makes decisions about the purchase of groceries that all family members will consume, or when several family members decide on the purchase of a new automobile. Finally, an ultimate consumer may purchase a good or service for use by an entirely different individual. This is the form of ultimate consumer activity that occurs when a parent buys clothing for a child or when someone buys a gift for a friend.

Industrial buyers make decisions about the purchase of goods or services to be used in operating a business or institution. This may be a manufacturing company, a service business such as a public accounting firm, a governmental agency such as a park district or the United States Air Force, or a private nonprofit organization such as a church or a community orchestra. In any of these cases, the distinguishing characteristic is that the goods or services will be used or consumed for organizational purposes rather than for personal enjoyment or need.

From our standpoint, either type of consumer—whether ultimate consumer or industrial buyer—can be described by the following definition: *Consumers are decision makers who choose among available alternatives to find products and services that they can use to best serve their own goals or the goals of others on whose behalf they are acting.*

*Consumer Advisors*     Promotional efforts are often aimed at influencing consumers indirectly through advice they receive from persons or organizations whose opinions they value. Such efforts are usually supplementary to promotion aimed at influencing consumers more directly. Such consumer advisors usually have no monetary interest in the final outcome of the consumer purchase decision, and are often referred to as "noncommercial information sources."

The nature and role of such consumer advisors can be summarized as follows: *Noncommercial information sources include all individuals, groups, or organizations from which a consumer may obtain facts or opinions about product alternatives but that act independently of sellers and have no commercial interest in the outcome of the purchase decision.*

**Mass Media as Noncommercial Information Sources.**   Two principal types of noncommercial information sources are of particular interest in the planning of many promotional programs. The first consists of *mass media vehicles,* such as newspapers, magazines, or television shows, which may serve as noncommercial information sources when they are transmitting information independently and not as advertising. The principal element in your promotional mix that is likely to be useful in gaining this type of voluntary and unpaid support from media vehicles is publicity effort.

**Professional Advisory Agencies.**   The second type of noncommercial information source that can be of importance in certain promotional situations is the *professional advisory agency.* In some cases, the professional advisory agency is an organization that specializes in providing such advice, as in the case of the Consumers' Union. In other instances, the advisory agency is an individual whose professional expertise in a specific field may be considered highly relevant in assisting a buyer to judge the value of a particular product. For example, the advice of a physician may be sought and followed in choosing among diet foods. Other types of professionals whose advice may have critical bearing on consumer decisions include architects (in selecting roofing materials) and county agricultural agents (in selecting fertilizers and herbicides). Special explicit promotional efforts are frequently made to influence professional advisory agencies. For example, a mouthwash manufacturer might send "detail persons" to call on dentists, trying to convince them that its brand is best for patients' oral hygiene needs and persuading them to distribute free samples.

It should be stressed that the ultimate goal of promotion to both of the above types of noncommercial information sources is to reach consumers. However, the route by which they are reached is indirect. It requires the cooperation of someone who has no connection with your firm and no profit-oriented interest in the sale of your product.

***Opinion Leaders.*** There is a potential third type of noncommercial information source that may merit your consideration. This type is composed of peers—people with whom your prospective customer frequently associates, such as friends and co-workers. Although peers may possess no special or professional expertise, some may serve as "opinion leaders," persons whose advice concerning some particular product category is respected by other consumers. Peers who serve as opinion leaders will be influenced by both your explicit and implicit promotion. Insofar as they are led to make recommendations for or against your brand, they are probably most influenced by your implicit promotion, resulting from their own personal experience with it. In Chapter 9, we will take a closer look at the issue of opinion leadership and the potential role it might play in guiding the design of your promotional program.

***Resellers—The Consumer Suppliers***

When you sell through some outside firm, you are using a reseller. Resellers may be retailers who resell to ultimate consumers, or wholesalers who resell either to industrial buyers or to other resellers. In all cases, resellers can be thought of as "consumer suppliers," because they help form the channel of distribution through which products and services reach the people who actually consume them. It is important to emphasize, however, that resellers do not buy or handle goods and services for the purpose of using them. Rather, their interest is in selling them to someone else at a profit. For this reason, there is a fundamental difference in the way resellers make decisions concerning your brand versus the way in which consumers make such decisions. The basic question asked by any consumer, either an ultimate consumer or an industrial buyer, is, "If I buy this, what will my use of the product do for me, my family, or my organization?" In contrast, the basic question asked by the reseller is, "If I buy or handle this product, will my customers be willing to buy it from me or my organization at a price and in a volume that provide me with a profit?"

Because promotion directed to ultimate consumers and industrial buyers is often more visible, there is a danger that the importance of promotion directed to resellers may be overlooked. When resellers are used in a distribution plan, promotion directed to them has two major purposes: (1) to assure easy availability of your brand to consumers, and (2) to induce resellers to add their own promotional support to your promotional efforts. Once again, this is an indirect route by which consumers are reached through your promotional mix.

*Availability.*   As pointed out earlier, no matter how favorably disposed a consumer may be toward a product, she or he cannot make a positive purchase decision unless that product is available. Most products are made available to consumers through resellers. For this reason, minimal reseller support in at least carrying your brand is generally essential to your success.

*Reseller Promotional Support.*   Resellers usually conduct their own promotional strategy programs. If at all possible, you would like to have them work in conjunction with you so that their efforts supplement yours. For example, if the reseller conducts an advertising program it would be to your benefit to have your brand included in that program. In the ultimate consumer goods market, favorable shelf space and store display can often have dramatic effects on sales of a particular brand. If you are able to convince a retailer to give your brand prominent and favorable positioning, the effects of all your other promotional efforts will tend to be magnified.

Reseller activities as they relate to your promotional goals can be summarized in the following definition: *Reseller activities are those decisions and support functions, undertaken by the independent wholesalers and retailers who handle your brand, that can affect consumer purchase decisions.*

Of course, not all products are sold through resellers. Some producing firms choose to sell directly to consumers, in which case no reseller activities are involved in the strict sense of the term. The activities that would normally be undertaken by wholesalers and retailers become the responsibility of the producing firm itself.

# A FRAMEWORK FOR ANALYZING PROMOTIONAL STRATEGY

Having dealt with the origins of promotion in terms of its organizational and competitive climate and having delineated the three broad categories of audiences toward which it may be directed, we are now ready to take a more complete look at the total field in which promotional strategy both originates and operates. Figure 4.2 illustrates in flowchart format one method of depicting both the forces that shape promotional strategies and the sequence of effects that those strategies are aimed at achieving.

*The Purpose of the Framework*

This framework will be the basis for organizing the discussion of promotion throughout the remainder of this book. It is designed to serve three primary functions. First, it dramatizes in a much simplified way the array of forces that must be considered in building a promotional program. Second, it provides a graphic means of viewing the interplay of those forces. Third, it can be a useful guide in analyzing the total structure of the environment in which you are working as you develop your strategy.

FIGURE 4.2 A
framework for
analyzing promotional
strategy

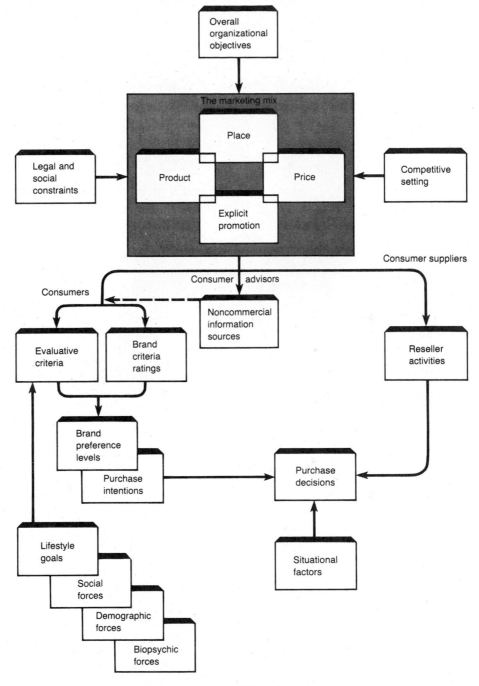

## The Consumer Field

The terms shown in the boxes at the top of Figure 4.2 were introduced in Chapter 1 (see Figure 1.2, p. 7), and the notion of three distinct audience types as broad targets for promotional messages was just discussed. Ten new variables are introduced in the lower portion of Figure 4.2. Taken together, these ten variables trace a pattern for examining the "consumer field." They outline an organized approach to exploring the path your persuasive communications will follow.

As depicted in the figure, the consumer field makes use of terms and relationships drawn from much more extended models of consumer behavior.[1] In the framework we are following, these variables and relationships are presented in abbreviated form and will be discussed with emphasis on their promotional applications rather than on their theoretical implications. However, even as we consider them in this abbreviated form, you may well question whether they are worth treating with so much formality and complexity. Consumers often seem to be making purchase decisions with little thought. Frequently, especially in the case of low unit value items, consumers may appear to be acting on the basis of impulse or habit rather than anything remotely resembling the sequence of consideration and logic implied in this framework. Importantly, the approach in Figure 4.2 is not intended as a set of rules to tell consumers how to make purchase decisions nor even as a pattern that describes how they will consciously put facts and actions together in every single case. Its purpose is to provide you with a systematic guide for analyzing the factors that can influence consumer decisions and, therefore, that should be influencing your promotional strategy design.

## Adapting the Framework to Specific Market Situations

In many cases, your analysis may lead you to conclude that one or two variables hold the key to strategy building in the particular promotional case with which you are dealing, while the others deserve little of your attention. Even when this is true, your initial consideration of the market situation from the perspective of the full pattern can have value in aiding you to discover and isolate such key variables with greater confidence. As one expert on consumer behavior puts the matter, ". . . [decision-making] models must be adapted to particular circumstances. Adaptation from the general model to specific markets requires research that will define those needs, perceptions, and attitudes most likely to influence the consumer's choice of particular brands. [However] the general model is essential in defining the important variables in the consumer decision process."[2]

By considering the full context of the consumer field you lessen the risk of jumping to an unwarranted conclusion or overlooking some aspect that could be crucial to your success. We shall return to this issue of directing attention to key variables in the consumer field after describing each of the variables in greater depth.

As suggested by the pattern of the framework, the ten variables in the consumer field can be thought of as forming an interactive system. Since your promotional messages act as inputs to that system, your ability to understand the nature of these variables and their interactions can serve as a valuable base for planning your promotion. In other words, though promotion is designed

*A Framework for Analyzing Promotional Strategy*

to influence the consumer field, the nature of the consumer field should also influence the design of promotional strategy. The more you know and understand about the variables in the consumer field as they apply in your particular marketing situation, the better equipped you will be to plan and act effectively. For this reason, Chapters 5–8 will discuss these variables in greater detail and illustrate ways in which you can both examine them and use the results of your examination to guide the structuring of the various elements in your promotional mix. It is appropriate at this point, however, to give introductory consideration to each of the variables in the consumer field and to their interactions with each other.

## CONSUMER FIELD VARIABLES AND THEIR INTERACTIONS

*Purchase Decisions*  In a narrow sense, a purchase can be viewed as an exchange involving the payment of money to acquire some type of good or service. For example, when a consumer buys a video game cartridge for $27.95 or pays $300 for a series of karate lessons, he or she has made a purchase decision. Most of the examples we will be considering illustrate promotional strategies aimed at influencing such "conventionally viewed" purchase decisions. This is because the majority of jobs in the promotional strategy field are also directed toward influencing such conventionally viewed purchase decisions.

Nonetheless, it should be stressed that, in a more extended sense, a purchase can involve other types of exchange situations[3] and the product or service can also involve such abstract things as ideas or charitable causes.

Under this broader definition, a purchase is the acquisition of anything desired by the purchaser through exchange of any one of a variety of payment forms including money, effort, or flattery. For instance, sometimes a person can be described as having "purchased comfort at the price of freedom."

The same promotional techniques applicable to purchases viewed in the strict, narrow, and conventional sense are also usually applicable in more broadly viewed purchase situations. The North Shore Animal League case offered you an example of this. Persons who contributed money to support the league's activities did not purchase a good or service in the narrow sense of the term. However, in the more extended sense they were "purchasing" something like an "enhanced personal feeling" or a "fulfillment of social participation." Considered from that aspect, the league could be regarded as a seller and the contributor as a buyer or consumer. Similarly, a political candidate may seek a voter's support in an election in exchange for the candidate's promise to work for certain causes or legislation desired by the voter. Again, from this point of view, the candidate could be thought of as a seller and the voter as a buyer or consumer.

Our description of consumers stressed the point that they can be viewed as decision makers choosing among available alternatives to best serve their own goals. With the broad definition of "purchase" in mind, the end objective of all promotional activity is to convince the consumer to make a favorable decision regarding the purchase of some particular market offering. For that reason, the box labeled "Purchase Decisions" in Figure 4.2 is pictured in the framework as the end result of all environmental forces and promotional activities.

*Lifestyle Goals*   The framework assumes that each purchase decision is made on the basis of satisfying or helping to satisfy some goal or goals of the purchaser. To put it differently, every time a purchase is made it means that some person or group of people decided the product or service involved delivers benefits that help fulfill his, her, or their goals better than other available alternatives. The term "lifestyle" began to appear in the marketing literature in the early 1960s.[4] Since then it has been used with a variety of slightly different meanings. It is used here with the following rather broad interpretation: "[Lifestyles are] the patterns in which people live and spend time and money. . . . Life-styles are learned by individuals as the result of many influences such as culture, social class, reference groups and the family. More specifically, however, life-styles are derivatives of a consumer's personal value system and personality."[5]

*Lifestyle Goals and Product Benefits.*   In pursuing their lifestyles, people develop and seek to achieve certain goals. Products and services, through the features and benefits they deliver to their users, can be one important means of attempting to reach those goals. On this basis the term "lifestyle goals," as it will be used in this book, can be defined as follows: *Lifestyle goals are consumers' expressions of their needs and wants, in terms of their basic objectives, to be accomplished through the purchase of goods and services.*

The following example illustrates one way in which such needs are translated into features and benefits sought by a prospective purchaser. "A man may be conservative and introverted by nature, but his wife has him in a group of extroverted people who wear the latest fashions. The man wants to be accepted, but detests the clothing worn by his friends. It is difficult to say what the man's behavior will be. He may compromise by purchasing the more conservative of the latest fashions."[6]

*Forces That Shape Lifestyle Goals.*   It is important for you to observe in the hypothetical example just given that an interaction between *underlying determinants* has occurred to produce a particular lifestyle goal reaction. In this case, the underlying determinants are a conservative and introverted personality interacting with exposure to an extroverted, fashion-conscious social group. The resulting lifestyle goal that has been generated is acquisition of status in the group coupled with continued self-expression of a basically conservative, individual nature. The goal, in turn, leads to an emphasis on certain types of features that may be sought in the purchase of clothing. In this instance, there would appear to be a strong possibility that the consumer would seek out clothing that somehow combined conservatism with up-to-date styling.

*Lifestyle Goals in Industrial Markets.*   To understand the application of lifestyle goal analysis techniques in the industrial buyer market requires special treatment. When industrial buyers are the targets of your promotional efforts, lifestyle goals can be most usefully thought of as combinations of the personal characteristics of the individuals representing the organization in the purchase decision and the "personality" of the particular organization involved. One observer has put the matter this way, "All companies have character. The nature of that character is sometimes difficult to appraise, but it is probably what determines the company's image—that new quality understood and so often discussed in today's sophisticated business climate . . . . [In the industrial field] buying motives are influenced by the buyer's personality, the character of the company and his or her position in that company."[7]

Thus, while the considerations of profit potential, productivity and/or efficiency usually loom large, in the making of industrial purchase decisions, the exact pattern through which these decisions will actually be made must be interpreted by considering the potential interactions between the organizational personality and that of its buying representatives. In consequence, promotional strategies must often be modified not only on a person-by-person basis but also on an organization-by-organization basis.

*Underlying Determinants of Lifestyle Goals.* As has been suggested, lifestyle goals result from a constellation of underlying forces that shape the general behavioral needs and desires of purchasers. The underlying determinants of lifestyle goals can be usefully classified in terms of three general types of forces as follows:

1. *Social forces* are those that evolve from a person's relations with other people and memberships in groups. Their major effects are generally studied in terms of culture, subculture, socioeconomic class, peer group relationships, and social role playing.
2. *Demographic* forces are those that are connected with statistically oriented characteristics customarily used to classify, describe, and study human populations. Prominent examples are age, sex, income, marital status, occupation, geographic location, family size, educational level, religion, ethnic or racial origins, and stage in the "life cycle."
3. *Biopsychic forces* are those that evolve from a person's innate needs as an individual human being. They are biological and/or psychological in origin. The most common approaches to studying them often make use of one or another theory of personality.

Lifestyle goals tend to be reactions to the composite effects of all three types of forces. Although it is possible to interpret consumer activities in terms of lifestyle goals without considering the underlying forces individually, there can also be value in assessing the impact of the separate underlying forces that shape the goals of consumers. This latter approach offers two main advantages for guiding promotional strategy development. First, the study of these underlying forces often provides the key to developing and understanding how lifestyle goal variations among consumers can be applied in the promotional planning process. Second, as a practical matter, promotional strategy is frequently based on finding consumers who can be measured in terms of their relationship to one or more of these underlying forces, rather than on measurement based on a total lifestyle typology. This is true in part because data on the underlying forces, especially those relating to demographic–economic variations, are usually more readily available than data on lifestyle goals per se. In addition, a promotional strategist may conclude that one or another of these underlying forces, for instance socio-economic class, may relate so strongly to product usage and imply so much about lifestyle goals that it deserves primary consideration.

*Evaluative Criteria*

*Evaluative criteria are the particular features that consumers seek in choosing among brands within a product category to achieve the benefits they desire.*

If your prospective customers make their purchase decisions to satisfy lifestyle goals, it follows that they will somehow have to compare competitive offerings on the basis of how well each delivers benefits that can help fulfill those goals. The term "evaluative criteria" has been coined to describe those aspects of specific product categories that consumers use to evaluate alternative brands on a comparative basis. For example, the "elimination of dandruff" might be one evaluative criterion used to compare different brands of shampoo. When the evaluative criterion, "ability to eliminate dandruff," is given high importance by a particular consumer, it is likely that such importance stems largely from some particular lifestyle goal of that person, such as upgrading his or her status in contacts with other people.

**The Role of Promotion in Shaping Evaluative Criteria.**   Although lifestyle goals are usually the most important factors in shaping consumers' evaluative criteria, it is also possible that explicit promotion may help shape consumers' views of those criteria by dramatizing the relationship between product features and enhancement of lifestyle objectives. For example, shampoos whose appeal centers around their ability to eliminate or reduce dandruff—such as Head and Shoulders or Selsun Blue—may not only stress this criterion in their advertising but also attempt to amplify its importance through their advertising messages. Thus, you will frequently see television commercials for such brands that link their strength on this evaluative criterion to a specific lifestyle goal of target audience members, such as achieving enhanced acceptance for the individual in social or romantic situations.

**Customer Variations in Emphasis Placed on Evaluative Criteria.**   Analysis of evaluative criteria and their relationships to lifestyle goals can suggest a rich field of opportunities for promotional strategy development in almost any product category. It can provide you with an important key to promoting your brand in a way that makes it distinctively different and attractive to some particular class of prospective customers. This is true because various groups of consumers often differ in terms of the amount of importance they place on specific evaluative criteria and, possibly, in terms of the lifestyle goals they associate with those criteria.

For instance, it is likely that all purchasers of executive jet aircraft consider speed and cabin capacity as relevant evaluative criteria and use them as guides in choosing among the models offered by competing aircraft manufacturers.

However, some prospects may place much more emphasis on speed than cabin capacity whereas others may feel that roominess for passenger comfort and working convenience is the higher priority feature.

Moreover, consumers may have both primary lifestyle goals and secondary lifestyle goals in mind when they are making a purchase decision. When all brands are thought to be equally efficient in delivering benefits that fulfill the primary goal, the purchase decision may be made on the basis of evaluative criteria related to secondary goals.

For an example, again consider shampoo as a generic product category. Presumably, the most basic and primary reason for purchasing shampoo is to get one's hair clean. If this were the only goal of interest to the consumer, the logical purchase decision choice should be made in favor of the brand that does this at the lowest price. Sometimes, purchase decisions may be made on that simple a basis. However, if we consider this product category in terms of a hierarchy of lifestyle goals, as a prospective purchaser may see them, secondary goals can come into play and the relevance of these secondary goals may vary a great deal among individuals. One of those secondary goals, the removal or prevention of dandruff, was mentioned above. However, there are a number of other lifestyle goals and resultant evaluative criteria that apply in the shampoo market. Examples of the divergent criteria that have been emphasized by specific brands in recent years include: "Making Short Hair Easier to Handle" (Short & Sassy), "Babying Your Hair With Gentleness" (Johnson's Baby Shampoo), "Repairing Split Ends" (Wella Balsam), and "Getting Rid of the 'Greasies' " (Agree).

***Evaluative Criteria and Market Segments.*** As the above examples illustrate, the market for a product category is usually not really one market at all. It would be more accurately described as a collection of submarkets, each delineated by the particular evaluative criterion or set of criteria that consumers in that submarket use to form opinions regarding the competing brands. This approach to viewing a market as a collection of submarkets has been formalized by the term "market segmentation."

***Evaluative Criteria in the Context of the Promotional Framework***

In summary, we can make the following statements about evaluative criteria: (1) Prospective purchasers make their purchase decisions on the basis of evaluative criteria that are related to their lifestyle goals. (2) Although some lifestyle goal or a combination of such goals forms the logical basis for each evaluative criterion used by consumers, it is also possible that explicit promotion can affect the amount of importance that people place on a given evaluative criterion. When this occurs, it is most commonly accomplished by promotion that stresses the relationship of the criterion to a preexisting lifestyle goal. (3) Both lifestyle goals and the meaning and importance of various evaluative criteria can differ greatly among buyers within the same general product category. (4) Competing brands are often promoted on the basis of quite different criteria, thus appealing to different market segments.

**Brand Criteria
Ratings**

*Brand criteria ratings are the collections of facts, as known, perceived, and interpreted by consumers, regarding how well each brand within a generic product category rates on each of the relevant evaluative criteria.*

In order to compare brands on evaluative criteria of importance to them, prospective purchasers have to somehow rate each of the brands they are considering on each of the relevant criteria. For instance, if we assume a given consumer places heavy emphasis on "dandruff prevention" as an evaluative criterion in the selection of shampoos, then he or she would have to form some kind of opinion as to how various brands of shampoo rate in terms of ability to prevent dandruff.

***Information Sources for Brand Criteria Ratings.*** To form ratings the consumer must both receive and process information about competing brands. This information could come from a variety of sources. Certainly the implicit promotional content of the brand, especially actual experience with its performance, is one potentially important information input component. Recommendations from noncommercial information sources such as physicians or beauty operators represents still another possibility. Much of the information is also likely to be provided by exposure to explicit promotional efforts of the competing brands. In the case of a shampoo, this will most probably be received in the form of advertising and sales promotion. In the cases of other product types, personal selling or publicity may play a role of equal or greater importance as information sources.

***Resellers as Brand Rating Information Sources.*** Consumers may also receive persuasive information from resellers that helps them form brand criteria ratings or helps shape the amount of importance they attach to various evaluative criteria. The promotional analysis framework shown in Figure 4.2 does not show this directly for two reasons. The first reason is concerned with an attempt to keep the illustration of that framework as simple as possible. The second reason stems from the unique role that resellers can play in the promotional program. Typically that role focuses primarily on the consumer purchase decision itself. It is so central to the whole process, and the reseller (or the equivalent extension of your own firm) is so critical in completing it, that reseller communication flows will be treated separately and viewed as centering around the actual purchase decision situation.

***Information Processing.*** In large measure, consumers' views of how well your product rates on relevant criteria will be based not only on how much and what kinds of persuasive information they receive but also on how they process that information. As a consequence, in order to develop effective promotional programs it is necessary to understand the general nature of consumer information processing. At a later point in the book we will be discussing the types of influences that are at work during consumer information processing and what these influences imply in terms of decisions regarding the design and transmission of promotional messages.

**Brand Preference Levels**

*Brand preference levels are consumers' rankings of the individual brands within a generic category, based on assessments of how well each brand rates on the evaluative criteria that the consumer regards as important.*

Presumably, a consumer's attitude toward your brand is somehow arrived at by comparing evaluative criteria (what that consumer wants from the product category) with brand criteria ratings (what that consumer perceives your brand as delivering). How the two might be compared and composed into a brand preference level will require further discussion later in Chapter 6. Again, the emphasis of that discussion will be upon the useful managerial purposes that can be served by analyzing a market in terms of attitude "composition" processes.

**Purchase Intentions**

*Purchase intentions are consumers' plans to act on purchase decisions, as those plans exist at some point in time before the actual purchase is made.*

The "purchase intentions" factor is the most abstract notion in the promotional framework with which we are working. Separating purchase intentions from brand preference levels may appear to be cutting things rather thinly, because purchase intentions should logically be direct outgrowths of those same brand preference levels. At first glance they might seem to be merely the same concepts, stated in different ways. Would a consumer not always plan to buy the brand for which she or he had the highest preference level?

Market research suggests the situation is not quite so simple. At least in many product categories, consumers may "go shopping" with several brands in mind, each brand having some chance (or probability) of being purchased. Consider a situation in which a consumer is choosing among five brands with which she is familiar. She ranks Brand A very highly but just slightly above Brand B. Brands C, D, and E have lower preference levels, but she still considers them "very acceptable." Over a period of time, will she shop with the loose intention of *probably* giving all of her business to Brand A, or *probably* dividing it between Brands A and B, or *probably* spreading it among all five brands with A and B getting disproportionately high shares?

As this question suggests, a variety of different patterns of purchase intentions could result from the same brand preference level situation. Recognizing this and treating purchase intentions separate from brand preference levels makes it easier for you to analyze how your total promotional strategy process is working.

**Situational Factors**

We have considered all of the items suggested by the general promotional framework except one. The remaining variable, termed "situational factors," is rather an untidy sort of thing with which to deal. However, recognition must be given to its existence, especially when you set out to analyze the results of certain promotional activities.

*Situational factors include all circumstances, existing at the time a consumer purchase decision is made, that are unpredictable and not subject to the influence of any of the sellers involved, but that can affect the decision process.*

For example, your advertising and sales promotion may have convinced a prospective consumer that your new product is probably best on all evaluative criteria that she or he weights highly in line with his or her lifestyle goals. The customer visits a retail store at which your sales force has persuaded the retailer to give you first-rate shelf positioning, use your point-of-purchase display materials, and feature a special price reduction. The sale should be yours, but is that a certainty?

The answer is "No," because there are a number of situational factors that may intervene and disrupt the outcome. Some immediate occurrence may put the consumer in a temporarily conservative mood, unwilling to try anything new at the moment. He or she may be distracted by other shoppers, the weather, or most any other happening, and reach for another brand out of sheer habit. Because you really cannot foresee, let alone influence, factors like these, little more will be said about them; yet they belong in our framework because marketing management must be aware of their potential impact, especially when trying to measure the effectiveness of promotional strategies through field research. Purchase intentions and reseller activities will not correctly predict consumer purchase behavior in every single case, even on a probabilistic basis, largely because of possibly countervailing situational factors.[8]

## PLANNING INPUT IMPLICATIONS FROM THE CONSUMER FIELD

As pointed out earlier, even if all or most of the other variables in the consumer field are playing some role in shaping purchase decisions in your product category, it is quite possible that one or two will stand out as key variables. Once you have investigated your market situation and found this to be true, you can often both simplify and expedite your strategy approach by concentrating the majority of your emphasis on those one or two variables. This is illustrated by the following examples.

*Fad Markets*

Consider the case of fad mechandise, which includes all product categories that are in vogue for a very short period of time and then quickly fall out of style. Outstanding examples include the Pet Rock in the late 1970s and Rubik's Cube in the early 1980s. The popularity of a fad item tends to be circular in nature. That is, its popularity breeds more popularity and the process induces geometric growth in demand. Consequently, the consumer field variable of major importance is likely to be that dealing with social forces.

Insofar as an evaluative criterion is applicable, it is probably a rather vague criterion, dominated by the impact of a social force that seems to be telling people that the reason to purchase a product is the fact that it is the "in" thing to do at the moment. Once the fad effect begins to diminish, it is unlikely that any amount of product improvement or explicit promotion can restore vitality to the item.

*Habit Buying*

Much more prevalent than the fad phenomenon is the existence of market situations in which routinized decision making or habit buying predominates.

Habit buying is characterized by "limitation or absence of (1) information seeking and (2) evaluation of alternative choices."[9] In other words, the consumer is not actively open to consideration of persuasive information on evaluative criteria or facts that could influence her or his brand criteria ratings.

A consumer may have compared brands on relevant evaluative criteria in the past, found one that seemed to be superior, purchased it, and determined that it was highly satisfactory. Following that, the consumer may decide to continue purchasing the same brand with little or no consideration given to alternative offerings. There appear to be two main reasons that explain why a consumer would do this.[10] The first reason concerns reduction of search effort. Especially for low-involvement, rather unimportant purchases, it can be appealing to rely on habit simply to make one's life less complicated. The second reason concerns reduction of risk. Remaining more or less loyal to a brand that has proved itself adequate can be a way of avoiding disappointment or embarrassment from switching to an untried brand. The latter reason may be especially critical in the case of high-involvement products that are quite important to the consumer.

When confronting a market in which habit buying is widespread, you may decide the key variable that requires your attention is purchase intentions. Habit buying essentially presumes that purchase intentions are high and firmly established for some particular brand or perhaps for a group of two or three brands. If yours is a brand that enjoys heavy sales through habit buying, you might want to consider an explicit promotional program that emphasizes maintenance and strengthening of your high purchase-intentions position. You may even avoid too much promotional stress on specific evaluative criteria and concentrate instead on more generalized "image retention" appeals. However, if yours is a brand that is struggling against competitors' brands that are entrenched through predominant habit buying, you may decide to seek methods to weaken or destroy existing purchase-intentions patterns. For example, you may consider using sampling or highly attractive coupon offers or a vigorous comparative advertising campaign or promotion of a new evaluative criterion never before promoted for your product category. In any event, it could be to your advantage to cause turmoil in the market in an effort to disrupt consumer complacency and initiate consumers' reconsideration of evaluative criteria.

*Impulse Purchases*

A final example that deserves mention is impulse buying. This is one form of unplanned purchase decision and is characterized by "a tendency to buy on whim, with little thought given to [the purchase]."[11] One illustration of a likely impulse purchase might be a novelty item that a consumer picks up while waiting in the checkout lane of a supermarket. In a pure impulse situation, evaluative criteria and even lifestyle goals may not be very critical considerations. The key issues may be situational factors and reseller activities. You can do little to influence situational factors although you may be able to anticipate the probability and nature of their occurrence in given settings. You may be able to do a great deal toward influencing reseller activities, however, and this may be the locus of stress in your planning. In particular, achieving good in-store displays may be the main aim of your explicit promotional strategy.

The three illustrations just cited—fads, habit buying, and impulse buying—by no means exhaust the possibilities that exist concerning the point of view you will want to take concerning variables in the consumer field. However, these illustrations demonstrate the fact that the variables must be considered in the context of the specific situation you confront. The framework for analysis that we are following is intended to guide your creativity and imagination, not to restrain it or force you into a rigid, routinized procedure.

## SUMMARY

The goal of all promotional activities is to persuade consumers to make favorable decisions concerning particular products being offered in the marketplace. As this book uses the term, a "product" need not be a tangible item such as a baseball or a can of soup. It can also be an intangible service, a corporate image, a charitable cause, or even an idea. Although much promotion is intended to reach the consumer audience directly, other promotional efforts may be aimed at reaching consumers indirectly through individuals or organizations whose advice and/or activities can influence consumer decisions. Beyond the consumer audience, then, the two additional broad audience categories to which promotional communications may be directed are consumer advisors and the resellers who serve as consumer suppliers.

The portion of your promotional mix that is aimed toward reaching consumers directly can be thought of as operating within a pattern of interacting variables that this book treats as "the consumer field." To discuss all aspects of promotion in the context of a coordinated and cohesive background, the rest of this book follows a "framework for analysis of promotion," which ties together the concepts of promotional antecedents, promotional audience types, and a sequential, interactive view of the variables in the consumer field. Each aspect of that framework will be considered both in terms of how it relates to the other aspects and how you can analyze it for input information that can guide you in developing an analytical and creative approach toward building a sound promotional strategy mix.

## DISCUSSION QUESTIONS

1. Why is promotion directed to resellers important in an overall mix? What might the implications be if a promotional strategy failed to take resellers into account?

2. What are some of the possible lifestyle goals that a product such as body lotion might satisfy? As an advertiser, to which goals might you appeal? How could these goals vary among market segments?

3. Implicit and explicit promotional elements are

blended to form a total promotional strategy. This total promotional strategy, in turn, can influence variables that ultimately affect consumer purchase decisions. First, distinguish between implicit and explicit promotion. Then briefly list and describe the variables that ultimately affect consumer purchase decisions.

4. Why is it important to distinguish between purchase intentions and brand preference levels?

5. What is the principal way in which promotion to resellers differs from promotion to ultimate consumers?

6. Why should a promotional strategist be concerned with the underlying determinants of lifestyle goals?

7. How can an industrial buying situation be influenced by "lifestyle"? What are the main components of such a "lifestyle"?

8. Evaluative criteria form the basis on which consumers rate various brands and decide which brands they prefer. Why then should a marketer be concerned with lifestyles? Cite the chief reasons why lifestyles are important and the impact lifestyles have on evaluative criteria.

9. What are noncommercial information sources? Give examples and discuss three different product categories in which they might be especially important.

10. Why can situational factors be important from the promotional strategist's viewpoint?

## REFERENCES

1. For two excellent examples of such extended models see the following: Henry Assael, *Consumer Behavior and Marketing Action* (Boston: Kent Publishing Company, 1981); and James F. Engel and Roger D. Blackwell, *Consumer Behavior*, 4th ed. (New York: The Dryden Press, 1982).

2. Assael, *Consumer Behavior and Marketing Action*, p. 24.

3. Richard P. Bagozzi, "Toward a Formal Theory of Marketing Exchanges," in *Conceptual and Theoretical Developments in Marketing*, ed. O. C. Ferrell, Stephen W. Brown, and Charles W. Lamb, Jr. (Chicago: American Marketing Association, 1979), pp. 431–447; and O. C. Ferrell and J. R. Perrachione, "An Inquiry into Bagozzi's Formal Theory of Marketing Exchanges," in *Theoretical Developments in Marketing*, ed. Charles W. Lamb, Jr. and Patrick M. Dunne (Chicago: American Marketing Association, 1980), pp. 158–161.

4. William Lazer, "Lifestyle Concepts," in *Toward Scientific Marketing*, ed. Stephen A. Greyser (Chicago: American Marketing Association, 1963), pp. 130–135.

5. Engel and Blackwell, *Consumer Behavior*, p. 188.

6. C. Glenn Walters, *Consumer Behavior, Theory and Practice*, 3rd ed. (Homewood, IL: Richard D. Irwin, Inc., 1978), p. 186.

7. John W. Rice, *Successful Selling* (Englewood Cliffs, N.J.: Prentice-Hall, Inc., 1983), pp. 9–11.

8. For an expanded discussion of this topic see: Jagdish N. Sheth, "A Field Study of Attitude Structure and Attitude Behavior Relationship," Faculty Working Paper No. 116, College of Commerce and Business Administration, University of Illinois, July 1973.

9. Assael, *Consumer Behavior and Marketing Action*, p. 53.

10. *Ibid.*, p. 54.

11. *Ibid.*, p. 514.

# CHAPTER FIVE

# Purchase Decisions as Planning Inputs

## FOCUS OF THE CHAPTER

In this and the next three chapters, we will be considering planning input factors from the consumer field of our general framework for analysis that you can examine to organize your view of your market. Your information concerning these factors gives you an intelligence report from which to start building an effective promotional mix.

This chapter introduces and illustrates some of the most basic planning input data you can use to guide your thinking—figures on previous sales or the results of past purchase decisions. In addi-

tion, we will discuss three concepts closely associated with understanding and interpreting the strategy implications of purchase decisions. These three concepts are market segmentation, product differentiation, and the product life-cycle. Market segmentation and product differentiation will be the initial subjects covered because they provide such important conceptual bases for organizing your study of all the planning input factors. The product life-cycle will be the final subject covered because of its potential importance in translating observations of certain purchase decision patterns into the guides for marketing action.

# SECOND STAGE MARKET POSITIONING

As pointed out in Chapter 1, the first stage in positioning your brand in the marketplace is determination of the general product category into which it should be placed. In doing this, you automatically define the set of existing brands with which you must compete. The second stage of market positioning is determination of a means to distinguish your product from these competitive offerings. In this stage, you normally seek to promote your brand in terms of its differential advantage or ability to serve the needs and wants of some target consumer group in a superior manner. Basic approaches for initiating this process are commonly outlined in relation to methods of locating your best available route toward market segmentation or product differentiation.

*Market Segmentation and Product Differentiation*

When the term was first introduced, the technique of "market segmentation" was described in relation to another technique called "product differentiation." It is important to recognize that both techniques can be useful in promoting products and that they can be used either separately or together. We will begin with a discussion of product differentiation and then move to a discussion of market segmentation that includes illustrations of combined usage of both techniques.

*Product Differentiation.* Product differentiation has been described as a technique that "is concerned with the bending of demand to the will of supply. It is an attempt to shift or to change the slope of the demand curve for the market offering of an individual supplier."[1]

This definition can be interpreted as implying three major points regarding a "pure" differentiation technique, that is one which is *not* used in conjunction with market segmentation.

**1.** Your brand is meant to serve a very broad, general market that more or less includes everyone who buys the generic product category. If groups of consumers in that market have special needs or desires, you concentrate on convincing those consumers to accept your product as it is, even though it may not exactly fit some of those needs or desires. In other words, you try to serve a number of segments, without specifically tailoring your product to meet the special desires of any individual segment.

**2.** You are usually in competition with brands very much like your own. At least in terms of functional features, your brand and the others are reasonably close substitutes if not almost identical.

**3.** The biggest differences between brands are likely to lie in surrogate cues, such as brand name and package designs. Along with these, competitors will rely on differences in explicit promotion, such as unique slogans and advertising programs or varied approaches in personal selling techniques.

An example of a virtually pure product differentiation approach can be found in the "standard" cola beverage field. Three major brands compete nationally. It would be untrue to say they are exactly the same, but they are probably very close substitutes in the minds of most consumers.[2] Their advertising suggests little in the way of clear-cut functional features that would make one of them better than another for some specific groups of consumers. They tend to compete on the basis of images largely created through strong advertising campaigns. This implies no criticism of the standard cola brands. In fact, it represents both sound business practice and healthy competition in the free-enterprise system.

Incidentally, this also does not mean the cola companies think all consumers are equally good prospects for their brands. For example, certain age ranges and geographic regions include more heavy soft drink users than others. The cola producers know this and promote accordingly. However, all three major brands are more or less aimed at the same broad spectrum of soft drink consumers; they are not tailored to the special desires of a specific group.

*Market Segmentation.* Market segmentation can be defined as a technique that "consists of viewing a heterogeneous market (one characterized by divergent demand) as a number of smaller homogeneous markets in response to differing product preferences among important market segments. It is attributable to the desires of consumers or users for more precise satisfaction of their varying wants."[3]

In its most basic form, market segmentation can be interpreted to imply four major premises concerning strategy.

**1.** Your brand is *not* aimed at all users of the generic product category. It is aimed at only some of them. The consumers you seek to serve want emphasis on one or more evaluative criteria and/or lifestyle goals that are different from those sought by other consumers when considering brands in the product category.

**2.** Rather than starting with a product and trying to make everyone in the market like it, you start with the market. You try to locate an unmet consumer need. You then build a brand that fulfills that need. This usually would mean that you try to develop a significant difference from competing brands in at least one functional feature.

**3.** Your explicit promotion can now be built on genuine functional superiority in one or more aspects. You will still be concerned about issues such as surrogate cues, slogans, and advertising themes. However, they do not form the only foundation on which you are relying to distinguish your brand from competitors.

**4.** Possibly, but not necessarily, you will have the segment to yourself, at least for a while. If you are the first brand to offer the difference in product benefits, you may enjoy a short-term "monopoly" among consumers in the segment. If your brand is successful and the segment is reasonably large, you will generally be joined by competitors aiming at the same target market.

An example of market segmentation can also be drawn from the cola beverage field. A minority of cola consumers want a low-calorie beverage. The distinguishing functional feature is connected with the evaluative criterion "low-in-calories" or "sugar-free." The underlying lifestyle goal is a desire to reduce or "hold down" one's weight. When the first competitor introduces such a brand and explicitly promotes it, it strikes a responsive chord among consumers in the "low-calorie cola segment." The new brand attains a high-brand criterion rating on this functional feature and is off to a flying start. Not every cola drinker will want it, but a sizable minority will.

*Varieties of Segmentation Approaches*

In actual practice, market segmentation is not one single strategy. It really breaks down into several major forms and, as suggested above, can be combined with product differentiation to form a hybrid strategy. Furthermore, some of its forms can be combined to form still more variations. Some major variations worth considering are unique segmentation, segmented differentiation, lifestyle segmentation, subsegmentation, and occasion segmentation.

**Unique Segmentation.**    In its basic form, market segmentation seems to imply you have a segment all to yourself. If so, you have unique segmentation. When you are the first entrant in a segment this is likely to be true, at least for a while. Sometimes this may stretch into a long period. For example, the Polaroid Land Camera had the instantly-developed-photography segment to itself for many years.

The first diet cola brand was also uniquely segmented when introduced, but soon it was joined by other brands. The three major cola producers now compete in the low-calorie or diet segment just as they compete in the general cola market. Here again, the leading low-calorie brands are likely to be regarded by many consumers as close substitutes for each other. In other words, within this segment the rival entries again seem to be basing their promotion on something that looks partially like a product differentiation strategy. This sort of situation can be called *segmented differentiation,* and it is very common.

**Segmented Differentiation.**    The diet cola example illustrates a combination of market segmentation and product differentiation. If several brands are aiming at the same segment, stressing the same evaluative criteria, and are very much alike in functional features, they are actually "differentiating" within that segment. Each is trying to "bend demand" its way, but each is concentrating on the demand of a recognized subgroup of consumers.

The term "segmented differentiation" simply recognizes that you may not be the only brand featuring a particular blend of evaluative criteria and aiming at the same segment of consumers. This situation has three implications. First, your brand is not aimed at all users of a generic product category. It is aimed at only some of them. The consumers you seek to serve want emphasis on one or more evaluative criteria that are different from those that other segments of consumers want. Your explicit promotion is built around these functional differences. Second, you are nevertheless in competition with brands very much like your own that are aimed at much the same segment. Your brand and the others are reasonably close substitutes, if not almost identical. Third, to differentiate yourself from competitors in your segment you may be emphasizing slight variations of the same evaluative criteria that they are promoting. You may also be relying partly on differences in surrogate cues, such as brand name, package designs, or incidental product characteristics. Moreover, you are attempting to make your brand stand out from direct competitors through powerful explicit promotion—distinctive advertising themes, active sales promotion, and imaginative personal selling techniques.

In short, you are attempting to differentiate within your segment.

*Lifestyle Segmentation.* Although it has been implied that you will try to serve your chosen segment by starting with some clear difference in functional features, this is not always the exact route followed. A segmentation strategy can also start from a focus on consumer differences in lifestyle goals. This could mean that you build a unique product to serve those goals.[4] It could also mean that your basic product is much like those of your competitors; however, your explicit promotion is interpreting it in terms of a specific set of lifestyle goals that are different from the goals pictured by your competition. You are really segmenting on the basis of unique promotional claims rather than unique product features.

To illustrate this latter approach, consider the diet cola example once more. Suppose that two brands are both sugar free and each contains only one calorie per twelve ounces. One is appealing to people who are weight conscious. Its advertising and sales promotion feature weight control as a lifestyle goal. The other might "segment" toward an adolescent market more concerned about skin problems than weight problems and emphasize its lack of sugar. Alternatively, it might aim its messages toward the mothers of young children and emphasize the benefits of better health and less tooth decay. In short, then, the same functional features could appeal to different groups of consumers for different reasons. Those different reasons, or lifestyle goals, could provide your basis for segmentation.

*Subsegmentation.* If you can differentiate within a segment, can you also segment within a segment? Of course. Again using the diet cola market, let's see how this could work. Regular colas may contain 156 or more calories per twelve-ounce serving; diet colas usually contain one calorie or less. Many people in the diet cola market might feel they are giving up a great deal of taste to obtain the lower calorie count. Maybe they would be willing to compromise.

If you studied the market and found there was a fair-sized part of the low-calorie cola segment that felt this way, you could "subsegment." Perhaps your new brand would feature thirty calories per twelve-ounce can but "fuller taste" than the other diet brands. Instead of "bending demand" to a one-calorie cola through explicit promotion, you would be treating the low-calorie segment as one characterized by "divergent demand." It could be made up of still smaller "homogeneous markets," each differing further in product preferences.

*Occasion Segmentation.* Thus far we have been assuming that consumers in a segment always remain in that segment, their lifestyle goals are constant, and they are consistent in seeking functional features. However, this idea has been challenged. It has been pointed out that each person faces a variety of situations in the course of living. Even when considering items within the same product category, an individual consumer's choice of brands may change as the situation, mood, or occasion changes.[5] One marketing commentator has offered this illustration, "When [my colleagues] talk about shampoos . . . I want to know whether the ideal they are asking me about is my ideal when I am on holiday sea bathing [or] my ideal when . . . shopping has to be done as quickly as possible."[6]

If an individual may seek somewhat different benefits from a product category to fit different occasions, this fact provides you with another opportunity to search for a unique positioning scheme for your brand. For example, a few years back Michelob beer chose to position itself in this fashion. Its campaign theme—"Weekends were made for Michelob"—implied that people who drink other brands of beer during the week are looking for "something special" on weekend occasions. After the successful use of this theme, Michelob broadened its occasion appeal with a new campaign that suggested, "Put a little weekend in your week."

If you were promoting that compromise diet cola—more calories but more taste—you might want to tie those features to occasions such as parties, weekends, or meals. In doing this, you would simply be recognizing that people could move in and out of the segment as the occasion changes.

## The Limits of Segmentation

To follow any segmentation scheme profitably, the consumer group at which you aim must have both sufficient size and reachability.

**Sufficient Size.** The segment must be large enough to generate a profitable volume. If you segment too far, you will be appealing to only a handful of consumers, which would be feasible only if you were selling a very high-priced product that could be customized to fit individual needs. For example, there may be a segment of consumers who want a sugar-free cola that contains ten calories per twelve ounces, is enriched with vitamin C, has a slight hint of orange flavoring, and a below-average carbonation level. Yet these customers may be so few in number that you would go bankrupt trying to serve them.

**Reachability.** Even if your segment is sufficiently large, it will not be a promotionally viable segment unless it is economically reachable. Suppose that there were a million people who wanted the kind of cola just described, and that they will each buy an average of ten dollars' worth of product per year. Is that workable? If they all lived in or around the same geographic area—say New York City—it might be. If they were scattered across the country, it might not be. It would probably cost too much to reach them with both explicit promotion and physical distribution of the product.

## Bases for Segmentation

If you are going to locate segments, where do you start looking? It has been suggested that the bases for segmentation strategies fall into two categories: general consumer characteristics and product-related consumer characteris-

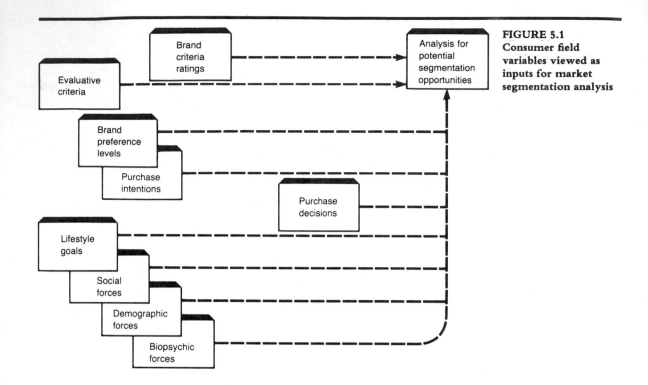

**FIGURE 5.1**
**Consumer field variables viewed as inputs for market segmentation analysis**

tics.[7] General consumer characteristics include social forces such as social class and culture; demographic forces such as family size, age, and geographic location; biopsychic forces such as personality or physical needs; and lifestyle goals including the various "occasions" that may occur in pursuing living patterns. Product-related consumer characteristics include attitudes toward existing brands such as brand preference levels and purchase intentions; product knowledge in the form of brand criteria ratings; factors such as usage levels, brand loyalty, and store loyalty, which are aspects of purchase decisions; and evaluative criteria or specific benefits sought from the product.

As illustrated in Figure 5.1, this means that most of the variables in the consumer field of the promotional framework we are following can provide potentially useful bases for segmentation. In consequence, the issue of segmentation approaches will keep reappearing as we deal with these variables in this and the next three chapters.

The ideal situation for any brand would be unique segmentation based on a genuine difference in a functional feature. Given this situation and a sizable group of consumers who place high importance on the evaluative criterion associated with that feature, the rest of your promotional mix is much easier to handle. However, it is more likely that you will be dealing with or helping to build a brand that is different from competitors, but not sufficiently different to control a clear market segment completely. You will be looking for ways to capitalize on such differences as you have through explicit promotional techniques. An advertising agency executive has put it this way:

*Purchase Decisions as Planning Inputs*

The advertising [or other promotional] strategist rarely has to worry about marketing entities that are inferior; rather, his challenge is that he must formulate strategies about entities that are not differentiated enough from their competitors. [8]

## PURCHASE DECISIONS

Whether you are aiming at a large market that may really contain several overlapping segments, an existing market segment that is already served by several brands, or a newly discovered segment in which your brand will be the first entry, formulation of strategy starts with a study of the consumers you expect to serve. The variables in the consumer field give you points of reference to guide your study. The most basic of these variables is that concerned with purchase decisions and therefore it is the starting point for our discussion of planning input factors.

Convincing customers to buy your brand is the goal of your efforts. In that sense, purchase decisions are the results of promotional strategy processes. Then how can you also use them as your starting point? The answer is in the dimension of time. Your goal is concerned with future purchase decisions. Your starting point is what you can learn from past purchase decisions.

*Sales Leave Trails*    When a consumer makes a purchase, her or his action "registers" and there are several aspects from which the results can be studied. Five such aspects can be especially important to you because they convey highly significant information about purchase decision patterns that consumers have followed in the past (Figure 5.2). These five aspects are as follows:

**FIGURE 5.2 Five aspects of past purchase decisions as planning inputs for strategy development**

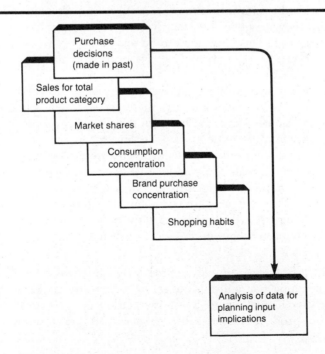

1. Sales trends and total sales for the generic product category
2. Market shares held by competing brands
3. Consumption concentration or the "heavy buyer" approach
4. Brand purchase concentration or "brand loyalty" versus "brand switching"
5. General shopping habits, the "where and when" of consumer purchase behavior

Because they are so important to marketing planners, data relating to all five are regularly collected by syndicated research services for a number of product categories. In particular, several services provide these data on a subscription or fee basis for such ultimate consumer goods fields as foods, beverages, drugs, and cosmetics. Figure 5.3 summarizes information on some of these services and the purchase decisions data they can provide.

*Sales Trends for the Generic Product Category*

The most basic question concerning past purchase decisions is "What is the size of the total market for my product category and how has it been changing in recent years?" The answer to this question is vital for two reasons. First, in setting your target sales goal you will generally be aiming at obtaining some percentage of the total existing or predicted market. To know what that percentage will amount to in dollars, you must have some estimate of total market size. Among other things, this will help define an upper limit on the budget you can afford to allocate for promotion. Second, knowing how the market has been changing—whether total sales are rising, falling, or holding steady—may influence your decision on how much you want to invest in future promotional dollars. To a large extent, the sales trend of past years gives you a basis for anticipating what is going to happen in the future.

When the sales for a generic product category are increasing each year, firms tend to be optimistic about promotional investments. When sales are declining, they may decide to switch promotional emphasis toward other product categories. This tendency can be related in part to the concept of a "product life cycle," a topic that will receive further discussion at the end of this chapter (see p. 128).

Yearly sales for three representative product categories are shown in Figure 5.4. These examples illustrate three very different situations. The market for cigars is fairly large, but has been showing a consistent downward trend. The market for dry cat foods is smaller but experiencing rapid growth. The market for coffee is extremely large; its downward movement is not quite as serious or consistent as that for cigars, but does suggest a general weakening of demand. As a promotional strategist for a brand entry in one of these categories, such size and trend figures are important starting points for your planning. However, they must be combined with other planning input data before you can fully interpret them in terms of suggested promotional possibilities.

*Market Shares*

Having ascertained sales volume size and trends for the market category, the next thing you will want to know is how the market is divided among competitive brands. Figure 5.5 shows market shares for selected years for the same three product categories just mentioned. If you are attempting to increase sales

**FIGURE 5.3 Examples of purchase decisions data available from commercial research firms**

| Data Available | Research Firm | | | |
| --- | --- | --- | --- | --- |
| | A.C. Nielsen Co.; Northbrook, IL | MRCA; Stamford, CN | SAMI; New York, NY | Simmons Market Research Bureau; New York, NY |
| Estimates of total product category sales | Yes | Yes | Yes | No |
| Market share estimates | Yes | Yes | Yes | No. However, estimates of percent of total consumers using brand are available |
| Consumption concentration | Not in standard Nielsen reports | Yes | Yes (in some studies) | Yes, including breakdowns by Heavy/Med/Light users; also information to determine the demographic characteristics of the decision maker |
| Brand purchase concentration | Not in standard Nielsen reports | Yes | Yes (in some studies) | Yes |
| Shopping habits (outlet types and seasonality) | Yes | Yes | Yes | No |
| Types of items covered | Food and drug products | Food products, household care items, textiles | Retail grocery store products | Automobiles, books, records, restaurants, women's apparel, health care items, food products, games, toys, household care items, tobacco products, home furnishings, banking, investments, insurance and credit card usage, travel, appliances, hair care items, and beauty aids |
| Standard sample size | 1,600 supermarkets | 7,500 households in basic sample; various sample sizes used for individual projects | Varies from market to market | 15,002 adults aged 18 and over, selected on a probability basis |
| Geographic coverage | 36 metropolitan areas | Civilian households throughout the continental United States | Audits in 45 metropolitan market areas; scanner data in 4 markets | 48 continental states of the United States |
| Method of data collection | Store inventory audits and scanner data | Mail-in purchase diaries completed by consumers | Warehouse inventory audits and store scanner data | Personal interviews (3-phase interviews over a 1 year period) |
| Frequency of reports | Bimonthly/weekly | As ordered | 4-week reports generated from warehouse data; weekly reports from scanner data | Yearly report |

*Note:* The information above is based on various published materials available at the time this book was written. Details concerning data available from these firms may change over time.

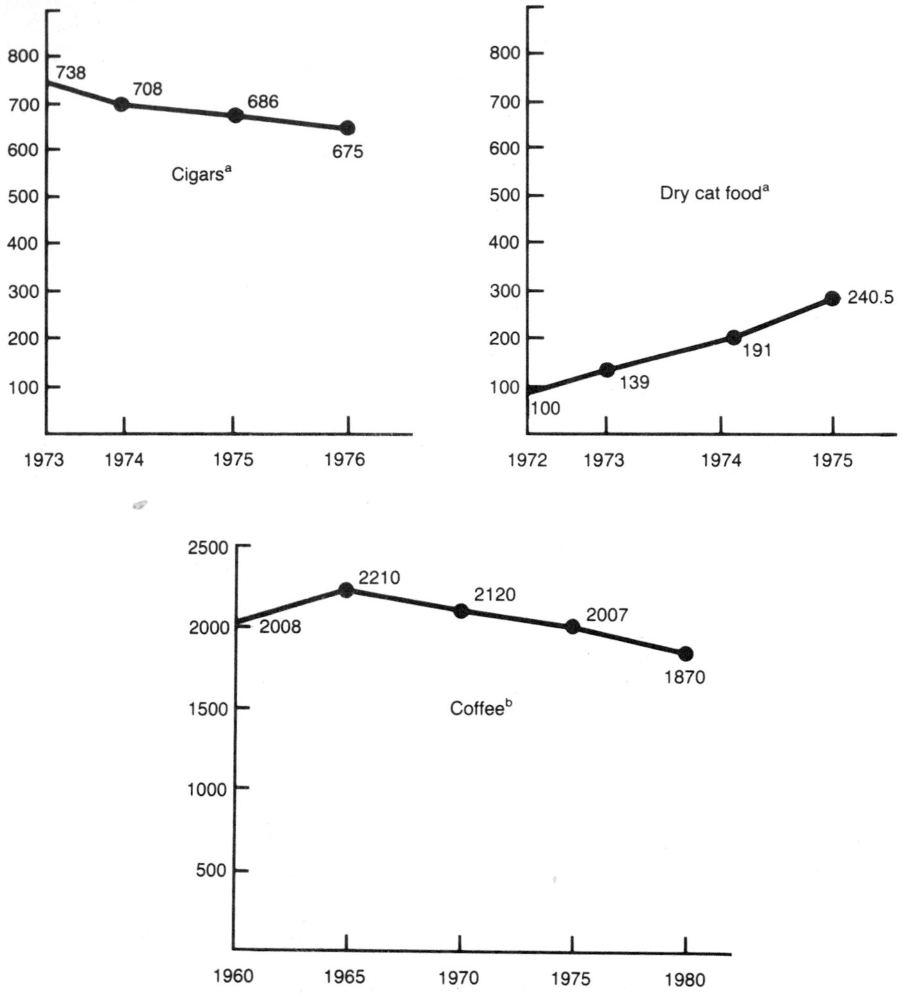

**FIGURE 5.4 Sales trends in selected product categories**

Cigars[a]

- 738 (1973)
- 708 (1974)
- 686 (1975)
- 675 (1976)

Dry cat food[a]

- 100 (1972)
- 139 (1973)
- 191 (1974)
- 240.5 (1975)

Coffee[b]

- 2008 (1960)
- 2210 (1965)
- 2120 (1970)
- 2007 (1975)
- 1870 (1980)

[a] Measured in millions of dollars.
[b] Measured in millions of pounds.

*Sources:* Data on cigars and cat food prepared by Maxwell Associates, Division of Wheat First Securities, Copyright by Maxwell Associates and reproduced with permission. Data for coffee sales reported by A. C. Nielsen Co. and published in *Tea and Coffee Trade Journal*, January 1981, p. 28.

for an existing brand or introduce a new brand you will probably be trying to change such market share figures. Your promotional efforts may draw new users into the market, but in most cases your brand probably will be getting the majority of its sales by luring them from competitive entries. In assessing your situation, you have two related questions to consider. How likely is it that you can attract customers away from their presently preferred brands? In consequence, how large a market share can you expect to achieve?

Considering share patterns as they have existed in the past gives you a basis for making some initial estimates. For example, in the coffee market the leading brands were holding rather steady in shares during the period shown.

**FIGURE 5.5 An illustration of market shares data**

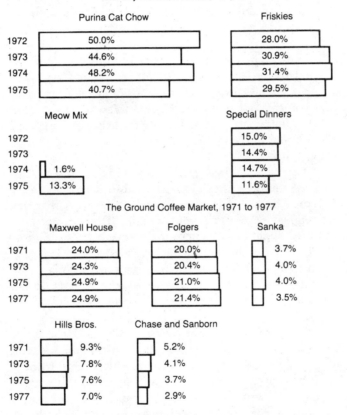

The Cigar Market, 1972 to 1976[a]

| | King Edward | Muriel | Dutch Master | White Owl | Robert Burns |
|---|---|---|---|---|---|
| 1972 | 15.0% | 11.4% | 6.4% | 6.7% | 6.7% |
| 1973 | 15.1% | 10.8% | 6.5% | 6.3% | 6.3% |
| 1974 | 13.4% | 10.5% | 6.7% | 6.7% | 6.1% |
| 1975 | 15.9% | 9.9% | 6.7% | 6.7% | 5.8% |
| 1976 | 16.4% | 10.1% | 7.1% | 6.0% | 5.3% |

[a]Includes only brands that had at least a 6% market share in 1972

The Dry Cat Food Market, 1972 to 1975

| | Purina Cat Chow | Friskies |
|---|---|---|
| 1972 | 50.0% | 28.0% |
| 1973 | 44.6% | 30.9% |
| 1974 | 48.2% | 31.4% |
| 1975 | 40.7% | 29.5% |

| | Meow Mix | Special Dinners |
|---|---|---|
| 1972 | | 15.0% |
| 1973 | | 14.4% |
| 1974 | 1.6% | 14.7% |
| 1975 | 13.3% | 11.6% |

The Ground Coffee Market, 1971 to 1977

| | Maxwell House | Folgers | Sanka |
|---|---|---|---|
| 1971 | 24.0% | 20.0% | 3.7% |
| 1973 | 24.3% | 20.4% | 4.0% |
| 1975 | 24.9% | 21.0% | 4.0% |
| 1977 | 24.9% | 21.4% | 3.5% |

| | Hills Bros. | Chase and Sanborn |
|---|---|---|
| 1971 | 9.3% | 5.2% |
| 1973 | 7.8% | 4.1% |
| 1975 | 7.6% | 3.7% |
| 1977 | 7.0% | 2.9% |

[a]Includes only brands that had at least a 6% market share in 1972.
*Source:* Data prepared and copyrighted by Maxwell Associates, Division of Wheat First Securities. Reproduced with permission.

Two of them—Maxwell House and Folgers—dominated the market, claiming roughly forty-five percent of the business. Only one other brand, Hills Brothers, held over five percent. About forty percent of the volume went to minor brands not listed in Figure 5.5, many of them regional in distribution or sold under private labels. There was a small decaffeinated segment served mainly by Sanka.

Suppose you were a brand with a low and shrinking market share, such as reported here for Chase and Sanborn and Hills Brothers. How could you promote your product to improve your position? First of all, your past pattern of market shares gives you one reading on the effectiveness of your past promotional strategies. If you have been aiming and budgeting for increases, you know that some drastic changes are probably needed. Second, you would be especially interested in studying the strategies of major brands that have been holding or expanding their shares. Are similar strategies suitable for you, or is there an appropriate counter—strategy that might be more effective? What initial clues do such market share figures suggest about the evaluative criteria that consumers are seeking?

Market share figures alone cannot give you complete answers. However, they can aid you in beginning to assess your position and searching for ways to improve it.

*Consumption Concentration*

In many product categories consumption is "concentrated." This means that a relatively small percentage of the population accounts for a relatively large percentage of the sales. In terms of developing promotional strategy, this tells you that not everyone is going to be an equally good prospect. Therefore, in beginning to plan your mix, it helps to sort your market out in terms of current usage levels.

**The "80-20" Principle.** The existence of consumption concentration is well recognized in the industrial goods market, where it is sometimes referred to as the "80-20" principle. Basically, this says that you can often expect to get eighty percent of your volume from twenty percent of your accounts. Although the exact percentages may vary from product to product, it remains true that industrial accounts can usually be categorized as to potential. Large firms or institutions are important users. Smaller firms or institutions are less important. Industrial buyers can be analyzed on a one-by-one basis, and can be individually rated as to consumption concentration.

**Consumption Concentration in Widely Used Product Categories.** The fact that consumption concentration exists in markets for ultimate consumer goods may be less apparent. Some products seem to be so widely used that it becomes easy to take the view that "almost anyone is a good prospect for this item." Actually, even in such widely used ultimate consumer product categories as coffee and chewing gum, a surprisingly small percentage of people account for a very high percentage of the sales. In still other product categories such as cigars and cold remedies, consumption concentration is remarkably pronounced. Figure 5.6 illustrates the phenomenon for all four of these product groups.

If you are promoting chewing gum, your market is broad in one sense but fairly narrow in another. Almost sixty percent of the adults in the United States chew gum. However, almost two-thirds of the gum volume comes from roughly seventeen percent of those adults. If you are promoting cigars, your market is narrow in one sense and very narrow in another. Only about

**FIGURE 5.6 Some examples of consumption concentration by product categories**

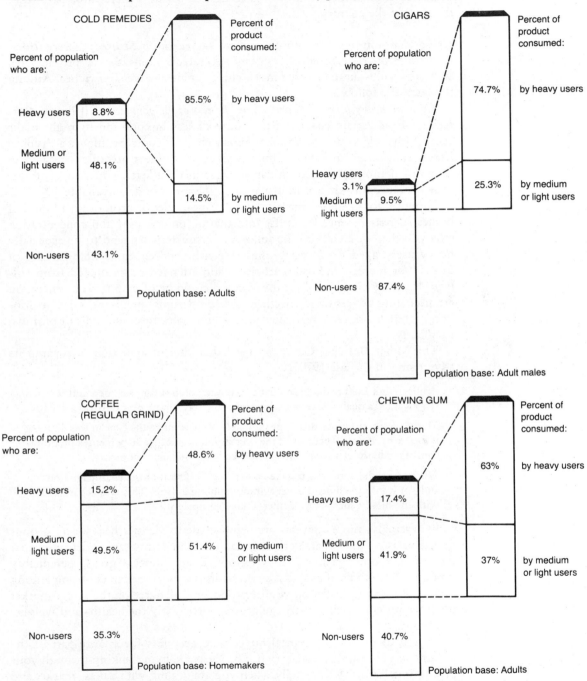

Source: TGI and Simmons Market Research Bureau Data, *Progressive Grocer*, July 1979, pp. 58, 66, 137, and 142.

one out of every eight men is a cigar smoker. Furthermore, the bulk of the business—almost three-fourths—is accounted for by a mere three percent of the men in the country.

***Using Consumption Concentration Data to Search for Strategy Alternatives.*** Consumption concentration suggests several questions that a promotional strategist will want to consider in searching for alternative approaches. Among these are the following:

*How are heavy users "different" from the rest of the population?* If heavy users tend to have certain characteristics more or less in common it might make sense to handle your promotional approach with some profile of a "typical heavy consumer" in mind. Typical heavy consumers are often defined in terms of demographic determinants—age, income level, educational status, etc.—because this kind of information is the most readily available.

Suppose, for example, that you were responsible for promoting a brand of tissues such as Kleenex or Puffs. Information on consumption concentration tells you that women with the following characteristics tend to be especially heavy users: aged 35–44 years, married with children, household income of $18,000 or more, employed part-time, and attended or graduated from college. Keeping this general profile in mind could be of help to you when you are preparing advertising, selecting package designs, preparing sales promotion materials, or deciding which stores your sales force should call on most frequently.

The Miller Brewing Company used this kind of approach to revamp its advertising in the late 1970s.

> [Miller High Life] had a high quality, country club image for men and women who wanted a quality beer but who, unfortunately, drank beer only occasionally.
>
> Market research shows that approximately 80 percent of the beer in this country is drunk by about 30 percent of the beer drinkers and <u>that</u> 30 percent is predominantly made up of young, blue collar working men and women.
>
> What had to be done was to take Miller High Life out of the champagne bucket and put it into the lunch bucket without spilling a drop. This was accomplished with the highly successful "Miller Time" campaign. [9]

Increasingly, more attempts are being made to identify heavy-user groups on the basis of other characteristics in addition to demographic determinants. Among the other characteristics examined are lifestyle goals, personality types, and the kinds of evaluative criteria heavy users seek in choosing among brands. For example, frozen yogurt producers "all agree on the target market for frozen yogurt—the 18–25 age group, particularly the health- and weight-conscious."[10]

Trying to picture the typical buyer who accounts for a large part of the volume in your product category can be a great help in thinking through your promotional strategy, especially when you are dealing with a mass market and are out of direct contact with your customers.

*Are there unserved segments within the heavy-user group?* This question starts from an almost opposite position than the first question. Suppose again that you are trying to sell a brand of tissues. When you look at the facts and figures, you see that not all heavy users fit the same profile. (As a practical matter, they usually do not.) Although women with the characteristics noted above tend to be heavy users, there are also other heavy users with entirely different characteristics. Perhaps they are younger (or older) and have lower incomes. Perhaps they are not homemakers or not female.

If competitors' promotional mixes are all more or less directed to the typical heavy user, you may want to aim at a less typical group or at least at an open group that competitors seem to be ignoring. This is roughly the approach taken by Sara Lee in the case described in Chapter One.

*Are lighter users being overlooked?* In a way, this is a variation on the second question. Assuming that lighter volume consumers are best reached through promotional strategies that are different from those for heavy users, and assuming that your competition generally is aiming toward the latter, then there could be a wide open opportunity for you among light users.

In some cases this could mean that you are deliberately willing to limit your market share possibilities. You would probably expect to get only a portion of the business from people who are not very heavy users, which almost certainly means your share of the total volume would be relatively small. Although many firms would not accept the idea of settling for a low share, it has been pointed out that "[there] are countless examples of low-market-share companies that nevertheless triumph where giants have huge market preserves: Schweppes with only 1.5% of the hotly competitive soft drink market; . . . Mohawk Rubber in tires; Steiger Tractor which goes toe to toe against Deere and J. I. Case; Midland Glass, that capably holds its own against giants such as Owens-Illinois; and feisty little Quaker State Oil in lubricants."[11]

*Is there some way to convince non-users to start using the product?* This question probably presents you with your greatest promotional challenge. It suggests that if you study the people who do not now buy any of the brands in your product category, you may be able to open up an entirely new and large market segment. It amounts to an attempt to increase generic demand. You will recall from Figure 5.6 that over eighty-seven percent of American men do not smoke cigars. Over forty percent of American adults do not chew gum and almost forty-five percent do not use cold remedies. If you were responsible for marketing one of these products, you might want to learn who the non-users are, why they do not use the product, and what sort of other characteristics they have that make them different from both heavy users and light users. Your next job would involve a search for product benefits to meet their special lifestyle goals.

You might expect to see an approach like this being followed by a company that has a very large share of the existing market. Especially if the total size of that market is weakening, such a firm might try to find ways to attract new users. Think of the regular, ground coffee market in relationship to General Foods. That company sells two of the leading coffee brands, Maxwell House and Sanka. The combined shares of all its coffee brands have been estimated to account for over one-third of the total market. It might be difficult to obtain a greater total market share percentage. You begin to encounter buyers who are

**TABLE 5.1 Coffee consumption trends in the United States (selected years)**

| Year | Percent of Persons Drinking[a] | Pounds Per Capita (Annually) |
|------|------------------|------------------|
| 1970 | 74.7 | |
| 1970 | | 13.9 |
| 1971 | | 13.7 |
| 1972 | | 13.6 |
| 1973 | | 13.5 |
| 1974 | | 13.1 |
| 1975 | 61.6 | 12.8 |
| 1976 | 59.1 | 11.7 |
| 1977 | 57.9 | 10.5 |

[a]Varies from percentage in Figure 5.6 because different population bases are used.
*Source: Advertising Age*, June 26, 1978.

pretty much committed to other brands they have used for years, to private-label brands with a low-price appeal, or to regional brands with a strong local following.

Furthermore, with its large total market share General Foods has a big stake in preserving a healthy coffee market; the success of the generic product category is important to the company because it is so important in that product field. If company executives look a bit further than total generic sales, however, they will see drop-offs in both the percentage of Americans drinking coffee and per capita consumption, as shown in Table 5.1.

Suppose that the drop-offs are especially pronounced among younger consumers. The company might decide to search for ways to appeal to young, non-users of coffee. A good start would be to learn what people in this non-user group look for in a beverage (the evaluative criteria) and how they rate coffee on these points as compared to other beverages (the brand criteria ratings). The result could be the introduction or revised explicit promotion of brands such as Mellow Roast (less bitterness, lower price), Brim (caffein free but with a "youthful, innovative" image), and The International Line (instants with added non-coffee flavoring such as "Irish Mocha Mint").

Non-users of the product category might be a difficult group to convert to your brand, but in some situations the potential size of the market to be gained could make it a very worthwhile effort.

**Brand Purchase Concentration**

Market share figures tell you how much of the market is going to your brand and its competitors. They do not tell you how individual customers are dividing their purchases among the various brands. This information is especially valuable in product categories in which the unit value of each sale is rather small and customers repurchase the product fairly often.

On the one hand, a consumer could be completely "brand loyal." This would mean that every time that consumer buys the product he or she will choose the same brand. Brand purchases in this case are totally concentrated.

**FIGURE 5.7 Brand purchase concentration**

| Percentage of purchases each customer in each group gave to the brand over some extended time period | The "brand loyal" situation | | | | | The brand switching situation | | | | Total market share for this brand |
|---|---|---|---|---|---|---|---|---|---|---|
| | Customer group I (25% of total market) | Customer group II (30% of total market) | Customer group III (30% of total market) | Customer group IV (15% of total market) | | Customer group I (25% of total market) | Customer group II (30% of total market) | Customer group III (30% of total market) | Customer group IV (15% of total market) | |
| **Brand A** | 100% | | | | | 30% | 25% | 25% | 16⅔% | 25% |
| **Brand B** | | 100% | | | | 30% | 20% | 40% | 30% | 30% |
| **Brand C** | | | 100% | | | 30% | 40% | 20% | 30% | 30% |
| **Brand D** | | | | 100% | | 10% | 15% | 15% | 23⅓% | 15% |

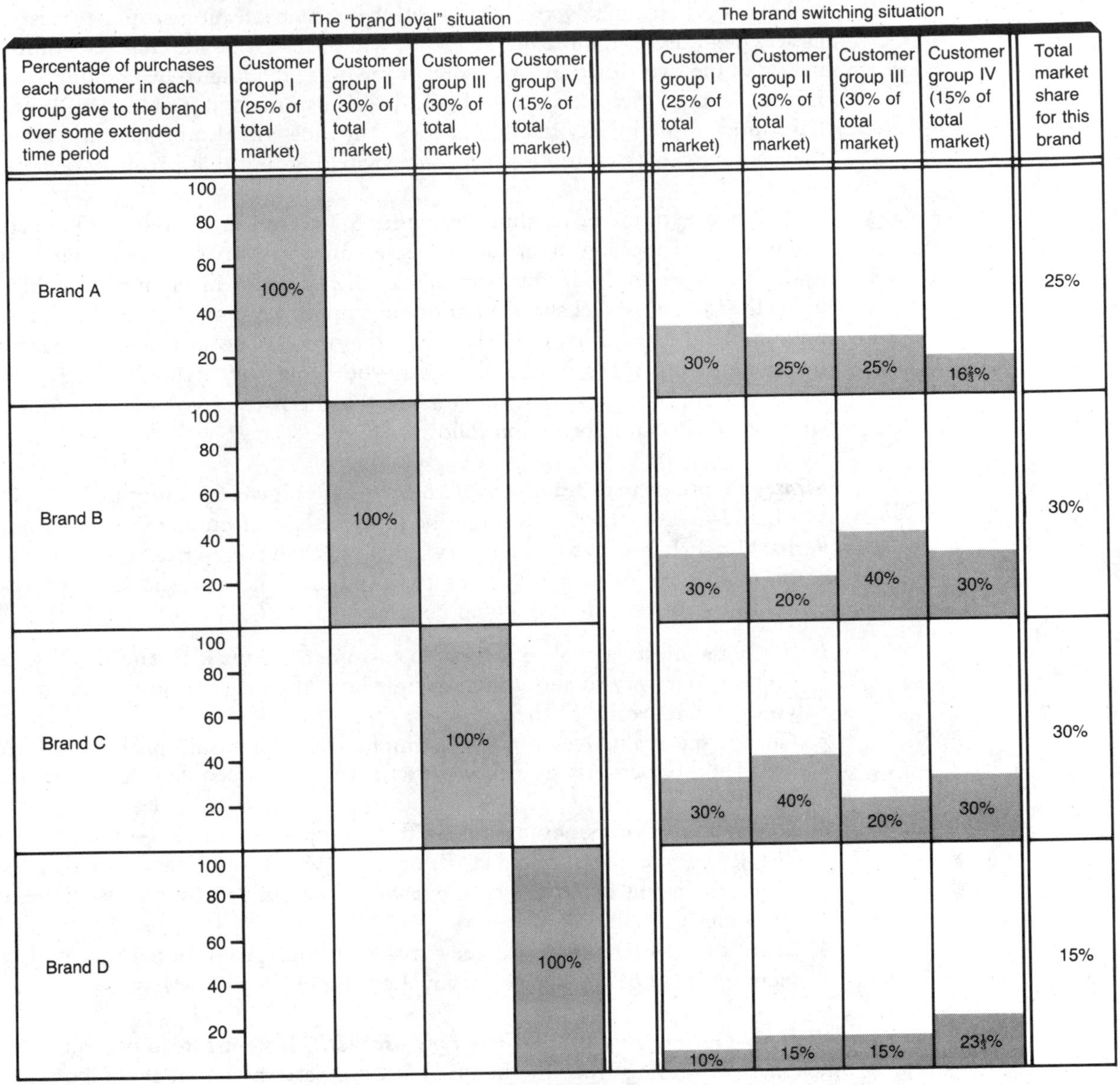

On the other hand, a customer could follow a constant "brand switching" policy. Each time the product is purchased, a different brand is selected. Brand purchases in this case are totally dispersed. Figure 5.7 shows how four competing brands could be holding the same market shares from two completely different types of brand purchase concentration situations.

In each case illustrated in Figure 5.7, the market shares for the four brands are the same. Brand A gets twenty-five percent, brand B gets thirty percent, brand C gets thirty percent, and brand D gets fifteen percent. However, the way they achieve those shares could be quite different. In the first situation, all customers are totally brand loyal. In the second, all customers want to keep switching. It is unlikely that brand purchase concentration in practice is so clearly delineated. In most markets, you will probably be looking at a combination of the two situations, with one or the other tending to be predominant. Every competitor will have some brand-loyal customers, but some brands will have much more loyalty than others. Most brands will also be gaining part of their business from customers who keep switching, but that part may be large or small.

The two extreme possibilities in Figure 5.7 are meant merely to illustrate some ways of looking at brand purchase concentration to assess your best options. For example, if you were marketing brand D in Figure 5.7, which holds the lowest market share, your options might be somewhat different in a predominantly brand-loyal market than they would be in a predominantly brand-switching market. In either case you would want to discover why customers are acting as they are. Some of the alternatives you could consider after you had such information follow.

### Strategy Options in a Brand-Loyal Market.
If you were promoting brand D in a brand-loyal market, you might be facing a case of unique segmentation. Perhaps each brand is stressing very different evaluative criteria that fit the lifestyles of very different types of people. Some of the basic strategy approaches worth considering would be these:

1. Study the lifestyle goals of people in customer groups I, II, and III. Try to find a better way to show these people how the benefits now stressed by your product really fit their needs.
2. Change the evaluative criteria you emphasize. You would probably try to broaden those criteria to include benefits sought by people in groups I, II, and III.
3. Develop an entirely new brand—a fifth entry in the market—that would directly compete with brand A, B, or C but would not interfere with sales of your existing brand D because it would be built to fit a very different consumer group.
4. Leave things pretty much as they are. Plan your promotional mix with a view toward holding the brand-loyal customers you now have.

### Strategy Options in a Brand-Switching Market.
If your fifteen percent market share is coming from the brand-switching pattern shown at the bottom, you are receiving some business from all consumers, but not very much from any of them. Two of the possible reasons for this could be that you are in something like an "occasion-segmentation" situation or that the brands are differentiated but are still seen as very close substitutes for each other. Depending on what your study revealed, some of the promotional strategies worth considering might include the following:

1. Attempt to extend the occasions for which your brand is considered appropriate. For example, Swift's has tried to extend the sales of its "Butterball

Turkeys" beyond the traditional holiday occasions by advertising them for use on occasions such as summertime cookouts.

2. Try to strengthen your degree of differentiation. For example, if your brand seems to be getting a low rating on a certain evaluative criterion, you might test the possibility of some redevelopment of the functional feature underlying that criterion. You could then turn to a strong advertising campaign with a "new and improved" product theme.

3. Take advantage of a possible novelty-seeking situation. Especially when brands are seen as close substitutes for each other, there is reason to believe that some consumers may switch back and forth just to break the monotony. This could be a form of "novelty seeking," which is a desire to do something different.[12]

If you have reason to think the latter situation is a factor in your market, you might want to capitalize on it rather than try to change it. One way to do this without altering your product is to put more emphasis on in-store displays and other sales promotion techniques. This would give prospects who might make purchases on impulse more reasons to act favorably toward your brand.

These are just some of the possible routes you might consider. Which route you finally chose would depend on learning much more about your market than merely the brand purchase concentration patterns. However, these patterns can aid you in working out some initial ideas to help you decide what else you need to know.

*General Shopping Habits*

Purchase decisions have been considered thus far mainly in terms of what products and brands people buy or how they concentrate purchases among various brands. In contrast, the study of shopping habits is concerned with where and when customers buy products. The most important questions regarding the *where* of shopping habits generally revolve around the types of outlets from which consumers usually buy. The most important questions regarding the *when* of shopping habits are likely to revolve around the times of the year during which consumers buy most heavily. Although these aspects of shopping habits will vary for every product category, some specific examples can illustrate how the information might be used.

*Types of Outlets.* Suppose that as a promotional strategist for a cosmetics company you are looking at shopping habits by outlet types as shown in Table 5.2, and that hair care items are important parts of your firm's total line. If sales of your brands are following the general industry pattern, food stores would be delivering fifty percent of your shampoo business but only fifteen percent of your hair coloring volume. The largest part of the latter market would be coming from drugstores.

If your sales by outlet types did not follow or approximate this pattern you would have to decide whether that was good or bad. For example, if you were securing fifty percent of your shampoo volume from drugstores and only twenty-five percent from food stores it might mean that your sales force was extremely effective in working with druggists, ineffective in working with

**TABLE 5.2 Hypothetical sales percentages of hair care products by retail outlet types**

|  | Drug-stores | Food Stores | Mass Outlets | Other |
|---|---|---|---|---|
| Hair Coloring | 50% | 15% | 35% | 0% |
| Hair Sprays | 20% | 40% | 30% | 10% |
| Shampoos | 25% | 50% | 20% | 5% |

grocers, or both. In any case, comparing sales for your brand and its competitors by outlet types assists you in deciding where personal selling or other promotional efforts should be directed, studied, or improved.

*Examining Trends in Sales by Outlet Types.* Sales by outlet types are not necessarily static. Consumers may change shopping habits and retailers may change the amount of emphasis they give to different product lines. For example, the perfume market has traditionally been based mainly in department stores and quality drugstores. Currently, this market is reportedly characterized by more supermarket and chain drugstore purchasing.[13] The traditional outlets have been dominated by brands that are prestige oriented, high priced, and backed by rather small national advertising efforts. They tend to be sold on a personalized clerk-service basis. The currently expanding outlets for perfumes are characterized by self-service and more frequent emphasis on low prices. As a result, observers see much potential for greater development of lower-priced, mass market perfume brands backed by strong national advertising, which would be something quite different than the standard promotional approach of this industry.

*Seasonal Sales Patterns.* In many product categories, there are pronounced sales peaks and valleys throughout the year. Some months are especially good, some rather poor.[14] For instance, consumer demand for cold tablets peaks in October and January, with both months running about thirty percent above average. In contrast, the market for barbecue sauce has only one peak, which occurs in the spring, when sales run at better than seventy-five percent above average. After that, the latter market gradually drops downward until the next spring. Promotional efforts, especially advertising, personal selling, and sales promotion are logically geared to take advantage of seasonal sales patterns. In some cases, manufacturers may attempt to stimulate off-season business. More commonly, they attempt to "strike while the iron is hot." In any case, knowing your seasonal patterns plays an important part in helping you decide on the timing of your promotional efforts.

## THE PRODUCT LIFE CYCLE

The concept of a product life cycle (PLC) has been one of the most discussed topics in marketing. Figure 5.8 illustrates one frequently described view of the

FIGURE 5.8
Generalized prod-
uct life cycle curve
relationships

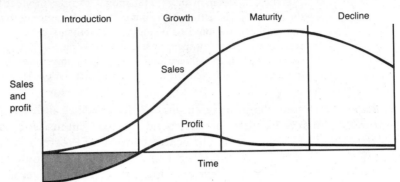

Source: Haas, Robert W., *Industrial Marketing Management*, Second Edition (Boston: Kent Publishing Company, 1983), p. 171.

classic life cycle curve.[15] As shown there, products can be thought of as something akin to living organisms. They are born (or introduced), grow, mature, and eventually decline and die. The key measurement that defines each of the stages is the sales curve.

The classic product life cycle pattern is often described in the following way. During the introduction stage, sales are moving upward but at a slow rate. In the growth stage they climb at a rather rapid rate. In maturity the sales curve goes through three phases: (1) "growth maturity," a period when sales are still increasing but at a very slow rate; (2) "stable maturity," a period when sales are holding constant; and (3) "decaying maturity," a period when sales slowly start to fall. Finally, there is the decline stage, with sales dropping at an accelerating rate.

As indicated in Figure 5.8, profit margins generally peak long before sales reach their high point. In the very early introductory stage, profits are negative because of the high costs required to develop the market. For a short but very happy period in the growth stage, the early investment pays out handsomely. The innovating firm either has a growing market to itself or, at worst, shares it with a few competitors. As more competitors enter the market, however, there are pressures on prices and probably a need for heavier promotional budgets to offset competitive claims. These forces cause profit margins to drop.

## *Implications for Promotional Strategy*

A number of writers have sought to use the PLC as a guide for designing portions of the promotional mix. For instance, life cycle stages have been suggested as being pertinent to the selection of advertising media. In this respect it has been written that "if the product is in the introductory stage . . . media should be chosen that reach a large number of people very quickly. If the product is in the maturity stage, media should be chosen that very selectively reach the target market so that 'waste' is minimized."[16]

Other suggestions involve directions for changing approaches to various promotional elements as the life cycle proceeds, as in the following quotation:

*The Product Life Cycle*

[S]mall increases in quality [of functional features] produce large increases in sales during the introduction stage, but as the product moves toward the decline stage, the market's response to quality improvements declines considerably. Pricing reaches its greatest impact in the maturity stage but drops off in importance in succeeding stages. Advertising remains quite important throughout and packaging appears as the element to stress in the saturation [stable maturity] stage. [17]

## Reservations about the Usefulness of the Product Life Cycle

Despite the positive emphasis it has received in textbooks and articles, some marketing practitioners sound less than enthusiastic when the subject of the PLC is discussed. The board chairman of Procter and Gamble put his feelings in very clear-cut terms when he stated, "I am sometimes asked what is our theory on the life cycle of products, and my answer is very simple. We don't believe in it! I don't mean to say we haven't had brands die—we have—but in each case we failed to do our job."[18]

Two staff members of a major advertising agency have expressed much the same view. They suggest that overreliance on the life cycle approach could lead to a self-fulfilling prophecy of doom, and argue that the life expectancy of a product is in large measure the result of promotional strategy. They conclude that to turn things around and plan promotional strategy on the basis of life expectancy traps you into a vicious circle. In their words, "Clearly, the PLC is a dependent variable which is determined by marketing actions; it is not an independent variable to which companies should adapt their marketing programs. Marketing management itself can alter the shape and duration of a brand's life cycle."[19]

Despite such negative comments, however, there are some good reasons for taking a close look at the PLC when studying promotional strategy. For one thing, it is a simple truth that monitoring sales curves is an important guide to evaluating your past results and planning your future actions. Sales curves are the most basic pieces of information you can obtain about purchase decision patterns. As pointed out above, the PLC is really built around such sales curves. It is one way of analyzing them. Even if you decide you do not want to put too much reliance on it, it is worth considering. Among other things, the PLC can suggest some modified approaches that may be valuable to you.

Furthermore, though some marketing people recommend against it, others say they find the PLC useful. The general manager of Armstrong Cork has written, "I believe [thoughtful managers] will continue to use the PLC concept . . . . I cannot accept the implication that the PLC should be abandoned as a management tool."[20]

## The Product Life Cycle and Promotional Planning

If you are considering the use of life cycle analysis, you should start by recognizing that there are almost always three different types of life cycles involved in a single promotional situation.

1. *The life cycle of the generic product category.* For example, there are the life cycles of automobiles or dentifrices as total product categories.
2. *The life cycle of general product forms or basic variations within the generic product category.* In the automobile category these would include convertibles,

**FIGURE 5.9 Life cycle stages of various products**

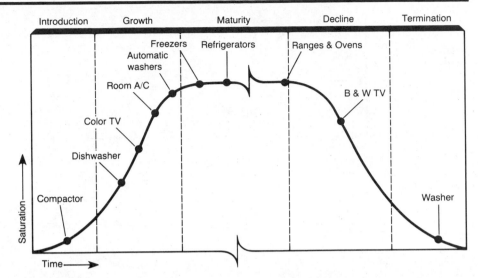

*Source:* Smallwood, John E., "The Product Life Cycle: Key to Strategic Marketing Planning," *MSU Business Topics,* Winter, 1973, p. 30.

sports cars, and station wagons. In the dentifrice field they would include toothpastes, tooth powders, and liquid tooth cleansers as well as fluoride versus nonfluoride dentifrices.

3. *The life cycle of various brands in the product category,* such as Buick, Ford, Studebaker, and Packard in the automobile category or Ipana, Pepsodent, Crest, and Pearl Drops in the dentifrice category.

*Life Cycles of Product Categories and Product Forms*

Your final interest is in the sales of your brand. However, those sales will be tied in some way to the life of some generic product category and to the product form in which your brand is marketed. Figure 5.9 shows one writer's view of where some product categories and product forms were located in their life cycles in the 1970s. Assuming these general locations are accurate, the information might help a major appliance manufacturer to initiate general promotional planning. For instance, wringer washers would probably be written off with respect to much promotional investment. They appear to be dying items. (In fact, this is the way they are treated in practice.) Compactors and dishwashers might be given attention and promotional investments far out of proportion to their current sales because of their potential future demand by consumers.

*Variations in Life Cycle Curve Patterns.*   Before drawing any firm conclusions about promotional strategies, you should consider the fact that not all products follow a neat, "normal" PLC sales curve over time. A number of variations in curve patterns have been described in marketing studies.[21] Two such possible alternatives are shown in Figure 5.10. As they suggest, past sales trends will not always predict future sales directions because those directions could take a variety of different paths. For instance, it is at least remotely

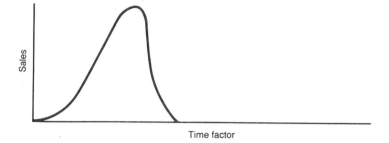

Rapid growth
followed by
rapid decline

Sales

Time factor

**FIGURE 5.10 Alternative product life cycle curves**

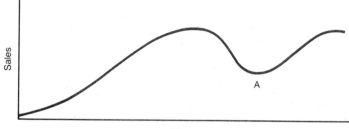

Decline
followed by
renewed growth

Sales

A

Time factor

possible that cigars, though currently a declining product category, are at point A on the type of curve shown in the lower portion of Figure 5.10, in a valley but due for an upturn.

***Analyzing Reasons for Changes in Life Cycle Curves.*** In summary, the evidence suggests that life cycles are worth studying, but are not always clearly predictable for the future, even when you are thinking in terms of a generic product category or a general product form. Furthermore, they should not be viewed as "automatic." Certainly, your promotional planning should not be treated as automatic, or based simply on past sales curves. Life cycle patterns are more appropriately used to help answer such questions as, "Why are the sales curves changing as they are? What should be done about it?"

It was recommended in Chapter 4 that buyers are best viewed as decision makers who choose among available alternatives to best serve their own lifestyle goals or those of others for whom they are acting. If this is true, the reasons for sales curve changes, or for product life cycles, must lie in the way consumers believe various products satisfy lifestyle goal needs. Two actual cases follow in which promotional strategists saw product categories with static or declining sales, asked why and then decided to enter the market with a new brand designed to reverse the downward PLC trend by serving consumer needs more effectively.

The first case involves the grocery field and the company is H. J. Heinz. Its director of new product development studied both product sales trends and competitive behavior. His conclusion was that many fast-growing categories attract too many new brand entries. The result can be a violent struggle for market shares and a dismal profit picture. With that in mind he began examining slow-growth and no-growth areas—mainly products in the stable maturity stage of the life cycle. His premise was that a weakening life cycle for a product category might be the result of ineffective marketing efforts. It might signal an opportunity to innovate rather than a reason to retreat. One commentator on the case wrote, "The chili market stood out like a burnt enchilada. Sales were roughly $140 million and relatively static. Heinz researched the products already in distribution and discovered widespread consumer dissatisfaction, principally with the inferior quality of the meat."[22]

At this point, Heinz decided to send a new brand entry into a static, saturated market. The product, "Chili Fixins," was carefully developed, researched, and backed with heavy advertising and sampling campaigns. The strategy worked. In one survey of retailers, "Chili Fixins" was voted the top new product of the year.

The second example involves a product category in the decline stage. One company decided to compete with a new form of the product and met with some unexpected results. The category was laundry starch. The company was the Boyle-Midway Division of American Home Products. The new product form was spray starch in an aerosol can. It was introduced to the market when the major existing brands were downgrading promotional efforts because consumers were no longer starching clothing and sheets. The starched-look was out of vogue, yet the new brand became an instant success. As one writer described the situation, "Had America returned to the starched-look? No. As is often the case, consumers used the product for something the marketers had not anticipated. Spray starches, later research revealed, were used because they made ironing easier. The products acted as dampening agents, helped eliminate wrinkles, and provided lubricity for the iron."[23]

These illustrations are not meant to imply that product categories in the stable maturity or decline stages always offer good opportunities for new brand entries. The critical issue is analysis of consumer needs, wants, and goals and of the competitive product alternatives available to serve them. Through such analysis you can find clues as to why sales are behaving as they are. Then you can begin considering your promotional alternatives.

## Life Cycles of Individual Brands

Even when sales for product categories are growing rapidly or holding firm in the maturity stage, individual brands may be dying. Especially in markets for low-unit value, ultimate consumer goods (toothpastes, toilet soaps, breakfast cereals, etc.), it is common to talk about increasingly short life cycles. Yet some brands have been top sellers for many years, and are still very robust.

In the toilet soap field, the current best-selling brands are Dial and Ivory. Dial was introduced in 1948; Ivory in 1879. This means that one market leader is over thirty-five years old. The second has been a major brand for more than a century. These are hardly exceptions. There are an abundance of brands that have been thriving for generations, for example, Hershey chocolate bars, Crisco shortening, Ford automobiles, Maytag washers, Otis elevators, and John Deere tractors.

Then how can anyone talk about short life cycles?

For one thing, the average life cycle looks short because so many brands die very young. Their peak sales levels are low and are reached quickly. They are soon withdrawn from the market as failures but their short lifespans pull down the average. Although Dial and Ivory have been leaders for years, a number of rival soap brands have come and gone in rapid succession. Between 1955 and 1970, twenty-two new toilet soaps were put on the market.[24] They included such names as Spree, Choice, Veto, Blossom, and Goddess, and all were entries from major soapmakers. Reportedly, only five out of the twenty-two were ever able to attain a market share above five percent.

***Extending a Brand's Lifespan.*** Brands that continue to live far beyond their normal life expectancies usually have two things in common. First, they were introduced with distinctive and superior functional features that appealed to some large group of consumers. Second, they have been carefully tended over the years. Their functional make-up has often been changed to keep pace with consumer tastes and desires, and explicit promotion has been reformulated to reposition or reinforce the brand's image.

In the case of products like elevators, tractors, and washing machines, the redevelopment of functional features over a period of years is so dramatic that it is easy to see. Among lower-priced package goods, the changes can be much more subtle, but just as vital to maintaining a high market share. For example, consider how alert promotional strategists work to prolong the lifespan of Dial soap. "Dial's profile is monitored yearly, and the product tested against other brands. Management never forgets that the first Dial users are now approaching their 70's. And while the heaviest Dial users fall into the 35-to-50-year-old spread, management concentrates on a younger segment as insurance against an early retirement of the soap."[25]

The monitoring of Dial soap includes reappraisals of customers' preferences not only in the functional features of the product but also in terms of such surrogate cues as shape, fragrance, and package design. For instance, in one year the company tested fifty-six different shades of aqua, pink, and gold and then introduced new color variations into the Dial soap line on the basis of *current* consumer preferences. In short, Dial soap remains alive because (like most other market leaders), it is constantly reviewed for improvements that will better suit consumers' changing lifestyle goals and tastes. A Procter and Gamble executive put it in the following way:

> To keep an established brand healthy and growing over the long term, the successful marketer must continually anticipate changes in the marketplace and must continually improve the product and marketing plans to capitalize on those changes. . . . [For example, the Tide laundry detergent] which we are selling today is importantly different from the Tide product which we introduced in 1947. It is different in its cleaning performance, sudsing characteristics, aesthet-

ics, physical properties, [and] packaging. In total, there have been 55 significant modifications in this one brand during its [first 30 years of life]. [26]

### Rejuvenation through Explicit Promotion.
Apart from making changes in basic implicit promotion, you can extend the life cycle of successful brands through revisions in explicit promotion. Often this is based on product improvements, as is evident from the many "new and improved" advertising appeals you see.

In many cases, however, a better approach to advertising or personal selling can revive a faltering brand with little or no change in the basic product. This assumes you already have a good product. It also assumes that you have studied your target consumer group to learn what kind of messages will convince them that your brand has the evaluative criteria they seek. An illustration is provided by still another critic of the product life cycle:

> Brand managers should forget the product life cycle concept [according to an executive of a major advertising agency]. "Managers curtail advertising and other marketing activities and, as a result, kill off brands that could be profitable for many more years." . . . An example, he said, is Charmin, a one-ply toilet tissue which was a dying product until Procter and Gamble developed the Mr. Whipple advertising. [27]

*An Extended View of Life Cycle Analysis*

Perhaps the main criticisms of the product life cycle approach can be summed up this way. The critics do not seem to quarrel with the idea that markets change or that a product that fails to reflect market changes is likely to die. They do seem to be challenging the idea that the death of a brand is inevitable simply because it has been on the market for a certain number of months or years or even if sales have been falling. Their point is that promotion—both implicit and explicit—can be redesigned to fit market changes. Ideally, this would be done by constantly monitoring consumers and competitors while the brand is still strong, and on this basis making appropriate revisions in the promotional mix. Even when a brand has begun to go into decline, it may be worth saving.

Brands can be "reborn" through new promotional efforts. One writer has offered an extended and somewhat colorful view of the product life cycle from a managerial perspective. Its sequential flow is shown in Figure 5.11. In terms of our current discussion, the interesting parts of this PLC approach are the "introduction" and "ongoing" stages. The suggestion is that by "repositioning," you can put your brand into something like a new introduction stage. It is possible, therefore, that by monitoring the market and readapting your promotional strategies, you can "reintroduce" your product over and over again.

Only when your analysis convinces you that there is no hope of rebirth, should you accept the "twilight" stage. At that point you will probably decide to cut back on development and promotion, and be content to simply "milk" the brand for whatever declining sales and profits it will produce. But that point may not come for many years; or it could come in a few months.

**FIGURE 5.11 A dynamic, managerial view of the life cycle concept**

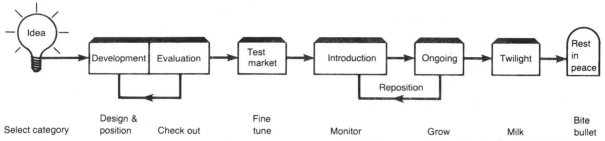

Source: Little, John D. C., "Decision Support Systems for Marketing Managers," *Journal of Marketing*, Summer, 1979, p. 12. Reproduced with permission.

## SUMMARY

Market segmentation involves the idea that consumers differ in terms of exactly what features and benefits they want from a particular product. Ideally, in applying a segmentation policy, you begin by examining consumer desires. If you find a segment of consumers whose particular needs and desires are not well served by existing brands, you tailor a brand to meet those needs and desires. The rest of your promotional program is built from there. In practice, segmentation seems to have several variations that can overlap with each other. Some of these variations include the following:

1. *Unique Segmentation.* Your brand is the only one serving a particular segment.
2. *Segmented Differentiation.* Your brand serves a particular consumer segment but competes with rather close substitutes that serve the same segment.
3. *Lifestyle Segmentation.* Your brand may be quite similar to competitors in terms of functional features. However, your explicit promotion interprets those features differently from competitors' promotion to show how they fit the unique lifestyle goals of a particular segment.
4. *Subsegmentation.* Your brand takes segmentation one step further than competitors and "segments within a segment."
5. *Occasion Segmentation.* Your brand aims at the same consumers as other brands but is positioned for use in specific situations. You promote with the idea that your target market will use your brand in some occasions, but use competitive brands in others.

In searching for open segments, the planning inputs from the consumer field are logical starting points for your analysis. Purchase decisions, as a planning input, deal with what, how, where, and when consumers have bought in the past. There are five major aspects of such behavior that can aid you in considering promotional options for the future. These are: (1) sales trends for your generic product category; (2) market shares; (3) consumption concentration; (4) brand purchase concentration; and (5) general shopping habits.

Analyzing purchase decision patterns can suggest questions and possibilities regarding your promotional strategy alternatives. These questions and possibilities must then be considered in the light of what you know about competitive promotional strategies. Combined with information on the other planning inputs, they can guide your creative thinking.

The product life cycle is a much discussed approach that relates to purchase decision patterns. It deals essentially with the nature of sales curves over time. These sales curves may involve generic product categories, product forms, or individual brands.

Some writers feel that by examining your "stage in the life cycle" you can get almost automatic guidance for promotional planning. Other writers see the product life cycle approach as a useless or even dangerous technique. The point of view taken in this text is that the concept can be a useful one if the following points are recognized: (1) the PLC curve can take a variety of forms; (2) the amount of time involved in a life cycle—even for different brands of the same product—can vary tremendously; (3) brands can be "reborn" or "recycled" so that their lives are stretched over very long periods; and (4) life cycle curves actually reflect changes in consumers' wants, needs, desires, and perceptions. On this basis, it is suggested that sales curves must be analyzed in terms of other market data. When this is done, even a declining sales curve may signal a promotional opportunity rather than a reason to withdraw from the market.

## DISCUSSION QUESTIONS

1. Five different varieties of market segmentation approaches were discussed at the beginning of the chapter. Now suppose that you are the marketing manager for a large well-recognized computer firm that is introducing a new line of computers built exclusively for home use. You have several competitors offering essentially the same product; however, your brand has one exclusive though minor difference. Utilizing the concepts introduced under each variety of market segmentation, briefly explain why you would or would not use that technique.

2. Why is it important to study consumer purchase decisions when beginning to devise a promotional strategy? What are the major aspects of purchase decisions and in what terms should they be studied?

3. What is meant by "consumption concentration"?

Summarize the findings of consumption concentration for coffee, chewing gum, cigars, and cold remedies. What questions do these findings suggest for developing an appropriate promotional mix?

4. Heavy-user groups are often identified on the basis of demographic variables. What are some of the other determinants used in defining a heavy-user group? Which variables would be most appropriate in defining a "typical" user of a new cable TV system featuring informational, cultural, and educational programs? List them in order of importance and explain why you ordered them that way.

5. Consider the brand purchase concentration patterns shown in Figure 5.7. Distinguish between "brand-loyal" and "brand-switching" consumer purchase patterns. What are some of the promotional strategies worth considering in the "brand-loyal" situation?

6. Suppose you are interested in entering the parcel delivery service market. At present the market is dominated by three major competitors and the market seems to be declining, according to many analysts. What information might you want to consider before entering the market, and how might your parcel delivery service be effectively promoted?

7. Discuss occasion segmentation in terms of how it might be applied in marketing perfume, coffee, breakfast cereals, and cold remedies.

8. Assume you are selling a product with sharp seasonal sales fluctuations. Sixty percent of total product category sales occur in April and May.

The remaining forty percent are spread fairly evenly over the remaining ten months. How might this affect your advertising strategy?

9. Cigars appear to be in the decline stage of the product life cycle. What strategy alternatives does this suggest for existing brands? What factors, if any, could lead to renewed growth for this product category?

10. Nine consumer field variables were listed as potential bases for market segmentation approaches. Discuss each of these as it might be used as a base for segmenting the market for vitamin/mineral preparations.

## REFERENCES

1. Wendell R. Smith, "Product Differentiation and Market Segmentation as Alternative Marketing Strategies," *Journal of Marketing,* July 1956, p. 4.

2. Frank M. Bass, Edgar A. Pessemier, and Donald R. Lehman, "An Experimental Study of Relationships between Attitudes, Brand Preference and Choice," *Behavioral Science,* November 1972, pp. 532–541.

3. Smith, "Product Differentiation and Market Segmentation as Alternative Marketing Strategies," p. 4.

4. Alfred S. Boote, "Market Segmentation by Product Values and Salient Product Attributes," *Journal of Advertising Research,* February 1981, pp. 29–36.

5. Alfred E. Goldman, "Occasion Segmentation Can Help You in Profiling Market," *Marketing News,* 6 April 1979, p. 1.

6. J. A. Burdus, "Attitude Models—The Dream and the Reality," in Philip Levine, ed. *Attitude Research Bridges the Atlantic* (Chicago: The American Marketing Association 1975), p. 161.

7. Burton Marcus, et al., *Modern Marketing Management,* rev. ed. (New York: Random House, 1980), p. 125.

8. William M. Weilbacher, *Advertising* (New York: Macmillan, 1979), p. 186.

9. Miller Marketing Show (Milwaukee: Miller Brewing Company, 1979–80), pp. 4–5.

10. Bernice Tinkleman, "Though Marketing Methods May Be Various, Frozen Yogurt Makers Aim At Same Target Markets," *Marketing News,* 2 December 1977, p. 4.

11. "Market-Share-ROI Corporate Strategy Approach Can Be an Oversimplistic Snare," *Marketing News,* 15 December 1978, pp. 6–7.

12. Edmund W. J. Faison, "The Neglected Variety Drive: A Useful Concept for Consumer Behavior," *Journal of Consumer Research,* December 1977, pp. 172–175.

13. James P. McKinley, "Shelf Space Battle Driving Cosmetics into Food Stores," *Chemical Marketing Reporter,* 27 February 1975, pp. 47–52.

14. SAMI Size and Trend Report, *Progressive Grocer,* July 1979, p. 56.

15. Much has been written about the product life cycle and it has been presented in a number of modified versions. Articles of special interest include:

George S. Day, "The Product Life Cycle: Analysis and Application Issues," *Journal of Marketing,* Fall 1981, pp. 60–67.

Gerard E. Tellis and Merle Crawford, "An Evolutionary Approach to Product Growth Theory," *Journal of Marketing,* Fall 1981, pp. 125–132.

George F. MacKenzie, "MacKenzie: On Marketing's 'Missing Link'—The Product Life Cycle Concept," *Industrial Marketing,* April 1977, pp. 42–43.

John A. Weber, "Planning Corporate Growth with Inverted Product Life Cycles," *Long Range Planning,* October 1976, pp. 12–29.

Ben M. Enis, Raymond La Garce, and Arthur E. Prell, "Extending the Product Life Cycle," *Business Horizons,* June 1977, pp. 46–56.

16. Robert C. Anderson and Thomas E. Barry, *Advertising Management* (Columbus, Ohio: Charles E. Merrill, 1979), p. 262.

17. Burton Marcus, et al., *Modern Marketing* (New York: Random House, 1975), p. 611.

18. Edward G. Harness, *Some Basic Beliefs About Marketing* (Cincinnati OH: The Procter and Gamble Company, 1977), p. 18.

19. Nariman D. Dhalla and Sonia Yuspeh, "Forget the Product Life Cycle Concept," *Harvard Business Review*, January–February 1976, p. 105.

20. R. H. Caldwell, in "Letters to the Editor," *Harvard Business Review,* March–April 1976, pp. 148, 150.

21. David F. Midgely, "Toward a Theory of the Product Life Cycle: Explaining Diversity," *Journal of Marketing,* Fall 1981, pp. 109–115.

22. Curt Schleier, "Heinz Reverses Poor Image in New Product Development," *Product Marketing,* May 1977, p. 23.

23. Robert S. Wheeler, "Marketing Tales With a Moral," *Product Marketing,* April 1977, p. 43.

24. Barbara Johnson, "Dial: How a Number One Product Stays on Top," *Product Marketing,* February 1977, p. 27.

25. *Ibid.,* pp. 28–29.

26. Harness, *Some Basic Beliefs About Marketing,* pp. 15–16.

27. "Product Can Live Longer, Say 3 Marketers: Not So, Says Fourth," *Marketing News,* 18 September 1978, p. 19.

# CHAPTER SIX

# *Consumer Attitudes as Planning Inputs*

## FOCUS OF THE CHAPTER

This and the next two chapters continue the discussion of planning inputs for promotional strategy. They draw heavily on some basic ideas from the behavioral sciences that can serve as useful points of reference in your decision making. This chapter deals with consumers' attitudes and attitude formation processes in terms of their relevance to designing your promotional program.

## APPLYING BEHAVIORAL SCIENCE TO PROMOTION

The coverage in these chapters is *not* intended to be a complete review of the literature on consumer behavior. Especially during the last two decades, many academicians have made highly interesting contributions to this field.[1] A sizable proportion of these contributions relate to basic research meant to serve as a foundation for further study rather than as a direct guide to the implementation of business practice. Although such material is intellectually rich and stimulating, the majority of it is not immediately germane to the development of promotional programs. Therefore, in selecting theories and research findings to be included here, major emphasis has been placed only on those contributions that relate most closely to the methods observed and discussed in the business world.

Though the subjects we will be discussing are relevant to business decision making, promotional strategists often arrive at their decisions without using theories or terms quite as formal as those we will use in presenting these subjects. For example, we will be suggesting rather strict definitions for "attitudes," "personality," and "culture," even though each of these words tends to be used much more loosely in the business world. Importantly, you should recognize that the ideas with which we shall deal are applicable in the practice of promotion, even though our descriptions of them will often be framed in a much more rigid structure than most business executives might use.

In addition, it should be emphasized that, while examples will be presented to explain how you might actually put the concepts into action, they are not meant to present precise or unqualified recommendations concerning specific research techniques. The intention is to acquaint you with potentially valuable approaches to analysis and creativity. When there are differences of opinion concerning the research methods that should be used to gather and interpret data, footnote references to further discussions of research procedures are provided for those interested in pursuing the topic.

# CONSUMER ATTITUDES

*Attitudes and Marketing*

For marketing purposes, attitudes can be distinguished under two general headings: (1) consumer attitudes toward lifestyle goals, and (2) consumer attitudes toward products and brands. Many attitudes toward lifestyle goals can be described as having "centrality," being deep-seated or firmly anchored in a person's self-concept—her or his way of living and thinking. Consider such differing views as:

> "It's important to keep yourself feeling and looking young," versus "People should look and act their age."

> "It's wrong for women to work outside the home while they still have small children around the house," versus "Being a wife and mother should not deprive a person of fulfilling herself through a career."

> "To be popular you have to go along with the crowd," versus "People will respect you most if you stick to your guns and are true to your own values."

Attitudes like these may be very strongly rooted and difficult to change, at least through the techniques emphasized in this book. However, attitudes toward lifestyle goals are rarely the kind promotional strategists try to influence directly; rather, they are usually recognized as facts with which the promotional strategist works but does not attempt to alter. You build messages mainly to fit such centralized, lifestyle attitudes, not to change them. Centralized attitudes of this sort will be discussed later in our coverage of lifestyle goals and their underlying determinants, the subject of the two chapters following this one.

Attitudes toward products and brands, the second general type of attitude and the topic of the present chapter, are usually considered to have much less centrality and to be much more susceptible to change.[2] When a person is vigorously opposed to mothers with small children pursuing careers outside the home, any argument you raise against that person's position may be met with strong resistance, misperceived, or tuned out completely. But what if the same person has the attitude that Oil of Olay works better than Rose Milk in keeping her skin soft and youthful looking? It seems much less likely that you would encounter formidable opposition when you presented your case for Rose Milk. You still might not succeed in changing her brand preference, but the odds are that you would at least receive a fair hearing and have a better chance to sell your idea.

## The Purpose of Studying Attitudes

Understanding consumers' attitudes toward products and brands is an issue of importance to you as a promotional strategist. Of special concern are their attitudes toward (1) your product category in general, (2) your brand in particular, (3) competing brands in your product category, and (4) alternative product categories that could serve the same needs. The more you know about such attitudes, including how they are formed and the techniques through which they can be analyzed, the better equipped you will be to change them (if they are unfavorable or nonexistent toward your brand), upgrade them (if they are only moderately favorable) or better capitalize on them (if they are favorable but not resulting in as high a level of sales as they should).

Despite its importance in the development of promotional strategy, the term "attitude" does not appear in any of the boxes of the general framework for analysis which we are following (see Figure 4.2). This is because the issue of attitudes toward products and brands revolves around four separate variables in that framework. This chapter will deal with those four variables shown in Figure 6.1 in terms of both their relationships to each other and their implications as planning input factors. We will begin by considering brand criteria ratings, brand preference levels, and purchase intentions. The role played by evaluative criteria will be considered later in the chapter.

## Attitudes: What They Are

One formal definition of an attitude is as follows: "An attitude is a mental and neural state of readiness to respond, organized through experience, exerting a directive and/or dynamic influence on behavior."[3]

The average consumer would probably give a much shorter and less complex definition. A fairly typical statement might be, "An attitude is the way I feel about something." However, if we asked several consumers about their attitudes toward various brands of a specific product such as coffee, we could get answers such as the following:

> Mr. A: I think Folger's is very good because it has such a rich flavor, but I also like Maxwell House and I usually buy one of those two.

> Mrs. B: I don't think there's very much difference between most brands, so I generally buy the one that is on sale, if it's one of the brands I like.

> Ms. C: I drink too much coffee and it's starting to make me jumpy. I'm thinking of trying Brim. It's supposed to be caffein-free.

FIGURE 6.1
Consumer field
variables relating
directly to customers'
attitudes toward
products and brands

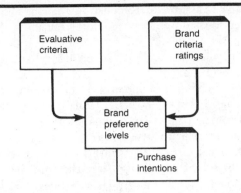

When you hear answers like these, you know that attitudes involve more than just "feelings." Examined closely, such statements begin to explain why the formal definition of attitudes is so complex.

## Components of Attitudes

Because the word "attitude" really implies several different things, psychologists often divide attitudes into three components: (1) the cognitive or perceptual component, (2) the affective or feeling component, and (3) the conative or intentions component.

**The Cognitive Component.**   "The cognitive or perceptual component represents a person's <u>information</u> about an object."[4] Note that the key word in this definition is "information." Such information can be of two general types: (1) information that the object—in our case the brand or product—exists, or (2) information about specific aspects of the brand as <u>perceived</u> by the individual. We will say more about the first type of information—sheer awareness that a brand exists—later. As to information of the second type—perceptions concerning specific aspects of the brand—you can see that this is part of what Mr. A and Ms. C were implying when they said, respectively, "Folger's . . . has such a <u>rich flavor</u>" and "Brim . . . is supposed to be <u>caffeine-free</u>."

**The Affective Component.**   "The <u>affective or feeling component</u> deals with the person's <u>overall feeling</u> of like <u>or dislike</u> for a situation, object, person, policy, idea, <u>and so forth</u>."[5] When Mr. A said, "Folgers is <u>very good</u> . . . but I also like Maxwell House," he was expressing overall feelings, ranking the brands on a like–dislike scale, although not a very precise one. Folger's ranks highest, followed by Maxwell House. In other words, that portion of Mr. A's statement was a report on the affective component of his attitude.

**The Conative Component.**   "The <u>conative</u> or <u>intentions</u> component refers to the person's gross behavioral expectations regarding the objective."[6] In other words, it is what he or she plans to do as a result of his or her overall feeling. In loose fashion, this is the component Ms. C was reflecting when she said she was "thinking of trying" Brim and what Mr. A had in mind when he said he usually bought Maxwell House or Folger's.

**The Relationship Between the Components**

It seems reasonable to assume that a consumer's plans to buy a particular brand (conative or intentions component) would be related to that consumer's overall feeling about the brand (affective or feeling component), which in turn should be based on the information that consumer has about the brand (cognitive or perceptual component). This is what our general framework for promotional analysis is saying. No one box contains the word "attitude" because several boxes are needed to show the relational system of attitude components. The terms used to name those components in the framework apply more to promotional practice than to behavioral theory. However, when translated into the psychological terminology just introduced, the following may be concluded: (1) "brand criteria ratings" are the equivalent of the cognitive or perceptual component; (2) "brand preference levels" are the equivalent of the affective or feeling component; and (3) "purchase intentions" are the equivalent of the conative or intentions component (Figure 6.2).

*Order of Influence.* In the general framework, these three variables are shown as influencing each other in the sequence discussed—brand criteria ratings influence brand preference levels, which in turn influence purchase intentions. Not every promotional strategist would agree that the promotional situation is always quite that simple or that things must follow that exact order. For example, the issue of habit buying was mentioned in Chapter 4. It could be argued that once consumers fall into a pattern of habitual purchase intentions they might "learn" to like what they have been buying as much as to buy what they like. In other words, there could be more complex interplays between these three variables than our one-way sequence suggests. Nonetheless, as a promotional strategist your major entry point among these three variables is most likely to be through persuasive information that changes brand criteria ratings. Based on this assumption, the sequence suggests a logical way to begin considering a strategy approach. Because your goal is a sale, or a purchase decision, we will first take a closer look at the attitude component closest to that goal, purchase intentions, and then work back through the sequence.

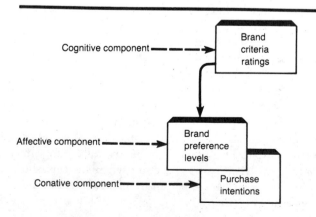

FIGURE 6.2 Attitude components as represented in the framework for promotional analysis

*Consumer Attitudes as Planning Inputs*

**Purchase Intentions and Purchase Decisions**

Our imaginary coffee drinkers seemed to be implying something about brands they intended to buy, but only in a very loose fashion. Suppose we asked Mr. A to be more specific about how "usually" he bought Maxwell House versus Folger's and, more to the point, how "usually" he thought he would be doing so in the future. If we could induce him to express this in terms of probability of purchase—how many chances out of a hundred for each brand—we would have a tighter and more quantified measure of purchase intentions. He might even extend his list a bit and say something such as "the chances are about fifty (out of one hundred) for Folger's, thirty for Maxwell House, ten for Chock Full o' Nuts, and ten for Sanka." Would this be a measure of attitude? It would certainly be a measure of one component, and an important component at that, if it accurately predicted how much of each brand he bought over time.

The issue of how accurately attitudes in general predict behavior such as purchase decisions is disputed.[7] However, when the conative or intentions component is isolated and used as the predictor of behavior the evidence is much more positive.[8] Indeed, some marketing research practitioners have found that under certain conditions purchase intention measures can predict market shares rather well: "If the intention measure is 'yes-no' toward a single purchase of a single brand, prediction is likely to be very weak. . . . *But if the intention measure is probabilistic . . . [and is applied to] a series of purchases, prediction can be quite strong.*"[9]

On this basis, if a market survey discovers a segment of consumers with purchase probabilities such as those reported by Mr. A, market shares for that segment over time should be approximately fifty percent for Folger's, thirty percent for Maxwell House, and so on, for as long a period as those probabilities hold and assuming segment members are average in terms of consumption concentration.[10] One reason a market researcher might want to measure purchase intentions is to predict changes in market shares before they actually take place. One reason that you, as a promotional strategist, might be interested is that they could help give you an advance reading on the effectiveness of your strategy before you were able to measure it through sales response.

**Capitalizing on Purchase Intentions Levels**

Viewing purchase intentions as probabilities rather than certainties can be important in building your total promotional strategy mix. For example, consider the following consumer survey that classifies purchase intentions probabilities in broader terms.

*Purchase Intentions Survey.* As shown in Figure 6.3, the researchers who conducted this survey had consumers classify brands into sets.[11] The *total set* includes all of the brands that are readily available to the consumer. The *awareness set* includes all the brands of which the consumer has any knowledge at all, as measured by his or her unaided listing of brand names. The *unawareness set* includes all the remaining brands in the total set not listed by the consumer. The *evoked set* includes all the brands of which the consumer is aware and says that she or he considers buying. The *inept set* includes all the brands of which the consumer is aware but would absolutely not consider

**FIGURE 6.3 Sets of brands based on consumer attitudes**

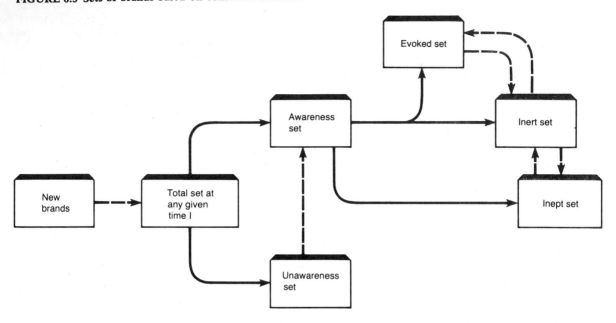

*Source:* Adapted from Chem L. Narayama and Rom J. Markin, "Consumer Behavior and Product Performance: An Alternative Conceptualization," *Journal of Marketing*, vol. 25 (October 1975), p. 2.

buying anytime at all. The *inert set* includes the remaining brands of which the consumer is aware. Apparently the consumer feels rather neutral about these but would not absolutely refuse to buy them.

On a probability of purchase basis, the evoked set might be translated as "rather high probability," the inert as "rather low probability," and the inept set as "no chance." The results of the survey, as they apply to brands of beer are shown in Table 6.1.

***General Implications of the Survey Data.*** Some points worth considering about the pattern of such results are these. The average person was not even

**TABLE 6.1 Purchase intentions measured by number of brands in each set**

|  | Average Number for All Consumers Questioned | Maximum Number Given by Any Consumer Questioned |
| --- | --- | --- |
| Awareness Set | 10.6 | 24 |
| Evoked Set | 3.5 | 13 |
| Inert Set | 4.7 | 15 |
| Inept Set | 2.4 | 18 |

*Source:* C. L. Narayama and R. J. Markin, "Consumer Behavior and Product Performance: An Alternative Conceptualization," *Journal of Marketing*, vol. 25 (October 1975), p. 3.

close to being aware of all the brands available, at least when awareness is measured on the basis of freely naming the brand without any assistance. Out of an apparently possible twenty-four brands, the average person named only about eleven. Although there were some people who indicated that they would consider only one brand in their high probability "evoked set," on average most appear to be more open minded. The typical person is willing to buy any one of three or more different brands. If the high probability and low probability sets are combined, the average acceptable number of brands comes out to be slightly over eight. In this same survey, although the actual numbers were somewhat lower, the general pattern was similar for toothpaste, mouthwash, and deodorants.

*Promotional Implications of the Survey Data.* Figure 6.4 displays the survey results when specific beer brands are classified on the basis of the percentages of potential customers who (a) know about the brand (the awareness set), (b) give it a high purchase intention probability (the evoked set), (c) give it a lower but still possible purchase intention probability (the inert set), and (d) give it a zero probability, no chance of purchase (the inept set). At least among these individuals, Budweiser had an advantage over three competitors, in both "top-of-mind" awareness and high-probability purchase intentions. This should give it a higher market share. If the others want to increase their shares, one promotional strategy course would be to attempt to change consumer attitudes so that their brand is moved into the evoked set of more prospects.

Another approach is to take better advantage of any positive purchase intention position you have at present. A brand such as Miller appears to have some chance among fifty-eight percent of these consumers, which is not all that far below Budweiser's total chance among sixty-nine percent. Although Miller's proportion of the market with high-order purchase intentions is much lower, anything it can do to "bias" the final outcome in its favor might give it a higher market share than the original purchase probabilities would predict.

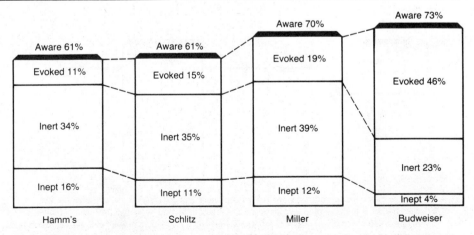

FIGURE 6.4 Four brands of beer compared on purchase intentions sets

*Source:* Adapted from C. L. Narayama and R. J. Markin, "Consumer Behavior and Product Performance: An Alternative Conceptualization," *Journal of Marketing*, vol. 25 (October 1975), p. 4.

*Consumer Attitudes*

***Maximizing the Conversion of Purchase Intentions into Purchase Decisions.***
If a prospective purchaser gives your brand a twenty percent purchase intentions probability, this does not mean she or he will necessarily buy it one time
out of every five. As any successful gambler knows, probability has no memory. Losing the sale this week, on a twenty percent probability, will not
increase your chances for next week. Conversely, winning the sale this week
will not lower them for the future. In your situation as promotional strategist,
this means that each time that person is shopping, you have a twenty percent
chance of making a sale. Part of your job is making that rather low chance pay
off as often and as profitably as possible.

For mass-marketed, heavily advertised merchandise sold through middlemen, the most logical way to increase payoff from any positive level of purchase intention, however high or low, is by gaining assistance through reseller
activities such as recommendations, better shelf-positioning, displays, or point-
of-purchase sales promotion pieces. As Figure 6.5 reminds us, this is what our
general framework for analysis is saying in part. This issue will be given more
extended attention when we deal with explicit promotion—especially personal
selling and sales promotion—directed to resellers (see Chapter 19). Even when
you have built a strong purchase intentions level, reseller support is often
essential for market success.

**Brand Preference Levels and Purchase Intentions**

***Intervening Factors Between Preferences and Intentions.*** As a general rule,
should you expect that people intend to buy what they like—that brand preference levels will predict purchase intention probabilities? What about all those
people who "like" Rolls-Royce automobiles, Chris Craft cruisers, and jewelry
by Cartier, yet have absolutely no intention of buying such brands in the
foreseeable future? In trying to link brand preference levels to purchase intentions, you first have to qualify your prospects by asking such questions as the

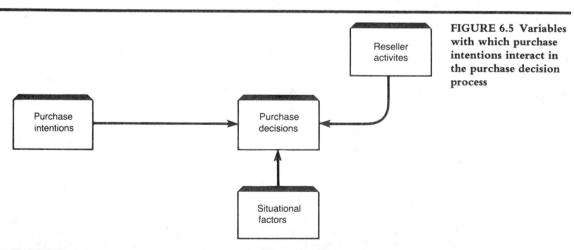

FIGURE 6.5 Variables
with which purchase
intentions interact in
the purchase decision
process

Purchase intentions are normally probabilistic in nature and combine with other factors in the
determination of the final purchase decision. In particular, favorable reseller activities can often be a
vital coexisting factor if you are to capitalize fully on any positive purchase intention level your brand
may possess at the start of the decision process.

following about your target customers. Are they actually in the market for the product class at all? Can they afford the item? When price is included as a consideration, do their brand preference levels still hold? As one text on salesmanship states, "Outstanding sales people spend their time selling the most promising prospects, whereas weak salespeople try to sell to anybody."[12]

It is also true that people sometimes intend to do things they do not seem to like. Quite probably, there have been times when you intended to study for an exam or visit a dentist, even though such activities do not rate all that highly on your preference scale. However, in these situations, what you "like" is not the activity itself but what it will help you attain—a college degree or relief from a painful tooth. The activity you intend to undertake is simply a price you must pay to get what you do like. This suggests that predicting purchase intentions from brand preference levels requires consideration of other factors.

***Discrepancies in Relationships Between Preference Levels and Intentions Levels.*** Even when those other factors are accounted for, preference levels may not produce intention levels on a direct, one-to-one basis or even on a clear rank-order basis. For example, suppose we wanted to dig a bit more deeply into attitudes of consumers toward the brands of beer discussed above. We ask a respondent to give us (1) an overall, brand preference level for each brand on a nine-point scale (nine being highest) and (2) a purchase intentions probability level on a "chances out of one hundred" basis. The brand preference ratings come out this way: Hamm's = 9, Schlitz = 8, Budweiser = 6, and Miller = 3.

Would you now feel confident that the *purchase intentions* level for Schlitz is very close to that for Hamm's, whereas that for Budweiser is two-thirds as high and that for Miller about one-third as high? This would be one possibility but there are many others. This same person could express a purchase intentions probability of seventy percent for Hamm's and thirty percent for Schlitz—a far different ratio than that for "overall liking." He or she could also give both Budweiser and Miller zero probabilities, rank ordering them the same for purchase intentions though not for "overall liking" level. At the same time, it does not seem likely that this customer would have as strong purchase intentions for a low-ranked brand as he or she has for a high-ranked brand unless we have overlooked something such as price, availability, or social influence.

Despite all these complications it is not illogical to assume that the more your promotion raises brand preference levels the more it tends to raise purchase intentions. The relationship, however, is not one of absolute necessity or direct ratio.

***Implications for Promotional Strategy Planning.*** What does all this mean to you as a promotional strategist, again assuming you are dealing with a mass marketing situation? It suggests that, if you want to measure the effects of your promotion on attitudes and are in a position to order a market survey, you would be well-advised to secure information on *both* purchase intentions and brand preference levels. The former is likely to be a better predictor of market shares while the latter gives you a reading on how much progress you are making toward improving your market image in a manner that should induce higher purchase intention levels in the future.

**Brand Criteria Ratings**

Our general framework for promotional analysis considers consumers to be information processors who obtain their information from several sources and use it to rate brands on the benefits of interest to them. Sometimes they may actively seek out that information. At other times they are passive information receivers. The initial type of information they generally acquire is sheer awareness—knowledge that the brand exists. A second type is knowledge about specific aspects of the brand, *as they perceive those specific aspects*—their brand criteria ratings. When trying to uncover the reasons behind consumers' overall brand preference rankings, it can help to try disaggregating the attitude. When you do this, you are asking the question, "What does the consumer perceive and believe about separate aspects of this brand that make her or him think it is good, bad, or in-between?" There are a variety of techniques to analyze this question. One especially useful approach is multivariate statistical analysis that produces a perceptual mapping of consumers' component brand perceptions. Some examples of such perceptual mapping studies will be given to help illustrate how consumers' interpretations of various qualities of a brand can blend to produce a general perception of that brand's status vis-à-vis competitors. Our discussion will not go into detail regarding the statistical methodology involved; for more extended treatment of that issue you may wish to refer to more statistically specialized sources.[13]

**Perceptual Mapping of Criteria Ratings**

The results of a study done by a major commercial research agency using multivariate statistical analysis lends itself well to illustrating the nature of brand criteria ratings.[14] Figure 6.6 illustrates these results. Based on a sample of 499 male beer drinkers, the study compresses the respondents' beliefs about several different attributes to a single point for each brand.[15] These data come from an entirely different survey than that referred to in Figure 6.4. However, for purposes of illustration, let us imagine there is some reasonable relationship between the two. Taken together, they suggest that once people are aware a brand exists, and assuming they have any sort of interest in it, they start processing communications to form impressions as to where it stands on relevant evaluative criteria. Those impressions become their brand criteria ratings.

**Comparing Brands on Specific Criteria Ratings and General Positioning.** Again, the point beside each beer brand name in Figure 6.6 represents a statistical compression of ratings on several different evaluative criteria. To obtain a rough approximation of how brands compare on any single criterion, you can draw a perpendicular line from the points beside brand names to the arrowed line (vector) for that feature. Figure 6.7 shows how this would work if you wanted to compare the way the average person rated Schlitz, Miller, Budweiser, and Hamm's on how "light" they are. In this case, consumers' brand criteria ratings, at least on average, say that Miller was seen as being the

FIGURE 6.6
Perceptual mapping of
brand criteria ratings

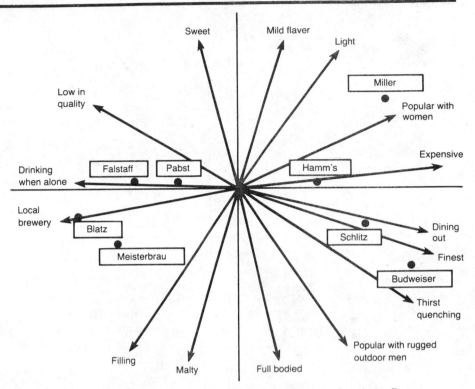

*Source:* B. Sherak, *Consumer Segmentation and Brand Mapping* (New York: Market Facts, Inc., p. 5).

"lightest" followed by Hamm's, Schlitz, and Budweiser. This kind of diagram also tells a marketer how his or her brand is generally positioned in consumers' minds, relative to other brands. The closer together two brands appear on the diagram, the more generally alike they appear to consumers. Here, Schlitz and Budweiser are seen by consumers as somewhat similar to each other, whereas Hamm's, and especially, Miller are seen rather differently.

*Relationships*
*Between Brand*
*Criteria Ratings*

Figure 6.6 also demonstrates that pieces of information can be related to each other in consumers' minds. How consumers rate a brand on one quality could affect the way they rate it on another. The arrowed lines are vectors. The closer two vectors are to each other, the more those two evaluative criteria tend to be related in consumers' perceptions. For example, the vectors for "mild flavor" and "light" are close to each other. This suggests that when a beer drinker rates a brand highly on lightness, it is likely that he or she also thinks of it as having a very mild flavor.

Sometimes the vectors point in almost opposite directions, such as "light" and "filling." When this happens, they are telling you that the two features tend to be thought of almost as opposites to each other. When someone rates a beer as "very light," it is probable that person will also think of it as very "nonfilling." The in-between situation in which two vectors are at approximately a ninety degree angle suggests that consumers usually do not see much

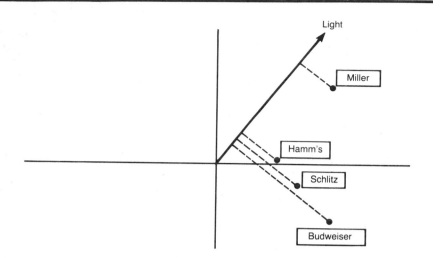

**FIGURE 6.7**
**Comparing four**
**brands of beer on**
**relative "lightness"**

relationship at all between those two features. For instance, the way someone rates a brand on "lightness" does not seem to have much bearing on how the same person will rate it on "quality" and, oddly enough, a beer that is regarded as "popular with women" is not necessarily seen as being "unpopular with rugged outdoor men."

***Analyzing the Promotional Implications of Perceived Criteria Relationships.***
The way consumers relate evaluative criteria might or might not offer some challenges to a promotional strategist. Consider the following case. Some years after the above study was done, one brewer attempted to popularize low-calorie beer. The first attempt was rather unsuccessful. The strategy that ultimately succeeded promoted the brand as "light" and "nonfilling." So far no problem, but suppose your target market is also demanding a "full-bodied" beer. "Full-bodied" and "light" are not exactly seen as opposites, but they are negatively related. When you say your brand is "light and nonfilling" you could be convincing people it is *not* full-bodied. That might be injurious to sales.

How do you surmount this problem? You can take your choice of many strategies. One might be to picture the brand as being "popular with rugged outdoor men," because consumers are likely to perceive a close relationship between this and "full body." This is just about what Miller's did in its successful promotion of Lite beer. They could even point to a lifestyle goal to explain why those rugged men wanted a light beer—because it is less filling it helps you move faster and continue being "rugged."

Now that you have some familiarity with this type of analysis, you may want to try your hand at the same type of strategy making. Figure 6.8 presents a similar sort of analysis from a different survey. This time the comparisons are between product categories rather than brands within the same category. Suppose you are a marketing manager for a particular brand of paper towel. You want to position your product as being "clothlike," even though it is made of paper. If possible, you want customers to think of it as being very much like a rag or sponge. Because you have great control over all elements in the promotional strategy mix—including both implicit and explicit promotion—you can start as far back in the promotional process as you would like to get the job done. What strategies are open to you? What do you think you might do?

**Perceptual Mapping of Market Segments**

Figure 6.9 demonstrates an interesting extension of the perceptual mapping approach that incorporates the concept of market segmentation. Among other things, this technique has the advantage of providing you with some preliminary and tentative estimates of the relative sizes of consumer groups likely to be attracted by various combinations of evaluative criteria.

In this case, the product category is a prepared food item. Consumers were asked to report their brand criteria ratings for six existing brands in the product category on eight evaluative criteria. Again, the criteria are shown as arrowed vectors. The brands currently on the market are labeled A through F and their perceived, composite ratings are shown by the points bearing those labels. In addition, consumers were questioned about their perceptions of a new brand being considered for introduction. In the figure, this is labeled as the "test product." The respondents then ranked their overall brand preference level for each brand. The data collected in the survey were next processed by a

**FIGURE 6.8
Perceptual mapping of bathroom cleaning products**

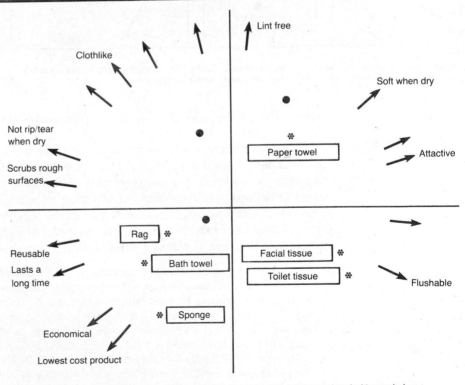

*Source:* Burke Marketing Services, Inc., Cincinnati, OH, copyrighted material reproduced with permission.

*Consumer Attitudes*

153

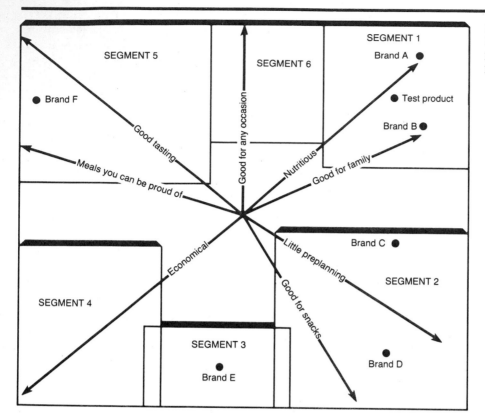

**FIGURE 6.9**
**Perceptual mapping to position a new food product**

Source: Adapted from Henry Assael, "Evaluating New Product Concepts and Developing Early Predictions of Trial," *Marketing Review*, May 1975, p. 13. Reprinted with permission from *Marketing Review*.

series of multidimensional computer programs to plot the information as shown in Figure 6.9.

As depicted there, the analysis suggested there were six market segments of consumers, each designated by a box. Segments were delineated by plotting each respondent's location on the map so that he or she was placed closest to his or her most preferred brand and farthest from the least preferred brand. The size of each box serves as an indicator of the relative number of consumers estimated to be in each segment. Some potential implications of these data, in terms of their use as planning input factors, were described as follows:

> First [this analysis] provides management with a picture of the market for the concept [of the proposed new brand] and competitive brands. It suggests there is a danger of competing head-on with brands A and B. On the other hand, there may be room for the concept since all three brands are positioned to the largest segment. Secondly [this analysis] shows the concept as closely positioned to appeal to nutritional benefits, a positioning intended by management. Third, the analysis provides implications for new product possibilities by defining "gaps" in the perceptual space. The most obvious is the failure of any product to be perceived as "good for any occasion," (breakfast, main meal, in-between meals). A

product positioned so it can be eaten at any occasion may best appeal to segment 6. In addition, the map shows a need for an economical snack since consumers in segment three are buying two different brands to fulfill snacking and economy benefits. [16]

## Limitations of Perceptual Mapping Techniques

As the author of the above survey points out, there are a variety of methodological limitations associated with perceptual mapping. These relate both to the procedures by which the data are gathered and to certain assumptions regarding the statistical procedures used to produce the mapping pattern.[17] In general, these limitations suggest that perceptual mapping is best treated as an initial and tentative planning input technique that can be used to suggest various options in the development of promotional strategy. In choosing among those options, further market analysis and/or market testing is likely to be required. Nonetheless, by combining relationships between perceived brand criteria ratings and brand preference levels, perceptual mapping can offer you a valuable starting point for your total decision process.

## Ideal Points

How highly your prospects see your brand as rating on a particular attribute is one thing. How highly they want their brand to rate on that same attribute could be something else. If the product category is automobiles and the feature is gas mileage, you would think the feeling should be, "The higher the better," unless high gas mileage makes people suspicious concerning things such as power and acceleration. The same should be true of "processing speed" in a computer or "durability" in an industrial grinding wheel. However, suppose the feature is "sudsiness" in a laundry detergent, "size" in a bulldozer, or "heaviness" in a perfume? Is it still going to be a case of the more the better? Quite possibly the answer is "No." When there is reason to believe your prospects have some idea of how much of any quality is "right," you will want to assess their information perceptions in terms of how closely they think your brand matches their "ideal point" on each meaningful feature, rather than just how highly you rate on the feature.[18]

## Brand Criteria Ratings, Evaluative Criteria, and Brand Preference Levels

*Variations in Importance Placed on Product Features.*  Suppose you were selling wristwatches and spent a great deal of time, money, and effort convincing prospective buyers that your brand was antimagnetic. Suppose your prospects all believed you and stored this brand criteria rating in their memories. Whenever questioned on the matter of antimagnetism in wristwatches, they would quickly give your brand the top score. There should not be any "ideal point" problem. It would hardly seem possible that your product could be too highly antimagnetic.

However, suppose also that these customers really did not care whether their wristwatches were antimagnetic—or did not care very much. Then your promotion of the feature would probably do little or nothing to raise your brand preference level or purchase intentions, or to produce favorable purchase decisions. In short, you would be promoting a functional feature that does not yield sales. It is hardly a new idea that customers may think some functional features are more important than others. One of the world's foremost management consultants has cautioned that ". . . what the producer or supplier thinks the most important feature of the product to be . . . may well be relatively unimportant to the customer."[19]

***The Process of Brand Preference Level Formation: Composition Rules.*** In recent years, experts who study consumer behavior have begun examining more formally the relationships between the following: (1) what people know and believe about a given brand's evaluative criteria ratings, (2) how important they view each evaluative criterion as being to them, and (3) how these two variables interact to produce overall feelings toward the brand. Using the terms of the general framework we are following, this examination translates into studying the process by which brand criteria ratings combine with evaluative criteria weightings to form brand preference levels (Figure 6.10).

The term "composition rule"—or "multiattribute model"—is used to describe this process. A composition rule is the presumed decision process by which consumers compose or put together their ratings and weightings to give an overall ranking to each of the brands among which they are choosing. The consideration of composition rules can be of value in the design of promotional strategy because it can suggest techniques of planning and executing promotional programs to heighten their effectiveness.

***Some Preliminary Qualifications Concerning Composition Rules.*** Before beginning our discussion some qualifications are in order. All composition rules assume that consumers are making choices by processing information. However, at least one leading theorist on consumer behavior has challenged this idea and proposed that in many instances there may be no real processing of information prior to a purchase.[20] After an extensive study of published data on prepurchase information search, one team of writers seemed to support this challenge with the conclusion that "for many purchases a decision process never occurs, not even on the first purchase."[21] They offered several explanations as to how this could happen. These included purchases made out of immediate necessity; those made in response to social forces such as cultural or peer group norms, recommendations of friends, or imitation of other people; purchases based on preferences acquired in childhood; and purchases made on a random basis. Nonetheless, they also tempered their conclusions with the following commentary:

> It would be an oversimplification, however, to characterize purchasing behavior as either involving predecision processes or not. While this may be an accurate characterization of some purchases, in general, we should allow for combination or "hybrid" strategies whereby choice and nonchoice are used; e.g., personal recommendations can be combined in various ways with limited search and evaluation. Indeed, future research may reveal that such hybrid strategies are the most common type of prepurchase behavior. [22].

This view is compatible with the overall implications of the framework we are following and with the admonitions pointed out in Chapter 4 when the concept of the consumer field was introduced. As noted there, some purchase

*Consumer Attitudes as Planning Inputs*

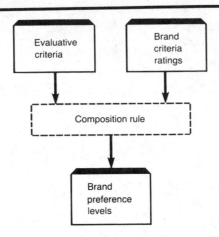

**FIGURE 6.10 The role of the composition rule in attitude processes**

decisions may be based on such patterns as fads or impulse buying. In market settings where these are the prevalent patterns, you may be concerned mainly about social forces or reseller support and only secondarily about evaluative criteria, brand criteria ratings, and composition rules. Habit buying presents still another setting in which your strategic starting point may lie elsewhere even though evaluative criteria, brand criteria ratings, and composition rules may be issues that merit study in your total planning process. Again, the amount of emphasis you place on any of the variables in the consumer field will differ depending on the particular decision influences dominant in your market. As one expert puts the matter, "The amount of search for information for a given product is contingent on the nature of the product (high risk or high price will generate more search), the situation (an involving situation will generate more search), brand attitudes (weakly held attitudes will generate more search)."[23]

Despite the fact that composition rules may be part of a hybrid consumer decision processing procedure, they deserve your consideration because they offer one valuable form of structured approach to analyzing your market. Again, your *total* analysis must be tailored to fit the specific promotional setting you face. With that caveat in mind, we shall look at what these rules are and what strategies they might suggest.

## THE NATURE OF COMPOSITION RULES

Suppose we are selling liquid floor wax. Our brand, Zipshine, competes mainly with two others, Glitter and Marvel Mop. In a market survey, we ask a user about his evaluative criteria, which are the features he seeks in choosing among brands within the floor wax category and how much weight or importance he gives to each. We do this by listing features and having him divide one hundred points between them. The more points, the more important the feature. Zero points would mean he does not even consider that feature when choosing a brand. We also ask this user about brand criteria ratings, which are

**TABLE 6.2 An example of evaluative criteria weightings and brand criteria ratings**

| Evaluative Criteria | Consumer's Importance Weighting for This Criterion | Brand Criteria Ratings (Ratings of Brands on Each Criterion) | | |
|---|---|---|---|---|
| | | Zipshine | Glitter | Marvel Mop |
| Cleans as it polishes | 20 | 2 | 2 | 4 |
| Goes on easily with little rubbing or buffing | 30 | 6 | 8 | 8 |
| One application lasts a long time | 10 | 3 | 2 | 3 |
| Resists scuffing | 15 | 7 | 4 | 3 |
| Gives a bright shine | 25 | 6 | 5 | 3 |

the facts (as known, perceived, and interpreted by him) regarding how well each of these brands rates in terms of his evaluative criteria. We do this by having him grade every brand on a scale from one (rates very poorly) to nine (rates very well).

If these weightings and ratings came out as shown in Table 6.2, could you predict this person's brand preference levels? To do so, you would have to know the process by which he combines the evaluative criteria weightings with brand criteria ratings. This is the process that we are terming a composition rule. A number of composition rules have been suggested.[24] We will concentrate on three that are both widely discussed and seem to be clearly reflected in actual promotional strategies. They are (1) the linear-compensatory rule, (2) the lexicographic rule, and (3) the conjunctive rule.

*The Linear-Compensatory Composition Rule*

This is the most widely investigated and talked about composition rule and some researchers have found it can predict brand preference levels rather well for certain product categories.[25] In its most general form, the rule can be stated in this way: When shaping a brand preference level the consumer does the following

1. Compares and rates brands on each criterion that has any importance to that consumer
2. (Possibly) weights each brand criterion rating for each brand, according to the importance the consumer puts on that feature
3. Allows a brand to compensate for low ratings on some evaluative criteria by getting high ratings on others
4. Combines the ratings on all criteria for each brand (using weighted ratings if applicable) to determine a brand preference level

Different writers have suggested variations in the arithmetic method used with this rule. The approach we will use in our example is probably the most

**TABLE 6.3 An example of a linear-compensatory procedure**

| Evaluative Criteria | Consumer's Importance Weighting for This Criterion | Brand Criteria Ratings (Ratings of Brands on Each Criterion) | | |
|---|---|---|---|---|
| | | Zipshine | Glitter | Marvel Mop |
| Cleans as it polishes | 20 | 2 (40) | 2 (40) | 4 (80) |
| Goes on easily with little rubbing or buffing | 30 | 6 (180) | 8 (240) | 8 (240) |
| One application lasts a long time | 10 | 3 (30) | 2 (20) | 3 (30) |
| Resists scuffing | 15 | 7 (105) | 4 (60) | 3 (45) |
| Gives a bright shine | 25 | 6 (150) | 5 (125) | 3 (75) |
| Total scores | | 505 | 485 | 470 |

commonly talked about and one of the simplest. It assumes the customer does something that amounts to multiplying each of the brand criteria ratings by the weighting she or he puts on that evaluative criterion, and then adding the results. The brand with the highest total attains the highest preference level, followed by the brand with the next to the highest total, and so on. Table 6.3 presents an illustration of the procedure, using the ratings and weightings introduced in Table 6.2.

The numbers in parentheses are simply the products of each importance weighting multiplied by the rating for each brand. The total scores were calculated by adding the weighted ratings in parentheses. If this is the way our interviewee is forming preference levels for floor wax, Zipshine should be his highest-ranked choice, followed in order by Glitter and Marvel Mop. Because Zipshine is our brand we win, but notice that Zipshine is not top rated on all features. In fact, both competitors outscore our brand on the most important evaluative criterion of ease in application. We also rate poorly on cleaning ability. We are making up for these shortcomings by fairly high ratings on "bright shine" and "scuff resistance." In short, we are compensating for rather low brand criteria ratings on some features by attaining rather high ratings on others. This is why the rule is called "compensatory." We are best on an "all things considered" basis.

When first considering composition rules, and especially in the case of the linear-compensatory model, you would not be out of line if you said, "Hey! Wait a second. I've bought all kinds of things in my life and even when I've gone through a conscious decision process, I've never gone to the trouble of thinking out all these weightings and ratings, let alone multiplying and summing them."

The composition rule approach is not meant to duplicate *exactly* what the consumer is doing. It is an attempt to simulate in a general way how brand

*The Nature of Composition Rules*

159

preference levels can be developed by consumers. The simulation procedure does two things that consumers would not ordinarily be expected to do. First, it treats very formally a decision procedure that consumers would usually treat in a much less formal or even casual fashion. Second, it quantifies weightings and ratings that consumers would usually handle in a nonquantified way. For example, if you thought Zipshine was "good" at resisting scuffs or felt that ease of application was "important," you would probably not try assigning numbers to "good" and "important."

Of course, in some industrial buying situations buyers might actually use formal, quantitative techniques to rate alternatives. Ultimate consumers might come close to using them when purchasing an important or expensive item such as a house or an automobile. However, even if consumers are reaching their opinions on a very loose, informal, and nonquantified basis, they must be using some kind of information and criteria to judge brands if they are following any type of decision process at all. It is quite possible that the way consumers make decisions in ranking alternative brands amounts to something very like a linear-compensatory approach, even if they do not consciously think of it that way.

As mentioned earlier, various analysts have proposed approaches to handling this composition that differ from our example. Some of these differences suggest using another technique when asking consumers to weight the importance of the criteria,[26] not multiplying the ratings by the weightings,[27] and not using addition to combine the ratings.[28] One commercially applied research technique, called "conjoint analysis," employs a very similar approach without even asking consumers to supply weightings and ratings directly.[29] Our purpose here is not to go into extensive discussions about research methods but simply to present the general idea of the rule.

**Promotional Strategy in a Linear-Compensatory Market**

If you think your customers are using something like a linear-compensatory rule, one logical approach you might want to consider is as follows: *Dramatize each one of a number of evaluative criteria on which your brand is strong, stressing those that are most highly weighted. Aim for the market segment that looks for your combination of criteria.*

***Applications in Personal Selling.*** Do "real world" promotional strategists actually use this kind of reasoning? If you are waiting to hear a brand manager, an advertising copywriter, a salesperson, a sales promotion specialist, or a publicist say "linear-compensatory," you may have a long wait. At least at this point in time, it is mainly an academic term. However, that does not mean that practicing promotional strategists do not use the same line of reasoning. One study of sales representatives for an industrial product found a significant relationship between their success in selling and their ability to analyze individual customer preferences using a linear-compensatory technique.[30] Some very practically oriented advice given to salespersons seems to suggest the same model without using the term. For example:

There may be many features to your specific product or service, each relating to a specific need, problem or interest. Combined, they represent the total features. . . .

**FIGURE 6.11 Advertisements whose structure is consistent with a linear-compensatory approach**

Courtesy American Motors Corporation, Chevrolet Motor Division, and the Ford Motor Company.

You [the sales representative] normally present each feature separately so that you answer these two questions:

1) What is it?
2) What does it do? You can explain and briefly demonstrate, adding further interest and conviction by letting [your prospect] do it. [31]

*Applications in Advertising.* Applying a parallel strategy in advertising might mean that when you are limited by space or time in single ads you would want to distribute your dramatizations over several advertisements, overlapping them under a common campaign theme. Among advertisers, it is not uncommon to see product categories in which most competitors appear to believe one or another of the composition rules predominates with customers. As illustrated in Figure 6.11, marketing executives responsible for selling low-priced and medium-priced automobiles often employ an approach that suggests they think their prospects are using something like a linear-compensatory rule, even though neither the executives nor the customers are likely to use the term "linear-compensatory" to describe it.

**The Lexicographic Composition Rule**

If one specific evaluative criterion is especially important to a consumer and one brand satisfies that criterion better than any other brand, why not stop the decision process right there? This is the basis of the lexicographic rule. *The consumer orders the evaluative criteria by weightings and uses the first (highest weighted) to judge alternative brands. Only if no clear distinction can be made between brand ratings using that criterion does he or she introduce the second. Each consumer proceeds through the list until a distinction can be made.*

To see how this would work, reconsider the results of the interview with the liquid floor wax customer. This time we will arrange the evaluative criteria

*The Nature of Composition Rules* 161

**TABLE 6.4 An example of a lexicographic procedure**

| Evaluative Criteria | Consumer's Importance Weighting for This Criterion | Brand Criteria Ratings | | |
|---|---|---|---|---|
| | | (Ratings of Brands on Each Criterion) | | |
| | | Zipshine | Glitter | Marvel Mop |
| Goes on easily with little rubbing or buffing | 30 | 6 | 8 | 8 |
| Gives a bright shine | 25 | 6 | 5 | 3 |
| Cleans as it polishes | 20 | 2 | 2 | 4 |
| Resists scuffing | 15 | 7 | 4 | 3 |
| One application lasts a long time | 10 | 3 | 2 | 3 |

in the order of importance he gave them, from high to low, because that is the order he would presumably use in establishing a brand preference ranking under this rule.

This time we do not have to do any multiplying or adding. We only have to compare the ratings. Our brand, Zipshine, loses on the very first feature. Because this consumer feels it is not as easy to apply, and that is the criterion he weights most heavily, we are probably going to be ranked no higher than third in his overall brand preference level ordering. Glitter and Marvel Mop tie on this feature. Therefore, he is unable to make a clear distinction between them without moving to the next criterion, "Gives a bright shine." Here Glitter comes out ahead. Thus, his brand preference level rankings should be Glitter, Marvel Mop, and Zipshine in that order—much different than the linear-compensatory result even with the same weightings and ratings.

As with the linear-compensatory situation, the lexicographic rule might require more complex interpretation than we are giving it here. For example, it is possible that a consumer would fail to see enough difference between a rating of 8 and a rating of 6 to make a clear distinction. In this case, Zipshine would still be in the running as he moved to his second highest criterion. If the user does not interpret a weighting of 30 (for easy to apply) as having *significantly* more importance than the weighting of 25 (for a bright shine), we would also be kept in the running.

*Promotional Strategy in a Lexicographic Market*

Again, our interest is in the general concept and what it would imply for promotional strategy, not in the intricacies of the research problems. Some investigation has suggested consumers may well be using a lexicographic method to compare brands in certain product categories.[32] One logical approach you should consider in building your strategy for a lexicographic market is as follows: *Dramatize one evaluative criterion—or possibly a select few—on which your brand is strong. Aim for the market segment that weights that one (or few)* most heavily. *Let implicit promotion provide the consumer with information that your brand has acceptable levels on the other criteria.*

***Applications in Personal Selling.*** "Lexicographic" is another word you are not likely to hear too often in sales offices, advertising agencies, or corporate headquarters. However, as with "linear-compensatory," marketing practitioners often give or use advice that seems to presume a lexicographic market situation. For instance, in terms of advice for personal selling strategy, it seems to be reflected in the following recommendation for closing a sale: "Sometimes a prospect will be particularly anxious to obtain one special feature in a product, or sometimes a product will have a feature that competition cannot match. . . . In either case, the single feature close may be the best method for the salesperson to use."[33]

***Applications in Advertising.*** In advertising, strategists for certain product categories seem especially prone to frame appeals on what seems like an interpretation that their customers are using a lexicographic rule. Leading dishwashing detergents have often been advertised on a lexicographic basis. For instance, Procter and Gamble offers three such brands, each advertised with heavy emphasis on a single feature: Joy makes your dishes "shine," Ivory helps your hands stay "young-looking," and Dawn "cuts through grease" (Figure 6.12).

***The Conjunctive Composition Rule***

This rule assumes the customer is unwilling to buy a product that is clearly deficient on even a single feature that has any importance to her or him.[34] To attain the sale, your brand must meet or surpass some minimum standard on every evaluative criterion that has a weighting above zero. *The consumer sets up critical cutoff points for each evaluative criterion and requires the brand to meet or surpass all cutoff points before the brand is even considered.*

If we thought our floor wax customer might be using the conjunctive rule, we would have to ask him one more question during the interview: "Will you please give me a number for each feature that shows the lowest level of performance you would be willing to accept on that feature and still consider the brand?" We will add a column at the right of the table to accommodate his answers to that question and have another look at all the data (Table 6.5). By comparing his brand criteria ratings with his minimum acceptable ratings, we see that Zipshine and Glitter are both unacceptable on the very first criterion. They are so poor in cleaning ability that he will not accept either one, and his first choice will be Marvel Mop. Our weak points did not hurt us under the linear-compensatory rule, but now one of them does.

***Promotional Strategy in a Conjunctive Market***

What if a large part of the market felt as the imaginary consumer does? If the trouble with Zipshine is in the functional aspect of implicit promotion, that is, if it really does not clean nearly as well as Marvel Mop, we would probably want to change its basic formulation. We could then introduce "New Improved Zipshine—With Added Cleaning Power." If our lab tests showed Zipshine's functional cleaning ability to be just as good or even better than

**Your Joy shows.**

*What a nice reflection on you.*

FIGURE 6.12 Examples of advertisements whose structure is consistent with a lexicographic approach

1. (MUSIC UNDER THROUGHOUT) RITCH: I feel sick.

2. TOM: Four pancakes, six sausages and three eggs are inclined to have an adverse effect on your body, Ritch.

3. RITCH: It's not the pancakes, it's all these greasy dishes. How are we ever gonna get 'em clean?

4. MARV: Let's not panic. We've got Dawn. Look.

5. Dawn scatters grease.

6. It fights hard

7. to take grease out of the way. Help keep it away.

8. See? Dawn got the grease.

9. RITCH: Look what I found on the moose.

10. MARV: So wash it. RITCH: After four million greasy dishes?

11. This looks as good as the one you washed earlier. And my hands don't feel greasy.

12. Mm, mm, grilled trout. Uh, who's gonna clean 'em?

13. MARV: I clean the dishes.

14. TOM: And you clean the fishes. (LAUGHTER)

15. ANNCR: (VO) Dawn takes grease

16. out of your way.

**TABLE 6.5 An example of a conjunctive procedure**

| Evaluative Criteria | Consumer's Importance Weighting for This Criterion | Brand Criteria Ratings | | | Minimum Acceptable Rating for This Criterion |
|---|---|---|---|---|---|
| | | Zipshine | Glitter | Marvel Mop | |
| Cleans as it polishes | 20 | 2 | 2 | 4 | 3 |
| Goes on easily with little rubbing or buffing | 30 | 6 | 8 | 8 | 4 |
| One application lasts a long time | 10 | 3 | 2 | 3 | 3 |
| Resists scuffing | 15 | 7 | 4 | 3 | 2 |
| Gives a bright shine | 25 | 6 | 5 | 3 | 3 |

Marvel Mop's, we would face a perception problem. Perhaps it would help to change surrogate cues that could influence perceptions of functional features. On that basis we might want to check out things like odor or color or even the name. If these do not seem to be a problem, we should examine our explicit promotion—the advertising, the sales promotion, and possibly even the kind of publicity our brand is receiving. Is there something wrong with our themes or message techniques?

Now suppose we have corrected the problem, whether through changes in functional features, surrogate cues, or explicit promotion. We have brought things around to where this interviewee, and other prospects like him, would give us a rating of 4 on "cleans as it polishes." By the conjunctive rule, this would leave our customer without a clear first choice. Both Zipshine and Marvel Mop now pass on all criteria. Only Glitter is ruled out because it still does not meet his standards on "one application lasts a long time." Now the question is which of the two would he prefer—Zipshine or Marvel Mop?

This question illustrates one of the problems with the conjunctive rule. If more than one brand meets the standards, the rule is incapable of predicting brand preference levels beyond general winners and losers. For this reason, it is often regarded as a screening procedure or a first test. All brands that pass the conjunctive test are then evaluated by another test, such as the linear-compensatory or lexicographic test.[35] In this case, if Zipshine could be made to pass on cleaning ability, it and Marvel Mop would be compared by a second rule. If that rule were linear-compensatory, Zipshine would be the highest-ranked choice. If it were lexicographic, Marvel Mop would be the highest-ranked choice.

As with the other rules, consumers may be using something like a conjunctive approach without the precision or formalities suggested by these hypothetical figures. The conjunctive line of reasoning is implied when people make such statements as: "Zipshine is great in lots of ways but it doesn't get the marks off my floors," or "Florsheim shoes are really good but they're awfully expensive."

Another possible use of the conjunctive rule is in a situation in which consumers are not completely clear about the features they want or how to assess relevant evaluative criteria. For instance, when the Survey Research Center at the University of Michigan queried people about features they looked for in selecting major appliances—refrigerators, television sets, washers, and stoves—thirty-nine percent said, "No specific features."[36] This might mean they had some evaluative criteria in mind but just could not name them. It could also mean, however, that they were comparing brands on the basis of "overall quality," seeking satisfactory ratings on every relevant criterion, even though they were not entirely clear on the specific criteria that spelled out overall quality. Especially when a product category is rather technical, complex, and infrequently purchased, this scenario might not be unusual.

What sort of technique would a "conjunctive market" suggest for your promotional approach? One logical strategy would be as follows: *Dramatize overall superior quality rather than specific evaluative criteria per se. Use specific criteria in passing, largely as examples of overall quality possessed on all criteria dimensions.*

*Applications in Advertising.* The conjunctive rule has been a common approach to advertising in a variety of product categories. Automobile tires provide an example. As shown in Figure 6.13, Goodyear has emphasized overall quality under the slogan, "We've got the blimp behind us." General Tire has done much the same thing with the slogan, "Sooner or later, you'll own Generals," and Michelin has promoted its reputation with the headline, "Michelin put America on radials." The conjunctive rule may also help explain the success of techniques like the Good Housekeeping Seal and celebrity testimonials, which suggest the brand "passes muster" on all pertinent features.

*Applications in Personal Selling.* In personal selling, recognition of a conjunctive approach—or perhaps a conjunctive screening process—occurs when handling customer objections to your brand. For example, consider the following advice:

> When competition indicates to the prospect that it fails to be impressed by some aspect or characteristic of the salesperson's product, competition is probably planting an objection—or at least a doubt—in that prospect's mind. It is this type of product feature which must be covered fully and favorably in the main story. . . . The clearer, more logical, and more complete the story is, the less important a prospect's objections become. If the prospect's attention is monopolized by the mountain of plus-points and the small pile of minus-points, the prospect will be inclined to consider the objections he had planned to make too insignificant to mention. [37]

**Other Composition Rules**

A complete list of composition rules hardly ends with these three. However, these are probably the most heavily discussed rules and in the author's view

*Consumer Attitudes as Planning Inputs*

**FIGURE 6.13 An example of an advertisement whose structure is consistent with a conjunctive rule**

From the corporate advertising campaign of the Goodyear Tire & Rubber Co.

they are the three with the clearest implications for promotional strategy. Nonetheless, you may want to verify this for yourself, studying rules such as the disjunctive and dominance models,[38] and attempting to work out the strategic options they could suggest.

*A General Note on Changing Brand Preference Levels*

Because brand preference levels result from a combination of the consumer's evaluative criteria weightings and brand criteria ratings, there are two basic ways you can go about trying to change them. The two can be used either separately or in conjunction with each other. One way involves promotion aimed at persuading prospects that your brand excels in delivering features and benefits that match the evaluative criteria those prospects *already* consider as important. In essence, this means that you build your strategy to influence brand criteria ratings. The other way involves promotion aimed at persuading prospects to upgrade the amount of importance they place on one or more applicable evaluative criteria. In essence, this means that you build your strategy to influence prospects' weightings of evaluative criteria on which your brand is especially strong.

It is generally concluded that the first method—proving your brand's merits on evaluative criteria that are already considered as important by your target consumers—is the easier of the two.[39] The rationale underlying this view is that evaluative criteria are mainly outgrowths of lifestyle goals rather than effects of promotion per se. For this reason, if they are to be successful at all, promotional strategies aimed at changing evaluative criteria weightings must show how the benefits of your product affect those goals. For example, when the Seven-Up Company introduced Like Cola in 1982 it aimed at convincing consumers that they should place importance on an evaluative criterion new to the cola beverage field at that time, "caffeine free." The advertisements that promoted this new criterion were heavily oriented toward a related lifestyle theme, in this case the lifestyle role of "good parent." One writer interpreted these commercials in the following way:

> They initially focus on what a child needs (such as every kid needs a dream, lots of love, encouragement, etc.), and then, as action abruptly stops on the child for several seconds, an announcer notes "But there's something they don't need. They don't need caffeine. That's why we created a cola with no added caffeine." Copy says Like gets its excitement from full, rich cola taste, unlike the leading colas that add caffeine. [40]

We will consider potential relationships between evaluative criteria and lifestyle goals more fully in the next two chapters. This relationship is also an issue in the decision charts to be introduced in the appendix to this chapter. When you reach a box in one of these charts that suggests upgrading an existing criterion or introducing a new criterion, you might want to consider what could be involved in using underlying lifestyle goals to establish the criterion as being relevant to your prospects' needs and desires.

## SUMMARY

There are two main types of attitudes the marketing strategist must consider: (1) consumers' underlying attitudes toward lifestyle goals and (2) consumers' attitudes toward specific products and brands. This chapter concentrated on the second variety—the kind usually regarded as the easier to change and also the kind that most promotion actually tries to change.

An attitude toward a specific brand can be thought of as having three components: (1) what the consumer knows (or perceives or believes) about specific features of the brand—brand criteria ratings, (2) how the consumer "feels" about the brand on an overall basis—the brand preference level, and (3) what the consumer plans to do as a result of that overall feeling—purchase intentions. For promotional planning purposes, it can be useful to think of the components as affecting each other in the order just shown.

Purchase intentions tend to be probabilistic in nature, giving you some high or low probability of a sale before the purchase actually occurs. One aspect of a sound promotional strategy mix is concerned with making the most of whatever chance you have. Another aspect of the mix is concerned with raising your chances, or upgrading purchase intention probabilities by improving preference levels for your brand. To do this it is helpful to understand (1) how your brand is now seen as rating on specific evaluative criteria, and sometimes, how consumers may see these features as being interrelated, (2) how much weighting your target market places on the various evaluative criteria, and (3) what kind of "composition rule" customers use to combine these ratings and weightings to form overall brand preference levels.

Based on your understanding of these points, your task is to devise a strategy to build up your brand's ratings on significant features and/or to increase the importance consumers place on evaluative criteria that your brand emphasizes. Some initial suggestions for using composition rules as starting points for strategies were presented. The appendix that follows carries these suggestions further to illustrate one approach toward using composition rules to search out promotional opportunities.

## DISCUSSION QUESTIONS

1. You are a promotional strategist for a consumer goods manufacturing firm. The marketing research team assigned to measuring purchase intentions for one of your new brands has just notified you that sales are likely to decline in the future. However, your boss is reluctant to increase your promotional budget now, before the sales figures are in. Using the techniques outlined in the chapter, describe how you would convince him that a change in promotional strategy was needed.

2. Research for a mass-marketed, heavily advertised final consumer product reveals the following attitude data for the three leading brands.

| Brand A | Brand B | Brand C |
|---|---|---|
| Aware 54% | Aware 75% | Aware 69% |
| Evoked 15% | Evoked 35% | Evoked 20% |
| Inert 20% | Inert 25% | Inert 30% |
| Inept 19% | Inept 15% | Inept 19% |

Discuss the purchase intentions probabilities for each brand in terms of being positive or not positive. As product manager of brand C, what is the most logical way to increase payoff from your level of purchase probabilities?

3. Suppose you are the brand manager for an instant cocoa beverage that is tremendously popular with children. The product also has a very high nutritional value, which as yet has gone unpromoted. Market surveys have revealed that the major perceived brand benefit of your product is "rich taste." This attribute is also positively related to "dark color." Now you are interested in reaching the adult market. However, most adults view the instant cocoa generic product category as being strictly for children. How might you promote this brand given that the specific adult segment you are trying to reach is health conscious? Remember, you must be careful not to alienate the children's market segment.

4. Assume you are a real estate sales manager. One of your newer salespeople has come to you for advice on selling a particular home to a young couple. According to the salesperson, the couple is having difficulty choosing between the home your real estate firm is offering and a home offered by another firm. Structurally, the homes are nearly identical. However, your firm's house is located in a quiet neighborhood close to excellent schools and shopping facilities. The competing firm's home is located in a more exclusive neighborhood, yet farther away from schools and shopping centers. (The homes also have an identical price tag.) Briefly outline the promotional strategy you would tell the salesperson to use, and identify the composition rule that is involved.

5. Your firm is entering a market where there is only one other competitor. Your product, a mouth-

wash for dogs, is significantly different from your competitor's mouthwash on a number of features—your mouthwash prevents tooth decay, kills germs that cause colds, and leaves the dog's mouth smelling fresh for hours. It also dissolves hairballs. Your competitor's mouthwash does not do any of these things as well as your brand (if at all). There is only one problem. In tests, dogs hated the taste of your brand and refused to gargle. Dogs love the taste of brand X. What should you do now? Which if any of the composition rules provides a solution?

6. Look through recent issues of the following magazines: *Time, Newsweek,* and *U.S. News and World Report.* Select four product categories heavily advertised and attempt to determine which composition rules are being used for each category.

7. Choose one of the brands of beer shown on the left-hand side of Figure 6.6 (p. 151). Draw up and defend a tentative plan for repositioning the brand.

8. Based on the description of factors that influence the intensity of information search activity for various product categories, choose three such categories and explain how each of those factors might apply.

9. Assume you wanted to raise the amount of importance consumers place on two of the evaluative criteria listed for floor wax—"long-lasting" and "resists scuffing." Give examples of techniques you might use to do this.

10. You want to study consumer attitudes toward your brand. What general instructions would you give to the research personnel who are going to conduct your field survey?

## REFERENCES

1. To sample a variety of the classical work that has been done in this field see James U. McNeal and Stephen McDaniel, eds., *Consumer Behavior: Classic and Contemporary Dimensions* (Boston: Little, Brown & Company, 1982); Richard J. Lutz, ed., *Contemporary Perspectives in Consumer Research* (Boston: Kent Publishing Company, 1981); and Harold H. Kassarjian and Thomas S. Robertson, eds., *Perspectives in Consumer Behavior*, 3rd ed. (Glenview, IL: Scott, Foresman and Company, 1981).

2. For a more extended discussion see Carl E. Block and Kenneth J. Roering, *Essentials of Consumer Behavior* (Hinsdale, IL: The Dryden Press, 1979), pp. 343–344.

3. George S. Day, "Theories of Attitude Structure and Change," in S. Ward and T. S. Robertson, *Consumer Behavior: Theoretical Sources* (Englewood Cliffs, NJ: Prentice-Hall, Inc., 1973), p. 306.

4. *Ibid.*, p. 308.

5. *Ibid.*

6. *Ibid.*, p. 309.

7. Leon Festinger, "Behavioral Support for Opinion Change," *Public Opinion Quarterly*, vol. 28 (1964), pp. 404–417.

8. Martin Fishbein and I. Ajzen, "Attitudes and Opinions," in P. H. Mussen and M. R. Rosenzweig, eds., *Annual Review of Psychology* (Palo Alto, CA: Annual Reviews, Inc., 1972), pp. 188–244; and Leon G. Schiffman and Leslie Lazar Kanuk, *Consumer Behavior,* 2nd ed. (Englewood Cliffs, NJ: Prentice-Hall, 1983), pp. 207–209.

9. John Pavasars and William D. Wells, "Measures of brand attitudes can be used to predict buying behavior," *Marketing News,* vol. VIII, no. 19 (11 April 1975), p. 6.

10. For a more extended discussion of this concept see Frank M. Bass, "The Theory of Stochastic Preference and Brand Switching," *Journal of Marketing Research*, vol. XI (February 1974), pp. 1–20. For an application to generic product categories see C. Joseph Clawson, "How Useful Are 90-Day Purchase Probabilities?," *Journal of Marketing,* vol. 35 (October 1971), pp. 43–47.

11. Chem L. Narayama and Rom J. Markin, "Consumer Behavior and Product Performance: An Alternative Conceptualization," *Journal of Marketing,* vol. 25 (October 1975), pp. 1–2.

12. Charles A. Kirkpatrick and Frederick A. Russ, *Salesmanship,* 6th ed. (Cincinnati: Southwestern Publishing Co., 1976), p. 233.

13. See Joseph F. Hair, Jr., Rolph E. Anderson, Ronald L. Tatham, and Bernie J. Grablowsky, *Multivariate Data Analysis* (Tulsa, OK: Petroleum Publishing Co., 1979), and Susan F. Schiffman, M. Lance Reynolds, and Forrest W. Young, *Introduction to Multidimensional Scaling* (New York: Academic Press, 1981).

14. B. Sherak, *Consumer Segmentation and Brand*

*Mapping: A Methodological Study* (New York: Market Facts, Inc., undated).

15. For a more extended description of the technique used, see Richard M. Johnson, "Market Segmentation: A Strategic Management Tool," *Journal of Marketing Research,* vol. VIII (February 1971), pp. 13–18.

16. Henry Assael, *Consumer Behavior and Marketing Action* (Boston: Kent Publishing Company, 1981), pp. 458–459.

17. *Ibid.*, pp. 459–460.

18. For a very good discussion of ideal points see Frank M. Bass, Edgar A. Pessemier, and Donald R. Lehmann, "An Experimental Study of the Relationship between Attitudes, Brand Preference, and Choice," *Behavioral Science*, vol. 17 (November 1972), pp. 532–541.

19. Peter F. Drucker, *Managing for Results* (New York: Harper & Row, 1964), p. 96.

20. Harold H. Kassarjian, "Presidential Address, 1977: Anthropomorphism and Parsimony," in H. Keith Hunt, ed., *Advances in Consumer Research*, vol. 5 (Ann Arbor, MI: Association for Consumer Research, 1978), pp. xii–xiv.

21. Richard W. Olshavsky and Donald H. Granbois, "Consumer Decision Making—Fact or Fiction?" *Journal of Consumer Research*, September 1979, pp. 93–100.

22. *Ibid.*, p. 99.

23. Assael, *Consumer Behavior and Marketing Action*, p. 493.

24. For an excellent and extended discussion see Kenneth R. MacCrimmon, "An Overview of Multiple Objective Decision Making," in James L. Cochrane and Milan Celeny, *Multiple Criteria Decision Making* (Columbia, SC: University of South Carolina Press, 1973), pp. 18–44.

25. See for example Frank M. Bass and W. Wayne Talarzyk, "An Attitude Model for the Study of Brand Preferences," *Journal of Marketing Research*, vol. IX (February 1972), pp. 6–9.

26. Paul Busch, Ronald F. Bush, and Joseph E. Hair, Jr., "The Generality and Concurrent Validity of the Importance Component in Multi-Attribute Models," in Kenneth C. Bernhardt, ed., *Marketing: 1776–1976 and Beyond* (Chicago: American Marketing Association, 1976), pp. 616–621.

27. John H. Lindgren and Leonard J. Konopa, "A Comparative Analysis of Multiattribute Models," *Journal of the Academy of Marketing Science*, Fall 1980, pp. 374–389.

28. Jagdish N. Sheth, "Brand Profiles from Beliefs and Importances," *Journal of Advertising Research*, vol. 13, no. 1 (February 1973), pp. 37–42. Also see C. Michael Troutman and James Shanteau, "Do Consumers Evaluate Products by Adding or Averaging Information?," *Journal of Consumer Research*, vol. 3 (September 1976), pp. 101–106.

29. Paul E. Green, J. Douglas Carroll, and Stephen M. Goldberg, "A General Approach to Product Design Optimization via Conjoint Analysis," *Journal of Marketing*, Summer 1981, pp. 17–37.

30. Barton A. Weitz, "Relationship Between Salesperson Performance and Understanding of Customer Decision Making," *Journal of Marketing Research*, vol. XV (November 1978), pp. 501–566.

31. Allan Reid, *Modern Applied Salesmanship,* 2nd ed. (Glenview, IL: Scott, Foresman and Company, 1975), p. 256.

32. Frederick A. Russ, "Consumer Evaluation of Alternative Product Models," Unpublished doctoral dissertation, Carnegie-Mellon University, 1971.

33. Kirkpatrick and Russ, *Salesmanship*, p. 31.

34. For a study describing an interesting variation on a conjunctive approach see James R. Bettman, "A Threshold Model of Attribute Satisfaction Decisions," *Journal of Consumer Research*, vol. 1 (September 1974), pp. 30–35.

35. MacCrimmon, "An Overview of Multiple Objective Decision Making," p. 31.

36. Eva Mueller, "A Study of Purchase Decisions. Part 2. The Sample Survey," in I. H. Clark (ed.), *Consumer Behavior. Vol. 1. The Dynamics of Consumer Reaction* (New York: New York University Press, 1955), p. 49.

37. Kirkpatrick and Russ, *Salesmanship*, pp. 370–371.

38. Philip Kotler, *Marketing Management*, 4th ed. (Englewood Cliffs, NJ: Prentice-Hall, Inc., 1980), pp. 159–162.

39. Richard J. Lutz, "Changing Brand Attitudes through Modification of Cognitive Structure," *Journal of Consumer Research*, vol. 1, no. 4 (March 1975), pp. 49–59; and James F. Engel and Roger D. Blackwell, *Consumer Behavior,* 4th ed. (Hinsdale, IL: The Dryden Press, 1982), pp. 430–432.

40. Nancy Giges, "Seven-Up Chief Believes Time Right for Like Cola," *Advertising Age*, 20 March 1982, p. 2.

*Summary*

171

# APPENDIX TO CHAPTER SIX
# USING COMPOSITION RULES TO SEARCH FOR STRATEGY OPTIONS*

As noted in this chapter, all of the issues relating to the intricacies of composition rules have not yet been settled by the researchers who have investigated them. In its present form, however, the logic of the composition rule approach as a technique of studying consumer decision making can serve as a useful basis both for surveying markets and for generating ideas regarding tentative strategy alternatives. To illustrate how you might apply it in considering promotional possibilities, this appendix will describe an options-search program. Essentially, this is a structured approach to assessing the types of composition rules that might be used by potential consumer segments in your product category, and then using that assessment to initiate study of implied market openings given the existing competitive environment.

The discussion will use the dentifrice market as an illustrative product category and draw on historical data describing that market as it existed in the 1970s. The advantage in drawing data from this period is that a considerable amount of published information is available to support the illustration. We shall begin with a hypothetical situation that places you in the role of a promotional strategist facing a specific problem.

## THE OVERALL PROMOTIONAL GOAL

You are a marketing manager with a large, multibrand consumer-goods company. One of your firm's products is Maxident, a toothpaste that has held a very large share of the market for over a decade. Within the past year, competitors have introduced two new brands and your sales have begun to slip badly. Your company's management has determined to reposition Maxident within the product category. Your job is to find the best way to do it. You want to start by reviewing and considering all of the options open to you in terms of new positioning strategies. How should you organize your options-review program?

The illustration of how you might proceed begins with the flowchart in Figure 6A.1. Step 1-1 calls for a

general gathering of facts on your market. Steps 1-2 and 1-3 bring up two questions with which you must deal before you can work with the composition rules themselves. These are (1) the possible effects of social pressure in the formation of brand preferences and (2) the possibility of occasion segmentation. Because the existence of either can affect your total approach to working with composition rules, we shall begin by discussing each of them briefly.

### Social Influence

Although the basic composition rule approach assumes that people rate brands, form attitudes, and act on those attitudes rather independently of other people, in some product categories it is possible that one or all of these factors are shaped in whole or in part by social influence. Especially where brand choice decisions are more or less in public view, consumers may avoid or accept certain brands because of what other people may think, despite their own appraisals of those brands. If, for example, you were selling automobiles or tennis rackets, this might be a serious issue. Potential implications of social influence will be described in greater detail in the following chapter. At this point we shall merely stress that if you know social influence is widespread in your market, you will want to analyze it and determine how to handle the situation. In that case, you would answer "Yes" to the question in step 1-2 and move to step 1-4.

### Occasion Segmentation

As pointed out in Chapter 5, an evaluative criterion important in one usage situation may be unimportant in another, even to the same consumer. Your answer to the question in step 1-3 will depend on your assessment of the product category with which you are working. For instance, considering automobiles as a generic category, your answer would probably be "Yes." The same individual might want a small, compact car for maneuverability and good gas mileage in city driving, but a large, heavy car for roadability, comfort, and power on the highway; an ornate, luxuriously appointed car for social occasions, but a simple, rugged, four-wheel-drive vehicle for fishing and camping trips; a flashy, high-

*The text and figures in this appendix are adapted from an article by the author that appeared in *Business*, July–August 1981, pp. 16–24.

**FIGURE 6A.1 A general options–search program using composition rule analysis**

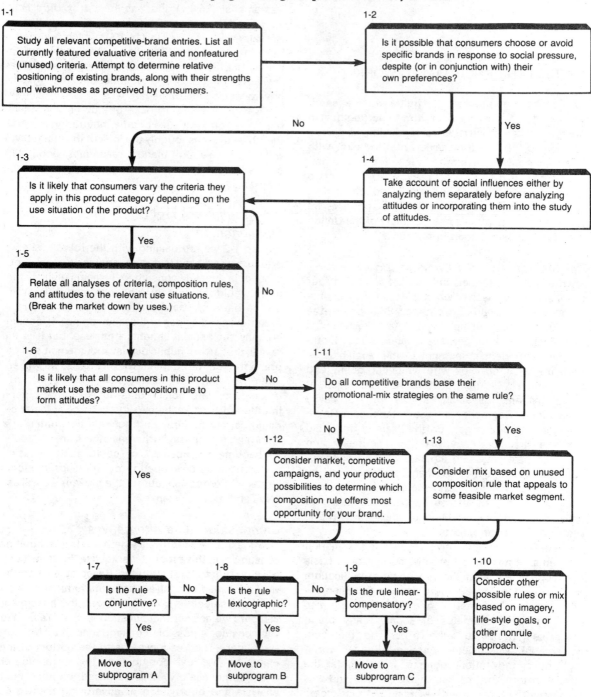

performance sports car for individual use, but a sedate, spacious station wagon for family vacations and grocery shopping.

## PUTTING THE PROGRAM TO WORK

To show how the program can guide you in a search for strategy options, we will return to our toothpaste example. Our objective is to reposition Maxident. Again, step 1-1 calls for a review of the market, with emphasis on evaluative criteria featured by competing brands. In actual practice you would want to spend considerable time and careful thought on this, but to keep the illustration as brief as possible we shall settle for a rather terse summary of the United States toothpaste market in the 1970s.

### The Market—A Brief Background
A writer once described this market as having four major segments, each of which placed heavy emphasis on specific evaluative criteria.[1] Segment 1—the "sensories"—looked mainly for taste, refreshment, a clean-feeling mouth, perhaps a "stimulating" toothbrushing experience. Segment 2—the "sociables"—were mainly concerned with whitening ability and stain removal. Segment 3—the "worriers"—sought dental hygiene, especially in the form of cavity prevention. Segment 4—the "independents"—examined brands largely on the basis of price, did not take specific evaluative criteria seriously, and might be best classified as skeptical and nonemotional. A possible fifth segment not mentioned by this analyst could be "young sociables"—concerned about clean breath and sex appeal, too young to have stain problems, beyond the "cavity-prone years," but not yet parents.

An advertising executive looked at the market segments somewhat differently, though on a basis not inconsistent with the preceding classification. He suggested three very broad segments—"therapeutic," "cosmetic," and "all other." He also provided some estimates of segment and brand shares as they existed in the 1970s.[2] The "therapeutic segment" was virtually identical with the "worrying," decay-prevention segment. It was by far the largest in terms of market shares (64.9%) and was dominated by three brands—Crest (37.1%), Colgate (20.0%), and Gleem (7.8%). The "cosmetic segment"

included both the freshness and whitening appeals—the "sociables" and "young sociables." It was smaller (25.8%) and was served by Ultra Brite (8.1%) and Pepsodent (3.6%), each using a whitening appeal, and by Close-Up (14.1%), which featured a fresh-breath appeal. The "all other" category included brands with combination appeals as well as "sensory" (MacCleans) and "independents" (mainly private labels). Its total share was 9.3%.

Over time, some of these brands have been repositioned on evaluative criteria, but during much of the 1970s this was roughly the look of the market. We will assume we have made a reasonably good start on the issues raised in step 1-1 and move into the program.

### Social Influence and Occasion Segmentation
At step 1-2 we are dealing with the role that social pressure may play in brand choice. Because our product is privately consumed, it seems unlikely that users would feel forced to choose a specific brand on the basis of social conformity. In fact, there is even published evidence that they do not.[3] Consumers may seek social benefits from use, but it is the results that are on public display, not the name of the brand that delivered them. On this basis, we will answer "No" and move to step 1-3.

Do customers look for different evaluative criteria in different toothpaste-use situations? For instance, could certain features and benefits be wanted in a "morning toothpaste," whereas others are wanted in a "bedtime toothpaste," or could such occasion preferences be developed through our promotional strategy? Perhaps so, but for the present we will say "No" and move to step 1-6.

### Composition Rule Alternatives
The question at step 1-6 is whether it is likely that all consumers in this product market use the same composition rule to form attitudes. Based at least on the very brief market analysis presented earlier and on types of campaigns common among toothpaste advertisers we answer this question with a "Yes." (We will consider a possible consequence of a "No" answer later.) The Yes moves us to the bottom of the chart. Is the rule conjunctive, lexicographic, or linear-compensatory? Again, based on that brief analysis and observation of advertising themes as they existed at that point in time, the lexicographic

strategy seems to best describe how brands competed in this market.

Admittedly, this is open to interpretation. However, most toothpaste advertisers during this period seemed to rely on dramatizing one or possibly two evaluative criteria. When two were used, one tended to be the dominant feature, the other either a compatible or secondary feature. Although this was hardly an absolute rule, it was a rather predominant practice. If we answer "Yes" to step 1-8—"Is the rule lexicographic?"—we switch to subprogram B. This route will explore lexicographic possibilities.

## Lexicographic Options

The full subprogram for lexicographic possibilities is presented in Figure 6A.2. The first step in the subprogram calls for consideration of segmentation possibilities and then raises the question of whether we would have a lexicographically oriented segment all to ourselves. Based on our previous analysis, we would have to say "No" and move to step 2-3. In examining the evaluative criteria covered previously, those most featured during the relevant time period seem to be the following: (1) prevention of tooth decay (stannous fluoride), (2) whitening ability, (3) brightening ability, (4) taste, refreshing quality, and enjoyment in use, and (5) breath-freshening quality.

There are other possible criteria that might appeal to some feasible segments. Logical candidates include the following:

1. Ease of application or use (perhaps a packaging feature)
2. Low in abrasiveness, will not harm tooth enamel
3. Foaminess for more thorough cleaning
4. Stimulation and medication for healthier gums
5. Germ- and bacteria-killing ability—a general oral-hygiene appeal rather than mere decay prevention.

Each of the last five criteria has been used to some extent at some time, but in the 1970s none was featured as the lead appeal by any heavily promoted, major brand. Whether there is really a feasible segment—large, easily reached, and readily persuaded—for any of these or for other new appeals is an open question. At various times some brands have dramatized such criteria as functional packaging features and low abrasiveness in a lexicographic fashion and without much success. However, you might see a stronger, unused evaluative criterion (or

a better technique for dramatizing one of these). In this case answer "Yes," and move to step 2-4. If you answer "No," move to step 2-5, which asks, "Can we surpass competition on a major criterion?"

Crest is the most notable historic example of a brand that answered "Yes" to this question very successfully. Decay prevention was an evaluative criterion that had been promoted for many years before Crest was first introduced. Crest was able to demonstrate superiority via stannous fluoride and acceptance by the American Dental Association.

Following Crest's highly successful market entry, competitors entered the market with the same credentials. However, based on its history and experience in the field, Crest was able to communicate superiority on its featured criterion. In answering "Yes" with respect to your brand, you would have to assume you could convince a consumer segment that Maxident is superior to a current market leader on that leader's featured appeal. For example, you would have to show that Maxident delivers greater cavity prevention than Crest, more whitening ability than Pepsodent, or more breath-freshening ability than Close-Up. If you do not believe this is possible, move to step 2-7, which asks, "Can we equal competition on the major criterion and surpass it on another criterion of high importance?"

A brand that answered "Yes" quite successfully is Aim. Aim's basic introductory message implied the brand matched Crest on cavity prevention (it contained the same stannous fluoride), then added a secondary feature, better taste. The total benefit package was framed as a parental appeal—"perhaps even fewer cavities because your children will brush even longer." Essentially this is still a lexicographic approach. It concentrates on one benefit supplied by a combination of two features; one feature is dramatized and the second is treated as a supporting appeal.

If you are unable to answer "Yes" at step 2-7, you can move to step 2-9, which calls for upgrading a low-weighted criterion. The difference between the question here and that in step 2-3 depends on your assessment of current consumer weightings of evaluative criteria. Step 2-3 assumed there was a segment waiting for the feature you dramatized. Step 2-9 assumes your promotional campaign must both dramatize your ability to deliver the benefit and also upgrade a segment's weighting on that criterion. This is probably a more difficult assignment and, as

**FIGURE 6A.2 Options search in a lexicographic market**

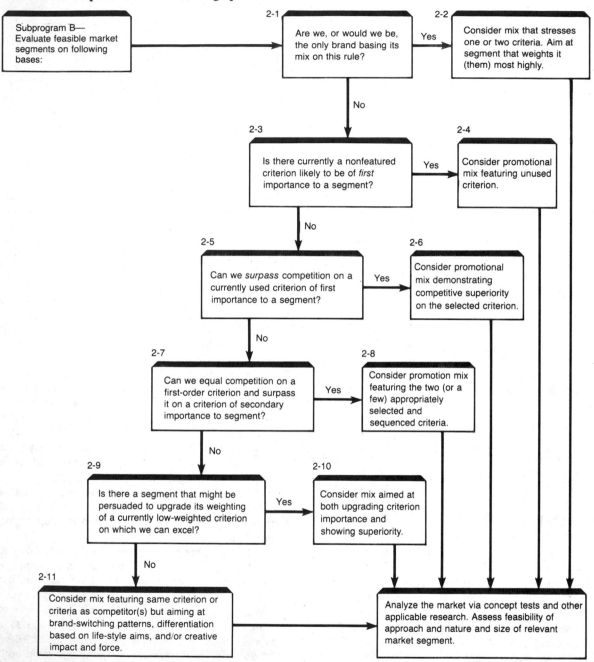

Subprogram B—
Evaluate feasible market segments on following bases:

**2-1** Are we, or would we be, the only brand basing its mix on this rule? — Yes → **2-2** Consider mix that stresses one or two criteria. Aim at segment that weights it (them) most highly.

No ↓

**2-3** Is there currently a nonfeatured criterion likely to be of *first* importance to a segment? — Yes → **2-4** Consider promotional mix featuring unused criterion.

No ↓

**2-5** Can we *surpass* competition on a currently used criterion of first importance to a segment? — Yes → **2-6** Consider promotional mix demonstrating competitive superiority on the selected criterion.

No ↓

**2-7** Can we equal competition on a first-order criterion and surpass it on a criterion of secondary importance to segment? — Yes → **2-8** Consider promotion mix featuring the two (or a few) appropriately selected and sequenced criteria.

No ↓

**2-9** Is there a segment that might be persuaded to upgrade its weighting of a currently low-weighted criterion on which we can excel? — Yes → **2-10** Consider mix aimed at both upgrading criterion importance and showing superiority.

No ↓

**2-11** Consider mix featuring same criterion or criteria as competitor(s) but aiming at brand-switching patterns, differentiation based on life-style aims, and/or creative impact and force. → Analyze the market via concept tests and other applicable research. Assess feasibility of approach and nature and size of relevant market segment.

*Consumer Attitudes as Planning Inputs*

**FIGURE 6A.3 Options search in a conjunctive market**

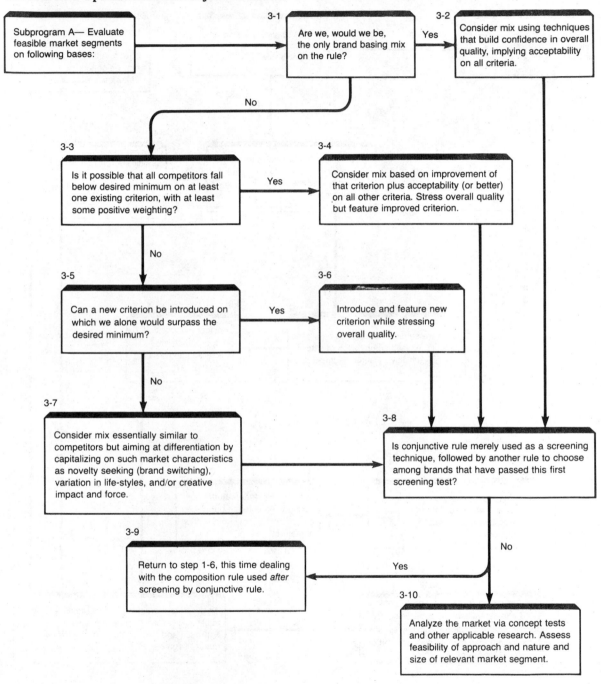

**FIGURE 6A.4 Options search in a linear-compensatory market**

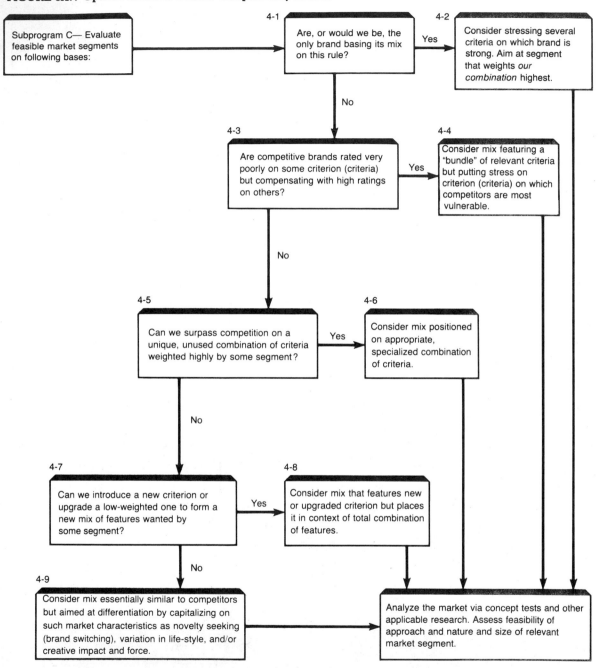

Subprogram C— Evaluate feasible market segments on following bases:

**4-1** Are, or would we be, the only brand basing its mix on this rule?

Yes → **4-2** Consider stressing several criteria on which brand is strong. Aim at segment that weights *our combination* highest.

No ↓

**4-3** Are competitive brands rated very poorly on some criterion (criteria) but compensating with high ratings on others?

Yes → **4-4** Consider mix featuring a "bundle" of relevant criteria but putting stress on criterion (criteria) on which competitors are most vulnerable.

No ↓

**4-5** Can we surpass competition on a unique, unused combination of criteria weighted highly by some segment?

Yes → **4-6** Consider mix positioned on appropriate, specialized combination of criteria.

No ↓

**4-7** Can we introduce a new criterion or upgrade a low-weighted one to form a new mix of features wanted by some segment?

Yes → **4-8** Consider mix that features new or upgraded criterion but places it in context of total combination of features.

No ↓

**4-9** Consider mix essentially similar to competitors but aimed at differentiation by capitalizing on such market characteristics as novelty seeking (brand switching), variation in life-style, and/or creative impact and force.

→ Analyze the market via concept tests and other applicable research. Assess feasibility of approach and nature and size of relevant market segment.

suggested in the preceding chapter, is one that requires deeper analysis of lifestyle goals.

For instance, assume you agreed with the analyst who described fluoride-toothpaste users as "worriers." At least one consumer-advisory agency has suggested that stannous fluoride may not be of great benefit to persons over twenty-five years of age.[4] Might it be possible to mount a promotional campaign downgrading fluoride to those over twenty-five who are "worriers" and upgrading another health feature such as germ- and bacteria-killing ability? This is at least one of the alternatives you may wish to consider.

Should you still feel unable to answer "Yes," you are at step 2-11. This suggests you might want to meet a competitor head-on if you feel your market is prone to brand switching, or if you can give a different lifestyle twist to the same evaluative criterion. You might feel your existing brand name or strategic superiority in carrying out a promotional program would be sufficient to give you a successful entry, even though your brand is not unique in terms of evaluative criteria.

As a case in point, Colgate toothpaste has been on the market since 1877 and has been repositioned many times. It was the market leader in 1960. When Crest received acceptance of its cavity-fighting claim from the American Dental Association, Colgate was hit hard and displaced. In 1969, Colgate attained the same acceptance and in large measure its promotion since then has met Crest head-on, although Colgate sometimes adds an additional appeal such as taste. Colgate's initial repositioning approach looked much like a step 2-11 strategy. In addition to a long-established name, Colgate relied on heavy promotional impact. Its initial attempts to reposition featured Captain Kangaroo, a "cavity-fighter" kit for children, 30 million samples to United States homes, and 100,000 kits to dentists.[5]

### Other Options

Return to Figure 6A.1, the basic search program. You may have disagreed with or at least questioned some of the yes or no decisions that have been suggested. For example, is a "Yes" answer possible, at least for some market segments, at step 1-3, which asks about possible occasion segmentation? Could you convince at least a portion of the large group of fluoride-toothpaste users that fluoride is right for brushing before going to bed, but your brand, the breath freshener, is best for morning brushing or before social occasions?

At step 1-6 we assumed that all consumers use a lexicographic rule. Is it possible that some segment, perhaps the "worriers," includes latent prospects for a conjunctive approach? If so, you would move to Figure 6A.3. At step 3-1 you would probably decide Maxident would be the only heavily promoted brand basing its mix on this rule. Alternatively, at step 3-3 you might determine that questions could be raised about minimum levels of low-weighted criteria (e.g., abrasiveness, germ-killing ability, foaminess, medication). If you could quickly show that only Maxident surpassed all minimum standards on these you might have a viable start toward successful repositioning.

## SUMMARIZING THE APPROACH

The possibilities do not end here. Our analysis of promotional variations for toothpaste did not lead us into a linear-compensatory subprogram. A potential route through such a subprogram is shown in Figure 6A.4. You may decide that another composition rule holds the key—or that none does. Even in the latter circumstance, following an analytical program of this sort should help you marshal your facts and provide the basis for other lines of strategy development.

Although flowcharts sometimes give the appearance of forcing their users into a mechanistic routine, the emphasis of the search program suggested here is on the discovery of new, creative approaches. It is meant to help promotional planners find additional options for their consideration, rather than limiting them to predetermined answers. In considering the merits of those options, research techniques that underlie composition-rule studies are available to assist in developing concept tests and other investigations of market feasibility.[6] An approach such as this options-search program can assist marketing management in its quest for promotional alternatives by blending observable practice with developments in theoretical research. In today's fast-changing and increasingly competitive marketplace, the two may form a very effective combination.

## APPENDIX REFERENCES

1. Russell Haley, "Benefit Segmentation, a Decision Oriented Tool," *Journal of Marketing*, July 1968, pp. 30–35.

2. Charles Fredericks, "Aim Toothpaste vs. Crest and Colgate," *Proceedings of 1974 Regional Conventions* (New York: American Association of Advertising Agencies, 1974), pp. 1–14.

3. Joel B. Cohen and Arnold M. Barban, *An Interactive Consumer-Product Typological System: A Progress Report and Partial Evaluation*, Working Paper No. 12 (University Park, Pennsylvania: College of Business Administration, Pennsylvania State University, 1970).

4. "Toothpaste," *Consumer Reports*, April 1972, p. 251.

5. "Dentists Endorse Colgate Formula," *Business Week*, October 11, 1969, pp. 46–47.

6. For some examples see:
   Kenneth R. MacCrimmon, "An Overview of Multiple Objective Decision Making," in James L. Cochrane and Milan Celeny, *Multiple Criteria Decision Making* (Columbia: University of South Carolina Press, 1973), pp. 18–44.
   Paul E. Green and Yoram Wind, *Multiattribute Decisions in Marketing* (Hinsdale, Illinois: Dryden Press, 1973), Ch. 2.
   Peter L. Wright, "Use of Consumer Judgment Models in Promotion Planning," *Journal of Marketing*, October 1973, pp. 27–33.

# CHAPTER SEVEN

# *Social Forces as Planning Inputs*

## FOCUS OF THE CHAPTER

In this and the next chapter, we will consider the types of guidance that you can obtain by studying lifestyle goals. In the scheme we are following, these goals are understood to be shaped by three types of forces—social, demographic, and biopsychic (Figure 7.1).

Many marketing people have come to believe that lifestyle goals are best studied as a single, total entity. In other words, there has been something of a trend toward researching rather generalized information on consumers. That information often sweeps across social, demographic, and biopsychic forces, and also includes facts on such additional points as general attitudes and product usage patterns. This approach is usually called "psychographics."

We shall come back to the idea of obtaining planning input data through psychographic analysis at the end of the next chapter. First, we will take separate looks at social, demographic, and biopsychic forces—the underlying factors that influence lifestyle goals. This chapter concentrates on social forces, and proceeds from the definition introduced in Chapter 4. *Social forces are those that evolve from a person's relations with other people and memberships in groups. Their major effects are generally studied in terms of culture, subculture, socioeconomic class, peer group relationships, and social role playing.*

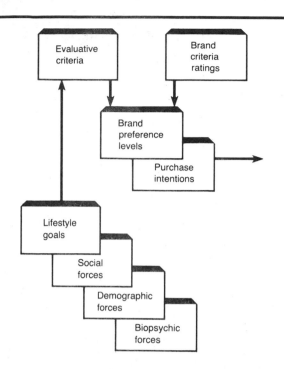

**FIGURE 7.1 Lifestyle goals and underlying determinant forces viewed in the framework for analyzing promotion**

## SOCIAL FORCES AND PURCHASE DECISIONS

There is little doubt that most of us are greatly affected by our relationships with other people. However, do such relationships influence each and every product we buy? At first glance, some products seem to have little or no social meaning. For example, when you buy antifreeze for your automobile it is unlikely that anyone knows or very much cares what brand you buy. On this basis, you might expect that there is no social influence on your choice of an antifreeze. Yet even in a case like this, a promotional strategist might find some type of potential, underlying social meaning and give you a social reason for choosing the particular brand that he or she is promoting.

A few years ago, the television campaign for one brand of antifreeze began by showing a smug motorist chanting, "Prestone, Prestone, who needs Prestone?" As the commercial continued, this same motorist was shown with his car stalled in the middle of bitterly cold weather. A group of friends in his car began chanting, "Prestone, Prestone, you need Prestone." In short, even a seemingly nonsocial product such as antifreeze can often be given social interpretation. If you do not use the "right brand" you may be embarrassed in front of other people. If you do use the "right brand" you may be more socially successful, that is, more admired by the people with whom you identify.

*Searching for Socially Based Appeals*

Consider products such as beer and razor blades. The basic reason for choosing a brand of beer would seem to be that the user thinks it tastes good and quenches his or her thirst. The basic purpose of a razor blade is to shave one's beard with a minimum of discomfort. However, like many products, beer and razor blades can take on strong social meaning and are often promoted largely on the basis of such meaning. While watching a Superbowl telecast, one sociologist analyzed the commercials for these products and described what he saw in the following way:

> The beer advertisement first prepares us for the introduction of the beer. We see a rowing team of all men. The camera focuses on their muscles—the strength and power of the men becomes clear, but they all take directions perfectly from their leader. The importance of strict obedience is coupled with victory, and victory coupled with being a man. The beer is introduced as being the well-earned reward, with the concluding comment, "It's sort of good to be with men who won't settle for second best."

> The razor blade ad follows a similar pattern. The blades are tungsten, but they are not introduced until they are associated with a powerful steelworker drilling through tough tungsten steel. His shirt sleeve is cut short, (and ragged) to reveal his muscles. Sparks bounce off his helmet. He balances himself above the city drilling the steel that makes the city (a far cry from "softer hands with Dove"). Now the tungsten blades can be introduced. They are "blades as tough as steel, for men with tough beards." [1]

Products can serve purposes that go far beyond the immediate and apparent reason for their use. Some of those purposes are related to social forces—the way consumers are affected by the people around them and the way they want to be seen by those other people.

With this in mind, it is worth considering your brand in terms of potential social factors that may be linked with its use, even though these factors may sometimes seem remote. After examining the situation, you may decide social forces play such a small role in influencing consumers' evaluative criteria weightings that they are not worth much consideration. However, you will usually be well advised to think the issue through very thoroughly before reaching that conclusion. In doing so, you may discover some new and important promotional appeals with which to build your persuasive communications package.

## CULTURE

"Culture" is a commonly used term with a variety of meanings. Two sociologists once listed 164 different definitions of the word.[2] A reasonable working definition for our purposes can be stated as follows: *"A culture is the configuration of learned behavior and results of behavior whose component elements are shared and transmitted by members of a particular society. [In marketing situations, that society is typically a nation or a closely related group of nations.]"*[3]

It has been pointed out that national culture is not found in museums or formed by graduate schools or universities. It is composed of the common daily habits and patterns in the lives of the people, and of mutual interests in entertainment, sports, news, and even advertising. In other words, people who live in the same nation tend to share some very broad-scale notions. This does not imply that all of those people are the same in every respect. It does mean that taken as an entire group they are likely to hold, or at least be influenced by, certain habits and points of view that make them somewhat different from people in other nations.

**Cultural Factors and Promotional Practices**

To illustrate how cultural factors can be studied and utilized for promotional strategy, we will proceed from "the inside out." Because this book is being written mainly from the perspective of American promotional strategy, it will be assumed that the "inside" is the United States. The "outside" is the rest of the world. Therefore, we shall first discuss broad-scale American cultural patterns in terms of their promotional implications. Then we shall move to a consideration of the more finely delineated social aspects existing within the American culture. Finally, we shall look at cultural differences as they can affect promotion on an international basis.

## THE AMERICAN CULTURE

A number of analysts have proposed lists of characteristics that tend to dominate American national culture. For example, one expert on consumer behavior noted such national traits as humanism, egalitarianism, materialism, achievement, stress on individualism, admiration of youthfulness, and emphasis on promptness.[4]

**Diversity Within American Culture**

The people within any particular national culture can react in different ways to general cultural norms. Of course, this includes Americans. Anyone familiar with the United States realizes that not all Americans are humanistic, materialistic, or individualistic. These may be *general* norms of American culture but individuals respond to them in varying degrees and in different ways. Although generalizations concerning dominant cultural features can be useful starting points for your thinking, you will ultimately have to analyze specific cultural patterns that affect your specific product category and your specific target consumer group.

**Changing Patterns in American Culture**

All cultures are subject to shifts and modifications over time. The pace of such cultural change can be very gradual or very rapid. Many observers feel that contemporary American culture is not only changing more swiftly than most foreign cultures, but is undergoing more rapid and widescale change than American culture itself has undergone in the past. Rapid cultural shifts can suggest opportunities for emphasis on new products, stress on new evaluative criteria, and development of new promotional approaches. Among the important cultural trends noted by one marketing researcher are the following:

> Trend toward more liberal sexual attitudes: The relaxation of sexual prohibitions and the devaluation of "virtue" in the traditional sense among women.

> Trend toward . . . rejection of institutionalized religions and the substitution of more personalized forms of religious experiences characterized by the emergence of numerous small and more intimate religious sects and cults.

Trend toward acceptance of stimulants and drugs: Greater acceptance of artificial agents (legal and illegal) for mood change, stimulation, and relaxation, as opposed to the view that these should be accomplished by the strength of character alone.

Trend toward greater tolerance of chaos and disorder: less need for schedules, routines, plans, regular shopping and purchasing; tolerance of less order and cleanliness in the home, less regular eating and entertaining patterns.

Trend toward new forms of materialism: The new status symbols and the extent of de-emphasis on money and material possessions.

Trend toward return to nature: Rejection of the artificial, the "chemical," the man-made improvements on nature; the adoption of more "natural" ways of dressing, eating, and living. [5]

A commercial consulting firm has dubbed the changing patterns of American culture the "new Narcissism." Based on their studies they conclude, "The ramifications of the 'new Narcissism' are many, including less pressure to conform, tolerance of diversity, single person and child-free households, personalization, customization, permissive sexual attitudes, insensitivity to drugs, concern for privacy and safety, inner gratification, status, a glut of specialized publications, and the need for fun and enjoyment to compensate for unfulfilling employment."[6]

Again, the promotional implications of such trends must be interpreted in terms of the particular product and target market with which you are dealing. In some cases, one or another cultural trend may be important. In other cases, they may have little or no meaning. To better understand how cultural changes might affect the process of promotion, consider the following examples.

***Are McDonald's Hamburgers Replacing Organized Religion?*** At least one anthropologist takes the view that increased rejection of traditional religious institutions may be causing people to seek substitute forms of "spiritual comfort." In particular he cites the popularity of the McDonald's fast-food chain as an example. In his view, in a chaotic and disruptive cultural environment, the traveling or uprooted American can obtain something akin to a comforting and reassuring religious experience by heading for the local golden arches of McDonald's. "The menu is located in the same place, has the same items, and has the same prices . . . we know what we are going to see, say and hear from that first request for a Big Mac to the final 'Have a nice day.' . . . Every move is ritualized like a religious service."[7]

Admittedly, this is simply one person's interpretation of what is happening. It is also an interpretation that might come as somewhat of a surprise to marketing executives of the McDonald's chain. However, the very general possibilities are worth considering. When important cultural institutions lose much of their power and attraction it is not unusual for people to seek replacements to fulfill the essential human needs formerly served by those institutions. These substitutes may be packaged in highly disguised forms. By implication, this opens up potential promotional opportunities for those marketers who can provide consumers with such substitutes, even if they take the form of something so simple as nation-wide consistency in menus and architectural design.

***Will Future Appliances Be Smaller?***   Changes in the nature of the family as an institution and especially the shift to smaller household sizes have prompted one observer to predict the onset of some widespread marketing changes. In particular, he foresees the need for smaller appliances to suit smaller households. He also sees a developing growth market for tools designed especially for use by women and "products that are increasingly convenient . . . and also adaptable for more specialized situations."[8]

***Will Advertising Become Even More Sexually Explicit?***   The use of sexual appeals in promotional strategies is hardly new. What is changing in response to trends in the American culture is the degree of openness and extent of detail with which sexual appeals are now presented. As one writer points out, "One advertiser uses a headline 'Clean is Sexy,' a statement which would have been regarded in poor taste a decade ago. Another advertiser uses the headline 'What to wear on Sunday when you won't be home until Monday' with the implication of a young woman spending the night with a young man."[9]

***What Does Increased Drug Use Imply for Promotional Strategy?***   According to at least one market study, the expanding use of mind altering drugs will affect future promotional approaches. In the opinion of the analysts, the ever growing proportion of the American public that has used marijuana, cocaine, or LSD will be attracted by promotional strategies that recognize the experience of such drug use. In their view, "Products and ads will have to afford these individuals a sensory experience if they are to be effective. Also, marketers must develop new ways of escaping reality and modifying mood."[10]

***How Can the Study of Cultural Trends Help You Sell a Soft Drink?***   As reported in one business journal, the changing themes of Pepsi-Cola advertising have long been guided by sociological investigations of shifts in the American cultural mood. In the late 1960s, Pepsi ads were built around the slogan, "You've got a lot to live and Pepsi's got a lot to give." The theme of these ads was intended to provide prospects with a "soothing respite from grim contemporary issues" such as civil rights struggles and antiwar protests. It was followed by "Join the Pepsi people, feelin' free," which was introduced during a period highlighted by the Watergate scandal, inflation, and the energy crunch, and was meant to "momentarily free people from their everyday problems."

Research showed that the 1970s was the "decade of self." Egocentrism was promulgated and popularized via numerous self-help books and movements. To keep its advertising in tune with the national mood, Pepsi's slogan became, "Have a Pepsi day." The "Pepsi day" ads implied that the issue of importance was personal self-gratification. Toward the end of the 1970s sociological research revealed the beginning of a revised national mood, and in 1980 a new slogan was introduced—"Catch that Pepsi spirit, drink it in." The 1980 campaign centered around the idea that, rather than being mainly concerned with themselves, Americans were looking toward more "togetherness" and a sharing of experiences with others. The new national mood was seen as a response to such things as the 1976 bicentennial celebrations and the Iranian hostage crisis. In "Pepsi spirit" ads, scenes featured affection and sentiment for others: "A professional baseball player returns triumphantly to his home town; a European father is reunited in this country with his son and family; a young Texan hires a sky writer to deliver a marriage proposal."[11]

*American Culture and Promotional Planning*

The United States tends to be characterized by broad cultural norms, but it also seems subject to rapid changes and trends. Both the overall nature and the patterns of change can be useful factors to consider for their possible promotional implications. In particular, recent shifts in American cultural norms have produced some interesting speculations concerning their effects on consumer needs and responses.

All such interpretations must be related to the particular product category and target market with which you are working. Neither general cultural characteristics nor current cultural trends are going to affect everyone in the United States or every product in the United States in the same way. For example, though many observers feel that changing sex roles—especially as they alter women's attitudes—demand revised promotional approaches to the female market, one pair of researchers makes the following important point, "While a number of critics have maintained that advertising is not moving fast enough in correctly portraying women's changing role in society, it is desirable to point out that over 50% of married women are not working outside of the home and a substantial percentage of those employed still consider their role as homemaker as important."[12]

In short, when you are attempting to estimate the way in which cultural norms or current changes in cultural norms may affect your strategic planning, you will be well advised to examine them on a product-specific and segment-specific basis.

## SUBCULTURAL INFLUENCES

*The Nature of Subcultures*

Like the word "culture," the term "subculture" has been given a number of slightly different definitions by various writers. For our purposes, we will use the following definition: *"A subculture is a segment of a culture which shares distinguishing patterns of behavior."*[13]

As generally interpreted for marketing purposes, this definition has three implications. First, a subculture includes a rather large group of people, for example, all blacks in the United States. This large size usually makes it impossible for all members to be in direct contact with each other. In fact, the typical member is likely to have direct communication with only a very small percentage of the other individuals who comprise the subculture. Second, although most members do not know each other personally, all are socially influenced by the total group. This is because each of them, consciously and actively, identifies with everyone else within the subculture. They tend to share some similar norms and beliefs that differ from those of the culture as a whole. Subcultural norms may not guide every aspect of a member's behavior, but will affect at least some. Third, because a subculture is also part of a larger culture, it is not entirely independent. Its members are concurrently influenced by the norms of the culture in general. They may add to those norms or modify them or perhaps react against some of the major cultural norms.

*Relevance of Subcultures to Promotional Planning*

Subcultural differences may or may not be important when you are working on promotional strategy for a particular brand. Such differences can be especially important if subcultural norms (1) affect the extent to which your general product class is used, (2) affect the specific set of lifestyle goals with which use of your product is associated, (3) affect the amount of emphasis that consumers put on various evaluative criteria, or (4) affect the manner in which explicit promotional messages are received, including the ways in which differences in wording, creative details, salesperson acceptance, or media usage may influence interpretation of your promotional messages.

*Bases of Subcultures*

Subcultures can be built around or related to a variety of characteristics. Those most often thought to have possible marketing implications include ethnic or racial origins, social class, age, and geographic location. Most of these characteristics were used as illustrations of demographic forces when those were defined in an earlier chapter. Now we seem to be transferring them to another category and designating them as social forces. The fact is that subcultures tend to originate from demographic factors. However—and very importantly—such factors do not necessarily form subcultures in and of themselves.

This distinction is not merely a philosophical fine point. On the contrary, it highlights a situation to which you should be alert. Some groups of consumers who can often be distinguished on the basis of certain demographic factors can also be distinguished on the basis of unique types of socially anchored attitudes and behavior. People in such groups are not merely alike in demographic terms, but are also alike in social or subcultural terms because they identify with each other and distinguish themselves from the general population. Still other groups of consumers who can also be distinguished on demographic bases are not generally thought of as subcultures because they do not identify with each other in any serious social sense that affects their behavior.

For example, Americans of Jewish, Hispanic, or black ancestry are commonly described as forming subcultural groups. This is because a great many blacks, Jews, and Hispanics think of themselves as belonging to a separate category of people with whom they want to identify. They actively share certain socially important interests and attitudes with other subculture members. In contrast, Americans of English or German ancestry are usually not considered as subcultural groups. The assumption is that the majority of them do not identify with each other in a way that resembles a social entity. Rather, they are essentially socially independent of each other. Presumably, most persons of English or German ancestry are so deeply assimilated into the general American culture that they have lost most of their ethnic distinctiveness. In similar fashion, and for the same general reasons you will frequently hear discussions of a "youth subculture," but rarely if ever will you hear references to a middle-aged subculture.

When you are promoting to a group that is distinguished as a subculture you may have some divergent social forces to consider that run much deeper than the mere surface variations of demographics. Such social forces can provide you with both problems and opportunities. Perhaps you will have to use specialized language, modified appeals, or more selective advertising media to reach subculture members. You may even want to design a special product to meet unique subcultural needs. Many of these decisions depend on what you are selling or where you are selling it. In illustrating how subcultural structures might influence promotional strategies, the following discussion is limited to subcultures based on either ethnic origins or social class.

# ETHNIC SUBCULTURES

**Black Americans as a Subcultural Market**

Because of its size, the most frequently discussed subculture in the United States is that composed of black Americans. One writer points out that, though blacks constitute only about twelve percent of the United States population, they tend to be very heavy consumers in certain product categories.[14] By some estimates, they account for twenty-eight percent of soft drink sales and twenty-three percent of shoe sales. Are differentiated promotional approaches often needed to reach black Americans? Observers disagree, but there is a strong body of opinion which holds that many marketers could profit by giving specialized attention to the black subculture.[15]

*Specialized Products for Black Consumers.* In some cases, serving black prospects may involve starting with the implicit portion of the promotional mix, in other words, designing products with functional features that supply the special needs and lifestyle goals of black Americans. For example, Sperry-Remington has introduced an electric shaver built especially for black men. Its cutting mechanism was engineered to meet the shaving problems presented by "extremely curly facial hair." The advertising campaign for the product has made use of contemporary and black-oriented radio stations along with insertions in four major black magazines.[16]

The makers of women's cosmetics have also become aware of the need for special products for blacks. Both skin color and physiological differences make many white-oriented cosmetic items unsuitable. After researching the market, a number of firms including Avon and Revlon have introduced full lines of cosmetics for black women. Separate advertising campaigns tailored to relate to the black consumers' needs, interests, and attitudes have been developed and run in selected media vehicles.[17]

*Special Considerations in Explicit Strategies.* Even when the basic product is sold to both black and nonblack consumers, there is a fairly broad consensus that when black buyers make up a significant percentage of your potential market, black-oriented media are more effective as a means of achieving a favorable response from black prospects because they identify themselves with such media.[18]

Another issue that often crops up when an advertising campaign is aimed at a combination black and nonblack audience is the question of whether ads should be "integrated." One group of writers summed up their survey of the available data in these words: "Based on the existing research evidence, we can conclude that (1) all-black advertisements, and to a lesser extent, integrated advertisements will be favorably perceived by black consumers. (2) such ads will not automatically cause negative reactions in whites though specific ads should be tested prior to utilization, and (3) favorable response to the advertisement is not a certain indicator that a favorable sales response will follow."[19]

## The Hispanic Subculture

Hispanic Americans, who can be loosely defined as persons with Latin-American origins, are becoming a consumer group of growing interest to United States marketers. There are several reasons for this. Foremost among these reasons is the large size of the Hispanic population, estimated at over 18.5 million people.[20] A second reason is its continuing growth which, according to some observers, will make it the nation's largest minority within the next two decades.[21] Furthermore, because a high proportion of Hispanic Americans are concentrated in such major urban areas as New York, Los Angeles, Miami, and Chicago, they are relatively easy to reach through specialized appeals and specialized media. Although Hispanic household incomes still lag behind the national average, the evidence suggests they are rising more rapidly, largely owing to the trend toward more working wives in Hispanic households.[22]

A variety of distinctions have been drawn between Hispanics and the "typical" American consumer. The outstanding difference is that the majority of persons identifying with the Hispanic subculture use Spanish as a first or second language. This suggests one major promotional variation that is often vital when aiming at this market, which is the transmission of your messages in Spanish. However, Hispanics have also been identified with certain other differentiating characteristics. For example, they tend to be younger and to have larger family units than the United States average.[23] It has also been noted that their household units tend to be highly cohesive. One observer notes, "The macho stereotype is one myth that is quickly dispelled by research. Major product and lifestyle decisions are made by husband *and* wife, not by a man unilaterally. . . . Another aspect of Latinos we must acknowledge is their pride. The deference they pay to their past and tenacity with which they hold to their heritage underscore the pride these people feel."[24]

Although Hispanics are heavy users of television, viewing both English-language and Spanish-language stations where they are available, it has been noted that the medium they use most often is radio.[25] In large measure, this orientation toward radio is an outgrowth of ethnic tradition, since it is the most heavily used medium in much of Latin America.

Although it is possible to cite a variety of generalizations about the Hispanic market, it should also be emphasized that there is heterogeneity within its ranks. A major aspect of difference stems from the diversity of countries to which the subculture members can trace their roots. An estimated sixty percent have Mexican backgrounds. Fourteen percent identify with Puerto Rico, six percent with Cuba, and the remaining twenty percent with other Central or South American nations. In consequence, Hispanics vary in their precise interpretations of heritage as well as in language nuances. There are also gradations in income levels, educational backgrounds, and length of residence in the United States.

A number of firms have succeeded in reaching the Hispanic market by tailoring messages specifically for its members. For example, realizing that Hispanic Americans are heavy patrons of fast-food restaurants—making purchases at such outlets at twice the national rate—Kentucky Fried Chicken developed a special campaign to reach groups in Hispanic areas.[26] Based on its research, the franchise chain determined that Hispanics put more emphasis on the intrinsic quality of the chicken itself as opposed to its mode of preparation. As a result, it replaced its "We Do Chicken Right" slogan with one more meaningful to Latin consumers—"The Chicken of Chickens."

In another example, a chain of paint stores serving the southern California area directed a special promotional campaign toward the Hispanic population. The reasoning behind its Hispanic-oriented advertising was described as follows: "Strong cultural and family ties will be the focus of Spanish-language commercials designed for Standard Brands Paint Company's Hispanic media campaign. The . . . company will spend $600,000 beginning early this year, mainly on Spanish-language TV and radio programming. Recent in-depth Hispanic market media tests and follow-up studies indicate the company and Hispanic market are compatible."[27]

As a final example, because beer has been reported as the most popular drink among Hispanic Americans it is not surprising that major American brewers have made intense efforts to reach that market.[28] For example, Schlitz has reportedly stepped up its appeal to Hispanics by promoting itself on the basis of a "blended lifestyle." The essence of the appeal rests on the recognition that many Hispanics have lives that move between the Spanish-speaking and English-speaking subcultures. To back up its campaign, Schlitz not only has added Hispanic sales representatives and customized advertising but has become a heavy participant in events such as Hispanic street festivals, scholarship programs, and fund-raising events.

*The Jewish Subculture*

American Jews are usually thought to form a distinct subculture. However, the extent to which this influences their purchasing patterns may be less widespread than it is among blacks and Hispanics. One author suggests that the "American Jew is becoming more identifiable with the rest of American society. The growing conformity has altered even forms of living which have throughout the ages been directly tied with Jewish religious and social views. As the attachment to Jewish values becomes slightly weaker with each generation distinctive purchasing behavior becomes less discernible."[29]

For many or perhaps most marketing purposes American Jews may not form a unique consumer group. However, there seem to be some exceptions, the most notable of which exists in the category of food products. Not only do many Jews prefer or demand grocery items identified as "Kosher," but there are also variations in food usage patterns other than those related to religious practice. As a case in point, one study found Jewish families tended to reject prepared cake mixes and dehydrated soups, were comparatively light users of frozen dinners and desserts, and often heavy users of instant coffee and tea as well as fresh vegetables and meat. Because many Jews apparently do have subcultural preferences in their eating patterns, it is not uncommon for major United States food producers to construct extra advertising campaigns directed to the Jewish market. The specific food items involved may be the same as those promoted to Americans in general, but separate and additional promotions are built to reach the Jewish market through specialized vehicles. For example, the Best Foods Division of CPC International runs special advertising for its regular brands such as Mazola corn oil in such publications as the New York Jewish Week and the Los Angeles B'nai Brith Messenger to deliver advertising messages aimed especially at this market. In turn, it alerts its sales force to the planned appearance of such advertisements so that they can use this information to help gain added reseller support from grocery outlets with a large Jewish clientele.

A thought-provoking, though highly tentative finding regarding a unique characteristic of the American Jewish community could be of some importance to firms that are introducing new products.[30] A research study suggested that Jewish consumers may be much more prone toward innovation and have greater influence as opinion leaders than their non-Jewish counterparts. To the extent that this is true it could be taken to imply that by directing heavy emphasis toward reaching members of the Jewish subculture in the early phases of a brand's introduction, you might be able to hasten its market acceptance. Presumably, not only might members of this subculture be more responsive to the idea of trying a new brand, but assuming they found it to their liking and adopted it they could also hasten acceptance by others through word-of-mouth endorsements.

**Other Ethnic Subcultures**

The black, Hispanic, and Jewish populations by no means exhaust the variety of ethnic subcultures which exist in the United States. It has been noted that as part of the general American cultural trend there has been something of a widespread return of ethnic pride among diverse nationality groups. For promotional strategists, it is worthwhile to consider the possibility that a special appeal to Italian Americans, Polish Americans, Swedish Americans, or any one of a number of other groups might be feasible. For that matter, even though we dismissed them as "nonethnic" earlier, it is not entirely impossible that a group such as English Americans or German Americans might respond favorably to an ethnic identification theme in certain situations.

# SOCIAL CLASS AS A PLANNING INPUT

American tradition has enshrined the ideal that all people are created equal. However, even in a society dedicated to egalitarianism the population tends to be stratified into a system of social rankings. Sociologists have formalized the study of the social-ordering pattern by proposing the existence of status categories designated as social classes.[31] For our purposes, social classes can be defined as follows: *Social classes are very broad groupings of individuals who hold roughly similar status levels in society, arranged in a hierarchy from low through middle to upper class divisions.* A less formalized description of what is implied by the concept has been expressed as follows:

> I would suppose social class means where you went to school and how far. Your intelligence. Where you live. The sort of house you live in. Your general background, as far as clubs you belong to, your friends. To some degree the type of profession you are in—in fact, definitely that. Where you send your children to school. The hobbies you have. Skiing, for example, is higher than the snowmobile. The clothes you wear . . . all of that. These are the externals. It can't be (just) money because nobody ever knows that about you for sure. [32]

As hinted in the above quote, the amount of money earned or possessed tends to affect social class status, but it is usually not the only variable involved in most class categorization schemes. Nonetheless, it should be noted at the outset that whereas some research has pointed to social class as a viable segmentation variable,[33] other analysts have concluded that it may be more meaningful to group consumers by income levels and ignore the idea of social class.[34] A logical explanation for these opposite findings is that they are outgrowths of differences between the product categories studied. By inference, social class may provide a sensible segmentation frame for some product categories and brands but have little or no utility for others.

To explore the feasibility of employing social class as a technique for assisting in your development of promotional strategy, we will begin with some evidence of how it has been or might be related to marketing situations. Following that we will examine some of the more basic issues involved in the general concept of social class, including methods you might use to assess its potential for applicability in your particular promotional setting.

*Applications of Social Class in Promotional Strategy*

As noted above, the usefulness of social class as a planning input factor may be dependent on the particular product category and brand with which you are working. There seem to be some significant lifestyle preferences that attach to various social classes. These in turn could affect the evaluative criteria customers emphasize and/or the lifestyle goals to which promotional messages can most effectively be related. For example, differences in leisure time preferences have been associated with social class status. Diversions such as tennis, bridge, ice skating, and concerts are favored by middle-class and upper-class individuals whereas members of the lower classes are likely to be more involved in fishing, bowling, pool, and drive-in movie attendance.[35]

One sociologically oriented market analyst has advanced the interesting proposition pictured in Figure 7.2. He points to tentative evidence linking

**FIGURE 7.2 An interpretation of the social class structure of food symbolism**

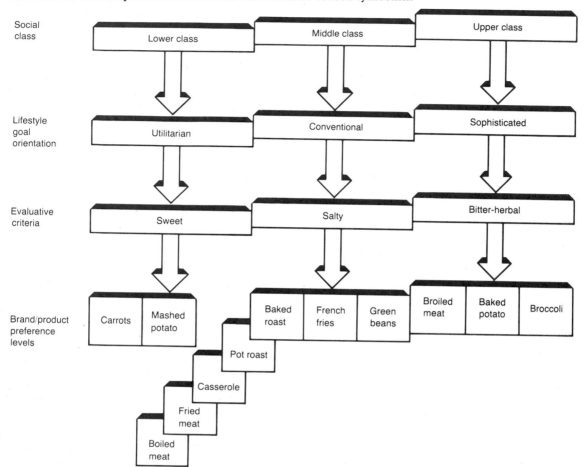

Source: Sidney J. Levy, "Interpreting Consumer Mythology: A Structural Approach to Consumer Behavior," *Journal of Marketing*, Summer 1981, p. 57.

social class to food preferences through a system of intermediate causal factors.[36] In terms of the general framework for promotional analysis which we are following, the suggestion is that the social class aspect of social forces greatly influences particular lifestyle orientations. In consequence, certain evaluative criteria are indirectly shaped by social class standards, which in turn affect specific product choices. By inference, a promotional strategist who has analyzed this flow of influences could be in a much better position to devise specially tailored messages aimed at the particular social class group. Knowledge of the existence of such a causal flow would enable you to relate your product to the criteria of importance to particular social class members and to embed your appeal in the background of lifestyle goal qualities with which it is connected.

***Differences in Promotional Appeals and Media Preferences.*** Variations have been found in terms of how social class members use and interpret advertising media and messages. It appears that the higher the social class, the less time spent with television and the more time spent with magazines and radio.[37] In still another study, lower-status individuals were shown to respond especially well to advertising that concentrated on solving everyday problems in a very practical way and used heavy visual appeal and activity. As for television program types, whereas soap operas, situation comedies, and quiz shows seem to have an especially strong appeal to lower social class members, the middle and upper classes tend to favor shows featuring current events and drama.[38]

***Brand Positioning by Social Class.*** In Chapter 3 reference was made to the successful promotion of Perrier water on the basis of social status. Essentially, the Perrier campaign was aimed at the upper-middle class. In developing such a campaign, information regarding the interests, habits, and social goals of your target consumers can be extremely valuable as a starting point for developing your promotional mix. In fact, the tone of Perrier's approach suggests they used generalized social class data to help choose such things as advertising vehicles, a spokesperson, and "proper" sports with which to associate their name.

You saw still another illustration of a promotional campaign with social class underpinnings in our discussion of consumption concentration in Chapter 5. As pointed out there, the Miller Brewing Company formulated its repositioning approach on the basis of data which revealed that eighty percent of the beer in the United States is consumed by roughly thirty percent of the beer drinkers in the country and that these heavy consumers are predominantly young, blue-collar workers. With such information in hand, Miller set out to "take Miller High Life out of the champagne bucket and put it into the lunch bucket." The essence of the resulting campaign was built around activities that match or appeal to the lifestyle interests of individuals whose social status can be described as upper-lower class.

***Relationships Between Social Class and Product Preferences.*** A study that related preferences in living room furnishings to social class status revealed an interesting and rather pronounced pattern of style preferences among those persons surveyed.[39] For example, bulky furniture, bright walls, translucent curtains, and floral carpet designs appear to have shown rather strong association with low social status. On the other hand, plain curtains, picture windows, and modern furniture were more typically associated with high social status.

Another team of researchers conducted a survey to determine whether upper-class, middle-class, and lower-class women would vary in their stereotyped opinions about the nature of persons who bought particular brands of products. They examined brands in seven product categories hypothesized to differ from each other in terms of their "value-expressive dimension" based on the findings of previous research.[40] The value-expressive dimension (VED) refers to the product category's capacity to communicate symbolically in a social sense. For example, automobiles were considered to be high in terms of VED. Washing machines and vacuum cleaners were considered to be moderately high. Brassieres, deodorants, and laundry detergents were considered to be low VED categories. In reporting the results, the researchers concluded the following:

> Overall, these results refute the contention [of some analysts] that differences in social class have disappeared because of common exposure to mass media . . . . The highly value-expressive product categories had many brands with significant differences in user stereotypes while the utilitarian had few. Moreover, for highly value-expressive products the product categories themselves were perceived as different by the upper and lower social classes. [41]

*Bases for Social Class Measurements in Promotional Applications*

It was suggested in the informal commentary quoted earlier (see p. 193), social class "can't be (just) money because nobody ever knows that about you for sure." In practice, there are a number of variables that can be used to measure social status. Some of these are demographic variables such as educational level, occupation, and income. Others are primarily lifestyle-related variables such as type of residence and club memberships. In considering social class in terms of how it can be measured and what relationship it may have to promotional decision making, the sequential flow between influencing forces as shown in Figure 7.3 can serve as a useful benchmark. The model depicted there is predicated on the assumption that there are a series of cause and effect relationships that produce a particular social lifestyle pattern. The model begins with the assumption that the socioeconomic status of one's parents has a direct and positive bearing on a person's educational attainment. In turn, educational level has a direct effect on occupational level, which has a positive association with income level. To the extent that income level either encourages certain actions or imposes constraints on one's lifestyle, the chain culminates in a variety of behavioral patterns that tend to be considered as appropriate for a given social class position. For our purposes, these aspects of lifestyles and the series of causal factors that produced them might be interesting insofar as they are reflected in consumer purchase behavior.

The model depicted in Figure 7.3 is not presented as an absolute statement of an inevitable and invariant pattern. Rather, it is introduced because the illustrated flow sequence provides some very useful points of reference from which to initiate consideration of the complexities involved in working with and attempting to measure social class. In particular, the model serves as a backdrop for discussing three critical issues: (1) the comparatively flexible nature of the American social structure, (2) the rather weak relationships between demographic forces customarily used to describe and measure social class status, and (3) the resulting alternative measurement techniques that can be employed.

***The Flexible Nature of the American Social Structure.*** Although the model begins with the notion of a clearly ordered set of cause and effect variables, the American social structure is hardly as rigid as that ordering would imply if interpreted strictly. In medieval Europe, for example, it might be true that the status of one's parents determined everything that followed and led to a predictable and inescapable lifestyle for most people. Even in contemporary American society, it is likely that a child in a wealthy family will be en-

**FIGURE 7.3**
**Dimensions of social status as influences on purchase decisions**

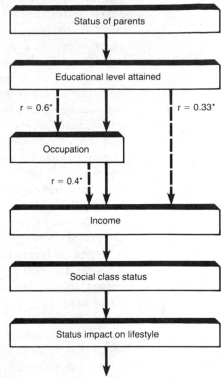

Possible implications relative to purchase influences — e.g., brand preferences, stress on particular evaluative criteria, media usage habits, etc.

*Correlation coefficient between indicated variables where 1.0 would indicate perfect correlation, while 0 would indicate no correlation.

*Sources:* The first five functional relationships are based on those suggested in R. W. Hodge and P. M. Siegel, "The Measurement of Social Class," *International Encyclopedia of the Social Sciences* (Glencoe, IL: Free Press, 1968) p. 332.

couraged and supported with respect to educational attainment in a way that a child raised by parents existing at the poverty level will not be.

The vast majority of people, however, fall somewhere in between these two extremes. Furthermore, even at the extremes themselves, though the outcome may be heavily influenced by family environment, that outcome is not an absolute certainty. In short, there is mobility in the American societal framework. People can rise or descend from one level to another. In turn, this suggests that persons in any given status category may harbor aspirations of moving to another and their current lifestyles may be influenced by those aspirations.

*The Positive but Rather Weak Relationships Between Demographic Factors, Social Status, and Consequent Lifestyle Behavior.* Figure 7.3 presumes that occupational level is a direct outcome of educational level and, in turn, that income level is a direct outcome of occupational level. As indicated by the correlation figures shown on the diagram, there is some evidence that these relationships do indeed exist. However, the data also suggest that those relationships are far from absolute. At least one study found a correlation of 0.6 between education and occupation and a correlation of 0.4 between occupation and income. When the association between educational level and income level was studied directly, the correlation was 0.33. In other words, the more years of education an individual possesses the more likely it is that the individual will enjoy both a higher occupational status and a higher income. However, this is far from being a certain or assured outcome. Sheer number of years in school is not the only factor leading to increased job prestige or earning capacity. Furthermore, an individual's income is not necessarily totally commensurate with the prestige level of that person's job or profession.

These findings should be considered if and when you are attempting to delineate a market in terms of social class. At least as represented in the pattern we are considering, using data on education alone or on gross occupational status alone might result in misleading conclusions regarding social lifestyle status. As mentioned earlier, it has been argued that one solution is to refer directly to income level as a rather easily measured demographic indicator of social class and consequent lifestyle. However, this option also risks the possibility of reaching a faulty conclusion. As one team of writers has pointed out, "A college professor or lawyer may have the same income as a truck driver or plumber. Nonetheless, it is likely that their consumption process for a variety of products will differ."[42]

*Alternative Methods of Measuring Social Class.* As emphasized earlier, the major marketing issue involved in the question of social class is concerned with status-associated lifestyle patterns that affect product use and brand choice. Because these patterns and the social status that determines them are rather cumbersome to measure directly and in depth, a number of systems have been advanced for ascribing social status to an individual on the basis of more easily gathered data. Specifically, a common procedure is to infer social class status by using one or some combination of the presumed causal variables shown in Figure 7.3. To illustrate the nature of these systems, we will look at three proposed methods. The first uses four variables, the second uses two, and the third uses only one.

*The Warner Four-Factor system* is based on pioneering socioeconomic studies and is one of the earliest and most fully documented approaches. It divides people into six classes using an index based on four measurements. The measurement factors are occupation, source of income, house type, and dwelling area. The socioeconomic classes defined by the method are shown in Table 7.1, along with some generalized interpretations of characteristics associated with each social class. These interpretations are meant to provide you with merely a rough sense of the pattern of this approach. Although the Warner method is not heavily employed in current marketing research efforts, it none-

**TABLE 7.1 An example of one generalized interpretation of social classes**

| Social Class | Predominant Income Levels | Types and Examples of Occupations | Representative Residential Descriptions | Income Sources |
|---|---|---|---|---|
| Upper-upper and lower-upper | Usually extremely high | Very high-level executives, officials, and professionals (e.g., heads of large corporations, top medical and legal specialists) | Often multiple residences (e.g., urban townhouse, country estate, etc.) | May be partly from high salaries and/or fees. However, usually derives mainly from possessed wealth (e.g., dividends, interest, and capital gains) |
| Upper-middle | High | Professional and managerial positions (e.g., lesser corporate executives, doctors, lawyers, successful independent business owners) | Expensive and stylish homes in fashionable suburbs or neighborhoods | Mainly from current occupational efforts in form of fees, commissions, bonuses, profits, and salaries |
| Lower-middle | Moderately high to moderately low | "White-collar" jobs (e.g., small business owners, sales representatives, office personnel, low-level supervisors) | Comfortable homes in "good" suburbs or neighborhoods | Typically from salaries that tend to be stated as a monthly pay rate |
| Upper-lower | Above average to moderately low | "Blue-collar" jobs (e.g., mechanics, truck drivers, coal miners, heavy equipment operators) | Plain homes, often in mass-built developments or older neighborhoods | Wages that are most often based on hourly pay scales |
| Lower-lower | Low to extremely low | Unskilled manual labor (e.g., migrant farm workers, hotel maids, casual day labor) or chronically unemployed | Substandard housing in rural or poorest urban areas | Hourly or day wages and piece work payments (also public aid) |

theless merits your consideration for two reasons. First, it provides an illustration of an attempt to combine measurements of several factors in order to secure a more accurate description of social class status. In other words, it recognizes the existence of inconsistencies between variables affecting social class. Second, because a number of in-depth sociological surveys have been based on the Warner method, descriptions of a variety of lifestyle patterns can be associated with each of the classes that the method defines.[43] For the most part, these descriptions can be related to promotional implications only on an indirect basis, if at all. However, they do offer broad views of behavioral differences that some observers see as being associated with various social class levels.

*The Hollingshead Two-Factor system,* which has had strong impact on sociological investigations of status, uses only two factors, occupation and education, in its measuring procedure.[44] Occupational groupings similar to those shown in Table 7.1 are assigned graded scores ranging from one to seven. Educational levels ranging from less than an elementary school education through attainment of a graduate degree are also graded on a one through seven scale. Both measurements are then weighted and combined to produce an index score that places a person in one of five social status categories. Like the Warner method, the Hollingshead approach can be related to published descriptions that go into some detail regarding general lifestyles associated with each status category. If you wish to analyze your market through field research, the Hollingshead method has the advantage of greater simplicity. Not only does it call for only two pieces of information on each person questioned but the information required is less detailed and more likely to be readily supplied by respondents than that needed in the Warner method.

*The Duncan Socioeconomic Index* is one of the most easily operationalized approaches to establishing social class designations and relies solely on occupation as status indicator.[45] It was previously noted that gross occupational categories might not serve well as highly reliable predictors of status-related lifestyle patterns. However, the Duncan approach is designed to upgrade predictive power through a much more finely detailed calibration procedure. Some 435 occupations are covered in the index. Each has been assigned a numerical score in the 0 to 100 range, with scores having been precalculated on the combined bases of education required for and income potential associated with that occupation. As illustrations, dentists are rated at 96, optometrists at 79, bus drivers at 24, and barbers at 17. A prime appeal of an indexing system such as this is its potential as a market research tool. Because occupational data are usually more readily and economically attainable than detailed lifestyle information, the Duncan approach suggests a potentially viable shortcut technique in field research efforts. At the same time, the cautions noted earlier regarding the far-from-perfect correlation between occupation and social status lifestyle connotations must still be borne in mind.

**Working with Social Class in Your Promotional Planning**

Three pertinent points can be drawn from the foregoing review of social class. First, the opportunity for successful use of a social positioning strategy is demonstrated by examples such as Perrier water and Miller beer. Second, the available published research evidence suggests that the feasibility of such a positioning strategy is directly associated with the value-expressive dimension of your product category. Third, there are a variety of methods available to group individuals into social status rankings. None of these methods is likely to be an absolutely perfect predictor of class-oriented lifestyle behavior. However, any of them can provide you with some useful guidelines for market measurement.

Based on these three points, a sensible procedure to follow in considering the possibility of promoting your brand on the basis of social class would begin with an analysis of the product category in which you are competing. If your product category is inherently high in its power to serve as a mechanism for communicating social symbolism, you may be especially interested in investigating the possibility of a social class promotional approach. Even in cases in which the value-expressive dimension of your product category is not pronounced, you might wish to further analyze buying patterns and market attitudes toward individual brands before abandoning your search for social positioning opportunities. In many ultimate consumer goods lines, data available from syndicated research services can provide you with valuable clues regarding social-class implications that may affect your product category and the particular brands within it. For example, the Simmons service outlined in Chapter 5 includes information on product and brand usage by income, educational, and occupational breakdowns. Through comparison and cross classification of these figures, you can develop preliminary opinions regarding the opportunities that might be generated through a class-oriented strategy.

Assuming you determine that social class may be worth consideration as an important planning input factor, you are left with the task of identifying class groupings and relating them to present or potential preferences, as well as to lifestyle behaviors linked to particular social strata and related to use of your product. To do this you have a choice of classification techniques. There is no absolute answer as to which you should use, but it is the opinion of this author that the Duncan index may provide you with your best starting point because of its comparative simplicity.

*Promotional Implications of Social Mobility and Aspiration Levels*

Some writers have suggested that social-class factors could prove even more valuable as a promotional guide if a greater amount of imagination were applied in analyzing them. One interesting suggestion involves the high degree of mobility and aspiration that characterizes the American social system. Because of this, a person in any given class might identify with some alternative social class. Very often this means that an individual aspires to a higher social class than he or she currently enjoys. For example, someone who measures out as part of the lower-middle class might want to become or be thought of as part of the upper-middle class. As one pair of writers has put it, "For some reason, the literature on social class and consumer behavior has assumed social class to be a stable trait. This is evidenced not only by the ignoring of post-social classes but also ignoring the effects on consumption of aspirations to a higher social class."[46]

There is little published evidence of how social mobility might be related to purchase behavior and used as a planning input factor in promotional strategy. One type of possibility is illustrated by a specialty liquor product. As shown in Figure 7.4, the brand in question has been given the disguised name "Bayou Rum." In practice, it is not really a rum; and though the true name will remain disguised, you might not be too far wrong if you thought of it as being something like a bourbon whiskey with a character somewhat like a liqueur or cordial. Our question is, "Can social class, viewed in conjunction with an aspiration-level perspective, help us define the natural market for this drink?"

The actual social class position of the people surveyed was first determined by using standard measurement variables such as those we have been discussing. In addition, respondents were classified according to aspired social class based on the way in which each thought of himself or herself—regardless of what the standard measurements revealed. This dual classification procedure

## Blended bourbon

| Actual and aspired class categories | Estimated percent in category using product |
|---|---|
| 1. Lower class with lower class aspirations | 47% |
| 2. Lower class with upper or middle class aspirations | 38% |
| 3. Middle class with lower class aspirations | 38% |
| 4. Middle class with middle class aspirations | 29% |
| 5. Middle class with upper class aspirations | 19% |

## Scotch whiskey

| Actual and aspired class categories | Estimated percent in category using product |
|---|---|
| 1. Lower class with lower class aspirations | 11% |
| 2. Lower class with upper or middle class aspirations | 7% |
| 3. Middle class with lower class aspirations | 19% |
| 4. Middle class with middle class aspirations | 24% |
| 5. Middle class with upper class aspirations | 31% |

## Bayou rum

| Actual and aspired class categories | Estimated percent in category using product |
|---|---|
| 1. Lower class with lower class aspirations | 11% |
| 2. Lower class with upper or middle class aspirations | 17% |
| 3. Middle class with lower class aspirations | 19% |
| 4. Middle class with middle class aspirations | 17% |
| 5. Middle class with upper class aspirations | 10% |

**FIGURE 7.4 Using a dynamic view of social class to define a market position**

*Source:* Adapted from Morris J. Gottlieb, "Segmentation by Personality Types," in Lynn H. Stockman, ed., *Advancing Marketing Efficiency* (Chicago: American Marketing Association, 1959), pp. 148–158.

produced the five categories shown in Figure 7.4, ranging from lower class· with lower-class aspirations to middle class with upper-class aspirations. The percentages in each category using three different types of liquor were then compared. Perhaps not too surprisingly, purchases of scotch whiskey were found to be positively related to social status whereas purchases of blended bourbon displayed an inverse relationship. Interestingly, these purchase patterns tended to be influenced not only by actual class position but also by the interaction effect of actual plus aspired class position. Taking both of these factors into account seems to have produced a more sharply detailed portrayal of the market.

As for Bayou Rum, the strongest natural market appears to be among lower-class persons who aspire to higher status and middle-class persons with no aspirations toward higher status. Armed with this information, the promotional strategists for Bayou Rum reportedly felt much better prepared to determine the best positioning for the brand as well as the type of messages and media most likely to reach the target market effectively. This more dynamically oriented view of social class seems to be rarely applied in promotional practice. However, it may represent an approach worth your consideration in some market situations.

## SOCIAL ROLE PLAYING IN PEER GROUP SETTINGS

Cultural and subcultural norms affect and influence individual behavior. However, the actual behavior occurs in much smaller social settings. The groups in which people interact on a day-to-day and face-to-face basis are called peer groups or reference groups. They are mainly built around social activities, family relationships, and work situations. In every small group in which a person participates with other people, he or she can be thought of as playing a particular role. *"A role is a prescribed pattern of behavior expected of a person in a given situation by virtue of the person's position in the situation."*[47]

As one writer has pointed out, "The number of roles which a person may perform is infinite . . . and [varies] for each individual. There are those traditional roles such as father, mother, and doctor. There are general roles, such as child, and girl, and there are specific roles such as secretary to Mr. Jones."[48]

From the standpoint of developing your promotional strategy, two points are worth noting concerning the issue of social role playing. First, the notions of culture, subculture, and social role playing are not totally independent of each other. There can be interplays of influence between them and those interplays can have significance for promotional planning in some situations. Second, the product you are promoting may be strongly related to one or more specific types of role playing situations. If this is true, it would be prudent to consider your brand's potential for assisting prospects in playing those roles. As one analyst has observed:

> Products are vehicles for conveying the impression one tries to impose on the audience. Each product conveys a symbolic representation through its perceived appearance. Effective marketers should mold their product into an image that

will fit properly into the "setting" surrounding the consumer's perceived role expectations. . . . To provide the consumer with the proper "props" to perform his [or her] role, marketers should be aware of their product's image and should shape that image to match the consumer's self image. [49]

This can often be accomplished by using explicit promotion to portray your brand in a way that dramatizes its power to aid a prospect in playing a desired role more effectively, as the following illustrations will demonstrate.

*Promoting Bowling Balls as Role-Appropriate*

For example, suppose you are promoting a brand of bowling balls. You know your product is used in a very distinctive and particular type of social situation. Some intuitive thinking or consumer surveys will probably tell you that your prospects have fairly sharply defined expectations of the roles they play or would like to be seen playing when bowling. You might want to identify your product with norms and beliefs consistent with the social class attitudes of the typical bowling league member at whom you are aiming. Perhaps this means an upper-lower class tone. Then you might seek to demonstrate as convincingly as possible exactly how your product will help its user "fit in" as an admired and well-liked member of a bowling team.

*The Instant Coffee Case*

Some product-role relationships may require more imagination and/or field research to uncover. A classic example is the often-cited study involving the initial promotion of instant coffee. Sales were sluggish in the early years, even though taste tests showed most consumers could not detect the difference between instant and drip grind. Therefore, taste did not seem to be the major problem. Initial advertising campaigns had emphasized the convenience of using instant coffee. At first glance this seems to make good sense because convenience is the evaluative criterion that clearly distinguishes instant from regular coffee. Unfortunately, this type of convenience was apparently viewed by many prospects as being inconsistent with the role of the "good housewife." When asked to describe a hypothetical housewife who included instant coffee as one of the items on her shopping list, a typical response was, "I think the woman is the type who never thinks ahead very far—the type who always sends junior to the store to buy one item at a time. Also she is fundamentally lazy."[50]

As a practical matter, the convenience of instant coffee does its own implicit promotional communicating rather effectively because it involves a functional feature that is self-demonstrating. Just using instant coffee tells you it is more convenient than the regular variety. What really needed support, via explicit promotion, was the role-appropriateness of the product. When promotional strategy was changed to provide such support through advertising, sales volume began to accelerate. Rather than stressing convenience, the revised campaign showed instant coffee being used by a housewife who was praised by her husband and family for serving such delicious coffee. She did not buy instant coffee primarily to make her own life easier. She chose it as something especially good to serve to the other members of her family.

Interestingly, some years after the original survey, a follow-up study was done to see whether people still regarded instant coffee users as poor performers of their housewife role.[51] The results revealed that regular coffee was now rated as somewhat old fashioned and out-of-date. In other words, the role-appropriateness of instant versus regular coffee had almost become reversed.

**Other Examples of Role-Related Promotional Themes**

Of course, regular grind coffees can also place themselves in the context of the superb housewife role. Folger's has employed the character of Mrs. Olson to show women how they can demonstrate their domestic skills and receive the admiration of husbands and friends. Mrs. Olson's secret lies in using mountain-grown coffee "because that's the richest kind." Other products promoted on a similar theme include such things as mixes that produce cakes which people refuse to believe are not "made from scratch," and fabric softeners that cause husbands and children to comment on how good their clothes feel and how fresh they smell.

Housewifery is only one of many roles which can be "better played" by using the "right brand." Some others that have been promoted include: the liberated woman role illustrated by Virginia Slims ("You've come a long way baby"); the upwardly mobile executive role illustrated by advertising for a popular brand of scotch ("As you're fighting your way to the top, it helps to have a taste of what's up there"); the girlfriend/boyfriend role illustrated by television commercials for breath mints ("If he kissed you once, will he kiss you again?"); the good husband role illustrated by advertising for a life insurance company ("Tell your bride you just guaranteed her financial security"); and the socially proper friend role illustrated by Hallmark's reminder to use their greeting cards ("When you care enough to send the very best").

**The Use of Role-Oriented Themes**

The above list shows just a few of the roles people play and a sampling of the ways in which products can be portrayed as helping them play those roles. In considering the use of role-playing themes, there are four major points you should bear in mind.

1. *The Relevance of the Product Usage Setting.* Although any product can be presented and dramatized in the context of a specific role setting, some products probably lend themselves much more naturally to this technique than others. Coffee, cake mixes, scotch whiskey, breath mints, fabric softeners, cigarettes, life insurance, and greeting cards all seem to have very prominent social aspects. Therefore they are extremely well adapted to such treatment. Products such as insecticides, ball bearings, typewriters, or toothache remedies may not fit into this approach quite as readily. Your first consideration must be the product itself and the nature of its most logical usage settings.

2. *Communication Needs and Potential.* Even when you can relate your product to role playing, you may prefer to let your audience infer the connection rather than openly portray it for them. Perhaps you will feel the relationship between evaluative criteria and role enhancement is so apparent that it needs no overt dramatization. Perhaps you will decide your product fits so many different role-playing situations that tying it to only one or two of them may cause prospects to feel it is inappropriate for the others. If this were true, you

might find that the role-playing approach needlessly limits your usage potential.

**3.** *Cultural Consistency.* You will want to be certain that the evaluative criteria you stress along with the lifestyle situation and the role interpretation you portray are all consistent with the cultural and subcultural norms of the market segment you are trying to reach.

**4.** *Applicability Beyond Advertising Situations.* The illustrations we have been discussing are drawn from advertising. You should be aware that the same considerations of role-playing potential are applicable in all other phases of promotional strategy. For example, as you will see when we come to the chapters on personal selling (Part III), effective salespeople know how to translate a product's features into specific benefits that fit roles which are most important to the individual customers with whom they deal.

## PROMOTIONAL STRATEGIES IN FOREIGN CULTURES

*Language as a Cultural Barrier*

One of the most apparent differences between national cultures is language. At first glance, language differences seem so obvious as to need little further discussion. For instance, if you are attempting to promote your brand to prospects in Finland, certainly you will have sufficient sensitivity to realize that your advertising and other promotional materials should be translated into Finnish. If you plan to establish a sales force in Brazil, you will recognize that it is highly preferable if not mandatory that your salespeople be fluent in Portuguese. However, though broad differences between languages are obvious, there can be less apparent subtleties in the way languages are used and such subtleties can be easy to overlook. To recognize them, a communicator must understand not merely the vocabulary and rules of grammar but also a great deal about the culture in which the language is spoken.

*Examples of Language Problems*

The rapid growth in multinational marketing over the last quarter century has produced its share of promotional blunders because of language mix-ups. In Brazil, an American airline promoted its on-plane lounge facilities as "rendezvous lounges." Unfortunately, the Portuguese interpretation of "rendezvous" implies a "private room hired for sexual activity."[52] After Pepsi Cola had been quite successful in the United States with the slogan "Come alive with Pepsi," the company decided the same approach should be appealing to Germans. Unfortunately, the original German version came out with the unintended meaning "Come alive out of the grave with Pepsi."[53] Colgate introduced a new toothpaste named Cue. In the United States, the word Cue carries a desirable connotation. In France it is a word with pornographic implications.[54]

Even if you are dealing with another English speaking nation, you may have trouble with subtle language differences. The meaning of English words can change between cultures. A British automaker promoted its sports model with the promise that it would "go like a bomb." In the United Kingdom the word "bomb" has a positive meaning. The company planned to use the same theme in the United States until it learned that Americans take a dim view of things that "bomb."[55]

As these examples suggest, you cannot simply prepare a promotional communication in English and then make a literal translation into another language. Ideally, you begin by preparing an original message in the foreign language with full consideration of the cultural context of that language. As one expert has said, "Translate thoughts, not words. What you want is an exact equivalent in the thought process of the other language."[56]

*Differences in Lifestyle Goals*

Lifestyles in one's own culture often seem so logical and normal that it is difficult to believe that anyone living anywhere in the world would not respond to the same lifestyle appeals. For this reason, acting on the assumption that the same techniques and appeals can sell your product anywhere in the world is a frequently committed promotional error. Ironically, another type of error which is not infrequent in cross-cultural marketing situations results from assuming exactly the opposite—that just because people in other countries speak a different language and follow different cultural patterns, they will automatically reject appeals which produce favorable results at home. Put simply, no predetermined conclusions are safe. You must investigate each promotional situation separately. You may be surprised by both similarities and differences in consumer response.

*Successful Domestic Strategies Can Fail in Foreign Cultures*

If you are interested in examples of promotional techniques that worked well in one nation but failed in another you can find many. Here are a few illustrations.

***They Want Soft Hands in the U.S.A. but Ultraclean Dishes in Germany.***[57]   In the United States, liquid dishwashing detergents are often sold on the principal evaluative criterion of gentleness to the user's hands. Lux is one brand that has been successful with this appeal. Because the "soft hands" campaign worked so well with American housewives, Lux assumed German housewives would respond the same way. They did not. According to an advertising creative director, the "soft hands" approach was rejected by German housewives because Germans tend to take a "super housewife" attitude. As a result, they are much more concerned about a brand's cleaning power and much less concerned about its cosmetic benefits than are Americans. The advertising executive summed things by saying, "[In Germany] our problem was to make Lux tougher. We thought a five minute pre-soak could be the answer. Once the thrust of the campaign was changed to fit the super housewife image, which research told us the German housewife wanted to be, the product's German sales records improved."[58]

***Do North Americans and South Americans Feel the Same About a Man's Hairstyle?***[59]   It is not unusual for hair care products in America to be promoted on the basis of how your hair is noticed by others. This seems to work well whether the target consumer is male or female. When one United States company decided to introduce its men's hair products into South America, its campaign theme was built on the idea that users would be noticed and admired because their hair would call attention to itself.

In the Caribbean countries this strategy worked. However, in Argentina the results were different. Research revealed cultural rejection of such an appeal. The typical Argentine man felt it was wrong to call attention to himself by means of hairstyle. As a result, the campaign in Argentina was changed to stress neat hair that does *not* call attention to itself. In short, the important evaluative criterion as interpreted by the Argentines was almost the exact opposite of the desired benefit as interpreted by other people in the western hemisphere. With a specially built campaign, the brand became successful in Argentina.

***How Should You Use a Laundry Presoak?***   In the two cases above, the only aspect of the marketing mix that required modification was a portion of the explicit promotion—the advertising appeal. You may have to go farther back than this in your promotional mix to deal with a variation in cultural preferences and beliefs. One such situation follows in which not only the advertising but also a surrogate cue of the product itself had to be changed. The product was a laundry presoak with stain-removing enzymes. The country was Peru. The advertising campaign, which was highly effective elsewhere, showed "little cartoon enzymes with big mouths nosily 'eating' dirt from clothes."[60]

Peruvian women were willing to try the product, but unlike their counterparts in other cultures, most of them did not purchase it a second time. Consumer studies showed the basic problem was cultural. The traditional method of laundering in Peru involved boiling clothes prior to washing. The TV commercials' emphasis on the need for powerful action to remove dirt reinforced the cultural belief in the need to boil clothes. So far, so good. Peruvian women bought the brand and added it to the boiling water. Unfortunately, the boiling water killed the enzymes. Because this destroyed the ability of the brand to remove stains, it meant that in trial use situations the product failed to deliver the benefit the advertising had promised. People bought it once but did not repurchase it because of disappointment in its performance.

The advertising problem became one of not merely persuading people to try the brand but also instructing them regarding its proper use. To solve the problem, promotional strategists turned to another aspect of the Peruvian culture. Fresh lemons were traditionally used as stain removers and customarily used before the boiling process. Therefore, the presoak was repositioned as a lemon-related item. To stress the point the brand was given a lemon scent. Like any surrogate cue, this did not alter performance but did influence consumers' perceptions of performance. The cartoon characters of the television commercial became "bio-lemons." They still ate dirt from the laundry but their appearance, in keeping with cultural traditions, convinced purchasers they could get the job done without the boiling water. According to a published report: "Peruvian women, who had watched their grandmothers use lemon to remove stains, bought the product and used it properly."[61]

***Does a Cavity-Prevention Appeal Sell Toothpaste?***[62]   In many markets, the leading dentifrice brands trade heavily on their ability to reduce tooth decay.

Because teeth are teeth the whole world over, you would expect the appeal to work with most anyone, most anywhere. However, this is not the case. One company with heavy multinational experience and a solid position in the toilet goods field gave up on Latin America for its cavity-prevention toothpaste. Decay prevention simply was not a major evaluative criterion most Latin Americans looked for when selecting a dentifrice. After a year of heavy advertising and personal selling efforts, the brand was withdrawn from these markets. As compared to the fifteen percent share it had been able to garner in the United States, the full year's efforts and investment had brought it up to only a three percent share in Latin America.

**The Small, Family Farm Is Not an International Ideal.** An American manufacturer of farm equipment found that unexpected cultural reactions can also occur in industrial marketing. A commonly stressed evaluative criterion in selling farm equipment and many other industrial products is economy in use. To make this point, the farm equipment company developed an advertising campaign using testimonials. In the United States the campaign, which was built around endorsements from small farmers who had enjoyed good experience with the product line, was a big success. In Europe, it was a failure. European dealers and distributors explained, "Most of our farms in Europe are small to begin with. When you stress 'smallness' so much, our customers think you are talking about peasants. And who likes advice from them."[63]

In short, people around the world can respond quite differently to any given promotional approach. Should you assume there is no such thing as a "worldwide" appeal? Taken to its extreme, this might imply that every promotional program must be individually tailored to each prevailing national character.

*Successful Domestic Strategies Can Succeed in Foreign Cultures*

An expert in the field of international advertising, though admitting that variances between cultures can often impose a requirement for tailoring your promotional strategies on a national basis, also points to the foolishness of automatically stereotyping nations with respect to their promotional needs. "When, eventually, we learn that the similarities . . . in other countries far outweigh the differences, we can concentrate on universally acceptable advertising practices rather than attempting to make different ads every time we cross a border . . . . Oh, there are certain differences that must be respected . . . . But [there are] few that would make it undesirable to run in Italy an ad that has been successful in Scandinavia."[64]

His advice is, "Let the differences between countries be the exception not the rule," and there is abundant support for this point of view. One study compared both attitudes and shopping behavior among working and non-working wives in France and the United States. In presenting her findings, the author concluded, "In brief, while cross-national differences are, on the surface, greater than within-country differences . . . a closer examination shows that observed differences probably reflect differences in the retail environment rather than underlying attitudes and preferences."[65]

Many marketing people agree that cross-cultural differences can be overemphasized, possibly defeating attempts at sound multinational promotional strategies. One executive expressed his experiences in these words: "There are more similarities among worldwide consumers than dissimilarities. In addition to the basic human physiological needs for food, shelter, etc. most people have similar psychological needs such as status, recognition within peer groups, etc. The human mind seems to work much the same way for Malaysians and Nigerians as it does for Americans and Europeans."[66]

One ad agency president feels that local promotional strategists may often overestimate local cultural differences. "A typical immediate reaction of a local agency, however international in outlook, is: 'But what you've been doing in your country won't work in our country.' This always was wrong, and it is still 99% wrong."[67]

This executive points to an American firm planning to advertise its hair-care product in England. The English agency advised that the successful American television commercial was "too hard-sell for the gracious English people." The sponsoring company did some consumer research to investigate that opinion. Contrary to the agency's view, British consumers liked the commercial. They thought the actors were English rather than American. Crossing the Atlantic from the other direction, an American agency once told its British client, the producers of Wilkinson razor blades, that Wilkinson's reputation as a sword-maker might impress the rest of the world but would never sell razor blades in the United States. As things turned out, "the blade's U.S. sales did not really take off until the international sword campaign was introduced into this country."[68]

## ANALYZING FOREIGN MARKETS

Should you change your promotional strategy for foreign markets or keep it the same as your domestic approach? The record of past experiences provides no quick and easy answer. Sometimes you may need an entirely different approach; sometimes little more than a good translation. Attempting to categorize entire nations in broad terms—such as "materialistic" or "elitist"—may not be of much help when you are trying to sell a specific product such as toothpaste or razor blades. The basic question is "How does my product fit into the lives of the consumers who form my most logical target market?" Cultural differences may or may not affect relevant lifestyle goals as you move from country to country. Furthermore, local marketing experts may not be able to help you without some locally conducted market studies. After all, instinct alone is not always reliable when used by an American marketing executive to predict response in the American market. Why should instinctively based decisions be any more reliable in foreign markets?

*Working from a Product-Specific and Segment-Specific Point of View*

A sensible plan to follow is one that examines differences between national markets in terms of the specific product category with which you are working. Additionally, when working with a foreign market, you should not lose sight of the market segmentation approach you use in your home market. It is likely that your foreign market will also be divided into segments. Some data from multinational consumer studies will illustrate these points.

**FIGURE 7.5**
**A comparison of national attitudes toward selected lifestyle behavior issues (full agreement shown in percentages)**

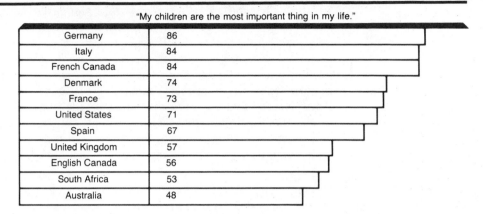

"My children are the most important thing in my life."

| Country | % |
|---|---|
| Germany | 86 |
| Italy | 84 |
| French Canada | 84 |
| Denmark | 74 |
| France | 73 |
| United States | 71 |
| Spain | 67 |
| United Kingdom | 57 |
| English Canada | 56 |
| South Africa | 53 |
| Australia | 48 |

"A house should be dusted and polished 3 times a week."

| Country | % |
|---|---|
| Italy | 86 |
| United Kingdom | 59 |
| France | 55 |
| Spain | 53 |
| Germany | 45 |
| Australia | 33 |
| United States | 25 |

"Everyone should use a deodorant."

| Country | % |
|---|---|
| United States | 89 |
| French Canada | 81 |
| English Canada | 77 |
| United Kingdom | 71 |
| Italy | 69 |
| France | 59 |
| Australia | 53 |

*Source:* Joseph T. Plummer, "Consumer Focus in Cross-National Research," *Journal of Advertising,* November 1977, pp. 10–11.

*Lifestyle Orientation Differences Between Nations.*    As shown in Figure 7.5, there appear to be pronounced national variations in predominant attitudes toward selected lifestyle goals. Notice that all the countries surveyed are considered to be members of the western world. In other words they are essentially more similar to each other than they are to such nations as China or Kenya. Even so, a glance at the survey findings suggests the following: (1) if you were selling furniture polish, a campaign that emphasized the need for household neatness would probably be much better received in Italy than in the United States; (2) if your appeal is based heavily on the idea that buying your brand of breakfast cereal will show other people that the purchaser is a "first rate parent," it may be far more successful in Germany than in Australia; (3) in selling a deodorant, a socially oriented campaign will probably work much more effectively in French Canada than in France.

***Lifestyle Orientation Differences Within Nations.*** Before accepting conclusions based on very generalized information, you should also notice that the data in Figure 7.5 hint at differences within each nation as well as between nations. For example, another way of reading responses to the statement "A house should be dusted and polished three times a week" is to say that the majority of British housewives think it is true, but a sizable minority disagree. What we are looking at is the potential for market segmentation. If it is important to recognize the existence of market segments on a domestic basis—and most marketing experts think it is—then it is equally important to consider potential segments among foreign consumers.

*If Changes Are Needed, What Needs Changing?*

Having analyzed a foreign market on a product-specific basis, and having taken segmentation possibilities into account, you may or may not see a need to change some portion of your strategy in that market. If you find a need for change, you should recognize that variations in your promotional approach may take place on one or both of two levels: (1) differences in basic appeal, and (2) differences in the details of the creative presentation.

***Differences in Basic Appeal.*** The basic appeal—or buying proposal—usually centers on certain evaluative criteria and lifestyle goals. For example, the strategy change for Lux dishwashing detergent in the German market focused on a switch in basic appeal, from "soft hands" to "super-clean dishes."

***Differences in Creative Presentation Techniques.*** The creative presentation involves the particular style, design, and theme through which you present your appeal or buying proposal. For example, the solution to the promotional problem of the laundry presoak in Peru required an extensive change in the details of the creative presentation. The basic appeal of stain removal remained the same.

One writer reported that basic appeals, or stress on particular criteria and lifestyle goals, can be very successfully transferred from country to country with little or no change more than fifty percent of the time. "If the target audience has certain general levels of interest in a product, they must then also be shown to agree on the specific benefits. Very often they do."[69]

On the other hand, this same researcher found that the specific details of creative presentation are much less likely to be transferable with little or no change. "A preponderance of the executives surveyed felt that creative presentations do not travel across geographical boundaries nearly as well as buying propositions. Less than 30% of all advertising campaigns are used outside of the market for which they were first produced [with no changes in creative techniques]."[70]

*Foreign Cultures and Your Promotional Planning*

Summing things up, we can make the following seven generalizations:

**1.** Among the various nations of the world there are some broad differences in habits, lifestyles, attitudes, and beliefs. These differences tend to prevail among a high proportion of the people in one country or another.

2. Language is the most apparent type of difference. Basic language differences may seem obvious, and therefore easy to handle. However, it is quite possible to make serious mistakes in translation because of subtle variations in the interpretation of words and phrases among your target consumer groups. When using a foreign language, remember that you are aiming at translating ideas, not just words.

3. Sometimes deep-seated cultural traditions can influence the way in which people judge products or messages about those products.

4. When cultural traditions do influence the perception of your product, your strategy may need drastic changes in basic appeal, starting with stress on entirely different evaluative criteria. In other situations, your appeal may be the same but require a different approach in creative presentation.

5. To determine whether changes in strategy are necessary at all—and if so what kinds of changes you will need—you should study the foreign culture on a product specific basis. What traditions or beliefs among designated target consumers could affect the way in which they might react to your particular product and brand, its features and the messages about them?

6. Just as there are market segments among American buyers, so also can you expect to find segments in foreign markets. In other words, all buyers in a country such as Brazil do not want exactly the same thing any more than all buyers in a market such as the United States want the same thing.

7. Local experts in foreign markets can prove helpful to you. However, they have no more certainty of intuitively knowing what local customers want than American experts have concerning American consumers. If at all possible, you should secure feedback from consumers themselves to gauge the effectiveness of your promotional strategies before you launch a full-scale campaign.

# SUMMARY

Social forces derive from an individual's interactions with other people. From the viewpoint of promotional strategy, social forces are potentially meaningful because they can affect lifestyle goals and consequently help you decide which evaluative criteria you should stress and how you should structure your promotional messages. The three levels of social forces discussed were culture, subculture, and social role playing in peer groups.

Culture is the broadest level of social force. Cultural norms are customs, behaviors, and beliefs that prevail among a very large group of people. For marketing purposes this very large group is typically a nation or a closely related group of nations. Different cultures may or may not require stress on different evaluative criteria or different lifestyle goals. You can only judge this by relating a specific product to a specific culture. Generally, experts seem to feel that the same promotional appeals—the amount of stress you put on particular evaluative criteria—can be transferred from country to country more than fifty percent of the time. However, the executions of those appeals (e.g., creative advertising formats or sales presentations) are much less likely to be accepted in overseas markets without at least some change.

When marketing within your own national culture you may find it helpful to consider both the general norms of that culture and the current cultural trends or national moods. The importance of these will depend on how they relate to the specific product category and consumer segment with which you are working. A number of experts forecast some interesting trends in the American culture that offer thought-provoking possibilities for promotional strategy approaches.

Subcultures are large groups of people within cultures. Prominent subcultures within the United States include black Americans and Hispanic Americans. Even though they may not know each other personally members of a particular subculture tend to influence each other because so many of them seek group identification and share some important norms.

Social classes were also identified as types of subcultures. As with any other subcultural group, members of a social class tend to influence each other through group identification and shared norms. However, especially within American society, there is also a sense of mobility within the social-class structure. For this reason, you may want to consider your prospective customers on both an "actual class" and an "aspired class" basis.

As with culture, the importance of subcultural variations is likely to vary depending on the product category with which you are working. However, the needs and desires of various subcultural groups are well worth some investigation. When you do find differences between subcultures that might relate to your product category or your promotional approach they can provide you with valuable insights to guide either implicit promotion, explicit promotion, or both.

The final level of social force discussed was social role playing in peer group settings. A role is a more or less standard pattern of behavior expected of a person in a given situation. Roles usually are associated with small peer groups, and are built around such things as social activities and work settings. Any given person is likely to play a variety of roles, which can be influenced by particular cultural or subcultural forces. In many cases, the use of your product could be strongly associated with the playing of a particular role or set of roles. When this is true, one possible promotional approach is to dramatize the role-product relationship.

Social forces can often provide you with important clues even when they are examined apart from the other types of forces that may influence lifestyle goals. Increasingly, however, the trend among many marketing practitioners is toward studying lifestyle goals as a totality including social forces in the study but combining them with information on demographic, biopsychic, and other relevant factors.

## DISCUSSION QUESTIONS

1. Your firm is interested in penetrating the European market with its latest product, Widgets. Widgets are enormously popular in the United States, partly because of the clever advertising strategy devised by your agency. The vice president of marketing has asked you to outline some

techniques for making sure the same promotional strategy will "go over" in Europe. What is your response?

2. The chief promotional strategist for your firm has asked you to evaluate the feasibility of introducing a popular domestic men's cologne into the Italian market. You briefly visited Italy several years ago and received the impression that all Italian males are "macho," and therefore would not be receptive to the clean-cut, boyish image of your product's fragrance. However, you decide to investigate the market more carefully. What approaches should you use?

3. A United States manufacturer of coffee has successfully built an advertising scheme around a theme that stresses the "healthful benefit" of its caffeine-free product. The print and television advertisements featured a woman executive espousing the noticeable effects on her lifestyle after switching to this brand. Outline and briefly describe the two basic ways the promotional strategy might be modified to fit a foreign market.

4. The chapter mentioned several trends in the American culture and a few examples of how such trends might affect specific promotional practices for a few product categories. How might such trends affect promotion for other product categories such as automobiles and men's clothing?

5. What do you think of the interpretation cited concerning McDonald's role as a source of "spiritual comfort"? Assuming this was true, what changes in product design and/or explicit promotion would you suggest for competitive fast food chains?

6. Do you see evidence that any marketers are actually placing increased emphasis on developing "new ways of escaping reality and modifying mood" as one observer was quoted as suggesting?

7. If you were promoting a product such as shaving cream, what specific strategies do you think you might want to consider or investigate to improve your ability to reach the Hispanic market?

8. Subcultural differences may or may not be important to you when you are working on a promotional strategy for a particular brand. When are subcultural differences most likely to be important (the chapter outlined four situations)? Why are some groups of people distinguished on demographic bases but not generally thought of as subcultures?

9. Define the notion of role playing and explain why one individual may play multiple roles. What implications does this have for designing an effective promotional strategy?

10. A foreign manufacturer of subcompact automobiles decided to introduce its brand into the American market. The advertising strategy stressed the gas-saving qualities of the car and positioned the car in the lower-middle class segment of the United States population. More specifically, the ads showed the car in role-playing situations that might be encountered by members of the lower-middle class segment. The car failed to reach targeted sales volume over the next few years and was withdrawn from the market. What explanations can you offer for the car's failure? What advice would you give to the manufacturer if the automobile were to be reintroduced into the American market?

## REFERENCES

1. Warren Farrell, *The Liberated Man* (New York: Random House, Inc., 1974), pp. 89–90.
2. A. L. Kroeber and C. Kluckhohn, *Culture* (New York: Vintage Books, 1952), p. 357.
3. Ralph Linton, *The Cultural Background of Personality* (London: Routledge & Kegan Paul, Ltd., 1947), p. 21.
4. Kenneth E. Runyon, *Consumer Behavior,* 2nd ed. (Columbus, OH: Charles E. Merrill Publishing Company, 1980), pp. 97–98.
5. Daniel Yankelovich, "Yankelovich Describes Types of Trends," *Marketing News,* 17 May 1971, pp. 7–8.
6. "Environmental Scanning Provides Scenario for America in 1980's," *Marketing News,* 7 September 1979, p. 3.
7. *Moneysworth,* 14 March 1977, p. 2.
8. "J. W. T. research director says, 'Shifts to skepticism, activism, individualism, are affecting products, ads,'" *Marketing News,* 10 February 1978, p. 8.
9. Roger D. Blackwell, "Changing American Lifestyles: Implications for Marketing Strategy," *Business Proceedings,* Series #40, 1977, p. 207.

10. "Environmental Scanning Provides Scenario for America in 1980's," p. 30.

11. Bill Abrams, "Pepsi Sociologists Detect New Mood," *The Wall Street Journal,* 5 February 1980, p. 12.

12. Louis C. Wagner and Janis B. Banos, "A Woman's Place: A Follow Up Analysis of the Roles Portrayed by Women in Magazine Advertisements," *Journal of Marketing Research,* May 1973, p. 214.

13. Thomas S. Robertson, *Consumer Behavior* (Glenview, IL: Scott, Foresman and Co., 1970), p. 99.

14. B. G. Yovovich, "Marketing to Blacks," *Advertising Age,* 29 November 1982, p. M-9.

15. Herbert Allen, "Grass Roots Involvement Touches the Market's Heart," *Advertising Age,* 29 November 1982, p. 10.

16. "Norelco Aiming to Slice into Wet Share Market," *Advertising Age,* 9 June 1980, p. 4.

17. "Avon Aims New Line, Ad Effort at Fast-Growing Black Market," *Advertising Age,* 28 July 1975, p. 57; and L. Baltera, "Ultra Sheen Losing Luster Under Revlon Pressure," *Advertising Age,* 11 July 1977, p. 1.

18. "Minority Readership Poll," *Advertising Age,* 22 September 1980, p. 38; and G. J. Glasser and G. D. Metzger, "Radio Usage by Blacks: An Update," *Journal of Advertising Research,* April 1981, pp. 47–52.

19. Del I. Hawkins, Kenneth A. Coney, and Roger J. Best, *Consumer Behavior: Implications for Marketing Strategy* (Dallas: Business Publications, Inc., 1980), p. 133.

20. Renee White Fraser, "Dispel Myths Before Trying to Penetrate the Hispanic Market," *Marketing News,* 15 April 1982, p. 7.

21. "Hispanic Households Quickly Becoming Like Rest of U.S. Population," *Marketing News,* 2 October 1981, p. 1.

22. *Ibid.*

23. *Ibid.*

24. Fraser, "Dispel Myths Before Trying to Penetrate the Hispanic Market," p. 1.

25. *Ibid.,* p. 7.

26. *Ibid.*

27. "Marketing Briefs," *Marketing News,* 26 January 1979, p. 2.

28. Theodore T. Gage, "Luring the Hispanic Dollar," *Advertising Age,* 15 February 1982, p. M-11.

29. C. Glenn Walters, *Consumer Behavior: Theory and Practice,* 3rd ed. (Homewood, IL: Richard D. Irwin, Inc., 1978), p. 468.

30. Elizabeth C. Hirschman, "American Jewish Ethnicity: Its Relationship to Some Selected Aspects of Consumer Behavior," *Journal of Marketing,* Summer 1981, pp. 102–110.

31. For an excellent discussion of the basic issues involved see M. L. Warner, Marchia Meeker, and Kenneth Eels, *Social Class in America: Manual of Procedure for the Measurement of Social Status* (New York: Harper & Row Publishers, 1960), pp. 36–39.

32. R. P. Coleman and L. Rainwater, *Social Standing in America: New Dimensions of Class* (New York: Basic Books, 1978), p. 20.

33. For examples see J. W. Slocum and H. L. Matthews, "Social Class and Income as Indicators of Consumer Credit Buying," *Journal of Marketing,* April 1970, pp. 60–64; J. H. Myers, R. R. Stanton, and A. F. Haug, "Correlates of Buyer Behavior: Social Class Versus Income," *Journal of Marketing,* October 1971, pp. 8–15; J. H. Myers and J. F. Mount, "More on Social Class Versus Income as Correlates of Buying Behavior," *Journal of Marketing,* April 1973, pp. 71–73.

34. For examples see R. D. Hisrich and M. P. Peters, "Selecting the Superior Segmentation Correlate," *Journal of Marketing,* July 1974, pp. 60–63; James H. Myers and Jonathan Gutman, "Lifestyle: The Essence of Social Class," in William D. Wells, ed., *Life Style and Psychographics* (Chicago: American Marketing Association, 1974), pp. 235–256.

35. D. W. Bishop and M. Ikeda, "Status and Role Factors in the Leisure Behavior of Different Occupations," *Sociology and Social Research,* January 1970, pp. 190–208; W. R. Cotton, Jr., "Leisure and Social Stratification," in G. W. Thielbar and Saul D. Feldman, eds., *Issues in Social Inequality* (Boston: Little, Brown & Company, 1972), pp. 520–538.

36. Sidney J. Levy, "Interpreting Consumer Mythology: A Structural Approach to Consumer Behavior," *Journal of Marketing,* Summer 1981, pp. 49–61.

37. J. P. Robinson, *How Americans Use Time* (New York: Praeger Publishers, 1977), pp. 103–106.

38. Sidney J. Levy, "Social Class and Consumer Behavior," in J. W. Newman, ed., *On Knowing the Consumer* (New York: John Wiley and Sons, 1966), p. 62.

39. Edward Auld Laumann and James S. House, "Living Room Styles and Social Attributes: The Patterning of Material Artifacts in a Modern Urban Community," *Sociology and Social Research,* April 1970, pp. 321–342.

40. V. Parker Lessig and C. W. Park, "Promotional Perspectives of Reference Group Influence, Advertising Implication," *Journal of Advertising,* February 1978, pp. 41–47.

41. J. Michael Munson and W. Austin Spivey, "Product and Brand User Stereotypes among Social Classes," *Journal of Advertising Research,* August 1981, p. 42.

42. Hawkins, Coney, and Best, *Consumer Behavior: Implications for Marketing Strategy,* p. 152.

43. See W. Lloyd Warner, *American Life, Dream and Reality* (Chicago: The University of Chicago Press, 1962).

44. A. B. Hollingshead and F. C. Redlich, *Social Class and Mental Illness* (New York: John Wiley and Sons, 1958).

45. See P. M. Blau and O. D. Duncan, *The American Occupational Structure* (New York: John Wiley and Sons, 1967); and Albert J. Reiss, Jr., et al., *Occupations and Social Status* (New York: Free Press, 1961).

46. Gerald Zaltman and Melanie Wallendorf, "Sociology, The Missing Chunk or How We've Missed the Boat," in Barnett A. Greenberg and Danny N. Bellenger, eds., *Contemporary Marketing Thought* (Chicago: American Marketing Association, 1977), p. 237.

47. T. Shibutani, *Society and Personality* (Englewood Cliffs, NJ: Prentice-Hall, Inc., 1961), p. 46.

48. James U. McNeal, *Dimensions of Consumer Behavior,* 2nd ed. (New York: Appleton-Century-Crofts, 1969), pp. 10–11.

49. Charles D. Scheuwe, "Selected Social Psychological Models for Analyzing Buyers," *Journal of Marketing,* July 1973, p. 34.

50. Mason Haire, "Projective Techniques in Marketing Research," *Journal of Marketing,* April 1960, pp. 649–656.

51. Frederick E. Webster, Jr. and F. Von Pechman, "A Replication of the Shopping List Study," *Journal of Marketing,* April 1970, pp. 61–63.

52. D. A. Ricks, J. S. Arpan, and M. Y. Fu, "Pitfalls in Advertising Overseas," *Journal of Advertising Research,* December 1974, p. 48.

53. K. Lynch, "Adplomacy Faux Pas Can Ruin Sales," *Advertising Age,* 15 January 1979, p. s-2.

54. H. Martyn, *International Business: Principles and Problems* (New York: Collier-Macmillan, 1964), p. 78.

55. James Killough, "Improved Payoffs from Transnational Advertising," *Harvard Business Review,* July/August 1974, p. 108.

56. Robert F. Roth, "In Search of the Perfect Translation," *Industrial Marketing,* January 1979, p. 52.

57. A. D. Lowenthall, "Too Soon or Too Late, Good Ideas, Products Can Fail Here, Overseas," *Marketing News,* 10 March 1978, p. 3.

58. *Ibid.*

59. "Transplanted Market Strategies May Not Work in Latin America," *Marketing News,* 7 April 1978, p. 8.

60. *Ibid.*

61. *Ibid.*

62. Killough, "Improved Payoffs from Transnational Advertising," p. 103.

63. *Ibid.*

64. Robert S. Trebus, "Reaching Overseas Business Market: No Stereotypes, Please," *Industrial Marketing,* July 1978, pp. 48–52.

65. Susan P. Douglas, "Cross-national Comparisons and Consumer Stereotypes: A Case Study of Working and Non-working Wives in the U.S. and France," *Journal of Consumer Research,* June 1976, p. 19.

66. David R. McIntyre, "Multinational Positioning Strategy," *Columbia Journal of World Business,* Fall 1975, p. 108.

67. "Ad strategies that work in one market are often good in others," *Marketing News,* 10 March 1978, p. 9.

68. *Ibid.*

69. Killough, "Improved Payoffs from Transnational Advertising," p. 106.

70. *Ibid.*

# CHAPTER EIGHT

# Demographic Forces, Biopsychic Forces, and Lifestyle Goals

## FOCUS OF THE CHAPTER

In addition to the social forces discussed in the preceding chapter, the lifestyle needs and goals of your prospects can be related to demographic and biopsychic forces. Each of these has been used to help define and describe market segments in various product categories. Demographic data are probably the type of information most commonly used in examining consumer groups. Furthermore, as mentioned earlier, there has been something of a trend toward combining the information pertaining to social, demographic, and biopsychic forces to obtain a composite view of lifestyle goals as they affect the way consumers respond to promotional appeals. This composite approach is often termed "psychographics." This chapter will examine demographic and biopsychic forces separately, and conclude with a discussion of psychographics.

## DEMOGRAPHIC FORCES

*Linking Demographics with Lifestyle Goals*

Demographic forces are those that are connected with statistically oriented characteristics customarily used to classify, describe, and study human populations. Prominent examples are age, sex, income, marital status, occupation, geographic location, family size, educational level, religion, ethnic or racial origins, and stage in the life cycle.

Demographic data can provide you with a highly useful starting point for exploring alternatives in terms of evaluative criteria, advertising media, and sales presentations you should consider in developing your promotional strategy mix. As noted in Chapter 7, such data can often be related to other lifestyle goal forces. For instance, if you know that sales of your product are heavily concentrated in certain occupational or income groups, you may want to build a strategy that appeals to the social-class standards associated with people in those occupations and income levels.

*Demographic Market Definition.* As an illustration of how demographic data can be interpreted relative to lifestyle goals, consider the case of developing a promotional strategy for diamond engagement rings. Annual sales, in the United States, are estimated at 900 million dollars. DeBeers, Limited has an eighty percent market share of the diamonds used in these rings. Naturally, DeBeers is interested in increasing demand for the generic product category. In planning its promotional approach, DeBeers began with a profile defined in terms of two demographic features—age and marital status. The specific demographic profile of the target group is single women and men between the ages of 18 and 24. Working from this demographic base, DeBeers then analyzed lifestyle aspects relating to that demographic profile which affect the purchase of engagement rings.

> [An important] marketing condition in the engagement ring field is that a pre-marriage couple is faced with more purchase demands in one period than ever before in their lifetimes. Some short-range alternatives to the diamond ring are: no ring at all, fancy luggage, an expensive honeymoon or another gem (only 5% select this option). Some longer range objectives may be a place to live, appliances, a television set, audio equipment or a new car. . . . Obviously, the expectancy of receiving a diamond ring over other items must be strongly encouraged with advertising. [1]

Working from this view of demographics and associated lifestyle goals, DeBeers was ready to develop creative themes, choose advertising vehicles, and plan its reseller support program.

*Linking Demographics with Consumption Concentration*

In Chapter 5 it was pointed out that analysis of consumption concentration involves aggregating customers into groups based on the amount of a given product category that they purchase. When linked with demographic data, consumption concentration analysis can provide you with some very worthwhile clues to aid in conceptualizing strategy options. Table 8.1 illustrates some demographic differences that have been found to exist between light buyers and heavy buyers in selected product categories. Information of this sort can help you develop a general description of consumer groups based on volume of purchases. This description can serve as a useful base from which to visualize the lifestyle needs and interests of a user group of particular interest to you and relate them to your brand's image and features.

To obtain such data you may want to have a special market survey conducted or you may choose to buy data from a syndicated research service that

**TABLE 8.1 Light and heavy buyer groups compared on demographics**

| Product | Description | |
|---|---|---|
| | Light Buyers | Heavy Buyers |
| Catsup | Unmarried or married over age 50 without children | Under 50, 3 or more children |
| Frozen orange juice | Under 35 or over 65, income less than $10,000, not college grads, 2 or less children | College grads, income over $10,000, between 35 and 65 |
| Pancake mix | Some college, 2 or less children | 3 or more children, high school or less |
| Candy bars | Under 35, no children | 35 or over, 3 or more children |
| Cake mix | Not married or under 35, no children, income under $10,000, T.V. less than 3½ hrs. | 35 or over, 3 or more children, income over $10,000 |
| Beer | Under 25 or over 50, college ed., non-professional, T.V. less than 2 hrs. | Between 25 and 50, not college grad., T.V. more than 3½ hrs. |
| Cream shampoo | Income less than $8,000, at least some college, less than 5 children | Income $10,000 or over with high school or less education |
| Hair spray | Over 65, under $8,000 income | Under 65, over $10,000 income, not college graduate |
| Toothpaste | Over 50, less than 3 children, income less than $8,000 | Under 50, 3 or more children, over $10,000 income |
| Mouthwash | Under 35 or over 65, less than $8,000 income, some college | Between 35 and 65, income over $8,000, high school or less |

Source: Frank M. Bass, Douglas J. Tigert, and Ronald T. Lonsdale, "Market Segmentation: Group versus Individual Behavior," *Journal of Marketing Research*, August 1968, p. 267.

gathers information on consumers on a continuous basis. An example of the material available from one such service is reproduced in Figure 8.1.

***The Relationship Between Demographics and Product Use.*** The data in Figure 8.1 give you a view of how typical users—or typical heavy users—are often defined by general demographics. One key statistic is the index shown in column D. The index tells you how consumers in a particular demographic class compare with consumers in general in terms of product usage. For example, suppose you are in charge of promoting a brand of toothpaste and want to determine whether there is a relationship between heavy toothpaste use and age. When you analyze usage among all adult females you will find that 33.4 percent of them are heavy users. Then, when you examine the thirty-five to forty-four age bracket, you will find that 37.1 percent are heavy users.

The index is found by dividing 37.1 percent (the percentage of thirty-five to forty-four year olds who are heavy users) by 33.4 percent (the percentage of all females who are heavy users). In this case, the result is 111. An index of one hundred would suggest that people in the demographic group use the product to about the same extent as the population as a whole. Since this index is above one hundred, it tells you that someone between thirty-five and forty-four years of age is more likely to be a heavy user than the average person.

Another important way of analyzing these data is to work with the "%

*Demographic Forces, Biopsychic Forces, and Lifestyle Goals*

FIGURE 8.1 A page
from a typical SMRB
marketing report

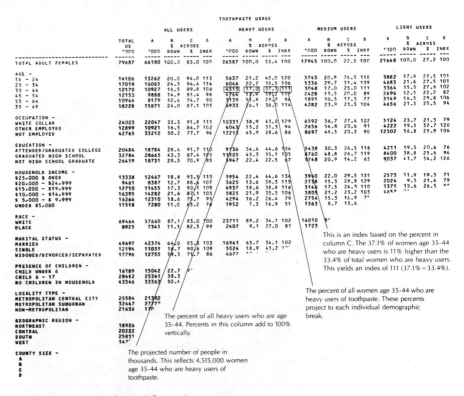

The percent of all women age 35-44 who are
heavy users of toothpaste. These percents
project to each individual demographic
break.

This is an index based on the percent in
column C. The 37.1% of women age 35-44
who are heavy users is 11% higher than the
33.4% of total women who are heavy users.
This yields an index of 111 (37.1% ÷ 33.4%).

The percent of all heavy users who are age
35-44. Percents in this column add to 100%
vertically.

The projected number of people in
thousands. This reflects 4,515,000 women
age 35-44 who are heavy users of
toothpaste.

*Source:* Simmons Market Research Bureau, Inc.
   These illustrative data were taken from a SMRB Marketing Report. The headings reflect adult female users of tooth-
paste grouped by total, heavy, medium, and light users.
   Users of individual brands are reported in the same manner as heavy, medium, and light users of the product category.

Down" column—column B. This takes into account not only the degree to
which the product is used by the average person in the group but also the effect
of group size. It tells you the percentage of all users (or heavy, medium, or
light users) who fall into each specified demographic category. For example, in
this case, about forty-four percent of all heavy users are between eighteen and
thirty-four years of age. Young people make up a very large part of the
toothpaste market.

As Figure 8.1 demonstrates, you can make the same "Index" and "%
Down" comparisons for a variety of demographic factors. The toothpaste
market, as an example, tends to be slanted toward people who are young, in
white collar occupations, rather well educated, and above average in income.
This information can be highly valuable to you when you are designing a new
brand, forming an advertising appeal, or making some other promotional
decision. Of course, you may not always want to confine your interest to the
heavy-user group. If your competitors are overlooking the light users and if
those light users have some special lifestyle goals or stress different evaluative
criteria, it is possible that you might transfer your interest to this group. In
other words, you may have found a tentatively profitable, open market
segment.

*Demographic Forces*

# FAMILIES AS DEMOGRAPHIC UNITS

Because such a large share of ultimate consumer goods is purchased within the setting of a "nuclear family," the family is an important demographic unit for many marketing studies. The nuclear family unit can be characterized in the following way:

> The nuclear family normally refers to a group of at least two adults of opposite sex living in a socially approved sexual relationship, with their own or adopted children. Occasionally, there may be only one adult present or there may be or may not be children present. The key term of the definition is "normally." Variations from the normal pattern exist as exceptions (for example, the widowed partner who continues to hold the family together). [2]

One frequently suggested approach to analyzing markets is by use of a "family life cycle" classification system. This is not the only approach available. However, because it is so widely discussed, we will use it to demonstrate some of the ways in which demographic analyses might influence your promotional planning. Our coverage of the topic will be sequenced as follows. We will begin with a general description of the family life cycle approach. This will be followed by illustrations of types of relationships between life cycle stages and consumer buying patterns. Next, some pertinent trends in the demographic factors underlying this approach will be discussed. Finally, we will look at ways in which marketers can respond to those trends in terms of revising their promotional strategies.

***The Family Life Cycle***

The family life cycle approach is a method of classifying consumer household units on the combined demographic bases of age, marital status, and nature of the nuclear family unit. A variety of schemes have been suggested for interpreting family units in terms of life cycles or stages. The format to be discussed here is especially interesting because it recognizes that it is not uncommon for people today to move back and forth between some of these stages. In this respect, it is more flexible and dynamic than most other family life cycle analysis formats. Figure 8.2 illustrates the format. The three bracketed areas of that illustration divide households into age groups based on the age of the household head.

No family life cycle categorization system can account for all possible variations in household types and stages that exist. For example, the scheme shown in Figure 8.2 does not take account of people who never marry. Neither does it take number of children into consideration, nor is any distinction made between families in which both spouses are working versus those in which only one spouse is employed. Of course, these and other variations could affect lifestyle goals. For this reason, you may have to look beyond the basic categories you see in Figure 8.2 to obtain a complete picture of your market.

***Buying Patterns Associated with Life Cycle Stages***

Certain patterns of purchasing tend to change as people move through the family life cycle.

## FIGURE 8.2 Modernized concept of family life cycle stages

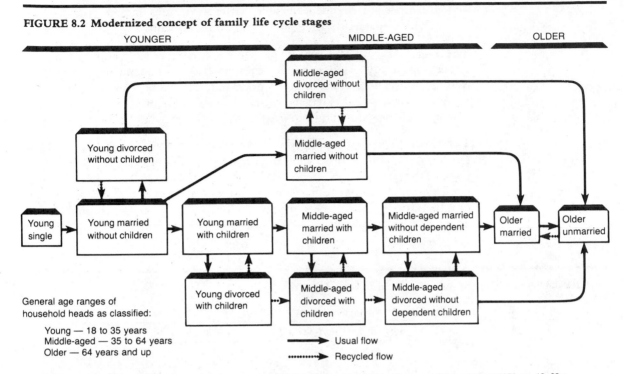

YOUNGER          MIDDLE-AGED          OLDER

General age ranges of
household heads as classified:

Young — 18 to 35 years
Middle-aged — 35 to 64 years
Older — 64 years and up

→ Usual flow
••••••••► Recycled flow

Source: Patrick E. Murphy and William A. Staples, "A Modernized Family Life Cycle," *Journal of Consumer Research*, June 1979, pp. 12–22.

**The Younger Stages.** *Young singles* are generally characterized as having comparatively modest incomes and economic resources. Their buying habits tend to concentrate rather heavily on nondurable items such as food, clothing, and entertainment. In addition, they are often seen as forming an especially good market for travel and automobiles. *Young marrieds* without children are typically portrayed as enjoying greater affluence than young singles because both partners are usually working. They are important buyers of many types of durable goods such as furniture, appliances, and automobiles. *Young marrieds with children* may be somewhat less well off financially because, at least traditionally, the wife has stopped working. They form a sizable market for appliances and other durable goods as well as single family homes and, of course, child care needs.

**The Middle-Aged Stages.** *The middle-aged married* are often significantly better off financially than their younger counterparts, either because the husband's occupational situation has improved or because the wife has returned to work. As conventionally pictured, they are likely to increase their purchases of food items, cleaning supplies, and such recreation-oriented goods as bicycles, sports equipment, and pianos. As people move into the *middle-aged without children* stage, their disposable income tends to reach its maximum. Purchases that are especially frequent include better furniture, bigger automobiles, travel, hobby materials, gifts, and home improvements.

**The Older Stages.** The later stages—*older married* and *older unmarried*—are rather commonly given grim descriptions. Diminished income because of retirement impels a return to more modest housing. Illness and the infirmities of aging can demand extensive financial outlays for prescription drugs and patent medicines in addition to general medical services.

**Variability Between Families Within the Same Life Cycle Stage.** It should be pointed out that the descriptions of these stages are highly general. Within each stage of the family life cycle, you will find households which are quite different from each other in terms of other demographic characteristics. As an illustration, Figure 8.3 classifies percentages of United States households on the combined bases of age of household head and income. This analysis, using constant

**FIGURE 8.3 Diversity of income ranges within age categories**

*Distribution of Households by Income and Age, 1980–1990*

*Annual Household Income Before Taxes: All figures in 1980 dollars*

| | Total House-holds | Under $5,000 | $5,000–10,000 | $10,000–15,000 | $15,000–20,000 | $20,000–25,000 | $25,000–35,000 | $35,000–50,000 | $50,000 and Over |
|---|---|---|---|---|---|---|---|---|---|
| **1980** | | | | | | | | | |
| Households: Millions | 79.7 | 8.1 | 12.4 | 11.1 | 9.7 | 9.9 | 14.0 | 9.4 | 5.1 |
| Distribution | 100.0% | 10.2% | 15.5% | 13.9% | 12.2% | 12.4% | 17.6% | 11.8% | 6.4% |
| Percent of Total | | | | | | | | | |
| Household Income | 100.0% | 1.1% | 5.2% | 7.2% | 9.8% | 12.0% | 23.0% | 21.8% | 19.9% |
| **Distribution: Households** | | | | | | | | | |
| by Age of Head | 100.0% | 100.0% | 100.0% | 100.0% | 100.0% | 100.0% | 100.0% | 100.0% | 100.0% |
| Under 25 | 7.8 | 10.8 | 10.8 | 12.5 | 10.9 | 7.2 | 4.7 | 2.1 | 0.4 |
| 25–34 | 23.0 | 12.4 | 14.8 | 24.0 | 30.1 | 29.5 | 29.5 | 23.4 | 12.5 |
| 35–44 | 17.9 | 7.9 | 9.8 | 12.9 | 14.6 | 22.9 | 24.4 | 26.6 | 26.4 |
| 45–54 | 15.5 | 7.6 | 8.5 | 10.6 | 13.3 | 15.6 | 18.6 | 25.7 | 32.5 |
| 55–64 | 15.7 | 14.7 | 14.1 | 15.3 | 15.4 | 15.1 | 15.9 | 16.6 | 21.2 |
| 65 and over | 20.1 | 46.6 | 42.0 | 24.7 | 15.7 | 9.7 | 6.9 | 5.6 | 7.0 |
| **1990** | | | | | | | | | |
| Households: Millions | 96.8 | 7.8 | 14.8 | 12.1 | 11.2 | 9.9 | 17.7 | 13.7 | 9.6 |
| Distribution | 100.0% | 8.1% | 15.3% | 12.5% | 11.6% | 10.2% | 18.3% | 14.1% | 9.9% |
| Percent of Total | | | | | | | | | |
| Household Income | 100.0% | 0.8% | 4.4% | 5.9% | 7.8% | 9.1% | 21.6% | 22.8% | 27.6% |
| Distribution: Households | | | | | | | | | |
| by Age of Head | 100.0% | 100.0% | 100.0% | 100.0% | 100.0% | 100.0% | 100.0% | 100.0% | 100.0% |
| Under 25 | 6.6 | 11.5 | 9.1 | 10.4 | 8.9 | 7.1 | 4.5 | 2.6 | 0.6 |
| 25–34 | 23.6 | 14.5 | 15.4 | 22.7 | 30.6 | 31.0 | 30.3 | 24.3 | 15.4 |
| 35–44 | 22.0 | 10.9 | 11.5 | 15.9 | 19.1 | 22.5 | 28.9 | 32.0 | 31.1 |
| 45–54 | 14.6 | 9.0 | 7.2 | 9.4 | 11.3 | 13.5 | 16.7 | 20.1 | 30.1 |
| 55–64 | 12.7 | 11.0 | 11.2 | 12.7 | 11.5 | 12.9 | 11.8 | 14.4 | 16.6 |
| 65 and over | 20.5 | 43.1 | 45.6 | 28.9 | 18.6 | 13.0 | 7.8 | 6.6 | 6.2 |

*Source:* Fabian Linden, "At the End of the Eighties," *Across the Board*, March 1981, p. 51.

*Demographic Forces, Biopsychic Forces, and Lifestyle Goals*

dollars and estimates prepared for the National Industrial Conference Board, forecasts both an upward shift in average purchasing power and a significant increase in the thirty-five to forty-four age range through the decade of the 1980s. It also demonstrates the degree of variability in the relationship between these two demographic forces. For example, the data substantiate the view that households in the top age bracket tend to fall into the lowest income brackets. However, the figures also indicate that a sizable number of households in the top age bracket remain in the upper income groups and that there are wide variations in income levels within the middle age brackets. Outlooks on life and modes of purchase behavior are likely to vary greatly depending on these additional demographic factors as well as the basic family life cycle stage.

*Shifts in Demographic Forces Associated with the Family Life Cycle*

*Family Life Cycle Trends.* Despite the continued prevalence of the traditional household pattern, some important changes are taking place in American society. In introducing the modernized family life cycle flow of Figure 8.2, its originators listed several of these changes as reasons for considering the use of their somewhat more complex approach in preference to the older and simpler life cycle approaches that have been employed in the past.[3] A list of some of these changes follows:

**1.** *Declining family size.* Increasingly, married couples are deciding either to postpone having children or plan to have no children at all. On this basis you would expect the future to find a higher proportion of people in the young married and the middle-aged married without children stages.

**2.** *An increasing divorce rate.* The divorce rate in 1981 was more than twice that of 1970 and more than three times that of 1960.[4] This has been accompanied by a high rate of second and subsequent remarriages. However, the remarriage rate seems to be declining. On that basis it has been surmised that the middle and older age brackets may be increasingly made up of divorced individuals.

**3.** *Increasing postponement of first marriages.* In 1981, an estimated fifty-two percent of American women aged twenty to twenty-four years had never married, compared to only thirty-six percent in 1970. For men in the same age group, the figures were seventy percent in 1981 versus fifty-five percent in 1970.[5] With the tendency of people to begin marriage later in life, the young single group may increase substantially not only in terms of size but also in terms of average level of affluence.

Concurrent with such trends, there is a general aging of the American population. As shown in Figure 8.4, the heaviest rates of growth will tend to be in the thirty-year-and-over age brackets for the rest of this century.

*Promotional Responses to Demographic Changes*

The anticipated trends toward more young singles, smaller family sizes, more divorced persons, more late marriages and life-long singles, and a generally aging population provide some excellent illustrations of how demographics can affect promotional planning.

| | Age group | | % Decrease | % Increase |
|---|---|---|---|---|
| 1980 to 1990 | Under 15 | (+9.3) | | |
| | 15-19 | (−17.7) | | |
| | 20-29 | (+0.6) | | |
| | 30-39 | (+34.3) | | |
| | 40-40 | (+39.4) | | |
| | 50-64 | (−1.1) | | |
| | 65 and up | (+27.6) | | |
| 1990 to 2000 | Under 15 | (+2.4) | | |
| | 15-19 | (+11.7) | | |
| | 20-29 | (−13.9) | | |
| | 30-39 | (−3.0) | | |
| | 40-49 | (+31.2) | | |
| | 50-64 | (+26.5) | | |
| | 65 and up | (+10.2) | | |

**FIGURE 8.4 Projected changes in the U.S. population—1980 to 2000**

Source: *Current Population Reports*, series p-25, no. 922, October 1982, United States Department of Commerce, Bureau of the Census.

Such demographic trends are likely to result in a decreased emphasis on many product categories. Among these are multi-bedroom homes, infant care products, and items that appeal mainly to children and teenagers. On the other hand, the same trends should lead to increased markets for a variety of luxury items aimed at young singles, childless couples, and to some extent, the wealthier members of the older age group. Examples of such items are convenience foods, prestige furniture, more extensive vacation packages, health spas, and tennis clubs. A few more specific illustrations follow that indicate how some of these demographic forces reshape promotional strategies.

*Promoting Breakfast Cereals to "Consenting Adults."* One business publication reported, "So far this year Kellogg has introduced five new cereal brands—more than have ever been launched in a single year . . . as part of a stepped-up and redirected marketing campaign aimed at getting faster growing, older consumer segments to begin eating as much cereal as younger groups do."[6] With declining proportions of children and teenagers, the cereal companies have begun to revise their implicit promotional strategy for new product development. In place of past emphasis on presweetened cereals, the revised thrust is on introducing cereals with high-fiber content and relatively low-fat and calorie content, which are more appealing to adults. Beyond functional feature changes, the promotional direction in breakfast cereal strategy includes a change in surrogate cues. "Packages [for most newly introduced brands] no longer carry pictures of gremlins or pixies to grab kids' attention. A box of adult-aimed Total, for example, carries enough charts and statistics to satisfy a computer programmer."[7]

This strategy requires revision of the explicit promotional mix. In one such

*Demographic Forces, Biopsychic Forces, and Lifestyle Goals*

change, "television advertising is on early-evening news shows or afternoon soap operas, rather than on Saturday morning cartoons."[8]

The revised age profile of the American population has brought new life to some cereal brands that were in the decline stage of their life cycles. In 1980 Quaker Oats, one of the most long-established brand names in the country, revived its television advertising schedule after a ten-year lapse. The reason was that Quaker Oats rates highly on evaluative criteria of special interest to adult consumers. As that segment of the market increases in size, Quaker's sales are starting to grow with it, and its promotional strategy is being revised.

***Wider Blue Jeans.*** Levi-Strauss and Company has reaped a rich harvest of sales for "Levi's," its trade name for blue jeans. Levi's have been on the market since the nineteenth century, but the dramatic surge in their popularity began with younger consumers during the 1960s and 1970s. During that time teenagers made Levi's a household word. The nation's changing age profile impelled a redirection of promotional strategy for the company. One of its vice-presidents put the issue this way, "As the baby-boom kids continue up the age ladder, either we will go with them or somebody else will."[9] The result is the addition of a new Levi's line with some modification in functional features. Billed as "Levi's for Men," the new version is "cut to fit a man's build with a little more room in the seat and thigh." This revision in implicit promotional emphasis is also accompanied by new advertising themes and new media approaches.

***More Attention to Upper Age Brackets.*** A number of observers feel that promotional strategists have missed major opportunities by not paying closer attention to the lifestyles and product benefit needs of older consumers. As this segment of the population grows in size, there are signs the oversight is being corrected.

> Helena Rubinstein is offering a new line of skin care products for women over 50, called Madame Rubinstein; Leeming Pacquin Division of Pfizer is test-marketing New Season, a shampoo conditioner for "people over 50" and Noxzema's Cover Girl, a leading brand for young women, has introduced the Moisture-Wear makeup line for older women, which includes Moisturizing Wrinkle-stick. . . . At least two manufacturers that found fame and fortune in the youth market have recently been marching to a different drummer: Gerber Products which had a long standing habit of saying "Babies are our business, our only business," has dropped the tagline, since it started selling life insurance to the older generations. Its new motto: "Gerber now babies the over-50's." And Wrigley, whose gum has satisfied four generations of youngsters is now turning out a product for the denture set—stick-proof Freedent. [10]

To improve their capability of analyzing the untapped opportunities that may exist among older consumer groups, it has been suggested that marketers examine the answers to three basic questions.

> [1.] Compared to when they were younger, do people over fifty-five have different functional and psychological needs and wants, the identification of

which could lead to the successful marketing of new products and services, as well as new ways of positioning brands?

[2.] Are the self-images of the people over fifty-five inconsistent with how they are portrayed in advertising?

[3.] Do people over fifty-five have specific leisure time activities and interests that represent an untapped market for the media? [11]

Although it is essential that you pay close attention to demographic segments whose proportions of buying power are growing, it is equally essential to recognize that any sizable demographic segment is worth considering in terms of its special marketing needs and promotional opportunities. For example, though the teenage market may decline in relative size during the 1980s, it will continue to form a large and important segment of the population. Although the numbers of divorced and life-long single people may increase, traditional nuclear families will continue to exist and be heavy buyers of many product categories. In short, the same issues that prompt the three questions listed above regarding older consumers are worth raising about all demographic customer groupings that may form a significant part of the prospect segment for your product.

## FAMILY PURCHASE DECISION PROCESSES

Although the proportion of traditional nuclear families may be declining, the fact remains that the majority of people in the country still live in more or less traditional family settings. In 1981, over sixty-four percent of Americans aged twenty years or more were married and living with their spouses. Over seventy-five percent of those under eighteen years of age were living in a household with two parents.[12] For this reason, the family remains an important source of influence on many buying decisions, and marketers continue to be interested in family units and the purchase choice processes taking place in such units. Figure 8.5 is a schematic guide to analysis of the types of influences family structures may exert on the purchase of your product. First, it should be recognized that when one member of a family buys a product, the product itself may be consumed in any one of three general ways:

1. *On an individual basis by an individual family member, although not necessarily the one making the purchase.* A shopping trip to the drugstore by one family member may include the purchase of shaving cream, nail polish, and acne remedy. Even though this is, in a sense, a family purchasing situation, the products are probably intended for individual use, not group use. Presumably the shaving cream is likely to be for the father or son, the nail polish for the mother or daughter and the acne remedy for a teenage daughter or son.

2. *By all or most individuals in the family on a group basis.* Many grocery items fall into this category. For example a shopping trip to purchase pork sausage, instant mashed potato mix, and ice cream probably involves goods intended for joint consumption by family members.

3. *By the household unit rather than by its members individually.* The buying of

**FIGURE 8.5  A model of family decision making**

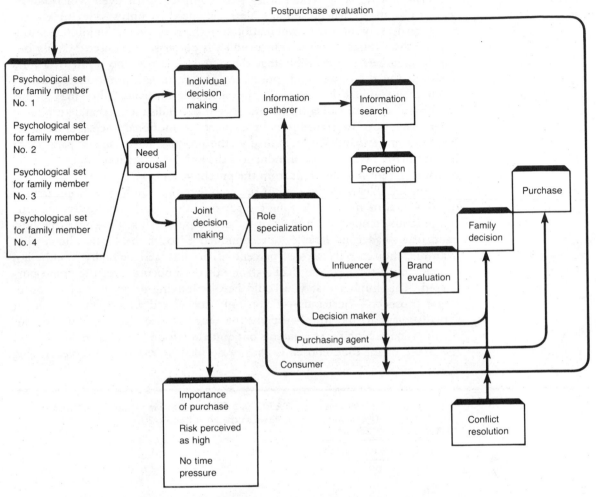

Source: Henry Assael, *Consumer Behavior and Marketing Action* (Boston: Kent Publishing Company, 1981), p. 349.

items for home operation and maintenance fall into this category. Illustrations might include floor polish, household cleaners, living room furniture, and appliances.

Regardless of how the item is to be consumed, the buying decision may be either individual or joint. An individual decision is one made by a single family member. A joint decision is one in which several family members participate or exert some influence. In the latter case, Figure 8.5 illustrates that the various members of the family can influence each other through interactions of their "psychological sets." In other words, each family member may bring her or his lifestyle goals, evaluative criteria weightings, brand criteria ratings, and so on to the decision-making process regardless of whether the item will be individually consumed, jointly consumed, or consumed by the household as a unit.

*Family Purchase Decision Processes*                            229

As a promotional strategist, you may have to consider more than just the question of who acts as the family purchasing agent or even which family member is the actual consumer. You will need to know who makes the purchase decision or what combination of influences interact in joint decision-making discussions. Even if your product is purchased and used by only one family member, it is possible that the brand chosen is the result of a joint decision. On the other hand, purchases for group consumption could be a result of individual decisions. For instance, the husband/father may decide what brand of catsup all family members will eat. This means that determining where and how to transmit your explicit promotional messages requires knowing more than who buys or uses the product. The issue of paramount importance is "who makes or influences the purchase decision" and that could be someone entirely different from the purchaser or even the user.

Table 8.2 illustrates the kind of research data that can help you in carrying out this kind of analysis. Among the persons surveyed in this study, the wife of the family tended to do most of the actual purchasing. However, the husband often had considerable "direct influence" over the brand choice. For example, though only sixteen percent of the husbands actually bought hot cereals, thirty-three percent had a strong direct influence over the brand purchased. This implies that you could be overlooking an important group of target prospects—husbands—if you only considered which family member actually went to the store—usually the wife. Notice also that husband influence is quite high for some items but quite low for others. As an illustration, the brand of cat food chosen is usually decided by the wife. However, dog

**TABLE 8.2 Who makes the purchase and who influences the brand choice?**

|  | Purchased by | | Direct Influence Over Brand Choice | |
|---|---|---|---|---|
|  | Wife | Husband | Wife | Husband |
| **Cereals** |  |  |  |  |
| Cold (unsweetened) | 84 | 16 | 71 | 29 |
| Hot | 84 | 16 | 67 | 33 |
| Packaged lunch meat | 73 | 27 | 64 | 36 |
| Peanut butter | 81 | 19 | 74 | 26 |
| Scotch whiskey | 35 | 65 | 18 | 82 |
| Bar soap | 85 | 15 | 64 | 36 |
| Headache remedies | 67 | 33 | 67 | 33 |
| Cat food (dry) | 66 | 34 | 81 | 19 |
| Dog food (dry) | 76 | 24 | 59 | 41 |
| **Fast-food chain** |  |  |  |  |
| hamburgers | 68 | 32 | 55 | 45 |
| Catsup | 75 | 25 | 68 | 32 |
| **Coffee** |  |  |  |  |
| Freeze-dried | 68 | 32 | 62 | 38 |
| Regular ground | 74 | 26 | 65 | 35 |
| Mouthwash | 72 | 28 | 56 | 44 |

*Source:* "Purchase Influence Measures of Husband/Wife Influence on Buying Decisions," Haley, Overholser & Associates, Inc., New Canaan, CN, January 1975, in "Buying Study Called Good Support Data," *Advertising Age,* 17 March 1975, p. 52.

food brand choices are apt to be influenced by the husband in a high proportion of families.

*Children's Influence*  Table 8.3 shows what a research team found when they questioned a sample of mothers concerning the influence their children had on purchases. Both the frequency with which children attempt to influence purchases and the percentage of cases in which parents accept their decisions are quite high for some types of products. For example, breakfast cereals, snack foods, candy, soft drinks, and Jell-O are product categories in which children have significant impact on buying decisions.

**TABLE 8.3 Children's influence on mother's purchases (children aged 5–12)**

| | Frequency of Requests by Children | Percentage of Yielding by Mothers |
|---|---|---|
| **Relevant foods** | | |
| Breakfast cereal | 1.59 | 87 |
| Snack foods | 1.80 | 63 |
| Candy | 1.93 | 42 |
| Soft drinks | 2.01 | 46 |
| Jell-O | 2.80 | 36 |
| Overall mean | 2.03 | |
| Overall percentage | | 54.8 |
| **Less relevant foods** | | |
| Bread | 3.16 | 19 |
| Coffee | 3.94 | 1 |
| Pet food | 3.36 | 7 |
| Overall mean | 3.49 | |
| Overall percentage | | 9.0 |
| **Durables for child's use** | | |
| Game, toy | 1.65 | 54 |
| Clothing | 2.52 | 37 |
| Bicycle | 2.61 | 8 |
| Hot wheels | 2.67 | 22 |
| Record album | 2.78 | 24 |
| Camera | 3.80 | 2 |
| Overall mean | 2.67 | |
| Overall percentage | | 29.4 |
| **Notions, toiletries** | | |
| Toothpaste | 2.39 | 39 |
| Bath soap | 3.17 | 9 |
| Shampoo | 3.28 | 16 |
| Aspirin | 3.79 | 4 |
| Overall mean | 3.16 | |
| Overall percentage | | 17.0 |
| **Other products** | | |
| Automobile | 3.57 | 12 |
| Gasoline brand | 3.70 | 2 |
| Laundry soap | 3.72 | 2 |
| Household cleaner | 3.76 | 2 |
| Overall mean | 3.69 | |
| Overall percentage | | 1.75 |

Frequency of requests are on a scale from 1 (often) to 4 (never).

*Source:* Scott Ward and Daniel B. Wackman, "Children's Purchase Influence Attempts and Parental Yielding," *Journal of Marketing Research,* August 1972, p. 317.

When the opinion of more than one family member influences the choice of a product or a brand, any or all stages of your promotional strategy planning process can be affected. In terms of advertising, for example, it may mean that your creative strategies and media schedules should be designed to appeal simultaneously to a variety of family members. Alternatively, it could mean you will want to consider separate campaigns—each to entirely different family members.

This latter strategy is demonstrated in Figure 8.6. Because mothers and children both influence the selection of its Hostess line of sweet baked goods, ITT Continental Baking Company actually runs separate campaigns to reach those two separate audiences. The mother-oriented campaign emphasizes wholesomeness as an evaluative criterion. It dramatizes the way in which Hostess products can help a mother play her role as a good parent. The child-oriented campaign emphasizes taste as an evaluative criterion and shows Hostess products in situations to which children can easily relate.

Mother-oriented commercials are shown during weekday and evening television programs. Child-oriented commercials appear mainly during programs with a heavy concentration of children in their audiences. The pair of coordinated campaigns sell the product to both partners in the decision-making process, communicating to mothers and children separately with messages tailored to their respective interests.

## BIOPSYCHIC FORCES

Even when two people are very much alike on the basis of demographic and social factors, they may be very different from each other in terms of specific behavior patterns and physical needs. There are serious people and light-hearted people, tall people and short people, active people and passive people, and so on. These personal characteristics combine to make each of us unique and different from anyone else on earth. They are the biopsychic forces. *Biopsychic forces are those that evolve from a person's innate needs as an individual human being. They are biological and psychological in origin. The most common approaches to studying them often make use of one or another theory of personality.*

*Biological or
Physical Differences
Among Consumer
Segments*

Some biopsychic determinants are biological or physical in nature. Throughout this book we have been considering examples of brands aimed at target markets based on specialized physical needs that some people have and others do not. Head and Shoulders Shampoo, mentioned in Chapter 4, has found a large market among people who have problems with dandruff. Datril and Tylenol, mentioned in Chapter 2, both serve people who have unpleasant physical reactions to regular aspirin. Freedent chewing gum appeals to people with restorative dental work or who wear dentures.

The drug and cosmetic fields represent promotional areas in which intense attention is paid to the possibility of developing special products and special appeals based on physical characteristics. For instance, because the skins of different people can react quite differently to the sun, a variety of suntan preparations are available for different "complexion segments." One brand of toothpaste, Sensodyne, is marketed especially for people who have tender gums. However, opportunities for segmentation based on physical needs are by no means limited to drugs and cosmetics. They are worthy of consideration in a wide variety of product categories, such as appliances and sports equipment for people who are left-handed, clothing for people who are unusually tall, and foods for people who have weight control problems.

As suggested in our definition, the most frequently discussed approaches to studying biopsychic forces involve personality theories, which investigate the purely psychological aspect of individual differences. Rather little has been published concerning distinctions based on physical differences. Perhaps this is because the research findings concerning market segments based on physical differences do not ordinarily evoke surprise. However, you should remain alert for any untapped segmentation possibility based on physical or biological characteristics that may exist within your product category. In some cases, these could be associated with some other lifestyle determinant. An example is Freedent chewing gum that tends to be associated with age levels. In other cases, however, a physical characteristic with potential promotional applicability might be relatively independent of any other lifestyle determinant. Examples are provided by previously cited physical characteristics which produce markets for dandruff remover shampoos and specialized varieties of suntan lotions.

|  |  |
|---|---|
| ***Personality as a Biopsychic Force*** | The term "personality" is commonly used in everyday life. Most people generally use it in what psychologists classify as a "social stimulus" sense. This means it is used to describe an individual primarily from the perspective of how she or he is viewed by other people relative to social relationships. For example, one way of describing someone's personality in a social-stimulus sense is to say the person has a "good personality" or a "great personality." This, of course, means that the individual meets and interacts well with other people. In another social-stimulus application, you frequently hear people described in terms of one or a few outstanding personal characteristics. As an illustration, you might describe a friend as being "ambitious and enthusiastic but a little too pushy." Either type of description of an individual's personality essentially refers to what you and other people can infer about the person by observing how he or she acts. |
| ***A Structural Approach to Personality*** | Psychologists view personality in a more extended and complex way. In contrast to the rather simple, social-stimulus sense, they attempt to define and measure personality in a structural sense. This means they probe beneath the overt behavior of a person and seek to discover what sort of internal mental and emotional structure is generating that behavior. A helpful definition of personality in the structural sense is as follows: *"Personality is the dynamic organization within the individual of those psychophysical systems that determine his/her characteristic behavior and thought."*[13] The implications of this definition have been explained in these words: |

> Personality is something and does something. It is not synonymous with behavior or activity; least of all is it merely the impression that this activity makes on

**FIGURE 8-6 Promoting to multiple decision makers within the family**

(SILENT)

MOTHER: Do your homework.
SON: Oh, Mom.

MOTHER: Wear your raincoat.
DAUGHTER: Oh, Mother.

MOTHER: Not now, after we eat.

You want to be soft, you gotta be firm.

There's a right time for snacks, and I say when,

then I insist on Hostess, because they're always so fresh.

Chocolatey Cup Cakes,

tender Fruit Pies,

Golden Twinkies Snack Cakes with creamed filling.

Fresh wholesome Hostess meets my tough standards.

So when I say yes -- It's Hostess.

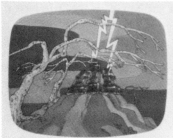

(MUSIC UNDER)
(SFX: THUNDER, LIGHTNING)

GIRL: This house isn't haunted, is it?
(SFX: CRASH)

BOY: Do something, Fruit Pie the Magician.

FRUIT PIE: My wand...
BOY: We're falling!

FRUIT PIE: Oh, drat! So are the Hostess Fruit Pies and...Twinkies Cakes.

GIRL: I wanna go home.

TWINKIE: That's easy! Yahoooo!
BOY: Twinkie the Kid.

BOY & GIRL: Saved!

FRUIT PIE: Now for Hostess Fruit Pies. Apple and Cherry.
TWINKIE: And Twinkies.

GIRL: Creamed filling.

BOY: Real fruit filling.

EERIE VOICE: You get a big delight in every bite of Hostess Fruit Pies and Twinkies Cakes.

others. It is what lies behind specific acts and within the individual. The systems that constitute personality are in every sense determining tendencies and when aroused by suitable stimuli provoke those adjustive and expressed acts by which the personality comes to be known. [14]

*Applying Personality as a Segmentation Technique*

The rationale for the appeal of personality segmentation to promotional strategists is apparent. If people's minds work in different ways, these differences may influence what they buy and why they buy it.

*The Anheuser-Busch Experiment.*[15]   To discover how personality differences might affect beer preferences, Anheuser-Busch sponsored a study among consumers. Several fictitious new brands of beer were developed. Each was actually just the same beer presented under a different name and label.

Advertisements were created to make each fictitious brand especially appealing to a different personality type. For example, one brand was positioned for the "reparative drinker," who is an individual defined as being middle-aged and feeling that he or she has much more basic ability than his or her accomplishments have demonstrated. The reparative drinker rationalizes that lack of personal accomplishment is due to unselfishness. In other words, this individual believes himself or herself to have put aside self-interest and sacrificed for other people. In consequence, he or she has not been as successful as might have been possible. The strategy behind the advertising designed to appeal to "reparative drinkers" was based on the assumption that such persons drink beer as a reward for self-sacrifice and a solace for lack of achievement.

Other personality types studied included the "social drinker" who drinks beer as part of friendship situations; the "indulgent drinker" who drinks to compensate for serious failures in life while blaming those failures on the environment; and the "oceanic drinker" who also drinks to compensate for perceived failures but attributes those failures to his or her own shortcomings.

A set of television commercials—based on the lifestyle goals of each personality type—was shown to 250 people. Each person then sampled the various beers and was asked to list brand preference levels and also to complete a short test concerning personality characteristics. Most people gave the highest preference level to the beer that was advertised to match their own personality characteristics and lifestyle goals. Most also rated another brand as absolutely terrible and "not fit to drink." Because all brands were precisely the same in terms of functional features, the inference is that these people were rating the brands in terms of perceived relationships to their own personality characteristics. On this basis, it would seem that individual personality differences might indeed yield strong clues to guide promotional strategies, at least for some product categories.

Despite positive evidence from the Anheuser-Busch experiment and similar studies, the usefulness of personality research in marketing practice remains a highly controversial topic. Most attempts to relate personality and consumer behavior have been based on one or another of several existing personality theories. To say that there are several theories—not just one widely accepted theory—indicates part of the problem that must be confronted in applying personality research to promotion.

One of the first questions you must consider is "Which theory should I follow?" A variety of psychological models have been utilized in attempting to study consumers. Most of them fall into one or the other of two general approaches: the intrapsychic approach and the trait approach. Let's look at how you might apply each type of approach.

*Intrapsychic Approaches to Personality*

Intrapsychic approaches are aimed at "determining those events which take place 'inside' the other person."[16] They tend to look at parts of internal psychological mechanisms and then attempt to describe how those parts interact. Among the intrapsychic approaches most frequently mentioned or studied in connection with consumer behavior are those of Kurt Lewin, Carl Rogers, and Sigmund Freud.[17] The one that has received by far the most attention is Freud's psychoanalytic theory, which will be used to illustrate how you might use an intrapsychic approach in considering your promotional options. It is chosen as the one to be illustrated for two reasons. First, it can produce some highly interesting and imaginative views of why consumers buy certain products and brands. Second, it is clearly the one that has had the most impact on many practicing promotional strategists, especially those concerned with product design and advertising.

*An Intrapsychic Approach Using Freudian Theory*

According to Freud's psychoanalytic theory, the human mind can be thought of as being divided into three components—the Id, the Ego, and the Superego—that interact with each other. Figure 8.7 shows one way of depicting the relationships that these three components have to each other and to three "levels of awareness"—the conscious, the preconscious, and the unconscious. To demonstrate how Freud's ideas might possibly be utilized in promotional settings, we must begin with a highly condensed description of the theory.

***The Id, the Ego, and the Superego.*** According to Freud, the Id is the first and most basic part of the individual's personality system. The Ego and the Superego attain their "psychic energy" from it and to a large extent exist to serve the needs of the Id. Short and simplified descriptions of the three components can be stated as follows.[18] The Id comes into being with a person's birth. It contains a mass of instincts built around bodily needs such as hunger, thirst, and sexual activity. It presses for comfort, pleasure, and relief from tension. However, it cannot cope with the outside world in fully satisfactory ways. The Ego develops out of the Id. It is able to deal with the "real world" in a conscious and intelligent way. Although it exists to satisfy the demands of the Id, it can also hold the Id in check. The Superego develops out of very early relationships with other people, especially one's parents. Unlike the Ego, which may attempt to postpone the desires of the Id but not to thwart them, the Superego can actually work to inhibit the impulses of the Id if they violate its moral and social code. Once developed, the Superego can punish an indi-

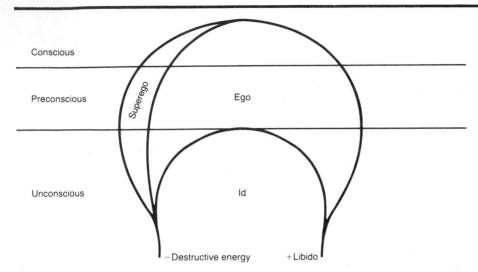

FIGURE 8.7
Schematic
interpretation of
Freudian personality
components

*Source:* Benjamin B. Wolman, *The Unconscious Mind: The Meaning of Freudian Psychology* (Englewood Cliffs, NJ: Prentice-Hall, Inc., 1968), p. 49.

vidual for doing or even thinking about things regarded as "immoral" or "antisocial."

*Levels of Awareness.* Notice that Figure 8.7 depicts the Id, the Ego, and the Superego operating at three different levels of consciousness or awareness. The conscious level includes all of the facts, feelings, and information of which an individual is immediately aware and knowingly recognizes at any particular point in time. For example, right now, you are conscious of all the items shown in Figure 8.7. (At least you should be.) The preconscious includes all of the thoughts, feelings, and facts of which a person is not particularly aware at the moment but which she or he can bring into consciousness without much difficulty. For example, later today or tomorrow you will not be immediately conscious of the items you are now looking at in Figure 8.7. You will have other thoughts and feelings on your mind. However, if you want to—or have to—you should be able to bring this information out of your preconscious and into your conscious without much trouble. The unconscious is a very different type of entity. It is a reservoir of wishes, needs, desires, and instincts of which an individual is totally unaware in any conscious sense. Furthermore, it is impossible for a person to bring any of this material into consciousness in its real and true form. The only way unconscious thoughts can enter your consciousness is in disguised or symbolic form.

*Relating Freudian Theory to Promotional Strategy*

This last part of the theory regarding the unconscious mind could be extremely important for promotional strategy. Notice that all of the Id, a very large part of the Superego, and even some portions of the Ego are operating at the unconscious level. Then recall that what is happening at that level can be brought into consciousness only in disguised or symbolic form. This suggests that you might be able to use very subtle, symbolic communication techniques

238          *Demographic Forces, Biopsychic Forces, and Lifestyle Goals*

to appeal to your prospects' unconscious needs and motives and your audience would not be consciously aware of why these needs and motives were being "stirred up." In other words, you *might* be able to communicate at an unconscious level and convey ideas that your audience would logically reject or against which its members would probably counterargue if they were consciously aware of what was happening.

The key terms for any potentially successful use of unconscious appeals are "subtle" and "symbolic." If your appeal is open and direct, it is no longer an unconscious appeal. Once your prospect is aware of what is involved, she or he will evaluate it on a fully conscious and presumably fairly rational basis. For example, consider the many promotional appeals relating in some way to sexual situations. On the basis of Freudian theory, these would presumably be most effective if they induced unconscious excitation of the Id. However, the power of this effectiveness depends on being able to communicate at a purely unconscious level. One team of writers has offered the following illustration:

> Freud based most of his theory on the idea that sexuality pervades all of our thoughts and actions. If this is true, it is important to include implicit sexual content in appeals. . . . For example, the shape of a container can have sexual implications and the use of sexually attractive people in advertisements has become commonplace. Such advertising, however, should remain at the symbolic level and not be so blatant as to be offensive or ridiculous. Some advertisements are so obvious in their appeal to sexual motives that the symbolic appeal is lost. . . . In fact, Freud would probably judge this as violating the Principle of Complication, which states that the more hidden the true motive . . . the better the work of art and the more easily and comfortably people will respond to it. [19]

So far, so good! As a practical matter, however, just how are you supposed to think through and develop these very subtle, unconscious symbols? How might all of this work in practice? We really have to rely on speculation rather than fact for examples at this point, at least if you demand that facts be incontrovertible and scientifically demonstrable. However, some of that speculation is rather fascinating and may help you do some imaginative thinking. Two examples follow that use very well-known brands and discuss some possibly unconsciously oriented symbols that may have helped to promote those brands successfully. One brand is Ivory soap. The other is the Hershey chocolate bar.

### *Does Ivory Soap Offer Special and Unconscious Appeals to Superego Needs?*
In Chapter 5 you read that Ivory bar soap celebrated its one hundreth birthday in 1979. After a full century on the market it is still a top seller. While other brands have come and gone, Ivory has endured and continuously prospered. Could there be any Freudian symbolism connected with Ivory soap and its implicit and explicit promotion which has helped it do so well? Because this is a product used for bathing and washing, we can start looking for an answer in what one Freudian-oriented market analyst has to say about these activities.

> Bathing and washing . . . seem to have an effect of moral purification. Thus, Pontius Pilate washed his hands, indicating that he did not want to be held responsible for the crucifixion of Jesus. Baptism is a sort of washing and in

certain religions the priests must wash themselves completely before starting the ritual service. Nor has the symbolic significance of washing and bathing been entirely lost in our modern times. One respondent reported that after taking a bath, she "feels like an angel." After bathing, people feel cleaner in a moral, as well as a physical sense. [20].

Now consider some surrogate cues relating to Ivory soap. It is white, which is traditionally the color of purity—and it is *pure* white. Even its odor might be described as pure—not really perfumed but rather clean and gentle. The name Ivory itself could conjure up an image of purity and goodness. In fact, Harley Procter was reportedly inspired to name his soap Ivory while he was attending a church service. He took the name from a passage in the Bible. Furthermore, Ivory soap floats. Perhaps, even this would suggest something gentle and good, if not downright angelic.

Some of Ivory's historically famous advertising appeals have included such slogans as "99&44/100% pure" and "Gentle enough for a baby's skin." Its association with babies was probably meant simply to convey an aura of gentleness. However, babies are often thought of as being guiltless and free of sin. Is it possible that some of this latter imagery rubbed off on the brand itself?

Some observers suggest that just such implicit and explicit promotional factors may have helped Ivory soap tremendously through their unconscious symbolic communication. If someone told you to use Ivory soap to rid yourself of guilt feelings arising from your Superego, you would shrug it off as absolute nonsense. However, if the communication were framed in disguised and symbolic form, it might well work, at least according to certain interpretations of Freudian theory.

### Do Hershey Chocolate Bars Have a Special Unconscious Appeal to Some Need of the Id?

To speculate about how disguised symbols might apply in selling milk chocolate, we again have to start with an interpretation of what the eating of chocolate might imply on an unconscious level. One such interpretation states, "There are considerable elements of reward and guilt in the pleasure connected with chocolate. Chocolates are impulse items; there is relatively little planning done in their purchase. . . . In almost all civilized countries chocolate is remembered from childhood days as a reward for good behavior. This carries over into adult life."[21]

One way to apply this interpretation is to connect the impulsive purchase of chocolate to instinctive needs of the Id. These could be related to very early memories of being fed and cared for by one's mother. After all, we are talking about childhood rewards and *milk* chocolate. In this product category, Hershey has been astoundingly successful. Their chocolate bar is an extremely long-lived brand that has maintained a large market share while many other competitors have come and gone. For most of its extensive lifespan, Hershey accomplished all this with little or no formal advertising. It was not until the 1960s that Hershey milk chocolate bars were very actively advertised.

Could there be something unconsciously symbolic about this brand that has helped it over these many years? Some observers say "Yes." The presumed clue is in the brand name itself. If you give imaginative scrutiny to that name, you will see that it has the unique character of being a double feminine—"her" and "she." If you are now willing to relate that double feminine to the unconscious need for "motherly affection and comfort" then you might feel the brand name (a highly subtle and accidental aspect of implicit promotion) has given Hershey a tremendous advantage in unconscious appeal.

*Motivation Research*

In the 1950s, a Freudian approach to obtaining consumer feedback was popularized under the name "Motivation Research." (Not all motivation research is Freudian-based, but much of it is.) Although somewhat less popular today, motivation research studies are still in use, especially as guides to developing advertising strategies. Generally, motivation research projects rely on rather small samples of consumers and unstructured interrogation techniques.[22] One idea behind many such studies is to let respondents talk rather freely on the assumption that they will reveal their unconscious needs and motivations. Motivation research has received a fair share of criticism, some of which is based on moral grounds. Does anyone really have the right to delve into consumers' unconscious minds for the purpose of selling toothpaste, razor blades, or pantyhose? Another criticism is based on pragmatic grounds. Is it actually possible to probe someone's unconscious thoughts in a short interview and come up with anything usable, assuming you accept Freudian theory in the first place?

The reason for mentioning motivation research at this point is to help prepare the way for the later discussion of psychographics, which has largely replaced motivation research as a field of interest for marketing practitioners. In contrast to nonstructured interviews and reports that avoid the use of numbers (two characteristics of motivation research), psychographic studies are usually well structured and the results are quantified.

*Comments,*
*Observations, and*
*Other Points of*
*View*

Assuming you accept Freudian notions concerning promotional appeals, you should be able to learn from examples such as those of Ivory soap and Hershey milk chocolate and then "go and do likewise." First a few words of caution— or perhaps some dashes of cold water—are in order.

*The Importance of Conscious Appeals as Opposed to Unconscious Appeals.* There is absolutely no evidence that either the makers of Ivory soap or the makers of Hershey bars ever planned things as depicted in the scenarios described above. If any such unconscious communications are really taking place in either of these cases, it is accidental and coincidental. The fact is that both companies have applied sound and straightforward marketing principles over the many years of their success. These revolve around much less dramatic but effective and very consciously oriented promotional techniques. They begin with brands that have excellent and desired functional features, and include sound competitive pricing practices, widespread availability, well-conceived explicit promotion, and updating of the brands over time to keep pace with changes in the environment. Put simply, even if there is any hint of truth to those suggestions about unconscious symbolic stimuli connected with either brand, the unconscious appeal would probably account for only a very small fraction of the total success story.

*The Unproved Nature of Freudian Theory.* Although there are many experts who accept most or all of Freud's psychoanalytic theory, there are even more who reject much or all of it. After all, it is only one of many existing personality theories. Furthermore, neither it nor any other theory can be absolutely demonstrated to be true or false. As two of the country's leading psychologists point out:

> The fact of the matter is that all theories of behavior are pretty poor theories and all of them leave much to be desired in the way of scientific proof. Psychology has a long way to go before it can be called an exact science; consequently, the psychologist [or the promotional strategist who wishes to use psychology] must select [from] the theory that he or she intends to follow for reasons other than those of formal adequacy and factual evidence. [23]

In short, Freudian theory may provide a fairly accurate description of what goes on in the human mind, but then again it may not. Speculation concerning Freudian symbols in promotional communication, as in the cases of Ivory soap and Hershey chocolate bars, may be correct, partly correct, or absolutely incorrect. If you choose to use Freudian theory or any other intrapsychic personality approach, your choice will have to be made in the absence of absolute proof. You must make your decision and take something of a chance.

*Intrapsychic Approaches as Catalysts to Creativity.* Of course, even a theory that is not absolutely true might still help you develop a very effective promotional strategy. This could happen for a number of reasons. For one thing, at the very least, any of these approaches can encourage the generation of ideas concerning ways to examine markets and search for new opportunities. Each of the intrapsychic theories—and perhaps Freudian theory in particular—can be a great aid in stimulating your imagination. Thus, an intrapsychic personality approach may serve a highly useful purpose simply by acting as a catalyst for your own creative talents.

Although Freudian theory has been used to illustrate the intrapsychic approach, it is only one of a number of such theories that have been suggested as potentially applicable to marketing. You may wish to examine some of the alternative models before making your own decision regarding whether any of them might be of assistance in the formulation of your promotional planning.[24] In any event, if you opt for an intrapsychic approach, you should be aware of both the limitations and the possibilities.

**Trait Approaches to Personality**

A trait approach tends to concentrate on uncovering the nature of more or less ongoing psychological characteristics—"traits"—that exist within individuals and form their personalities. The general hypothesis is "that there are enduring, stable personality differences which reside within the person and the determination of these is the best means of predicting human behavior."[25]

Trait approaches are usually less concerned with the basic structures of personality and more concerned with behavioral patterns. "The trait approach to personality study holds an effective theory can be built by finding, in the total behavior of a person, certain patterns of action that are broader than a single, specific and non-recurrent act but less complex than his total behavior."[26]

Perhaps at some time in your life you have been or will be required to take a formal, written personality test in which you answer a great many questions about your feelings, behavior, and experiences. If so, the chances are that the test will be based on or at least related to some trait theory of personality. For the most part, attempts to apply a trait psychology approach to consumer analysis seem to be more extensively favored by marketing academicians than by marketing practitioners.

As with intrapsychic approaches, there are a variety of trait approaches from which to choose. Each of them usually begins with a list of characteristics that, when taken together, are meant to provide a usable description of the important aspects of an individual's personality. Trait approaches are typically statistically based. That is to say, they enable the researcher to obtain numerical scores for each person and for each trait. It is then possible to correlate these scores with such variables as an individual's product or brand preference levels, evaluative criteria weightings, or reactions to different types of promotional appeals.

*Procedures for Measuring Traits.* Information on traits is most often gathered by means of a paper and pencil test made up of questions that have been developed to measure each of the traits involved. These tests have usually been analyzed for validity and reliability before being put into widespread use. Figure 8.8 illustrates the traits that are measured by one such test, Cattell's "Sixteen Personality Factor Questionnaire."

*The Status of Trait Tests in Consumer Research.* Other trait tests that have been used in consumer research include the California Personality Inventory, the Edwards Personal Preference Schedule, the Gordon Personal Profile, the Minnesota Multiphasic Personality Inventory, and the Thurstone Temperament Schedule. While a wide variety of approaches have been utilized, mainly on an exploratory basis, to search for possible links between specific traits and various aspects of consumer behavior, the total results of all this research are anything but impressive, at least in terms of demonstrating strong relationships between personality types and behavior in the marketplace. One team of writers conducted an extensive review of the findings and commented, "The correlation or relationships between personality test scores [using trait tests] and consumer behavior variables such as product choice, media exposure, innovation, segmentation, etc., are weak at best and of little value in prediction."[27]

*Examining the Problems of the Standard Trait Approaches*

Does this mean that personality—or at least the trait approach to personality—offers no potential applicability in assessing lifestyle goals, evaluative criteria, or brand preference levels? Not really. Even those who have published critical reviews of past research seem to feel that individual personality differences are worth considering when analyzing consumer segments. In speculating on why past studies have not uncovered more significant relationships, three major reasons tend to stand out.

First, most standard personality trait tests were designed for purposes or types of people much different from those of interest in typical consumer

**FIGURE 8.8 Example of the trait approach: Cattell's sixteen source traits**

*I. Primaries*

| Factor | Low Sten Score Description [1–3] | High Sten Score Description [8–10] |
|---|---|---|
| A | *Reserved*, detached, critical, cool, impersonal<br>Sizothymia | *Warmhearted*, outgoing, participating, interested in people, easy-going<br>Affectothymia |
| B | *Less intelligent*, concrete-thinking<br>Lower scholastic mental capacity | *More intelligent*, abstract-thinking, bright<br>Higher scholastic mental capacity |
| C | *Affected by feelings*, emotionally less stable, easily upset, changeable<br>Lower ego strength | *Emotionally stable*, mature, faces reality, calm, patient<br>Higher ego strength |
| E | *Humble*, mild, accommodating, easily led, conforming<br>Submissiveness | *Assertive*, aggressive, authoritative, competitive, stubborn<br>Dominance |
| F | *Sober*, prudent, serious, taciturn<br>Desurgency | *Happy-go-lucky*, impulsively lively, enthusiastic, heedless<br>Surgency |
| G | *Expedient*, disregards rules, feels few obligations<br>Weaker superego strength | *Conscientious*, persevering, proper, moralistic, rule-bound<br>Stronger superego strength |
| H | *Shy*, restrained, threat-sensitive, timid<br>Threctia | *Venturesome*, socially bold, uninhibited, spontaneous<br>Parmia |
| I | *Tough-minded*, self-reliant, realistic, no-nonsense<br>Harria | *Tender-minded*, intuitive, unrealistic, sensitive<br>Premsia |
| L | *Trusting*, adaptable, free of jealousy, easy to get on with<br>Alaxia | *Suspicious*, self-opinionated, hard to fool, skeptical, questioning<br>Protension |
| M | *Practical*, careful, conventional, regulated by external realities<br>Praxernia | *Imaginative*, careless of practical matters, unconventional, absent-minded<br>Autia |
| N | *Forthright*, natural, genuine, unpretentious<br>Artlessness | *Shrewd*, calculating, socially alert, insightful<br>Shrewdness |
| O | *Unperturbed*, self-assured, confident, secure, self-satisfied<br>Untroubled adequacy | *Apprehensive*, self-reproaching, worrying, troubled<br>Guilt proneness |
| $Q_1$ | *Conservative*, respecting established ideas, tolerant of traditional difficulties<br>Conservatism of temperament | *Experimenting*, liberal, analytical, likes innovation<br>Radicalism |
| $Q_2$ | *Group oriented*, a "joiner" and sound follower<br>Group adherence | *Self-sufficient*, prefers own decisions, resourceful<br>Self-sufficiency |
| $Q_3$ | *Undisciplined self-conflict*, careless of protocol, follows own urges<br>Low integration | *Controlled*, socially precise, following self-image, compulsive<br>High self-concept control |
| $Q_4$ | *Relaxed*, tranquil, torpid, unfrustrated<br>Low ergic tension | *Tense*, frustrated, driven, restless, overwrought<br>High ergic tension |

*Source:* Adapted from R. B. Cattell, H. W. Eber, and M. M. Tatsuoka, *Handbook for the Sixteen Personality Factor Questionnaire (16 PF)*, Champaign, IL: Institute for Personality and Ability Testing, 1970, pp. 16–17. (1982 Printing) Reprinted by permission of the copyright owner. All rights reserved.

*Demographic Forces, Biopsychic Forces, and Lifestyle Goals*

surveys. If a test was originally prepared to help psychologists work with someone who is emotionally disturbed or to assist a job counselor in giving advice on career planning, why would the traits it measures have any relevance to determining what is important to consumers when they shop for automobiles or shoes? The traits measured by the standard tests are often very general. There is no special reason to think they might be connected with ways in which people choose between brands. One writer has observed,

> "Careful examination reveals that in most cases, no appropriate thought is directed to *how* or especially *why* personality should or should not be related to that aspect of consumer behavior being studied." (Emphasis added) [28]

Second, the behavioral impact of any particular personality trait is likely to be situation-specific. As an illustration, consider the trait of "Humble" versus "Assertive" in the list of traits in Figure 8.8. Suppose that a person measures out as highly assertive. How might that affect the kind of features and styling which that individual would seek when buying clothing, if it affected them at all? In all probability, you would have to know the specific situations and occasions the person had in mind for wearing the clothing before you could associate assertiveness with clothing choices. Attempting to assert oneself in a business situation might call for a much different type of wearing apparel than would be suitable in trying to assert oneself in a social situation. Put more formally, one writer has suggested that it is "more correct to conceive of personality as a moderator variable whose function is to moderate the effect of environmental change in the individual's behavior."[29]

Third, consumer attitudes and decisions that are related to personality may also be influenced by other concurrent behavioral factors. In the last two chapters, we have been discussing a variety of lifestyle forces. Personality is just one of these and its consequences may be affected or even dominated by one or more of the others. Again considering the trait of assertiveness, ask yourself whether the exact manner in which a person expresses assertiveness, might not depend on subculture, role-playing needs, and even such factors as age and income level. In most buying situations, it seems reasonable to anticipate finding a number of characteristics acting in concert to influence the outcome. If this is true, a logical corollary implies that the importance of personality, relative to such other influences, could vary among different product categories. In some instances personality might be the single most critical lifestyle force and merit your special and separate consideration in planning promotional strategy. In other cases it might be influential only in union with other aspects of behavior, or perhaps its proportion of influence may be so subordinate as to merit little or no consideration.

**Trends in Personality-Related Research Approaches**

***Customized, Product-Specific Studies.*** Sophisticated approaches have been devised to probe the relationship between consumers' behavior and personality traits. The Anheuser-Busch study described earlier is an excellent example of such a refined application of a trait approach. That experiment was the culmination of an intensive project aimed at isolating the lifestyle underpinnings of drinking behavior. The investigators did not begin with a haphazard assumption that personality type *might* be an influence on variations in reasons for drinking and therefore affect responses to variations in advertising appeals. Rather, their initial assumption was "that we would not be able to evaluate advertising messages adequately without knowing *why* people drink beer and, more generally, alcoholic beverages."[30] They then analyzed past research on drinking, which led to their hypothesis that personality was indeed a dominant influence and that pre-researched trait patterns might delineate distinctive segments of drinkers. Their trait-measurement instrument was then carefully devised on the basis of intensive field investigations and custom designed to measure the specific trait patterns pertinent to situations in which alcoholic beverages are consumed. In short, the study was based on a customized test measuring only relevant traits, it was situation-oriented, and it was applied in a product category where careful pre-study had revealed that personality type could play a highly important role in influencing consumers' behavioral patterns.

## PSYCHOGRAPHIC ANALYSIS

An increasingly popular trend in market research is toward psychographic analysis, which treats personality only as one potential component in the mix of factors that influence buyers. The goal of most psychographic studies is to achieve a more complete concept of the individual that transcends mere personality factors and considers the impact of the total blend of forces affecting lifestyle goals.

*The Background of Psychographics*

In our consideration of Freudian psychoanalytic theory, mention was made of motivation research. Then we discussed attempts to use personality trait approaches to achieve a better understanding of consumers. Psychographics or lifestyle analysis has been described as an outgrowth of both the motivation research and the trait approaches. However, it differs from each of these techniques in several important respects.

In contrast to the rather loose procedures of motivation research, psychographics uses a more structured questionnaire procedure. Its results can usually be stated numerically as percentages or ratings. For this reason, it is generally considered to be more precise than motivation research. Although it often employs techniques that are somewhat similar to those used in trait studies, psychographic consumer research does not rely on standard personality tests. Instead, it uses questionnaires that are tailored to the needs of the particular marketing situation.

Apart from these differences, psychographic research is vastly different from typical motivation research and trait studies in one very important additional aspect. It does not limit itself to personality data. Psychographic research reports often include information on demographic-lifestyle forces, social forces, attitudes, brand usage, and circumstances related to the way a consumer buys and thinks about particular products. In terms of our general framework for analyzing promotional strategy, psychographic or lifestyle research studies can be described as being concerned with both lifestyle goals and the complete pattern of underlying forces that affect those goals. Moreover, many psychographic studies go even further and try to relate lifestyle goals to segmented preferences for certain types of evaluative criteria as well as brand preference levels, purchase intentions, and purchase decisions.

**A Closer Look and Some Examples**

As with most of the terms we have been discussing, "psychographics" is ascribed somewhat different meanings by various writers and researchers. It really amounts to a collection of techniques that can be used in a variety of ways to suit particular planning needs. For our purposes it will be defined as follows: *Psychographics is a type of research aimed at describing lifestyle goal patterns as they relate to consumer purchase behavior. It makes use of combinations of data on biopsychic and/or social forces along with relevant information on attitudes, interests, and activities of consumers. These are often supplemented with information on demographic forces.*

Not every psychographic study analyzes all of the factors mentioned in this definition. However, the general philosophy behind psychographic research is that it is useful to consider a mixture of relevant factors to secure a rather complete picture of consumers' lifestyles and lifestyle goals as they pertain to purchase decisions and decision making. To illustrate the types of consumer descriptions that can emerge from such analyses, we will consider the results of two psychographically oriented market studies. The first deals with heavy users of shotgun ammunition. The second compares people who shop at discount stores as opposed to those who do not.

*The Psychographics of Heavy Users of Shotgun Shells.* Heavy buyers of shotgun ammunition, as compared demographically to nonbuyers, tend to be younger men with lower incomes and lower educational levels. On a social class basis they are more likely to be found in blue collar jobs and, by inference, to be associated with the upper-lower class. They also seem to be generally more attracted to violence, danger, and risk. In addition, a report on this group concluded that "it is obvious that hunting is not an isolated phenomenon but is associated with other rugged outdoor endeavors. Shotgun shell buyers not only like to hunt, they also like to fish and go camping. They even like to work outdoors."[31]

*The Psychographics of Discount Store Customers.* In a study that examined the lifestyle characteristics of retail shoppers, discount store customers were pictured as follows: "While discount store patrons were younger and better educated than non-patrons, their average income was less. The discount store shopper was also found to be more socially conscious than non-patrons."[32]

**Psychographic Research Techniques**

Figure 8.9 shows two portions of a questionnaire used in a psychographic study concerned with women's food shopping behavior. Notice that these questions center on attitudes and situational factors specifically related to food preparation and usage. The full questionnaire also sought information about demographic forces along with more general psychographic items dealing with role orientation, habits and attitudes, shopping goals, and purchase be-

**FIGURE 8.9 Examples of psychographic questionnaire items**

| Shopping Behavior Items | Food Preparation Items |
|---|---|
| I keep a running list of certain things such as staples, adding an item to the list when we run low on it. | At home we usually eat quickly prepared meals rather than more carefully prepared dishes of various flavors. |
| I watch for the lowest possible prices when I shop. | When I give a dinner party I feel my guests will judge me by the food I serve. |
| I use a list when shopping for food. | A wife who is not a good cook owes it to her husband to work at improving her cooking. |
| I buy the highest quality food available. | Cooking is very creative. |
| I compare labels to select the most nutritious food. | I am disappointed in myself when dinner is a flop. |
| I notice when products I buy regularly change in price. | I worry about my family's nutrition. |
| Before I go to do a big food shopping, I make a list of everything we need. | I feel good when I spend a lot of time making dinner for my family. |
| I shop for specials in food. | I like to serve unusual dinners. |
| If the store has very long lines that day I leave without buying anything. | Dishes cooked in wine or sauces appeal to me. |
| If a product isn't wholesome I won't buy it. | I am an excellent cook. |
| I keep a running list of everything we need, adding an item to the list when we run low on it. | I have better ways to spend my time than in grocery shopping and cooking. |
| | It is the wife's responsibility to keep her family healthy by serving nutritious meals |

Source: Mary Lou Roberts and Lawrence H. Wortzel, "New Life Style Determinants of Women's Food Shopping Behavior," *Journal of Marketing*, Summer 1979, pp. 28–39.

havior. In all, ninety-one psychographic items were examined. When the study was completed, the authors were able to divide shoppers into two major categories—"traditional orientation" and "contemporary orientation." Then they related these consumer types to general evaluative criteria as follows:

> Traditional Orientation was most highly correlated with "Concern for Quality," had a small correlation with "Price Minimization" and a negative correlation with "Concern for Time." This indicates that the traditional woman wants to provide high quality food for her family at a reasonable cost with little concern for the shopping and meal preparation time required. . . . The "Contemporary Orientation" showed a positive correlation with "Concern for Time," and "Empirical" shopping behavior. This reflects the use of primarily point-of-purchase information in an attempt to save time. [33]

**Broad-Scale Psychographic Studies**

Not all psychographic studies focus on consumers in the context of a particular product category. Some wide-ranging surveys have been conducted with the purpose of psychographically grouping the entire American population. For example, one report by the Newspaper Advertising Bureau classified American men into eight groups, which were summarized under such titles as the "quiet family man" (8% of the total males) and the "ethical high brow" (14% of total males).[34] At least two advertising agencies have been reported as having done similar broad-scale studies.[35]

*The VALS Program.* Perhaps the most comprehensive and intensely researched broad-scale approach is the VALS typological system.[36] VALS was

*Demographic Forces, Biopsychic Forces, and Lifestyle Goals*

developed by SRI International, a California-based research and consulting organization. The name "VALS" is an acronym for "values and lifestyles." The program was established in 1978 and is the product of approximately seventeen years of background research and development, drawing on the work of a variety of leading behavioral theorists.

Based on responses to questions concerning some thirty to forty demographic and attitudinal items, the VALS program places consumers into one of nine general categories. As shown in Figure 8.10 each of these categories can be associated with a general lifestyle pattern as well as a general buying-style pattern.

Importantly, the VALS program views each category as being potentially transitional in nature. In other words, it recognizes that an individual may move from one category to another and places emphasis on gaining insights into the process by which such movement occurs. Furthermore, the theory behind the program recognizes that each person retains elements of all the stages that have been passed through earlier. Thus, it allows for more refined and statistically sophisticated analyses of consumer response data where this seems desirable in order to pinpoint prospects' characteristics with greater accuracy.

VALS analyses can guide a number of promotional strategy decision areas. For example, by evaluating usage rates for your product category and the brands within it, as those rates vary among VALS-defined segments, you can sharpen your ability to locate target market groups offering the greatest potential for your promotional efforts. Following this, you can design advertising strategy to stress evaluative criteria and creative techniques most appropriate to your target segment, again using the VALS typology descriptions as your background. The VALS data can also assist you in selecting advertising media or designing premium offers, contests, and other sales promotion efforts.

## Applications of the VALS Program

A number of interesting promotional applications of the VALS program have been reported as being used by some famous names in American business. One illustration involves the Merrill Lynch stock brokerage firm. Several years ago, Merrill Lynch introduced an advertising campaign built around the theme, "Bullish on America,"[37] which was dramatized by picturing a herd of bulls. VALS-based research found that perceived connotations associated with a herd of bulls appealed most strongly to the VALS segment designated as "belongers." However, the market segment at which the campaign had aimed was composed mainly of people who fall into the "achievers" segment. The "herd theme" was found to have little appeal to this group. So, Merrill Lynch switched its campaign theme to a lone bull and the slogan, "A Breed Apart."

Another user of VALS is the New York Telephone Company, which has applied the typology to guide its product planning, pricing, and personal selling procedures. In the words of New York Telephone's market manager, "We now have engineers, costing people, researchers, etc., all speaking the same language—the language of the VALS typology."[38]

For example, the company found that the variety of telephone styles it offered customers had a different strength of appeal for persons in various

## FIGURE 8.10 The VALS typological system

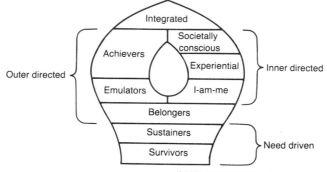

NEED-DRIVEN, who buy more out of need than choice, include

| | Survivors | Sustainers |
|---|---|---|
| % of population | 4% | 7% |
| Lifestyle | Struggling for survival | Hopeful for improvement over time |
| | Distrustful | Concerned with security |
| Buying style | Price dominant | Price important |
| | Focused on basics | Want warranty |

OUTER-DIRECTED, who buy with an eye to appearances and in accord with established norms, include

| | Belongers | |
|---|---|---|
| % of population | 35% | |
| Lifestyle | Preservers of status quo Seek to be part of group | |
| Buying style | Do not want to try something new Heritage brand buyer | |
| | Emulators | |
| % of population | 10% | |
| Lifestyle | Upwardly mobile Emulate rich and successful | |
| Buying style | Conspicuous consumption Sacrifice comfort and utility for show | |
| | Achievers | |
| % of population | 23% | |
| Lifestyle | Materialistic, comfort-loving Oriented to fame and success | |
| Buying style | Luxury and gift items Like "new & improved" but not radically changed products | |

INNER-DIRECTED, who buy to satisfy their self-expressive, individualistic needs, include

| | I-am-me |
|---|---|
| % of population | 5% |
| Lifestyle | Transition between outer and inner directed Very individualistic |
| Buying style | Impulsive Trendy products |
| | Experiential |
| % of population | 7% |
| Lifestyle | Seek direct experience Intense personal relationships |
| Buying style | Process over product Interested in what product does for them, not what it says about them |
| | Societally conscious |
| % of population | 9% |
| Lifestyle | Simple, natural living Socially responsible |
| Buying style | Discriminating Want true value and environmentally sound products |

INTEGRATED are rare people who have melded power of the Outer-directed with sensitivity of the Inner-directed. Their lifestyle is one of tolerance and self-assurance; their buying style is oriented to ecologically sound, esthetically pleasing, one-of-kind products.

*Source:* SRI International, Menlo Park, CA. Reprinted with permission.

*Demographic Forces, Biopsychic Forces, and Lifestyle Goals*

FIGURE 8.11 Using VALS segments to define the market for various styles of telephones

| General Style of Phone | VALS Segments to Which Particular Phone Models Appeal | | |
|---|---|---|---|
| | Belongers | Achievers | Etc. |
| Romantic | Phone M Phone A Phone C | | |
| Character | | Phone R Phone Y | |
| Message Center | Phone T | | |
| Contemporary | | | |

Source: "Properly Applied Psychographics Add Marketing Lustre," Marketing News, 12 November 1982, p. 10.

VALS groupings. These findings, presented in Figure 8.11, also suggested that the available telephone designs were often competing with each other for the same consumer segment and were thus resulting in low sales for each of the competing types. For example, three telephone styles with a "romantic design" were found to appeal mainly to "belongers," whereas no "romantic" telephone style appealed to "achievers." The conclusion was that no cell (as shown in this figure) should have more or less than two products in it. As a result, the company began designing phones of each style to appeal to each VALS category. New York Telephone also introduced a training film for its sales personnel that describes the VALS target segments. The film attempts to instruct sales personnel to listen for key words used by a customer which can help identify that person's probable VALS orientation. The sales representative then works from the hypothesis that certain types of telephone styles and company services will or will not be especially appealing to that customer.

**The "Competitive Frame" Approach to Psychographic Analysis**

One expert in the field has suggested an interesting and useful guide to planning psychographic studies; it is shown in Figure 8.12. In commenting on her outline, she emphasizes the importance of conducting your study from the perspective of your generic product class and your competitors' promotional strategies. "A study for a prepared pudding would have different coverage if the competition were defined as other prepared puddings than if it were defined as all desserts; one for a soft drink would be different if limited to soft drinks rather than extended to all beverages. The Competitive Frame definition is key then in a psychographic study."[39]

Notice how the consumer research structure in Figure 8.12 provides you with a guide for combining the planning input factors that we have been discussing in this and the three preceding chapters. Analysis of such data provides an aggregate of coordinated information from which to begin your promotional planning process. Examples of what such compilations look like are shown in Figure 8.13 (page 253).

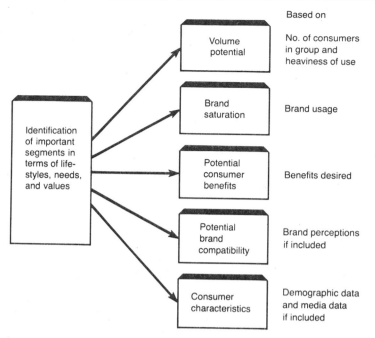

Based on

Volume potential — No. of consumers in group and heaviness of use

FIGURE 8.12 The "Competitive Frame" approach to psychographic studies

Identification of important segments in terms of life-styles, needs, and values

Brand saturation — Brand usage

Potential consumer benefits — Benefits desired

Potential brand compatibility — Brand perceptions if included

Consumer characteristics — Demographic data and media data if included

Source: Ruth Ziff, "The Role of Psychographics in the Development of Advertising Strategy and Copy," in William D. Wells, *Lifestyle and Psychographics*, (Chicago: The American Marketing Association, 1974), p. 144.

*Putting Psychographic Information to Use*

Lifestyle studies have been credited with forming the basis for successful promotional strategies for brands ranging from Irish Spring soap to Oldsmobile automobiles. Even a product as prosaic as heavy-duty hand soap can be subjected to psychographic analysis. A study on this very product "concluded that the current users of heavy-duty hand soap were women who were most comfortable in the confines of their own homes, with home and family as the focus of their lives."[40] It also discovered they regarded themselves as "gatekeepers" (information sources and decision makers) for their families and shopping experts. Their general lifestyles centered around simple, traditional, and conservative views. Furthermore, they were found to have anxieties about cleanliness in general. This background information held several implications for the promotional campaign.

First, it was decided that the mother should be placed in the role of gatekeeper and that all family members should be included in the advertising. Second, it was decided that there should be a demonstration of how the product works to remove dirt and this demonstration should be conducted in an everyday situation in an authoritative style. Finally, it was decided, since the target audience approached most things in a simple and straightforward manner, the basic claim would best be made in that way too. . . . The campaign was built around the idea that children, with their half-hearted attempts to wash their hands, must often be required to make several trips to the bathroom. Thus they need a heavy-duty hand soap to get out all of the dirt the first time. The campaign included all members of the family (in one commercial even the grandmother was included) and placed the mother as the gatekeeper. [41]

*Demographic Forces, Biopsychic Forces, and Lifestyle Goals*

**FIGURE 8.13 An example of psychographic research output: two types of automobile buyers**

| TYPE ONE | |
|---|---|
| **What they are like** | **What they want** |
| — Know little about cars<br>— Uninvolved in cars, driving, maintenance<br>— Apprehensive about cars<br>— Need reassurance that car will run well<br>— Car make and dealer important<br>— Get pleasure from appearance of car | — Trust in manufacturer and dealer<br>— Dependable car<br>— Good engine performance<br>— Good handling qualities<br>— Good styling<br>— Minimum maintenance |
| **Who they are** | **What they do** |
| — Older<br>— Better educated<br>— Higher incomes | — More own Chevrolets, Pontiacs, Oldsmobile<br>— Choose on trust in make; styling<br>— Own more cars; recent models |

| TYPE TWO | |
|---|---|
| **What they are like** | **What they want** |
| — Know a lot about cars<br>— Involved in cars and maintenance<br>— Enjoy driving<br>— Are power oriented in driving<br>— Want to be in control when driving<br>— Believe in differences between makes | — Powerful cars for driving control<br>— Top engine performance<br>— Good handling qualities<br>— Cars made by major companies |
| **Who they are** | **What they do** |
| — Younger<br>— Middle class in income and education | — More own a Ford, fewer a Chevrolet/AMC<br>— Drive more powerful cars<br>— Choose on engine performance, styling |

*Source:* Ruth Ziff, "The Role of Psychographics in the Development of Advertising Strategy and Copy," in William D. Wells, *Lifestyle and Psychographics* (Chicago: The American Marketing Association, 1974), pp. 145–146.

**Comments and Cautions**

You are almost certain to find disagreement and controversy regarding the usefulness of any market research technique. It is understandable that not everyone is completely convinced of the value of psychographic research.

**Questions Concerning Reliability.** Questions have been raised concerning the reliability of lifestyle questionnaire results. Those who raise this issue are asking whether the results are stable over time. Will the same psychographic questionnaire produce the same results if repeated in studies of the same consumers on several occasions? Or will you obtain different results each time because people vacillate in their opinions and views? At least one pair of researchers was not entirely satisfied with the reliability of some psychographic tests which they checked. But even though they questioned the precision of psychographic studies, they also stated, "The conclusion is not entirely discouraging, however. When one inspects the degree of individual random response to items in the stable and lasting psychographic dimensions, most respondents appear to vary unsystematically, but by only one response category from the pretest and post-test."[42]

***Using Psychographics in Concert with Other Analytical Tools.*** The use of psychographics is one way to fulfill some of your planning input needs. Like any other information gathering technique, psychographics exists to help you reach your goal of building an optimum promotional mix. It is not a goal in and of itself. The research vice-president of a major advertising agency offered the following sound advice on this point: "Don't fall in love with techniques—segmentation, psychographics, brand mapping, problem tracking, etc., and lose sight of the issue. No single technique can solve all of the problems. . . . The first thing to do is identify critical marketing issues. Then, be creative in selecting the research techniques which can address them. Finally, be thorough and rigorous in applying them."[43]

***Translating Psychographic Findings into a Communication Design.*** In the final analysis, neither psychographics nor any other analytical technique really builds your promotional mix. They are all merely devices to help you construct a base from which to work. You are still faced with the problem of interpreting the results and then developing a promotional program based on that interpretation. In short, you are still left with the task of creating a communication package using the results of consumer analysis—psychographic or otherwise. Different promotional strategists are likely to come up with quite different promotional programs even when they start with the same survey results. Some programs will work. Some will not. For example, consider the following case in which psychographic data reportedly led to an unwise promotional decision.

> Leo Burnett once had psychographic data indicating that women who bought TV dinners tend to lead hectic lives and had trouble coping with everyday problems. Burnett, thereupon, came up with an ad for Swanson [frozen dinners] showing a run-down woman flopping into a chair just before her family is to arrive home and demand dinner. Suddenly realizing that she has a problem, she gets the bright idea of cooking a TV dinner. "We couldn't have made a worse mistake," confesses . . . the Senior Vice President and Director of Research. "The last thing those ladies wanted to be reminded of is how tired they are." [44]

To put your planning input data to work in a persuasive communication package, you must understand the principles of communication techniques and the methods you can use to implement those principles. Approaches to doing that will make up the topics of the next eleven chapters.

# SUMMARY

Data on demographic forces are probably the most widely available and widely employed types of information in marketing practice. They can frequently be related to more general types of lifestyle goals and used to identify customer groups by rate of usage.

In markets for ultimate consumer goods, the nuclear family is often the basis for organizing demographic data. Certain demographic trends within the American population and family structure provide good examples of how data on demographic forces can be applied in promotional planning. For example, overall aging of the population is bringing about changes in strategies for a number of companies and product categories.

Biopsychic forces are highly individualized in nature. They may involve either physical differences or psychological differences among consumers. Although little has been written about the marketing implications of physical differences, they can be important bases for differentiating among prospects in a number of product categories. Drugs and cosmetics are notable examples. However, physical differences are worth your consideration in many other situations as well. Much has been written about the implications of psychological aspects of biopsychic forces and two broad approaches to studying personality differences have been widely attempted in marketing: intrapsychic approaches and trait approaches. Probably the most frequently discussed intrapsychic approach is based on Freud's psychoanalytic theory, which, though controversial, has intrigued quite a number of promotional strategists and researchers. Among other things, it has been used to develop some interesting though unproved ideas about how promotional techniques might convey symbolic messages to the unconscious mind. The users of Freudian approaches generally work with loose, nonstructured questionnaire techniques and avoid statistical analysis. They prefer to interpret their results in purely verbal descriptions.

In contrast, the trait approach normally makes use of structured, standardized paper and pencil tests to measure individual personality characteristics or traits. Trait approaches usually produce quantified (or numerical) results that can then be related to various aspects of consumer behavior. Many trait studies of this type have been done. Unfortunately, the results of such studies are usually not very impressive. This does not necessarily mean that personality differences have nothing to do with what people buy or why they buy it. The opinion that currently prevails among those who have studied the results of trait research can be summarized as follows:

1. Specialized and custom-made trait tests are needed to measure the specific traits that might relate to consumer purchase behavior. Most of the standard tests were designed for other purposes.
2. The effects of any particular personality trait may change as the purchase situation changes. Therefore, the specific purchase situation has to be considered in the study.
3. Personality forces blend in with other lifestyle forces to affect consumer preferences. In other words, lifestyle goals are likely to be shaped by a

mixture of social, demographic, and biopsychic forces, which include but are not limited to personality differences.

One of the major results of such conclusions has been the growth in popularity of psychographics. There is no such thing as a standard psychographic study. The designs of such studies vary widely among different researchers. In general, however, psychographic studies tend to include social, demographic, and biopsychic forces in defining consumer groupings. They can also include items relating to such other factors as usage situations, evaluative criteria, and existing brand preference levels.

Psychographics has been credited with helping promotional strategists develop successful programs for a number of brands in widely different fields. The technique has also drawn its share of criticism. With respect to your use of psychographics or any other research approach, a reasonable piece of advice was suggested: Be carefully selective in your reliance on research techniques, focus on your particular marketing problem, and do not become infatuated with the research method you use.

You must also remember that research data can only assist you in starting to build your promotional mix. Even with the best consumer research available, you still face the task of formulating an effective communication approach, and this requires that many decisions be made. The handling of those decisions will be the topic of the next several chapters.

## DISCUSSION QUESTIONS

1. Discuss methods of linking demographics with consumption concentration. What is the primary purpose of studying demographics?
2. Several illustrations of promotional responses to demographic trends were discussed. Using the information on major demographic trends discussed in the text, outline some suggestions and modifications for a promotional strategy to be used by a manufacturer of camping equipment.
3. The fact of the rapidly growing mature market raises three basic questions that apply to all significant demographic groupings. List these questions and propose at least one example that applies to each question.
4. Name and briefly discuss the components of the personality as postulated by Freud. How do these components relate to the level of awareness? What level has the most significant effect on promotional strategies?
5. Discuss how the trait approach differs from intrapsychic approaches. What are the major shortcomings of traditional studies of the trait

approach to personality as applied to marketing situations?
6. Comment on the usefulness of "the competitive frame" when using the psychographic approach to studying promotional problems.
7. Draw up a list of tentative suggestions for applying the VALS segmentation technique to the marketing of the following product categories: automobiles, furniture, men's toiletries.
8. Study current examples of advertising and try to find at least two that seem to make use of Freudian psychological principles. Discuss their probable effectiveness in terms of the points raised in the chapter.
9. Discuss possible techniques for influencing various family members in the promotion of soft drinks, peanut butter, and dog food.
10. According to one observer whose views were presented in the chapter (see p. 254), the "tired housewife" commercial for Swanson's frozen dinners was not well received by target audience members. Working from the same general psychographic description, suggest more appropriate advertising approaches.

# REFERENCES

1. "De Beers Consolidated Mines, Ltd.," *Advertising Campaign Report Newsletter* (New York: American Association of Advertising Agencies, April, 1978).

2. Kenneth Runyon, *Consumer Behavior*, 2nd ed. (Columbus, OH: Charles E. Merrill Publishing Co., 1980), p. 164.

3. Patrick E. Murphy and William A. Staples, "A Modernized Family Life Cycle," *Journal of Consumer Research*, June 1979, p. 17.

4. *Population Characteristics: Marital and Living Arrangements*, series P-20, no. 372, June 1982, U.S. Department of Commerce, Bureau of the Census.

5. *Ibid*.

6. "Kellogg: Still the Cereal People," *Business Week*, 26 November 1979, p. 82.

7. "Food in the A.M.," *Time*, 31 March 1980, p. 53.

8. *Ibid*.

9. "The Over-the-Thrill-Crowd," *Time*, 28 May 1979, p. 39.

10. *Grey Matter*, vol. 49, no. 1 (New York: Grey Advertising, Inc., 1978).

11. *Ibid*.

12. *Population Characteristics: Marital and Living Arrangements*.

13. Gordon W. Allport, *Pattern and Growth of Personality* (New York: Holt, Rinehart and Winston, 1967), p. 28.

14. Gordon W. Allport, *Personality: A Psychological Interpretation* (New York: Holt, Rinehart and Winston, 1937), p. 48–49.

15. R. L. Ackoff and J. R. Emsoff, "Advertising Research at Anheuser-Busch, Inc.," *Sloan Management Review*, Spring 1975, pp. 1–15.

16. Robert M. Liebert and Michael D. Spiegler, *Personality: An Introduction to Theory and Research* (Homewood, IL: The Dorsey Press, 1970), p. 36.

17. For an excellent description of Lewin's theory and its possible implications for marketing see Harold H. Kassarjian, "Field Theory in Consumer Behavior," ed. Scott Ward and Thomas S. Robertson, *Consumer Behavior: Theoretical Sources* (Englewood Cliffs, NJ: Prentice-Hall, 1973), pp. 118–140.
   For an excellent description of Roger's theory see Calvin S. Hall and Gardner Lindzey, *Theories of Personality*, 3rd ed. (New York: John Wiley and Sons, 1967), pp. 279–309.
   For some examples of consumer studies based on Roger's theory see E. Laird Landon, Jr., "Self Concept, Ideal Concept and Consumer Purchase Intentions," *Journal of Consumer Research*, September 1974, pp. 44–51; and B. C. Hamm and Edward W. Cundiff, "Self-Actualization and Product Perception," *Journal of Marketing Research*, November 1969, pp. 740–742.

18. For a more extended discussion see Hall and Lindzey, *Theories of Personality*, pp. 31–73.

19. Gerald Zaltman and Melanie Wallendorf, *Consumer Behavior: Basic Findings and Management Implications*, 2nd ed. (New York: John Wiley and Sons, 1983), pp. 402–403.

20. Ernest Dichter, *Handbook of Consumer Motivation* (New York: McGraw-Hill Book Company, 1964), p. 193.

21. *Ibid.*, p. 331.

22. For a more extended discussion of the types of qualitative survey methods used in motivation research see Danny N. Bellenger, K. L. Bernhardt, and J. L. Goldstucker, *Qualitative Research in Marketing* (Chicago: American Marketing Association, 1976).

23. Hall and Lindzey, *Theories of Personality*, p. 69.

24. For an especially good summary of a variety of applicable intrapsychic theories see Scott Ward and Thomas Robertson, eds., *Consumer Behavior: Theoretical Sources* (Englewood Cliffs, NJ: Prentice-Hall, Inc., 1973), pp. 45–199.

25. Liebert and Spiegler, *op. cit.*, p. 95.

26. E. Earl Baughman and George S. Welsh, *Personality: A Behavioral Science* (Englewood Cliffs, NJ: Prentice-Hall, Inc., 1964), p. 335.

27. Harold H. Kassarjian and Mary Jane Sheffet, "Personality and Consumer Behavior: One More Time," in Edward Mazze, ed., *Marketing: The Challenges and the Opportunities* (Chicago: The American Marketing Association, 1979), p. 203.

28. Jacob Jacoby, "Personality and Consumer Behavior: How Not to Find Relationships," Purdue Papers in Consumer Psychology, no. 102 (Purdue University, 1969).

29. Masao Nakanishi, "Personality and Consumer Behavior: Extensions," *Proceedings of the Association for Consumer Research* (1972), pp. 61–65.

30. Ackoff and Emsoff, *op. cit.*, p. 5.

31. William D. Wells, "Psychographics, A Critical Review," *Journal of Marketing Research*, May 1975, p. 198.

32. William O. Bearden, Jessie E. Teel, Jr., and

Richard M. Durand, "Media Usage, Psychographic and Demographic Dimensions of Retail Shoppers," *Journal of Retailing,* Spring 1978, p. 71.

33. Mary Lou Roberts and Lawrence H. Wortzel, "New Life-Style Determinants of Women's Food Shopping Behavior," *Journal of Marketing*, Summer 1979, p. 36.

34. Wells, "Psychographics, A Critical Review," p. 201.

35. Peter W. Bernstein, "Psychographics Is Still An Issue On Madison Avenue," *Fortune*, January 1979, pp. 78–84.

36. For much more detailed discussions of VALS see T. C. Thomas and S. Crocker, *Values and Lifestyles—The New Psychographics* (Menlo Park, CA: S.R.I. International, 1981); and Arnold Mitchell, *The Nine American Lifestyles* (New York: Macmillan Publishing Co., 1983).

37. "A New Way to View Consumers," *Dun's Review*, August 1981, pp. 42–46.

38. "Properly Applied Psychographics Add Marketing Lustre," *Marketing News*, 12 November 1982, p. 10.

39. Ruth Ziff, "The Role of Psychographics in the Development of Advertising Strategy and Copy," in William D. Wells, ed., *Life Style and Psychographics* (Chicago: The American Marketing Association, 1974), p. 143.

40. Joseph T. Plummer, "Application of Life Style Research in the Creation of Advertising Campaigns," in William D. Wells, ed., *Life Style and Psychographics* (Chicago: American Marketing Association, 1974), pp. 166–167.

41. *Ibid.*

42. Alvin C. Burns and Mary Carolyn Harrison, "A Test of the Reliability of Psychographics," *Journal of Marketing Research,* February 1979, p. 37.

43. "Feigin Offers Research Do's, Don'ts in Marketing to 'Me-Generation'," *Marketing News*, January 1979, p. 4.

44. Bernstein, "Psychographics Is Still An Issue On Madison Avenue," p. 84.

# CHAPTER NINE

# *Models to Guide Communications*

## FOCUS OF THE CHAPTER

All forms of promotion involve persuasive communication. The more thoroughly you understand your audience, the more effectively you can communicate. For this reason, much of our discussion thus far has dealt with ideas to help you discover and analyze the people in your target market.

However, as was stressed at the end of the last chapter, knowing your audience and communicating with your audience are two different things. In the case of Swanson's frozen foods, the advertising people knew a great deal about the prospects at whom they were aiming. Yet when they attempted to communicate with consumers, their efforts misfired.

# BUILDING PERSUASIVE MESSAGES TO ACHIEVE MARKETING OBJECTIVES

To acquire a sense of the challenges you will face in developing promotional communications, you may want to take another look at the lifestyle descriptions of automobile buyers presented in Figure 8.13 (see p. 253). Now suppose you are trying to develop either an advertising program to reach these people or a program to train automobile salespeople to sell to such customers in the showroom. To put your knowledge about the market to work, you must know how to build specific promotional messages and how to communicate those messages effectively. Communication techniques will be the subject of this and the following ten chapters. We will begin with some models that can help you understand the nature of communication in general and the ways in which audiences have been found to react to particular communication techniques. The main models that will be discussed are the following: (1) a general model of communication based on the "Category Theory," (2) a multistage interactive communications flow model, (3) classical conditioning and reinforcement learning models, and (4) the cognitive dissonance model.

## A GENERAL MODEL OF COMMUNICATION

Based on the work of a number of investigators, a more or less generalized communication model is rather widely discussed in marketing literature. We will consider a version of that model that has two highly important aspects. First, it emphasizes the fact that the target audience is a part of the communication process. This means that the audience actually has a hand in shaping the total communication. Second, the model divides the communication process into separate activities, which makes it easier for you to consider the variety of alternative communication tools that are available. We will begin with a review of the background and reasoning behind this model. Then we can discuss ways in which it can assist you in framing your promotional strategy.

*"Bullets" versus Categories*

At one time, communication was widely considered to work somewhat like a bullet. As a communication expert has said, "The audience was typically thought of as a sitting target; if the communicator could hit it, he would affect it."[1] However, as researchers began undertaking intensive studies of audience reactions to communications, they discovered that the "bullet" theory simply was not accurate. Precisely the same message could mean quite different things depending on who was receiving it.

One example of such a study involves the television program "All in the Family." The leading male character on the show was Archie Bunker whose behavior was intended to communicate the foolishness of being narrow-minded and prejudiced. He was pictured as being crude, shallow, and oafish. Is this the message the audience perceived? Well, that all depends. Many viewers saw Archie for what he was intended to be. However, others saw him as being logical, sensible, and even something of a hero. In short, the meaning communicated by Archie Bunker depended in large measure on the frame of reference of each particular audience member. Put in more general terms, the total message depended as much on the way the audience processed it as upon the way the program's creators constructed it.[2]

Studies like this have led most communications theorists to discard the "bullet" theory. It has been replaced by the *category theory*. The premise underlying this revised view is that different categories of people can receive, decode, interpret, and respond to your message in quite diverse ways.

> [As audience responses to communications were studied] it became quickly apparent that most college-educated people had different tastes from those of elementary school graduates, young people from old, males from females, city people from rural people, rich from poor, and so forth. As the [category] theory became more subtle, it was found that people who held different clusters of attitudes or beliefs would choose differently and react differently from those who held different clusters. As the theory was examined still more carefully, it became apparent that the groups people belong to had something to do with their communication habits, and these memberships led them to choose and react to messages in such a way as to defend the common norms of the groups they value. [3]

As a result of such findings, many experts agree "that it is now necessary to think of the communication process as two separate acts, one performed by a communicator and one by the receiver, rather than as a magic bullet shot by one into the other."[4]

***The Model and Its Two Major Sections***

The general model of communication we will follow is diagrammed in Figure 9.1. To emphasize the category theory approach, the model is divided into two major sections. The upper portion—or sender section—deals with message preparation and transmission by the communicator. The lower portion—or receiver section—deals with message processing by each audience member. Our chief interest is in what you, as a sender, should know about proper handling of components in the sender section in order to induce a positive response by your target audience members as they process your message in the setting depicted in the receiver section.

***Components of the Model***

There are eleven components of our communication model that require discussion. These are as follows:

1. Intended promotional message
2. Perceived promotional message
3. Communicator (or source)
4. Encoding symbols
5. Communication medium
6. Potential noise
7. Reception
8. Decoding
9. Interpretation
10. Response
11. Feedback

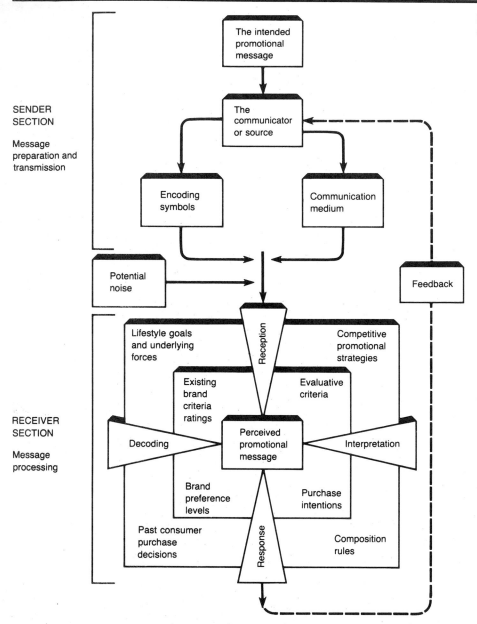

FIGURE 9.1 A general
communication model .

**SENDER
SECTION**

Message
preparation and
transmission

The intended
promotional
message

The
communicator
or source

Encoding
symbols

Communication
medium

Potential
noise

Feedback

Reception

**RECEIVER
SECTION**

Message
processing

Lifestyle goals
and underlying
forces

Competitive
promotional
strategies

Existing
brand
criteria
ratings

Evaluative
criteria

Decoding

Perceived
promotional
message

Interpretation

Brand
preference
levels

Purchase
intentions

Past consumer
purchase
decisions

Composition
rules

Response

*Source:* Adapted from a format proposed in William P. Dommermuth and Neil Richardson, "Corrective Advertising: A
Descriptive Model to Explore Relationships between Its Intended, Actual and Measured Effects," in John H. Summey
and Ronald D. Taylor, ed., *Evolving Marketing Thought for 1980* (Carbondale, IL.: Southern Marketing Association,
1980), p. 389.

We will begin with a brief description of the eleven components. Then more extensive discussion will be given to ways in which you can handle the components under your immediate control, those in the sender section.

**The Message—Intended and Perceived.** Notice that the term "promotional message" appears at two different points in Figure 9.1 and is qualified by two different modifiers. The *intended* promotional message is shown at the very top of the sender section of the model. The *perceived* promotional message is shown at the center of the receiver section. This double listing emphasizes the idea that the communication process is two separate acts, one performed by the communicator and one by the receiver. In other words, the message you intend to send and the message as processed by the receiver could turn out to be two quite different things. You do not want this to happen. A major aim of the general communication model is to provide you with a checklist and some guidelines to help ensure that it does not.

**The Communicator, the Encoding Symbols, and the Communication Medium.** Once you have decided what you want to say—your intended promotional message—there are three main areas of decision making you must consider.

1. Choosing the communicator or source—the person or organization that will be identified by the audience as originating and/or delivering the message.
2. Choosing the encoding symbols—the words, pictures, gestures, and other symbols you will use to transmit your intended message.
3. Choosing the communication medium—the vehicle you will use to transmit the message to the audience. For example, in the case of personal selling, the communication medium is the sales representative. In the case of advertising, the communication medium is usually some mass communication channel such as a newspaper or television program.

**Potential Noise.** As your message travels to your intended receiver, it may encounter obstacles that interfere with the receiver's message processing. Such forms of interference are commonly called "noise." Noise is any factor which impedes or distorts message processing. It includes such things as competing messages or situations in the receiver's environment that hamper clear reception. These might be called "external noise." Noise can also be built into the message itself. For example, some parts of your total message might actually distract your receiver and take away from or even obliterate the main message you are trying to deliver. When this happens, it can be described as "internal noise." Generally speaking, noise is something you want to eliminate, reduce, or overcome. Illustrations of how you can deal with noise will come up again in our more extended discussion of the sender section of the communication model.

*Reception, Decoding, Interpretation, and Response.* These are the major components of the receiver section. They form an outline of the way in which audience members process communications. You might want to think of them as the mechanics by which the audience decides what to do with your promotional message. It is important that you understand as much about these components as possible because such understanding will help you make more judicious decisions about the components you can control—those in the sender section.

Notice in Figure 9.1 that the four major receiver components are embedded in a field of preexisting conditions such as lifestyle goals and beliefs about evaluative criteria. Taken together, these conditions represent all of the points discussed in the previous four chapters. In Figure 9.1, they are simply represented as a field of forces which help determine if and how your message reaches the receiver. They are there to remind you that you are not simply communicating *to* an audience; you are communicating *with* an audience.

*Reception.* Before your prospect can process your message, he or she must receive it. There are two underlying requirements for *reception*. The first is *exposure*. To achieve exposure, your message must be "placed" or delivered in such a way that your prospect sees or hears it. The second requirement has to do with *attention*. Once exposed, your prospect must pay heed to the message.

Insofar as attainment of exposure is concerned, the critical aspect of strategy centers around the communication medium. For instance, you can initiate exposure by running a commercial on a television show or by sending a sales representative to call on a prospect. Exact techniques for getting message exposure to your target consumers depend on the specific promotional element involved. In the case of advertising, exposure strategy is largely connected with the media planning process. In the case of personal selling, exposure strategy is often closely related to a procedure called "prospecting." Because such techniques vary by promotional element, discussion of them will be deferred until later chapters in which we deal with each element of explicit promotion on an individual basis.

Mere exposure of your message does not guarantee that it will be received in any meaningful sense. After exposure, your prospect must focus attention on the message before genuine reception can occur. This does not happen automatically. For example, according to one estimate, fewer than thirty percent of the people who are exposed to a typical television commercial actually pay attention to the message being transmitted.[5] There are some rather widely accepted techniques you can employ to achieve attention. These and some of the problems connected with them will be explored in the discussion of encoding symbols (see p. 268).

*Decoding.* After receiving your message, your prospect must decode it. This means that he or she must determine the meaning of the words, pictures, and other symbols you are using. At first glance, there would seem to be no great challenge in choosing symbols that can be readily and accurately understood by your audience. In practice, however, your message can encounter some serious problems at this point. The basic cause of such problems is that the same words, pictures, and other symbols may mean different things to different people.

To give an extreme example, if you send your message in Latin, most Americans will not be able to decode it because they do not understand the symbol system. It may mean something to some people, but means nothing to most. Admittedly, no promotional strategist is very likely to transmit in a language that is completely foreign to the audience. However, even when the receiver and sender share a common language, words can convey quite inconsistent images. The same is true of pictures or any other type of symbol being used. The "All in the Family" example is just one illustration of how people who share the same language and even the same general cultural background can decode the same set of words and pictures and arrive at quite different understandings of what they have heard and seen.

With this in mind, it is important that you anticipate the kind of decoding process your receiver will use. Then you have to choose symbols that will produce the sort of understanding that you desire. Techniques for doing this will also be explored in our discussion of encoding symbols (see p. 274).

*Interpretation.*    Once a person has received and decoded your message, she or he will interpret it to see whether it has any potential value for her or his lifestyle situation. If the answer is "No," there is little reason for your prospect even to consider taking the kind of action you are recommending. In other words, your message may be received and understood but still achieve nothing in terms of improved brand preference level or purchase intention.

Of course, sometimes the value in the message may jump right out at the prospect. Suppose you are dealing with a customer who places extremely high importance on gas mileage as an evaluative criterion in automobiles. The make of car you are promoting delivers ninety-five miles to the gallon. Once you achieve good reception and decoding of your message, a favorable interpretation may occur immediately. However, many and perhaps most promotional benefits are not self-evident to receivers. Your brand's differential advantage over the competition may be slight, or your prospect may be unclear as to just how its value fits into his or her life. Furthermore, when you are attempting to change someone's buying habits you may run into active resistance. In the interpretation phase, your receiver may "fight the message." One observer has noted, "As for the receiver, he comes with his defenses up (to the extent, at least, that he perceives the persuader as manipulative). He is prepared to be skeptical. He has faced persuasion before. He asks, 'What is there for me in this message?' He comes with a set of needs he wants to satisfy, and a set of beliefs and attitudes, some relatively flexible but many of which he is prepared to defend stubbornly."[6]

We will later consider ways to ensure that your message demonstrates clear value to your prospect and that it is designed with a view to overriding potential resistance (see p. 278).

*Response.* The term "response" refers to the total effect that your message has on a receiver. It is the change in attitude brought about by the perceived message. Depending on if and how your intended message was received, decoded, and interpreted, response might range anywhere from total disinterest or rejection of everything you have communicated to a strong desire to purchase your brand as quickly as possible to an actual, immediate purchase.

*Feedback.* "Feedback" refers to measurement by the sender of the type of receiver processing that the communication has engendered. This might be measurement in terms of response. For instance, if your prospect buys your product, you have a gross measure of feedback. Your intended message has achieved its purpose. However, in many cases, the response might not be an immediate sale, but merely an improved preference level for your brand which paves the way for a future sale. Measurement of this second type of response would also provide you with feedback.

Furthermore, because our model treats receiver processing as a sequence of activities—reception, decoding, and interpretation, as well as response—there are other types of feedback for which you should be alert, in addition to response. For example, in trying to determine how your message is getting through, you should also be trying to secure answers to such questions as the following. Is the receiver paying enough attention to my message to ensure *reception*? Does she or he understand the symbols I am using sufficiently well so that I am getting proper *decoding*? Is my message being favorably *interpreted* in relationship to what this customer wants in the way of benefits?

In short, feedback concerning all four major components in the receiver section of the communication process can be of value to you because it can help you plan, adjust, and refine your handling of components in the sender section. In the case of personal selling, your opportunity to obtain feedback is immediate and direct, though this does not necessarily mean it is easy to achieve. In mass communication efforts such as advertising, analysis of feedback often requires special research efforts.

# THE SENDER SECTION

Again, the components in the sender section of the communication model are those over which you have direct control. We will assume you have determined what you want to say in your intended message and that you are now faced with decisions concerning the communicator, the encoding symbols, and the communication medium.

*The Communicator or Source*

There are usually at least two message sources involved in promotional communications. The first is the *message sponsor,* which is typically the business firm marketing the brand. The second is the *message presenter,* such as a sales representative or a television personality. Hence, you generally must consider a dual source effect. The major characteristics that have been found to influence audience reaction to either type of source—message sponsor or message presenter—include credibility, attractiveness, and power.[7] We will consider what each of these characteristics involves and how you can use them to improve your communication strategies by capitalizing on positive source effects.

***Source Credibility.*** Credibility is the degree to which your receiver senses that the message source is believable. Not surprisingly, message senders who are regarded as highly credible are generally thought to be more effective in creating a favorable reaction, though there may be exceptions to this rule as it applies in certain advertising situations (see Chapter 14). Credibility itself seems to depend largely on two factors. The first is the perceived *expertise* of the source. The second is the perceived *trustworthiness* of the source.

In part, and especially as they apply in personal selling situations, both factors may relate to a communicator's appearance and personality. Some people just naturally seem to impress others as having great expertise and as being trustworthy. More often, however, a reputation for expertise and trustworthiness is the result of direct and conscious efforts made by promotional strategists. Successful companies put great effort into training their salespeople to be experts and keeping them up-to-date on important developments in their field. Very often companies also reinforce the sales staff with a home-office staff of experts who can assist in answering customers' questions and solving their problems.

In advertising, it is common to see messages presented by sources who were chosen as spokespersons because they are either widely recognized as experts, considered as highly trustworthy, or both. Celebrity testimonial ads are often based on this premise. For example, in the early 1980s when Firestone wanted to refurbish its image, which had been damaged by some extremely bad publicity, it turned to Jimmy Stewart. Through a long career in motion pictures, Stewart had come to be thought of as a decent, trustworthy, and therefore credible source. The television campaign in which he appeared for Firestone was built around the company's early history in pioneering the development of quality products. It was aimed at producing a strong and positive dual source effect. Stewart, as message presenter, reflected credibility through trust. Firestone, the message sponsor, was portrayed in terms of its historical technical achievements to strengthen credibility in terms of both trust and expertise.

***Source Attractiveness.*** Attractiveness refers to a receiver's desire to identify with the message sender. The degree of attractiveness that a source will have for any particular audience is thought to derive largely from one or more of three factors—similarity, aspired similarity, and familiarity. This means that, if possible, you should choose as your message presenter, someone who is:

1. Very much like your prospect in important and easily observable respects, for example age, lifestyle interests, social class
2. The kind of person your prospect aspires to be, for example a skilled athlete or an admired wife and mother
3. Well known to your prospect through past association

The characteristic of attractiveness and the underlying bases of attractiveness will surface at various points in our consideration of personal selling (Chapters 10–12). For example, attractiveness is one of the qualities often considered in the selection of new salespeople. Attractiveness is also a consideration when choosing a message presenter to represent you in advertisements. For instance, commercials directed at housewives frequently take great pains to portray a lead character who is very much like the women with whom she is communicating. Celebrity commercials illustrate another application of the attractiveness principle. When matched with the right audience segment, the celebrity may possess both aspired similarity and convey a sense of familiarity.

*Source Power.*   Power implies that the message sender is seen as having the ability to punish or reward the message receiver. Rather little has been written about this in the literature on promotion, perhaps because the idea is not as widely applicable in situations involving promotional communications as in certain other communication settings. As a case in point, in a work environment a supervisor clearly has some power over the employees whom she or he directs. On this basis, the supervisor's message should carry extra weight, which makes a positive response more likely.

Could a sales representative or an advertising personality hold a similar kind of power? Well, perhaps not to the same degree. The capacity of these individuals to control punishments and rewards would seem to be more limited and of a different sort altogether. However, this does not mean that the presenter of a promotional message is never seen as having any power. Especially in face-to-face situations such as personal selling, the sales rep may command a certain degree of social control. Under certain conditions a customer may feel the need for approval and the salesperson may be in a position either to reward the receiver by giving such approval or punish the receiver by withholding it.

In mass communications such as advertising or publicity, strengthening the message presenter's appeal through a sense of power is more difficult because no person-to-person contact is involved. Therefore, it is less likely that your customer will think of your spokesperson as being able to reward or punish directly, even in a strictly social sense. However, when we look at a learning model, later in this chapter, we shall see that audience members sometimes seem to be drawn into mass communication settings in a highly personal or vicarious way (see page 291). If your receiver is, in fact, drawn into the communication and identifies with one of the characters in the advertisement, and your spokesperson in the ad is able to punish or reward that character, you may instill somewhat of a "transferred source power effect." On this basis, a sense of potential punishment or reward might be associated with your spokesperson even though that spokesperson has no direct contact with the receiver.

**Choosing Encoding Symbols**   Encoding is the manner in which you put your intended message into symbolic form—mainly words and pictures. Your approach to this is best guided by considering how your receiver will process those symbols. We previously identified the three initial processing steps as reception, decoding, and interpretation. Each of these steps suggests specific guidelines you should consider when encoding your message. For this reason, encoding guidelines will be discussed as (1) techniques of securing attention to improve reception, (2) techniques to achieve clear understanding by your receiver to ensure proper decoding, and (3) techniques of increasing the likelihood of strong, positive interpretation by your receiver.

## Techniques of Securing Attention

A stimulus is something that incites action. Once your message is exposed to a prospect, you want to initiate the action by capturing and retaining that person's attention. Therefore, you are looking for an effective opening stimulus.

In the strict sense, obtaining a prospect's attention means he or she tunes out or ignores all competing stimuli and concentrates totally on what you are communicating. You may not be able to secure attention in such a strict or absolute sense. However, you would like to come as close to doing this as you can. Remember, you are trying to secure attention in an atmosphere where there is generally a great deal of external noise—competing stimuli that threaten to draw attention away from you. There are two main ways to overcome such external noise and secure attention. The first relies on the physical impact of the stimulus. The second relies on the reward attraction of the stimulus.

**Attention Through Physical Impact of the Stimulus.** All *techniques that use physical impact* are based on a stimulus that is somehow different from surrounding stimuli. Because the stimulus is different, it tends to "reach out" and attract the receiver. Viewed the other way around, this approach often involves techniques that make it hard for a receiver *not* to give you attention. Four of the most frequently used physical impact techniques are intensity, novelty, contrast, and motion. (See Figure 9.2.)

**1.** *Intensity* is achieved by stimuli that physically dominate surrounding stimuli. They may be bigger, louder, brighter, more colorful, and so on. In any case, they strike the receiver's senses with greater force. Some examples are a full color advertisement as opposed to a black and white advertisement, a package which is larger than neighboring packages on the same shelf or that uses bolder colors and designs, and a sales representative with an especially strong, deep, and resonant voice.

**2.** *Novelty* results from using stimuli that are highly unusual. They attract attention by arousing curiosity. Some examples include an advertisement which is printed upside down or that features a rarely used type of artwork or color combination, a package design that is out of keeping with the typical design used in the product category (such as a powdered laundry detergent packaged in a bottle rather than a box or in a round box rather than a rectangular box), and a sales representative who dresses in an unusual fashion or makes use of an imaginatively different sales technique.

**3.** *Contrast* is being different from surrounding stimuli without necessarily being intense or highly unusual. To employ contrast, a promotional strategist must examine the surrounding environment and search for approaches that are

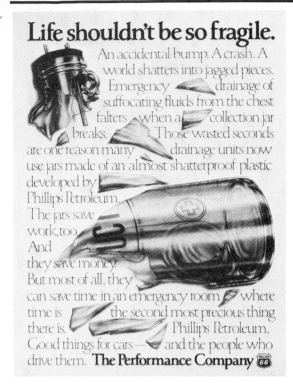

Life shouldn't be so fragile.

An accidental bump. A crash. A world shatters into jagged pieces. Emergency drainage of suffocating fluids from the chest falters when a collection jar breaks. Those wasted seconds are one reason many drainage units now use jars made of an almost shatterproof plastic developed by Phillips Petroleum. The jars save work, too. And they save money. But most of all, they can save time in an emergency room where time is the second most precious thing there is. Phillips Petroleum. Good things for cars — and the people who drive them. **The Performance Company**

Courtesy of Phillips Petroleum Company.

**FIGURE 9.2 Achieving attention through physical impact**

*This advertisement for Phillips Petroleum combines intensity (large type for body copy), contrast (unusual layout style), and motion (the shattering jar).*

not being widely used by competitors. Stimulus techniques using contrast can achieve their purpose in a more subtle manner than those using intensity or novelty. They win attention by calling for comparison. Some examples are a black and white advertisement in a publication featuring mainly four color ads, a package that is printed in much more quiet colors than its neighboring competitors on the shelf, and a sales representative who deliberately keeps the presentation restrained and almost understatedly calm because she or he knows that most rival sales personnel tend to rely on dramatic, forceful presentations.

**4.** *Motion* tends to attract attention because basic instinct tells people to be alert for movement in the environment. Movement can suggest an impending occurrence that may call for a quick response. As a promotional strategist, you can capitalize on this instinctive response tendency by deliberately building or increasing the amount of physical movement in your message pattern. Some examples include television commercials designed with heavy emphasis on activity and movement, such as body and hand gestures of the characters portrayed, changes in camera angles, and imaginative ways of putting action into the display of trade names and slogans; moving signs and displays in stores where the product is sold; and a personal sales presentation in which the

*Models to Guide Communications*

sales representative makes deliberate and planned use of hand and body actions to hold sustained attention for various selling points. Alternatively, he or she may use simple sales aids such as pointers or chalk boards that help inject more motion possibilities into the presentation.

***Some Comments on Physical Impact Stimuli.***   Each of the physical impact mechanisms for securing attention can be useful, and each is worth considering as a means of ensuring better reception from your receiver. All of them can enhance your effort to break through excessive external noise. However, they are not always unmixed blessings. Sometimes they relate directly to the basic message you want to convey. Sometimes they do not. When they do not, they may spawn a type of noise of their own—internal noise—which draws attention to the physical stimulus but distracts from the essential communication you wish to transmit. These techniques must therefore be used with caution. Some rules of thumb that govern the use of such stimuli are as follows:

1. If possible, choose a physical impact stimulus that blends in or fits with the rest of your total promotional strategy. For example, a powdered laundry detergent packaged in a bottle might get attention, but also might confuse customers unless you can relate that packaging to the rest of the benefits you offer. If you are trying to say that your brand gives customers the advantages of both powdered and liquid detergents, the unusual packaging could not only get more attention, but also help you make your basic selling point. However, it must be part of a total communication that explains the relationship between the packaging and the benefits.
2. When the stimulus is "artificial"—drawn into the situation even though it has little or no relationship to your basic selling message—use it with care. Consider not only its attention-getting power but also its total effect, especially the degree to which it might create internal noise.
3. When you have doubts about the total effect that will be created by such a stimulus, try to test the technique on a representative group of target prospects. Then study the feedback to see what the stimulus is doing both *for* your message and *to* your message.

***Attention Through Reward Attraction of the Stimulus.***   Physical impact techniques almost force themselves on the receiver, who can hardly avoid them. In contrast, techniques that attract attention by offering a reward cause the receiver to expend effort and willingly give you the attention your message needs.

*Reward techniques* initiate an attention-arousal process by featuring something of interest to the receiver. For example, if someone told you she could show you how to become a millionaire in sixty days, would you pay attention to her? It is quite likely that you would and, furthermore, she would not really need potentially distracting devices such as intensity or contrast to capture that attention. There are two general types of reward techniques used as attention-

**THESE OLD POSTCARDS CAN HELP YOU NAME ONE OF THE LARGEST LIFE INSURANCE COMPANIES IN AMERICA.**

Lincoln. It's a name you remember.

We're Lincoln National Life. For 75 years now, we've been meeting Americans' insurance needs. That makes us one of America's most experienced life insurance companies.

In fact, today, we're among the top 1% of the more than 1,800 life insurance companies in this country.

And, we have nearly 4,000 agents who make us easy to remember—by preparing life, disability income, group, and retirement programs just right for you, your family, your business and your future.

Lincoln National Life. For millions of Americans who buy insurance, we're the name that's easy to remember.

*The Lincoln National Life Insurance Company, Fort Wayne, Indiana.*

*A member of Lincoln National Corporation.*

**LINCOLN NATIONAL LIFE**
**WE'RE EASY TO REMEMBER.**

Courtesy of Lincoln National Corporation.

**FIGURE 9.3 Securing attention through a borrowed reward**

*Lincoln National Life draws on a theme of historical interest to secure attention for both the name and the size of the company.*

getting stimuli, a "borrowed" reward technique and an "inherent" reward technique.

A variety of subjects may be of great interest to persons in your target audience but they may have little or nothing to do with the product you are selling. When you use one of them as an attention-getting mechanism, you are in a sense *"borrowing" a reward*. Pictures of babies or beautiful women are subjects often used as borrowed rewards. The effectiveness of this technique in securing attention is suggested not only by its frequent use, but also by experimental research evidence. For example, in one test an audience was shown advertisements that were similar in every respect except for the amount of clothing worn by the female model in the ad. The reported results were as follows: "A manipulation check demonstrated that three of the more intense versions [with the erotic illustration] had stimulated considerably higher activation than their milder counterparts."[8]

Your potential list of borrowed reward attractions is certainly not limited to babies and attractive models. (See Figure 9.3.) Depending on the nature of your audience you may wish to consider borrowing interest from such subjects as baseball, scuba diving, space travel, and many others. In any case, the underlying principle is that you reach out for something largely unrelated to your basic message in order to draw attention to that message.

As with the attention-getting techniques that involve physical impact, there is the risk of distracting the receiver from the intended message. In other words, borrowed rewards may help you pierce external noise only to create internal noise and distortion of their own. One writer who has made an intensive review of studies on message processing by receivers offered the following observation:

> [C]onsumers who only process an advertisement's sensory features (e.g., a waterfall, a pretty scene, or a well-dressed person), without processing the semantic information in the ad and relating it to what they know about the product category, presumably will not recall the claims presented when they attempt to make a choice. In that sense, advertisements can err in actually encouraging sensory rather than semantic processing by their very nature. [9]

If you locate a topic that has high, natural interest to your prospect and also relates clearly to your basic promotional story you have an *inherent reward*. You can use it to arouse your audience's attention by making it a prominent part of your message. Like a borrowed reward, an inherent reward will induce attention by drawing the receiver to the message rather than forcing the message on the receiver. Beyond this, it has an important additional advantage in that it will not create internal noise.

Because it is compatible with your basic selling presentation, an inherent reward will reinforce rather than confuse the meaning of the full communication. For this reason, it is likely to represent your best line of attack for securing attention. But first you must find strong attention-getting rewards that relate to your brand. There are many different ways in which you can go about searching for an inherent reward to use as an attention getter. These range from pure creative imagination to rather sophisticated consumer research studies. To illustrate the general idea of how you might look for an inherent reward, one specific type of search process will be described that has been used with success by a major advertising agency. It is called the "Benefit Chain."

The basic structure of a benefit chain is shown in Figure 9.4. The data for this analysis technique are based on responses from a sample of consumers. Each consumer begins by listing two functional benefits that he or she associates with a basic functional feature of the brand. For example, if the product is a laundry detergent and if the feature is a special disinfectant ingredient, the customer would begin by listing two functional benefits of that ingredient. Then, each consumer is asked to list two practical benefits he or she will receive from each of the two functional benefits. This process continues until a chain of benefits is depicted. At the end of the chain, the consumer is really listing "the emotional payoff" or inherent lifestyle reward produced by the basic functional product feature.[10]

Something like a benefit chain approach can enable you to discover an

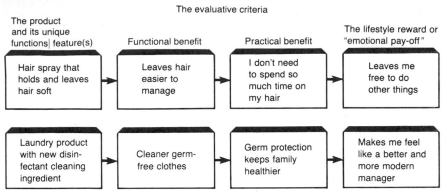

The evaluative criteria

The product and its unique functions| feature(s) | Functional benefit | Practical benefit | The lifestyle reward or "emotional pay-off"

Hair spray that holds and leaves hair soft → Leaves hair easier to manage → I don't need to spend so much time on my hair → Leaves me free to do other things

Laundry product with new disinfectant cleaning ingredient → Cleaner germ-free clothes → Germ protection keeps family healthier → Makes me feel like a better and more modern manager

**FIGURE 9.4 Finding inherent reward approaches through Benefit Chain\* analysis**

*Source:* Adapted from Shirley Young and Barbara Feigin, "Using the Benefit Chain for Improved Strategy Formulation," *Journal of Marketing*, July 1975, p. 73.
\*The Benefit Chain is a copyrighted technique created by Hal Lee, management consultant, New York City, © 1970, Hal Lee.

inherent reward which will not only serve as an attention getter but also help you define the complete structure of your promotional approach. Once you determine a relationship between your brand's functional features and final emotional payoffs of high and immediate interest to your receivers, you can aim at gaining attention by opening your communication with the lifestyle payoff. Exactly how you present that payoff depends on the specific element of promotion with which you are working. For example, in personal selling you would probably use it to start your approach. In advertising you would probably use it to build a headline or to open a television commercial.

*Mixtures of Attention-Getting Techniques.* In theory, your best route to capturing attention is the inherent reward approach. In practice, however, physical impact and borrowed reward methods are very commonly used. This suggests that many promotional strategists believe—on the basis of experience—that the power of these last two methods is often needed to penetrate the external noise barrier, especially in advertising situations. Of course, the various techniques are not mutually exclusive. They can be used together. For example, even when your message begins with a promise of inherent reward, you may wish to augment its power by coupling it with some physical impact and/or borrowed reward technique.

**Techniques to Ensure Proper Decoding**

*The Potential for Confusion of Symbolic Meaning.* Promotional messages must be transmitted by means of symbols—words, pictures, gestures, and so on. As noted earlier, symbols can present problems because the interpretation of their meanings can vary from person to person. For example, consider the word "gusto." "Gusto" is a symbol. It stands for something; but for exactly what does it stand? The question is more than hypothetical. In fact, it produced what has been described as a tragedy for a major American brewer and its advertising agency.[11]

The story as reported in the press goes this way. The company's agency created a very successful series of advertising campaigns for Schlitz beer. All the advertisements were built around the word "gusto." For example, one campaign featured the slogan "Reach for all the gusto you can get." Despite the apparent success of the campaigns, the company felt there might be trouble brewing along with the beer. As pointed out in our earlier discussion of culture, there can be changes in national values over time. During the 1970s, one such change in the American culture was the move toward "lightness." This brought about the introduction and promotion of such products as light cigarettes, light gravy, light corn chips, light margarine, and light beer. Schlitz became curious about what "gusto" might mean to customers who seemed so intrigued with "lightness."

In the mid 1970s the company conducted some research to discover the answer. The findings suggested that consumers decoded "gusto" as meaning "heavy tasting." In a market dominated by appeals to "lightness," Schlitz did not want to employ a key symbol that implied "heaviness." The agency also conducted some separate consumer research on the same topic. Its findings indicated that "gusto" was decoded by consumers as implying "a certain verve or zest." Because "verve" and "zest" seemed completely in line with the national "lightness mood," the agency wanted to continue featuring the word "gusto." Schlitz wanted to discontinue it.

"Gusto" was deleted from Schlitz advertising, and a completely revised campaign format was introduced. After some slippage in market share and some further research, it was decided that perhaps "gusto" had not been as negative as the first studies indicated. On the contrary, the third survey suggested that consumers thought of "gusto" as virtually meaning "Schlitz." A new campaign was instituted to reinstate the idea that "Schlitz has gusto." In line with what you just read about the need to secure attention, much effort was put into finding powerful borrowed interest and physical impact techniques to accomplish this objective. According to one published report, "The strategy of the commercials . . . was to be 'interruptive', meaning the commercials 'should be able to arrest your attention and cut through what all the other [beer advertisers] are saying.' It should say, 'Hey, I'm not just another beer commercial.'"[12]

The strategy was implemented by featuring ultra-macho Schlitz drinkers who threatened immediate physical destruction to anyone who "tried to take their gusto away." The new approach not only drew attention but also drew criticism as one of the "most disliked commercial campaigns in advertising history." Again according to the same report, "The campaign came to be regarded at the company as 'a great tragedy—really, really bad.'"[13]

So much for the tragedy. Now, what does "gusto" really mean and how can you go about ensuring that your audience decodes your meaning properly in a world where there is disagreement over the interpretation of such symbols? To answer this question we must consider the nature of symbolic interpretation.

**Denotations and Connotations.**    A *denotation* is the strict meaning of a word as you find it defined in a dictionary. Even at this level, many common words have a variety of meanings. For example, the word "soft" can mean "subdued," "deficient of hardness," "sentimental," "easy," or "weak." Not only can the denotation—or strict dictionary definition—actually turn out to be a variety of different definitions, but words can acquire secondary meanings that go beyond strict dictionary definitions. These secondary meanings are termed *connotations*. An example of the way connotations can be formed and the way they can affect the receiver's decoding process is given by the following piece of advice suggested for use in personal selling situations.

> Understanding may be blocked by the unwitting use of words and phrases that have emotional overtones for the other person. "Home made" might cause a favorable feeling or response in one person, because the expression elicits in him an image of apple pie baked by mother for Sunday dinner. For another person it might be a reminder of impoverished youth when the family could not afford "storebought" clothing. Another person might give the term a meaning of less than adequate or perfect. [14]

Now, what about the denotations and connotations of "gusto"? If you consult a standard dictionary you will probably find that the word "gusto" has two denotations. The first is "hardy or keen enjoyment." The second is "individual taste or liking." If you reexamine the Schlitz story you will see that neither of these exact dictionary meanings appeared in the research findings. What did appear were connotations—secondary meanings that have come to be associated with the word "gusto."

***Methods of Clarifying Symbolic Meanings.*** As demonstrated above, symbol systems are often somewhat vague and unstable as to precise meanings. Fortunately, there are some actions you can take to minimize the potential confusion that may be present in the symbols you are using.

1. *Analysis of Your Target Audience.* The meaning of a word—especially in the connotative sense—often depends on the receiver's background and past experiences. Put another way, the same word can conjure up different images for different people. The following example involving an advertising campaign that used the word "stroked" shows what kind of decoding variations you may get from different audience groups.

> The [Bic Razor] commercial shows a young man's wedding day. His sly uncle tells him to use Bic and be stroked in the morning. At the wedding, his bride-to-be announces that he got stroked that very morning and now will get stroked every morning. The groom looks embarrassed as well he might. . . . When this commercial was shown to samples of younger and older women, the meaning of the word "stroked" was decoded quite differently. . . . The young women found such suggestive insinuations embarrassing when others were present and offensive at all times. However, the older women saw nothing offensive in the Bic commercial and some thought it was quite cute. . . . When the connotation was explained to them, the older women would pause, look puzzled, furrow their brows, and then say, "ohhhhh . . . they couldn't mean . . ." [15]

In personal selling situations you can consider each prospect on an individual basis. You can think of what a word is likely to mean to the particular person to whom you are talking. You can also use techniques to encourage immediate feedback and learn what meaning is being put on the words and other symbols you are using.

When dealing with advertising, sales promotion, or publicity, you have to think in terms of a mass audience. You are unable to handle things on a person-to-person basis. However, you can start by attempting to define your target consumer group as carefully as possible. Then, based on that definition and perhaps some field research you can reason out, in advance, the possible variations in meaning which you may anticipate from different types of receivers. After you have done that, your next step is to choose words and other symbols on the basis of what they mean to the particular group of receivers at whom you are aiming.

2. *Setting Symbols in Context.* "Context" refers to how a particular word or other symbol interacts with the other symbols in the message. To show how this works, we will invent a new word—"grellec." If you know what this means *when you see it out of context* you know more than an English language dictionary can tell you. There is no such English word. However, once you see it in even very brief context it can begin to acquire meaning for you. "He adjusted the sleeve on his grellec." "One lone grellec was perched on a limb at the top of the tree." "The cook heated up some left-over grellec in a sauce pan."

Context—or perhaps the absence of it—could be the reason for the different meanings given to the word "gusto" in the Schlitz market studies. In the commercials themselves, "gusto" not only had its own basic meaning but also the meaning conveyed to it by the total context of the advertisement. For example, picture a setting in which a strong and handsome sea captain returns from an exciting voyage. Once on shore, he joins his crew in a happy gathering of adventurous and active men and reaches out for a bottle of Schlitz beer. Simultaneously, a voice advises you to "Reach for all the gusto you can get." The word "gusto" is now assuming a virtually unmistakable meaning. The context makes it almost impossible to decode it improperly.

The issue of context raises questions about the research which suggested that "gusto" meant "heavy tasting" to consumers. If respondents were asked to react to the word "gusto" without seeing it in the total commercial context it might not be surprising to discover they were giving it a different meaning than the commercial had conveyed. In essence, you could obtain misleading feedback about the decoding of the word because you were presenting it in a different context.

Consider still another example of how context can clarify the meaning of symbols. A range of possible meanings that could apply to the word "soft" was given earlier. In selling toilet tissue, softness tends to be the main evaluative criterion promoted. However, if you use the word "soft" or "softness" what will it imply to your prospects? One way to assure that it takes on the meaning you intend is to surround it with a reinforcing contextual setting.

You may recall from an earlier chapter that the Mr. Whipple campaign is credited with restoring Charmin sales to an upward growth pattern. A key element in the success of those ads was their use of context to clearly define and dramatize the meaning of "soft." The image sought for

Charmin is soft in the sense of gentle, comfortable, and a bit luxurious, which was attained by the use of the term "squeezably soft" and the context of a supermarket setting. The shoppers cannot keep themselves from squeezing the Charmin because its softness is so enjoyable. In one sense these commercials may be outlandish, but they accomplish their objective. They assure the proper decoding of the intended message with very little chance for misunderstanding. They dramatize the meaning of softness through unmistakable context.

3. *Multiple Symbolic Reinforcement.* The third technique for assuring proper decoding is to reiterate major message points with each repetition using a different but synonymous symbol. In essence, this amounts to using one symbol to define another so there can be no doubt about the meaning. The multiple symbols might consist of different words, as in "softness that is gentle and luxurious." Alternatively, you can use two different symbol forms such as words and pictures to reinforce and clarify each other. Laboratory experimentation has demonstrated that words paired with pictures can be much more effective than either used alone.[16] Like the meaning of words, the meaning of pictures is not necessarily constant. Different viewers can decode the same picture in different ways. However, words and pictures together can put each other into proper perspective so that there is little room for improper decoding of either.

You see a good example of how this can work in Figure 9.5. Each of the key words in this ad—"flat and fluffy"—has a variety of meanings in both denotative and connotative terms. Similarly, each of two dominant pictures could take on a variety of meanings. However, when the word symbols are combined with the picture symbols, it is almost impossible to misread the intended meaning.

## Techniques of Increasing Strong, Positive Interpretation

In promotion your purpose is to persuade. Securing attention and clear understanding is necessary to that purpose. However, your goal is not reached until your receiver is convinced your brand offers benefits that fit his or her needs and that will clearly fulfill a meaningful lifestyle goal. In other words, you need positive interpretation of your message which causes your prospect to say, "This sounds like something I should buy." Creating a communication that culminates in such interpretation requires an understanding of the factors we have been considering in past chapters, especially the lifestyle goals which cause people to place importance on particular evaluative criteria.

Techniques such as psychographics can help you discover the lifestyle goals on which you should concentrate. Once you discover them, you are left with questions concerning specific aspects of message structures you can use to dramatize the positive relationship between buying your brand and achieving lifestyle goals. Some of the main alternatives from which you can choose follow.

### Rational versus Emotional Appeals.
There is no absolutely firm or universally accepted line of demarcation that divides rational appeals from emotional appeals. In general, however, the difference can be stated as follows. *A rational*

FIGURE 9.5  An illustration of multiple symbol usage

In this advertisement, words and pictures are used to "cross-define" each other, so that the meaning becomes easy to decode correctly.

Courtesy of Procter & Gamble Company.

*appeal* is made to the prospect's *logic*. It tends to review specific brand benefits and possibly their relationships to lifestyle goals on a point-by-point basis. It provides strong "reasons why" for choosing your brand. Your receiver should be able to interpret your message on an "intelligent" basis. *An emotional appeal* is made to your prospect's *feelings*. It is often aimed at arousing a basic drive, such as fear, guilt, self-pride, or a desire to escape from the problems of reality.

You might expect that the choice between a rational versus an emotional appeal would depend to some extent on the type of product you are selling. Rational appeals would seem to be naturally suited to products that prospects study rather carefully before buying. Examples might be home appliances, automobiles, and heavy industrial equipment. On the other hand, when you are promoting low unit-value items, especially those bought for personal and immediate satisfaction, it might seem that emotional appeals would fit the situation better. Examples in this latter category include such things as lipstick, chewing gum, and cigarettes.

However, the relationship between type of product and type of appeal is often far from clear. For instance, consider the advertising of cigarettes. Some brands, such as Marlboro, use an appeal that seems largely if not entirely emotional. Little is said about the brand's distinct advantages. Instead, the advertisements seem to be aimed at emotions—association and identification with the "Marlboro Man" and the rugged imagery of the wide open spaces. However, other brands of cigarettes promote distinct features, such as low tar and nicotine content, and present a detailed and point-by-point sales argument that assumes the prospect wants to think things through on a logical basis.

Even in the industrial market, which is generally thought to be more "rational," emotional appeals can be used effectively. A group of industrial magazines did a survey on buying practices of industrial buyers and reported, "Fear is one of the major influences in industrial buying . . . . The buyer is afraid of displeasing his stockholders, his board of directors, his boss, or his associates. He doesn't want to lose face or look bad."[17] A finding such as this suggests that emotional appeals might be much more effective in industrial selling situations than most promotional strategists currently realize or admit.

The fact is that you can choose to use either a rational appeal or an emotional appeal with most any type of product. In the end, your choice is probably going to rest largely on how you evaluate your audience. Your critical question becomes, "Given the particular prospects with whom I'm working, should I stress hard facts and logic or should I use an emotional appeal to reach their 'feelings'?" Fortunately, you are usually not faced with an absolute either-or type of choice. Rational and emotional appeals are not mutually exclusive. They can be combined. In fact, many advertisements and sales presentations are built on a blend of the two types of appeals.

When you do include an emotional appeal in your message, you need to remember that emotional reactions can be complex and unpredictable. For this reason, emotional appeals can sometimes be self-destructive, especially if overdone. To illustrate a way of analyzing the potential effect of an emotional approach, we will look at one such type of appeal that has been heavily researched. This is the "fear appeal."

Some of the earliest experiments on the effects of fear appeals suggested that low-level fear messages brought about more positive responses than high-level fear messages. Later studies showed just the opposite.[18] Why the difference? One explanation advanced for these contradictory reports is the hypothesis that a fear appeal really produces two quite different kinds of reactions— "facilitating effects" and "inhibiting effects." The facilitating effect strengthens the response to your message because it arouses feelings that help "drive the message home." The inhibiting effect does the opposite. It causes audience members to resist or defend against your message because it is unpleasant to be confronted with fear. If you create too high a level of fear your audience may "tune you out" or deny the threat you are suggesting. Furthermore, if you are too successful in arousing a gravely severe fear, you may make it impossible for the receiver to believe that your product can really help overcome such a serious danger or threat.

Figure 9.6 illustrates how the two effects can work together but in opposite directions, at different levels of fear arousal. When you are considering the use of a fear appeal, the interactions suggested in this diagram can be useful in

FIGURE 9.6 Opposing
effects of fear appeals

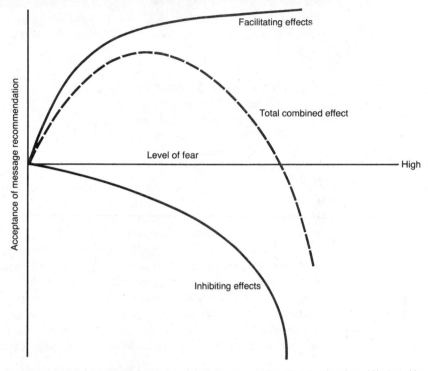

Source: Adapted from Michael L. Ray and William C. Wilkie. "Fear: The Potential of an Appeal Neglected by Marketing," *Journal of Marketing*, January 1970, pp. 54–62.

analyzing your situation. By thinking in terms of two separate effects you should be in a better position to consider or perhaps research the results you are likely to obtain from each type of effect. Your optimum goal would be a message built in such a way as to achieve maximum facilitation with minimum inhibition. Above all, you want to avoid raising the level of inhibition to the point at which your prospect no longer believes your product could possibly solve the problem you are raising.

***Implied versus Explicit Conclusions.*** In any communication there are likely to be things you say and things you leave unsaid. In working with promotional messages, this raises a question as to whether your message should contain a "conclusion." In other words, should you clearly tell the receiver how the message should be interpreted and what he or she is supposed to do about it? Your alternative is to omit the conclusion on the theory that audience members would prefer to make their own interpretations and decisions.

As with fear appeals, research on conclusion drawing has produced mixed results. In an early and often-quoted study it was found that clearly stating the conclusions produced much more effective persuasive results than leaving conclusions to the imagination of the audience.[19] However, this view has been challenged on various grounds. For example, one writer suggests that conclusion drawing may have a boomerang effect among some prospects.[20] Especially if they feel the drawing of a conclusion is an attempt to limit their freedom of choice, many people may "turn off" and actively resist what you are saying.[21]

***Two-sided versus One-sided Presentations.***   In a one-sided message, you speak only about those points on which your brand is superior. You admit to no weakness. In a two-sided message, you deal with both the strong points and the weak points of your brand. Which is the better technique? Again, you will find mixed opinions.

Early studies seemed to suggest that two-sided messages were preferable.[22] Thus, if your brand is inferior in some ways to competitive offerings, you would be well advised to come right out and admit it. Of course, you would also want to follow that admission quickly with an explanation of why those defects are not important, or perhaps why they are far outweighed by the superior benefits you offer in other respects. If you will think back to the discussion of composition rules in Chapter 6, you will see that this would amount to an all-out linear compensatory approach.

Although the two-sided approach frequently occurs in personal selling, it is something you rarely see in advertising. The results of at least one study suggest that, possibly, more two-sided approaches should be used in advertising. Part of the report on the findings runs as follows:

> [The experiment] compared the effectiveness of one-sided and two-sided radio commercials for three different kinds of consumer products: floorwax, gas (for cooking), and automobiles. . . . The two-sided commercial was more effective in changing attitudes in all three cases . . . and was particularly effective under these conditions:
>
> 1. Two-sided commercials are more effective with more intelligent consumers.
> 2. Two-sided commercials are more effective with users of competitive products.
> 3. Products of greater psychological value benefit more from two-sided commercials than products of lesser value. (I.e., the more a consumer has to lose, if he makes a mistake, the greater the appeal of two-sided arguments.)
> 4. Two-sided commercials are more resistant to counterclaims. Six weeks following the experiment it was found that those exposed to two-sided arguments maintain the attitude change that took place following the commercials to a greater degree than those exposed to the one-sided commercials. [23]

Two major reasons have been advanced to support the greater success potential of two-sided appeals as observed in the above experiment. First, they increase the credibility of the message sender. Second, they tend to reduce resistance or "counter-argumentation" by message receivers.[24]

***Order of Presentation of the Major Points of Your Message.***   When you are preparing a personal sales message or writing a piece of advertising, some of the things you have to say may involve evaluative criteria that are extremely important to your prospects. Others may deal with somewhat lower-weighted criteria. Moreover, your brand may have a significant and easily demonstrated advantage on some criteria. On others, you may have a very trivial advantage, a doubtful advantage, no advantage at all, or even a slight disadvantage. Assuming you have a number of such mixed things to say, in what order should you arrange your presentation?

Once more the investigation of this question has produced mixed results.[25] After reviewing the evidence one group of writers concluded that, despite inconsistencies among published studies, some logical guidelines exist for promotional strategy:

> First, the initial presentation of the strongest argument may have a stronger effect on attention, attraction and receptiveness to subsequent arguments. Moreover, material presented first is usually best learned. On the other hand presentation of successively weaker arguments may tend to diminish the over-all persuasive effect of the message. Therefore, saving the strongest arguments for last may boost reception when it is most needed. [26]

The general recommendation that emanates from this view is that the most critical elements of your message, such as brand name and key selling points, should be presented early in the message and quite probably repeated near the end, because these are the two points at which the most learning takes place.[27]

## A MULTISTAGE INTERACTIVE COMMUNICATIONS FLOW MODEL

Up to this point we have been considering communication merely in terms of the relationships between a sender and an individual receiver. In practice, however, a communication transmitted to one receiver may also have indirect effects on other persons who obtain information about the message from the initial receiver. In other words, the communication process can also be viewed in terms of its more extended effects through social interaction. This is especially applicable in the case of communications sent via mass media such as advertising or publicity. The emergence of models pertaining to this second aspect of communication effects has paralleled the evolution of the category theory out of the older bullet theory. In the present case, a sequence of three models has emerged, with each model more or less supplanting its predecessor. In the order of their emergence these three models can be designated as follows: the one-step flow model, the two-step flow model, and the multistage interactive model. Even though the last named approach represents the latest and most advanced thought on the situation, there is merit in looking briefly at its two predecessors in order to better appreciate the possible intricacies of extended communication flows.

*The One-Step Flow Model*

The mass media such as radio, television, and magazines were once thought to influence people directly and only directly. The upper portion of Figure 9.7 shows how this would look in graphic form. The communication is initiated by the mass medium. Each person in the audience receives, decodes, and interprets the message on an individual and independent basis. Presumably, he

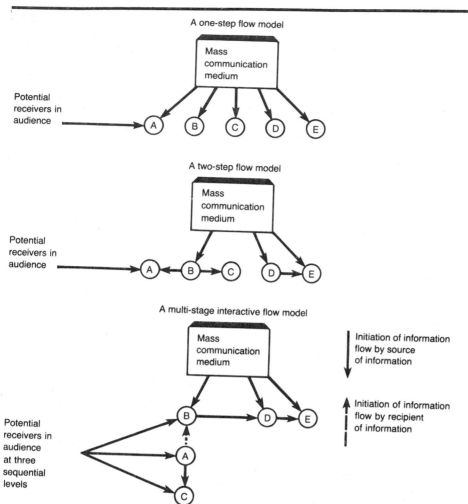

FIGURE 9.7 The evolution of models dealing with the effects of mass communications on groups of receivers

or she then responds to the message on an individual basis, and if successfully persuaded, that individual accepts and follows the opinion espoused via the mass communication effort.

**The Two-Step Flow Model**

Research undertaken some years ago began to cast doubt on the direct–flow idea. A number of communication studies suggested that the mass media often operate on a two-step basis. A simple illustration of how that two–step flow might look is shown in the middle section of Figure 9.7. In this case, it is assumed that only three of the five people involved actually received the message from the mass media. One of them, B, initiated a further personal communication that passed the information on to two additional people, A and C, who were not exposed to the original mass medium message. D and E, the two remaining individuals, were both receivers of the original message.

However, at a later point in time, D initiated conversation that influenced E's interpretation of and response to that message.

The basic concept of the two-step flow model has been summarized as follows: "Individual decisions are influenced less often by direct exposure to mass media than by the opinions of other people. [Those other people who influence decisions] are more likely to be exposed to relevant mass media, than are the people whom they influence."[28] By inference, while the mass media can be powerful carriers of information, their power often works in conjunction with more personalized information flows initiated by influential audience members such as those represented by B and D in our illustration. These people are termed "opinion leaders."

## The Multistage Interactive Flow Model

The two-step model served as the foundation for still further study of communication effects, which revealed that opinion leaders are not necessarily forceful initiators of communications. Rather, in many instances their opinions are responses to queries initiated by the people with whom they communicate.[29] Furthermore, there is no absolute dichotomy that distinguishes individuals who communicate opinions to others from those who receive information from others. Opinion leaders may also be opinion seekers. In fact, one survey found that the majority of receivers were also communicators and the majority of communicators were also receivers.[30] Still other investigation has suggested that the length of interpersonal communication flows may stretch through three or more levels rather than merely two.[31]

Such analysis of communication flows has led to the view that communications initiated by promotional efforts can move through the target audience in a more complex fashion than was once assumed. The intricacy of the resulting multistage interactive model makes it much less adaptable to illustration by the relatively simple type of diagrams we used for the one-step and two-step models. A sampling of representative multistage interactive communications is depicted in the lower portion of Figure 9.7. Although it hardly captures the full complexity of the model, it does convey a sense of the model's implications. As shown there, audience members B, D, and E are the only persons who received the information directly from some mass communications medium, just as in our example of the two-step flow. However, from this point on the situation is less simple. Individual B functions as both a passive opinion leader whose advice is sought by A, and as an active opinion leader who initiates advice to D. Meanwhile person A, who was never exposed to the original promotional message, is nonetheless both influenced by it because of the advice sought from B and serves as an opinion leader because of the advice that A gives to C, forming a three-stage sequence.

It is helpful to recognize the overall interactive configuration of the second-tier and third-tier information transfers that, as this last model suggests, can take place on an interpersonal basis after your message has made its primary impression through some nonpersonal vehicle such as a newspaper, magazine, or television program. Recognition of these potentially extended communication effects alerts you to the fact that the power of your promotional presentation may be magnified, distorted, or otherwise altered by an informal yet intricate interpersonal network that is not easily observed. In most instances it probably will not be feasible for you to attempt detailed study of that network. However, whenever you have reason to believe that such a communication flow is operating in your market, you will wish to consider the role that might be played by opinion leaders and the strategies you might adopt to make that role both positive and strong.

*Opinion Leadership*   If a multistep information flow is occurring in your market, opinion leaders are especially valuable people to reach. For instance, if you could run your advertising in vehicles most used by opinion leaders and design your messages to be especially appealing to them, you should be able to multiply the effect of your advertising dollars. This would happen because each opinion leader you convinced could play a pivotal role in continuing the information flow and reinforcing favorable response tendencies among your target consumer group. However, opinion leaders are hard to identify. A variety of studies have indicated four major points about the nature of opinion leadership.[32] First, it appears to be a widespread trait. Most people are opinion leaders for at least one or a few product categories. Second, opinion leadership is not especially related to social status. For example, it is not safe to assume that persons enjoying relatively higher social positions will be any more influential than those on a lower rung of the social hierarchy. Third, among any particular group of people, different individuals may serve as opinion leaders for different types of situations. In other words, just because someone is an opinion leader in one area does not mean that person can be regarded as a general opinion leader. Fourth, when you attempt to find out who is an opinion leader and who is not, you may have a difficult time of it. Opinion leadership is not always easy to spot. As one analyst has observed, "In the first place, consensus 'leadership' is of the casual everyday, face-to-face variety. It is usually so invisible and inconspicuous that it would be actually more accurate to call it, 'guidance'."[33]

***Opinion Leadership and Mass Communication Strategy.***   How can you use the concept of opinion leadership in building your promotional programs? One approach that is frequently suggested is to create a feeling of opinion leadership in your advertising. For instance, it is not uncommon to see television commercials built around the idea of one person giving advice to another person. Essentially such an ad is trying to create a "simulated opinion leader." Another suggested approach is the development of campaigns that are likely to be "talked about." Anything in an advertisement that can generate conversation among your prospects could be helpful in intensifying the multistep flow process.

***Opinion Leadership and Personal Selling.***   Although the multistage flow model was originally a mass communication concept, its use in promotional situations may be more applicable when face-to-face communication is involved. In other words, it might be easier to apply in personal selling than it is in advertising. Because salespeople work with customers on a one-to-one basis, they are in a much better position to determine which prospects are more likely to be opinion leaders. For instance, suppose a sales representative is calling on twenty different industrial accounts in a given city. With some study of the situation, she may learn that two or three of those accounts either give guidance to people in the other firms or are looked to as examples to follow. Once such a discovery has been made, the sales representative could devote a good deal of extra time and effort to the accounts that play leadership roles.

In the next chapter, an industrial sales representative will tell you that he does not try to sell to any customer by pointing out that a competitor has bought his firm's product. This is because he senses a degree of jealousy among customers in his market. Nevertheless, it could well be that, without the sales representative ever mentioning it, the fact that firm A is using his brand makes it much more likely that firms B, C, and D will be more interested in trying it because they have respect for the judgment of firm A. In other words, firm A may be acting as something akin to an opinion leader and therefore be worth special sales attention.

## LEARNING MODELS

Promotional messages educate people concerning products and services. From this point of view they can be regarded as learning experiences. This does not imply that a sales representative or an advertising copywriter should consciously attempt to play the role of teacher. The setting and the atmosphere in which promotion takes place is much different from the setting and the atmosphere in which most formal education takes place. However, the idea that exposure to a promotional message is a type of learning experience suggests that certain learning principles might be useful in working out your design for promotional strategy.

To survey some of the possibilities, we will first define two distinctly different types of learning. Then we will consider classical conditioning theory, which deals with a potential learning sequence often discussed in connection with certain types of promotion. Following that, a reinforcement model will be explored in terms of its promotional applications.

*Intentional Learning and Incidental Learning*

Two distinct and quite different types of learning have been identified as intentional learning and incidental learning.[34] *Intentional learning* involves the planned and deliberate acquisition of knowledge and skills. It tends to center around conscious study or practice. You know you are doing it. For example, when you are preparing for an examination, you are engaging in intentional learning. The same thing is true when you are obtaining training in something like automobile repair or playing soccer. Your learning process is called intentional because you are "set" or "intent" to learn. Your efforts are clearly directed toward a purpose, and you are an active and alert participant in the process.

*Incidental learning* is quite different. It involves learning that takes place without the express intention or planning of the individual. For instance, if you turn on a shower and are rewarded with a dose of painfully hot water, you have just "learned" something. From then on you will probably test a shower for temperature before standing under it. However, your learning experience was anything but intentional. It happened as a result of an unplanned *incidental* happening. Much of what people learn really occurs on this kind of incidental basis. For example, you learn appropriate ways of acting toward other people because when you behave in the right way you tend to receive a good response. For the most part, you learn those appropriate ways of behaving on an unplanned or incidental basis.

**The Two Learning Types in Promotional Situations: High-Involvement versus Low-Involvement Decision Making**

From the standpoint of promotional planning, the distinction between intentional and incidental learning suggests you should consider both the amount of interest people have in your product and the circumstances in which your message will be received. Then you should try to determine whether the total situation is more likely to involve intentional learning or incidental learning. One writer has made the point in the following way:

> Most advertising messages are presented to people who either are doing something or relaxing. Usually the television viewer is relaxing before the screen, the radio listener is doing something else, the outdoor poster viewer is getting to his destination, the magazine or newspaper reader is not primarily searching the advertisements. Thus, the audience members do not sense the advertisements with an intent to learn, [and therefore, they tend to learn on an "incidental" basis]. [35]

Therefore, a model of intentional learning apparently does not apply to advertising—or does it? In some cases, intentional learning does apply regardless of the specific medium in which an advertisement is placed. In other words, a person may watch television passively but suddenly begin to pay attention to a commercial for a certain product or service. This type of situation is likely to occur when the consumer is in the process of considering a purchase in a product category that she or he regards as being *"high involvement"* in nature. For example, someone planning to buy a new automobile or a home computer is likely to be concerned about making the best brand choice and therefore highly interested in deliberate acquisition of information.

When you believe your product and your selling situation put your prospect into a high-involvement, intentional learning mode, you will probably want to plan a promotional message based on an easy-to-follow set of facts. In other words, you want to make your presentation conducive to study. You can expect to hold your prospect's attention because he or she is "intent to learn." You are fitting your message to the purpose of the audience.

When your product and selling situation are *"low involvement,"* the learning that occurs may take place on an incidental basis. For example, consider commodities such as chewing gum, breakfast cereal, and shaving cream. Do people learn about them through deliberate and intentional study or do they learn about them largely through incidental experience? If you think the answer is through incidental experience, you may want to consider a learning approach based on a stimulus-response concept. Let's look at how this might be done.

*Classical*
*Conditioning*
*Theory*

When you hear the term "stimulus-response," you probably think of Ivan Pavlov. Using a technique known as "classical conditioning," Pavlov taught a dog to salivate at the sound of a tone. He began with food powder as the original stimulus, which when presented to the dog, caused a natural physiological response—salivation. Then by pairing the presentation of food powder with the sounding of a tone, Pavlov eventually taught the dog to salivate at the sound of the tone alone.

After a sufficient number of trials, the dog's mouth would water just at the sound—a conditioned stimulus—without the original, natural stimulus of food powder being present. The result is called a conditional response. A diagram of how classical conditioning works is shown in Figure 9.8. Also shown there is an example of how you can use roughly the same approach in promotional situations by pairing your product with some stimulus that your prospect has previously learned is desirable. We will now turn to a more extended learning model related to classical conditioning but introducing some additional factors and giving you more possibilities with which to work in incidental learning situations.

*A Reinforcement*
*Learning Model*

A simplified version of this model is shown in Figure 9.9. The essential question at issue is: If an individual is exposed to a particular stimulus, what is the likelihood that he or she will respond in some predictable way?[36] In marketing terms that question might apply in the following way. Suppose that you are selling a particular brand of product—say a carbonated beverage. A consumer sees a display of your brand (the stimulus) in a store. What determines how likely it is that she or he will purchase your brand (the response) as opposed to buying a competitor's product or not buying at all?

***H, K, D, and V.*** The reinforcement learning model says that the likelihood of a response favorable to your brand is affected by four factors. As labeled in Figure 9.9, these factors carry the designations H, K, D, and V. Factor H (think of it as habit) deals with the matter of how many times this person has made this response in the past and has been rewarded for making the response. Factor K deals with the size of each of those rewards. Does the subject see them as being large rewards or small ones? Factor D (think of it as drive) deals with the needs of the subject at the time he or she is exposed to the stimulus. For example, if we are talking about a carbonated beverage display, does the person see it at a time when he or she is thirsty or planning a party or at a time when the person is not in the mood for soft drinks? Factor V deals with the power and the visibility of the stimulus itself. For example, is the display sign large or is it small and easy to miss?

***Cumulative Effects of the Four Factors.*** The essential idea is that, all other things being equal, the likelihood of achieving a favorable response will in-

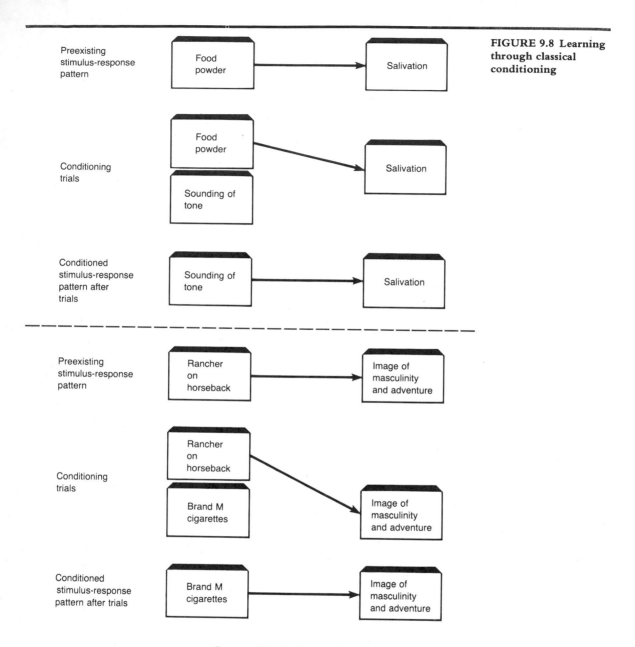

**FIGURE 9.8 Learning through classical conditioning**

crease as factors H, K, D, and V increase. In other words, the greater the number of past reinforced training trials, the bigger the amount of past reward, the stronger the drive, and the more powerful the stimulus, the more likely it is that the person will respond positively to that stimulus. (You also see a broken line leading from Habit to Drive and labeled: "Increase in novelty-seeking drive." We will come back to this later.) As you probably guessed by looking at Figure 9.9, the factors involved can be controlled very nicely in laboratory experiments dealing with lower animals such as mice or

*Models to Guide Communications*

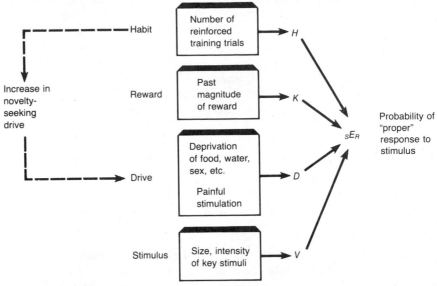

**FIGURE 9.9 A reinforcement learning model**

Habit — Number of reinforced training trials → H

Increase in novelty-seeking drive

Reward — Past magnitude of reward → K

Drive — Deprivation of food, water, sex, etc. / Painful stimulation → D

$_sE_R$

Stimulus — Size, intensity of key stimuli → V

Probability of "proper" response to stimulus

*Source:* Adapted from Michael Ray, "Psychological Theories and Interpretations of Learning," in Scott Ward and Thomas Robertson, eds., *Consumer Behavior: Theoretical Sources* (Englewood Cliffs, NJ: Prentice-Hall, Inc., 1973), p. 62.

guinea pigs. In those situations, you can pretty well set up H, K, D, and V to suit your purpose. Therefore, you can teach the animal to respond in a certain way when given the right stimulus.

***Relationship of the Reinforcement Model to Promotion.*** Can the same principle be applied to promotion? Reconsider the carbonated beverage example. In broad terms the model is telling you that the more often your customer has used your brand in the past (H) and enjoyed it (K) the more likely that person is to buy it in the future, especially if you give it promotional prominence (V) and if the person feels a strong need for a soft drink (D).

Your promotional strategy might therefore be to develop a truly good product that delivers a genuine reward, to promote it heavily so that people try it as often as possible, and to make certain that it is prominently displayed. So far, so good. That sounds like a coherent approach to promotional strategy. However, would you really need a learning model to reach this conclusion? Wouldn't your common sense tell you approximately the same thing? Well, if this was all the model could tell you, you would hardly need it. Your own native intelligence and reasoning ability should get the job done. However, there is something else that the reinforcement model may be telling you that goes beyond mere common sense and could be of critical assistance to you in some promotional situations.

***Vicarious Practice.*** To understand the additional inference that can be drawn from the model we will have to introduce one more hypothesis from psychological research findings. This is the proposition that learning can occur through "vicarious practice." For example, when you see someone do something and then see that person being punished or rewarded for doing it, you tend to learn by example. What is happening in such a situation can be loosely described as vicarious practice, the process by which an individual is influenced through incidental learning by observing what happens to other people.

Furthermore, research findings suggest that people who watch a movie often "identify" with an actor in the movie. When they do, they more or less feel as though they themselves are experiencing what that actor is experiencing. When the person in the movie is rewarded for a certain kind of behavior, many audience members are more likely to make that same kind of response in a similar situation. When the actor in the movie is punished for making a certain kind of response, the viewer is less likely to make that type of response.[37] In other words, on a vicarious basis—by seeing what happened to someone else with whom she or he identifies—the viewer appears to have been run through something very much like a reinforcement training trial.

***Application of the Model.*** On this basis, promotional messages such as television commercials might also function as reinforcement learning trials. As a promotional strategist, you can determine the timing and the nature of such commercials and hence exercise a high degree of control over all four of the factors shown in Figure 9.9. The following is an illustration of how you might put this strategy into use when building a TV campaign.

First, choose as the characters in your advertisements people with whom your audience can easily identify so that you encourage a maximum vicarious experience effect. Second, work on factor H, that is, aim at building as much of a response-reward habit as you can through heavy repetition. One way to do this is to follow a "massed practice" schedule, which means clustering your advertisements so that you generate a large number of exposures within a fairly short period of time. Third, work on factor K by showing a very great and immediate reward for using your brand, or perhaps, a great punishment for *not* using your brand. Show as many variations of immediate rewards or punishments as you can. For example, if you are selling a carbonated beverage, the person who drinks it can be pictured as enjoying immediate refreshment and good taste as well as enhancing the fun and pleasure of a lively social occasion.

Next, work on factor D. Try to tie into or excite an appropriate drive. Your messages probably will be more effective if they reach the receiver when he or she is in a preexisting drive state that relates to the use of your product. For instance, a commercial for sleeping pills will probably be an especially strong reinforcement experience if it reaches someone who has just spent a sleepless night. An advertisement for food should have its strongest reinforcement effect if it is shown to someone who is hungry at the time it is presented. Aside from influencing the timing of advertising, the desirability of associating your message with a potent drive state might influence the way you build your ads. Anything you can do to intensify a relevant drive through the construction of your message should increase the reinforcement process. (We will have more to say about this later in connection with "subliminal advertising"; see p. 294.)

Finally, work on factor V. Make your brand stimulus powerful. Advertising does not normally achieve its results immediately; rather, the message it presents is usually stored in memory for future use. This means that you might want to coordinate your ad with a stimulus that is likely to occur in the person's regular environment at a point when he or she is in a position to buy your brand. If all goes well, that stimulus should "pop up," to bring the reinforcement scene back to life. Such a stimulus might simply be a store display that your prospect will see when she or he goes shopping. It could also be a normal life occurrence which the prospect is likely to experience. As an illustration, if you were promoting milk, your advertising strategy might be to picture people drinking milk on their coffee break. Show them as being happy and rewarded for what they are doing and set the stimulus in place with a slogan such as "When it's time for a coffee break, make yours a milk break."

***A Hypothetical Illustration.*** Do advertisers really use techniques like these? Are some ads built along reinforcement theory lines? The best way to determine your own answer to these questions is to pay close attention to the advertising you see, especially some of the television commercials. At least a few of them seem to be following patterns that closely approximate principles of the model. If you wanted to put those principles into action, how might you go about doing it in more specific terms? As a purely imaginary illustration, suppose you are promoting a particular brand of traveler's checks. You know the following things about the reasons and circumstances that cause people to buy in your product category.

1. Traveler's checks are used when a person is going to be away from home, probably on a fairly long trip.
2. They have to be bought *before* the person leaves home and are often bought at a bank.
3. Many people experience anxiety and agitation when planning a long trip. It is always possible to encounter trouble far away from home. It would be especially uncomfortable to be financially embarrassed should trouble occur.
4. There is an element of fear involved in making the purchase, fear that one's money or traveler's checks might be lost or stolen.
5. If they were lost or stolen, one would want help in a hurry. It could be worrisome and even dangerous to be stranded in a strange place where no one ever heard of the brand of traveler's checks one just lost.

Now, recalling that you are trying to instill incidental learning through vicarious experience, what kind of format could reinforcement theory suggest for your television commercial? You might possibly want to introduce the commercial by exciting a relevant drive state in the viewer. Perhaps you can do this by showing people in a compartment on a train in Europe. For them, it is a strange and far-away place. They are about to be visited by a customs inspector and something is wrong. They are searching frantically through their luggage. When the official opens the door of their compartment, they appeal to him for help. It turns out that they have lost their traveler's checks. He asks what brand of traveler's checks they were carrying. Unfortunately, it is not the "right" brand. (The right brand, of course, is the brand you are selling.)

Because these people did not "respond" properly when they bought their traveler's checks, they are going to be "punished." In other words, they are going to receive a negative reward. The official looks at them with scorn. He shrugs and walks away. He refuses to help because they made the wrong purchase decision—they did not buy the brand you are selling and he lets them know it. The scene switches to a bank in the United States. A man appears to tell you how you can avoid such punishment. All you have to do is respond properly when you receive the "stimulus." The logical stimulus in this case is a sign or display in a bank advertising your brand of traveler's checks. After all, if you are going to take a long trip, you will probably have to visit a bank first. So, we will have the man give a final bit of advice. While he is standing in a bank next to such a sign or display, he can say something such as, "Don't make a big fool of yourself. The next time you travel, be sure you are carrying Amalgamated Traveler's Checks."

The only thing left to do is to run that commercial on television frequently enough to give your prospects a large number of reinforced training trials. (Of course, those trials are all vicarious. Your prospects are acquiring experience by watching what happens to other people.) If something like this could be feasible for a product such as traveler's checks, it might work for a number of other products as well. For instance, it might be useful in building brand preference levels for such things as upset stomach remedies and decaffeinated coffee. Just to see what might happen, why not try building some imaginary commercials for those products using reinforcement principles?

*Drive States and Subliminal Stimulation*

There has been a good deal of interest in a controversial phenomenon termed "subliminal perception." Generally, when you think of messages, you consider symbols you can consciously see or hear. However, it is also possible to transmit symbols in a manner which puts them below the threshold of normal perception. When this happens, the message is termed "subliminal." *A subliminal message is one that is transmitted in such a way that the person receiving it is not consciously aware of the message. This usually means that the symbols involved are too faint or too brief to be clearly recognized. However, they are still powerful enough to have an effect on the receiver.*

If the symbols involve sound, the subliminal message may be in the form of very soft sounds mixed in with nonsubliminal louder sounds. If the subliminal message is visual, it may be something that is presented so quickly or so vaguely that the receiver cannot consciously recognize it. For example, one writer has suggested that a liquor firm buried the letters s-e-x in an advertisement picturing a gin drink,[38] but buried them so skillfully that the average person would not notice them until they were pointed out to her or him. Because the essential objective of subliminal techniques is to deliver a message that is just below an individual's perceptual threshold, there is one immediate problem. Perceptual threshold levels vary among audience members; thus, symbols that are subliminal to one person may be consciously perceived by another. Then again, those same symbols may not be perceived at all—subliminally or otherwise—by still a third person. For this and a diversity of other reasons, the feasibility of employing subliminal perception is debatable.[39]

Most marketing textbooks dismiss the subject rather tersely.[40] Therefore, if you decide that subliminal communication simply will not work, you are in very good company. After an extensive study of the published evidence regarding subliminal techniques, including those tested in promotional applications, one psychologist concluded, "The notion that subliminal directives can influence motives or actions is contradicted by a large body of research evidence."[41]

However, if you consider the reinforcement model just discussed, you may have second thoughts. Although there is disagreement on the subject, at least some published research suggests two potential characteristics of interest concerning subliminal stimuli.[42] First, at least on a limited basis, it may be possible for such symbols to influence a receiver without the receiver being aware of them. They may not always affect all receivers but they can often affect many receivers. Second, when they do influence a receiver, they seem to work on drive states. In other words, some researchers have reported that subliminal stimuli may make the receiver at least marginally more hungry, more thirsty, more fearful, and so on. This could conceivably make that person more susceptible to the message that follows.

This is hardly the same as saying you can persuade people to do something by a direct subliminal command. However, there is at least an outside possibility that by increasing the receiver's drive state subliminal cues could play one small part in building a stronger persuasive communications package. Therefore, perhaps subliminal techniques should not be dismissed too quickly.

*The Novelty-Seeking or Variety Drive*

The reinforcement learning model shown in Figure 9.9 also suggests something potentially meaningful to promotional techniques that involve heavy and long-term repetition. This is illustrated by the broken "novelty-seeking drive" line. The relevant hypothesis holds that "inhibition builds up with repetition and [must be] subtracted from reaction potential."[43] In terms of promotional application, this means that as you repeat your message you increase the likelihood of a positive response to your stimulus only up to a point. Beyond that point, repetition can begin to generate a drive of its own. The drive involved has been called by several different names. These include "novelty seeking," "the variety drive," and "satiation or curiosity." Basically, they all imply that people simply get tired of the "same old thing."

The existence of such a drive has been demonstrated in laboratory experiments with lower animals. Even when such animals are well rewarded for making the proper response to the stimulus, they eventually become bored. Then they decide to make a different response, despite the fact that it may not produce the same level of reward.[44]

What does the novelty drive suggest for developing your promotional strategies? There are at least four main types of possibilities you should consider: (1) novelty as an opportunity for new brands, (2) novelty as a means of prolonging product life cycles, (3) novelty in formulating advertising campaign strategy, and (4) novelty in the use of sales promotion techniques.

***Opportunities for New Brands.*** In writing about novelty seeking, one expert has advanced the following suggestion:

> With this variety drive, it becomes unlikely that any manufacturer can exert a Svengali effect upon purchasers. Even though a consumer is completely satisfied with the brand he is buying, he occasionally buys another brand, just for the "hell of it." This represents a promising advertising strategy for new products. Rather than trying to switch dissatisfied customers to your brand, simply encourage them to buy the new product as a change of pace. This would have a much broader appeal where present brands are well entrenched. [45]

***Novelty Seeking and the Product Life Cycle.*** In Chapter 5 we discussed the product life cycle concept. The novelty-seeking or variety drive may provide one explanation of why some brands have such long life cycles, whereas the lives of others are so short. The long-lived brands are frequently those that are constantly revamped and remodeled. For instance, recall what was said about Dial soap. Because changes are continuously made in its implicit promotional mix, consumers are given much less chance to become bored and wander off to other brands.

The implication is that you should consider making changes in your product *while it is still at its peak sales level*. Despite the fact that large numbers of people are enthusiastic and responding favorably to your product, its very success may be breeding a force that will eventually work against you. Waiting for a drop in sales before you initiate changes may mean that you have waited too long.

***Novelty and Advertising Campaign Strategy.*** The novelty or variety drive also holds some implications for planning your advertising campaigns. It helps explain why even the best advertising campaigns wear out. People simply experience satiation owing to overexposure to the same learning pattern. In consequence, most successful campaigns are built around a continuous theme, but are made up of separate ads which provide variety within that theme. In planning advertising strategy, then, you can strengthen your position by taking this drive into account and carefully building variations into your campaign approach.

***Novelty and the Use of Sales Promotion.*** One of the strongest available routes for injecting novelty and change of pace into your promotional program involves the element of sales promotion. As mentioned in Chapter 3, such techniques as displays, coupons, and contests are excellent devices for putting added interest into a promotional plan. As one example, part of your effort toward developing a completely coordinated promotional mix should consider how sales promotion techniques can be used to help your sales representatives cope with novelty seeking on the part of their customers.

## THE COGNITIVE DISSONANCE MODEL

A cognition can be defined as *a belief or item of knowledge*. Dissonance can be defined as *discord or inconsistency*. Cognitive dissonance, then, refers to the proposition that a person may have beliefs or items of knowledge that are inconsistent with each other. If this is the case, it is expected that such dissonance is psychologically uncomfortable, in which case the person will seek to reduce dissonance.[46] The type of cognitive dissonance usually talked about in connection with promotional situations is termed "post-decision dissonance." Figure 9.10 shows one way to envision how this might operate in the marketplace.

*The Potential for Dissonance Following Purchase Decisions*

Many purchase decisions are based on prior comparison between brands. After comparison, a decision is made and one of the brands is purchased. Following the purchase, it is possible the consumer might have second thoughts. Perhaps she begins to think that the brand she did not buy was superior on some evaluative criterion to the brand she bought. Such speculation could lead the purchaser to reconsider the decision. Perhaps she will begin to lose some confidence as to whether the brand she purchased was really the best choice. If such uncertainty arises, dissonance exists.

She would like to think she bought the best brand but now she thinks she could have made the wrong choice. As a result, she is "uncomfortable." One logical way for a purchaser to reduce the discomfort of dissonance is to search for additional information. The evidence seems to be that when people do search for such added information they are likely to look for facts, figures, and opinions that support their original purchase decision.[47] In this sense, once you have won the sale, dissonance is working for your brand. That is, your purchaser would like to be convinced your brand was the best choice because she has already committed herself to it. In fact, in one study it appeared that the higher the original level of post-decision dissonance, the greater the level of brand loyalty produced for the brand that was chosen.[48]

As depicted in Figure 9.10, post-decision dissonance is not likely to be a major factor following every single purchase decision. In many cases, the consumer may see no need to reconsider the purchase decision. In general, it is expected that "the magnitude of post decision dissonance is an increasing function of the general importance of the decision and the relative attractiveness of the unchosen alternatives."[49] In marketing terms this indicates that the greatest possibility for dissonance exists when *major* purchases are made, purchases involving relatively expensive or socially sensitive items. For example, the purchase of an automobile, a high-priced article of clothing, or a piece of heavy machinery might provoke a degree of post-decision dissonance.

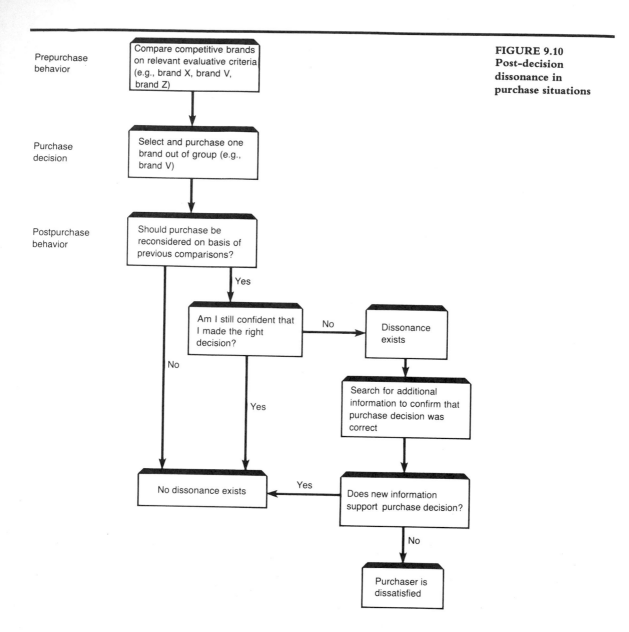

FIGURE 9.10
**Post-decision
dissonance in
purchase situations**

It seems unlikely that the purchase of something like a loaf of bread or a tube of toothpaste would provoke very much.

*Applying
Dissonance Theory
in Promotional
Planning*

The most important implication of dissonance theory for promotional practice is the inference that explicit promotion may still have a vital task to perform after the sale has been made. This is because your customer may still be searching for information to confirm the wisdom of what he or she has done. In that case, you would want to be especially alert to opportunities for making positive and reassuring information available.

***Applications in Personal Selling Strategy.*** Personal selling probably provides the greatest opportunity for utilizing dissonance theory. As you will see in the next chapter, one pattern often recommended to sales representatives includes stress on the "follow-up," which is a post-sale visit by the salesperson. Its main goal is to ensure that the product is performing properly and to answer any questions that may arise concerning its use. However, the follow-up also provides an excellent opportunity to deal with potential dissonance problems. An effective salesperson should be on watch for any second thoughts the customer might have and be prepared with a planned program of reassuring information.

***Applications in Advertising Strategy.*** Dealing with dissonance through advertising is a somewhat different matter. It is unlikely that much of your advertising will be planned primarily to aid in dissonance reduction. However, it may be serving as a dissonance reducer for some recent purchasers at the same time that it is carrying your message to people who have not yet purchased your brand. In other words, you might want to think of advertising as both a means of attracting new customers and a means of reassuring recent purchasers.

The Ford Motor Company has reportedly gone further than this and actually designed some of its advertising *specifically* for the purpose of reducing dissonance among recent purchasers.[50] The evidence suggests that such overt attempts to reduce dissonance are successful only if handled with caution. In one study involving the purchase of a refrigerator, a follow-up letter aimed at dissonance reduction seemed to be successful. However, a follow-up telephone call actually seemed to raise dissonance and lower customer satisfaction with the brand. Perhaps this may have happened because a telephone follow-up seemed so unusual that it raised suspicions concerning possible problems with the product.[51]

## SUMMARY

In the category theory of communication the audience is understood to play a very active part in the communication process. This means that the same message may mean different things to different receivers. To make this idea operative, the general communication model presented in this chapter considered the communication process in terms of eleven components: the intended promotional message, the perceived promotional message, the communicator or source, the encoding symbols, the communication medium, potential noise, reception, decoding, interpretation, response, and feedback.

An important part of your task as a promotional strategist is to ensure that your promotional message reaches your receiver with its meaning properly conveyed. If you are successful the perceived promotional message will be the same as your intended promotional message. To ensure that they are the same, you must begin by understanding as much as you can about the way receivers process messages. The mechanics of this processing can be thought of in terms of four components of the above model; these are reception, decoding, interpretation, and response. You can then develop an effective design for the sender components, which are under your control; these are choice of a communicator, choice of encoding symbols, and choice of the communication medium. This chapter was mainly concerned with the first two—the communicator and the encoding symbols. More detailed discussions about the communication medium will be pursued in the chapters that follow.

Three major factors that can have a positive influence on the effectiveness of a particular communicator are credibility, attractiveness, and power. As for the choice of encoding symbols and the encoding process itself, a general outline was suggested that focused on affecting three critical components in the receiver section of the model—reception, decoding, and interpretation. The techniques relevant to improvement of reception center around the physical impact of the stimulus and/or the reward attraction of the stimulus. Techniques to improve decoding revolve around your analysis of the target audience, the setting of symbols in context, and the use of multiple symbols. Techniques of increasing strong, positive interpretation involve such choices as rational versus emotional appeals, implied versus explicit conclusions, two-sided versus one-sided presentations, and order of presentation of selling points.

The multistage interactive flow model suggests that many people in your market may receive your communication or be influenced in their interpretation of it through opinion leaders. Distinguishing opinion leaders from nonleaders may be difficult, especially in mass communications situations. However, there are worthwhile steps you can take to put some of the power of opinion leadership to work for you.

Promotional messages can be thought of as educational experiences for consumers. Hence, the use of learning models was suggested as a way to explore certain promotional possibilities. If you want to follow this approach, your first step is to determine whether your product is likely to involve intentional learning or incidental learning. Especially in the case of incidental learning, some interesting possibilities to consider are the classical conditioning theory and the reinforcement learning model. The prospective use of a reinforcement model raises further issues. One of these is the use of subliminal techniques as a means of exciting drive states. A second is the existence of a variety drive or a drive for novelty seeking.

Subliminal perception is a highly controversial issue in terms of both ethics and practical workability. The issue of the workability of subliminal communication is a disputed point. The position taken in this chapter is that the possibility of using subliminal techniques should not be dismissed too quickly. They may produce some results at least in a limited, drive-excitation sense.

The main promotional implication of the cognitive dissonance model is that promotion may have a significant role to play after you have made the sale. This will occur when customers continue to search for post-purchase information to reassure themselves that they have made the right brand choice.

All of the concepts covered in this chapter are more or less general. They sweep across a variety of promotional elements, especially the explicit elements of personal selling, advertising, sales promotion, and publicity. Our next objective is to look at those explicit elements individually and to see how these and other principles apply in more specific terms.

## DISCUSSION QUESTIONS

1. Explain the reasoning behind the bullet theory. What theory replaced the bullet theory and what is the general reasoning behind the newer theory? Can you think of an advertising message that failed because it operated on the bullet theory principle?

2. Discuss the major components found in the receiver section of the general communications model. How are these components related to the category theory?

3. It is your job to select a spokesperson for your company's advertising campaign. What factors must you consider in your selection of a source? Do you think Chrysler Corporation successfully met these criteria with their selection of Lee Iacocca as a spokesman?

4. Analyze the following advertisement in terms of the effectiveness of the message presenter (source):

   The advertisement is targeted at teenage girls who are just beginning to date. In the scenario, a young, extremely attractive teenage girl is surrounded by an admiring group of basketball heroes. She has just made the cheerleading squad thanks to her bright, shiny, bouncy hair. During the ad, the cheerleader recounts her lonely, unpopular days when she had dull, lifeless hair. But *now*; thanks to Brand X Shampoo . . .

5. Use the concepts of "internal noise" and "physical impact stimuli" to explain why an advertisement that used a circus elephant to get attention for a men's shaving cream did not effectively gain reception from the receivers. What could be done to correct the situation?

6. Clarify the differences between physical impact techniques and the "reward" techniques described in your text. Which type of reward techniques do you think would be most suitable for an ad featuring frozen gourmet dinners? Why?

7. Using the concept of the Benefit Chain, try to generate some inherent reward approaches for the ad in question number 5.

8. Discuss the three main techniques an advertiser may use to ensure that the audience is properly decoding the promotional message.

9. Describe the techniques you would suggest for increasing strong, positive interpretation of an ad for the following restaurant: The restaurant is rather bland and nondescript in atmosphere (but *clean*) and is in an out of the way spot. However, the specialty of the restaurant—barbecued ribs—are superior to the competitors' ribs, because they contain a higher ratio of meat to bone. Additionally, they are not more expensive, owing to the low overhead of the small restaurant. Why did you choose the techniques you did?

10. (A) What is the main difference between the category theory of communication and the multistage interactive flow model? (B) What are some of the problems advertisers encounter when they try to use the concepts of the latter model in preparing a mass communication message? (C) What are some ways to design persuasive messages that incorporate the concept of the multistep flow model?

11. Use the principle of novelty seeking to examine the implications for advertisements that involve heavy and long-term repetition.

# REFERENCES

1. Wilbur Schramm, "The Nature of Communication Between Humans," in Wilbur Schramm and Donald F. Roberts, *The Process and Effects of Mass Communication*, rev. ed. (Urbana, IL: University of Illinois Press, 1972), p. 8.

2. Neil Bidmar and Milton Rokeach, "Archie Bunker's Bigotry: A Study in Selective Perception and Exposure," *Journal of Communication*, Winter 1974, pp. 36–47.

3. Schramm, "The Nature of Communication Between Humans," p. 9.

4. *Ibid.*, p. 10.

5. James F. Engel, Martin R. Warshaw, and Thomas C. Kinnear, *Promotional Strategy*, 5th ed. (Homewood, IL.: Richard D. Irwin, Inc., 1983), p. 56.

6. Schramm, "The Nature of Communication Between Humans," p. 44.

7. For a much more detailed discussion of source characteristics and their relationship to promotional messages see Dorothy Cohen, *Consumer Behavior* (New York: Random House, 1981), pp. 328–340.

8. Werner Kroeber-Riel, "Activation Research: Psychobiological Approaches in Consumer Research," *Journal of Consumer Research,* March 1979, p. 245.

9. James R. Bettman, "Memory Factors in Consumer Choice: A Review," *Journal of Marketing*, Spring 1979, p. 38.

10. Shirley Young and Barbara Feigin, "Using the Benefit Chain for Improved Strategy Formulation," *Journal of Marketing,* July 1975, pp. 72–74.

11. Joseph M. Winski, "Tragedy of 'Drink Schlitz or I Will Kill You'," *Chicago Tribune,* 8 August 1978, pp. 1 and 13.

12. *Ibid.*, p. 13.

13. *Ibid.*

14. W. D. E. Crissy, William H. Cunningham, and Isabella C. M. Cunningham, *Selling: The Personal Force in Marketing* (New York: John Wiley and Sons, 1977), p. 253.

15. "TV ads sexual offensiveness depends on appropriateness, audience, other factors," *Marketing News,* 24 March 1978, p. 7.

16. Allan Paivio and A. D. Yarmey, "Pictures vs. Words as Stimuli and Responses in Paired-Associate Learning," *Psychonomic Science,* May 1966, pp. 235–236.

17. "Penton Presentation Shows Facts, Figures and Fear Plays Roles in Industrial Buying," *Marketing News*, 18 November 1977, p. 8.

18. Irving L. Janis and Seymour Feshbach, "Effects of Fear—Arousing Communications," *Journal of Abnormal and Social Psychology,* January 1953, pp. 78–92; Michael L. Ray and William L. Wilkie, "Fear: The Potential of an Appeal Neglected by Marketing," *Journal of Marketing*, January 1970, pp. 54–62.

19. Carl I. Hovland and Wallace Mandell, "An Experimental Comparison of Conclusion-Drawing by the Communication and by the Audience," *Journal of Abnormal and Social Psychology,* July 1952, pp. 581–588.

20. Jack W. Brehm, *A Theory of Psychological Reactance* (New York: Academic Press, 1966), Chapter 6.

21. James F. Engel and Roger D. Blackwell, *Consumer Behavior* 4th ed. (Hinsdale, IL: The Dryden Press, 1982), p. 476.

22. C. I. Hovland, A. A. Lumsdaine, and F. D. Sheffield, *Experiments on Mass Communication,* vol. 3 (Princeton, NJ: Princeton University Press, 1948), Chapter 8.

23. Edmund W. J. Faison, *Advertising: A Behavioral Approach for Managers* (New York: John Wiley and Sons, 1980), pp. 238–239.

24. See E. Walster, E. Aronson, and D. Abrahams, "On Increasing the Persuasiveness of a Low Prestige Communicator," *Journal of Experimental Social Psychology,* 1956, pp. 325–342; and G. J. Szybillo and R. Heslin, "Resistance to Persuasion: Inoculation Theory in a Marketing Contract," *Journal of Marketing Research,* August 1973 pp. 396–403.

25. For some examples see H. Sponberg, "A Study of the Relative Effectiveness of Climax and Anti-Climax Order in an Argumentative Speech," *Speech Monographs,* vol. 13 (1946), pp. 35–44; H. Gilkinson, S. Paulson, and D. Sikkink, "Effects of Order and Authority in an Argumentative Speech," *Quarterly Journal of Speech,* vol. 40 (1954), pp. 183–192; and H. Gulley and D. Berlo, "Effect of Intercellular and Intracellular Speech Structure on Attitude Change and Learning," *Speech Monographs,* vol. 23 (1956), pp. 288–297.

26. Engel and Blackwell, *Consumer Behavior,* p. 481.

27. Herbert E. Krugman, "Memory Without Recall, Exposure Without Perception," *Journal of Advertising Research,* August 1977, pp. 7–12.

28. Elihu Katz and Jacob J. Feldman, "The Debates in Light of Research: A Survey of Surveys," in Sidney Krause, *The Great Debates: Background of the Perspective Effects* (Bloomington, IN: Indiana University Press, 1962), p. 33.

29. Johan Arndt, "Selective Processes in Word-of-Mouth," *Journal of Advertising Research,* June 1968, pp. 19–22.

30. Charles W. King and John O. Summers, "Dynamics of Interpersonal Communication," in Donald F. Cox, ed., *Risk Taking and Information Handling in Consumer Behavior* (Boston: Division of Research, Graduate School of Business Administration, Harvard University, 1967), pp. 240–264.

31. Jagdish N. Sheth, "Word of Mouth in Low-Risk Innovations," *Journal of Advertising Research,* June 1971, pp. 15–18.

32. See C. W. King and J. O. Summers, "Overlap of Opinion Leadership Across Consumer Product Categories," *Journal of Marketing Research,* February 1970, pp. 43–50; and Stephen A. Blumgarten, "The Innovative Communicator in the Diffusion Process," *Journal of Marketing Research* (February 1975), pp. 12–18.

33. Paul Lazarsfeld, "Who Are the Marketing Leaders?", in James U. McNeal, ed., *Dimensions of Consumer Behavior* (New York: Appleton-Century-Crofts, 1969), p. 163.

34. Frank W. Schneider and B. C. Kintz, "An Analysis of the Incidental-Intentional Learning Dichotomy," *Journal of Experimental Psychology* (January 1967), pp. 85–90.

35. Steuart H. Britt, "Applying Learning Principles to Marketing," *MSU Business Topics,* Spring 1975, pp. 5–6.

36. J. Paul Peter and Walter R. Nord, "A Clarification and Extension of Operant Conditioning Principles in Marketing," *Journal of Marketing,* Summer 1982, pp. 102–107.

37. Albert Bandura, "Vicarious Processes: A Case of No-Trial Learning," in L. Berkowitz, ed., *Advances in Experimental Social Psychology,* vol. II (New York: Academic Press, 1966), vol. 2, pp. 1–55.

38. Wilson B. Key, *Subliminal Seduction* (New York: New American Library, 1973), pp. 4–5.

39. For a complete and good discussion, see N. F. Dixon, *Subliminal Perception: The Nature of a Controversy* (New York: McGraw-Hill Book Company, 1971).

40. For examples, see Del I. Hawkins, Kenneth A. Coney, and Roger J. Best, *Consumer Behavior: Implications for Marketing Strategy* (Dallas: Business Publications, Inc., 1980), p. 257; Engel and Blackwell, *Consumer Behavior,* p. 296; and Harold W. Berkman and Christopher C. Gilson, *Consumer Behavior: Concepts and Strategies* (Encino, CA: Dickenson Publishing Co., 1978), p. 261.

41. Timothy E. Moore, "Subliminal Advertising: What You See Is What You Get," *Journal of Marketing,* Spring 1982, p. 38. (This article will also provide you with an excellent review and bibliography on the subject.)

42. Joel Saegert, "Another Look at Subliminal Perception," *Journal of Advertising Research,* February 1979, pp. 55–57, and Sandra H. Hart and Stephen W. McDaniel, "Subliminal Stimulation—Marketing Applications" in James U. McNeal and Stephen W. McDaniel, eds., *Consumer Behavior: Classical and Contemporary Dimensions* (Boston: Little, Brown & Co., 1982), pp. 165–175.

43. Michael Ray, "Psychological Theories and Interpretations of Learning," in Scott Ward and Thomas S. Robertson, eds., *Consumer Behavior: Theoretical Sources* (Englewood Cliffs, NJ: Prentice-Hall Inc., 1973), p. 67.

44. Harry Fowler, "Satiation and Curiosity: Constructs for a Drive and Incentive—Motivational Theory of Exploration," in K. W. Spence and J. T. Spence, eds., *Psychology of Learning and Motivation,* vol. 1 (New York: Academic Press, 1967), pp. 152–277; W. N. Dember and H. Fowler, "Spontaneous Alternation Behavior," *Psychological Bulletin,* 55, 1958, pp. 412–428; and D. P. Schultz, "Spontaneous Alternation Behavior in Humans: Implications for Psychological Research," *Psychological Bulletin* 62, 1964, pp. 394–400.

45. Edmund W. J. Faison, "The Neglected Variety Drive: A Useful Concept for Consumer Behavior," *Journal of Consumer Research,* December 1977, p. 174.

46. Leon Festinger, *A Theory of Cognitive Disso-*

*nance* (Stanford, CA: Stanford University Press, 1957), p. 30.

47. For examples see J. Adams, "Reduction of Cognitive Dissonance by Seeking Consonant Information," *Journal of Abnormal and Social Psychology,* 1961, pp. 74–78.

48. Robert Mittelstaedt, "A Dissonance Approach to Repeat Purchasing Behavior," *Journal of Marketing Research,* November 1969, pp. 444–446.

49. Festinger, *A Theory of Cognitive Dissonance,* p. 262.

50. G. Brown, "The Automobile Buyer, Decision Within the Family," in N. Foote, ed., *Household Decision Making* (New York: University Press, 1951), pp. 193–199.

51. Shelby Hunt, "Post-Transaction Communication and Dissonance Reduction," *Journal of Marketing,* January 1970, pp. 46–51.

# PART THREE

# *Personal Selling*

# CHAPTER TEN

# *Personal Selling —Salespeople at Work*

## FOCUS OF THE CHAPTER

Personal selling was defined earlier as, "Oral presentation in a conversation with one or more prospective purchasers for the purpose of making a sale." In considering where and how it fits into the total promotional strategy mix, there are two major levels of personal selling to examine. The first is the *micro-level*, in which the sales process is viewed up close. Our concern here is with activities of sales representatives when they are actually making or preparing to make the oral presen-

tation. The second is the *macro-level,* which includes sales management and requires adopting a larger view of personal selling from the standpoint of overall company goals. Our concerns with this level include how much emphasis should be placed on personal selling, how other promotional techniques should be used to support the sales force, and how sales representatives should be assigned and supervised. This chapter will discuss personal selling at the micro-level. The two following chapters will discuss the macro-level.

# THE IMPORTANCE OF PERSONAL SELLING
# IN PROMOTIONAL PLANNING

Having an understanding of what salespersons do—how they go about organizing their selling strategies and dealing with customers on a face-to-face basis—is an essential part of understanding the total promotional process. It has been repeatedly stressed in this text that the components of the promotional strategy mix work together. The activities of the sales representative often form the final link in the process of promotion. He or she can activate all the other elements of the mix by obtaining reseller cooperation, securing support from persons who advise consumers or completing a sale to a consumer.

There are many varieties of selling jobs and various patterns have been suggested for developing selling plans. Regardless of the specific job or the specific pattern chosen, all salespersons face problems and opportunities that are different from those confronting any other type of promotional strategist. In this chapter, we will begin with some criticisms of personal selling, which both illustrate challenges facing sales representatives and set the stage for discussing what effective selling entails. Next we shall look at ways to classify and distinguish between various types of personal selling jobs. Following that we will consider actual examples of how four salespersons from very different product and market categories handle their work. Finally, we will discuss four specific patterns that have been suggested for analyzing and planning sales contacts. Those patterns will be related to the work descriptions given by the four salespeople and to general concepts and principles covered in other sections of the text.

*Criticisms of Personal Selling*

Promotion in all forms is subject to criticism. Advertising probably receives the lion's share of abuse, but personal selling also draws fire. In any situation in which persuasion is involved, the persuader may be convincing people to do things that others consider to be wrong or may be using techniques that critics see as being overly emotional and socially undesirable. However, personal selling often faces a further accusation that is less frequently leveled at the other promotional techniques—that much of it is amateurish and ineffective.

For example, the head of a firm which specializes in training sales personnel has expressed his belief that "the art of personal selling probably has reached an all-time professional low in the United States."[1] In justifying that conclusion he cites a survey of some 10,000 buyers concerning specific purchases they had made. The study findings revealed the following:

- Eighty-two percent did not recall the name of the salesperson one year after the date of purchase because of a lack of follow-up.

- Sixty-three percent said they would not buy from the same salespeople or companies again, and cited "neglect" and "indifference" as the reasons.

- Ninety-six percent said the salespeople did not ask for a commitment on an order form, apparently because they "lost control" of the selling situation.

- Eighty-eight percent said the salespersons did not present or demonstrate products they were selling, and appeared to be selling price instead of product.
- Eighty-nine percent said the salespeople did not know their product.

In another case, the marketing vice-president for a major American consumer goods corporation expressed his criticism by saying, "Many corporations have become victims of some of the lowest levels of individual sales performance on record. . . . One obvious reason is that major corporations have improved their other marketing abilities sufficiently to create advertising campaigns and media promotions that compensate for lack of aggressive, forceful [personal] selling."[2]

*Positive Implications of the Criticisms*

The purpose of beginning with criticisms is *not* to start you off with a negative attitude. On the contrary, if you look carefully at these criticisms you will see they really imply some highly positive things about personal selling.

Customers often want assistance from qualified salespersons. The complaints that surfaced in the survey quoted above suggest that the buyers were disappointed by the inertia of the sales representatives, not by their over-aggressiveness. A well-informed sales representative who studies the customer's problem and deals with the prospect candidly is an asset in the purchase decision process. This book stresses the view that buyers are information processors and seekers. They want information if they think it will help them solve problems or fulfill goals. Because of its face-to-face, personalized nature, personal selling is often able to supply information in detailed fashion, tailored to the specific problems of an individual customer in a way no other promotional technique can possibly match.

Personal selling requires skill, knowledge, energy, and often a good deal of creativity. It is not something "just anyone" can do. It is rarely something that can be done well without training, experience, and planning. At its highest level, it is a very professional activity. Further, if many people in sales positions are not sufficiently knowledgeable about what they are doing, as some critics claim, the opportunities for individuals with the right mix of talents are tremendous.

As the second critic above pointed out, other promotional techniques—notably advertising—can be substituted to some extent for deficiencies in sales force abilities. Ideally, however, a good salesperson recognizes the power of the other promotional elements and puts that power to work for her or him. For instance, rather than letting advertising replace you, you can capitalize on the job it has done in building positive customer attitudes and make advertising work for you rather than instead of you.

*Categories of Salespeople*

Almost 6.5 million persons are employed in some type of selling job in the United States.[3] In a field as big as this, there are bound to be wide variations in the types of work actually done by salespeople. Various lists have been drawn up to categorize selling jobs. No such list is perfect or even complete. Many tend to duplicate categories as well as have inconsistencies among job descriptions within categories. The typing scheme we will use has both defects because there is no reasonable way to avoid them.

Our scheme lists seven classes of salespeople.[4] The need for genuine promotional skill generally increases as you move from the beginning of the list to the end, but even this generality will require some qualification later.

**1.** *Route Salespeople.* Persons in this category make deliveries on a routine basis in connection with their selling activities. Examples include individuals who deliver bread, soft drinks, and similar items to retail outlets as well as those who deliver such products as heating oil and newspapers to homes. Because their work revolves around a sale, they are technically involved in personal selling. In general, however, they do very little to originate sales via persuasive communication. Primarily, they concentrate on serving established customers rather than developing new business.

**2.** *Sales Clerks.* This group is composed of people who work in retail stores or wholesale outlets. Most occupations involve the taking of orders rather than active initiation of sales effort. In some cases, for example in supermarkets, the job can be virtually limited to ringing up the sale on the cash register. However, there are many instances in which the sales clerk has a genuine promotional role to play. We will discuss one such example shortly.

**3.** *Detail People.* Individuals in this category normally do not take or solicit orders in a direct sense. Their activities center on promoting a product and convincing the prospect either to place the order with someone else or to specify the product for purchase by another person. For example, in the pharmaceutical field, detail people call on doctors to inform and persuade them concerning the merits of new drug items. If their efforts are successful, the physician will prescribe the drug for his or her patients. The actual sale will occur at a pharmacy, but its origins can be traced back to the efforts of the detail person.

**4.** *Account Representatives.* This term is frequently used to designate salespeople who call on retailers and wholesalers. In general, the accounts on whom they call are currently doing business with the firm they represent. The function of the account representative is to make certain the customer is being properly serviced and very often to secure increased reseller support.

**5.** *Industrial Sales Representatives.* The work of individuals in this group is concerned with selling products to be used in the operation of a business. Normally, it does not require a high degree of technical expertise regarding the operation of that business. The products involved tend to be items presently used by the business entity, such as raw materials, supplies, and small machinery items. The task of the industrial sales rep is to acquire that business for his or her firm. Frequently, the salesperson does this by providing additional services to the customer or through skillful contract negotiation.

**6.** *Sales Engineers.* Like the industrial sales representative, the sales engineer sells to industry. However, he or she is usually technically trained and, beyond merely selling a product for which the customer has a preexisting demand, becomes involved in more creative sales activities. The sales engineer may supply a good deal of expertise to help a customer analyze a problem and then recommend an item that will solve it. Sales engineers are especially active in fields such as heavy industry and high technology.

**7.** *Creative Salespersons.* The distinguishing characteristic of the creative salesperson is his or her ability to help the customer visualize a need for an item or a service. Often, the product is an intangible, such as insurance, advertising, or an executive development program. Alternatively, it may be a relatively expensive tangible commodity that is highly innovative from the standpoint of the customer involved. Examples in this latter category are executive aircraft and industrial robots. Because the offering is intangible and/or innovative, the sale requires much more intense and imaginative persuasive effort than transactions handled by the previously listed categories of salespeople.

*Promotional Needs and Opportunities Related to Category*

When promotion was defined in Chapter 1, the words "communicate" and "persuade" were emphasized. Accordingly, the degree to which people in any of the above categories can be called promotional strategists depends upon the extent to which they communicate and persuade. Some positions included in the list, for example that of the supermarket checkout clerk, probably do not provide much opportunity for persuasive communication, even if an individual wanted to attempt it. Other positions, such as the selling of advertising services, may absolutely demand it if the person intends to achieve even moderate success. Between these two types of positions there are a multitude of levels in which some salespeople are behaving like genuine promotional strategists while others are not. In part, the criticisms quoted earlier reflect a fairly widespread feeling that too many people involved in personal selling positions are content to limit themselves to product delivery or order taking when they have an opportunity to be active in persuasive communication.

To an extent, our seven-level sequence of classes of salespeople reflects the results of varying treatments of the promotional mix as discussed in Chapter 3. In the case of the lower levels, the mixes have often been built with heavy reliance on advertising, sales promotion, publicity, and/or the implicit promotional content of the merchandise itself. Where the promotional mix calls for a sales position at the upper end of the list, however, there is often less that can be done through these other elements of promotion. Sometimes products must be tailored or engineered to the specific needs of the customer. Sometimes prospects demand a great deal more information and demonstration than they could possibly be given through the more impersonal promotional techniques. Sometimes prospects are extremely passive and simply will not purchase unless contacted and convinced of their need on a face-to-face basis. When any of these conditions exists, the absolute necessity for effective personal selling is obvious. However, even when such compelling factors are not present, personal selling is commonly required to capitalize on the strength built up by other forces in the promotional mix.

# FITTING PERSONAL SELLING INTO THE PROMOTION MIX —THE MICRO-LEVEL

Whenever a salesperson has an opportunity to play the role of promotional strategist (or persuasive communicator), rather than being limited to mere order taking, all the factors of our general framework for promotional analysis become relevant, but with a unique twist. As suggested in Figure 10.1, personal selling is an *individualized* explicit promotional element. The other three explicit elements (advertising, sales promotion, and publicity) are primarily mass communication methods. They can be tailored on a group or market segment basis, but almost never on a customer-by-customer basis. Personal selling must almost always be handled on an individually tailored basis. This presents some special oppportunities and also some special challenges.

*Coordination with Other Promotional Elements*

Although only a portion of the entire promotional framework flowchart is represented in Figure 10.1, all the variables in the total framework are implied and are very much relevant to the salesperson acting as a promotional strategist. The first implication of importance is that personal selling is part of an explicit promotional mix which, in turn, stems from a completely integrated marketing strategy process. As one team of observers has said, "Every personal sale can be divided into two parts: the part done by the salespeople and the part done for the salespeople by the company. For example, from the standpoint of the product the company should provide the salesperson with a product skillfully designed, thoroughly tested, attractively packaged, adequately advertised, and priced to compare favorably with competitive products."[5]

Part of the initial and continued training that companies should provide to their sales forces deals with these and other aspects of the full promotional mix which form the starting base for personal selling activities. Although the company is likely to give its field representatives briefings on planning input factors—such as relevant evaluative criteria and how they relate to lifestyle goals—it is also up to the salesperson to secure as much additional information as possible on a prospect-by-prospect basis. Because this is a customized promotional technique, the sales representative can attempt to discover the pattern of emphasis given to various evaluative criteria, to determine the types of lifestyle goals behind that pattern, to check for existing brand preference levels and brand criteria ratings, and to test for purchase intention levels, especially in connection with preparations to "close" the sale—*all on a purchaser-by-purchaser basis.*

These kinds of information gathering account for much but not necessarily all of the preparatory work shown as "Precustomer contact activities" in Figure 10.1. Essentially, this is the salesperson's strategy planning phase. However, the information gathering process continues into the strategy execution phase, "Individualized customer contact activities." At this juncture the salesperson is in a position different from that of any other promotional strategist. He or she can survey the customer directly and make on-the-spot adjustments in promotional strategy approaches.

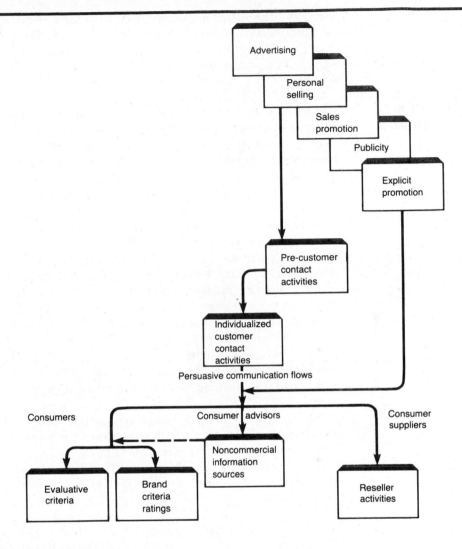

**FIGURE 10.1 Personal selling in the explicit promotional mix**

## EXAMPLES OF PERSONAL SELLING

A variety of strategy patterns have been suggested to guide salespeople. In these suggested patterns, personal selling has been treated as everything from a football game[6] to a sophisticated "process model."[7] To develop a background for exploring some frequently recommended selling patterns, we will first consider the accounts of four salespeople describing how they handle their jobs. The names are fictitious and the companies are not identified, but everything else is quite factual. For the most part, even the words are those used by the people involved.

Although these descriptions will not cover all seven of the salesperson categories previously defined, they will deal with four distinct levels of selling intensity. The salespeople involved are an inside order taker who deals directly with ultimate consumers, a detail salesperson who works mainly with physicians, a sales engineer who calls on many different industrial buyers, and a service salesperson who sells to both ultimate consumers and industrial buyers.

**Mr. Altein Sells Women's Shoes**

Jim Altein is a salesman in a retail shoe store that is located in a shopping mall and carries items in the middle-price ranges. Jim has been a shoe salesman for over thirty years, and has worked in a number of different stores. Generally, he has been compensated on a straight commission basis. Currently he receives an eight percent commission on all his sales. Jim feels the commission system is fine. It has allowed him to earn an excellent income and be directly and immediately rewarded for his effort. His description follows.

"One thing I've found is that customers are different by time of day. In the morning, you're usually dealing with more serious buyers. They really intend to make a purchase. They usually don't have much time to spend on it. Up until about noontime, I work with that in mind. In the afternoon and evening, many women are coming in to look more than to buy. You can take more time with them but you also have to sell harder. While traffic increases in the afternoon, your chances of making a sale with any one customer go down. For that reason, you have to be careful that you're not wasting time. When I get a customer who seems to be just shopping to pass the time, I usually attempt a 'trial close.' I say something which more or less forces the issue. Depending on how I read that customer's response, I may either go on with the sale or cut things short.

"We do have some steady customers, people you get to know. For the most part, though, I'm making a fresh start every time someone walks in the store. When I first see a customer, there are some things I quickly check. All of them help me decide what kind of shoes to show her and what features to emphasize. This is what amounts to my preapproach—my first planning information to help me handle the sale. The main things I check out are (1) how old the lady is, (2) whether she is dressed conservatively or stylishly, and (3) the quality of the shoes she's wearing.

"Of course, the standard opening line, in this business, is something like, 'May I help you?' or 'Is there something I can show you?' I probably open this way as much as anybody else. However, if a woman is looking at a particular pair of shoes when I approach her, I'll try to start the conversation by saying something about them. Naturally, I'm going to say something complimentary. The next thing I try to do is find out what that customer is looking for. Some people are mainly interested in fit and comfort. Others are going for style. Sometimes a woman wants a shoe to wear for a very particular type of occasion. In other cases, she may want one that goes with different kinds of clothes and is right for a wide variety of situations.

"Once I think I've figured out what it is she wants, I'm ready to bring out several pairs for her to try on. It's important to show her an assortment. Even if she just asks to see a particular pair we have in the window, she's more likely to buy if you give her a chance to do some picking and choosing. This is true whether you're dealing with an afternoon shopper with plenty of time or a morning customer who's probably in more of a hurry. The styles I bring out are those I think will deliver what that particular person is looking for. My sales talk is based on the same idea. I put the stress on the features in which she seems to be especially interested.

"Some of the shoe companies give us poster-size copies of their ads. If a customer is very style conscious and I have such a poster on the styles I'm showing her, I'll bring out the poster. For example, it might be a young woman and the style might have been advertised in *Seventeen*. Showing her the poster can really help sell her on that pair of shoes. It can be a good way to close the sale.

"Another thing I try to do is sell myself—to let people know I'm there to help in every way I can. Whenever possible, I try to get customers to sit down and put on the shoes. Sometimes a shopper will say she simply wants to look without trying them on. If you can convince her to try wearing them, you're on your way to making a sale. Many salespeople simply hand the shoes to the customer. I always offer to put them on for her. It's just one more way of demonstrating that you want to be helpful.

"I try to sense when a customer is ready to buy. If she seems really interested, I try hard to close the sale by reassuring her and quickly going back over the points that seemed to impress her. But you have to be careful. You can push too hard and lose the sale completely. I used to work in a mall that had almost two dozen shoe stores. When I worked there I was concerned about letting customers get out of the store because they usually wouldn't come back. But here your best bet is to be friendly, let her go, but also let her know you really want to help her make the right choice."

**Miss Brussi Sells Pharmaceutical Products**

Five years ago, right after she graduated from college, Marilyn Brussi went to work for a major pharmaceutical firm. After finishing a training program, she was assigned to cover a three-county sales area. It includes one moderately sized city plus a number of smaller towns. Miss Brussi is paid on a salary-plus-bonus basis. Her year-end bonus is based on company sales in her territory and is figured by a rather complex formula. She also is given a company automobile and an expense account for traveling. Here is how she describes her job.

"The work I do is called 'detailing.' It involves making calls on doctors, hospitals, drugstores, and wholesalers to promote the company's products. We're primarily an 'ethical' drug company, so the emphasis is on prescription business. Doctors are critical to our success. For this reason, most of my time is spent selling them on the idea of prescribing our products.

"When I started with the company, I took over all the accounts of the person who had worked the area before me. Since then I've kept updating accounts—learning when a new doctor or new drugstore moves into my territory. If a physician opens a practice in my region, I try to get all the information I can on him or her. This goes onto an account card and a copy of that card is sent to company headquarters. If a new drugstore opens, my job is to get them set up with an opening order, making sure they have an adequate supply of our products. I don't actually write the order myself, but send it in to our wholesaler.

"As for calls on physicians, much of what I do depends on how many people are in the waiting room. If there are a number of patients waiting, I know I won't have much time to make my presentation. Consideration of a doctor's time is important and, for that matter, you also have to consider the nurse's time. If the nurse lets you in late in the day, for example, you want to make sure you don't talk so long that the staff stays after hours. If you do, you may find it hard to get in the next time.

"I try to establish at least some personal rapport with the physician at the beginning of the call. However, I don't push too much personal conversation unless the physician seems to encourage it. The doctor's time is likely to be short. Above all, I try to be myself and be honest. If you aren't, pretty soon your customers will see through you and you'll be finished. I have to build a continuous sense of trust. If one of my customers gets the idea that I'm a phony—or worse, thinks I lied or misrepresented a product—I'm finished with that account.

"My heaviest selling effort occurs when we are introducing a new drug. When you first present it, the company wants you to secure the physician's promise that she or he will prescribe it. However, things rarely work out that way. I usually try to rough out the full story on the first call. Instead of a commitment to prescribe, it's more likely that I'll encounter questions and objections. I'll talk about the product as long as the doctor wants. When I see that he or she wants to stop, I leave some samples and literature and say goodbye.

"Right after that I go to my car and write out everything I told that doctor about the drug. Then I make notes on the questions and objections that were raised and also on any points that seemed to arouse special interest. Before I make my return call, I'll prepare myself to cover the questions and objections that came up. I'm also ready to stress the features that seemed to get the most response.

"Because so many physicians are specialists, you have to consider how any new drug fits into the doctor's specialty. Even among practitioners in the same field, you'd be surprised at the differences as to interest in different aspects of product performance. Although you say essentially the same things to all customers, there's a big variation in the points you want to emphasize. The company has a staff of medical people and other researchers whom I can contact for any answers that I might not have. On my follow-up calls, I'm ready to deal mainly with the points in which each particular doctor seemed especially interested and to answer the questions he or she raised.

"As a practical matter, it's likely to take me half a dozen visits or more before I can actually secure a commitment to prescribe. As soon as I obtain it, I call on the druggists in the area telling them that doctor so-and-so intends to prescribe the new drug. Then I'll write up an order so that they'll have it in stock when the prescriptions come in. Later I'll check sales records to see if the physician is actually using the product. If he or she is not, I'll make a note to mention the item again on my next visit and try to find out whether there are specific objections we haven't covered.

"To handle my job, I have to be something of an expert on drug products, both ours and those of our competitors. When I started this job I went through over six weeks of formal training. Not only do we have frequent further training periods, but I also must be certified by the company on every major new product. To get that certification, I have to study up on the product and pass a written test. If I don't pass with a grade of ninety or higher, I must take repeat exams until I make that kind of score.

"Of course, I put our products in the very best light I can. However, there are a couple of touchy aspects in this business. For one thing, you always have to remember the doctor is the expert—no matter how much you think you know. Second, we are required by law to reveal information we have about contraindications, such as side effects or other potential difficulties from using the drug.

"I'm backed up by strong support from the drug company. In addition to the brochures, samples, and test lab results that we give physicians, the company also advertises heavily in medical journals. Those ads, plus the good publicity we often get, start me off with at least some prestige. They can also serve as excellent openers or reference points during a presentation. I see my job as putting the final package together and moving the product over its last hurdle."

**Mr. Collins Sells Packings and Seals**

Tad Collins is an independent salesman—a manufacturer's representative. He sells for firms that compensate him on a straight percentage of sales basis. Tad pays his own expenses. His account of his work follows.

"I represent several companies. In a way I am one of their customers, because I can recommend the product of one company or another to the accounts I call on, but I don't take the idea that I am a customer too seriously. If I don't produce the kind of volume they think I should be getting, they'll take the lines away from me. My territory covers parts of three states and I call on about 265 different accounts. These are mainly manufacturing plants, chemical plants, rock quarries, coal mines, construction companies, and marine industries.

"Whenever you are pumping liquids or running them through valves you have a leakage problem. It is my job to know the best way to handle this and have the right product to do the job. I sell braided packings and mechanical seals. For many purposes braided packings will work well. They are made out of a wide range of materials and control leaks but don't completely prevent them. For more complex situations, you probably need a mechanical seal. There are a variety of seals available. For example, when you get into a situation in which you are pumping a flammable liquid or a dangerous chemical, you don't want any leakage at all. That may require a double mechanical seal with fluid in between that forms a total block to any leakage.

"The real buying decisions are made by the people who actually deal with the problems—the production department, maintenance department, utilities department, environmental control people, and safety engineers. These are my customers. I try to work with them to solve their troubles. Then they write purchase requisitions that go to the purchasing agent.

"Although I don't spend as much time with purchasing agents, I do call on them to let them know what is happening and to keep their goodwill. The PA's job is to select the best source for filling the requisition. Although they may not really know what the product actually is or what it is used for, they do make the final buys and can give the business to someone else if they want to. At the very least I have got two people to sell to—the person back in the plant and the purchasing agent up front.

"One question you run into is 'What do I really have to sell?' I have my products of course, but competitors have products that are often close or equal in quality. While I promote the quality of my products I know that I have to offer something more than that. The next thing you can try to sell is price. You could try to beat competition, but if you do it will simply backfire on you. A price advantage is just going to last a little while and then it is gone.

"The next thing you can sell is yourself. You want your customer to know that you are a good person to deal with, that you understand his needs, are friendly, and easy to get along with. Beyond that you have service to sell. When a customer is facing a problem, you have to know how to help him solve it. If it's a problem with one of your products, you have to be ready to hop right in to correct it. This means you need a lot of training yourself. You not only have to know what your products are but how they fit into various applications.

"Finally, the big thing we are finding you can really sell is *knowledge*—sophisticated solutions and training programs for your customers. We'll put on training schools for customers' employees. If it seems to make sense, I'll ask a factory representative to come down with me to make calls and show people how to use our products and get the most out of them. To give you an example, I once spent over six months, off and on, analyzing problems in one plant. As an illustration of their problems, they had eight seals burn out on a pump in one weekend. I studied the situation and showed them how to put it in correctly so that a seal would last for five months.

"In this type of selling you begin by losing money. You don't charge for all your advice and study. You don't charge for the training programs you put on for your customers either. On top of that, when you work the problem out and show them how to get longer life from your products, it really means you are going to sell them less. What you are doing of course is working to let them know they can count on you so you'll get their future business. Most of this is fairly high volume. As an example, the plant where I solved the burnout problem has about 450 pumps. Each uses a mechanical seal and each seal costs about $150.

"I try to set up a regular call schedule for each customer. How often I call depends on how big the account is and what kind of service they need. I know that the more you call the better chance you have to make sales and keep their business. Every time they see your face it reminds them to buy something from you. This is a dog-eat-dog business. If you want to keep your customers you'd better keep yourself in sight.

"While I'm always on the lookout for new business, you can make a mistake trying to get too many new accounts and forgetting about your old ones. As far as finding new accounts is concerned, the type of plants who would use our products are fairly easy to spot through manufacturer's directories or just trade talk. To get your foot in the door with a new account you have several possibilities. One is simply to get on their bidding list. Some companies are required to send out calls for bids and if you are on their list you find out what they want and take it from there. Another way to open up a new account is to call and see if they are satisfied with the kind of service they are getting right now. This educational thing, putting on training schools and seminars, is also a great way to get started with customers.

"The actual sales call almost always begins with friendly conversation, just shooting the breeze. This is not so much for determining facts about the customer or what he's looking for, but finding out what the person is like and trying to get him to like you. I even keep short notes on my account file card to remind me about their hobbies, families, and so on.

"The next thing I do is to find out what the customer is looking for by asking relevant questions. I generally do this from a problem angle, attempting to learn what problems that customer is trying to solve or what situation he's trying to improve. Every customer is looking for something different. One might be concerned about downtime, another about leakage, still another might be just looking to make his job easier. You find this out through natural conversation and simple questions. I also try to discover how much the customer knows about various products and the field in general by asking what brands he's familiar with, what he's used in the past, what has worked and what hasn't.

"In some ways, a sales presentation is like facing a guy with a loaded gun. Every time I can answer a question that's on his mind (whether he's asked it or not) it's like taking a bullet away. If you leave him with one bullet, he'll shoot you down. I like to find out how many bullets he has early on, then I'm ready to handle the rest of the call.

"I carry samples and use them during my presentation. They're good because the customer can see and handle the product. It gets them involved. The brands I sell are advertised in trade journals and sometimes one of them gets written up. I also carry copies of the journals because that's something else I can hand a customer while I'm making the presentation. It's excellent back-up material. I stay away from mentioning other companies that have used my brands because there's often jealousy among these companies.

"Naturally, because the needs of each customer are different, my presentations differ. I represent several lines with a variety of products in each, so my presentation really starts when I pick the products I know will match the benefits this particular customer wants. The rest of the presentation centers around those benefits.

"As to closing a sale, I play it by ear. I may be able to make a sale in five minutes or it may take five trips. Much depends on who I'm dealing with, whether the individual has the authority to actually purchase the item or whether it has to go to someone else for final approval. Most of the time, I try to get a definite yes before I leave but if I sense that the customer is becoming irritated or needs to get the supervisor's okay, I drop it. Quite frankly, I often come out with no order in hand, at least on that call."

## Ms. Durek Sells Insurance

Ruth Durek is a Certified Life Underwriter. She has been in the insurance business for about four years and represents one of the major companies in the United States. Before entering the insurance field, Ms. Durek spent over fifteen years in retail merchandising. She works in three main areas—selling life insurance policies to individuals, selling group life plans to business firms, and doing estate planning work. Here is her description of her work.

"Every day is different, depending on the customers I'm contacting or the type of problems that come up. I try to get to my office between 7:00 and 7:30 in the morning. The first order of business is paperwork, sales call preparation, and studying. As a matter of fact, I really spend more of my time preparing to sell than I do in actually talking with customers about a particular insurance plan. One of the main things I do early in the morning is keep up with changes in the tax laws. I have to be able to give my clients the best and latest information available, and the laws and court rulings are constantly changing.

"When I'm finished with the paperwork, I begin working on getting new leads. Prospecting, finding potential customers, is the lifeblood of the insurance business. This is also the thing that many insurance agents hate the most. I've met a good many people who have been selling insurance for ten, twenty, or even thirty years who still hate to prospect for new business. They don't mind making the sales calls. It's trying to find new customers that bothers them. But if you can't do it, you'll never be a success in this field.

"Prospecting is different for someone just starting out in the business as opposed to someone who's been selling insurance for awhile. A new person is asked to list approximately 300 names—people he or she knows. You don't have to know much more than their names to list them. From there, you start making 'cold calls.'

"A person who has been in the business awhile gets prospect names from talking with people in town—hearing about someone who has bought a house, is getting married, or having a baby, etc. The biggest source of names is referrals. If I make a call on someone (and even if they don't buy any insurance) I say something like, 'If you're satisfied with the way I've handled myself, I'd appreciate your giving me the names of people who would be receptive to this approach.' Usually, I try to get two or three names each time.

"Once you have a name, you attempt to find out more about the person. In part, you do this to assess his or her potential as an insurance buyer. For example, I don't like to call on anyone making less than $20,000 a year. I generally prefer people who own their own homes. This tells me they live more solid lives and save some money. I avoid job hoppers. People who already have insurance are the easiest to sell.

"My preapproach is really a continuation of the prospecting. Before I call on the individual, I do some further investigation, trying to get as much personal information as possible. I want to be able to talk that person's language. Next, I either write the prospect a letter or drop by to introduce myself. Later, I'll contact the prospect again to arrange a meeting time.

"To open the actual sales call, we're trained to use a 'standard sequence' approach. Most people who have been in the business for awhile don't use it verbatim, but may follow the sequence concept. The approach usually begins with 'relaxing conversation.' I talk about myself, my company, and what I sell. Then I invite the customer to ask me any questions he or she may have. If there are none, I start asking some questions of my own. I try to find out the following information:

1. What insurance coverage does the prospect now have?
2. Why was it purchased?
3. Is it enough to give adequate protection?
4. In what areas of insurance is he or she most interested?
5. How does the person feel about insurance?
6. What benefits does this person want from insurance?
7. How much premium can be afforded?

"Because I have ten or fifteen products available, I have to find out what the customer really needs to make the best match. During that first call, I determine whether I want to show something to the individual immediately or later. Usually, I wait until later to make a full presentation.

"The second call is made about two weeks after the initial conversation. From my first visit, I can determine whether a formal typewritten presentation is desirable or whether a more individualized, informal presentation is best. I base this decision on both the nature of the policy (big business, small business, personal, etc.) and the personalities of the individual customers. For instance, if the presentation is to a business and the people are stuffy, an overhead projector or flip chart might be used along with formal typewritten handout material. In another presentation, I might just use a table easel and a felt tip pen.

"There are about seventeen standard objections a customer may raise. I practice my presentation ahead of time, bringing up the objections and working on responses best suited to that prospect. By thinking them through beforehand, I can gather any necessary information, facts, and figures that fit the particular case. During the presentation, I'm preparing for my close. I try to make the presentation conversational and get the person to say 'Yes' as many times as possible. I'll ask questions and phrase them in such a way that the answer almost has to be 'Yes.'

"When I think I may have a pretty good probability of getting the sale, I begin attempting 'trial closes.' I may say something like 'Don't you think this would be a good plan?' If I've run through three or four trial closings and still haven't received a 'Yes' answer, I may move to what is called an 'implied consent' close. Here I assume the individual is going to buy. It's up to the customer to stop me. For example, I may ask about arrangements for a physical or request the individual's social security number for an application form.

"Most every morning, I call the home office of my insurance company. Often, these calls involve questions on claims. It's vital for me to give my customers this service. If I don't they won't stay with me or recommend me to other people. Another reason for calling the home office is to obtain technical advice, not so much on selling but on details of policies and plans.

"The company is excellent in terms of giving me support in the form of technical assistance, good insurance plans, national advertising, and selling materials to help me in my presentations. When it comes to finding customers, however, I'm strictly on my own. I have a territory assigned to me and a base quota that I'm expected to fill.

"The company starts all its representatives off with an extensive training program. You're told how to find leads, how to talk on the phone, how to handle face-to-face selling situations, and how to prepare your presentation. After that you work with an assistant manager and for the first couple of weeks you really watch rather than do anything yourself. Next comes the critical part when you start trying to sell on your own. The initial period is especially tough and many people simply can't make it.

"A few years back our company spent a great deal of money to study the type of background that makes the best insurance sales representative. After all their investigation, they concluded there was really no particular background that seemed to make any special difference. Personally, I think that success in this business depends on having a lot of personal enterprise and being able to set your own goals. In addition to that, you need training and a good company to back you."

## Some Generalizations

From the four accounts just presented, it is apparent that the range of activities which salespeople undertake varies greatly, depending on the field in which they are selling. For example, the amount of preparation put in before the sales presentation is extensive in some cases but very brief and informal in others. Mr. Altein had little chance to prepare when selling shoes. Ms. Durek spends more time preparing than actually selling. The intensity of the selling process tends to increase as you move from retail to detail to technical and finally to intangible sales situations. But, though there are differences, you also saw many similarities in the way these four people approach the selling process.

All four analyze each customer in terms of the benefits that particular person seeks. Jim Altein must do this very quickly by some visual observation and perhaps a few questions. The other three have the advantage of making repeated calls on the same customers. They have a much better opportunity to get a complete picture of the benefit package desired and they work hard at capitalizing on that opportunity.

All four try to select a product offering with implicit promotional features that closely match the evaluative criteria of importance to the prospect. Marilyn Brussi is least able to put stress on this point. Her job pretty much requires her to try selling each drug item to every physician who is a potential prospect. However, the other three salespeople have some control over the choice of product to be promoted, and they are very much aware that much of their success depends on making the right kind of match.

All four develop a customized oral presentation. They do not say the same things to each potential buyer. Presentations vary from prospect to prospect and are built around the set of evaluative criteria and lifestyle goals which appear to be of most interest to that person.

Finally, in one way or another, all four try to convince the customer to make a favorable decision—a commitment to buy the product. This sometimes means using very specific tactics to almost force a positive response from the customer.

In summing up these points, it is apparent that personal selling is clearly distinguished from all other promotional techniques by the fact that it represents the ultimate in market segmentation—analyzing and promoting to customers on an individual-by-individual basis.

## PATTERNS TO GUIDE PERSONAL SELLING TECHNIQUES

Because there are common threads running through all types of personal selling, general patterns have been proposed as guides that can be used by all sales personnel. We will look at four such proposals. The first cuts across both precontact and customer contact activities. The other three deal mainly with some specific ways of handling the customer contact process itself. The four strategy patterns to be reviewed are (1) the sequential activities pattern, (2) the stimulus-response pattern, (3) the AIDA pattern, and (4) the dynamic feedback pattern.

## THE SEQUENTIAL ACTIVITIES PATTERN

This is probably the most widely discussed and recommended pattern for personal selling strategy. It views the sales representative's activities as a sequential process, a series of steps to be followed in order. These steps begin before the actual presentation to the customer and continue after the sale is completed. The sequence of precontact and contact activities is shown in Figure 10.2.

The pattern is based on the premise that there is much more to personal selling than just meeting with a customer face-to-face and that there is a certain order to the way things must be done. The steps have been compared to links in a chain, each of which must be constructed properly if the others are to serve their purpose.

*Prospecting*

***Variations in Importance.*** Prospecting, the initial step in the sequence, involves finding potential customers—people who are very likely to buy your product once you can convince them of its benefits. Not all salespeople are deeply involved in this step. In many cases, the company may provide representatives with a list of accounts and expect them to update the lists as new prospects enter the area. This describes Miss Brussi's situation. Tad Collins, in the industrial field, is in much the same position. If either of them were

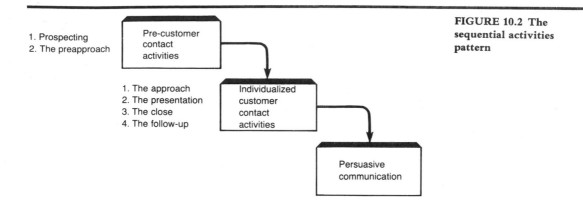

1. Prospecting
2. The preapproach

Pre-customer contact activities

1. The approach
2. The presentation
3. The close
4. The follow-up

Individualized customer contact activities

Persuasive communication

**FIGURE 10.2 The sequential activities pattern**

opening a new territory, prospecting would be an extremely important activity. Because both work in established territories, however, it does not involve all that much of their time.

In a strict sense, Jim Altein is not involved in prospecting at all. He deals with customers who find him rather than with customers he finds. If he were retailing a product such as automobiles instead of shoes, the situation might be quite different. To Ruth Durek, prospecting is the "lifeblood" of her business, and it is a task that many insurance people apparently find to be the most difficult aspect of their work.

***Methods of Prospecting.*** Prospecting can be accomplished in a variety of ways. Like Ms. Durek, many people in personal selling feel customer referrals are exceptionally valuable. Names may also come from various types of published lists and directories, including the telephone directory. Noncompeting salespeople—those selling to the same markets you serve but dealing in products that are not direct substitutes for yours—can be an excellent source for securing names and preliminary information on customers. Some prospecting is also done by "cold canvassing," simply going door-to-door or firm-to-firm and trying to determine whether each contact might offer a reasonable chance for making a sale.

***The Preapproach***

The idea behind the preapproach is that you should know as much about your prospect as you can possibly learn before you begin the actual sales contact.

***Qualifying Prospects.*** Usually, the first aspect of the preapproach is "qualifying" potential customers, by rating them as to the likelihood that working with them will be successful. For example, Ruth Durek uses some fairly easily obtained bits of demographic data to help her determine how much effort she wants to put into a sales call or whether she even wants to make a call on a particular person. Factors such as yearly income, marital status, home ownership, and whether the person currently carries insurance help her prescreen potential customers. Even Jim Altein does some prescreening when he attempts to sort out shoppers who are merely looking from those who have a more serious intention to purchase a pair of shoes.

*Personal Selling—Salespeople at Work*

***Obtaining and Analyzing Pertinent Information.***   However, there is more to the preapproach than merely distinguishing between good prospects and poor prospects. Ideally, every salesperson would probably like to know as much about each prospect as he or she could possibly learn. One view suggests, "Top flight salespeople often accumulate more information about their prospective customers than would be found in an FBI file. For example, it might not be important to anyone else, but the knowledge that Mr. Abbott, purchasing agent for the Steel Corporation of America, likes baseball, has a son in the Washington College crew, is allergic to onions, dislikes cigarette smokers, and collects wood carvings is invaluable to the salesperson."[8]

In one way or another, the accounts of all four salespeople emphasized the importance of obtaining information on customers before trying to sell. For Jim Altein this includes observation of age and mode of dress, followed by whatever else he can learn from conversation with shoppers. Marilyn Brussi places information on new prospects on file cards and keeps a written record of questions and reactions after each call. Tad Collins also uses a file card system to note information about his customers' hobbies, family, and so on.

Apart from simply gathering this information, the sales representative has to decide how it is going to be put to use during the actual sales call. This requires analyzing the information to prepare for the customer contact. Sometimes, as mentioned by Ruth Durek, the analysis is followed by an actual rehearsal of the sales contact procedure. Especially with an important sales call, it would not be unusual for a sales representative to rehearse the call very carefully attempting to anticipate both her or his role and that of the prospect.

## The Approach

***Importance of the Approach.***   The approach involves the first few minutes of the sales call. It is distinguished from the rest of the call because it is the time during which the salesperson "breaks the ice." In selling, as in many other fields, there is a common belief that first impressions are exceptionally important. Especially on your initial contact with any given customer, the approach is the time to make a good first impression.

During the approach the salesperson normally introduces himself or herself and also attempts to introduce the product to be presented. The objective of the approach is to attain the attention of your prospect, to establish a solid personal relationship, and to begin earning that customer's liking and trust. Then you try to secure as much additional information as possible about the goals and evaluative criteria your prospect regards as important. One observer has described the approach as "a sale within the sale—selling yourself and the interview. Unless you accomplish this presale successfully, your prospect may brush you off before he [or she] hears your full story."[9]

***Phases of the Approach.***   The same observer envisions the approach as usually covering less than the first five minutes of the sales talk and as being comprised of two distinct phases. These phases are as follows:

1. *The first seconds of the interview.* During this time your prospect decides that he [or she] will see you and hear your story.
2. *The balance of the approach time necessary* to obtain your objectives. During

this time you establish rapport, briefly introduce yourself, your company, your product or service, ask questions and get the prospect to tell you his [or her] problems or needs. [10]

The opening segment of the approach often has little to do with the actual promotion of the product itself. Ruth Durek described it as "relaxing conversation." Tad Collins called it "shooting the breeze." Marilyn Brussi referred to it as trying to establish "at least some personal rapport."

As Ruth Durek also indicated, many companies attempt to train their sales personnel to follow a more or less standardized approach, sometimes even word-for-word. Although the idea of a standardized approach can easily be carried too far, there is probably a good deal of sense in the idea of preplanning the opening of your sales interview, and then being prepared to make on-the-spot adjustments appropriate to the situation.

## The Presentation

**Objectives of the Presentation.** The presentation is the main part of the selling contact process; it is the point at which the salesperson goes into detail regarding product benefits that the brand offers and how those benefits relate to the lifestyle goals of the prospect. In practice, it might be difficult for an observer to tell exactly when the approach ends and the presentation begins. However, the presentation can be thought of as the "getting down to business" part of the sales call.

By this time the salesperson should have established herself or himself as a knowledgeable and trustworthy individual in the mind of the prospect. Something should also have been learned of the prospect's interests, needs, and desires. The job is now one of clearly demonstrating that your product can answer those interests, needs, and desires. During this stage the sales representative very often employs other elements from the firm's promotional mix—samples, brochures, copies of advertising material, and publicity references. You saw both Marilyn Brussi and Tad Collins making strong use of these and other techniques to add power to their presentations. You also saw Tad Collins talk about involving his prospects by having them touch and handle sample materials.

While these are examples of specific methods used in delivering the presentation, the essential core around which the presentation is built relates to our earlier discussion of attitude components. Each one of the four people you read about emphasized the importance of discovering how the various evaluative criteria are weighted by the prospect. Much of the work during the preapproach and approach stages was aimed at preparing for this. In the presentation phase, the salesperson puts this information to work to upgrade brand criteria ratings on important evaluative criteria and relate them to the lifestyle goals of the prospect.

**Handling Objections.** The salesperson is likely to encounter objections during the presentation. Tad Collins compared them to "bullets in a loaded gun." Ruth Durek felt she had them standardized down to a list of about seventeen. Marilyn Brussi made notes on them and if necessary sought technical assistance between calls so she would be ready to handle them on the next round. The ability to handle objections immediately illustrates a major difference between feedback possibilities in personal selling as opposed to feedback possibilities in an advertising situation. Confronting objections on a one-to-one basis is both a challenge and an opportunity that the salesperson has but the advertising planner does not have.

Tad Collins seemed to be suggesting that he tried to obtain a reading on every potential objection during the early part of the call, before the objection had even been openly raised. Then he hoped to cover the point in advance. In other words, he "took the bullets out of the gun." Ruth Durek, on the other hand, rehearsed her responses before the call but tailored them separately for each prospect. In both cases, however, they were personalizing their responses, rather than replying mechanically. The rationale behind recommending the personalized method to meeting objections has been stated in the following way:

> [Many salespeople have] been trained to give a specific answer to a specific question. This can be called the set-answer approach. This approach has one basic flaw. It does not necessarily follow that what the customer states is what [he or she] really means, nor is it possible for one set answer to an objection to be equally meaningful to all prospects. Thus a more accurate way to handle objections is to qualify or determine specifically what the individual means by [his or her] statement. [11]

In other words, the alert salesperson should amplify the feedback effect by probing further, if necessary, to clarify the prospect's reasoning and then frame an answer that best suits this specific case.

***Ending the Presentation Stage.***   If the sales interview is proceeding in a positive way, some decision ultimately has to be made as to whether the customer is ready to buy the product. In terms of the general framework for promotional strategy analysis which we are following, the salesperson has to decide (1) when the brand preference level has been raised to a sufficiently high point that (2) there is a very strong purchase intention probability. At this juncture, customer contact activity proceeds to the next step of the sequential activities pattern.

## The Close

The close is the move to actually complete the sale. At first glance, it may seem like a fairly automatic thing. If you have done a good job of opening the interview, via the approach, and then made a solid presentation, the customer should be ready to say, "I'll buy." Sometimes this happens.

However, most experts put great emphasis on knowing how to make certain that it happens. There are a variety of ways by which salespeople attempt to determine when it is time to close. In some cases the customer may be reacting so positively and showing such a high degree of interest that the signs are obvious. In other cases, salespeople probe the prospect's attitude by means of a "trial close" or an "implied consent close."

***Trial Closes and Implied Consent Closes.*** Ms. Durek gave a clear example of trial closing tactics. When she asks her insurance prospect, "Don't you think this would be a good plan?", she is really calling for feedback information on purchase intentions. A "Yes" answer means she should be able to begin writing up the policy. Notice in her case that if she does not receive a positive response, she may decide to force a close using her "implied consent" approach. However, also notice that Marilyn Brussi and Tad Collins said nothing about implied consent as a closing tactic. In fact, they both indicated there was a point at which the dictates of wisdom suggested no further attempt be made to complete the sale on that particular call. Their course of action was "Leave now, try later."

***Choosing Among Closing Tactics.*** The difference between the tactics of Ms. Durek and those of Miss Brussi and Mr. Collins derive largely from the fact that the latter two make continuous calls on the same customer. As Colllins pointed out, "I may be able to make a sale in five minutes or it may take five trips." Not only will they have future opportunities for a close, but their continuous customer relationships demand that they not take much chance of offending a customer by being too aggressive. When a tactic like implied consent backfires, Ruth Durek loses a sale, but Tad Collins or Marilyn Brussi could lose an account.

In short, as with most everything else in personal selling, closing the sale is very much a matter of the particular circumstances. The way it is handled depends on such factors as the nature of a product line, whether the salesperson is engaged in repeated calls on the same customer over time or whether each call is a more or less separate and one-time thing, and the personality and philosophy of the individual salesperson.

***Importance of Timing.*** Even granting these variations, it remains true that most successful salespeople follow a practice of somehow asking for the order. Furthermore, there is likely to be one particular point during the customer contact process when it is most appropriate to try concluding the sale. If you run past that time, or do not know how to handle it when it occurs, your chances of success decrease. The salesperson's task, therefore, includes both learning how to recognize the correct point for a close and learning procedures that work best with different situations and different customers.

*The Follow-up*

The follow-up involves customer contact after the sale has been made. It often includes services which ensure that the product is properly delivered and providing the benefits for which it was purchased. In many selling situations, especially at the retail level, it is simply impossible for the salesperson to do a follow-up. For example, Jim Altein is usually in no position to do it. However, recalling that customers buy goods and services to satisfy their needs, it stands to reason that anyone counting on repeat business or customer recommendations should try to make certain those needs are really being satisfied.

*Variations in Importance.*   Like the other steps in the sequential activities pattern, both the importance and the exact nature of the follow-up will vary with the type of product and market being served. It becomes especially crucial when the salesperson is in a position to provide advice that assists in the successful use of the product by the customer. A prime example is Tad Collins in his work with packings and mechanical seals. The follow-up is also important to Ruth Durek because her sales involve the promise of future benefit deliveries by the company she represents. As she pointed out, servicing customer claims is a vital part of her total selling activity.

*Motivation for Follow-up.*   From a sales management standpoint, motivating salespeople to be active in the follow-up stage may be much more difficult than motivating them to be effective in any of the other steps. The reason is that follow-up activity usually carries no immediate, direct incentive payment, such as a commission or bonus. Nonetheless, as one team of writers has pointed out, "The good follow-up is the key to building a loyal clientele which, ultimately, results in a handsome income for the salesperson. Satisfied customers voluntarily provide more business."[12]

## Comments on the Sequential Activities Pattern

The sequential activities pattern is probably the most frequently mentioned format for discussing personal selling in both textbooks and sales training manuals. The terms "prospecting," "preapproach," "approach," "presentation," and "close" are commonly used among selling professionals. They form a recognized method of organizing the overall selling process. If there is any danger or potential fallacy in the sequential activities pattern it stems from the possibility of taking a step-by-step sequence too literally. One sales management text warns, "If each of the steps in the process is not culminated successfully, the seller will fail to get the order. However, each step overlaps others and their sequence may be altered to meet the situation at hand."[13]

Following the pattern simplistically could lead to trouble. For example, information gathering is done largely during the preapproach and the approach phases, but it does not necessarily end there. You must continue to be alert for further clues relating to buyer preferences that might surface during your presentation or even during your attempt to close. As a practical matter, it is quite possible that a salesperson might move all the way to the close stage and then decide to return to a prior stage and repeat the sequence.

Furthermore, the sequential activities pattern seems to speak in terms of preparing for and making one call with a possible follow-up after the actual sale has been made. However, people like Marilyn Brussi and Tad Collins point out that five or six calls are frequently necessary before a sale is made. In a sense, the early calls may serve largely as preapproaches for later calls. This is not because the sales representative plans it that way, but because the interaction between buyer and seller often demands a more complex pattern than suggested by a simple step-by-step sequential process. The sequential activities pattern, then, is a popular, useful, and much employed technique that can provide a very workable basis for planning personal selling strategy provided you do not allow it to limit your vision and cause you to oversimplify your situation or lose flexibility in dealing with customers.

## THE STIMULUS-RESPONSE PATTERN

A description of classical conditioning based on concepts originally studied by Pavlov was presented in Chapter 9. The stimulus-response pattern in personal selling situations is related to that model, but it does not work in exactly the same way that either classical conditioning or reinforcement learning might work in mass communication situations. As used by salespeople, the basic idea of the stimulus-response pattern is that there are certain stimuli which can be provided by the salesperson to induce a fairly predictable and favorable response on the part of the customer. In other words, if the sales representative knows how to say and do the "right things," the prospect will respond the "right way" almost automatically.

*Examples of Stimulus-Response Applications*

The stimulus-response pattern applies in the customer contact segment of personal selling. It could be used as a technique through all of the steps in the contact phase of the sequential activities pattern. Presumably, there are "correct" things to say and do during the approach, the presentation, and especially the close to elicit the responses you seek. Figure 10.3 schematizes a situation in which the entire contact phase is mainly one of the salesperson leading the customer through a series of predictable responses.

Ruth Durek illustrated the stimulus-response pattern. For example, during her presentation she tried to prompt the prospect to say "Yes" as many times as possible. Her opinion is that this puts that person in the right frame of mind to accept her sales argument. Notice that she chose questions (stimuli) for which the answers (responses) almost had to be "Yes."

Her implied consent procedure to attempt the close is also a variation of the stimulus-response pattern. She assumes, for instance, that when asked about arrangements for a physical exam the prospect will be reasonably well "conditioned" to respond by setting a date.

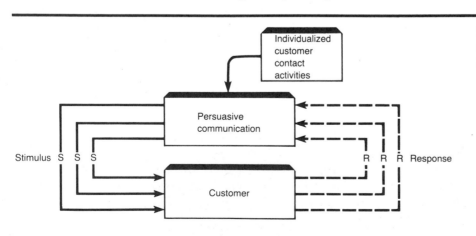

**FIGURE 10.3 The stimulus-response pattern**

In another situation, a person selling encyclopedias might decide that the key to success lies in stimuli related to prospects' fears of being viewed as bad parents. He or she could then prepare a selling strategy built on this proposition. For example, the presentation might incorporate repeated suggestions that, through buying the encyclopedias, parents can show neighbors, friends, and children that they really care about their parental roles. Stimuli could then be selected to reflect a prospect's prior conditioning toward concepts of good parenthood. These should elicit responses that positively influence the selling procedure.

*Limitations and Potential Hazards*

It was pointed out in the last chapter that there are some major differences between the way stimulus-response notions could be applied in personal selling as opposed to the way they might be applied in advertising. Again, if we are willing to accept the concept of vicarious learning, it is possible that some advertising could amount to a process that uses heavy repetition of stimulus-response-reward reinforcements to condition the audience.

It does not appear likely that the personal selling situation could really turn into such a reinforcement process. It generally lacks the same strength of repetition potential that is present in advertising and usually does not have the same power to induce a feeling of vicarious reward, at least not in the manner described in Chapter 9. Both in theory and in practice, the stimulus-response model as applied in personal selling seems to make use of existing, preconditioned responses. In other words, the salesperson does not "teach" the customer a stimulus-response pattern but relies on knowing that the customer's prior experiences have taught such a pattern.

This is exactly where Ruth Durek was placing her reliance. She chose questions which she felt the customer had been preconditioned to answer affirmatively, or she called for responses to questions with an "official sound"—arranging for a physical exam or giving a social security number. Again, these are stimuli to which many people have been more or less preconditioned to respond cooperatively. It has been pointed out, however, that there are major obstacles confronting a salesperson who overrelies on a stimulus-response pattern.[14] Some examples follow.

**1.** *Customers are different.* Because their backgrounds or preconditioning can vary greatly, not all customers will respond the same way to the same stimulus. The question or catch-phrase that works very well with one customer can fail miserably with a second and backfire badly with a third. For example, Ms. Durek's implied consent technique might produce an obedient response from one prospect but arouse hostility that ends the presentation from the next.

**2.** *Customers' drives and needs vary from time to time.* Even the customer who responded favorably the last time could balk when you use the same stimulus on a subsequent call. She or he may no longer be in the same mood.

**3.** *The salesperson usually lacks adequate control of the situation.* Recall that the learning model presented in Chapter 9 started with the assumption that the communicator was in somewhat the same position as a psychologist experimenting with rats or other lower animals. Although we are taking the view that the salesperson does not really do the conditioning, it is possible that someone using the stimulus-response technique could overestimate his or her control of the situation and perceive it as being similar to that of an experimental psychologist. Of course, this simply is not true. Your customers are likely to have as much if not more control of the situation as you. Therefore, overreliance on the method may mislead you very dangerously.

4. *The customer may be too complex and the approach too simple.* Especially when the salesperson starts with a predetermined list of stimuli, he or she may end by ignoring what is going on in the customer's mind. By following a strict stimulus-response pattern, you would be destroying your ability to receive feedback.

5. *It can prevent the salesperson from carefully studying prospects* and the kinds of interactions he or she has with those prospects. The stimulus-response pattern sometimes leads people into searching for magic words and phrases rather than analyzing each situation. When this occurs, the salesperson tends to obscure the reality of the situation—the needs, goals, and desired benefits of the prospect—and tries to achieve success through basically artificial techniques.

**Comments on the Stimulus-Response Pattern**

Even while stressing these limitations, it is still impossible to completely dismiss the possible applicability of stimulus-response methods as at least a part of the personal selling strategy in some situations. Ms. Durek, who used some stimulus-response techniques, did not seem to be over-simplifying matters, nor was she ignoring customer differences in preparing for her sales calls. On the contrary, she studied each sales call and planned it to aim carefully at that individual's particular needs, goals, and personality. Her stimulus-response mechanisms were simply a part of a total selling plan and usually a small part used quite carefully.

The other three salespeople did not mention the use of anything resembling the stimulus-response pattern. Presumably, if they rely on it at all, they do so only rarely. Especially when you are selling on a continuous basis and to prospects who are judging your offering with a professional eye, frequent attempts to arouse a favorable response by using a forceful stimulus could prove to be hazardous. Again, while Ruth Durek may be in a position to afford some occasional antagonism from an irritated customer, Tad Collins and Marilyn Brussi are not.

In summary, the stimulus-response pattern is worth some consideration. At best, however, it is likely to be merely part of a total selling pattern, and a small part applicable in only certain types of selling situations at that.

# THE AIDA PATTERN

This is one of the oldest patterns suggested for building a personal selling strategy and it views the salesperson as leading the prospect through a succession of four major mental stages—attention, interest, desire, and action. It

**FIGURE 10.4 The AIDA pattern**

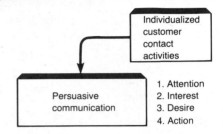

takes its name from the first letters of the stages it describes. Since being introduced over 50 years ago,[15] the AIDA formula has been and continues to be a favorite teaching technique among many sales trainers.

At first glance the four-stage series may seem to be another way of describing the adoption process model we considered in Chapter 3. It is not. Unfortunately, there is enough similarity of terms to make the two seem more like each other than they really are.

However, the AIDA pattern is built on premises very different from those of the adoption process model. The adoption process model assumes that consumers secure information from a variety of sources, usually over an extended period of time. Consumers then process this information to form opinions and attitudes toward various products and brands. The AIDA pattern, on the other hand, assumes that a salesperson or a piece of advertising leads a prospect through the four stages during one sales presentation. In other words it involves a very short period of time with only one source of information. From the perspective of sales planning, the AIDA pattern suggests the salesperson has a series of four hurdles to be overcome and that they occur in the order named. Figure 10.4 shows them in the context of the promotional analysis flowchart.

*Securing Attention and Interest*

The first goal in the AIDA pattern is achieving attention. It is quite possible that your prospect is apathetic or even antagonistic, in which case you must be prepared to do something to "break through," to get the customer to give you a hearing. Having succeeded in this, your next challenge is to arouse interest, to bring your customer to the point of having enough curiosity that he or she will want to hear more.

*Applicable Techniques.* The attention and interest stages are often seen as blending into each other. The specific techniques often recommended for achieving attention are very similar to those discussed in the previous chapter in connection with the general communication model—except that they are particularized to fit the personal selling situation. For example, one writer suggests "four factors of holding attention and interest" as follows:

- *Intensity.* Change the tone of your voice or the pace of your delivery, pause, or repeat yourself.
- *Contrast.* Employ verbal or illustrative differences to sharpen understanding

and awareness. For example, you can compare profit versus loss or cost versus savings.

- *Novelty.* Employ any novel or unusual attention-getting technique or device that keeps [your prospect] interested in you and your presentation.
- [*Borrowed Interest*]. Ask questions about personal or business subjects that interest your prospect; try to get [her or] him talking.[16]

*Building Desire*    Having accomplished your first two objectives, the AIDA pattern sees the next stage as building desire. Specific suggestions for accomplishing this usually involve special applications of the techniques suggested for increasing "positive interpretation" which we covered when discussing the general communication model in Chapter 9 (see p. 278). For example:

> Interest changes into desire when these events take place:
> 1. The prospect accepts the fact that a need or want exists.
> 2. The benefits to be gained from fulfilling that need satisfy his [or her] emotional buying motives.
> 3. The advantages of the benefit dominate [her or] his mind.[17]

*Prompting Action*    The last hurdle—securing immediate action—is related to the "response" portion of the general communication model. In the personal selling scenario, however, receiver response is quite different from response in a mass communications setting. The difference exists because mass communication usually anticipates a *delayed response* in terms of actual purchase decisions. An advertisement, for example, is normally not expected to close a sale. Rather, it is expected to aid in creating a favorable attitude that will produce a sale at some point in the future, but not at the exact moment the customer finishes reading, seeing, or hearing the ad. In contrast, salespeople should normally seek an *immediate, positive response.* As one observer has noted, "Very few prospects volunteer orders; they have to be asked for their business. Mere asking is not enough, however; you, as a sales representative, have to ask in such a way that you get a "yes, I'll buy now," instead of a no, a stall, or a put-off."[18]

*Relationships of the AIDA Pattern to the Sequential Activities Pattern*    The AIDA strategy not only parallels the general communication model to a large extent, but it is also a natural companion to the contact stages in the sequential activities pattern. Attention and interest relate to the approach, desire to the presentation, action to the close. The difference between these two patterns is that the sequential activities pattern places more emphasis on what the salesperson is doing, whereas the AIDA pattern views things from the standpoint of what is going on in the customer's mind. Both patterns are so frequently referred to and used by professional salespeople, and both have been part of the selling repertoire for so long, that their value is hardly in doubt.

Insofar as any weakness in the AIDA pattern is concerned, it is precisely the same as that discussed in connection with the sequential activities pattern. Viewing the selling process as a series of stages could lead to overlooking the fact that in some cases the seller may have to backpedal a bit because the buyer has backpedaled. In other words, AIDA followed to the letter and in mechanical fashion could cause you to be insensitive to feedback clues and to lose flexibility.

## THE DYNAMIC FEEDBACK PATTERN

*Rationale for the Dynamic Feedback Pattern*

Like all communication situations, personal selling settings are two-sided affairs. One side belongs to you as the salesperson. The other side belongs to your customers. It is a give and take arrangement. What your customer says and does is influenced by you, but what you say and do should also be influenced by your customer. The general communication model we considered in Chapter 9 stressed that the receiver segment of the communication process is just as important as the sender segment. Together, and only together, can they give meaning to your messsage. That model also highlighted the importance of feedback in guiding the sender to successful persuasion.

We have been emphasizing that a salesperson is in a highly advantageous position—relative to any other promotional strategist—because of the ability to obtain *immediate* feedback. The last pattern to be discussed is built around the feedback concept. It merges the major elements in the contact steps of the sequential activities pattern, the general flow of the AIDA pattern, and the dynamics or two-person interaction of the general communication model presented in Chapter 9.

The dynamic feedback pattern recognizes the importance of message decoding on the part of the receiver and suggests how the instantaneous feedback possibilities can be used to guide and if necessary redirect the selling sequence. It also has a built-in plan for gauging the components of attitude formation and using them to help determine your most logical persuasive route.

*Procedures for Application*

This pattern calls for the salesperson to chart her or his course by listening to and observing the customer. Figure 10.5 illustrates it in flowchart form. The sales contact process is not seen as a necessarily straightforward sequence of steps, but as a dialogue in which both the salesperson and customer take active parts.

The six oblong-shaped boxes running down the center of Figure 10.5 closely parallel, but also expand on the contact steps of the sequential pattern. For example, a separate survey step is singled out in box 2. Recalling what our four salespeople had to say earlier, this seems to be precisely in line with the practices each of them advocated.

*Utilizing Feedback.* Between each major step represented in the center of the figure there is a rectangular box suggesting that the salesperson should undertake some self-questioning before determining how to proceed. Following box 1, for example, if your approach has failed to secure the prospect's attention, the suggestion is that you may have failed to stimulate enough

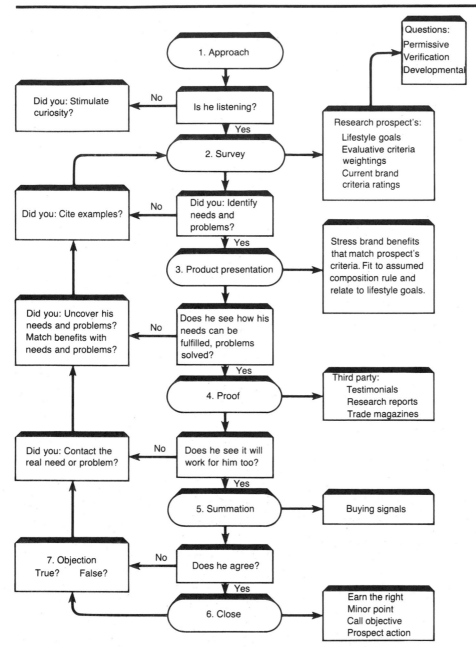

FIGURE 10.5
The dynamic feedback pattern

Source: Adapted from H. B. Rames, *The Dynamics of Motivating Prospects to Buy* (West Nyack, NY: Parker Publishing Company, 1973).

curiosity. Rather than moving forward through the planned sequence, you will have to back up and try a new approach.

Among other things, this pattern implies that misinterpreting feedback—assuming a "Yes" answer when the right answer should be "No," or vice versa—can cause you trouble. You not only have to be a good communicator but an astute interpreter of customer response. The boxes at the left contain questions you should ask yourself if your sale is not moving forward in smooth fashion. Depending on your judgment as to the correct answer, you would move back to one or another of the previous steps.

***Probing for Prospects' Attitudes.***   The boxes to the right in the figure expand on the specific actions you should be pursuing at each major step.[19] For instance, at the right of box 2 (the survey stage) the boxes suggest that you probe for your prospect's evaluative criteria weightings and lifestyle goals by using a variety of questions. In effect, these boxes summarize some points concerning the highly individualized market research that an effective sales representative gathers before moving into the presentation stage. You saw four salespeople describing how they did this, at the beginning of the present chapter. The importance of handling survey activity properly is stressed in practically every text on personal selling.

The survey stage puts you in a position to utilize the concepts concerning attitudes and attitude change procedures discussed earlier. Obtaining a clear picture of evaluative criteria weightings and, if possible, some notion of the likely composition rule that might be followed by this prospect equips you to build an effective product presentation.

***Selecting Evaluative Criteria for Special Emphasis.***   At stage three, the product presentation, you can match evaluative criteria with information about the benefits your brand delivers, putting your strength into the benefit or combination of benefits most relevant to this prospect. Some writers recommend that you not only check to see whether you are dealing with the right evaluative criteria, but actually *force* feedback that tells you whether you are successfully making the case for your brand's criteria ratings.[20] You may be dealing with pertinent needs and problems, but not conveying clear perceptions as to how your product can solve those needs and problems.

***Summarizing and Closing.***   When you are confident you have made your case, the dynamic feedback pattern suggests that you begin summarizing and watching for buying signals. At this stage you are really trying to estimate the probability that both the preference level and the purchase intention level for your brand are high and positive. When you sense agreement to your summation, you are ready to attempt a close. However, if your estimate of the situation suggests your prospect does not agree strongly enough to signal a high purchase probability level, you may have to return to an earlier stage of the pattern, perhaps even back to the beginning.

***Application over Several Sales Calls.***   Although Figure 10.5 implies that the entire process takes place during one sales call, it is quite possible and even probable that the stages and feedback analysis may stretch over a series of selling interviews. Based on what Ruth Durek said, she typically advances only to the survey stage on the first call. After that call, she prepares for a second visit that she hopes will proceed successfully through all six stages. For Tad Collins and Marilyn Brussi the situation is somewhat different. They may try to incorporate all six stages on one call, but it is more likely that the work will be distributed over four, five, or six calls with careful analysis of feedback both during and after each of those calls.

## SUMMARY

Selling jobs vary greatly. They range from situations in which the "salesperson" does little more than hand over merchandise in exchange for money to those in which the salesperson truly communicates and persuades the customer to purchase. Our concern is with those positions involving persuasive communication. A number of critics contend that many or perhaps even most salespeople are basically inept at handling their jobs. To the extent that this is true, it suggests the following:

1. There is a genuine need on the part of customers as well as of sponsoring companies for expert salespeople who can perform a service for *both*.
2. Personal selling at its best is a professional area requiring skill, knowledge, training, and aptitude.
3. The field holds much opportunity for those who are qualified.

The unique aspects of personal selling compared to other promotional techniques are the face-to-face individualized communication setting that allows the salesperson to treat virtually every customer as a unique market segment, and the aspect of direct and immediate feedback that allows a tailored and adjustable promotional presentation, which is guided by prospect reaction as it is in progress.

To help salespeople structure their activities, a number of different selling patterns have been advocated. The four reviewed in this chapter were (1) the sequential activities pattern, (2) the stimulus-response pattern, (3) the AIDA pattern, and (4) the dynamic feedback pattern. Each can provide valuable guidance to sales personnel, though none should be treated as an infallible formula. They represent structured guidelines rather than substitutes for situational thinking and individualized creative development.

The dynamic feedback pattern may be especially useful for analyzing and planning selling strategies because (1) it builds on major concepts from both the sequential activities pattern and the AIDA pattern; (2) it supplements these with clear recognition of principles from communication theory, such as the feedback process and the importance of message decoding by the receiver; (3) it incorporates ideas about the components of attitudes and the process of attitude formation—ideas that can be very useful in researching each customer prior to determining what to emphasize in the presentation; and (4) it avoids the danger of leading its user to the conclusion that the personal selling process will always move smoothly as a series of steps running in a predetermined sequence.

## DISCUSSION QUESTIONS

1. Discuss the general areas of feedback information a salesperson hopes to gain from the customer on a prospect-by-prospect basis. How is this feedback likely to influence sales techniques for each of the three distinct broad audience categories indicated in Figure 10.1?
2. Describe the similarities in the way the four salespersons in the text approached the selling process. What were some of the major differences?
3. Consider the precontact steps in the sequential activities pattern of personal selling. Which techniques described under each step might be most appropriate for a salesperson whose job is to persuade firms in a geographical area to join a nonprofit organization that tries to attract industry to that area? How might those steps differ for a salesperson who persuades individuals to buy nutritional supplements on a door-to-door basis?
4. List the objectives of the approach and presentation stages of the sequential activities pattern.
5. When is it appropriate to attempt a "close"?
6. Mary Smith has just completed a sales training course in selling health and beauty aids aimed specifically at women. During the course, Mary learned that women are often conditioned to say "No" automatically and that an effective way to make a sale is to ask the prospect a question to which a "No" reply is actually an affirmative response. Such a question might be, "Is there any reason why you cannot use this product?" A negative answer would imply consent to using the product. Mary tried this technique on her very first sales call and lost the sale. Outline some possible reasons why and describe the selling strategy pattern that this situation implies.
7. You are selling waterbeds and have just completed the survey stage in the dynamic feedback pattern. From this survey you have learned several things about the prospect's lifestyle goals: upwardly mobile, status seeker, conservative, and concerned with the aesthetics of the home environment. As far as waterbeds are concerned, your prospect, in his 40s, thinks that a waterbed might be too radical for his lifestyle. He places a great deal of value on comfort and appearance and owns a traditional, king-size bed. What is your next step in the selling process, assuming you are using the dynamic feedback pattern?
8. Describe how an automobile salesman might use each of the four selling patterns described to trade a customer up to purchasing a higher-priced car. Which do you think would be most effective?
9. Would you classify Jim Altein as a sales clerk or a creative salesperson? Explain your reasoning.
10. Although Tad Collins and Marilyn Brussi did not mention using the stimulus-response pattern, it seems possible that they might employ it on some occasions. Try to list three such occasions and discuss the feasibility of the approach in each.

## REFERENCES

1. Robert Evans, "Training, Employee Orientation Hike Sales Rep Performance," *Marketing News,* 13 November 1981, p. 1.
2. John C. Gfeller, "Five Keys to Better Salesmanship," *Nation's Business,* December 1970, p. 56.
3. U.S. Department of Commerce, *Statistical Abstract of the United States, 1982–83* (Washington, D.C.: U.S. Government Printing Office, 1982), p. 386.
4. For a more extended description of positions in personal selling see Richard H. Buskirk and Jack A. Wichert, "Careers in Marketing," in Steuart Henderson Britt and Norman F. Guess, eds., *Marketing Manager's Handbook,* 2nd ed. (Chicago: Dartnell Press, 1983), pp. 107–119.
5. Lawrence X. Tarpey, James H. Donnelly, Jr., and J. Paul Peter, *A Preface to Marketing Management* (Dallas, TX: Business Publications, Inc., 1979), p. 131.
6. John W. Rice, *Successful Selling* (Englewood Cliffs, NJ: Prentice-Hall, Inc., 1983), p. 39.
7. Barton A. Weitz, "Relationship Between Sales-

person Performance and Understanding of Customer Decision Making," *Journal of Marketing Research,* November 1978, p. 502.

8. Kenneth B. Haas and John W. Ernest, *Principles of Creative Selling,* 3rd ed. (Encino, CA: Glencoe Publishing Co., Inc., 1975), p. 146.

9. Allen L. Reid, *Modern Applied Salesmanship,* 2nd ed. (Glenview, IL: Scott, Foresman and Company, 1975), p. 201.

10. *Ibid.*

11. Joseph W. Thompson, *Selling: A Managerial and Behavioral Science Analysis,* 2nd ed. (New York: McGraw-Hill Book Company, 1973), p. 489.

12. William J. Stanton and Richard A. Buskirk, *Management of the Sales Force,* 6th ed. (Homewood, IL, Richard D. Irwin, Inc., 1983), p. 226.

13. *Ibid.,* p. 216.

14. Dan H. Robertson and Danny N. Bellenger, *Sales Management: Decision Making for Improved Profitability* (New York: Macmillan Publishing Co., Inc., 1980), pp. 31–34.

15. See David L. Kurtz and Louis E. Boone, *Marketing,* 2nd ed. (Hinsdale, Il: The Dryden Press, 1984), pp. 562–563.

16. Reid, *Modern Applied Salesmanship,* pp. 232–233.

17. *Ibid.,* p. 25.

18. *Ibid.,* p. 291.

19. For a much more extended discussion of such specifics and related aspects of the Dynamic Feedback Pattern see H. B. Rames, *The Dynamics of Motivating Prospects to Buy* (West Nyack, NY: Parker Publishing Co., 1973).

20. G. David Hughes and Charles H. Singler, *Strategic Sales Management* (Reading, MA: Addison-Wesley Publishing Company, 1983), pp. 94–95.

# CHAPTER ELEVEN

# Planning and Organizing the Personal Selling Program

## FOCUS OF THE CHAPTER

In one way or another most companies rely on people like Jim Altein, Marilyn Brussi, Tad Collins, or Ruth Durek to perform a critically important role in the promotional strategy process. They are the individuals who must persuade prospects on a person-to-person, face-to-face basis. Working together, such people form a "sales force."

*Sales management—personal selling viewed from the macro-level—deals with the tasks and decisions involved in organizing the personal selling element in the promotional mix.* Sales management can be divided into two broad aspects: (1) general planning and decision making regarding the role, the type, and the amount of personal selling effort to be undertaken by your firm and, (2) management of the sales force whose members will carry out that effort. This chapter will outline the major factors influencing both aspects of sales management. It will then concentrate on questions that affect the first aspect—the overall planning and organizing of your personal selling program. Chapter 12 will deal with management of the sales force.

Our main emphasis will be on a personal selling program carried out by field sales representatives (people who travel to and call on customers) rather than on salespeople who work inside some business establishment such as a retail store in which customers come to them. Usually, each field sales representative is assigned to a "territory." The results of that representative's work are measured ultimately in terms of "sales territory performance." However, total territorial performance is influenced not only by the effectiveness of the salesperson but also by a combination of other factors. Figure 11.1 outlines the mixture of determinants involved.

To initiate our consideration of sales management, we will discuss each of the factors included in Figure 11.1 and illustrate them by showing how they might apply to Marilyn Brussi, whose job was described in the preceding chapter.

*Company Marketing Effort—Other Promotion and Distribution*

No sales representative is likely to be effective for long unless she or he sells for a firm that provides solid back-up support. At the base of such support are competitive prices, appealing products and a method of distribution that delivers those products to resellers and consumers promptly and economically. In addition, the company should continually be considering ways to bolster personal selling efforts through other forms of explicit promotion. Figure 11.1 summarizes these factors in the boxes labeled "Product, price, and other Promotion" and "Distribution." They form parts of the "Company Marketing Effort" in the territory.

For our purposes, the issue of "Other Promotion" is especially pertinent. In her account, Miss Brussi referred to company advertising in medical journals, to publicity pieces about the firm's products, to brochures, and to samples. These make important contributions to her sales results and help set the tone for her own efforts. To place personal selling in the context of the total promotional mix, and to look at some examples of how it might be supported by other promotion, an important question we will want to examine is "What role should personal selling play in the total promotional mix and what support does it need from the other promotional elements?"

*Territory Workload—Account Characteristics and Geography*

A second factor that will influence a salesperson's performance is the territory workload. This has two main aspects: (1) the character of the accounts, which affects the amount of time a sales representative will have to spend working with each prospect to attain a given level of results, and (2) the geography of the territory, which determines how much time a sales representative must spend traveling between accounts.

*Character of Accounts.*   Differences in account characteristics usually revolve around the size of the accounts in the territory and the complexity of their needs. For example, Miss Brussi is probably calling on doctors with generally lower potential for prescription writing than you would expect in large, metropolitan areas. This has to be taken into consideration when setting goals for

**FIGURE 11.1 Determinants of sales territory performance**

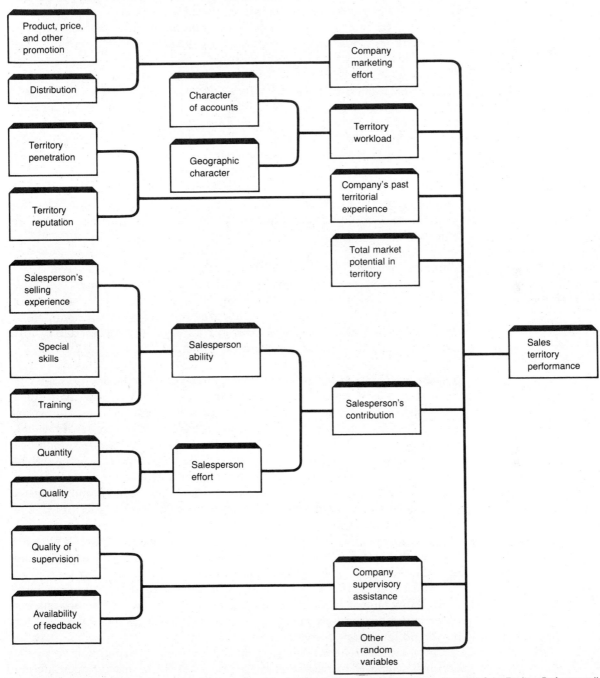

*Source:* Adapted from David W. Cravens, Robert B. Woodruff, and Joe C. Stamper, "An Analytical Approach for Evaluating Sales Territory Performance," *Journal of Marketing,* January 1972, pp. 31–33.

her activities. In other product lines, differences in account characteristics could be much more pronounced. For instance, salespeople in some territories could be calling on very large customers from whom each order produces a high dollar volume but who demand only a minimum amount of servicing. In other territories, salespeople might have to spend much of their time with smaller or more complex types of customers.

*Geographic Character of the Territory.* The geography of her territory is going to make a difference in Miss Brussi's performance. She covers a three-county area that is composed mostly of small towns. This means she has to spend a fair amount of time driving between calls. Her counterpart in an urban territory might be able to complete many more calls per day simply because the accounts are geographically concentrated.

To take territory workload into consideration, we will want to raise the following question: "How should our total market be divided into sales territories—considering account types and travel times—to maximize sales force efficiency?"

**Market Potential and Company Experience**

*Total Volume Potential of the Territory.* No matter how well she does her job, the market potential in Miss Brussi's area puts a ceiling on her sales attainments. To set her volume goals and to compare her performance with that of its other salespeople, her firm should start with a reasonable estimate of the total business available in Miss Brussi's territory. Then it must decide how large a share of this total it can realistically seek to achieve.

*The Firm's Competitive Strength in the Territory.* Total market potential in a territory is one thing. The likelihood that your company can attain some target share of it is another. That probability will be influenced by your company's "experience," which is the position it has carved out for itself through past performance. For instance, Marilyn Brussi is working in an established territory in which her company has been selling its products for a number of years. She started by taking over the accounts her predecessor had previously serviced. Her job is to build on previously established business and company position. To the extent that both are strong, her task is much easier. If Marilyn Brussi or any other salesperson were attempting to sell the same products in a part of the country where the firm had never done business before or where it had "weak experience" compared to competitors her performance level would probably be much lower, at least initially.

From a promotional strategy view, these issues suggest the following question: "How should we analyze each territory to determine the total market potential for our product category and a reachable market share potential for our brand, given our current and past position?"

Once a firm has considered (1) its full promotional mix relative to the personal selling element, (2) an appropriate territorial structure considering workloads, and (3) territorial market potentials and market share potentials, its promotional strategists are ready to ask "What sales objectives shall we set for each territory? How many salespeople do we need to achieve these objectives and what type of people do we need?" It is at this point that the direct contribution expected from each individual salesperson becomes an issue.

**Salesperson Ability and Effort**

Miss Brussi's direct input to sales of her firm's products is represented by the box in Figure 11.1 labeled "Salesperson's Contribution." As illustrated, her contribution is a consequence of both her basic ability and the amount of effort she puts into her work.

***Salesperson Ability.*** One aspect of her ability comes from the length of time she has spent on the job—five years of selling prescription drugs. Those years have sharpened her capacity to decipher customer needs and attitudes and to deal with them effectively. Her ability also comes from the special training that her company emphasizes. Not only did they start her off with a six-week period of schooling, but they continue to train her. This includes training in both new product developments and in improved selling techniques.

Very importantly, her past experience and training must blend with special skills and talents she brought to her position. Trying to find and hire people with the right kind of skills can be a major problem in sales management. Taken in total, these three factors—experience, training, and special skills—produce an "ability" configuration.

***Salesperson Effort.*** To make her ability effective, Marilyn Brussi has to combine it with quantity and quality of effort—energy and initiative. To do this, she must be motivated. The company's role in encouraging such motivation can take many forms. However, the most basic and probably the most important form of motivation is likely to be its compensation plan—how it rewards people for their performance.

***Managerial Influences on the Salesperson's Contribution.*** Although ability and effort are direct contributions of the individual salesperson, it is apparent that sales management decisions can influence those contributions in three main ways. It is the responsibility of sales management executives (1) to locate and recruit people with the needed skills and experience, (2) to see that they are properly trained, and (3) to set up a compensation plan that aims to maximize motivation while holding selling costs to a level that achieves the profit goals of the firm.

The full managerial question involved can be asked in the following way: "Given our sales objectives, what approaches should we take in hiring, training, and compensating salespeople?"

**Company Supervisory Assistance**

Like any group of employees, salespeople must be given guidance. Although Marilyn Brussi did not mention it, she reports to a district sales manager. Part of that manager's responsibility includes informing her about company objectives, going over any problems she may be having in handling her job, and evaluating her performance.

As we'll see later, there is some disagreement on how much supervision should be involved and exactly what forms it should take. Nonetheless, the need for supervisory assistance raises the following managerial question: "How should we set objectives for individual members of the sales team and then supervise them for purposes of guidance and evaluation?"

## SALES MANAGEMENT IN THE PROMOTIONAL STRATEGY PROCESS

Figure 11.2 illustrates a method of viewing sales management as a sequence of decision fields which blend into the full promotional strategy process. The questions that were just raised in our overview of sales management have been translated into calls for executive decision making. These are described in the boxes numbered 1 through 6.

Because problems and procedures vary from company to company and from time to time, there is no hard and fast order in which issues like these must be dealt with and answered. Figure 11.2 suggests one possible order, but this sequence may not be appropriate to each and every situation. It is intended mainly as a helpful way to start acquiring a sense of direction regarding the tasks of sales management. To illustrate possible ways to approach these decision areas, we will work through Figure 11.2 on a step-by-step basis. Steps 1 through 4 will be covered in this chapter; steps 5 and 6 will be treated in Chapter 12.

*Relating Personal Selling to the Total Promotional Mix*

Box 1 in Figure 11.3 recognizes a point that is emphasized throughout this book. Each promotional element should be designed to blend with and reinforce the other promotional elements as strongly as possible. In coordinating personal selling with the other elements, there are six questions to be considered: (1) How should the objectives of personal selling be defined, relative to the other promotional elements? (2) Should our personal selling effort be aided by increased emphasis on other promotional elements? (3) Should personal selling effort be increased—and other elements of explicit promotion increased along with it? (4) Should less personal selling effort be used and other promotional elements substituted to pick up the slack? (5) Should we concentrate on personal selling and virtually ignore other types of explicit promotion? (6) Should personal selling be eliminated as part of the promotional mix?

The last five of these questions call for "Yes" or "No" answers. The likelihood that you will want to answer "Yes" will probably decrease sharply as you consider each question in turn. Nonetheless, each is useful in appraising how personal selling fits in the total mix.

1. *How should the objectives of personal selling be defined, relative to other promotional elements?* Although promotional elements work together, their specific objectives can be somewhat different. To assure that your total program is soundly conceived, the objectives of each element should be spelled out carefully. Among other things, this enables marketing management both to assess results more clearly and to take appropriate corrective action if necessary. Knowing exactly what personal selling was intended to contribute in the total mix puts you in a better position to evaluate the direct contribution of your sales force more accurately.

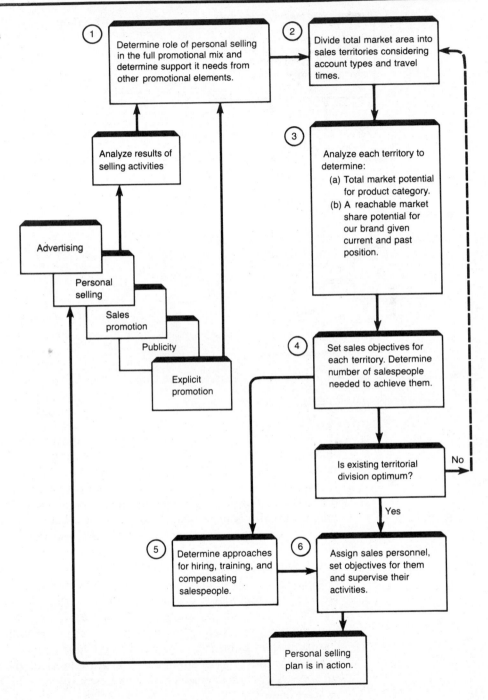

**FIGURE 11.2 Sales management viewed as a sequence of decision fields**

1. Determine role of personal selling in the full promotional mix and determine support it needs from other promotional elements.

2. Divide total market area into sales territories considering account types and travel times.

Analyze results of selling activities

Advertising
Personal selling
Sales promotion
Publicity
Explicit promotion

3. Analyze each territory to determine:
   (a) Total market potential for product category.
   (b) A reachable market share potential for our brand given current and past position.

4. Set sales objectives for each territory. Determine number of salespeople needed to achieve them.

Is existing territorial division optimum?

No

Yes

5. Determine approaches for hiring, training, and compensating salespeople.

6. Assign sales personnel, set objectives for them and supervise their activities.

Personal selling plan is in action.

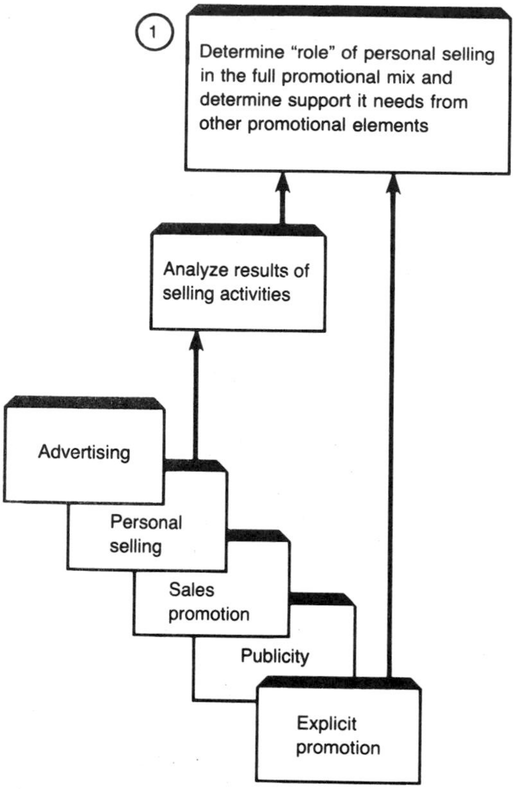

**FIGURE 11.3 Relating personal selling to the total promotional mix**

Box 1: Determine "role" of personal selling in the full promotional mix and determine support it needs from other promotional elements

Analyze results of selling activities

Advertising

Personal selling

Sales promotion

Publicity

Explicit promotion

For instance, it is possible that your salespeople are performing their assigned roles very effectively and yet sales volume is far below your targeted estimate. Perhaps the objectives assigned to the sales force were not the proper objectives needed to get the job done. Alternatively, perhaps one or more of the other promotional elements is not functioning effectively. By spelling things out in advance—stating specifically what your sales representatives are to accomplish—you are in a much better position to analyze their effectiveness.

Of course, the final goal of personal selling activity is to produce sales. However, the sales representative's role in achieving that aim may be somewhat indirect and highly dependent on other parts of the promotional process. As one pair of authors points out: "The positioning of the personal selling function within the corporate organizational structure will vary greatly among companies and industries. There is one possible generalization. The personal selling function tends to dominate advertising in industrial firms, but it shares equal or lesser roles than advertising in the consumer fields such as the grocery package industry."[1]

When personal selling is treated as the lead element, the position it usually holds among industrial goods producers, the objectives to be sought by the sales force may be stated in terms of actual dollar volume sales quotas and the securing of new customer accounts. In consumer goods categories, where advertising often serves as the principal means of communicating with prospects and sales are made through resellers, the sales representative's assigned role is usually one of convincing resellers to cooperate in the firm's efforts. In this latter instance, the objectives of the sales force may be spelled out in terms of securing prominent shelf positioning and displays in retail outlets as well as maintaining enthusiastic trade relationships.

2. *Should our personal selling effort be aided by increased emphasis on other promotional elements?* The basic issue here is one of maintaining the sales force at its present size but spending more money on another promotional element with the primary aim of boosting sales force effectiveness. While this approach is potentially applicable in any promotional mix, it can be especially useful when sales representatives carry the heaviest responsibility in the explicit promotional mix, that is, when personal selling is the lead element. The industrial goods field provides some excellent examples.

As an illustration, the Timken Company, which sells tapered roller bearings and specialty steel products, bases its explicit promotional strategy on a corps of highly trained sales engineers who call on industrial firms. Timken's purpose in advertising is primarily to support sales force activity. When the company added television to its advertising schedule, it did so because of television's capacity to enhance personal selling effectiveness. Most television viewers are not prospects for Timken products and the waste circulation is high; however, television is a powerful medium and was used to achieve a specific purpose. Carefully chosen spot commercials were scheduled to reach and impress key customers, and were run in ten metropolitan markets with high sales potential. They appeared during shows involving golf, professional football, and the Olympics. Their purpose was not to sell Timken products directly but to sell the sales representatives who would sell the products.[2]

Mary Kay Cosmetics turned to television advertising to supplement sales force efforts with a somewhat different goal in mind. Although it operates in the consumer goods market, Mary Kay also uses personal selling as its lead element. Its success has been built on the efforts of an extremely large contingent of part-time salespeople. In 1983 it was estimated there were close to 200,000 such individuals selling Mary Kay products, mainly through parties conducted in the homes of friends and neighbors. With a group this large and operating on a part-time basis, it is not surprising that sales force turnover is extremely high. In 1982, some 120,000 representatives reportedly either resigned or were discharged from the Mary Kay sales force. Because each lost salesperson can translate into lost customers, the company inaugurated a $6 million television advertising campaign. One objective of that campaign aimed at directing past customers to a currently operating Mary Kay beauty consultant, who can be found in the Yellow Pages of the telephone directory. In short, although it is customary to think of sales representatives as seeking out customers, Mary Kay uses advertising to help former customers seek out sales representatives.[3]

3. *Should personal selling be increased and other elements of explicit promotion increased along with it?* If the question concerns upgrading the size of your

personal selling organization to secure more business, it is possible that the answer should be, "Yes, but *only* if we also increase advertising and sales promotion to exploit the additional personal selling effort more fully." An example of the successful use of this approach is provided by Lanier Business Products, Inc. In the mid 1960s, the company was merely a distributor of dictating machines with its area of operation confined to the southern portion of the United States. At that point, total annual sales were about $12 million. By the 1980s Lanier was both manufacturing and selling a variety of office machinery products including dictating equipment, word processors, and copying machines. Its field of activities had expanded geographically to cover the entire United States as well as several foreign markets. Total revenues had risen to approximately $350 million per year.

In accord with the common practice of the industry in which it operates, Lanier uses personal selling as its lead element. However, it has also been an astute user of other promotional elements to supplement its sales force. When company executives first decided to move from regional to national distribution, they recognized the need to preestablish recognition for their sales force in areas where the firm's name was unfamiliar. To accomplish this they launched a national media campaign which included Arnold Palmer as the firm's spokesperson in radio, television, and print advertising. Another tactic employed by Lanier management as part of its territorial expansion program involves what has been described as a "saturation-selling blitz" technique. The core of this technique is to increase the size of the personal selling group in individual market areas, one at a time, with the concomitant support of that increase by intensive local advertising and sales promotion efforts. For example, when Lanier entered the New York metropolitan market it enlarged the size of its sales force by over twenty-five percent. To pave the way for sales representatives' efforts in New York, Lanier also ran a heavy local advertising campaign using radio, television, newspapers, magazines, and even car cards on subways and commuter trains. The firm's rationale is that a significant increase in personal selling effort should logically be accompanied by a parallel increase in supportive promotional efforts to develop a synergistic promotional response.[4]

4. *Should less personal selling effort be used and other promotional elements substituted to pick up the slack?* In an earlier chapter you saw that sales calls are expensive, with the average cost estimated at $106 (see p. 60). It is usually possible to reach the same customer with advertising with a much more modest expenditure. Of course, though cost comparisons are easy to make, comparisons of relative effectiveness are another matter. However, the lower cost of advertising can make it an attractive substitute for personal selling in dealing with accounts whose sales potential is rather small.

The Monarch Marking Division of Pitney-Bowes Corporation provides a case in point. It increased sales by decreasing the size of its sales force. The formula for its success was *substitution within the explicit promotional mix.*[5] An analysis of its selling expenses convinced management it was unprofitable to do business with seventy-six percent of its current customers when they had to be reached by personal sales calls. The solution? A catalogue was substituted for sales calls to low-volume accounts. The sales force was trimmed by thirty percent. Smaller customers were no longer called on unless they specifically requested information about a complex piece of machinery. Because the remaining sales staff could now spend more time with important prospects, it began attaining a larger share of their business. The lower cost of the catalogue also made it possible for the company to reach a much larger group of smaller customers.

5. *Should we concentrate on personal selling and virtually ignore other types of explicit promotion?* Large firms usually include at least some advertising in their explicit mix even if they place reliance on personal selling as their lead element. This is especially true of business entities that market their products mainly to ultimate consumers, but there are occasional exceptions. One such exception, mentioned in Chapter 8, involves Hershey chocolate bars, which rose to occupy a dominant market share with little or no advertising until the mid-1960s. The Shaklee Corporation provides a more recent example. Like Hershey, Shaklee eventually began to include advertising in its mix. However, the original and highly successful promotional strategy for the firm was one of almost total reliance on personal selling.

Shaklee sells nutritional products, personal care items, and household products through some 13,000 independent salespeople who contact consumers in their homes. Between 1968 and 1982, Shaklee's volume surged from an estimated $6 million to almost $472 million. During this time, Shaklee was competing with firms such as Amway and Avon, which use the same general distribution format but also support their personal selling efforts with a substantial amount of advertising. In contrast, during its period of most rapid growth, the only advertisements run by Shaklee were those in its own house organ. No conventional media advertising was used. In terms of explicit promotion, virtually total emphasis was placed on personal selling and sales training to sharpen representatives' effectiveness. The firm's president was quoted as saying that, "Someone else could copy our products and our sales plan, but they couldn't copy our salespeople."[6]

6. *Should personal selling be eliminated as a part of the promotional mix?* This approach is used by Publishers Clearing House, which sells magazine subscriptions. Personal selling has traditionally been a common way to solicit such subscriptions. Publishers Clearing House has substituted an unusual blend of direct mail advertising backed by sales promotion that, in turn, is reinforced by television advertising. The result is high volume with no personal selling involved.

Although Publishers Clearing House may represent an unusual case, it is not unique. Other firms have abandoned a conventional sales force even though they compete in industries where most companies rely on the efforts of sales representatives. One such situation involves an electronic data processing firm that sells management information systems. Company executives decided their product was too complex to be sold effectively with a conventional field sales organization. Instead, they invite potential customers to attend seminars at company headquarters. Prospects pay their own expenses. According to a published report, the approach has proved immensely successful.

"One notable sale was made to a hardworking wholesaler who already was a heavy user of computer services. The sale was negotiated between executives of the firms. No salesman was involved because the EDP firm does not have any sales force—nor does it intend to develop one. Management feels that its seminar approach is far superior to field selling."[7]

Another firm, Sather Cookie Company, was doing an annual volume of $2 million with a force of traveling salespeople covering a five-state area. When a disgruntled salesman quit his low-volume territory, Sather tried to salvage the lost business by telephoning its best accounts. To the company's amazement, response to the telephone approach turned out to be better than that which had resulted from face-to-face, personal selling. In consequence, Sather gradually withdrew its salespeople from the field and substituted telephone selling in their place. With the new technique, it was able to expand its market area and annual sales rose from $2 million to $44 million.[8]

The strategy followed by Sather has been given the name "telemarketing." It has been proposed that, especially in view of the increasing expense connected with personal selling, telemarketing along with such other techniques as demonstration centers and industrial stores offer alternatives that are potentially more cost efficient than conventional sales efforts in many situations.[9] It is highly unlikely that complete elimination of a conventional field sales force would prove to be a workable option for most companies that now rely heavily on field selling. However, the possibility of supplementing conventional efforts with one or more of the suggested alternatives may be well worth considering. Among other things, such consideration is likely to sharpen your reasoning concerning the basic role of personal selling in your promotional mix.

## Dividing Your Market into Sales Territories

Most field sales representatives work in an assigned territory which is geographically defined. One of your aims in determining your sales territory structure is to maximize the efficiency of your selling organization in terms of travel time. After allowing for weekends, holidays, and vacations the typical sales representative has about 235 days during the year in which to make calls and handle other aspects of her or his job. A sizeable portion of this time is often devoted to activities other than direct customer contact. For example, according to one estimate the average industrial salesperson is likely to spend approximately twenty-nine percent of his or her working hours handling such things as reports, paperwork, sales meetings, and service calls.[10] This reduces the remaining available time to approximately 167 days.

Table 11.1 demonstrates that traveling between accounts can erode a substantial portion of that remaining time. For example, a sales assignment that necessitates 25,000 miles of automobile travel would require the representative to spend nearly half of the 167 days moving between customers rather than calling on them. Furthermore, it would involve $5,375 in automobile operation costs. If that representative's travel requirements could be cut by 10,000 miles, the company would gain thirty-one days for actual contact work as well as save over $2,000 on automobile expenses. With figures such as these in

**TABLE 11.1 Examples of salesperson time and driving costs per year**

| Thousands of Miles of Business Travel | Salesperson Days Spent in Travel[a] | Cost of Operating Automobile[b] |
|---|---|---|
| 5 | 16 | $1075 |
| 15 | 47 | $3225 |
| 25 | 78 | $5375 |
| 35 | 109 | $7525 |
| 45 | 141 | $9675 |

[a]Based on an eight-hour working day and an average speed of forty miles per hour. Rounded to nearest full day.

[b]Based on estimated operating cost of 21.5¢ per mile for an intermediate-sized car as reported in John P. Steinbrink and William B. Friedeman, *Sales Force Compensation: Dartnell's 21st Biennial Survey* (Chicago: The Dartnell Corporation, 1982), p. 102.

mind, firms generally seek to assign sales personnel on a geographic basis that facilitates efficiency in moving between accounts.

When the total number of prospects to be contacted is rather small, territories can be quite large. Figure 11.4 shows a nationwide territorial scheme for a division of the FMC Corporation's Machinery Group. One sales representative was assigned to each of the eight territories shown on this map, with the "Blue Sky Country" (Montana, Wyoming, and the Dakotas) left open. When there are large numbers of customers and a greater need for sales call intensity, you will likely find much smaller basic territories built into some type of managerial sequence. For example, Best Foods, which markets such products as Skippy Peanut Butter and Hellman's Mayonnaise, has been reported to require a sales force of 400 people to do an adequate job of calling on grocery stores, wholesalers, brokers, and retail chain headquarters. Its personal selling organization is divided geographically into regions, which in turn are divided into districts. Each district is further divided into small marketing areas.

***Territories Set Up by a Strict Geographic Approach.*** If a firm chooses a strict geographic arrangement, it will have one representative selling all its products to all its customers in each basic territorial unit. The philosophy behind this system was expressed by an executive of Litton Microwave Cooking Products, who said "We have found that the best approach is to make a salesperson responsible for all accounts in a finite territory. . . . I don't believe in having salesmen running from Long Island to New Jersey. Travel time is too costly."[11]

Although geography still tends to play a dominant role in sales force organization, some observers feel that in an economic climate where the trend is toward bigness and centralization less emphasis should be given to geography as the basis for sales planning. One such observer has expressed this view as follows:

**FIGURE 11.4 A sales territory map for a firm with relatively few prospective accounts**

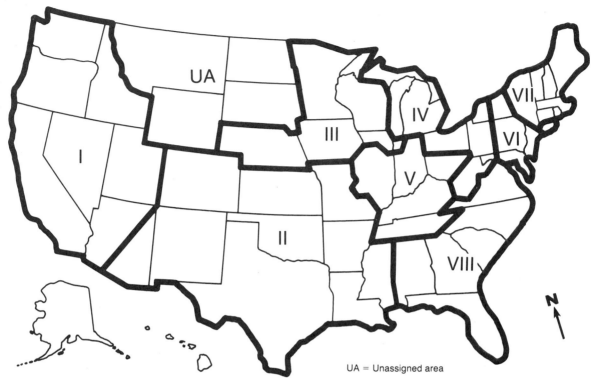

UA = Unassigned area

*Source:* Michael S. Heschel, "Effective Sales Territory Development," *Journal of Marketing,* April 1977, p. 43.

There are circumstances where the nature of the product or the market continues to justify a geographically structured sales organization. In an increasing number of selling situations, however, geography simply is not the strategic base for allocating sales efforts. . . . The bulk of traditional sales effort is directed toward individuals at local store units within specified territories, but, for many large businesses these individuals no longer have the authority to buy. . . . [It] becomes clear, therefore, that centralized purchasing demands a whole new approach to selling and a complete restructuring of many sales organizations. . . . No matter which task they perform [sales development or sales maintenance], salesmen can no longer afford to operate exclusively within traditional territorial boundaries. . . . Sales organizations must be flexible to meet the changing demands of a volatile market place. [12]

This point of view has led an increasing number of firms to turn toward nongeographic approaches. The two most frequently used alternatives are organization by type of product and organization by type of customer. These alternatives are often used in conjunction with a geographic approach, producing a hybrid structure for sales force assignments.

***Territories Set Up by Type of Product.*** If a company or one of its divisions produces a number of different products, it has the choice of either letting one representative sell all the products in a given geographic area or dividing the products into logical groupings and assigning a different salesperson to handle each group. For example, assume your firm has twenty different products and a sales force of 300 people. Using a strict geographic approach you could set up 300 separate territories in each of which one salesperson would handle all twenty items. Alternatively, you could arrange the products into, perhaps, four groups. Four separate sales forces would then be organized, one per product group. Each sales force might now be divided among 75 larger territories.

The advantage of assigning your sales representatives by product groupings is that it may make each salesperson more of a specialized expert. This procedure is often chosen when products are technically complex or when it is felt they require frequent and unique promotional attention. For example, Procter and Gamble has used six sales forces, one each for paper products, case foods, packaged soap and detergents, bar soap and household cleaning products, toilet goods, and coffee.

A possible disadvantage of this approach is the amount of increased travel time and customer duplication that may occur. Each territory will be larger in area, with more miles for all representatives to cover. Duplication in customer contact can sometimes lead to confusion and misunderstanding. In explaining why his company discontinued use of this approach, an executive of Robertshaw Controls pointed out, "We had four different sales forces calling on the appliance industry. If one salesman had gas controls, and the account needed electric, all too often we were out of luck."[13]

***Territories Set Up by Customer Types.*** Another possible variation in dividing sales territories is to have salespeople specialized by type of account. To achieve its strict geographic breakdown, Litton Microwave had the same salesperson calling on a variety of retail outlet types—appliance stores, department stores, and furniture stores—regardless of whether they were large or small, chain or independent. Another firm might decide that national chains have much different problems and needs than local, independent retailers or that department stores must be merchandised on a different basis than appliance stores. Using this line of reasoning, a separate sales force could be set up for each account type.

Again, the advantage to this approach is that it results in a sales force with greater expertise. This time the expertise involves an understanding of customer needs rather than specialized knowledge about individual products. The disadvantage of larger territories (increased travel time and customer duplication) remains. However, some firms feel this is more than offset by the improvement in customer orientation. Robertshaw Controls switched from ten separate product-oriented sales organizations to four sales forces, each of which serves a particular type of industrial group. As an executive explained, "We're trying to go from selling devices to meeting customers' needs."[14]

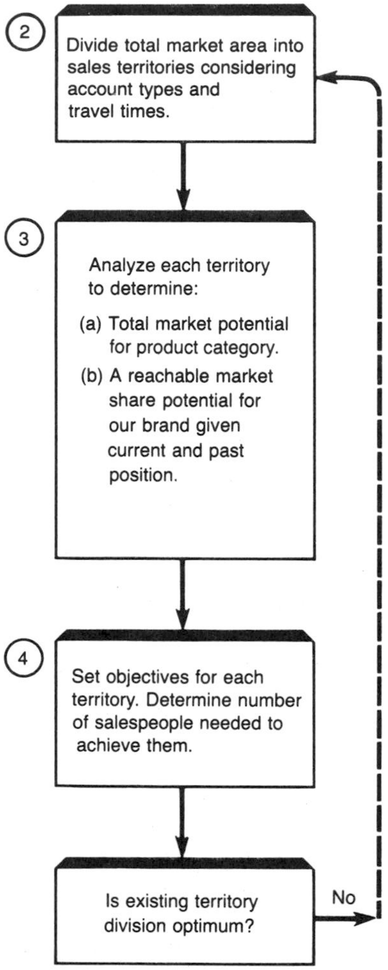

FIGURE 11.5 Appraising sales
territory structures

**2** Divide total market area into sales territories considering account types and travel times.

**3** Analyze each territory to determine:

(a) Total market potential for product category.

(b) A reachable market share potential for our brand given current and past position.

**4** Set objectives for each territory. Determine number of salespeople needed to achieve them.

Is existing territory division optimum?    No

***Drawing Up Territorial Boundaries.*** Although more centralized purchasing may be changing the nature of personal selling activities, it is still common practice to build sales territories with some sort of geographic definition. No matter how they have been designed—by strict geography, by product type, by customer type, or by some combination of these—all divisions of sales force assignments ultimately are groupings of current and prospective accounts.

These accounts differ in terms of volume potential. They also differ in terms of your probability of success in obtaining or retaining their business. In allocating your personal selling efforts and in setting territorial boundaries, such factors have to be taken into consideration. In other words, the steps of dividing your market into territories, analyzing territorial potential, and setting territorial objectives, are all interwoven. Figure 11.5 suggests that you start with some preliminary territorial boundaries. After you have analyzed your existing territories and set objectives, you should then ask "Is the existing territorial division optimum?" If the answer is "No," your next step is to redraw those boundaries into a more effective pattern.

# ANALYZING TERRITORIAL POTENTIALS BY ACCOUNTS AND DETERMINING OBJECTIVES

Because a salesperson's time is expensive, it is imperative to know not only which customers to contact but also which customers to avoid or give much less of your attention. It was mentioned earlier that the sales force for Best Foods is made up of 400 people (see p. 353). There are over 180,000 grocery stores in the United States. Even a 400-person force would be unable to handle all of them adequately. The company therefore concentrates on about 32,000 of those stores, only eighteen percent of the total. The reason is that the eighteen percent of the stores they call on do about seventy-two percent of the total grocery volume in the country.

*Classifying and Rating Accounts*

*Screening and classifying accounts* is a vital part of effective planning for personal selling. Figure 11.6 shows, in graphic form, a frequently used approach to classifying customers by sales potential. Known as the "ABC Rule of Account Classification," this approach holds that the top fifteen percent of your prospects are likely to account for about sixty-five percent of your volume. The middle twenty percent are likely to account for twenty percent of your volume. The remaining sixty-five percent will produce only fifteen percent of

**FIGURE 11.6 The ABC rule of account classification**

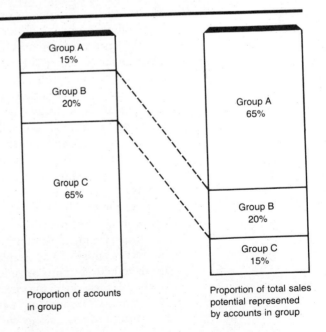

Proportion of accounts in group

Proportion of total sales potential represented by accounts in group

the total volume. The ABC rule is a somewhat more refined variation of the "80–20" principle discussed in Chapter 5. Although the exact percentage relationships may vary by company and industry, the reasoning underlying the rule suggests that you divide accounts into three categories—A, B, and C—and devote your heaviest sales call intensity to the high-potential A accounts and the least intensity to the low-potential C accounts.[15]

Many companies develop a formal system to rate accounts in a more finely delineated manner than the ABC rule. A sensible formal rating approach starts by considering the following:

1. The total potential of each account, which is the sales volume that would result if your firm could acquire a targeted proportion of the customer's business ranging from all of it to some stated fraction of it
2. The probability that your firm can acquire the targeted proportion of the customer's business
3. The sales effort—mainly selling time—that would be needed to secure the targeted portion of that business

In recent years, some firms have begun working with computer-based models, which start from an account rating system and output recommendations concerning the most profitable sales force allocation alignment. To illustrate the general nature of the procedures involved in a computer-based approach, we shall consider one example.

*A Computer-Aided Approach to Account and Territorial Analysis*

Figure 11.7 outlines one extensive and systematic computerized approach that can be employed to analyze accounts and then determine call frequencies and territorial sales assignments. This technique combines data regarding account characteristics, judgments on sales responses, facts about profit levels and time constraints, and a computer-based solution procedure.

The first decision that is required when following this approach involves the question of whether the analysis should be made on the basis of individual accounts or by account segments. The latter alternative might be chosen when an extremely large number of customers is involved, making an account-by-account analysis unduly cumbersome. For instance, in one reported usage situation, a pharmaceutical firm had its salespeople categorize physicians into four segments based on the extent to which each type of physician was likely to prescribe various drugs produced by the firm.[16]

A second question that must be resolved concerns the allocation of sales representatives' time to different products. Suppose that your firm markets ten different items. It is unlikely that your sales force can do an adequate job of promoting all of the products on any one call. Logically, the products chosen for most frequent promotional presentation should be those that have the highest promise of a substantial sales response. For a multiproduct firm which needs to take this into consideration, box 6 in Figure 11.7 calls for estimates of likely sales responses on a product-by-product basis. Estimated sales responses by accounts, account segments, and product categories are then fed into a computer program along with data on gross profits associated with the products being sold, the amount of time required per call, and the size of the

*Planning and Organizing the Personal Selling Program*

**FIGURE 11.7 A computer–aided approach to sales force allocation decisions**

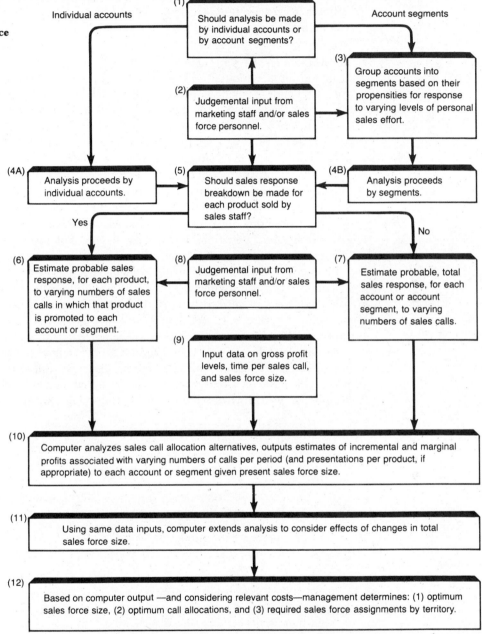

Individual accounts

(1) Should analysis be made by individual accounts or by account segments?

Account segments

(2) Judgemental input from marketing staff and/or sales force personnel.

(3) Group accounts into segments based on their propensities for response to varying levels of personal sales effort.

(4A) Analysis proceeds by individual accounts.

(5) Should sales response breakdown be made for each product sold by sales staff?

(4B) Analysis proceeds by segments.

Yes

No

(6) Estimate probable sales response, for each product, to varying numbers of sales calls in which that product is promoted to each account or segment.

(8) Judgemental input from marketing staff and/or sales force personnel.

(7) Estimate probable, total sales response, for each account or account segment, to varying numbers of sales calls.

(9) Input data on gross profit levels, time per sales call, and sales force size.

(10) Computer analyzes sales call allocation alternatives, outputs estimates of incremental and marginal profits associated with varying numbers of calls per period (and presentations per product, if appropriate) to each account or segment given present sales force size.

(11) Using same data inputs, computer extends analysis to consider effects of changes in total sales force size.

(12) Based on computer output —and considering relevant costs—management determines: (1) optimum sales force size, (2) optimum call allocations, and (3) required sales force assignments by territory.

*Source:* Based on adaptation of discussion in Leonard M. Lodish, ''A User-Oriented Model for Sales Force Size, Product and Market Allocation Decisions,'' *Journal of Marketing*, Summer 1980, pp. 70–78.

available sales force. (As the term is used here, "gross profit" refers to the difference between the cost and the selling price of products being marketed by the firm.)

***Input Data for the Approach.*** Figure 11.8 illustrates a format that can be used to begin implementation of the program. In this case, the analysis is handled on an account segment and product-by-product basis. Management and sales personnel begin with data concerning both historical sales records and projected future total volume for the category being considered. In this example, total sales for Product A among accounts grouped into Account Segment 1 are projected to grow at an annual rate of thirteen percent and reach $7,287,000 by 1982. The company in question currently holds a sixty-three percent share of the volume for this product in this account segment.

The individuals providing sales response estimates are next asked to quantify their opinions regarding the market share changes which would accompany designated variations in sales call levels. For instance, in the situation portrayed in Figure 11.8, the product in question is currently being represented at level 2—four sales calls (or details) during the period to each account within this account segment. Therefore, assuming calls are held at level 2, the sales index figure entered for year 1 is 100. The presumption is that maintenance of this sales call level would hold market share at its current rate. The question then becomes, "What would happen if we were to increase or decrease the number of times the product is represented to these accounts?" In the case being discussed, management was interested in analyzing volume and profit changes over a four year period. With that in mind, company personnel supplying the estimates were given the following instructions:

1. Start with the current level (four "details" or promotional presentations), then the zero level, saturation level and the other two policy levels.
2. For each level ask yourself two questions:
   a. If we follow this policy for four years what will our market share be in the fourth year?
   b. Starting with 1978's market share, how quickly will it increase or decrease to the ending level? [17]

The originator of the model we are discussing raises and then answers an important question that you may be asking yourself at this point:

A natural question about this procedure is "How good are the response estimates?" Our best answer is "better than nothing!" This procedure forces management to explicitly consider the sales and profit effects of alternative product/segment effort allocation. The final choice of allocation is made consistent with these assumptions. . . . This procedure is preferable to a situation where management makes decisions which may be inconsistent with its assumptions, by using past decisions or rules of thumb as a guide. [18]

***Program Output for the Approach.*** A portion of output from an actual solution procedure in which this program was applied is shown in Figure 11.9. Following the mathematical routine that it has been given to solve the prob-

**FIGURE 11.8 Format used to record input estimates for computer analysis**

Product A, Market 1                                                                    Growth Rate = 13%/yr.

Estimated Market Share:

| | '76 | '77 | '78 |
|---|---|---|---|
| | $3,500,000 | $3,955,000 | $4,469,150 |

Our Current Share: 63%

Our Principal Competitors X, Y, Z

| '79 | '80 | '81 | '82 |
|---|---|---|---|
| $5,050,000 | $5,707,000 | $6,449,000 | $7,287,000 |

| | | Year 1 | Year 2 | Year 3 | Year 4 |
|---|---|---|---|---|---|
| Zero Level | Sales = | _____ | _____ | _____ | _____ |
| Level 1 (2 Details) | Sales = | _____ | _____ | _____ | _____ |
| Level 2 (4 Details) | Sales = | 100 | _____ | _____ | _____ |
| Level 3 (6 Details) | Sales = | _____ | _____ | _____ | _____ |
| Saturation Level | Sales = | _____ | _____ | _____ | _____ |

*Source:* Leonard M. Lodish, "A User-Oriented Model for Sales Force Size, Product and Market Allocation Decisions," *Journal of Marketing*, Summer 1980, p. 77.

lem,[19] the computer proceeds through a series of steps. At each step, it adds people to the sales force and then estimates the total incremental or additional profit that will accrue to the firm with the relevant sales force size involved. It also estimates the marginal profit per call, which is the amount of profit that would be realized from the last additional call made available at the given sales force size. (Marginal profit analysis is discussed in greater detail in Chapter 20.) For example, at step number 7, the program has allocated a total of 95.1 people to the sales force and has estimated that the total incremental profits at that point would reach $9,474,000. The marginal profit anticipated for the last additional call made available to the firm with the sales staff at this size would be $31.30.

In the bottom portion of the figure, the program is outputting recommendations for the number of details or sales presentations which should be made for each product, given a total sales force size of 95 persons. Along with each recommended number of details, it again provides an estimate of the incremental or additional profit associated with that recommendation. For instance, among accounts that fall within segment A the program output recommends that product E be given five details whereas product B be given none. Although this implies that the firm may be foregoing a possible opportunity for increased profits from product B, the analysis suggests that any such opportunity loss will be more than offset by greater profit increases from more highly sales responsive items such as products C, D, and E. The objective is to maximize total profits by taking all products into consideration in terms of their sales responsiveness.

**Comments on Computer-Based Approaches**

The approach very briefly summarized above is only one of a number of computer-based methods that have been proposed for assisting management to make better decisions concerning the allocation of sales force efforts.[20] There are certain points that should be borne in mind when considering any of these approaches. First, there is no magic involved in the analytical procedures

**FIGURE 11.9 Output from a computer-based sales force allocation model**

*Interactive Computer Session for a Sample Problem*

*→ Allocate*
*For Which Year(s): > 4*
*For Which Segment(s): > All*
*Maximum No. of Salespeople to Allocate > 135*

*Allocation of Calls to Specialities, Y1982*

| *Step No.* | *Marginal Profit Per Call* | *No. of People Added* | *Total Incremental Profit (000)* | *Total People* |
|---|---|---|---|---|
| 1 | 196 | 6.3 | 1,959 | 6.3 |
| 2 | 155 | 8.0 | 3,940 | 14.3 |
| 3 | 77 | 6.3 | 4,708 | 20.5 |
| 4 | 75 | 4.1 | 5,203 | 24.6 |
| 5 | 58 | 4.1 | 5,588 | 28.8 |
| 6 | 45.8 | 22.5 | 7,228 | 51.4 |
| 7 | 31.3 | 44.0 | 9,474 | 95.1 |
| 8 | 25.3 | 6.3 | 9,728 | 101.3 |
| 9 | 19.0 | 8.0 | 10,746 | 109.3 |
| 10 | 14.1 | 4.1 | 10,839 | 113.4 |
| 11 | 9.1 | 6.2 | 10,929 | 119.6 |
| 12 | 4.6 | 4.1 | 10,960 | 123.8 |
| 13 | 1.3 | 6.2 | 10,972 | 129.9 |
| 14 | −1.4 | 6.2 | 10,959 | 136.1 |

*For Which Step Do You Wish to Report Detailed Allocation?* > 7

*Detailed Report of Allocation, Y1982*

*People Allocated* 95

Segment A

| *Product* | *No. of Details* | *Incremental Profit* |
|---|---|---|
| A | 2 | 768,090 |
| B | 0 | 0 |
| C | 4 | 595,195 |
| D | 3 | 396,537 |
| E | 5 | 940,584 |
| F | 0 | 0 |
| G | 0 | 0 |
| H | 1 | 1,195,300 |
| I | 1 | 763,790 |
| J | 0 | 0 |
| Total | 16 | 4,659,495 |

*Segment B*

| *Product* | *No. of Details* | *Incremental Profit* |
|---|---|---|
| K | 6 | 597,268 |
| L | 7 | 1,772,253 |
| M | 1 | 102,723 |
| Total | 14 | 2,472,243 |

*Source:* Leonard M. Lodish, "A User-Oriented Model for Sales Force Size, Product and Market Allocation Decisions," *Journal of Marketing*, Summer 1980, p. 73.

around which such programs are centered. The computer does an orderly, rapid, and precise job of working the arithmetic. It has the power to process a massive amount of data very quickly and thoroughly—a task that would be economically impractical without computer assistance. However, the basic power of any such technique lies in the logic and reasoning that goes into it. As implied by the quotation cited earlier, an important and advantageous side-effect of the use of such a formalized approach is that it forces some hard and clear thinking on the part of sales representatives and other marketing personnel involved in the estimation process.

Not every company will choose to analyze its sales force allocation efforts in quite as rigorous a fashion as computerized procedures usually demand. Some will choose to deal in a formal way only with major points such as initial estimates of the size and volume potential of the accounts being contacted and their likely response to persuasive efforts. Actual sales assignment decisions may be handled in a less formal manner. However, even if your choice is to use a simpler, noncomputerized approach, consideration of the decision steps and required information estimates outlined in Figure 11.7 can help you organize and analyze your personal selling program in a more effective fashion.

## SUMMARY

Sales management deals with the tasks and decisions involved in organizing and directing the personal selling element. It can be divided into (1) general planning and decision making for the personal selling effort and (2) management of the sales force.

An interplay of factors will influence your sales outcome in any given territory. These factors include direct contributions made by your firm and direct contributions made by the salesperson who represents your firm. When all are taken into consideration, they suggest six major issues to consider in planning and organizing your personal selling program.

1. Determining the role of personal selling in the total promotional mix and the kind of help it should receive from other elements
2. Dividing the total market area into sales territories
3. Developing methods to analyze the accounts in each territory and estimate the sales potential of each account
4. Setting sales objectives for each territory by starting with the estimates made in step 3, combining them with estimates of the effort required to achieve that potential, and then determining the most profitable way to allocate selling time (If necessary, this may also mean going back to step 2 and redesigning your territories)
5. Deciding on approaches to hiring, training, and compensating sales force members
6. Assigning salespeople to territories and supervising their activities

In relating personal selling to other promotional elements, it is helpful to spell out as clearly as possible the objectives that each element is intended to achieve and how they will fit together. This can aid you both in designing your program and in determining which element needs revision if that program is not performing as well as was expected. In most cases, the explicit promotional elements are blended to reinforce each other. In some cases, however, they may be used as substitutes for one another. For example, some firms have replaced a portion of their personal selling program with advertising, whereas others choose to rely almost entirely on personal selling with almost no support from the other explicit elements. Occasionally, you will encounter businesses which have achieved success by virtually eliminating personal selling in the conventional sense from their promotional mixes.

Because of the time and expense involved in traveling between accounts, geography is usually an important consideration in assigning sales representatives. In a strict geographic plan, only one company representative would be assigned to cover any given territory. Alternatively, a company might choose to have sales representatives specialize by type of product or type of account. Under either of the latter systems, there will usually be duplication of salespeople within territories. However, each salesperson will have more expertise in dealing with the special needs which the company may feel are important to its market.

The analysis of account potentials and the setting of sales objectives logically begin by considering (1) the total amount of business available from each account, (2) the probability that your firm can acquire some stated proportion of that business, and (3) the amount of selling effort that would be needed to make that acquisition.

Having done this, there are various ways to determine the time that should be spent on each account and the consequent, total number of people you will need to staff your sales force. One method, described in the chapter, is built around a somewhat rigorous computer program approach. Although it possesses no magical qualities, this approach points the way toward analyzing your information in a systematic fashion and forcing some clear and hard thinking on the part of sales representatives and their managers. For this reason, it can serve as a strong illustration of the logic that should guide your account analysis and determination of objectives.

## DISCUSSION QUESTIONS

1. Three factors that can influence a salesperson's performance are (1) the nature of the full promotional mix, (2) the territory workload, and (3) the company's past territorial experience. Discuss each in terms of how it can help or hinder a salesman's performance.

2. What underlying factors combine to shape the "salesperson's contribution to territorial volume"?

3. You are the marketing manager for a firm that currently relies almost exclusively on personal selling. Your firm is experiencing declining profits and it is your responsibility to revamp the promotional mix. Outline several strategies that you might want to consider.

4. Describe the major variations in sales territory

*Planning and Organizing the Personal Selling Program*

approaches. How would the following situation be handled under each variation? Sales force of one hundred persons selling five major product groups to four types of retailers.

5. With respect to the possible variations you outlined in the preceding question, discuss the factors you would consider in evaluating each alternative.

6. Bob Myers established his own business three years ago. After developing a highly successful volume through retail stores in a portion of one state, he expanded his marketing efforts to a four-state area. Bob decided the best way for his new sales force of five people to generate business would be to call on all prospective outlets in the four-state area. After six months, Bob is disappointed in the results and is thinking of dropping the sales force entirely. Comment on Bob's problem and make some recommendations to improve his situation.

7. List the factors that have led some firms to reduce or even eliminate conventional personal selling efforts. What trends do you think might develop in the future?

8. Why is geographic efficiency an important consideration in developing a sales force assignment plan and what arguments can be made against making it the issue of primary importance?

9. What issues should you analyze when classifying accounts for purposes of determining sales call frequencies?

10. What strengths and weaknesses do you see in the application of computer-based approaches to allocating sales force efforts?

## REFERENCES

1. G. David Hughes and Charles H. Singler, *Strategic Sales Management* (Reading, MA: Addison-Wesley Publishing Company, 1983), p. 16.

2. "Timkin: Well-prepared for Future Shocks," *Sales and Marketing Management*, 17 January 1977, pp. 40–42.

3. "Mary Kay Cosmetics: Looking Beyond Direct Sales to Keep Party Going," *Business Week*, 28 March 1983, p. 130.

4. See "Lanier Business Products," *Value Line Investment Survey,* 13 May 1983, p. 1117; "At Lanier a Better Mousetrap Isn't Quite Enough," *Fortune,* 26 February 1979, pp. 70–78; and "Lanier Business Products: Dictating to the Big Boys," *Sales and Marketing Management,* 17 January 1977, pp. 20–21.

5. "Pitney-Bowes: Now for the Good News," *Sales Management, The Marketing Magazine,* 10 December 1973, p. 3.

6. "Shaklee Corporation," *Value Line Investment Survey*, 4 March 1983, p. 1497; and Rayna Skolnik, "Shaklee Shares the Good Life," *Sales and Marketing Management*, 9 October 1978, pp. 33–36.

7. Alton F. Doody and William G. Nickels, "Structuring Organizations for Strategic Selling," *MSU Business Topics*, Autumn 1972, pp. 27–35.

8. "Sather Cookie Calling," *Sales and Marketing Management,* 7 February 1977, p. 14.

9. Benson P. Shapiro and John Wyman, "New Ways to Reach Your Consumers," *Harvard Business Review*, July/August 1981, pp. 103–110.

10. Robert W. Haas, *Industrial Marketing Management*, 2nd ed. (Boston: Kent Publishing Company, 1982), p. 246.

11. Rayna Skolnik, "Thou Shalt Not Cross Territory Lines at Litton Microwave," *Time and Territory Management (Special Report) Sales and Marketing Management*, 24 May 1976, p. 33.

12. Doody and Nickels, "Structuring Organizations for Strategic Selling," pp. 27–35.

13. "Robertshaw Controls: Dial 'R' for Reorganize and Reap," *Sales and Marketing Management*, 17 January 1977, pp. 22–23.

14. *Ibid.*

15. Hughes and Singler, *Strategic Sales Management*, p. 120.

16. Leonard M. Lodish, "A User-Oriented Model for Sales Force Size, Product, and Market Allocation Decision," *Journal of Marketing,* Summer 1980, p. 71.

17. *Ibid.*, pp. 76–77.

18. *Ibid.*

19. For a more detailed outline of the mathematical solution procedure involved see Lodish, "A User-Oriented Model for Sales Force Size, Product, and Market Allocation Decisions," pp. 77–78.

20. For descriptions of other computer-based sales force allocation approaches see Charles A. Beswick and David W. Cravens, "A Multi-Stage Deci-

sion Model for Sales Force Management," *Journal of Marketing Research*, May 1977, pp. 135–144; Leonard M. Lodish, "CALLPLAN: An Interactive Salesman's Call Planning System," *Management Science,* December 1971, pp. 25–40; Leonard M. Lodish, "A Vaguely Right Approach to Sales Force Allocation Decisions," *Harvard Business Review*, January/February 1974, pp. 119–124; and D. Montgomery, A. Silk, and C. Zaragoza, "A Multiple Product Sales Force Allocation Model," *Management Science,* December 1971, pp. 3–24.

# CHAPTER TWELVE

# Managing the Sales Force

## FOCUS OF THE CHAPTER

In Chapter 10 we discussed working patterns suggested for the actual planning and making of sales calls—the salesperson's job viewed close-up. In Chapter 11 we considered how a firm can organize its personal selling program—the general analysis and direction of overall company sales strategy. In a sense this chapter brings those two subjects together. It deals with methods of hiring, training, compensating, and supervising the people who must make the sales calls that make the company's strategy work. In terms of the decision areas in the sales management sequence represented on p. 368, we will be looking at steps 5 and 6 (see Figure 12.1).

## SOME UNIQUE PROBLEMS IN SALES FORCE MANAGEMENT

Managing a sales force presents a special type of administrative challenge. The author of one sales management text pinpoints the factor which makes sales management a unique administrative field in these words, "The big distinction between sales managers and other managers is that the selling task usually

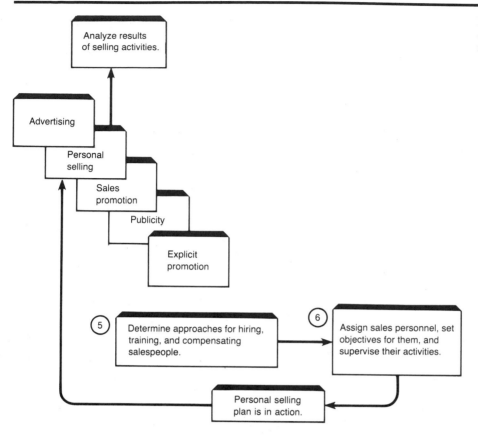

FIGURE 12.1 The
decision areas in sales
force management

Analyze results
of selling activities.

Advertising

Personal
selling

Sales
promotion

Publicity

Explicit
promotion

5   Determine approaches for hiring, training, and compensating salespeople.

6   Assign sales personnel, set objectives for them, and supervise their activities.

Personal selling
plan is in action.

allows an individual a great deal of freedom in how each day will progress. Salespeople do not work by a particular time clock."[1]

Sales managers must direct employees whose individual efforts can be especially critical to the success of the firm, yet whose activities usually take place out of the sight of any supervisor. The fact that sales representatives work on a more or less independent basis, coupled with the fact that proper conduct of their activities generally requires exceptionally strong motivation and initiative, demands that those in charge of the sales force must be especially skillful in selecting its members and influencing their performance.

## RECRUITING AND SELECTING THE SALES FORCE

This topic was introduced in Chapter 10 when Ruth Durek remarked that, "A few years back our company spent a great deal of money to study the type of personality background that makes the best insurance representative. After all their investigation, they concluded there was really no particular background that seemed to make any special difference."

Ms. Durek's company is not alone in being uncertain as to the exact qualities sales management should seek when recruiting new personnel. The turnover rate among new sales recruits tends to be high, and one major reason for high turnover is the hiring of people who are unable to handle the job. In a survey of 500 companies, it was found that fifty-two percent of business was brought in by only twenty-seven percent of the sales personnel. The same study showed that roughly thirty-two percent of the new salespeople hired had either quit or been fired by the end of their first year. It was expected that another eighteen percent would be gone by the end of the second year.[2] In commenting on the problem as it affects industrial selling one author suggests, "A reasonable assessment is that from 40 to 70 percent of industrial salespeople turn over annually. . . . What all these figures imply is that salesperson turnover is a very definite problem . . . [that] places great emphasis on more effective selection . . . by sales managers."[3]

Hiring a salesperson who fails means lost investment in training time and salary, lost sales, and disruption in territorial work loads. How then can you make an intelligent distinction between an applicant who is likely to succeed and one who is likely to fail? Tests of personality, intelligence, and sales aptitude are frequently used. Another common device is an application form that contains questions about "life history experiences." One extensive review of the research on these methods raised some serious questions about the amount of help they really provide, and in summarizing his analysis the author made the following important point:

> [P]rogress to date has clearly established that sales occupations should not be presumed to be homogeneous. Rather, research has indicated the need to recognize differences in various types of selling and to treat major product classifications separately if more accurate performance indices are to be developed. In fact, it may well be that predictors for one type of personal selling work may simply be of little value in a different personal selling setting. [4]

**Personality Tests**  Some of the most interesting attempts to improve sales force selection techniques have tried to isolate personality traits that will predict success.

For example, one widely quoted approach holds that there are two main traits essential to success—empathy and ego drive. The originators of this idea believe both traits can be easily measured by a paper-and-pencil test.[5] *Empathy* is the ability to sense, almost automatically and immediately, the way another person feels. Because much has been said about the need for salespeople to use feedback in their contact work, the notion that empathy is essential for sales success is appealing. *Ego drive* stems from a strong need and desire to succeed. It includes the ability to be spurred on rather than defeated by failure and rejection. This also seems to fit well with most descriptions of sales work. Field selling can include a good deal of loneliness and frustration, which call for a high degree of self-motivation on the part of sales representatives. However, not everyone has found a positive relationship between sales performance and these two personality traits. In fact one study reported a negative relationship.[6]

This is just one of a number of personality tests that have been used to screen sales recruits. It illustrates the point that there is much disagreement regarding the relevant personality traits for sales success and the merits of formal tests in discovering those traits. Part of the problem may lie in the way personality traits are defined and measured—the validity and comparability of the different tests being used. Another part of the problem may lie in the differences between various types of selling jobs. Each type may call for specialized traits rather than a "universal sales personality." At any rate, it is often suggested that such tests be used only with caution and only as one component of a total screening program.

## A Social Interaction Approach

Another view holds that you must consider more than just the personality traits of the prospective salesperson. You also must realize that her or his personality will react in some way with that of the customer. In one of the first studies to propose this idea it was noted, "The 'sale' is a social situation involving two persons. The interaction of the two persons, in turn, depends upon the economic and social, physical, and personality characteristics of each of them. To understand the process, however, it is necessary to look at both parties of the sale as a dyad, not individually."[7]

Later studies have suggested that selling effectiveness may be improved when customers and salespeople share certain personality characteristics or when customers feel they have something in common with the salespeople. The evidence available at this time is hardly conclusive. However, the possibilities are worth considering.[8]

One strategy this approach might suggest is that in assessing the types of salespeople you want to hire you should begin by considering the types of customers they will serve. On this basis, you would attempt to find salespeople who, among other things, most closely match those customers in personal characteristics and interests. A survey taken among the largest firms in the United States revealed that this is a highly popular approach. A number of the reporting firms indicated that they begin by researching clients and then seek salespeople with client-compatible profiles.[9] Another possible strategy is to seek salespeople with versatile personalities because not all their customers are going to be alike. An ideal sales representative might be the individual with wide-ranging interests and a multifaceted, adaptable personality.

## The Personal Interview as a Screening Device

In practice, much more reliance is usually put on personal interviews than on paper-and-pencil tests. A survey among sales executives revealed that interviews are typically ranked first in terms of helpfulness in screening applicants, whereas personality tests are ranked last among the selection tools studied.[10] A salesperson is rarely hired without an intensive interview and often he or she will be put through a series of such interviews. In the interview sessions, sales managers seem to be looking for qualities which might defy discovery through paper-and-pencil tests or application form answers. For example, characteristics frequently cited as important criteria in the recruiting process include such personal attributes as maturity, appearance, energy, drive, and emotional independence. These are all factors that might be hard to detect by any means other than a face-to-face interview.[11] Even in a personal interview, a highly skilled interviewer might be required to discern whether the applicant was really displaying genuine possession of these attributes rather than simply putting on a good show.

**An Example of a Multistage Screening Procedure**

What form might a complete screening take? We will look at one and see. In this case the firm is a television station and the product is commercial time. The sales manager is female and so are the applicants. Although the specifics of this screening are not going to fit every situation, the general approach is drawn from actual practice and will give you an idea of how a very intensive and apparently successful multistage procedure might be undertaken.

1. [We] talk with a large base of applicants in a short time to get a full sense of the potential available. I recently talked with forty on the phone, then had twenty-five in for personal interviews.
2. The top potentials stand out. The procedure continues until we hire one. I'll probably average no less than six meetings with the finalist to give her a sense of us. And for us to see her as a person. I vary the setting from formal office to the coffee shop to restaurant.
3. When we've really narrowed down, I turn final choices over with our sales team. I leave the room to encourage active exchange of questions and observations. It's beautiful to see group consensus on pluses and minuses. When they really like someone, it commits them to accept her on the team.
4. Next, we ask final candidate to take a nationally based three-hour sales aptitude test (cost: $35) to see if she falls within a high producing profile. Testing is administered by an outside training organization. I keep charts on indices of people we hire. So I have a feel for traits top billers share.
5. If married, meet with the husband. Give him a defined feel of the job, particularly the commitment in time and energy. Will he be an asset to your saleswoman socially and psychologically? The last thing you need is a jealous husband. Or a husband who thinks free enterprise and TV are national problems.
6. We slate a half-hour session with a psychiatrist to assess:
   Inner motivation of the individual for maximum selling.
   If the marriage is supportive and strong enough to stand a high pressure business with demands that take from home time. The last thing you need is a saleswoman with marital problems.
7. A thorough check of references and financial obligations. It's amazing what the question—"Would you hire this person again?"—brings to the surface. [12]

**Final Comments On Salesperson Selection Techniques**

The findings of academic researchers together with published reports of sales management practices do not provide you with fool-proof rules for screening sales recruits. However, they suggest some broad guidelines worth considering when setting up your screening procedures. These can be summarized as follows:

1. Start from your own selling situation. What is the role of personal selling in your promotional program? How has the job and its duties been defined? What implications do these factors suggest concerning the type of people needed by your firm?

2. Think in terms of the customers your salespeople will contact. There is

at least some reason to believe that the more personality and interest similarities your sales representatives and your customers share, the greater the chance of encouraging successful sales contacts. In any event, you want salespeople who are able to meet any unique challenges your customer group is likely to present.

**3.** The most critical part of the screening process is likely to be the personal interview. This means that you may wish to consider scheduling more than one such interview and using more than one interviewer. A sensible format involves thinking through the characteristics you are looking for before the interview, then planning your meeting in such a way that you acquire an adequate reading on those characteristics.

**4.** Application blank questions and paper-and-pencil tests, including personality and aptitude tests, may be useful. However, they are likely to be useful mainly as adjunct techniques rather than substitutes for effective interviewing procedures. Furthermore, the evidence suggests that you should interpret these test results carefully. Applicants with serious personality defects may not be successful in any selling job. Personality strong points do not necessarily seem to work the same way. A positive trait that is important in one type of selling may or may not be of equal importance in a different selling situation.

**5.** Keep a record of your successes and failures in judging prospectives salespeople. Be alert for new information and be ready to change your qualification standards when that information suggests a change is desirable. In an area such as this in which you find diverse opinions and little conclusive data, it makes good sense to maintain an open and inquisitive approach.

## SALES FORCE TRAINING

There are three critical issues in developing training programs for your sales force. They can be viewed as the "who, what, and how" of training strategy: (1) *Who* should be trained? (2) *What* information and skills should be stressed? (3) *How* should the format and method of conducting the program be handled?

**Who Should Be Trained?**

Most companies recognize that new and inexperienced salespeople need training and the typical firm invests a good deal of time and money in this effort. One survey reported the average training period for newly hired sales personnel requires 6.2 months and costs the sponsoring business $12,633.[13] There are also indications that an increasing number of companies are putting more emphasis on continued training for experienced members of their sales staffs. One team of observers suggests the most profitable payback from investments in sales training may come from programs for the best members of your existing sales team.

> The training session is . . . an important communication and educational experience for both the newly hired and the experienced salesperson. A wise management will develop special training programs geared to the unique needs of each of

these elements in the sales force. . . . Research shows that it is far more effective to focus on making good salespersons better than to try to bring the marginal salesperson up to above-average performance. The person who has taken the time to think about what makes a good salesperson and who is driven to learn more about selling will not only be among the company's best sales representatives, but will also get a great deal out of the formal class sessions and the discussions with fellow classmates in the sales clinic. One seminar requires that the sales manager certify that the people he is sending are in the top 25% of his sales force on overall performance. [14]

*Content of Training Programs— Information and Skills*

The subjects covered in typical training programs can be grouped under four general headings:

1. Information about the products of the company and its chief competitors
2. Information about the company's overall promotional policies and planning
3. Skills in analyzing markets and locating selling opportunities
4. Skills in communicating during selling situations

*Information About Products.* To be able to represent your company, your sales force must have expertise regarding the merchandise and services to be sold. In today's world of rapid technological change, this means that continuing training about product developments is often an absolute necessity. You saw this most clearly when Marilyn Brussi talked about her activities in selling drug products. Another aspect of product information as a sales training component was illustrated in the case of Tad Collins. Salespeople like Collins need information not only about changes in products but also about changes and new improvements in the way those products can be used by customers. As Collins pointed out, one of the most important things a sales representative may have to sell is knowledge that can assist customers in solving their problems through new and improved techniques.

*Information About the Company's Overall Promotional Planning.* Again, personal selling is part of a total promotional process. To make that total process work most effectively, salespeople should have as much information as possible about how other aspects of promotion will affect their activities. In the case of representatives who call on resellers, knowledge about forthcoming company advertising and sales promotion is vital because a large part of their work involves selling those promotional programs as a means of enhancing reseller support. In other cases, especially in industrial selling, explaining the total promotional program is essential because it helps your sales force to capitalize on the strength it can gain through company advertising, sales promotion, and publicity efforts.

*Skills in Analyzing Markets and Opportunities.* The techniques covered under this heading are largely concerned with "prospecting" and the "preapproach," discussed in Chapter 10. Their importance will vary with the type of sales job involved. It is at its highest when the salesperson's assignment calls for locating and screening prospects. In a sense, however, every salesperson should be a market analyst who is alert for new market opportunities and trained both to spot them and to develop a plan for exploiting them.

***Skills in Communicating During Selling Situations.*** These go to the very heart of the sales representative's job. Training in sales communication has traditionally revolved around the "approach, presentation, and close" stages of the "sequential activities" sales pattern described earlier. Increasingly, reports on sales training techniques suggest greater recognition that today's sales process more often revolves around something like the "dynamic feedback pattern." Salespeople are being trained to observe as much as to talk and to consult as much as to convince.

## Formats and Methods for Sales Training Programs

Sales training activities can be either informal or formal. Informal approaches tend to overlap with what is usually called "supervision of the sales force." They involve ongoing training and consultation that often concern specific selling problems or that are based on field observation of selling techniques.

Formal training programs generally have a specific and stated purpose and make use of some type of established educational format. For example, salespeople might be brought in for a two-day meeting on new selling techniques, or sales recruits might be given a three-week indoctrination program at company headquarters. Four general educational approaches frequently used in formal programs include the lecture method, the seminar or panel method, the "case" or "game" method, and role playing.

***Lecture Method.*** As its name implies, the lecture technique centers around a speaker who talks to members of your sales staff. In some cases, the speaker's lecture is built around a "motivational" or "inspirational" theme. The idea of this is not so much to teach salespeople specific pieces of information as to encourage them in their efforts. At least part of the thinking behind the use of inspirational speakers is that selling can be a lonely and frustrating experience when things are not going well. Because they usually work alone and away from colleagues or supervisors, sales representatives must have a good deal of stamina, enthusiasm, and self-reliance to meet these situations. Part of the motivational speaker's objective is to build up such qualities. Relatively little has been published in the way of studies evaluating the effectiveness of the motivational speaker. As often as not, you will find published comments proclaiming, "We don't do that anymore." However, many firms still include at least some motivational lectures in their total training format.

The more common lecture session has a company sales trainer or supervisor presenting factual information to trainees. The lecture approach is probably most effective and efficient when the topic involves straightforward material about products and promotional policies. It may be less effective when the objective is development of skills in analyzing markets or in communicating with customers.

***Seminar or Panel Method.*** The seminar revolves around a small group of salespeople discussing the training topics and often concentrating on problem aspects. The panel approach is a variation in which a small group discusses the topics before a larger group. Presumably, the panel members are persons with greater expertise than members of their audience.

***Case Method or Sales Games.*** A small group is involved in this method also, but in this instance group members deal with realistic selling problems and attempt to reach solutions. The feeling is that these approaches stimulate greater involvement by participants. They also tend to generate a higher level of original thinking.

***Role Playing.*** In a way, this is a variation of the sales game or case method. The distinction is that participants "act out" roles, usually concerning a sales communication situation. In published reports, the role playing approach is frequently mentioned with enthusiasm by sales executives. It is typically combined with one or more other methods, but the role playing portion is regarded as a key component. An example is cited below that describes a program for experienced sales personnel. The program is called "SST"— Systematic Selling Techniques—and the company reporting its use is Automatic Data Processing, which sells data processing services to a wide variety of business clients. "The salesperson learns how to listen for the proper clues in a selling situation . . . and what specific selling skill to use in each situation to move the prospect toward a buying decision. . . . After each skill is presented, the learning group moves into role playing that is carefully structured to reflect ADP's products and selling situations."[15]

More than simple, one-person role playing is involved in this program. The trainee is playing a role in response to feedback that he or she is receiving from a prospective customer. The model on which this program is based is much like the dynamic feedback pattern described in Chapter 10. Two writers have taken this dialogical concept one step further and introduced the notion of nonverbal communication—or body language—as feedback for salespeople. They offer the following report on an experimental study in which salespeople viewed videotaped sales situations:

> In the tape, various people in the prospect company can be seen and heard, but the salesman involved is kept off camera with only his voice presented. . . . Company salesmen of known competence were requested to assume the salesman's role in the film. They were then asked to indicate for each incident the cues obtained and what they discerned. . . . [The findings showed] no difference between high and low [performance] salesmen in their ability to interpret verbal feedback. . . . [However, the] successful salesman is apparently able to "decode" more of the nonverbal feedback than the less successful man. In addition, the high effect salesman is also able to take the information available at each point in the sale and to determine how favorable or unfavorable it is on the whole. [16]

Regarding possible implications for sales training, these researchers have concluded, "There should be actual skill building sessions in which, either through role-play or observation of a film, trainees have an opportunity to identify receiver reactions (both verbal and nonverbal) and to discuss how to adjust to them."[17]

## DEVELOPING A COMPENSATION PLAN

There are three main options available to you in choosing the way to compensate your sales force: (1) a straight salary, (2) a straight commission, and (3) a salary plus incentive or "combination plan."

*The Straight Salary Plan*

Under this arrangement, each salesperson is paid a fixed and stated amount of money per time period. Her or his income remains steady regardless of sales volume or specific quality of performance during that period. The company may sponsor special sales incentive programs such as contests from time to time. It may also provide discretionary bonuses, but these are not guaranteed and the amount of the bonus is not determined by any fixed method. In addition to such short-term incentive supplements, long-term incentive is provided to salaried people in the form of opportunities for salary increases and promotions.

*The Straight Commission Plan*

The straight commission method is somewhat similar to piecework payment. Salespeople are paid on the basis of some percentage of their sales volume. The more they sell the more they earn.

The commission system provides maximum incentive to secure immediate sales. It can also be adjusted to encourage sales of particular products that the firm is anxious to promote. For example, higher commission percentages can be placed on more profitable or slower moving merchandise. While the commission plan offers high incentive for immediate accomplishments, there is some question concerning its effect on long-term incentive and loyalty to the company. The tendency is for salespeople to be concerned about today's sales rather than working on accounts which might require long-term development.

A planned and preannounced bonus system is really a variation of the commission arrangement. The bonus is usually tied to achieving some level of sales rather than being paid in direct proportion to each sales dollar. The bonus may be calculated on the sales results of the individual or on the performance of a sales group. For example, a bonus system could be set up along the following lines: If total sales volume in territory X exceeds seventy-five percent of the assigned quota, two percent on all the "excess" sales dollars will be allocated to a bonus fund. All salespeople in the territory will participate in the bonus distribution in proportion to their base salaries.

*The Combination Plan*

This arrangement starts with a fixed base salary that is coupled with a preannounced and continuing incentive program based on performance. Generally this works out to be either salary plus a percentage commission rate on sales, salary plus bonus for sales over a predetermined quota, or salary plus commission plus bonus.

**FIGURE 12.2** Trends in sales compensation plans by percentages of firms using each type

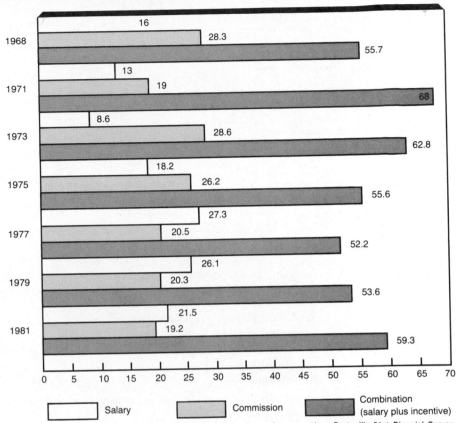

Source: John P. Steinbrink and William B. Friedman, *Sales Force Compensation: Dartnell's 21st Biennial Survey* (Chicago: The Dartnell Corporation, 1982), p. 13.

Figure 12.2 is based on a study of more than 330 companies employing over 16,000 salespeople. As you can see, the most common decision is to use some form of combination plan. However, each of the three alternatives tends to waver in popularity from year to year. If there were one plan that was clearly best, you would expect that all firms would choose that same plan and stay with it. Figure 12.2 suggests this is not the case.

*Factors Influencing Choice of a Plan*

In deciding on a compensation plan, you should begin by considering the objectives of importance to your company. The next step is to assess the effect which one or another of the compensation systems is likely to have on those objectives. The important objectives for most firms include the following:

1. High incentives to produce immediate sales
2. High incentives to build for long-range sales development
3. The ability of management to influence the mix of products sold, especially to promote new or high-profit products

| Which compensation plan is more likely to: | Straight Salary | Straight Commission | TABLE 12.1 Comparing the straight salary and straight commission plans |
|---|---|---|---|
| Provide high incentive for immediate sales | | √ | |
| Provide high incentive for long-range sales development | √ | | |
| Provide a strong means of influencing the mix of products sold | | √ | |
| Give management greater influence over nonselling activities | √ | | |
| Build sales force loyalty | √ | | |
| Give management maximum flexibility in redesigning sales territories | √ | | |
| Keep sales costs closely in line with sales volume | | √ | |

4. Strong managerial control over required nonselling activities such as setting up displays and solving customer problems
5. A company-loyal sales force composed of employees who plan a long career with the firm
6. Flexibility in realigning sales territories and shifting personnel to maximize effectiveness in the total market area
7. Effective control of sales costs in relationship to volume so that if sales should go down suddenly, costs will also drop to temper the squeeze on your profit

Table 12.1 compares the straight salary and the straight commission approaches in terms of which is more likely to achieve a favorable result toward each of the objectives just listed.

Because this table shows four check marks for the straight salary and only three for the straight commission does not mean the straight salary approach is always preferable. Each method has advantages and disadvantages, which suggests you would best begin by rating the importance of each objective as applied in your particular market setting before reaching your decision.

For example, in many technical selling situations sales efforts are complex and must proceed over a long period of time. A good deal of advice, service, and other nonselling activity can be involved. These situations frequently require teams of sales personnel, which makes it difficult to determine exactly who is responsible for the actual order. In a setting like this, you are more likely to find a straight salary plan in effect. At the opposite extreme, consider a company whose sales force sells encyclopedias door-to-door. Such things as long-range sales development, nonselling activities, and flexibility in reassigning personnel are not likely to be of much importance. The major issues are immediate sales and control of sales cost. The straight commission plan will work very well in this case.

In most situations, however, the issues may not be so clear. Your objectives may suggest that each plan has its advantages and the combination approach thus becomes more attractive. This is why it is used so frequently. Of course, choosing a combination approach still leaves you with the problem of determining just what kind of combination plan you will use. Again, the sensible way to make this decision is to begin by listing the importance you place on each objective, and then adjusting the balance in a way you hope will give you the best of both worlds.

## Competitive Level of Compensation

Deciding you will pay your sales force by salary, by commission, or by a combination is one thing. Deciding on the salary level, commission rate, or amount of bonus is another. When firms buy advertising space they are all subject to the same rate schedule. When firms compensate salespeople they may pay as much as, less than, or more than directly competitive companies. You have your choice.

Cost control suggests that you should set the level as low as possible. However, the need for encouraging enthusiastic field performance suggests that this could be a disastrously false economy. For example, one study compared the market effects generated by the sales organizations of two directly competitive companies. Company A's compensation ranges were consistently below those of Company B at all sales department position levels. The analyst conducting the study summarized his findings by observing, "Little wonder that Company A's sales force was regarded as substantially inferior by many major customers. And, because these major customers accounted for the bulk of the business, it is clear that Company A had very little chance of performing the job it should in the marketplace."[18]

Compensation levels vary both among industries and within industries. Table 12.2 displays some examples of such variations. For instance, it is likely

| TABLE 12.2 Annual compensation for sales representatives in selected product categories | Industry Classification | Middle-Half Compensation Range[a] | Median Compensation |
|---|---|---|---|
| | Beverages | $17,000–$28,500 | $18,000 |
| | Tobacco | $18,400–$23,776 | $19,000 |
| | Food Products | $23,000–$29,000 | $25,900 |
| | Iron and Steel | $25,000–$38,975 | $29,250 |
| | Office Machinery and Equipment | $30,000–$36,220 | $32,000 |
| | Autos and Trucks | $31,000–$35,575 | $33,000 |
| | Textiles and Apparel | $35,000–$45,000 | $36,500 |

[a]This is the range of the middle-half average total compensation for all sales reps reported by respondents, i.e., 25th–75th percentile.
Source: John P. Steinbrink and William B. Friedeman, Sales Force Compensation: Dartnell's 21st Biennial Survey (Chicago: The Dartnell Corporation, 1982), p. 24.

that you will be much better paid if you are selling apparel than if you are selling food products. To determine the proper compensation level for your sales force, industry comparisons such as this provide an initial guide. These must be coupled, however, with analysis of your own selling situation and needs. For example, if your company and its brands are well-known and well-accepted, you might decide to meet but not exceed competitive compensation levels. On the other hand, if yours is a firm that is not well established and needs extremely strong personal selling support to establish a foothold in the marketplace, just meeting competitive levels may not be enough.

## SUPERVISING THE SALES FORCE

You have made your decisions on sales force size and territorial assignments. You have set your strategies for hiring, training, and compensating your sales force. Your salespeople are now in the field. As with any group operating in an organizational framework, they need direction and leadership. Your market share and other objectives must be translated into working goals for individual sales representatives. To assist them in achieving those goals you need a plan for supervision.

*Factors Tending to Inhibit Interest in Supervision*

It has been suggested that supervision of the sales force is one of the more neglected areas of sales management and that there are several factors which contribute to this neglect.[19] One such factor involves the difficulty of measuring effects of supervision. Increasing the amount of direct guidance given to salespeople raises costs, yet any resulting increase in sales force productivity can be difficult to determine with precision. A second factor that sometimes leads firms to minimize sales supervision is the fact that it intrudes on selling time. The more supervision imposed on a salesperson, the more hours that person usually spends filling out reports, participating in conferences, or attending meetings, activities which reduce her or his customer contact time. Beyond these factors there is a common belief that good salespeople may resent close supervision. Part of the attraction of a career in personal selling is the sense of independence it can provide. Compared to most other employees, sales representatives have a much greater opportunity to plan their own time, use their own judgment, and work at their own pace. The people likely to do these things most effectively may be the very people who will most resent intrusion on their freedom.

One consequence of the attitudes that often prevail concerning sales force supervision is that there is little well-organized knowledge about the field. One team of analysts who studied the issue expressed its findings as follows:

Each sales executive works out his own ideas about how to manage a sales force from an assortment of "principles" he inherits from his predecessor, the customs of his industry, the expectations and demands of his superiors, and his own assumptions about what motivates salespeople and what leads to good sales performance. . . . Few theories and even less empirical knowledge are available about most aspects of sales [force] management. [20]

*Managing the Sales Force*

| | |
|---|---|
| ***The Need for a*** *** Supervisory Plan*** | Despite the paucity of clear-cut guidelines, each company must have some plan for supervising its selling team. The need for close field supervision generally tends to increase if any one or more of the following situations exists: |

1. The salesperson is relatively new and inexperienced or is performing at a below average level
2. The sales force is large, so that it is difficult for regional and national sales management to keep track of individual situations
3. Personal selling is extremely critical in the total promotional mix
4. Salespeople make repeated calls on the same accounts and each account is highly important to the company
5. Improper handling of contacts would reflect seriously on the company itself and might do long-term damage
6. It is impossible to build more or less automatic incentive plans into the compensation program without some system of personal evaluation

| | |
|---|---|
| ***Developing a*** *** Program for*** *** Effective Field*** *** Supervision*** | Figure 12.3 depicts a model that can assist sales managers in clarifying their thinking regarding the development of a supervision policy. It should be emphasized at the outset that neither the model nor the proposals that will accompany our discussion of it are meant to be treated as immutable or universal in character. Rather, they are intended as catalysts for stimulating your thinking concerning the sales supervision task. Both the model and the proposals stem from an extensive examination of theories and findings concerning individual and organizational behavior. |

***Major Components of the Model.*** The model centers around the salesperson's performance, as shown in the box at the middle of the diagram. That performance is assumed to be influenced mainly by three forces—motivation, aptitude, and role perceptions. *Motivation* refers to the salesperson's willingness and desire to expend effort and energy on the various activities required in his or her job. *Aptitude* refers to the ability to perform those activities effectively. *Role perceptions* are the salesperson's interpretations of the types of job behavior expected from him or her.

The last of these forces, role perceptions, can be examined on three bases—accuracy, ambiguity, and conflict. *Accuracy* is the extent to which the salesperson correctly understands the type of performance that company superiors seek. *Role conflict* deals with the issue of perceived incompatibility of demands on the salesperson. For example, if the company insists that she or he secure a certain type of response from a particular customer when the sales representative knows that customer will resent any attempt to evoke such a response, the sales representative is placed in a conflict role. *Ambiguity* relates to a feeling of uncertainty about task-performance standards. This may be uncertainty concerning what is expected of the salesperson, how to fulfill those expectations, or how job performance will be evaluated.

The model begins with the logical assumption that performance will be a function of the interaction between motivation, aptitude, and role perceptions. The task of sales supervision then becomes one of determining and applying

**FIGURE 12.3  A model of the determinants affecting a salesperson's performance**

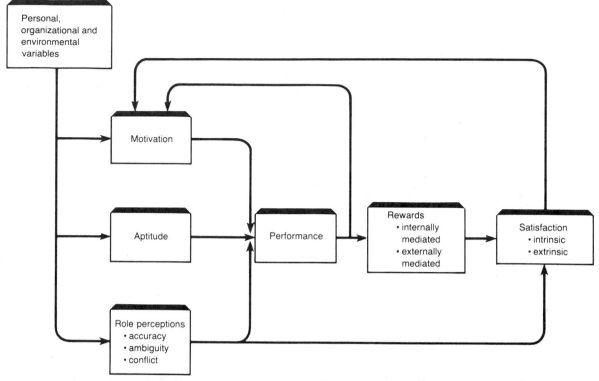

*Source:* Orville C. Walker, Jr., Gilbert A. Churchill, Jr., and Neil M. Ford, "Motivation and Performance in Industrial Selling: Present Knowledge and Needed Research," *Journal of Marketing Research*, May 1977, p. 158.

management practices that will affect those three variables in a positive manner. As shown in the box at the top left of Figure 12.3, it is recognized that organizational influences form only one source of input. Motivation, aptitude, and role perceptions will also be affected by personal and environmental variables which are largely outside the direct control of the firm. To demonstrate how a model such as this can assist in initiating and appraising sales supervision strategies, we will consider some proposals drawn from the original presentation. It is to be stressed that these proposals represent only a partial reflection of the model's potential. They are aimed at giving you an introduction to its concepts rather than a complete description of its depth.

***The Aptitude Component.***   As noted above, aptitude deals with the essential ability of the individual to perform the activities required in the selling assignment. If a person has an adequate understanding of what that assignment requires and is sufficiently motivated to perform the indicated tasks, he or she must also possess certain qualities needed for their fulfillment. Some individuals will possess those qualities in greater quantity than others. The exact combination of aptitudes that leads to successful performance will vary among

**FIGURE 12.4 Factors directly affecting the motivation component**

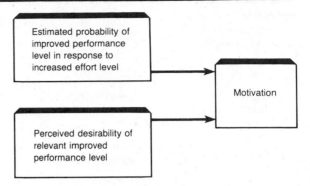

*Source:* Adapted from Orville C. Walker, Jr., Gilbert A. Churchill, Jr., and Neil M. Ford, "Motivation and Performance in Industrial Selling: Present Knowledge and Needed Research," *Journal of Marketing Research*, May 1977, p. 162.

different types of sales assignments. In consequence, a company should study its selling situation carefully and define aptitude on a "task-specific" basis. The critical question is, "What types of characteristics are most conducive to selling success given the nature of our product, our industry, and our customers?" Optimizing the effect of the aptitude component then becomes largely a matter of structuring procedures for selecting and training the sales force.

*The Motivation Component.* As shown in Figure 12.4, the model treats motivation as an outgrowth of two variables. The first is the salesperson's estimate of the probability that a given increase in effort will produce some corresponding improvement in job performance. For instance, a sales representative might consider the question, "If I spend five or six extra hours studying the needs of Customer X, how likely is it that I might be able to increase our volume from that account by ten percent?" The second variable is concerned with the salesperson's desire for improved performance in the goal that he or she is considering. As an example, the same salesperson might next ask, "Assuming I do increase the volume from Customer X by ten percent, how desirable would that be from my standpoint?"

The full model traces both of these variables back to their antecedents, or underlying determinants, and then offers proposals regarding the policies a firm can adopt to help shape them in a desirable fashion. Based on prior behavioral research findings, a number of action areas are suggested to improve the magnitude and accuracy of the salesperson's probability estimates and perceived desires for improved performance. Among these areas are the following:

1. Upgrading the salesperson's self-esteem, perceptions of work-related abilities, and proper understanding of his or her job requirements
2. Increasing the salesperson's sense of participation in determining the criteria by which he or she will be supervised and evaluated

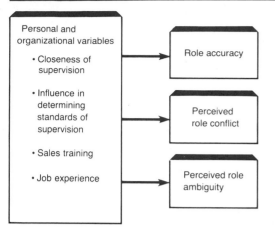

Personal and organizational variables

• Closeness of supervision

• Influence in determining standards of supervision

• Sales training

• Job experience

Role accuracy

Perceived role conflict

Perceived role ambiguity

FIGURE 12.5 Factors that influence the role perceptions component

*Source:* Adapted from Walker, Churchill, and Ford, *op. cit.,* p. 160.

**3.** Providing sales representatives with both the sense and reality of close supervision

This last proposition is especially interesting because, as was previously noted, it is quite frequently assumed that individuals attracted to sales work tend to resent close supervision.

***The Role Perceptions Component.*** The model represented in Figure 12.3 predicts that the presence of role conflict or role ambiguity or the absence of role accuracy will generally increase mental anxiety and reduce job satisfaction. Job performance may be negatively affected as a consequence. The underlying forces hypothesized as influencing these aspects of the role perceptions component are shown at the left of Figure 12.5. Once more, the model suggests that sales training and a participatory management style coupled with close supervision will have beneficial effects on all three aspects of role perceptions.

***Some Comments on the Model.*** The example just presented expounds the proposition that sales force supervision policies can be improved by systematically analyzing the factors that interact to influence an individual salesperson's performance. It is not meant to deal with the topic in extended detail. For this reason, our review of the model is abbreviated. Furthermore, as its originators have pointed out, the model itself is a pioneering attempt to encourage a more cohesive method of studying a complex field which has received little clearly organized study in the past. If sales management is a topic of special interest to you, you will want to examine the original model itself and consider its implications at greater length.[21]

In addition to helping you clarify your thinking regarding the proper course to take in supervising the sales force, a model of salesperson performance can assist you in analyzing empirical data concerning the effects that your company policies are actually having on sales force effectiveness. For example, working from a somewhat different model of salesperson performance, one analyst examined relationships between variables associated with selling success in a particular company. A highly interesting finding of his study was that job satisfaction did not necessarily improve sales performance, at least not in this case. In contrast, self-esteem on the part of sales force members was seen as a "key determinant." On the basis of his findings, the researcher was able to offer the following tentative guidelines in terms of setting up supervisory policies:

> [If] management's primary goal is to increase the performance of the sales force it would appear that resources should not be directed toward the enhancement of job satisfaction as a matter of policy. . . . Management should enhance self-esteem by regularly providing positive reinforcement in the form of personal recognition and monetary rewards, as well as socially visible acknowledgement of good performance . . . [And] finally, it is essential that accurate and complete feedback be provided as to attainment of goals and behavior of merit so that salespeople can make informed personal assessments in concert with their self-esteem. [22]

**Setting Goals for Sales Force Personnel**

As suggested above, the importance of setting clear goals for sales force members and providing meaningful feedback on progress in meeting those goals is a recurrent theme in reports on sales management practices. The authors of another study expressed these same ideas in the following way:

> This study's results suggest that the salesman should have considerable control over the means of accomplishing the job goals for which he is held responsible. Further, the goals and their importance should be made clear to the salesman. The salesman's supervisor should provide periodic feedback on how the salesman is performing in relation to what is expected of him. Rewards or penalties can be administered contingent upon the salesman's meeting his performance goals. [23]

An effective supervisory approach, then, should be constructed from a base of specific goals for sales personnel. These goals should complement the general promotional objectives you determined in the earlier stages of your personal selling plan. Further, they must be translated into clear and attainable tasks. Ideally, field personnel should be participants in the planning process.

*Viewing Goals in a Performance System Context.* Figure 12.6 illustrates a variety of goal types commonly set for sales personnel. Although the listings are merely illustrative rather than all inclusive, they depict some of the most frequent types of goals by which salespeople are evaluated. As displayed in this figure, goal types can be categorized in two dimensions—input goals versus output goals and qualitative goals versus quantitative goals. *Input goals* deal with the skills and efforts the salesperson expends to achieve results that will benefit the firm. *Output goals* deal with the actual achievement of such results. The goal types shown in the lower right-hand quadrant of Figure 12.6 repre-

| | Qualitative | Quantitative | |
|---|---|---|---|
| Salesperson Inputs | • Proficiency in selling techniques<br>• Knowledge of product line<br>• Understanding of customers and their needs<br>• Ability to communicate<br>• Enthusiasm and energy in making sales presentations<br>• Interpersonal relations skills | • Number of calls completed on:<br>  a) Established accounts<br>  b) Prospective new accounts<br>• Efficient control of time and expenses<br>• Measurable customer services—e.g., service calls, follow-up calls, response to complaints | **FIGURE 12.6 Sales personnel goals classified by input-output and qualitative-quantitative dimensions** |
| Salesperson Outputs | • Preparation and submission of accurate and useful field reports to company<br>• Assistance in solving customer problems<br>• Cultivation of customer confidence and acceptance<br>• Development of favorable customer attitudes toward salesperson's company<br>• Successful transmission of persuasive information | • Sales volume in unit dollars and/or market shares by<br>  a) Individual accounts<br>  b) Product types<br>  c) Total<br>• Gross profit dollars and/or percentages generated<br>• New accounts opened<br>• Upgrading of individual order sizes<br>• Attainment of reseller support as measured by shelf space and positioning, display set-ups, co-op advertising placed, etc. | |

sent the *final* end results sought from selling activities. However, it is important to recognize that their attainment is closely tied to achievements in the other three quadrants. For this reason, it has been suggested that goal setting should be viewed as a "systems engineering process."[24] Such a process requires that you first examine the full system of inputs and outputs, both qualitative and quantitative, and then develop a plan for sales force guidance and evaluation which takes account of all relevant components in the system.

***Translating Goal Types into Specific Goals.*** It should be stressed that the entries in Figure 12.6 represent *types* of goals, not specific goals per se. To be useful for purposes of sales supervision, each type of goal being used must be defined in much more detailed terms. For instance, suppose that "upgrading of individual order sizes" is set as a desirable quantitative-output type of goal for your sales force. To operationalize that goal, you must spell out such things as the size of increase to be sought in individual orders, the percentage of orders on which such increases should be sought, and, quite probably, a delineation of the customers or customer types from whom larger order sizes should be most logically obtainable.

***Criteria to Guide Determination of Appropriate Goals.*** A very sensible checklist has been suggested to help ensure that your goal-setting program produces a workable target plan for your sales representatives.[25] It stresses the need for goals that meet the following five criteria:

**1.** *The goals must be congruent.* Goals have to be in alignment with each other, not in conflict. For example, if a salesperson is instructed to (a) spend more time providing problem solving assistance to established customers, (b) work at opening up a significant number of new accounts, and (c) direct special attention to upgrading order sizes among established accounts—all at the same time—you may be building an impossible situation that forces the sales representative into frustration and the use of deception.

**2.** *Sales force goals must be compatible with overall company goals.* If the firm is operating on the basis of a carefully planned and coordinated promotional mix, as it should be, each personal selling goal should be evaluated in terms of its contribution to the overall aims of that mix.

**3.** *Goals must be specific.* If the objective is to increase dollar volume, the targeted percentage of increase should be defined along with the related salesperson input goals needed to attain it.

**4.** *Goals must be measurable.* At some point, evaluation is going to be required—evaluation of both the salesperson's performance and the value of the goals themselves. The standards of evaluation should be set in advance and be made known to the sales staff. For instance, if the output goal is to open new accounts, how are the results to be measured? Will performance be judged by the raw number of new accounts actually brought in, by the dollar volume generated from those accounts, or merely by progress toward laying the groundwork for future contacts with prospective customers?

**5.** *The goals must be understandable.* The language used in transmitting information about them should be clear, straightforward, and as simple as possible. The use of vague phrases such as "increasing customer confidence" is unlikely to produce very consistent results. It is more likely to generate misunderstanding.

***Reviewing Goals on an After-the-Fact Basis.*** Hopefully, your objectives will be achieved. However, sales supervision must anticipate the possibility that this will not always be the case. When results fall short of the target, three broad possibilities have to be considered.[26] First, goals may not have been realistic or attainable. If this is the problem, the goals must be redefined. Second, goals may have been realistic and attainable, but the salesperson's effort to achieve them may have been poorly executed. This presents a personnel problem. It usually calls for training and guidance by the supervisor, though in the extreme case it may require the replacement of the sales representative. Third, unforeseen and noncontrollable factors may have disrupted achievement of an otherwise attainable goal. This is particularly applicable in the case of goals that fall into the quantitative-output category. Competition may have lowered prices or stepped up promotion, or the economic condition in the sales territory may have taken a temporary turn for the worse. When

| Sales Representative | A 1983 Sales* | B 1984 Quota* | C 1984 Sales* | D % Change 1983 to 1984 | E % of Quota Achieved in 1984 |
|---|---|---|---|---|---|
| Rhonda Taylor | 529.2 | 520 | 531.8 | +0.5 | 102.3 |
| Alan Visch | 578.4 | 620 | 611.3 | +5.7 | 98.6 |
| Ron Somni | 632.6 | 650 | 636.7 | +0.6 | 97.9 |

*In thousands of dollars.

FIGURE 12.7
**Evaluating sales representatives on dollar volume of total sales**

this is the case, the sales supervisor has to decide whether the goal should still be considered attainable at some future point, or whether the entire situation needs rethinking.

## Evaluating Sales Force Performance

**Simple Analysis of Quantitative Outputs.** Figure 12.7 illustrates elementary data from which evaluations can be drawn concerning sales force performance in terms of basic, dollar-volume output goals. In the very simplest evaluation scheme, total sales volume for the year would be the only output considered. Given the situation outlined in this figure and using 1984 as the year in question, the applicable data are those shown in column C. Under this format, Ron Somni would receive the best evaluation, followed by Alan Visch, with Rhonda Taylor in third place. Of course, the weakness of using such a simple scheme is its failure to make any allowances for differences in volume potential between territories. A somewhat more advanced but still fairly simple procedure might use as its criterion percentage changes in sales volume from one year to the next. In this case, the figures in column D would be employed for evaluation purposes. The result would be that Alan Visch would rise to first place in the ranking because of his posting of a 5.7 percent increase in 1984 over 1983. Somni drops to second place with only a slim advantage over Taylor who remains in third position.

**Comparative Analysis of Quantitative Outputs.** Relying only on percentage increase or decrease figures requires that certain rather doubtful assumptions hold true. For one thing, it would have to be assumed that no changes in territorial potential had occurred between 1983 and 1984. An improved system can be developed by moving from simple analysis to comparative analysis. This requires establishing some reasonable yardstick against which the current year's results can be measured. A common method to accomplish this involves setting a quota for each sales representative for the coming year. For example, target quotas might be determined by analyzing territorial sales potentials following a computer-model analysis such as the one outlined in the preceding chapter. By incorporating account characteristics into the quota-setting procedure and allowing for economic changes that may occur in the various territories, the quotas can serve as reasonably good standards for making evaluative comparisons. Again with reference to Figure 12.7, the data that would be

*Managing the Sales Force*

applicable in a quota-based comparative evaluation format are in column E, which compares column C to column B. On this basis, Rhonda Taylor is in first place, followed by Alan Visch with Ron Somni dropping to last position.

*Composite Rating Systems for Analysis of Quantitative Goals.* If goals are being set in a full performance system context, as recommended in our earlier discussion, using sales volume as the only measure of goal achievement will be inadequate. For example, suppose that a firm wishes to emphasize not only dollar volume but also gross profit dollars. Suppose further that management wishes to direct efforts toward certain input goals which can be quantified, such as encouraging more calls on prospective new accounts with a view to expanding the future customer base. In this situation, some form of direction must be given to sales force members to guide them in allocating their own time and input efforts. Such guidance could be provided merely through verbal instructions without any specific numbers being used. However, a better procedure may be to provide such guidance through a composite goal rating system such as that outlined in Figure 12.8.

In this example, management has determined that three types of quotas will be used. Each is weighted differently to reflect the firm's priorities. Every sales representative is then assigned a quota for each of the three types of goals in the composite plan. The degree of attainment for each quota is again measured in percentage terms, just as it was in the case of the sales volume quota system. The percentage of quota achieved is then multiplied by the weighting factor assigned to that particular quota type. For example, because Visch achieved 98.6 percent of his assigned sales volume quota, and because dollar volume of sales is weighted at .3, his weighted score for the dollar volume quota is 29.6. His total weighted score for all three quota types is 109.7, placing him in the top position. In large measure, this is a reflection of the fact that he was exceptionally successful in exceeding his quota on gross profit dollars, which is the goal weighted most heavily in the composite plan.

| | | | Percentage of Quoted Types Achieved (and Weighted Percentages) by Sales Representatives | | | | | |
|---|---|---|---|---|---|---|---|---|
| Quota Type | Weighting of Quota Type | % | Taylor Weighted | % | Visch Weighted | % | Somni Weighted |
| Dollar volume sales | .3 | 102.3 | (30.7) | 98.6 | (29.6) | 97.9 | (29.4) |
| Gross profit dollars on sales | .6 | 97.2 | (58.3) | 116.5 | (69.9) | 89.4 | (53.6) |
| Calls on prospective new accounts | .1 | 99.0 | (9.9) | 102.3 | (10.2) | 101.7 | (10.2) |
| Total | 1.0 | | (98.9) | | (109.7) | | (93.2) |

FIGURE 12.8 A weighted composite rating system combining three quantitative goals

Although a composite system such as this gives salespeople a better sense of direction regarding their quantitative inputs and outputs, there are limitations to its use. As the number of goals increases, so does the complexity of the plan. Because an overly complex plan can produce confusion rather than guidance, the number of quota types involved should be held to some reasonable maximum number such as five or six.

*Evaluating the Achievement of Qualitative Goals.*   The authors of a sales management text have pointed out that concentration on purely quantitative goal evaluations can ignore the critical importance of certain qualitative goals. These latter goals may be of great significance to the firm over the long run, even though they have little effect on immediate sales and profits. In reference to them, the authors observed, "These [qualitative goals] include time devoted to developing a potential large account, to building long-term territorial good will for the company, or to developing detailed understanding of the capabilities of the firm's products. That is why many firms supplement sales and cost analysis with other measures that more directly reflect each sales representative's performance."[27]

*Managerial Ratings for Qualitative Inputs and Outputs.*   By definition, qualitative goals are not inherently numerical in nature. Because of this, there is almost always a degree of subjectivity connected with qualitative evaluations. The major responsibility for such appraisals typically lies with sales management personnel. The simplest qualitative evaluation procedure revolves around a descriptive, essay-type performance report prepared by the sales manager and likely to be rather imprecise in nature. This purely verbal approach has some serious deficiencies. As one pair of observers has noted, "many sales managers fall into some predictable pattern of being too harsh, too lenient, or too neutral in their comments so that the appraisal is not well balanced. Moreover, many evaluators are simply not very capable writers, so their use of words may fail to provide an accurate portrayal of the salesperson."[28]

*Qualitative Rating Forms.*   In view of the shortcomings associated with essay-type evaluations, many firms either supplement or replace them with more structured rating inventory forms. An example of such a form is shown in Figure 12.9. In this instance, each goal-related quality that is considered meaningful by the company is listed and followed by a sequence of adjectives. Alternatively, each listing could be followed by a numerical rating scale.

A more detailed rating instrument that has been advocated by a number of writers, is the "Behaviorally Anchored Rating Scale," or BARS system, illustrated in Figure 12.10. The goal-related output that is judged is the salesperson's preparation and submission of accurate and useful field reports. In contrast to the rather terse treatment this topic receives in the inventory rating form depicted in Figure 12.9, its appearance under the BARS system is accompanied by extended and precise descriptions of what constitute various levels of performance. These descriptions and their positionings along the ten-point

*Managing the Sales Force*

**FIGURE 12.9 A rating form for qualitative evaluation**

| | Poor | Fair | Average | Superior | Exceptional |
|---|---|---|---|---|---|
| Proficiency in selling techniques | ☐ | ☐ | ☐ | ☐ | ☐ |
| Enthusiasm and energy | ☐ | ☐ | ☐ | ☐ | ☐ |
| Preparation and submission of accurate and useful field reports | ☐ | ☐ | ☐ | ☐ | ☐ |
| Knowledge of product line | ☐ | ☐ | ☐ | ☐ | ☐ |

numerical scale are developed by examining the company's own experience plus assessments made by the sales personnel group itself.[29]

One of the arguments advanced for using a BARS approach is that it forces the evaluator to consider specific behaviors related to each dimension being studied, rather than generalizing on impressions of performance. A related advantage is that a BARS approach, or something akin to it, spells out the type of performance expected from each salesperson. As a result, the sales force has a more accurate understanding of management's expectations. Further, sales force members are also supplied with clearer feedback data regarding the supervisor's observations of past performance and areas toward which efforts for improvement should be focused.

***Extending the Scope of Performance Evaluation.*** An interesting method has been described for obtaining ratings on qualitative aspects of salesperson performance from customers or clients as well as company personnel.[30] The technique has reportedly proved both workable and useful for a number of firms, and centers around a fifty-item questionnaire. The responses recorded on the questionnaire are analyzed to create the Contingency Management System Sales Profile shown in Figure 12.11. As illustrated in the figure, the profile measures five qualities related to qualitative goals. Beyond the customary ratings provided by the sales manager, responses are also solicited from the sales representative plus his or her co-workers and a random sample of customers. Customer ratings are obtained from questionnaires mailed to approximately ten persons at firms currently called on by the representative. All customers submitting responses are assured their identities will not be revealed.

As indicated at the top of the figure, summary data are provided on the ratings in each profile category. The summary begins with "Self Scores," which show how the sales representative ranks herself or himself on each category. This is followed by a set of average scores tallied for all other people ranking the individual. The congruence ratio compares the sales representative's self-perception with the combined perceptions of all other raters. A ratio of 1.0 would indicate the sales representative's self-perception is consistent with the general perception of other evaluators. A ratio far in excess of this might suggest the salesperson does not perceive a deficiency that is apparent to

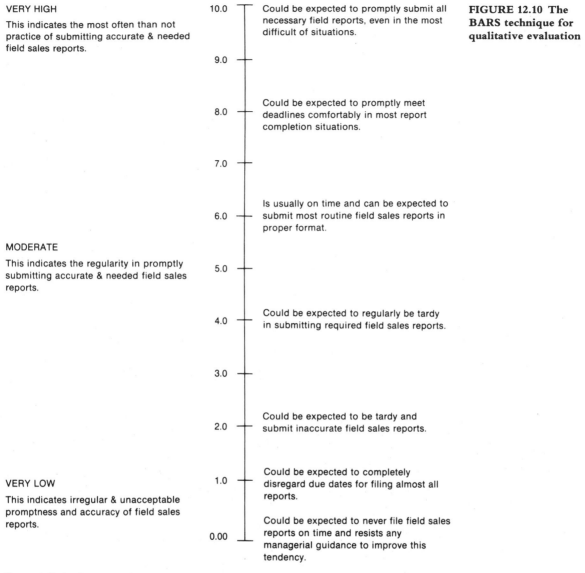

VERY HIGH

This indicates the most often than not practice of submitting accurate & needed field sales reports.

10.0 — Could be expected to promptly submit all necessary field reports, even in the most difficult of situations.

9.0

8.0 — Could be expected to promptly meet deadlines comfortably in most report completion situations.

7.0

6.0 — Is usually on time and can be expected to submit most routine field sales reports in proper format.

MODERATE

This indicates the regularity in promptly submitting accurate & needed field sales reports.

5.0

4.0 — Could be expected to regularly be tardy in submitting required field sales reports.

3.0

2.0 — Could be expected to be tardy and submit inaccurate field sales reports.

VERY LOW

This indicates irregular & unacceptable promptness and accuracy of field sales reports.

1.0 — Could be expected to completely disregard due dates for filing almost all reports.

0.00 — Could be expected to never file field sales reports on time and resists any managerial guidance to improve this tendency.

**FIGURE 12.10 The BARS technique for qualitative evaluation**

Source: A. Benton Cocanougher and John M. Ivancevich, " 'BARS' Performance Rating for Sales Personnel," *Journal of Marketing*, July 1978, p. 92.

the people with whom he or she deals. A ratio far below 1.0 would imply the salesperson may be underestimating his or her abilities. The "Efficiency Index" shows the relationship between this individual's rating and that of co-workers. Finally, the dispersion of individual scores provided by separate raters is depicted by the printout at the bottom of the profile.

The use of this approach takes place in the context of a total program that begins with a two- to four-hour seminar explaining its purpose and mechanics

**FIGURE 12.11 Printout of a contingency management system sales profile**

| CMS Measure Categories | Self score | Total other | Manager rating | Peer rating | Client rating | Congru-ence ratio | Efficiency index |
|---|---|---|---|---|---|---|---|
| Communication skills | 5.0 | 4.4 | 3.9 | 4.8 | 5.0 | 1.14 | 0.63 |
| Interpersonal relations | 4.7 | 4.4 | 3.7 | 4.6 | 5.7 | 1.06 | 0.63 |
| Product knowledge | 5.0 | 4.5 | 3.7 | 5.1 | 5.5 | 1.11 | 0.64 |
| Problem solving | 5.9 | 4.7 | 3.8 | 6.0 | 5.4 | 1.25 | 0.68 |
| Self management | 5.3 | 4.6 | 4.0 | 5.4 | 4.9 | 1.16 | 0.65 |
| Overall | 5.2 | 4.5 | 3.8 | 5.2 | 5.3 | 1.14 | 0.65 |

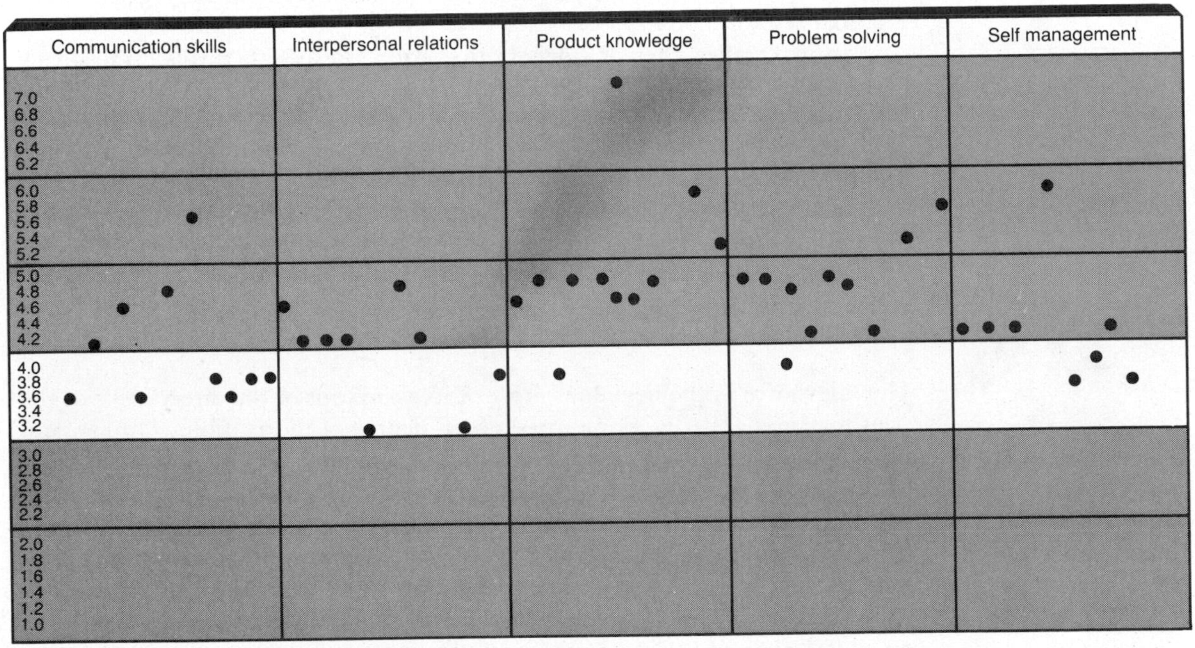

Source: Donald F. Harvey, "Managers Use Computer Profile System to Measure and Evaluate Sales-Rep Performance," *Marketing News*, 18 March 1983, Section 2, p. 12.

to both sales management and the selling staff. After the analysis has been completed, extended counseling sessions are held with each participating salesperson. The objective of the sessions and of the entire profiling technique is to provide feedback and guidance to participants. As the originator of this evaluation technique emphasizes, "It should be remembered that there are no 'good' or 'bad' ratings. . . . Rather, managers typically use the profiles to pinpoint specific areas in which sales reps need improvement."[31]

Among attendant side benefits cited for use of this method is the development of a clearer idea of selling behaviors that are likely to be well received by customers. This can potentially assist a company in developing more productive sales policies and sales training sessions.

*Supervising the Sales Force*

*Final Comments on Evaluation Systems.* Any procedure for evaluating personnel may be perceived by sales force members as having potentially threatening undertones. With this in mind, it is management's responsibility to ameliorate employee perceptions of the evaluation process by handling it in an open, positive, and constructive manner. Admittedly, if there is persistent evidence of unacceptably low performance, the salesperson must be replaced. However, the primary aim of a well-conceived program is provision of assistance and guidance to the sales force, not the thinning of its ranks. The intent is to enable sales representatives to upgrade their own abilities and increase their rewards. In consequence, it is essential that the evaluation system be accompanied by corresponding counseling, training, and reward systems. Additionally, active sales force participation should be encouraged at all stages, including goal setting.

As noted earlier, there is evidence that good salespeople thrive on feedback that equips them to control their own activities more productively. Furthermore, there is evidence that feedback and reward mechanisms which raise self-esteem in a realistic manner stimulate improved performance. Your total supervision plan, including the evaluation program, should be designed with these results in view.

## SUMMARY

The sales force in the field does most of its work out of the direct view of the sales manager. That work requires a high degree of motivation, stamina, and skill. For these reasons, managing the sales force presents some unique challenges, which revolve around techniques for hiring, training, compensating, and supervising.

A variety of tools are available to help you select new members of your sales force. These include interviews, application form "life history" items, and paper-and-pencil tests. The interview process is usually the most heavily relied on tool. Paper-and-pencil tests, especially those involving personality traits, may be helpful for back-up information. However, they are the most controversial and least used of the tools available at this time.

Suggestions for selection procedures include the following:

1. Define your own special selling situation and needs. Then, determine the qualities you will look for in selecting new people with your specific needs and goals in mind.
2. Think in terms of the customers your sales force will be contacting. There is some evidence that sales representatives are most effective when their personalities and interests relate well to the personalities and interests of their prospective customers.
3. Give special attention and care to building an effective interview procedure; aim at discovering whether the person being interviewed meets the criteria you established on the basis of your special needs, goals, and customer types.

4. Use paper-and-pencil tests—especially those dealing with personality traits—with care and as supplements to the interviews rather than as substitutes.

5. Keep a record of the methods you used and the results you obtained with an eye toward modifying your selection procedures as you gain more experience and knowledge. Because the "right qualities" to look for in a salesperson depend on the particular selling job involved, you should be ready to modify your approach and tailor it to your firm's unique situation.

Although it is common practice to conduct training programs for new and inexperienced salespeople, it can be argued that the firm will profit even more by investing in training for the best of its experienced sales representatives. Training may be aimed at increasing salespeople's information about products and their application, information about the company's overall promotional program, skills in analyzing markets, or skills in communicating with customers. It can use several types of training formats, among which are lectures, seminars or panels, the case method or sales games, and role playing. Each of these training formats has value. Your choice to some extent will relate to the particular aim you have in mind. It is not uncommon for a given program to use a combination of formats.

There are two main ways to compensate sales force personnel—on a salary basis or on a commission basis. (A bonus can usually be regarded as a special form of the commission plan.) These can be used individually as "straight plans" (straight commission or straight salary) or they can be used together in a "combination plan." The commission plan tends to be more effective in developing immediate sales, in influencing the mix of products sold, and in keeping sales costs in line with sales volume. The salary plan tends to be more effective in encouraging long-range sales development programs, in ensuring managerial influence over nonselling support activities, in building sales force loyalty to the company, and in providing more flexibility in redesigning sales territories.

To determine the appropriate form of compensation in your situation, you would do well to consider the relative importance of these advantages in your company's overall selling program. Very often you may choose some type of combination arrangement in an attempt to incorporate some of the advantages in each group. Beyond choosing a basic compensation plan, you must consider the level of compensation—dollars of salary or percentage commission per item sold. This will be affected mainly by competitive pay levels in your product category and by your own competitive position.

Supervision of the sales force presents some serious problems because field sales personnel usually work alone and, in a sense, independently. Although they are still in an embryonic stage, some interesting models have been proposed to help you structure your supervision program.

One sensible supervisory approach begins by translating company objectives into goals to be achieved by each sales representative. These goals can be thought of as forming a system of inputs and outputs having both quantitative and qualitative dimensions. Realistic goals must be (1) congruent with each other, (2) compatible with company goals, (3) specific, (4) measurable, and (5) understandable by the sales force. Management should also consider how it will interpret the situation and respond to it if the goals are *not* achieved.

Quantitative goal achievements can be evaluated by a variety of techniques. The simplest of these merely measures absolute sales results. More advanced techniques include comparisons of sales volume against previously set standards and composite ratings with separate goal types weighted on a priority basis. Qualitative goal achievements are often analyzed by essay-type reports. More useful routes to qualitative evaluations employ formal rating scales, which may include specific descriptions of the salesperson's behavior.

Ideally, the salesperson responsible for a territory should participate in the goal-setting process for that territory. Furthermore, he or she should be given an opportunity to review and analyze results with the sales supervisor. In an effective supervisory process, the salesperson is an active and informed partner in the process, and is not merely an executor of directions from superiors.

## DISCUSSION QUESTIONS

1. As sales manager for a business supply firm, you are in charge of screening applicants for your sales force. Evaluate the usefulness of paper-and-pencil tests as opposed to a personal interview. Write a memo to your boss explaining the broad guidelines you will use to set up your screening procedure.

2. Your district sales manager has a very poor record of recruiting successful salespeople. In discussing the problem with you he says, "I don't understand it! All of them scored very high on the personality tests and gave very impressive interviews! But they just didn't feel comfortable in the job—who knows why?" Comment.

3. Describe four general topics commonly covered in typical training programs. Discuss formats and methods most appropriate for communicating the content of each topic.

4. Name and describe the three main options in choosing a way to compensate your sales force. Then briefly list the objectives each compensation plan is likely to accomplish most effectively.

5. As sales supervisor for a new computer firm, you are responsible for setting up a compensation plan for your sales force. Your objectives are to keep sales costs closely in line with sales volume and provide high incentive for immediate sales.

Your major competitors offer a combination plan that is extremely generous. Which compensation plan do you think you should use? Should you set your compensation levels equal to those of your competitors? Why or why not?

6. You are field supervisor of a twenty-five person sales force. Your company, a manufacturer of construction equipment, has asked you to develop a more comprehensive program to monitor field activities. You fear that closer supervision might arouse resentment. How would you go about building a supervisory program to surmount this obstacle?

7. Models of salesperson performance are admittedly in an embryonic stage of development. Given this fact, how can any existing model be useful in a practical situation?

8. How do input goals differ from output goals and why are both types important to consider in a sales supervision plan?

9. What general guidelines should be applied in setting sales force goals?

10. Draw up rough examples of forms that behaviorally anchored rating scales might take for evaluation of the following types of qualitative goals: knowledge of product line, interpersonal relations, and assistance in solving customer problems. What advantages and problems do you see in evaluating these items by BARS?

# REFERENCES

1. B. Robert Anderson, *Professional Sales Management* (Englewood Cliffs, NJ: Prentice-Hall, Inc., 1981), p. 28.
2. Survey conducted by the Sales Executives Club of New York, *Business Week*, 1 February 1964, p. 52.
3. Robert W. Haas, *Industrial Marketing Management*, 2nd ed. (Boston: Kent Publishing Company, 1982), p. 251.
4. James C. Cotham, III, "Selecting Salesmen: Approaches and Problems," *MSU Business Topics*, Winter 1970, p. 71.
5. David Mayer and Herbert M. Greenberg, "What Makes a Good Salesman?" *Harvard Business Review*, July/August 1964, pp. 119–121.
6. Lawrence M. Lamont and William J. Lundstrom, "Identifying Successful Industrial Salesmen by Personality and Personal Characteristics," *Journal of Marketing Research*, November 1977, p. 526.
7. Franklin B. Evans, "Selling as a Dyadic Relationship—A New Approach," *The American Behavioral Scientist*, May 1963, pp. 76–79.
8. For examples see Edward A. Riordan, Richard L. Oliver, and James H. Donnelly, Jr., "The Unsold Prospect: Dyadic and Attitudinal Determinants," *Journal of Marketing Research*, November 1977, pp. 530–537; H. Lee Matthews, David T. Wilson, and John F. Monoky, Jr., "Bargaining Behavior in a Buyer-Seller Dyad," *Journal of Marketing Research*, February 1972, pp. 103–105; Arch G. Woodside and J. William Davenport, Jr., "The Effect of Salesman Similarity and Expertise on Consumer Purchasing," *Journal of Marketing Research*, May 1974, pp. 198–202.
9. Robert J. Zimmer and James W. Taylor, "Matching Profiles for Your Industrial Sales Force," *Business,* March-April 1981, p. 3.
10. Thomas R. Wotruba, "An Analysis of the Salesman Selection Process," *Southern Journal of Business*, January 1970, p. 47.
11. Douglas J. Dalrymple, *Sales Management Concepts and Cases* (New York: John Wiley and Sons, 1982), pp. 170–172.
12. Robin Brummett, "How to Pick an Ace Saleswoman," *Marketing Times*, May/June 1976, p. 12.
13. John P. Steinbrink and William B. Friedeman, *Sales Force Compensation: Dartnell's 21st Biennial Survey* (Chicago: The Dartnell Corporation, 1982), p. 12.
14. W. J. E. Crissy, William H. Cunningham, and Isabella C. M. Cunningham, *Selling: The Personal Force in Marketing* (New York: John Wiley and Sons, 1977), p. 417.
15. Bernard M. Kessler, "New Selling Skills for Today's Changing Marketplace," *Training and Development Journal*, November 1977, p. 39.
16. Gary M. Grikscheit and William J. E. Crissy, "Improving Interpersonal Communications Skill," *MSU Business Topics*, Autumn 1973, p. 65.
17. *Ibid.*
18. B. Charles Ames, "Build Marketing Strength into Industrial Selling," *Harvard Business Review*, January/February 1972, p. 55.
19. William J. Stanton and Richard H. Buskirk, *Management of the Sales Force*, 5th ed. (Homewood, IL: Richard D. Irwin, Inc., 1978), p. 327.
20. Orville C. Walker, Jr., Gilbert A. Churchill, Jr., and Neil M. Ford, "Motivation and Performance in Industrial Selling: Present Knowledge and Needed Research," *Journal of Marketing Research*, May 1977, p. 156.
21. *Ibid.*, pp. 156–168; also see Gilbert A. Churchill, Jr., Neil M. Ford, and Orville C. Walker, Jr., *Sales Force Management* (Homewood, IL: Richard D. Irwin, Inc., 1981), Chapter 9.
22. Richard P. Bagozzi, "Performance and Satisfaction in an Industrial Sales Force: An Examination of Their Antecedents and Simultaneity," *Journal of Marketing*, Spring 1980, p. 71.
23. Charles M. Futrell, John E. Swan, and John T. Todd, "Job Performance Related to Management Control Systems for Pharmaceutical Salesmen," *Journal of Marketing Research,* February 1976, p. 32.
24. Henry J. Porter, "Manage Your Sales Force as a System," *Harvard Business Review*, March/April 1975, pp. 85–95.
25. Donald W. Jackson, Jr. and Ramon J. Aldag, "Managing the Sales Force by Objectives," *MSU Business Topics*, Spring 1974, p. 54.
26. *Ibid.*, p. 56.
27. Churchill, Ford, and Walker, *Sales Force Management*, p. 519.
28. Rolph E. Anderson and Joseph M. Hair, Jr., *Sales Management: Text with Cases* (New York: Random House, Inc., 1983), p. 501.
29. A. Benton Cocanougher and John M. Ivancevich, " 'BARS' Performance Rating for Sales Personnel," *Journal of Marketing*, July 1978, pp. 87–95.
30. Donald F. Harvey, "Managers Use Computer Profile System to Measure and Analyze Sales-Rep Performance," *Marketing News*, 18 March 1983, Section 2, p. 12.
31. *Ibid.*

# PART FOUR

# *Advertising*

# CHAPTER THIRTEEN

# *Advertising Objectives, Decision Areas, and Organizations*

## FOCUS OF THE CHAPTER

The purpose of this chapter is to provide you with a broad overview of the fundamental nature of advertising and of the types of decisions and activities involved in planning your advertising program. The three chapters that follow will build upon this overview to discuss creative strategies and media strategies in more extensive detail. This chapter will also describe the two primary classes of organizations that specialize in the development of advertising programs—advertising agencies and advertising departments.

## THE GENERAL NATURE OF ADVERTISING

*Advertising is any paid form of nonpersonal presentation of ideas, goods, or services by an identified sponsor.* Like personal selling, advertising can be divided into a variety of different categories. In particular, its fundamental nature and immediate goals can be differentiated on the basis of (1) the type of audience to whom the messages are directed and (2) the type of firm sponsoring the

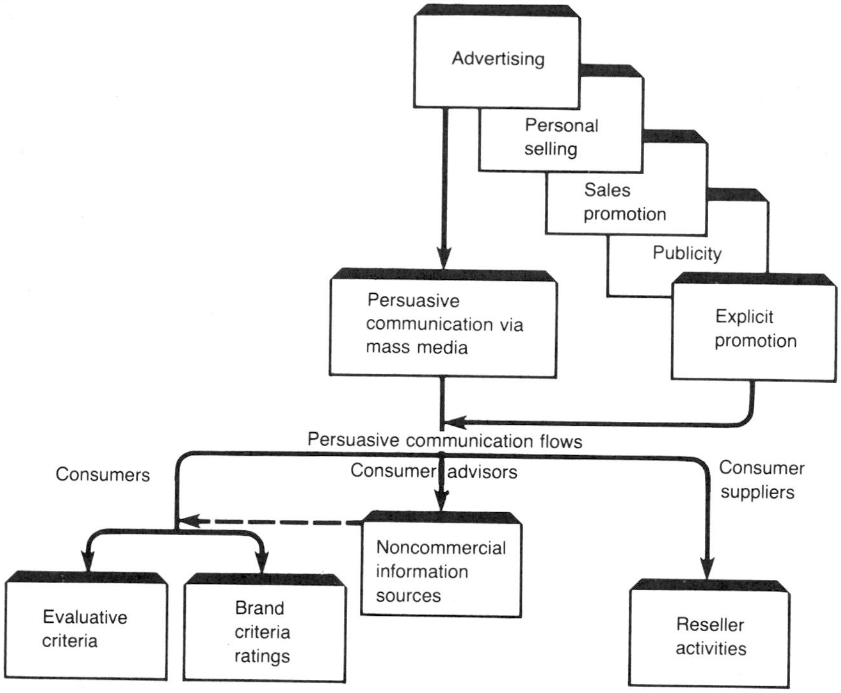

FIGURE 13.1 Advertising in the explicit promotional mix

advertisement. With this in mind, we will begin by examining each of these major breakdowns of advertising.

**Advertising Classed by Type of Audience**

In terms of the most broad kinds of audiences to whom it can be addressed, advertising can be categorized into three types. *Consumer advertising*, aimed at either ultimate consumers or industrial users; *professional advertising*, aimed at consumer advisors; and *trade advertising*, aimed at consumer suppliers, the resellers. Figure 13.1 illustrates these audience groups in relation to the framework for promotional analysis which we are following. The purpose of illustrating them in this way is to emphasize once more that advertising is normally one component working in conjunction with other explicit promotional elements. Together they form a coordinated communications mix intended to influence consumer purchase decisions. Again, if you view any of these three types of advertising in the full context of our general framework for analyzing promotional strategy, it becomes clear that they are all intended to have some final impact on purchase decisions. However, the route by which each influences such decisions is somewhat different.

**Consumer Advertising.** Consumer advertising is directed toward individuals or firms who buy a product to use it. The use to which the product will be put may be mainly for personal satisfaction (ultimate consumption) or may be mainly for the operation of some business or business-like organization (industrial consumption). In the latter case, the type of advertising involved is often referred to as "industrial advertising."

**Professional Advertising.** This is the name often given to advertising aimed at consumer advisors, noncommercial information sources from whom purchasers secure recommendations and opinions. Professionals such as physicians, dentists, agricultural agents, and architects can sometimes exert substantial influence in the process by which consumers rate various brands and make purchase decisions. Because such professionals are experts, the evaluative criteria they consider and the terms in which they want the criteria delineated may be much more comprehensive and sophisticated than those demanded by the consumers themselves.

**Trade Advertising.** This category includes all of the advertisements directed to consumer suppliers, the resellers. Since resellers view brands from a much different perspective than that of either consumers or professional advisors, the major emphasis of trade advertising is on improved profit potential. Usually, little or nothing is said about the evaluative criteria which are stressed in advertisements to consumers and professional advisors.

**Advertising Classed by Type of Advertiser**

There are two major types of advertisers—*national advertisers* and *local advertisers*.

**National or Manufacturer's Advertising.** The term "national" is used somewhat loosely in the advertising industry. It generally refers to advertisements for a brand which is sold or promoted on either a national or a regional basis. For example, if a firm produced and advertised a brand of ice cream which was sold only in the southeastern part of the United States, its advertising would still be considered "national." More accurately, then, national advertising really refers to advertising done by a manufacturer or other firm which *produces* a particular brand of product or service, as opposed to a reseller who mainly markets offerings produced by others.

**Local or Retail Advertising.** Local advertising tends to be very restricted in terms of its geographic coverage. It is usually run in advertising media which reach only a particular city or retail trading area. As the terms are commonly employed, "local advertising" and "retail advertising" are virtually synonymous. The general principles involved in building local or retail advertising are roughly equivalent to those involved in building national or manufacturer's advertising. However, retail advertising strategy often begins with the assumption that the manufacturer's advertising has presold consumers on the merits of the brand. Therefore, retail advertising usually places emphasis more on price and availability as opposed to an extended discussion of product features and benefits.

**Other Types of Advertising**

The customary division of advertisers into national and local categories hardly covers all of the possibilities. For example, there is also a category termed "classified advertising," which is often sponsored by individuals or businesses with special goals such as seeking employees or trying to find a lost dog. There is also mail-order advertising which may involve a retailer who does business on a national basis. Another possible variation is cooperative advertising, a hybrid type in which a manufacturer more or less joins forces with a retailer to sponsor the local promotion of a particular brand. We will talk more about cooperative advertising when we reach Chapter 19 and discuss reseller support. Aside from this exception, however, we are going to ignore these other types and concentrate on national and local advertising simply because they account for the bulk of advertising efforts with which most promotional strategists are most likely to be involved.

## ADVERTISING IN THE PROMOTIONAL STRATEGY PROCESS

Figure 13.2 depicts the outline we will follow to examine the major steps in the design and execution of advertising strategy and relate those steps to their place in the total promotional process. It parallels the outline introduced in Chapter 11 when we related sales management to the total promotional strategy process (see Figure 11.2). Box 1 calls for consideration of the entire promotional mix and the role that advertising should play in that mix. The six issues to be resolved at this point are exact counterparts to the issues raised in connection with the role of personal selling. They are as follows:

1. How should the objectives of advertising be defined relative to other promotional elements?
2. Should our advertising effort be aided by increased emphasis on other promotional elements?
3. Should advertising effort be increased, and other elements of explicit promotional effort be increased along with it?
4. Should less advertising effort be used and other promotional elements substituted to pick up the slack?
5. Should we concentrate on advertising and virtually ignore other types of explicit promotion?
6. Should advertising be eliminated as part of the promotional mix?

We are starting, as before, with consideration of possible substitutions and interactions among promotional elements in the total mix. The inherent nature of such substitutions and interactions among those elements—including advertising—was illustrated in some detail when we considered potential mix alternatives in connection with personal selling. Therefore, we need not go into the same kind of extensive detail at this point. Instead, we will take a different approach and look at how these six issues were handled in the successful promotion of one particular brand. The brand name and certain other specific details are disguised for proprietary reasons. The case was chosen because advertising was used as the lead element.

**FIGURE 13.2 Advertising in the promotional strategy process viewed as a sequence of decision fields**

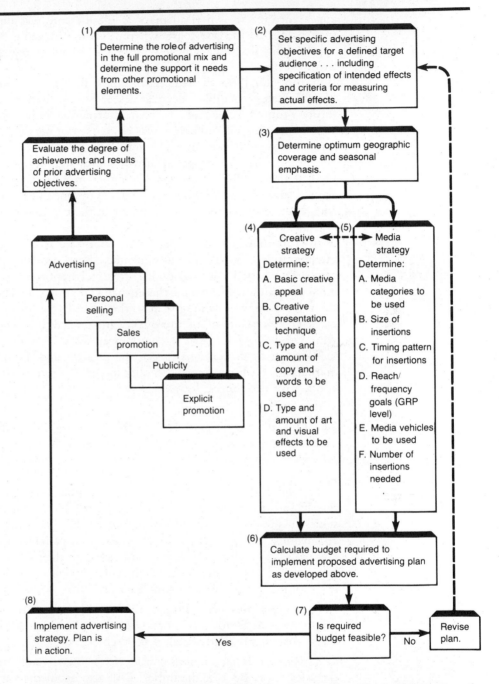

*Outlining an Advertising Strategy Approach —A Case Example*

The basic product is a rosé wine produced in northern Italy. Its history, and that of the winery in which it originates, date back for more than four centuries. In particular, it has attained a reputation for its unique semi-dry taste. The brand name of the wine is E'Suberante and it was first introduced into the United States in the late 1970s, when wine was gaining widespread popularity with industry sales volume rising rapidly. For the first several years after its appearance in the American market, E'Suberante was distributed mainly in major cities on the east coast, where it soon achieved a market share closely approaching that of a long-established and highly regarded rosé imported from Portugal.

In the early 1980s the American import firm that markets the brand in the United States assembled detailed research information to assist in shaping future promotional planning. That information indicated the primary consumer market for E'Suberante was composed of persons aged twenty-five to forty years who lived in large metropolitan areas or adjacent suburbs. In general, the heavy-user group had incomes significantly above the national median and could be categorized as upper-middle class in terms of actual or aspired social status outlook. They tended to dine out frequently and entertain friends or business associates at dinner in their homes several times during a typical month.

In-store influences often played an important role in determination of the brand selected. Such influences included both displays and information received from retail sales personnel. Price perceptions were also a meaningful influence. Although most purchasers had some roughly defined upper limit on the price they were willing to pay, they also had a lower limit. A low price carried connotations of inferior quality and tended to be a negative factor when wine was being purchased to entertain guests.

Working from their analysis of the product and the market, E'Suberante marketing executives aimed at a sales increase of twenty-five percent in dollar volume for the coming year.

### The Overall Promotional Mix for E'Suberante.

The following is a summarized list of the tasks assigned to various elements in the promotional mix to achieve the sales goal.

**1.** *Implicit Promotion—Surrogate Cues.* E'Suberante is packaged in a distinctive flagon-shaped bottle. Its label carries the colorful crest of the winery at which it is produced and the wording on the label is printed entirely in Italian. A separate, much smaller label at the bottom contains wording required by law to be in English. A slight modification in the label design was planned. Essentially, the major change was the enlargement of the winery crest to make it a more dominant aspect of the package.

**2.** *Implicit Promotion—Pricing.* E'Suberante was positioned to retail at approximately $4.50 for the 750 ml size. This placed it slightly above the Portuguese rosé that executives felt was its chief rival.

**3.** *Personal Selling.* Serious consideration was given to increasing the size of the sales force. Because the import firm also handled a variety of other wines and liquors which required attention from sales representatives, the amount of personal selling effort available for E'Suberante was felt to be below optimum. However, after extended discussion, it was decided to hold the sales force at its present size and target its activities more carefully toward retail outlets in which the potential for sales increases was especially strong.

**4.** *Sales Promotion.* A counter display piece featuring the E'Suberante crest and name was being made available to retailers. It had the look of an old-world, hand-carved artifact. It had been well received by retailers during initial efforts at placement. A small brochure was also planned, which would include both information on types of wines and their correct mode of use as well as a history of the E'Suberante brand itself. The brochure was to be made available to retailers for distribution to interested customers.

**5.** *Publicity.* E'Suberante's promotional staff was constantly on the alert for publicity opportunities. In 1980, the wine received a gold medal at an international fair in Brussels. Through a press release, the company was able to achieve excellent coverage of this award. The company was working with a California-based agency in an effort to have the brand appear in scenes of appropriate motion pictures.

**6.** *Advertising.* This was clearly the lead element in the E'Suberante strategy mix. In planning strategy for the coming year, company executives set out the following specific objectives for the advertising program:

**A.** To raise awareness of the brand's existence in the defined primary target market segment from its current level of fifty-six percent to at least seventy-five percent by the end of the year.

**B.** To make persons in that segment familiar with the pronunciation of the brand name so that they would feel at ease when ordering either in a restaurant or a clerk-service retail outlet

**C.** To accompany brand awareness with recognition of the product's special feature—its distinctive semi-dry taste

**D.** To enhance the social status of the brand by emphasizing the fact that it is imported and has a centuries-old reputation

**E.** To portray it as a wine to be enjoyed as part of a total, pleasant dining experience and as an appropriate accompaniment to any main course.

The advertising budget allocated to achieve these goals was $2.75 million, representing a thirty-five percent increase over the prior year.

***Relating Advertising to the Full Promotional Mix.*** Figure 13.3 highlights this step. To illustrate an approach to handling it we will discuss the manner in which E'Suberante's promotional strategists dealt with the six issues concerning the role of advertising in the total mix. Their decisions to our previously listed questions appear to have been as follows:

**1.** *Question:* How should the objectives of advertising be defined relative to the other promotional elements?
   *Answer:* Advertising is the lead element of our explicit mix. It should receive the primary emphasis in our planning.

**2.** *Question:* Should our advertising effort be aided by increased emphasis on other promotional elements?
   *Answer:* Only to a limited degree. Based on our evaluation of past results, any major increase in the promotional budget is likely to be most effective if it is spent on our advertising effort.

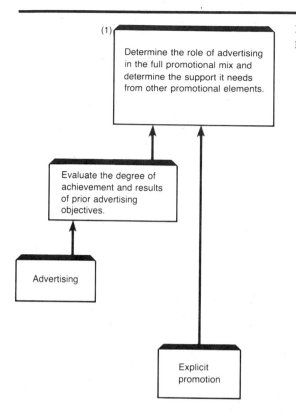

**FIGURE 13.3 Relating advertising to the total promotional mix**

(1) Determine the role of advertising in the full promotional mix and determine the support it needs from other promotional elements.

Evaluate the degree of achievement and results of prior advertising objectives.

Advertising

Explicit promotion

3. *Question:* Should advertising effort be increased, and other elements of explicit promotion increased along with it?
   *Answer:* Yes, the advertising effort should be increased. However, the general levels of effort in the other promotional areas can be left approximately where they currently stand.

4. *Question:* Should less advertising effort be used and other promotional elements substituted to pick up the slack?
   *Answer:* No. That will not work.

5. *Question:* Should we concentrate on advertising and virtually ignore other types of explicit promotion?
   *Answer:* No. Advertising may be our lead element but it clearly requires support from other promotional components.

6. *Question:* Should advertising be eliminated as part of the promotional mix?
   *Answer:* Absolutely not.

***Comments on the E'Suberante Strategy.*** Did the major decisions involved in this case produce an absolutely optimum promotional mix? Again, an optimum mix is a rather elusive target. You are normally striving to improve your position and move somewhat closer to the theoretical optimum. In the E'Suberante situation, a coordinated increase in the personal selling effort to achieve more intensive distribution coverage and reseller support might have

*Advertising Objectives, Decision Areas, and Organizations*

enabled the firm to capitalize more thoroughly on its increased advertising expenditures. We do not know if this would have produced better results. However, it is at least one of the alternatives worth some consideration.

More importantly, we do know two critical things about the E'Suberante promotional strategy. First, it placed very heavy emphasis on advertising. Second, it was highly successful in terms of sales results. For these reasons, it is also an interesting case to use as a means of previewing all of the subsequent steps in the advertising strategy process that are outlined in Figure 13.2. In this and the next three chapters we will be taking more extended looks at each of these steps. The manner in which they were handled in the E'Suberante case provides an opportunity both to introduce them and to set them in context.

## Setting Specific Advertising Objectives

After you have defined the role that advertising is to play in your total promotional mix, your next step is to determine the objectives your advertising is meant to achieve and the audience it is to reach (Figure 13.4). These objectives form the foundation on which your remaining advertising strategy decisions will be built. There is a good deal of expert opinion which holds that an ideal set of advertising objectives should meet three tests. First, they should be specific objectives. Second, they should be measurable objectives. Third, they should be objectives that are achievable by advertising alone. One analyst put it in the following way:

> Advertising of a product or a service must prove a success as advertising by setting specific objectives. Such general statements of objectives as "introduce the product to the market," "raise sales" and "maintain brand share" are not objectives for advertising. Instead, they are the objectives of the entire marketing program. . . . [The statement of objectives should indicate] (1) what basic message is to be delivered, (2) to what audience, (3) with what intended effect, and (4) what specific criteria are going to be used to measure the success of the campaign. [1]

Based on these guidelines, the statement of advertising objectives for E'Suberante wine rates rather well. Beyond extending brand awareness, the basic message to be delivered was defined as centering around a specific feature of the brand—its distinctive, semi-dry taste. Additionally, it was determined that the message should emphasize the imported nature and centuries-old reputation of the brand as well as its compatibility with any type of food. The target audience was designated on the basis of prior field research. The primary target group consisted of persons between the ages of twenty-five and forty years who were further delineated by such factors as actual or aspired social status and lifestyle characteristics. The major intended effect was partially defined by the positioning statement contained in the description of the basic message. More precise intended effects were defined in terms of increasing awareness of the product's identity to at least seventy-five percent of the primary target market and acquainting prospects with the pronunciation of the brand name to facilitate their asking for the product. As for the specific criteria used to measure actual effects, we shall review these when we come to a discussion of the box in our outline labeled "Evaluate the degree of achievement and results of prior advertising objectives."

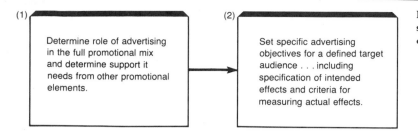

Determine role of advertising in the full promotional mix and determine support it needs from other promotional elements.

Set specific advertising objectives for a defined target audience . . . including specification of intended effects and criteria for measuring actual effects.

***Communication Goals versus Sales Goals.*** Very importantly, notice that the advertising goals specified for the E'Suberante campaign were mainly communication goals, not sales goals. The planning of the overall promotional strategy mix did start with a sales goal—a targeted increase of twenty-five percent in dollar volume. However, no single element in the promotional mix can achieve that sales goal by itself. Rather, each element must make a specific contribution toward the targeted increase. In the case of personal selling for E'Suberante, the contribution is made by securing the prescribed retail distribution coupled with proper shelf positioning and in-store displays. In the case of advertising, the contribution is made by building awareness and interest in the brand through delivery of messages promising desired consumer benefits and directed to a specific audience. Working in concert with implicit promotion, sales promotion, and publicity, the contributions of advertising and personal selling ultimately join in a confluence of persuasive communication effects. If properly conceived, executed, and coordinated, it is that confluence that will generate sales.

Paralleling the point made when we discussed objectives for personal selling, one of the advantages in stating clear objectives for advertising is that it improves your ability to assess results and correct any subsequently discovered weak points in your promotional mix. For example, should follow-up studies reveal that you achieved your advertising objectives but failed to reach your sales goal, you know that one of two very general things must be true. Either your advertising objectives were based on faulty assumptions regarding consumers' wants and needs or some other part of your promotional mix is not achieving the results originally intended. Knowing that one of these applies does not solve your problem. However, it does help you initiate your search for a solution.

***Translating Sales Objectives into Advertising Objectives.*** Again, E'Suberante set advertising objectives in terms of communication goals, not sales goals. This is the approach that many experts recommend and which this book recommends. Is it also the approach universally found in advertising practice? Not quite. When one analyst looked at published information concerning 135 "successful" advertising campaigns produced by forty leading American advertising agencies, he found that almost one-fourth of them used an increase in sales as a yardstick of success.[2] In other words, contrary to much expert advice, it is not at all uncommon for marketing executives to state advertising objectives and measure advertising results in terms of sales goals rather than communication goals.

Ideally, then, the top promotional strategy executive or team should work downward from a general sales goal to determine the specific communication goals which advertising must achieve as its contribution to that generalized sales goal. However, because actual practice frequently seems to contravene this recommended procedure, the task of translating a sales goal into a communication goal may devolve on a lower level promotional strategist such as an advertising manager. To see how that task might be approached at this lower level, we will consider a brief illustration. Although this illustration casts you in the role of an advertising strategist, it also outlines the type of sales-goal-to-communication-goal translation procedure that should have occurred earlier, at a higher level, in the total promotional planning process.

***An Example of an Objectives-Translation Process.*** Suppose you have been placed in charge of an advertising campaign for frozen orange juice. The marketing vice-president has told you that the objective of the campaign is to increase sales by twenty percent. To play your required part in reaching that objective, you must think in terms of communication possibilities. What is your best route toward helping achieve a twenty percent increase? Is it to persuade nonusers of your brand to begin using it or to convince current users to drink orange juice more frequently or perhaps to do both? Suppose further that your decision is to increase sales by convincing current users to increase their rate of orange juice consumption. The problem of achieving a twenty percent sales increase has now been transformed into a problem of communicating a specific message to a specific target audience. What can you say to current users to make them aware of the benefits they will reap from drinking orange juice more frequently? How can you relate those benefits to lifestyle goals of importance to your target prospects?

Thus, even if top management is determined to measure the results of advertising in terms of sales response, the actual implementation of advertising strategy must deal with communication objectives. Furthermore, it must also be recognized that advertising normally produces sales only in conjunction with other promotional elements. If advertising goals are set in a void, apart from goals assigned to other elements in the mix, proper alignment of the components in your program is being left somewhat to chance and proper interpretation of the effectiveness of each component is made less comprehensible.

*Determining Geographic Coverage and Seasonal Emphasis*

It is common to describe advertising budgets in terms of the number of dollars spent over the course of a year and across the entire nation. For example, the $2.75 million budget for E'Suberante was the amount spent throughout the United States during one year. However, speaking in terms of a national annual budget tends to obscure a very important point. The total annual national advertising effort is often divided unevenly among various territories and times of the year. This is done because sales potential and competitive settings can vary by territory and by season. Somewhere in your advertising

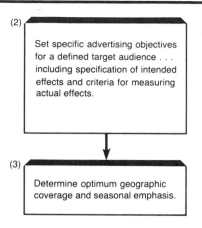

(2)

Set specific advertising objectives for a defined target audience . . . including specification of intended effects and criteria for measuring actual effects.

(3)

Determine optimum geographic coverage and seasonal emphasis.

**FIGURE 13.5 Determining geographic and seasonal emphasis for an annual advertising campaign**

planning you will have to decide where and when you want your ads to run. Box 3 suggests that the geographic and seasonal aspects of your plans should be considered early in the process (Figure 13.5).

*Geographic and Seasonal Allocations*

The E'Suberante case provides a good example of how proper geographical and seasonal emphasis can be determined. In terms of geography, E'Suberante began by concentrating in selected market areas. The advertising effort was gradually expanded to cover more regions. In its early years, less than one quarter of a million dollars was allocated for E'Suberante advertising and that sum was mainly concentrated in east coast metropolitan areas considered to be prime markets for this kind of product. Approximately five new markets on average were added each year as the total advertising budget was expanded and more complete retail store distribution was achieved. Eventually, E'Suberante was being heavily advertised in the top forty-two metropolitan markets of the United States, which account for well over half of the nation's total population. Thus, although this would be considered a national campaign, it was still fairly selective in terms of the portions of the country being emphasized.

E'Suberante strategists used a "flighting" technique for the seasonal aspect of their plan. Essentially, flighting refers to the practice of bunching up or concentrating your advertising during certain periods, rather than spreading it out more or less evenly through the year. The three flights for E'Suberante were in March, September, and November/December. Among these, the heaviest weight was given to the November/December flight because the Thanksgiving and Christmas holiday season is one of the best selling periods for wine. No advertising was run during the remaining eight months of the year.

*Developing Creative and Media Strategies*

The decisions discussed thus far are basically preliminary to the actual execution of your plan. In making those decisions you have answered four important questions that will guide the remaining pattern of your advertising strategy. First, *whom* do we want to reach? Second, *what* effects do we want to achieve? Third, *where* do we want to place our territorial emphasis? Fourth, *when* do we want the most advertising emphasis to occur? Having decided on who, what, where, and when you have one all-important question remaining.

*How?*

It is at this point that the actual formulation of your creative and media strategies begins to occur. In placing these two strategy areas side by side and connecting them with a double-headed, dashed line, Figure 13.6 emphasizes that they are far from independent of each other. For example, the general type of creative strategy you plan can influence the type of media strategy you will use. As an illustration, if your creative strategy is built around strong visual demonstrations of how your brand fits into people's lifestyle situations, it may virtually demand that your media strategy be built around television. On the other hand, if you start by deciding that radio will be your primary advertising medium, your creative strategy must be built around words not pictures, and the spoken word not the printed word. Even though we will discuss media strategy and creative strategy separately for purposes of simplification, we must recognize at the outset that they are interlocked in numerous ways.

As was mentioned earlier, discussions of creative strategies and media strategies will form the bulk of the material in the following three chapters. To preview those discussions, we will begin with a preliminary summary of the decision sequences suggested in boxes 4 and 5 of Figure 13.6. To illustrate the general thrust of the decisions involved we will continue using the E'Suberante case as an example.

**FIGURE 13.6 Major decision areas and coordination between creative and media strategies**

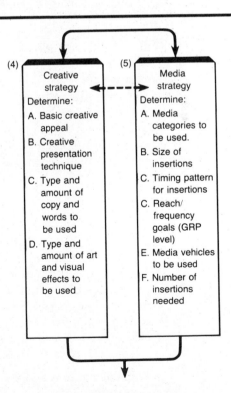

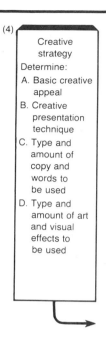

(4)

Creative strategy

Determine:

A. Basic creative appeal

B. Creative presentation technique

C. Type and amount of copy and words to be used

D. Type and amount of art and visual effects to be used

**FIGURE 13.7 Creative strategy development viewed as a sequence of decision areas**

**Development of Creative Strategy**

Figure 13.7 depicts a suggested creative strategy sequence that can be thought of in terms of two broad-gauge decision areas followed by two categories of more definitive tasks needed to implement the final creative plan. In its entirety, then, the sequence encompasses four stages. The first is the determination of the basic appeal—or buying proposal—that forms the core of your creative approach. The second involves determination of a creative technique to present the basic appeal. The third stage involves the writing of the individual advertisements—actually choosing the ideas and words that will be used to bring the appeal and presentation technique to life. Its counterpart is the fourth stage that involves the illustrating of the individual advertisements—creating the kinds of visual effects and/or artwork to be used in conjunction with the words.

*Basic Appeals and Creative Presentation Techniques.* Although these two terms received brief mention in our discussion of international promotional programs in Chapter 7, each merits more formal definition at this point.

The *basic appeal* or buying proposal is the central message of the advertisement. It is built around the reason or group of reasons why the message receiver should act in the way the advertiser is recommending, which usually means buying a particular brand. The basic appeal generally revolves around certain evaluative criteria and/or the lifestyle goals with which the product features and benefits are associated. In the E'Suberante case the basic appeal was conceived as follows:

**1.** E'Suberante is an *imported* wine with a centuries-old reputation (a type of feature).

*Advertising Objectives, Decision Areas, and Organizations*

**2.** It is a delicious rosé with a distinctive *semi-dry taste* (a feature which implies a benefit).

**3.** It *goes well with any food* and therefore you can feel socially comfortable in either ordering it or serving it (a benefit coupled with a lifestyle goal).

Having decided on your basic appeal, you are left with the question of exactly *how* it should be communicated. A *creative presentation technique* is the style and design of the message through which the basic appeal is presented. For instance, you might choose to present the same basic appeal using such varied techniques as humor, testimonials, or comparative advertising. In the E'Suberante case the decision was made to present the appeal using a creative presentation technique built around sophisticated humor and a celebrity spokesperson.

*Choosing Words and Illustrations.*   At this point your assignment becomes one of converting the advertising plan into the actual advertisements. This means working with the words and visual effects that will bring the appeal and technique to life. Because E'Suberante concentrated on radio as its only advertising medium, there were no visual effects to consider. The task was one of choosing the words and the people to deliver those words. After deciding on a creative presentation technique that would use sophisticated humor and a celebrity spokesperson, the advertising team set out to locate a well-known personality to bring this aspect of the creative strategy to life. The individual who was ultimately signed for the commercials was the star of a currently popular situation comedy series. Research data showed that she enjoyed extremely high public acceptance, especially among persons who most closely matched the description of E'Suberante's primary target market. The commercials themselves were built around incidents connected with either dining out or entertaining guests at a dinner party. Their tone was both consistent with the image of the spokesperson and the communication goals laid out in the initial decision-making process.

**Developing Media Strategy**

Your media planning can be thought of as involving six major steps (Figure 13.8). The first two are closely related to your creative strategy plan and may, in fact, be virtually fixed by that plan. The next four involve more detailed decisions concerning the kinds of audience coverage and timing impact at which you are aiming. Although there is no hard and fast order in which the decisions will always be made, one logical sequence might run as follows: Determine the general media categories to be used. Determine the size of the individual advertising insertions. Determine the general timing of those insertions. Determine desired reach and frequency goals, resulting in a GRP (Gross Rating Point) level. Determine specific media vehicles to be used. Determine the number of advertising insertions to be run.

**A Preliminary Look at the Media Planning Steps**

The terms and the issues involved in these planning steps will be covered at length in Chapter 16. At this point, we will introduce the general process by describing how several of these decision steps were handled in the E'Suberante case. First, we need definitions to clarify the meaning of two important terms, "media vehicle" and "media category."

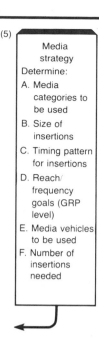

(5)

Media strategy

Determine:

A. Media categories to be used

B. Size of insertions

C. Timing pattern for insertions

D. Reach/ frequency goals (GRP level)

E. Media vehicles to be used

F. Number of insertions needed

**FIGURE 13.8 Media strategy planning viewed as a sequence of decision areas**

A "media vehicle" is a *specific carrier* of advertising messages. Examples would be *Cosmopolitan* magazine, *Popular Mechanics*, ABC's "Monday Night NFL Football," "Ryan's Hope," *The New York Times*, or the *Miami Herald*. Notice that each is a very clearly specified and individually identified message carrier rather than a general category of message carriers. In the case of radio and television, the vehicle may be specified in terms of station or network plus time of day or "daypart." For example, it might be designated as KYW radio/ morning drive time, or ABC (television)/weeknight prime time.

An advertising "media category" is a *broad grouping* of vehicles that all have the same general physical characteristics and capabilities. For example, magazines are a type of advertising media category. The magazine medium includes *Cosmopolitan, Popular Mechanics*, and a large number of other publications. Similarly, television, radio, outdoor advertising, and newspapers are all separate types of advertising media categories. Again, each of them includes a wide variety of different, individual media vehicles.

*A Preview of Media Strategy—The E'Suberante Case*

***Media Category and Insertion-Size Decisions.*** In the case of E'Suberante, the most basic media decision involved choosing radio as the principal media category to be used. Virtually the entire budget was scheduled for radio. This is a somewhat unusual approach for a large national advertiser of an ultimate consumer good. It is probably more common to see such advertisers use a combination of media categories. For example, an advertiser might decide to divide the effort among television, magazines, and newspapers. However, E'Suberante opted for what was essentially a one-medium concentration of effort and, in part, this was probably related to prior decisions regarding the

*Advertising Objectives, Decision Areas, and Organizations*

creative strategy to be followed. The insertion size was set at sixty seconds per commercial.

***General Timing, Reach/Frequency, and GRP Level Decisions.*** With regard to timing, you saw earlier that E'Suberante used a "flighting" plan with ads running during three periods of the year—March, September, and November/December. Because the topics can become somewhat complicated, we will defer defining "reach" and "frequency" until Chapter 16. These terms basically refer to how many of your prospects will be exposed to your advertising and how often they will be exposed. The combination of reach and frequency produces a measurement designated as Gross Rating Points or GRP level. In the E'Suberante case, the goal was ninety GRPs per week during the March and September flights, and 10 GRPs per week during the November/December flight.

***Specific Media Vehicles and Number of Insertions.*** E'Suberante's choices regarding specific vehicles within the radio medium were stated in terms of dayparts and station types. The radio stations chosen were mainly those featuring music and news formats that appealed to persons in the target segment. The particular dayparts selected were (1) afternoon drive time—3:00 PM to 7:00 PM, Wednesday through Friday; (2) evening—7:00 PM to 10:00 PM, Monday through Friday; and (3) weekend time—1:00 PM to 7:00 PM, Saturday and Sunday. As in any campaign whose media planning follows the outlined sequence, the required number of insertions is more or less fixed at this point, by previous decisions regarding the GRP level and the specific vehicles to be used. However, determination of the exact placement is anything but automatic. Rather, it can call for some complex procedures of analysis that will be illustrated in Chapter 16.

***Assessing Your Plan for Budget Feasibility***

Every element of explicit promotion requires a budget—a commitment of funds to carry out the programs you plan. So far we have been purposefully postponing discussion of how you should determine the size of your budget. The rationale underlying our postponement is based on the fact that promotional expenditures are intended to enable the various promotional elements to accomplish their specific assignments. For that reason, complete discussion of each element and its potential assignments should precede discussion of budget calculation. After each separate element has been covered, Chapter 20 will go into detail on the various budget-setting techniques that are widely talked about in connection with promotional planning. However, because your advertising program so often calls for spending a large sum of money that can vary a great deal from year to year, some brief initial remarks about budgeting are useful at this point. There are two general ways in which an advertising budget can be determined; they are the predetermined budget and the strategy-determined budget.

*The predetermined budget* is set *before* your advertising plan has been developed. In other words, before you even initiate work on the details of your advertising strategy, some kind of dollar limit is fixed as to how much money will be spent. There are a variety of approaches that can be used to arrive at a predetermined budget allocation. Regardless of which is used, the predetermined budget always puts a limit on your plan in advance of the actual development of that plan.

*The strategy-determined budget* works in reverse fashion. You start by building your strategy plan, using the outline just presented or something similar to it. When your plan is complete you calculate the amount it will cost to implement. In advertising, most of your expenses will go for media purchases: buying space and time. Some will involve creative expenses required to pay for things such as artwork, talent, and the production of television commercials. Importantly, with a strategy-determined budget, you start with no preset dollar figure. Your budget develops as you decide on your advertising needs.

Regardless of which general budgeting approach you follow—predetermined or strategy-determined—in the end you must somehow evaluate your plan in terms of the amount of money it will require.

### Assessing Feasibility of a Predetermined Budget.
If you are working with a predetermined budget and the plan requires more money than that budget permits, you must change something. The revision arrow from box 7 in Figure 13.9 tells you that the right way to do this is to go back to the beginning. This means examining your original advertising objectives to see whether they are realistic given the amount of money you have to spend. The important point is that you should reconsider the total advertising plan in the light of your budget limitation. This is a much wiser approach than simply cutting back on portions of your planned campaign and losing sight of your original objectives.

### Assessing Feasibility of a Strategy-Determined Budget.
If you are working with a strategy-determined budget, the total cost of your advertising plan must

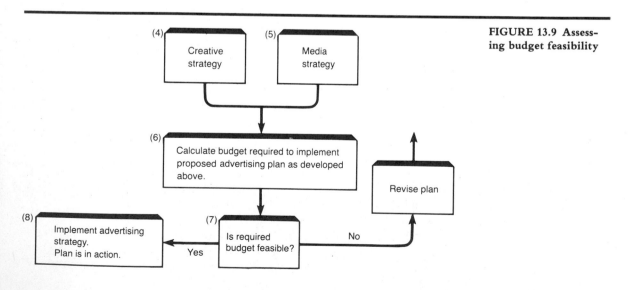

**FIGURE 13.9 Assessing budget feasibility**

*Advertising Objectives, Decision Areas, and Organizations*

**FIGURE 13.10 Implementation and evaluation of the advertising program**

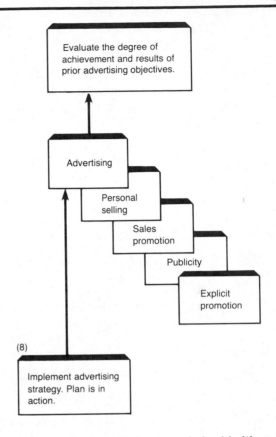

Evaluate the degree of achievement and results of prior advertising objectives.

Advertising

Personal selling

Sales promotion

Publicity

Explicit promotion

(8)

Implement advertising strategy. Plan is in action.

still be examined in terms of the availability of funds and the likelihood of earning an acceptable profit from the advertising investment. If your strategy-determined budget turns out to be unacceptably high, you should go back to the beginning and rework the entire strategy, just as recommended in connection with the predetermined budget. Again, you should not handle budget cuts on a piecemeal basis.

*Implementing the Advertising Program*

When you have an advertising strategy that appears to be both sensible and affordable, you are ready to implement your advertising program. This simply means actually building the specific advertisements and buying the necessary time and space to run them. The advertising portion of your promotional strategy mix is now in operation. As with any other promotional element, you will need to evaluate the results (Figure 13.10).

*Evaluating the Results of Advertising*

A successful evaluation plan assumes that you began with a clear statement of your objectives. As emphasized earlier, your objectives (at least in the ideal situation) should be stated as communication objectives, not sales objectives. It is true that you will also be interested in sales results. However, clearly understanding your communication objectives and being able to measure them will help you determine why you are or are not obtaining the sales results called for in your original marketing plan. For example, recall that the E'Suberante campaign had communications objectives expressed in terms of both building brand awareness and conveying certain specific items of knowledge about the brand (improving brand criteria ratings). After the campaign had been run, consumer surveys were conducted to evaluate its effectiveness in attaining those communications objectives among persons in the primary target prospect group. The survey results showed the following:

*Awareness.* In follow-up research at the end of the year, brand awareness had risen to seventy-eight percent. Virtually all of the respondents who were aware of the brand were reported as "feeling comfortable" with the pronunciation of its name.

*Brand Knowledge and Attitudes.* Eighty-six percent of the persons interviewed who were aware of the brand were familiar with the fact that it was characterized by a distinctive semi-dry taste. Ninety-two percent knew it was imported and had been in existence for several centuries. Seventy-nine percent identified it as a wine to be enjoyed primarily at dinner and as being proper to serve with any type of food.

The promoters of E'Suberante seemed to be achieving their stated advertising objectives. It is also true that they were achieving their sales objective, which ultimately is the issue of greatest importance. However, the check on the communications effects of the advertisements helps assure the firm that advertising is doing what it was intended to do as part of the total promotional mix.

# THE ORGANIZATIONAL FRAMEWORK FOR PRODUCING ADVERTISING

Now that we have taken a first look at the types of activities involved in building an advertising program, we will next look at the organizations and people who perform those activities. There are two main types of organizations which specialize in developing the creative strategies and media strategies needed to implement advertising programs. These are advertising agencies and advertising departments.

*The Advertising Agency*

Most national advertising and some local advertising is developed and placed by a unique type of marketing organization called an "advertising agency." In general, an advertising agency is an independent firm composed of experts in various phases of advertising such as copy, art, production, and media planning.[3] The basic services it provides have been outlined as follows by the American Association of Advertising Agencies:

1. A study of your product to determine its advantages and disadvantages and how it compares with competitors
2. An analysis of the present and potential markets for your product
3. A consideration of applicable distribution and sales techniques
4. A study of available advertising media that can be used to carry your messages

5. A formulation of a complete advertising plan
6. The execution of this plan through (a) preparing the advertisements, (b) purchasing media space and time, (c) mechanically preparing needed materials, (d) verifying insertions, (e) auditing and billing for the service
7. Cooperation with your sales force[4]

Many agencies offer services that go beyond this list. Examples of such additional services include marketing research studies, preparation of sales promotion and point-of-purchase materials, package design, and development of publicity materials. In short, although their activities center around advertising, the work of advertising agencies may extend into almost all areas of the promotional mix.

*The History and Structure of Advertising Agencies*

The advertising agency business first developed in the United States in approximately the middle of the nineteenth century. The original agencies were simply sellers of advertising space. It was only over time that they began to expand their functions and gradually make available the many services listed above. Because they began as sellers of space, agencies earned most of their revenues through commissions paid by the media vehicles whose space they sold. This commission came to be more or less standardized at fifteen percent.

For example, if an agency placed a client's ad in a newspaper and the cost of the newspaper space was $1,000, the agency retained $150 of that amount as its commission. As new types of advertising media emerged—such as radio and television—they also generally adopted the fifteen percent commission rate. There are some exceptions to the fifteen percent rule, however. As an illustration, outdoor advertising firms often pay the agency a commission of 16⅔ percent. An example of how the arithmetic works out under a typical commission arrangement is shown in Table 13.1.

*Services Provided Under the Commission System*

When it is operating under a commission plan, the agency provides many but not all of its services to the client at no additional charge. Services for which clients would be expected to pay separate charges include such things as finished artwork, the production of printing plates and videotapes, and the preparation of comprehensive layouts. Of course, the agency will also usually

---

**TABLE 13.1 Example of a "standard" advertising agency commission system**

*Billing to Agency by Media Vehicle*

| | |
|---|---:|
| Base charge for time or space | $50,000 |
| Less commission to agency (15%) | 7,500 |
| | 42,500 |
| Less cash discount if paid in ten days (2%) | 850 |
| *Net amount due to vehicle from agency* | $41,650 |

*Billing to Client by Agency*

| | |
|---|---:|
| Base charge for time or space | $50,000 |
| Less cash discount (2%) | 850 |
| *Net amount due agency from client* | $49,150 |

---

*The Organizational Framework for Producing Advertising*

421

make additional charges for services not directly connected with the placing of advertising in standard media vehicles. For instance, things like market research, publicity, and preparation of sales promotion materials are generally handled on a separate fee basis.

*The Agency Recognition System*

Historically, a commission was paid only to advertising agencies recognized by the advertising media. In other words, not just anyone could place an ad in a magazine, newspaper, or other media vehicle and expect to receive a fifteen percent commission. The essential standards an agency had to meet to gain recognition were the following:

1. It must be a bona fide independent organization, not under the ownership or control of either its advertising clients or any media vehicle.
2. It must keep all commissions received and not share them with either the client or the media vehicle.
3. It must be staffed with experienced and qualified personnel.
4. It must be financially able to cover the cost of all time and space purchases.[5]

In the mid 1950s, the U.S. Department of Justice took action that disrupted historically conventional industry practices, broke down these recognition standards, and brought about changes in methods of paying for agency services. These changes are considered more thoroughly below (see p. 426). First, however, we will discuss the *full-service agency* that developed under the traditional commission and recognition systems and which still serves as the general model for the agency business.

*The Full-Service Advertising Agency*

A traditional, full-service agency is equipped to handle all of the tasks and functions that were listed earlier. Because these include the possible preparation of sales promotion and publicity materials, such an agency is really involved in more than merely the advertising element of the mix. Its activities can even extend into the personal selling area in terms of the preparation of sales training materials and general cooperation with the client's sales force. In short, the full-service agency can become an important promotional partner of the client firm.

Agency organizational structures can be set up in a number of different ways. Figure 13.11 illustrates a general form that a typical full-scale agency might take. The agency departments with which we are most concerned are those listed under the titles Client Contact, Creative Services, Production, Media, and Auxiliary Services.

***Client Contact Activities.*** Account executives are the vital links between the agency and its clients. An account executive is directly responsible for working with one particular client or group of clients. She or he also supervises the work done within the agency on the client's behalf—not necessarily in a technical sense, but in terms of making certain that specialists within the agency produce work which meets the advertiser's needs. Ideally, the account executive should know as much about the client's market, competition, and

**FIGURE 13.11 General organizational pattern of the full-service advertising agency**

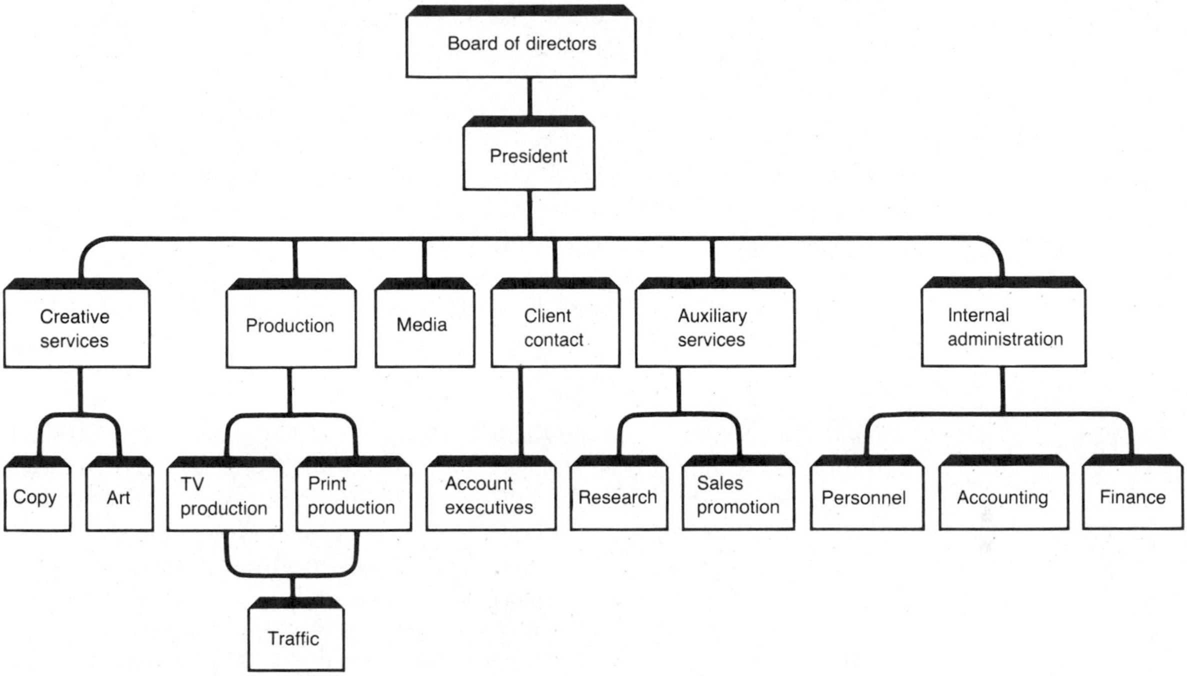

Source: Adapted from American Association of Advertising Agencies materials.

total promotional planning as do the members of the client's own marketing staff. The account executive should then be able to translate this information into an appropriate service program to be provided by the advertising agency.

*Creative Services—Copy.*    The words used in advertisements are referred to as "copy." The people who produce them are termed "copywriters." Many observers feel that these are the key people in the development of a successful advertising campaign because they usually initiate the actual creative work of building individual advertisements. At times they may be involved in determining the basic appeal or buying proposal that will be featured in the campaign. They are always deeply involved in questions concerning the way in which that appeal will be executed.

Although their chief responsibility is the wording of the advertising, copywriters often also prepare rough initial drawings that outline the general pictorial route that the ad is going to take. Customarily, copywriters are assigned on a more-or-less permanent basis to a particular account or group of accounts. Because of this, they acquire a good deal of expertise concerning the nature of the brand, its market, its competition, and its total promotional plan. The same copywriter often works on preparing advertising for all media categories. However, some agencies have separate staffs for print advertising on the one hand and radio/television advertising on the other.

***Creative Services—Art.*** The copy department is responsible for what an ad says. The art department is responsible for how it will look—the pictorial aspect of the advertising. In the case of print advertising, the art director and other members of the department prepare "layouts." These are the basic drawings from which the final artwork will be produced. They show what the total advertisement will look like. In making television commercials, the equivalent of the layout is called a "storyboard." This is a series of panels—something like a comic strip—that shows the scenes and types of action that the commercial will follow. Under each panel is the wording, or audio portion, which goes with that particular segment of the commercial.

In most cases, the art department does not produce finished artwork. Instead, it contracts with outside artists and photographers who produce the finished work based on the original layout. The client is then billed for the cost of this additional work done outside the agency.

***Production—Print.*** The copy has been written and approved. The finished artwork has been produced from the layouts. At this point, a print advertisement's final preparation becomes the responsibility of the production people in the agency. They work with outside suppliers such as typographers, photoengravers, and printers to have the ad set up in a mechanical form which the media vehicle can use to reproduce it. The engravings and other materials needed to print the finished ad are purchased by the agency on behalf of the client but usually paid for by the client firm itself. Among other things, the print production people are concerned with maintaining high quality in the materials they purchase for the client and obtaining those materials at a favorable price.

***Production—Television.*** Overseeing the production of television commercials requires special talents that are different from those we have been discussing. For this reason, it is usually handled by a separate department in the agency.

Most agencies do not actually produce television commercials. The work is done by outside studios and the cost of their services is another additional expense charged to the client. The agency's role is to hire the outside studio and supervise the work. The storyboard described earlier serves as the guide for the commercial. The television production department then chooses the people who will portray the roles shown in the commercial and decides on the types of settings needed to carry out the scenes within it. Finally, the storyboard is brought to life, videotaped, and edited.

***Production—Traffic.*** From what has been said so far about the creative activities of the agency, you can see that making a single piece of advertising can require much cooperation between different specialists in a number of departments. In each case there is a physical piece of advertising material that is scheduled to reach its audience at some prestated point in time. The people in the traffic department are responsible for making certain that the development of advertising materials is progressing properly so they will be ready by the deadline dates of the various media vehicles which will transmit them. In short, the traffic people ensure that the work gets out and gets out on time.

***Media.***   The media department works on choosing and buying the time and space required to carry the advertising. This is where most of the advertising budget is spent and the task of making all the choices and handling all the paperwork is a huge one.

Media specialists must be able to think in terms of the wide assortment of media vehicles available among the television stations, radio stations, newspapers, consumer magazines, business publications, farm publications, and outdoor services that exist throughout the country. They then attempt to choose those which will reach the right kind of audience with the right kind of effect at the lowest possible cost to the client. They must also devise schedules that deliver the ads in the timing pattern considered to be most effective and take into consideration the kind of audience overlap that will occur between different media vehicles. For example, if a commercial is run on two different television shows, how many people in the target market group will be watching only one of those shows and how many will be watching both? The media people must know the answer or at least be able to make a good estimate.

***Auxiliary Services—Research.***   To do an effective job of communicating with a mass audience you should have as much information about that audience as you can reasonably obtain before you prepare your advertising. Ideally, you should also have a means of securing information about the communication effects of your advertising after the advertising has been run. In the early days of the advertising business, both types of information were gathered on a rather informal basis, if at all. As more sophisticated research techniques became available, advertising agencies began using them to build better campaigns and to measure their results. This led to the addition of another type of expert within the organization, the research specialist. The talent of the research staff is used to gather and analyze market data and audience feedback.

Especially over the last quarter century, research departments have often extended their activities substantially. They no longer limit themselves to research aimed only at building better advertising but can also handle more broad-scale studies dealing with a client's entire marketing program.

Some of this research is original. That is, the entire study is designed, carried out, and interpreted by the agency's own people. In other cases the agency may design the study and then contract much of the remaining work to outside research firms. In still other cases the agency may buy complete research studies which were originated by independent, syndicated research firms. The role of the agency research staff, in this particular instance, becomes one of interpreting the information in terms of what it might mean to the client. Some research work may be provided to clients by the agency at no extra charge. When the work goes beyond normal advertising research, an extra fee will probably be involved.

**Auxiliary Services—Sales Promotion.** Sales promotion is not the same thing as advertising. However, it is similar in that it typically involves mass communication techniques. For this reason a similar sort of creative talent is usually required. Many agencies have extended their service packages to provide clients with assistance in developing such things as point-of-purchase display materials, retail promotions, contests, premiums, and sales brochures. The sales promotion department—sometimes known as the "merchandising department"—may also become involved in working with the client's sales management personnel to prepare training materials and sales development programs.

**Other Marketing Services.** The sales promotion department is a good example of how full-service advertising agencies often take part in much more than merely the advertising element of the promotional mix. A number of agencies are equipped to assist clients in still more promotional areas. For instance, they may have a public relations/publicity department, which is available to clients on a separate fee basis. Some agencies will work on projects such as package design and consumer product testing.

**Integrating the Various Agency Activities**

Although we have been looking at each of these departments on a separate basis, it is important to emphasize that agency personnel, drawn from a variety of departments, typically operate as a team in serving a client. In other words, one of the benefits of hiring the agency is that you gain access to a cooperative blend of skilled people with diversified backgrounds who pool their talents to help you build your promotional mix.

**Alternatives in Agency-Client Relationships**

At one time, virtually the only sensible route for a large national advertiser to follow was the use of a full-service agency, which was compensated mainly by the commissions it received from media vehicles. For example, if you spent $8 million a year to advertise your brand, the agency you hired would collect $1.2 million in commissions. Because of the commissions it earned, the agency was able to provide most of the services described above. It could also offer you supplementary services, at your option, for additional fees. Alternatively, if you chose to place your $8 million worth of advertising directly, bypassing the agency, you would not normally be able to receive the same commissions from the media vehicles. Therefore, you would have to pay for those services at your own extra expense.

As noted earlier, in the mid-1950s the government alleged that the agency commission system coupled with the agency recognition system violated federal antitrust law. Among the specific points to which the government objected were the following practices then followed by most media vehicles through their trade associations: (1) the setting up of uniform requirements for agency recognition, (2) the refusal to grant commissions to unrecognized agencies, (3) the charging of different rates to advertisers as opposed to the rates charged to advertising agencies, and (4) the establishment of a set commission rate fixed at fifteen percent.

Legal action was taken against the American Association of Advertising

Agencies and five trade associations representing the majority of station owners and publishers of media vehicles. The case was settled through consent decrees in which the various associations agreed they would no longer engage in any of the alleged activities. Essentially, this left agencies and advertisers free to work out any sort of compensation system they might choose. In many cases, those advertisers and agencies decided to leave things as they were. In other words, they concluded that the existing fifteen percent commission compensation arrangement worked well for both sides. However, others decided to adopt a different payment plan. The two main alternatives that resulted are the *fee system* and the *cost-plus system*.

**The Fee System.**   Under this arrangement, agency and client agree in advance on what services will be performed and what dollar fee will be charged. Usually this agreement is established for a period of one year. The agency will then rebate to the client all of the commissions it receives from the media vehicles. In place of commissions, the agency collects a straight fee from the client. For example, as an advertiser spending $8 million per year, you might negotiate a fee of $800,000 for the agency. Because the agency will now rebate its commissions from media vehicles, $1.2 million of your $8 million expenditure will be returned to you. In short, you appear to be $400,000 better off than you would be under a straight commission plan. Very commonly, however, the fee negotiation process may also involve a reduction in agency services. In other words, you pay less money but you also receive less service. For instance, it might be agreed that the agency will do less research on your account and limit its participation in such activities as sales promotion or developing sales training aids.

**The Cost-Plus System.**   The essential format of this arrangement is quite similar to the fee system. However, the amount paid the agency is based on what that agency has to spend for time and materials in working on your account, plus an allowance for overhead and profit. You then pay for the total amount involved and in turn receive a rebate of the commission.

**Choosing Between Agency Compensation Plans.**   There is disagreement as to which type of payment system is best for the advertiser. Switching from a straight commission plan to either a fee or cost-plus system puts the agency in the position of competing on price as well as on the basis of service. Some observers feel that either of the latter plans may save money for the advertiser only at the expense of losing valuable agency activities. An opposite view holds that payment on a fee basis rather than on a commission basis emphasizes the fact that advertising agencies are professional organizations similar to law firms or public accounting firms, which should have the effect of upgrading their efforts.

Immediately following the original consent decree, most advertisers continued to choose the traditional commission plan. In recent years, however, there has been a clear trend away from its use. According to surveys conducted by the Association of National Advertisers, sixty-eight percent of the responding firms were compensating their agencies by some form of traditional media commission arrangement in 1976. By 1979, that figure had dropped to fifty-seven percent. By 1983 it was reported to be down to fifty-two percent. Furthermore, the data released in 1983 indicated that, "Even those who continue to base payment on a percentage basis are not likely to use the 15% rule. . . . Large advertisers tend to pay less than 15%, while small advertisers and those using a broad range of agency services may pay much more than 15%."[6]

The commission system, then, still exists but is declining in popularity and increasing in complexity. From the standpoint of advertisers, the possible variations in compensation plans, which are now available, give them both more flexibility and, perhaps, more difficult decisions to make.

## Alternative Types of Agencies

Not only can advertisers now choose between different kinds of compensation plans, they can also choose among different kinds of agencies. The major alternatives available are the full-service agency (which has already been described), the in-house agency, the boutique agency, and the modular agency.

**The In-House Agency.** This is much like a full-service agency except that it is owned and controlled by the advertiser. Because the in-house agency collects and keeps all media commissions, the advertiser is now in a position to retain any profit that would normally go to an independent agency. In a sense, this reduces the expense of your advertising budget. Presumably, it could also give the advertiser closer control over all of the advertising activities. However, many critics believe that it has some serious drawbacks. For one thing, the inside agency is likely to be smaller and possess less diversity of talent. In addition, the advertiser loses an "outside point of view." Because all of the advertising personnel are company employees, they may bring a somewhat narrower and strictly company-oriented perspective to their work. Despite these limitations, quite a few important companies now use in-house agencies and the number appears to be increasing.[7]

**The Boutique Agency.** This is an organization that specializes in one part of the advertising process, but does not handle the full range of needed services. For example, during the 1960s "creative boutiques" began to appear. These are independent firms which specialize in copy and/or art but do not handle other activities such as media and research. Paralleling the creative boutiques, there are independent organizations which specialize in developing media plans only. Such agencies make it possible for an advertiser to be highly flexible in selecting outside assistance. For example, as an advertiser you could choose one firm to handle your creative work and another to do your media planning. Then you could consolidate all remaining activities within your own organization. Presumably you would be choosing each outside firm because it was especially strong in its particular area of expertise.

**Modular Agencies.** Some full-service advertising agencies will sell portions of their services separately. These have been given the name "modular" or "a la carte" agencies. For instance, you might decide to buy only art and copy services from one such agency. Then you could turn to a different modular agency for your media services. Of course, you could also combine certain services of a modular agency with other services purchased from boutiques or done on an in-house basis.

***Some Comments.*** The appearance of all these alternatives in agency types is relatively new. Like the alternatives in compensation plans, they provide advertisers with an opportunity for much more flexibility in program development. Of course, if various portions of the advertising task are turned over to a variety of different agencies, the advantages of a team effort possible with the full-service agency are lost. The client firm must also be able to coordinate the flow of work from several different sources. Still, some advertisers may feel that the gains offset any possible losses.

## THE ADVERTISING DEPARTMENT

An advertising department is a special unit within the advertiser's own firm. There are two broad categories of such departments—departments that replace outside agencies and departments that work with outside agencies.

***Departments That Replace Agencies***

If a firm does not use an outside agency, all of the tasks usually performed by a full-service advertising agency must be performed instead by the firm's own advertising department. The in-house agency represents a special case of an advertising department. To handle its responsibilities, this sort of advertising department tends to be structured along the lines of a miniature agency. Such departments are especially common among retail advertisers. Retailers tend to handle most if not all of their own advertising work for the following three main reasons:

**1.** *Much retail advertising demands extremely fast action.* The advertising staff of a department store may be preparing ads on Monday that are scheduled to run Thursday or Friday. Weather changes, merchandising needs, or special situations are constantly occurring which require the store to alter selling and advertising patterns quickly. For this reason, an advertising unit that is on the spot and in constant contact with the store's buyers and department managers is frequently best suited to do the job.

**2.** *Most retail advertising is noncommissionable.* Local retail advertising, especially that appearing in newspapers, is often billed at substantially lower rates than the rates charged to national advertisers. Because the rates are lower, the media vehicle will usually not pay a commission to any agency which places the advertising. Therefore, if they used outside agencies, retailers would have to pay them on a straight fee basis. The tendency of many retailers is to conclude that it is more economical to do the work themselves.

**3.** *Retailers often obtain a substantial amount of free outside help in handling their advertising.* For example, many manufacturers supply retailers with artwork, print materials, or videotapes. The media vehicles in which they run their advertising are often willing to give them creative assistance. Therefore, the retailer's advertising department often has a head start on its work which lessens the need for further outside help.

*Departments That Work with Outside Agencies*

Even if most of the details of designing and executing an advertising campaign are handled by one or more outside agencies, the firm which sponsors the advertising is likely to have its own internal advertising department as well. Such a department is usually headed by someone who carries the title of Advertising Manager, or possibly, Vice-President for Advertising. The individual who holds that position may report (1) directly to the chief executive of the firm (for example, to the president), (2) to the top marketing executive of the firm (for example, to the vice-president for marketing), or (3) to the company executive who is in charge of personal selling (for example, to the vice-president for sales). To an extent, the level to which the advertising manager reports tends to be a rough reflection of the importance placed on advertising in the firm's total promotional mix.

Because so much of the actual work will be done outside the company's own organization, the responsibility of the advertising manager and his or her staff tends to center around activities involving the interface between the company and its agency. Additionally, the company's advertising department will work with other units of the firm whose activities influence the total promotional mix.

The advertising manager should be thoroughly conversant with all aspects of the full marketing plan of which the advertising strategy forms one part. Ideally, he or she will have been a participant in the promotional staff meetings during which the entire program was designed. Most importantly, the advertising manager should understand the product, the competitive climate in which it is being sold, and the nature of the target market at which it is aimed. Starting from this base, she or he interacts with other experts within the company and the advertising agency to oversee fulfillment of all phases of campaign execution and its coordination with other elements in the promotional mix. In short, the company advertising manager and other department members should be promotional specialists who blend their expertise with that of colleagues in related fields to produce an integrated flow of persuasive communications.

# SUMMARY

Advertising, like personal selling, can take any one of three broad forms based on the type of audience involved. These are *consumer advertising, professional advertising*, and *trade advertising*. The intended end result of most advertising is its effect on purchase decisions. However, the exact nature and tone of your advertising will vary depending on which of these audience types you are addressing. On a type-of-advertiser basis, a number of different categories exist. The two categories of major interest to us are (1) "national" advertisers, who are producers of specific brands that may be sold on either a national or a regional basis, and (2) "local" advertisers, who are generally retailers doing business in a relatively limited market area.

Advertising should be considered in terms of its relationships and interactions with the other elements of your mix. Six broad questions were suggested to help guide this process; they are counterparts to the questions raised earlier with reference to personal selling. Following your resolution of these issues the development of your advertising strategy program should begin with a clear definition of your target market and a clear statement of the objectives of your program.

The objectives you set should be communications objectives rather than sales objectives because advertising usually does not achieve sales results all by itself. Your ideal set of objectives should be specific, measurable, and achievable by advertising alone.

With your target market clearly defined and your objectives clearly set, you will need to consider the type of geographic coverage and seasonal emphasis your advertising program will take. You then have a series of decisions to make in the two broad areas of creative strategy and media strategy. These two areas are separate in some respects but are clearly interrelated in others. They ultimately combine to form your total program.

The main decision areas in creative strategy development are the following:

1. Determination of your basic appeal or "buying proposal"
2. Determination of your creative presentation technique
3. Determination of type and amount of copy needed
4. Determination of type and amount of art and visual effects needed

The main decision areas in media strategy development are the following:

1. Determination of media categories to be used
2. Determination of size of insertions
3. Determination of timing of insertions
4. Determination of reach-frequency goals resulting in a "GRP level"
5. Determination of specific media vehicles to be used
6. Determination of the total number of insertions to be used

The decision areas for both creative and media strategies suggest a series of steps proceeding from major decision areas to narrower and more detailed decision areas. The exact sequence of decisions in practice may be somewhat different. You may often find yourself moving back and forth between decision areas as you fine-tune the details of your planning.

At the end, you will have a proposed advertising program, which must be examined in terms of budget feasibility. There are two major ways to determine an appropriate advertising budget—the predetermined budget and the strategy-determined budget. If you are working with a predetermined budget, feasibility centers around the following question: Is the cost of our proposed advertising program within the dollar limit that we previously established? If you are working with a strategy-determined budget, feasibility centers around a different question: Given the resources of our firm and the anticipated sales we hope to achieve, does the cost of our proposed advertising program "make sense"? More will be said about budget-determination techniques in Chapter 20. At this point, we are simply concerned about what happens if the cost of your proposed campaign does not meet the test of acceptability. If this is the case, you should rethink the entire program beginning with the advertising objectives. The alternative is to make piecemeal cuts in the proposed program, a course which is *not* recommended.

When you have decided that both the program and its cost appear sound and acceptable, you are ready to implement the program by actually preparing the advertisements and contracting for the needed time and/or space.

After the campaign has begun running, its results must somehow be evaluated. The ideal evaluation program is one that checks on the achievement of the same advertising objectives set at the beginning of your planning sequence. Again, these should be communications objectives rather than sales objectives. Depending on the type of feedback you receive from such evaluation, you may or may not want to alter the advertising program.

Much of the work of advertising planning and implementation is done by specialized experts in two types of organizations, the advertising agency and the advertising department.

The prototype of the advertising agency is the full-service agency. Traditionally, this has been an independent firm staffed with people having expertise in a variety of technical areas. At its best, the full-service agency becomes the promotional partner of the firm sponsoring the advertising. Often it is equipped not only to handle all of the activities described for the advertising strategy process, but also to provide services related to such other promotional areas as sales promotion, publicity, and even personal selling and product planning.

At one time, full-service agencies were compensated for their services largely on the basis of commissions they received from space and time purchases made in the various media vehicles. Because of legal action, the commission system is less dominant today than it once was. Alternative modes of paying agencies include a straight-fee basis and a cost-plus basis. The weakening of the commission system has also led to new types of agencies. Some of the newer alternatives to the full-service agency are the boutique agency, the in-house agency, and the modular agency.

There is disagreement as to whether an advertiser is better served by using the traditional full-service agency and traditional commission compensation system or by moving to one or another of the alternatives now available. In any event, advertisers now have both more flexibility and more decisions to make when working with advertising agencies.

An advertising department is a unit within the advertiser's own organization. There are two major types of advertising departments—those that replace agencies and those that work with agencies.

When the advertising department replaces an outside advertising agency, it often becomes a miniature agency of its own. The in-house agency is a special case of such a department. Departments that replace agencies are especially common in the retail field for a variety of reasons peculiar to that business category.

When the advertising agency works with an outside agency, much of the work of the department and the advertising manager who heads it centers around overall planning and coordination of activities. This means coordination both between the advertiser and the agency and coordination among various units within the advertiser's own firm. Like the outside agency, the inside advertising manager is likely to become involved in many related promotional areas. In other words, while specializing in advertising, she or he must be aware of and involved in the total promotional planning process.

## DISCUSSION QUESTIONS

1. The president of a long-established manufacturing company specializing in making jeans was concerned about competitive encroachment by other firms selling prestigious "designer" jeans. The president called the advertising manager into the office and made the following statement, "Our jeans are 'all-American' and traditional. None of that designer stuff for us! But I want to *regain market share!* That is to be *your* objective for this year! Come back with a plan." Comment.

2. Outline and briefly discuss the four basic stages in planning a creative strategy. Is the order important? Explain why or why not.

3. Charlie Forbes is marketing vice-president for a consumer products firm. He has allocated a fixed sum of money for advertising and all the other promotional elements. During the course of the year, the advertising director tells Charlie that the advertising budget is inadequate. Charlie replies, "Cut back on television advertising." Discuss the implications.

4. Calculate the billing to the client by an advertising agency working under a standard commission arrangement in the following situation: "Base time" charge of $100,000 by the media vehicle, with a two percent discount if paid in 10 days.

5. Outline the general organizational structure of a typical full-service advertising agency. Contrast the services offered by such an agency with those of a boutique or modular agency.

6. The chapter described three broad types of audiences to which ads can be targeted. Select two products from the following list and briefly describe how the advertising appeal for each product might differ across these audience types:
   1. Mouthwash
   2. Flea and tick collars for pets
   3. Aspirin-free pain relief medications

7. A national manufacturer of frozen foods is preparing to introduce a new line of frozen pancakes that are easier to prepare than the traditional mix. As marketing manager for the brand, you must propose assigned tasks for the various elements in the promotional mix. You wish to appeal to two distinct market segments: (1) "traditional" homemakers who do not work outside the home and (2) busy "career" homemakers who hold outside jobs. Using the E'Suberante case as a guide, briefly outline a possible strategy for each element in the explicit mix.

8. A manufacturer of high-quality children's clothing defined its advertising objective as follows: "Our objective is to reach mothers who are concerned about their children's appearance." Critique this objective and recommend specific changes.

9. Suggest several possible modifications in the creative presentation techniques outlined in the E'Suberante example, keeping the basic appeal the same.

10. Identify the six major steps in media planning. Can you think of any situations in which the sequence of decision steps might be modified?

# REFERENCES

1. Steuart Henderson Britt, "Are So-Called Successful Advertising Campaigns Really Successful?," *Journal of Advertising Research,* vol. 9, No. 2 (1969), p. 9.
2. *Ibid.*
3. See Philip Ward Burton and Reo Young, "Organization of the Advertising Agency," in Steuart Henderson Britt and Norman F. Guess, *Marketing Manager's Handbook*, 2nd ed. (Chicago: Dartnell Press, 1983), pp. 157–166.
4. Advertising Agencies—What they are, what they do and how they do it (New York, American Association of Advertising Agencies, 1976), pp. 10–18.
5. C. H. Sandage and Vernon Fryburger, *Advertising Theory and Practice*, 9th ed. (Homewood, IL.: Richard D. Irwin, Inc., 1975), pp. 634–635.
6. "The 15% media commission is on the way toward becoming a relic in ad agency compensation plans," *Marketing News*, 10 June 1983, p. 9.
7. *Media Decisions*, May 1976, pp. 118–120.

# CHAPTER FOURTEEN

# Developing Advertising Creative Strategy

## FOCUS OF THE CHAPTER

Advertising is often referred to as "salesmanship in print." From one perspective this is a useful analogy. In another sense, it is somewhat misleading. It is quite true that the ultimate goal of most advertising is much the same as the ultimate goal of most personal selling. Both are usually parts of a program aimed at influencing prospects to buy something or to do something. On this basis, roughly the same very broad principles apply. However, there are also substantial differences between these two promotional elements. For one thing, whereas sales representatives usually try to close the sale directly, most advertising tends to lay the groundwork for a sale that generally will occur later. Furthermore, in advertising you confront two disadvantages which sales representatives do not face. First, you are communicating with a mass audience which is diverse in nature and not visible to you. Second, you are not able to benefit from immediate audience feedback. This chapter will begin by examining techniques you can employ to deal with these problems. Then we will consider alternative, basic creative appeals and creative presentation techniques you can use in developing your strategy.

# THE GENERAL SETTING FOR CREATIVE PLANNING

**The Diverse Nature of Mass Communication Audiences**

The sales representative meets prospects one at a time and is in direct contact with each of them. Therefore, she or he is able to study and analyze each customer separately and then produce an individually tailored presentation. The advertising strategist not only deals with an unseen audience but must also speak simultaneously to a very large group of individuals who differ among each other in needs, viewpoints, and past experiences. Moreover, an advertising presentation has to be designed that will produce a favorable response from at least a reasonably large part of that diverse audience.

**The Lack of Immediate Feedback**

Feedback helps the alert salesperson adjust the message on an immediate and individualized basis as it is being received and processed. The advertising planner, who does not share this advantage, must have everything in place at the very beginning. In some cases, advertising may be pretested on a sample of consumers before it is actually run in the mass media, providing a degree of early feedback (see p. 696). However, in most cases it takes weeks or months before market research data become available to provide feedback; or it may never become available at all. In many instances, your only feedback will be sales results. These tell you rather little concerning the way that different parts of your message are being received, decoded, and interpreted.

This, then, is the general setting in which the creative people of the advertising world work. They are the writers, artists, and other specialists who must make the brand come alive, persuade prospects regarding its benefits, and generate favorable purchase intentions by rather brief messages carried through a variety of mass media.

# THE NATURE OF THE CREATIVE PROCESS

At the heart of any really effective and outstanding advertising campaign, you will find a fresh and imaginative creative plan. Because we opened our discussion of personal selling by acknowledging some criticisms that have been leveled at many salespeople, it seems only fair to point out that the current state of advertising creativity also has its critics. Again, we are referring to criticism concerning effectiveness rather than criticism of the ethics of advertising. The following is an example of such criticism coming from a man who is himself a creator of advertising:

> Today most advertising creativity is of the rubber stamp variety—straight out of the "advertising is an art" school [whose] graduates wear the same garb, go to the same hair dresser, attend the same creative seminars, use the same music arrangers and crib from the same source of material. So everything comes out looking and sounding alike—a creative collection of carbon copies. If you really want to get your advertising out of this rut, you have to do more than change agencies; you have to change your concept of advertising and the kind of creativity it calls for. [1]

Another advertising practitioner has said, "Creativity is art and instinct and some are naturally better at it than others. And this worries those of us less gifted. . . . Therefore, we see repeated attempts to reduce creativity to a formula when the only formula is to throw out the formula and to do something new."[2]

As these statements imply, neither this book nor any other can prescribe an absolute and infallible blueprint for you to follow when you are creating advertising. Certainly, you will want to start with a thorough understanding of your product, your target consumer group, your competition, and the role that advertising is intended to play in achieving promotional objectives. However, at some point, you must blend all this information together and infuse it with your own imagination and originality. Because the exact nature of this infusion process is unique to each creative strategist, different advertising professionals may arrive at quite dissimilar but equally effective creative plans, even when they all begin with the same product situation and factual background. Therefore, it is neither realistic nor desirable to suggest a universal, mechanistic routine for developing creative strategy.

However, it is both possible and useful to examine the major problems and options common to virtually all advertising creativity situations. In particular, it is important to consider procedures to initiate your creative efforts. One aspect of this initiation process involves techniques you can employ to aid you in visualizing your unseen audience and in acquiring a better feel for the kind of messages that will appeal to its members. Another aspect involves recognition of the broad categories of basic appeals and creative presentation options available to you.

## VISUALIZING AND UNDERSTANDING YOUR AUDIENCE

Although successful creativity demands an imaginative approach, mere intuition and cleverness can lead to disaster unless you are armed with prior knowledge concerning your audience members and their lifestyle goals. Because you will never see the overwhelming majority of your target prospects on anything like a face-to-face basis, it is quite possible to misjudge completely their likely response to your advertising unless you undertake some careful preanalysis. To illustrate this point, consider the following story of an imaginative creative approach that backfired because the advertising planners failed to understand their audience:

A European airline (which will remain nameless) once ran a pleasant campaign about the delights of its country, in which each ad concluded with a picture of a little girl who was supposed to be the child heroine "Heidi" of the movie by the same name. "Heidi wouldn't lie," the ad said.

Then the airline decided to change advertising agencies to get a new direction. Which they certainly did—the new campaign played off the old by featuring a seductive woman in each ad proclaiming, "Heidi Lied!" This European country, the ad implied, was really the place for hot night life, a swinging paradise.

The market reaction was quick and certain. The new campaign was anathema to the families who made up most of the tourist business, and, if it was meant to appeal to the male business travelers, it was a bit too blatant. All of one's associates would know exactly what was behind the request to go iron out the company business in that particular country. The campaign was dropped and the agency which produced it was later relieved of the airline account. [3]

## Methods of Analyzing Mass Audiences

If you never enjoy direct contact with your audience members how can you go about the process of understanding them? Most of the techniques to accomplish this reflect one of three main methods. One method involves starting with brand features and then reasoning outward to determine what those features would mean to your target consumer group. A second method begins with study of a very small, loosely drawn sample of target consumers on an informal but first-hand basis. Observations from this informal study are then extended to form an idea of what your total or primary audience is like. The third method involves working from statistical information based on more formalized, large-scale research studies. Some examples of how each approach might be undertaken follow.

## Starting with Brand Features and Reasoning Outward

One description of how you can use this approach has been phrased as follows:

Our search for the most effective creative strategy should begin with what we know best—our product. Our product has a number of physical attributes—such as taste, color, aroma, and texture—that can form the basis of our appeal. Very simply, then, we can list our product's features in one column and, next to each, a translation of that feature into a potential benefit for the prospective buyers. Then we do the same, as far as we can determine, for our competitors. What do they have that we don't? What do we have that they don't? [4]

Historically, some classic advertising campaigns have originated this way. For instance, the story is told of how one famous copywriter hit on a successful approach to advertising a brand of beer by studying the way it was bottled.

[He] observed that all of the returned beer bottles used by the brand were cleaned by live steam before they were refilled. He fastened upon this fact and created an advertising strategy based upon it. The strategy assumed that the purity of beer was of importance to consumers and that advertising about brand purity, based on the fact that the bottles to be refilled were cleaned with live steam, would provide a dramatic point of differentiation for the brand. [5]

## Informal Studies of a Small Sample of Consumers on a First-Hand Basis

Creative people sometimes seek to locate and talk with "typical consumers." Assuming the consumers you find are truly typical, and also assuming you can induce them to talk freely about the product and themselves, this could be one viable approach to help you visualize and understand that unseen, mass audience you are trying to reach.

Reportedly, the creative director for still another brand of beer used such an informal study approach with excellent results. His procedure was to visit various bars in the evening, observe heavy beer drinkers, and try to get to know them. His conversations with this very loosely drawn sample led to some conclusions about the lifestyle goals of the typical heavy beer drinker and about the role that beer plays in connection with those lifestyle goals. He concluded that there was a large target group made up of men who felt somewhat frustrated and let down by life. They tended to be dreamers rather than doers. They visualized themselves in much more powerful and bolder positions than they actually occupied. Based on this subjectively interpreted portrait of the prototype audience member, he developed a successful creative positioning. The brand was pictured as the beer drunk by men who had truly achieved the adventures and masculine success that was only dreamed of by the heavy users of the product.

*Focus Group Interviews.*   The focus group interview represents a more extended and methodical version of the informal study approach. A typical focus group is made up of eight to twelve consumers who are chosen because they are familiar with the product or topic to be discussed. A standard focus group procedure can last for one and a half hours or more and centers around a relatively free-flowing discussion by participants concerning attitudes toward a product, applicable evaluative criteria, reactions to advertising appeals, or some other matter of concern to the sponsoring firm. Although led by a professional moderator, the discussion itself is loosely structured and open-ended. After it is concluded, participants' statements and remarks are analyzed to interpret potential meanings for promotional strategy. Frequently, the session is recorded to facilitate later interpretation. The information gleaned from focus group studies and other informal, nonquantitative techniques can often provide fresh and valuable ideas. However, there are also certain cautions to be kept in mind in using such procedures. For example, one observer has offered the following commentary:

> Improperly conducted, focus groups can be worse than no research at all. Focus groups contain shy members reluctant to participate, small sample sizes, non-randomly selected members, and only participants able to spend at least 1½ hours at a central research facility. The moderator affects what group members say by the questions he asks, his facial expressions, and his background and training. Results often depend on who interprets the data and in what the interpreter considers important enough to report. . . . Despite the shortcomings, focus group interviews are extremely popular—so popular, in fact, that they may be "smothering" other more appropriate techniques. This inappropriate application happens, for example, when the results of focus group interviews lead to management decisions that should have used quantitative research results. This happens more than it should. Decision makers, it seems, are often prone to take focus group results and run with them. This is a misuse of qualitative research if the marketing problem can be better solved with quantitative research. [6]

**Working from Statistical Research Data**

This last approach uses survey data of the kind described in Chapters 5, 7 and 8. Such data can be analyzed to provide you with a numerically based audience profile. Normally, it is the outgrowth of a relatively large-scale and formally organized research effort. A variety of statistical procedures can be followed to interpret such data. To demonstrate a general approach, and simultaneously to point out some potential dangers, we will consider a very simple procedure. Our illustrative data base consists of demographic descriptions of the users of all-purpose household cleaners, as shown in Figure 14.1.

Assume that you have designated your target prospect group as female household heads who are heavy users of such products. To suggest how this kind of data might aid you in better visualizing and understanding your unseen audience, we will begin by extracting three selected demographic characteristics for analysis. (In actual practice, you would probably want a more complete analysis of the full array of characteristics to determine the most accurate profile of your target market. The characteristics ultimately chosen as relevant might include any of the types outlined in our earlier coverage of social, biopsychic, and demographic factors.) In our simplified illustration, we will work only with education, age, and number of children in the household.

Using these three characteristics along with information drawn from the basic report and shown in Figure 14.2, you might logically conclude that three major facts seem to stand out concerning heavy users. First, over seventy-five percent of them have a high school education or less. Second, almost half of them fall in the twenty-five to forty-four year age range. Third, almost two-thirds of them have children at home and under the age of eighteen years.

***Cautions Concerning the Use of Statistical Market Descriptions.*** A full discussion regarding the interpretation of statistically expressed market research data is an extensive subject that falls beyond the scope of this text.[7] However, two elementary issues concerning such interpretation merit comment because they so directly affect the examples that will be presented to illustrate how you might use these data in developing your creative strategy.

The first issue involves the procedure of combining separately measured characteristics to produce a composite profile. The second is concerned with the number of characteristics to be included.

***Combining Separately Measured Characteristics.*** Recall that our initial scan of the data on heavy users examined three demographic breakdowns separately and found that a majority or near-majority of users fall into a designated category within each of those breakdowns. Based on these separate measurements, it can be tempting but misleading to conclude that the preponderance of heavy users fit the following profile: "A woman between the ages of 25 and 44 with a high school education or less and with children at home and under the age of 18." However, this is not necessarily true. To ascertain the actual situation, we would have to reconsider the original data and analyze the three demographic breakdowns in conjunction with each other, not separately. For example, using the three categories that seemed predominant in our original scan of the data, our joint analysis procedure would determine the percentage of heavy users who fall into all three of these categories *simultaneously*.

Figure 14.3 presents a hypothetical pattern that could result from such analysis. To demonstrate how the profiling process can be extended beyond simple demographics, two additional descriptions involving social class and

# FIGURE 14.1 Demographic breakdowns in the all-purpose powdered cleaner market

| | Total Users | All Users | | | | Heavy Users | | | | Medium Users | | | | Light Users | | | | Non Users | | | |
|---|---|---|---|---|---|---|---|---|---|---|---|---|---|---|---|---|---|---|---|---|---|
| | '000 | A '000 | B % down | C % across | D index | A '000 | B % down | C % across | D index | A '000 | B % down | C % across | D index | A '000 | B % down | C % across | D index | A '000 | B % down | C % across | D index |
| All Female Homemakers | 64263 | 14960 | 100.0 | 23.3 | 100 | 1152 | 100.0 | 1.8 | 100 | 2706 | 100.0 | 4.2 | 100 | 11102 | 100.0 | 17.3 | 100 | 42275 | 100.0 | 65.8 | 100 |
| **Female Homemakers** | | | | | | | | | | | | | | | | | | | | | |
| 18–24 | 7235 | 1376 | 9.2 | 19.0 | 82 | 99 | 8.6 | 1.4 | 77 | 276 | 10.2 | 3.8 | 91 | 1000 | 9.0 | 13.8 | 80 | 4688 | 11.1 | 64.8 | 98 |
| 25–34 | 14780 | 3452 | 23.1 | 23.4 | 100 | 274 | 23.8 | 1.9 | 103 | 634 | 23.4 | 4.3 | 102 | 2545 | 22.9 | 17.2 | 100 | 10069 | 23.8 | 68.1 | 104 |
| 35–44 | 10937 | 2622 | 17.5 | 24.0 | 103 | 288 | 25.0 | 2.6 | 147 | 451 | 16.7 | 4.1 | 98 | 1882 | 17.0 | 17.2 | 100 | 7281 | 17.2 | 66.6 | 101 |
| 45–54 | 11645 | 3046 | 20.4 | 26.2 | 112 | 205 | 17.8 | 1.8 | 98 | 482 | 17.8 | 4.1 | 98 | 2359 | 21.2 | 20.3 | 117 | 7522 | 17.8 | 64.6 | 98 |
| 55–64 | 9333 | 2506 | 16.8 | 26.9 | 115 | 175 | 15.2 | 1.9 | 105 | 441 | 16.3 | 4.7 | 112 | 1890 | 17.0 | 20.3 | 117 | 6060 | 14.3 | 64.9 | 99 |
| 65 or over | 10333 | 1959 | 13.1 | 19.0 | 81 | 110 | 9.6 | 1.1 | 60 | 422 | 15.6 | 4.1 | 97 | 1426 | 12.8 | 13.8 | 80 | 6654 | 15.7 | 64.4 | 98 |
| Mid Income $25,000 or more | 10726 | 2918 | 19.5 | 27.2 | 117 | 201 | 17.4 | 1.9 | 104 | 541 | 20.0 | 5.0 | 120 | 2177 | 19.6 | 20.3 | 117 | 7000 | 16.6 | 65.3 | 99 |
| $20,000–24,999 | 5379 | 1382 | 9.2 | 25.7 | 110 | 145 | 12.6 | 2.7 | 151 | 248 | 9.2 | 4.6 | 110 | 988 | 8.9 | 18.4 | 106 | 3637 | 8.6 | 67.6 | 103 |
| $15,000–19,999 | 13122 | 3201 | 21.9 | 25.0 | 107 | 215 | 18.7 | 1.6 | 91 | 532 | 19.7 | 4.1 | 96 | 2534 | 22.8 | 19.3 | 112 | 8631 | 18.2 | 65.6 | 100 |
| $10,000–14,999 | 11721 | 2766 | 18.5 | 23.6 | 101 | 200 | 17.4 | 1.7 | 95 | 526 | 19.4 | 4.5 | 107 | 2041 | 18.4 | 17.4 | 101 | 7693 | 18.2 | 65.6 | 100 |
| $ 8,000–9,999 | 4884 | 1292 | 8.6 | 26.5 | 114 | 157 | 13.6 | 3.2 | 179 | * 225 | 8.3 | 4.6 | 109 | 911 | 8.2 | 18.6 | 108 | 3048 | 7.2 | 62.4 | 95 |
| $ 5,000–7,999 | 7788 | 1659 | 11.1 | 21.3 | 91 | 128 | 11.1 | 1.6 | 91 | 275 | 10.1 | 3.5 | 84 | 1256 | 11.3 | 16.1 | 93 | 5247 | 12.4 | 67.4 | 102 |
| Less than $5,000 | 10643 | 1661 | 11.1 | 15.6 | 67 | 106 | 9.2 | 1.0 | 56 | 360 | 13.3 | 3.4 | 80 | 1195 | 10.8 | 11.2 | 65 | 7020 | 16.6 | 66.0 | 100 |
| Household of 1 or 2 persons | 28889 | 6202 | 41.5 | 21.5 | 92 | 317 | 27.5 | 1.1 | 61 | 959 | 35.5 | 3.3 | 79 | 4925 | 44.4 | 17.0 | 99 | 18791 | 44.4 | 65.0 | 99 |
| 3 or 4 persons | 24492 | 6095 | 40.7 | 24.9 | 107 | 521 | 45.3 | 2.1 | 119 | 1222 | 45.2 | 5.0 | 118 | 4352 | 39.2 | 17.8 | 105 | 16167 | 38.2 | 66.0 | 100 |
| 5 or more persons | 10883 | 2663 | 17.8 | 24.5 | 105 | 313 | 27.2 | 2.9 | 161 | 525 | 19.4 | 4.8 | 115 | 1825 | 16.4 | 16.8 | 97 | 7317 | 17.3 | 67.2 | 102 |
| No children in household | 32616 | 7399 | 49.5 | 22.7 | 97 | 425 | 36.9 | 1.3 | 73 | 1165 | 43.1 | 3.6 | 85 | 5808 | 52.3 | 17.8 | 103 | 21127 | 50.0 | 64.8 | 98 |
| Children under 2 years | 5743 | 1304 | 8.7 | 22.7 | 98 | 185 | 16.1 | 3.2 | 140 | 285 | 10.5 | 5.0 | 118 | 834 | 7.5 | 14.5 | 84 | 3953 | 9.4 | 68.8 | 105 |
| 2–5 years | 10989 | 2434 | 16.3 | 22.1 | 95 | 213 | 18.5 | 1.9 | 108 | 601 | 22.2 | 5.5 | 130 | 1619 | 14.6 | 14.7 | 85 | 7445 | 17.6 | 67.8 | 103 |
| 6–11 years | 14389 | 3253 | 21.6 | 22.5 | 97 | 370 | 32.1 | 2.6 | 143 | 613 | 22.7 | 4.3 | 101 | 2249 | 20.3 | 15.6 | 90 | 9965 | 23.6 | 69.3 | 105 |
| 12–17 years | 15482 | 3832 | 25.6 | 24.8 | 106 | 369 | 32.1 | 2.4 | 135 | 714 | 26.4 | 4.6 | 110 | 2749 | 24.8 | 17.8 | 100 | 10207 | 24.1 | 65.9 | 100 |
| New England | 3251 | 941 | 6.3 | 28.9 | 124 | 136 | 11.8 | 4.2 | 233 | * 157 | 5.8 | 4.8 | 115 | 648 | 5.8 | 19.9 | 115 | 2107 | 5.0 | 64.8 | 98 |
| Mid Atlantic | 12497 | 3055 | 20.4 | 24.4 | 105 | 304 | 26.4 | 2.4 | 136 | 642 | 23.7 | 5.1 | 122 | 2109 | 19.0 | 16.9 | 98 | 8076 | 19.1 | 64.6 | 98 |
| East Central | 7312 | 2153 | 14.4 | 29.4 | 126 | 120 | 10.4 | 1.6 | 91 | 331 | 12.2 | 4.5 | 107 | 1702 | 15.3 | 23.3 | 135 | 4421 | 10.5 | 60.5 | 92 |
| West Central | 12616 | 3250 | 21.7 | 25.8 | 111 | 143 | 12.4 | 1.1 | 63 | 575 | 21.3 | 4.6 | 108 | 2532 | 22.8 | 20.1 | 116 | 7809 | 18.5 | 61.9 | 94 |
| South East | 13015 | 2353 | 15.7 | 18.1 | 78 | 198 | 17.2 | 1.5 | 85 | 375 | 13.8 | 2.9 | 68 | 1780 | 16.0 | 13.7 | 79 | 9378 | 22.2 | 72.1 | 110 |
| South West | 6549 | 1147 | 7.7 | 17.5 | 75 | 73 | 6.4 | 1.1 | 62 | 299 | 11.0 | 4.6 | 108 | 775 | 7.0 | 11.8 | 69 | 4702 | 11.1 | 71.8 | 109 |
| Pacific | 9023 | 2061 | 13.8 | 22.8 | 98 | 178 | 15.5 | 2.0 | 110 | 327 | 12.1 | 3.6 | 86 | 1555 | 14.0 | 17.2 | 100 | 5783 | 13.7 | 64.1 | 97 |
| Graduated college | 7256 | 1909 | 12.8 | 26.3 | 113 | 113 | 9.8 | 1.6 | 67 | 290 | 10.7 | 4.0 | 95 | 1507 | 13.6 | 20.8 | 120 | 4606 | 10.9 | 63.5 | 96 |
| Attended college | 8965 | 2467 | 16.5 | 27.5 | 118 | 167 | 14.5 | 1.9 | 104 | 385 | 14.2 | 4.3 | 102 | 1915 | 17.2 | 21.4 | 124 | 5506 | 13.0 | 61.4 | 95 |
| Graduated high school | 26886 | 6672 | 44.6 | 24.8 | 107 | 538 | 46.7 | 2.0 | 112 | 1261 | 46.8 | 4.7 | 111 | 4872 | 43.9 | 18.1 | 105 | 17722 | 41.9 | 65.9 | 100 |
| Did not graduate high school | 21155 | 3913 | 26.2 | 18.5 | 79 | 335 | 29.0 | 1.6 | 88 | 770 | 28.5 | 3.6 | 86 | 2808 | 25.3 | 13.3 | 77 | 14442 | 34.2 | 68.3 | 104 |

Source: Data selectively drawn from Simmons Report and reproduced with permission of Simmons Market Research Bureau, Inc.

*Visualizing and Understanding Your Audience*

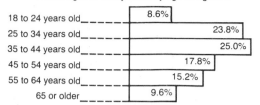

Percentages of heavy users by age categories:

| | |
|---|---|
| 18 to 24 years old | 8.6% |
| 25 to 34 years old | 23.8% |
| 35 to 44 years old | 25.0% |
| 45 to 54 years old | 17.8% |
| 55 to 64 years old | 15.2% |
| 65 or older | 9.6% |

Percentages of heavy users by educational categories

| | |
|---|---|
| Graduated college | 9.8% |
| Attended college | 14.5% |
| Graduated high school | 46.7% |
| Did not graduate high school | 29.0% |

Percentages of heavy users by presence and age of children in home*

| | |
|---|---|
| No children | 36.9% |
| Children under 2 years old | 16.1% |
| Children 2 to 5 years old | 18.5% |
| Children 6 to 11 years old | 32.1% |
| Children 12 to 17 years old | 32.1% |

*Total goes over 100% because respondents could fall into more than one category.

**FIGURE 14.2 Profiling a heavy-user group on selected demographic characteristics**

**FIGURE 14.3 Refining the statistical profile on a simultaneous-possession-of-characteristics basis**

| Base percentage of heavy users in category | Demographic or psychographic category | Decreasing percentage of heavy users who possess characteristic shown in category at left *and* also possess the characteristics shown in all previous categories |
|---|---|---|
| 75.7% | High school education or less | 75.7% |
| 48.8% | Aged 25 to 44 years | 42.1% |
| 63.1% | Have children at home | 39.3% |
| 46.1% | Take a "serious" attitude toward housework | 29.6% |
| 40.2% | Are upper-lower class in general outlook | 24.9% |

*Developing Advertising Creative Strategy*

personality have been included. Very importantly, Figure 14.3 emphasizes in graphic fashion the manner in which the size of any consumer category being defined will diminish as more characteristics are considered concurrently.

This is evidenced by the percentage figures at the right, each of which lists the proportion of heavy users who possess both the characteristic to the left *plus all* of the preceding characteristics. For example, the entry in the third row at the right indicates that only 39.3% of heavy users have a high school education or less *and* are aged 25 to 44 *and* have children at home. The three original characteristics of education, presence of children in the household, and age level do not describe the majority of these heavy users when these characteristics are considered on a simultaneous basis. They describe less than forty percent of them. Furthermore, even though the two added aspects of a personality trait and a social class outlook each describes a rather large part of the group when considered by itself, if all five characteristics are combined and considered simultaneously they characterize only one-fourth of the heavy-user group.

*Limiting the Number of Characteristics Used.* The second cautionary issue to consider follows from the issue just discussed. If you work with too many characteristics in defining a mass audience and then prepare advertising oriented very strongly to the defined group, but which may be much less well-received by persons outside the defined group, you may be risking rejection or misinterpretation by a large segment of your full audience.

For example, in our illustration almost forty percent of your heavy-user group is made up of women aged twenty-five to forty-four with a high school education or less and with children under the age of eighteen. Assuming your full analysis convinced you that this was a meaningful set of characteristics to consider, you might determine to give special emphasis to persons fitting this description. For instance, the situations depicted in television commercials as well as the spokespersons and language employed might be chosen with particular consideration to their probable acceptance by and influence on such individuals. However, you would also want to be careful that your advertising did not offend or convey a rejection-prone impression to prospects not meeting all three of these characteristics. After all, this latter prospect group still makes up over sixty percent of the heavy-user category.

Statistical data can provide you valuable assistance in visualizing your unseen audience. At the same time, you must recognize that it should be used with care and good judgment. In most advertising situations, what you say is going to be seen or heard by a large and diverse collection of prospects. The task is often one of making your message especially meaningful to the "typical" target consumer without turning away all of the others.

*Summarizing and Applying the Cautionary Points.* The issues just discussed suggest that there are two important points to be borne in mind during your mass audience visualization procedure. First, when defining your market statistically, it is desirable to keep your list of characteristics reasonably short, concentrating on those that describe a fairly large part of your market and which could clearly influence the way you should speak to that market. Second, though you may wish to create advertising that is especially appealing to some carefully defined group of consumers, you generally want to avoid advertising that appeals so narrowly to this group that it is meaningless or even offensive to prospects who fail to match all of the defined characteristics. Especially in the ultimate consumer goods field, there is almost no product that is bought only by one clearly definable type of person. In most cases, a variety of people buy the product, even though certain types may be especially likely to buy it—or to be heavy users—and therefore especially important to reach effectively. Parenthetically, while these points have been illustrated in the context of large-scale statistical studies, it should be emphasized that they are equally applicable in relation to the use of the small-sample, informal study approach that was described earlier.

The "Heidi Lied" campaign is an example of a creative plan that was too narrowly targeted; possibly the audience was defined by too many (or the wrong) characteristics. It received a negative response from the large group of people outside of that immediate target group. This does not have to happen. With some care and imagination you can usually produce advertising that strikes home with special force at a closely defined target group but still has the power to communicate positively to most of the people who do not fully fit into that group. Consider the following example involving the popular breakfast cereal "Wheaties."

["Wheaties" had been running a television campaign featuring famous athletes and] designed to regain brand awareness. It was aimed at a broad male audience—from 10 years old on up. After achieving the objective, General Mills wisely changed the campaign to motivate a more specific target group—pre- and early teenagers. The new campaign more directly reaches this market through the dramatization of a moment in a boy's life when he makes a breakthrough from boyhood to manhood. He's given an unexpected challenge by his father—taking a canoe through the rapids, breaking in a new horse, diving below the boat to untangle an anchor line. He accepts the challenge and there's a warm emotional tug at the end of each commercial keyed to the accomplishment of the resulting new father-son relationship. The musical theme "He knows he's a man and he's ready for Wheaties" is topped with the final frame super: "Are you ready for Wheaties?" [8]

This commercial says a great deal to its narrowly defined target group. To the many other people who do not fit the exact target definition but are still prospective purchasers, it still says something very positive.

## BASIC APPEALS AND CREATIVE PRESENTATION TECHNIQUES

As pointed out in the last chapter, the basic appeal or buying proposal is the central message of the advertisement that is built around the reason or group of reasons why the message receiver should act in the way the advertiser is recommending. The creative presentation technique is the style and design of the message through which the basic appeal is presented.

To examine the options available to you in these two creative decision areas, we will consider thirteen different basic appeals and eight different creative presentation techniques. The alternative basic appeals are as follows:

1. Overall brand quality
2. Specific brand features or features
3. Improvements or changes in the brand
4. Popularity of the brand
5. Economic appeals (such as a price advantage, savings in use, or profit through cooperation)
6. Special offers
7. Upgrading of customer satisfaction through information on how to use the brand
8. Solution to a consumer problem
9. Enhancement of the consumer's lifestyle
10. Enjoyment or self-gratification
11. Problem-plus-solution
12. Corporate image appeal
13. Advocacy or "editorial" appeal

The alternative creative presentation techniques to be discussed include the following:

1. Straightforward factual presentation
2. Comparative advertising
3. Proof-through-a-test
4. Brand personification
5. Slice-of-life dramatization
6. Spokesperson-centered advertising
7. Humor
8. Fantasy or playful exaggeration

**Additional Alternatives and Mixtures of Appeals and Techniques**

Because thirteen basic appeals have been designated, each of which could theoretically be expressed through eight different creative presentation techniques, the above listings might be construed to infer that there must be exactly one hundred and four possible variations in advertisement types. Such an inference would have to rest on at least two assumptions. The first required assumption would be that both sets of listings are complete, exhaustive, and unchallengeable—that there simply are no other possible appeals or techniques. The second assumption would be that it is impossible to combine two or more appeals and/or two or more presentation techniques in the same piece of advertising. Of course, both of these assumptions are absolutely incorrect. For this reason, before discussing the individual listings, it is appropriate to comment on the limitations inherent in any attempt to develop a classification structure that fully and accurately captures the diversity of advertising approaches available to you. Following that, it will be appropriate to comment on why and how our listing schemes can still serve a very useful purpose.

Both of our lists can be questioned on the grounds that they are somewhat arbitrary, incomplete, and oversimplified. In point of fact, there is no such thing as an official list of either basic appeals or creative presentation techniques. Other writers have proposed somewhat different lists; rarely are any two exactly the same. No matter whose list you are considering, it is always possible to find advertisements which defy placement with exact precision into any of the classifications to be found in that list. No list is likely to be totally complete. One reason for this lack of completeness is the virtually limitless potential for refinements and creative adjustments within each of the categories. If each such refinement or adjustment is interpreted as a category of its own, the list of alternatives becomes almost endless.

**Combinations of Appeals and/or Presentation Techniques.** Basic appeals are not mutually exclusive and neither are presentation techniques. Two or more appeals can be combined in the same advertisement. For instance, you might want to talk about an improvement or change in your brand that revolves around some specific brand feature that provides a solution to a consumer problem. Your advertisement would thus be structured around three interwoven appeals. In similar fashion, two or more creative presentation techniques can be combined in the same piece of advertising. For example, you might use a comparative technique that also involves humor as part of your total communication delivery strategy.

**The Purpose and Utility of the Listing Schemes.** At the outset, then, it is to be stressed that, if they are viewed narrowly and in isolation from each other, our thirteen appeal categories and eight presentation categories portray only a small fraction of the myriad mass communication styles open to you. Their usefulness lies in their ability to act as reference points which help to outline, in a very general manner, the wide spectrum of creative alternatives available. When considered in this sense, they can provide you with something akin to an inventory of broad advertising types from which you can draw examples to serve as catalysts in your own creative planning process.

Moreover, because research findings or commentaries have been published on some of the basic appeals and some of the presentation techniques, these listing schemes also facilitate consideration of such published materials in an orderly fashion. With this in mind, we will now consider the basic appeals and creative presentation techniques one at a time.

# BASIC APPEALS

*Overall Brand Quality*

An appeal based on overall brand quality does not emphasize either specific features of the brand or specific benefits to the user. If particular evaluative criteria are mentioned at all, such mention is made mainly in support of the general superiority or prestige of the brand. Advertisements that use this approach seem to be based on what was described in Chapter 6 as a "conjunctive composition rule."

## FIGURE 14.4 Overall brand quality appeals

*The emphasis in this advertisement for Hamilton watches is on total reputation built around an unsolicited letter from a highly pleased customer.*

*Although a few features are mentioned in passing, the major appeal of this ad is based on "general excellence."*

Advertisement courtesy of Hamilton Watch Co., Inc., Lancaster, PA 17604

Courtesy of Monroe Systems for Business

Figure 14.4 illustrates two examples that rely primarily on an overall brand quality appeal. This sort of advertising is used for a wide variety of items. For instance, it is often used in promoting such diverse merchandise types as high-fashion clothing and products intended for industrial use. At first glance, this approach seems to violate some of the points made in Chapter 9 when we discussed principles for building effective communications. It hardly makes use of anything resembling a "benefit chain analysis." It leaves interpretation rather largely in the hands of the receiver. However, there are several settings in which its employment could make good sense.

Apart from situations in which target prospects are assumed to be making decisions via the conjunctive composition rule, it is reasonable to speculate that an overall brand quality appeal would be most workable in either of two other strategy settings. The first of these exists when your advertising is merely meant to lay the groundwork for further promotional communications. For instance, in industrial selling programs you might be relying on sales representatives to deliver more specific messages about features and benefits directly to the prospect. The purpose of your advertising in this case could simply be to generate a base of prestige from which your sales representative can initiate those more specific promotional tasks. The second strategy setting exists when you feel you are dealing with an audience that prefers to draw its own conclusions. You will recall from Chapter 9 that openly stating your conclusion is generally felt to produce much more effective results than leaving the conclusion to the imagination of the audience. You will also recall that some analysts have challenged this view, at least as it applies to certain types of audiences or message reception conditions. Many strategists who opt for an overall brand quality appeal may be doing so because they feel their particular audience is not only able to draw its own conclusions but prefers to do so.

**Specific Brand Feature or Features**

A specific brand feature appeal talks about one or more evaluative criteria of a brand—usually functional features—but does not openly speak about the specific benefits such features will provide to the user. Figure 14.5 shows two examples. Like the overall brand quality approach, this technique seems to violate some of the principles discussed in connection with communication theories. The receiver is given little assistance in interpreting lifestyle meanings

---

**FIGURE 14.5 Specific feature appeals**

*This KitchenAid ad tells what the product will "do" and leaves "lifestyle interpretations" to the audience.*

*The copy in this advertisement for Honda concentrates on a variety of highly specific features.*

Courtesy of Hobart Corp. KitchenAid Division

Advertisement courtesy of American Honda Motor Co., Inc., Gardena, California, 90247

**FIGURE 14.6 Advertising based on brand change or improvement**

*Improved Realemon features a new "extra lemon taste."*

Realemon brand for reconstituted lemon juice is a registered trademark of Borden, Inc.

of the features. Again, the reasoning behind its use may relate to the possibility that conclusion-drawing by the communicator can be overdone in some cases. It is also possible that the promotional strategist feels that once the features have been stated the benefits that derive from those features are so apparent as to need no further explanation.

**Improvements or Changes in the Brand**

The improvements or changes appeal tells the audience there is something new and better about the brand. Figure 14.6 illustrates how this appeal can be used. Our previous discussion of "novelty seeking," in Chapter 9, explains much of the rationale behind the use of "new-and-improved" advertising. Changes can often help keep a brand alive. Advertising of this sort is a means of bringing those changes to the attention of customers and reviving their interest in your brand.

**Popularity**

A popularity appeal speaks in terms of the large number of people who use or prefer the brand or about a large increase in the number of users. At its strongest, such advertising says, "We're number one." The claim may be based on sales figures or consumer surveys. The basic message is, "More

*Basic Appeals*

people are using our brand. There must be a good reason and, therefore, you should probably be using it too." Figure 14.7 shows two examples of this technique.

At first glance, sheer popularity would not seem to be a very strong reason to choose a brand. Presumably, the focus of interest for most target prospects is on what the brand will do for them personally rather than the fact that a great many other people are using it. Of course, many advertisements that feature popularity also explain why that popularity is justified. In other words, popularity is emphasized merely as a prelude to presenting a more specific benefit-oriented appeal. Furthermore, in many product categories, popularity may almost legitimize the brand. Especially when you are competing in a product category which is socially visible, the fact that other people are using your brand in large numbers could imply that it is "correct," and therefore desirable, because of its social acceptance. Further, popularity—and especially a rapid increase in popularity—might suggest that the brand is thoroughly proving its merits. In other words, a prospect might infer that your brand could not be gaining in sales or holding its top position unless a great many

---

**FIGURE 14.7 Appeals built around popularity**

*American Airlines advertises that it has been voted "Number one" by frequent flyers for the fourth time in a row.*

*V.O. announces that among 3,000 imported whiskies it ranks first in sales.*

Courtesy of American Airlines

Courtesy of Seagram's V.O.

*Developing Advertising Creative Strategy*

**FIGURE 14.8 Varieties of economic appeals**

*The makers of Pella windows appeal to economy through use of their brand because of less energy consumption and maintenance costs.*

*In this retail ad, Sears announces special sale prices for a limited time only.*

*Here, a media vehicle is advertising to advertisers. The message: "Buy space in TV Guide to increase your market share and your profits."*

Courtesy of Pella Windows and Doors

Courtesy of Sears, Roebuck and Co.

Reprinted with permission of Triangle Publications, Inc.

people perceived it as rating highly in terms of critical and important evaluative criteria. On this basis, popularity tends to assure your prospect of your brand's superiority.

*Economic Appeals*

Economic appeals point out how purchase of your brand or acceptance of your advice will help people save or make money. Most such appeals fall into one of three major categories. The first category concerns saving money through a low initial price, including a "sale" or temporary price reduction. The second involves saving money through economy in the use of the brand. The third category of such advertisements promises that prospects can make money by using, selling, or promoting the brand. This last type is a commonly used appeal when advertising to business firms. Figure 14.8 shows you an example of each category. The reasoning behind any economic appeal is fairly apparent. Almost everyone is interested in saving or making money. In the case of price cuts, there is often an assumption that previous advertising has created a basic desire for the brand on the part of the consumer. A great deal of retail advertising, for example, does little but mention or show a brand and then speak in terms of some kind of temporary price reduction.

*Special Offers*

As pointed out when we discussed the adoption process model in Chapter 3, advertising is generally thought to be most effective in building awareness and interest. The other explicit elements, including sales promotion, tend to be

*Basic Appeals*

451

**FIGURE 14.9 Special offer appeals**

*L'Oreal is encouraging trial with a unique offer. In effect, the "coupon" is the front package panel from a competitor's brand, which helps assure that requests will come from persons who actually use this type of product.*

*Naturalizer encourages trial by means of a sweepstakes. No purchase is required but to enter the contest the prospect must visit a store where the brand is sold.*

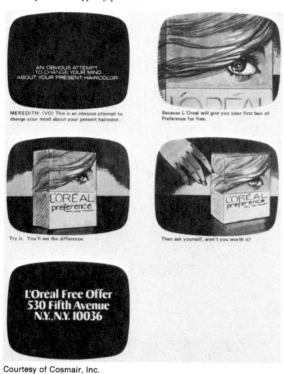

Courtesy of Cosmair, Inc.

Reproduced with the permission of Brown Group, Inc. Other reproductions are strictly prohibited.

more effective in moving prospects to trial of your product or to other forms of action. Because special-offer advertising is action oriented and very often seeks to encourage trial of the product, this category of appeal is usually combined with some sales promotion device, such as a coupon, a contest, or a rebate. Its objective is to impel action by offering a special reward if the prospect responds rather quickly (Figure 14.9). At least one study has suggested that special-offer advertising might also be useful in changing a product's image. In the case of "Koogle," a chocolate-flavored peanut butter, researchers noted that, "[Advertisements with a coupon offering a free sample] may help change attitudes and perceptions. We found that such an offer for Koogle peanut butter produced not only a shift from the childish image towards an adult image, but an increased improvement (greater acceptance) in the qualitative judgements of the product by an adult group that had received the sample."[9]

*Developing Advertising Creative Strategy*

| | |
|---|---|
| *Information on How to Use the Brand* | A "how-to-use" appeal assumes the prospect is interested in a presentation of detailed instructions and will be attracted by advertising that shows a way of fitting the brand into a particular usage situation or of improving the customer's skills in using or buying it. Figure 14.10 shows two ads which use this appeal. |
| *Solution to a Consumer Problem* | This appeal is based on the idea that your target consumer has a specific problem which she or he recognizes. The ad then shows how the problem can be solved by using the brand. Some writers describe this appeal as "product as hero," because the brand is often pictured as "coming to the rescue." Figure 14.11 shows how the solution-to-a-problem appeal can be used. |
| *Enhancement of Lifestyle* | Lifestyle enhancement appeals address the issue of what the brand can do to make you a better person. This can mean "better" in any of a variety of different ways—healthier, more popular, more successful in romance, a better parent, and so on. Enhancement appeals are especially common when advertising deals with the kind of role playing themes discussed in Chapter 7. Figure 14.12 shows examples of enhancement appeals. |
| *Enjoyment or Self-Gratification* | An enjoyment appeal focuses mainly on the sheer pleasure obtained from using the brand. It usually promises an almost immediate and highly personal reward. Figure 14.13 illustrates the use of the appeal. |
| *Problem-Plus-Solution Appeal* | A problem-plus-solution appeal is sometimes termed "negative advertising." It is built around the idea of emphasizing what will or could happen if the prospect does not use the brand or follow the advice presented in the ad. In a sense, it is really an extension or special case of the appeal that offers a solution to a consumer problem. The difference is that in the present approach the problem is emphasized whereas in the previously described solution-to-a-consumer-problem approach it was assumed the problem needed little or no such emphasis because target prospects were already aware of its existence. The situation depicted in the problem-plus-solution appeal, therefore, tends to center around a problem that the prospect currently may not recognize. In other words, the problem is introduced and dramatized in the advertisement. Then, the solution is presented. Figure 14.14 shows two examples of such advertising. |

Problem-plus-solution appeals have an element of fear arousal. The use of fear as a communication appeal was discussed at some length in Chapter 9. Importantly, you should recall from that discussion the proposed model of an interaction between a facilitation effect and an inhibition effect. Your suggested objective is to construct a message that recognizes the trade-off between maximizing the facilitation effect to arouse the prospect's sense of need and minimizing the inhibition effect to forestall message rejection by your audience or the arousal of disbelief in your brand's ability to cope with a serious problem. In essence, this places you in the position of aiming at a moderate level of fear arousal.

Reprinted with permission of The Pillsbury Company ©TPC

**FIGURE 14.10 The "how-to-use" appeal**

*As this ad illustrates, sellers of food products often employ "how-to-use" appeals that offer customers recipes and menu information.*

In addition to the issues raised in the earlier chapter, there are some other points that have been reported as having special meaning for the use of fear in advertising situations. For one thing, it has been found that the effects resulting from different levels of fear in a mass communication situation can vary depending on the nature of the audience. "In [a] particular case reported, the product being promoted was a group health insurance plan. Persons who were described as 'older liberals' and 'older blue collar blacks' responded more effectively to high fear appeals. The rest of the audience did not."[10]

In other words, if a mass audience is partitioned to permit examination of its separate demographic or psychographic segments, you may find that some segments seem to respond especially well to a high-level fear appeal whereas others do not. It has also been pointed out that at least in terms of fears concerning physical consequences as opposed to social consequences the effectiveness of a fear appeal can be directly related to the credibility of the communicator. "Increasing the threat of physical consequences increases persuasion only when source credibility is high. When the credibility of the source is relatively low, any level of fear arousal is non-persuasive."[11]

## Corporate Image

Corporate image appeals attempt to build or reinforce a positive opinion about a company in its entirety rather than about any specific product the company

*Developing Advertising Creative Strategy*

**FIGURE 14.10 (continued)**

*In this TV commercial, Valvoline featured a "how-to-use" appeal to tell prospects how to change their own oil. The ad also associated the brand name with do-it-yourself oil changes.*

(1) ANNCR (V/O): You don't have to be a genius to change your own oil and filter, and save yourself up to ten bucks.

(2) Valvoline Motor Oil shows you exactly how quick and easy it is with step-by-step instructions on the back of Valvoline cans.

(3) It's really quite simple, once you get the hang of it.

(4) Just see for yourself.

(5) Then do for yourself.

(6) No wonder more and more drivers are changing their own oil and filters . . .

(7) And changing to Valvoline.

(8) It's a smart way to save up to ten bananas. Without a lot of monkeying around. Right, Val?

Courtesy of Valvoline Oil Company, Lexington, KY

produces. Such appeals may be aimed at improving customer goodwill, investor confidence, employee enthusiasm, or general public acceptance. Two examples are shown in Figure 14.15.

**Advocacy or Editorial Appeals**

In recent years, a new term has been introduced to describe what amounts to a special extension of corporate advertising. The term is "advocacy advertising." In an advocacy appeal, the advertiser takes a position on a public problem or policy, which is usually related to its own business. The advertising attempts to rally public support for the position advocated by the company. Figure 14.16 shows you two advocacy appeals.

**FIGURE 14.11 Solutions to consumer problems**

*The problem is a headache. The solution is Bayer Aspirin. The effectiveness of the solution is dramatized by the "before-and-after" faces.*

Courtesy of the Bayer Company

*The current social emphasis on fitness finds many people actively searching for nutritionally sound foods. In this ad, Campbell's points to how it can help you find one solution to fulfilling nutritional needs.*

Reproduced with permission of Campbell Soup Company.

FIGURE 14.12 Lifestyle enhancement appeals

*Scoundrel dramatizes its part in aiding the user to play a desired lifestyle "role."*

Scoundrel photograph courtesy of Revlon, Inc.

*On an elegant note, Lenox suggests how its crystal and china can help you attain a desired lifestyle.*

Courtesy of Lenox China, Crystal

**FIGURE 14.13 Advertisements using enjoyment or self-gratification as the main theme**

*Anheuser-Busch pictures the enjoyment of Natural Light beer with good food.*

Courtesy of Anheuser-Busch, Inc.

*For luxurious enjoyment, fine furs have an uncompromising appeal.*

Courtesy of The Christie Brothers

Corporate image advertising, especially that using an advocacy appeal, presents some special challenges to promotional strategists. These advertisements do not usually call on the audience to undertake a specific action such as buying a particular product or service. Instead, they seek to change or modify basic and general attitudes existing among audience members. In many cases such attitudes may be deep-seated, strongly held, and highly resistant to change. In other instances, they may involve peripheral issues of little interest to audience members. Either circumstance poses problems for persuasive communication efforts. As a consequence, such advertising not only requires adroit handling but it may also take a good deal of time to achieve its purpose. One leading advertising executive has commented that most corporate advertising fails because the sponsoring corporation neither clearly defined the goal of the advertising nor continued the campaign long enough to attain results. He observed, "Stop and go is the typical pattern for corporate advertising. . . . What a waste of money. It takes time, it takes years, for corporate advertising to do a job. It doesn't work over night—even if you use television. . . . Corporate advertising should avoid the verbal and visual cliches of Madison Avenue. It should use the quiet graphics and the sober language of editors—not ad men."[12]

According to at least one published report, corporate advertising can achieve significant and even very difficult objectives if it is continued over a sufficiently long time period and carefully monitored to obtain communication feedback. One example of a successful corporate campaign is provided by International Telephone and Telegraph Corporation, which began such a program in the mid 1970s. Four years after its inception, the campaign was still in progress and received the following evaluation:

> At the time the corporate campaign started, ITT was beleaguered with a rash of adverse publicity, stemming from allegations of shady international and domestic operations. . . . ITT [used] magazines such as the newsweeklies and business publications "to catch the infrequent television viewers." [To reach the television audience, ITT used] a variety of 30- and 60-second commercials. . . . [Based on feedback from market surveys done over the course of the campaign] corporate advertising has improved the public's opinion of ITT markedly, judging from a tracking study using January, 1974 as a benchmark. Among the findings: ITT has begun to "close the gap" in favorable ratings compared with other corporations, and ITT is viewed more favorably than other conglomerates. [13]

## CREATIVE PRESENTATION TECHNIQUES

The basic appeals listed above all deal with the central *theme* of the advertising message—*what* the message is trying to say. In contrast, creative presentation techniques deal with the central *style* of the message—*the manner* in which the message is presented. We will now consider the eight major technique types identified earlier.

**FIGURE 14.14  Problem-plus-solution appeals**

*This ad suggests you might unknowingly be making a bad impression because you have dandruff. Head and Shoulders can help you overcome the problem.*

1. SING: IT'S SO EASY...

2. ...TO CATCH SOMEONE'S EYE...

3. ...AND SO EASY TO LOSE IT.

4. IT'S SO EASY TO GET THEIR ATTENTION...

5. ...AND SO EASY...

6. ...TO LOSE IT.

7. ANNCR (VO): Why risk letting the itch of dandruff...

8. ...be what they notice most...

9. ...when it's so easy to control..

10. ...with Head & Shoulders.

11. Head & Shoulders does an...

12. ...exquisitely beautiful job of keeping that little itch under control...

13. ...so all they'll notice is hair that's soft,...

14. ...shiny, and captivatingly clean. It's so easy to lose that itch and keep their attention with Head & Shoulders.

15. SING: IT'S SO EASY!

**FIGURE 14.14** (continued)

*This insurance advertisement warns of unsuspected problems that can occur if you misunderstand the terms of your policy. It then provides a solution through an offer of free booklets explaining insurance coverage to aid prospects in avoiding potential pitfalls.*

Copyright, Utica National Insurance Group, Utica, New York

**Factual Presentation**

A factual presentation technique relies mainly on a straightforward statement of points to carry the basic appeal. Little or nothing is done to embellish the presentation through humor, comparison, demonstration, or other communication formats. Figure 14.17 shows two ads that are primarily factual in their style.

**Comparative Advertising**

In a comparative presentation technique, your brand is related to one or more competitive brands. Figure 14.18 illustrates how the technique can be used. There are a variety of different ways in which you can develop a comparative presentation. The alternatives can be analyzed from the perspective of two dimensions—*intensity of comparison* and *direction of comparison*. *Intensity of comparison* refers to how openly and prominently you identify competitive brands. *Direction of comparison* refers to the posture you assume relative to competitors, which can be either "associative" or "differentiative." In an associative comparison, you are trying to demonstrate that your brand is similar to some

### FIGURE 14.15 Corporate image appeals

*Gould Electronics speaks of both its current accomplishments and its growth strategy.*

"There's a new kind of tactical sonar that can detect submarines at greater distances than ever before possible. And the sub can't tell it's being watched. Which electronics company received the contract?"

"Gould."

Gould is concentrating its interrelated technologies and products in six rapidly expanding electronics markets: high-performance 32-bit minicomputers, factory automation, test and measurement, medical instrumentation, defense systems, and electronic components and materials. Over the next decade, these worldwide markets should outpace the rest of the electronics industry. For more information about our growth strategy, write: Gould Inc., Department A, 10 Gould Center, Rolling Meadows, IL 60008.

**GOULD** Electronics

Advertisement, Courtesy Gould Inc.

*Mapco wants the public to realize what it is doing in the field of energy development.*

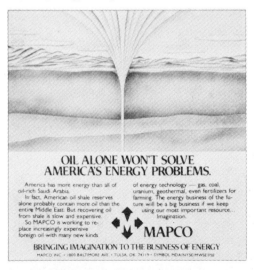

**OIL ALONE WON'T SOLVE AMERICA'S ENERGY PROBLEMS.**

America has more energy than all of oil-rich Saudi Arabia.

In fact, American oil shale reserves alone probably contain more oil than the entire Middle East. But recovering oil from shale is slow and expensive.

So MAPCO is working to replace increasingly expensive foreign oil with many new kinds of energy technology — gas, coal, uranium, geothermal, even fertilizers for farming. The energy business of the future will be a big business if we keep using our most important resource... Imagination.

**MAPCO**

**BRINGING IMAGINATION TO THE BUSINESS OF ENERGY**

MAPCO INC. · 1800 BALTIMORE AVE · TULSA, OK 74119 · SYMBOL MDA/NYSE/MWSE/PSE

Courtesy of Mapco, Inc.

## FIGURE 14.16 Editorial or advocacy appeals

*A portion of this advertisement talks about a specific product made by Warner and Swasey. However, the main theme of the ad raises questions about the overabundance of government agencies and regulations.*

> "He has erected
> a multitude of new offices,
> and sent hither swarms
> of officers to harass
> our people and eat out
> their substance."

*The Declaration of Independence.*

He who? F.D.R.? L.B.J.? Richard Nixon? Jimmy Carter?

No! King George III. A New Dealer 200 years ahead of his time.

References to the repetitious nature of history aside, isn't it ironic that the same complaints are heard in the streets today?

We've come a long way in a little over 200 years. From TEA and taxes to HEW, EPA, OSHA and taxes.

Indeed, we've come full circle. From a government of men to a government of laws to a government of regulations. Regulations made by bureaucrats not readily accountable to the people whose interest they "serve."

Once a government declares its intention to assume the responsibility for healing all the social and economic ills of the nation, there's no way the people can simultaneously maintain their independence.

The VFR vertical turning machine is the newest development of Warner & Swasey's G.A. Gray Company subsidiary. Designed for machining medium-sized parts, the VFR features superior machine rigidity through its unitized, stress-relieved steel monostructure. The highly accurate VFR can deliver up to 100 HP cutting capability.

**WARNER & SWASEY**

Productivity equipment and systems in machine tools, textile and construction machinery

Courtesy of Warner and Swasey

*The Savings and Loan Association urges public support for tax incentives to encourage more savings.*

# Why can't you buy the home you want? Or sell the home you have?

Your ability to buy or sell a home depends on the amount of mortgage money available at the time. And most of that money comes from Savings & Loan Associations.

But there is now an alarming shortage of mortgage money, due to a combination of shortsighted regulation, inflation and an antiquated tax system.

Even worse, there seems to be a concerted effort within the Government to dismantle home financing institutions in general—and the Savings & Loan business in particular—despite the fact that they are the main sources of mortgage lending.

If this situation is allowed to continue, homeowners will never again have the security of knowing that their homes will maintain their value, or that they will be able to translate that value into cash when they need it.

The U.S. Government must devise tax incentives and other ways to encourage people to save a larger share of their income for the creation of more capital for reindustrialization and housing.

If the U.S. fails to act soon, we simply won't be able to maintain our current standard of living. And the Government will have failed its people.

If you agree that homeownership should once again be a top priority in this country, write to us at the address listed below.

We guarantee that your views will be communicated.

THE SAVINGS & LOAN FOUNDATION

**If we all speak up, Washington has to listen.**

The Savings and Loan Foundation Inc.

**FIGURE 14.17 Factual creative presentation technique**

*Deutz sells diesel engines to industry. In this advertisement, the company blends a variety of appeals, which are all presented in a straightforward factual style.*

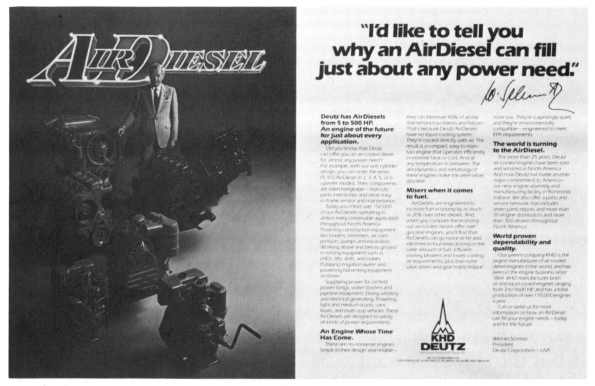

Courtesy the Deutz Corp.

competitor. For example, Ford Motor Company once advertised its Granada automobile by stressing its similarity to the Mercedes-Benz. In the more commonly used differentiative comparison, you are trying to demonstrate that your brand is different from and superior to one or more competitive brands. For example, both ads shown in Figure 14.18 are differentiative. The major cross-classifications of comparative techniques analyzed on the basis of these two dimensions are shown in Figure 14.19.

Comparative advertising of the low-intensity variety, in which the competing brand is not openly named, has been widely used for many years. Moderate and high-intensity comparisons, which openly identify competitors are much newer in terms of popularity. Their use was given strong impetus in the early 1970s when officials of the Federal Trade Commission urged television networks to change their policies and allow the open identification of competing brands in comparative advertising. A further spur to their popularity resulted from the success of a comparative campaign conducted for the Schick electric shaver. According to some reports, that high-intensity comparative

**FIGURE 14.17** (continued)

*The basic appeal in this ad is to personal enjoyment. The presentation technique is detailed and factual in nature.*

Courtesy Bermuda Department of Tourism

advertising effort helped raise Schick's market share from eight percent to twenty-four percent.

It is generally agreed that since the early 1970s there has been a rapid increase in the use of advertising which both compares and names competing brands. Is this good or bad? People who have studied the facts are divided in their opinions. One analysis conducted by a major advertising agency led to this conclusion:

> Our study of television commercials that named names suggests that there is little to be gained from this type of advertising for the advertising industry, the advertiser, or the consumer. The only one who may benefit is a competitor who is named in the advertising. It must be remembered, however, that these findings must be limited to 30-second television commercials for packaged goods. Different effects may be found for other media, such as print. [14]

Based on an experimental study, another researcher concluded, "Contrary to the opinion held by many advertising people, no evidence was found that a [high–intensity] comparative advertisement is more effective than its conventional 'Brand X' counterpart in projecting for the sponsoring brand an image

## FIGURE 14.18 Comparative advertising techniques

*Anacin's advertising appeal is based on a single brand feature (essentially lexicographic in nature). The presentation technique is comparative with competitors' brands openly identified, but the other brands are "toned down" in the illustration to provide "moderate intensity" comparisons.*

*Crest's appeal is based on a variety of features. The presentation technique is comparative but the competitive brands are not openly identified. In other words, it is rather a "low-intensity" comparison.*

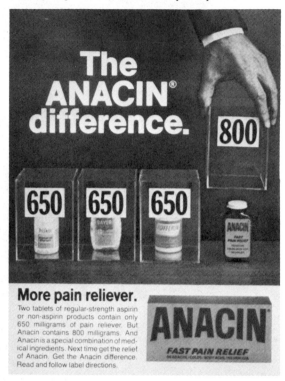

Courtesy Whitehall Laboratories

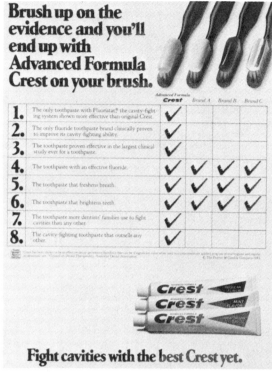

Courtesy of The Procter & Gamble Company

of competitive proximity to the industry leader."[15] However, based on his own experience, the president of a major advertising agency who sees things differently has stated, "Despite risks, a majority of advertisers and broadcasters seem to agree that dramatic advantages in creative selling are possible with this [comparative advertising] technique."[16]

The author of still another experimental study interpreted her findings this way:

An advertiser who expects to increase advertising effectiveness via a comparative strategy may want to look closely at the particular objectives, competitive situations, and the context of the advertisement before making a decision to advertise comparatively. The results of this study indicate that the relative effectiveness of comparative advertisements is not straightforward, but multivariate and likely to be influenced by other variables in the advertising environment. Comparative and non-comparative advertisements are not significantly, differentially effective for purchase intentions, claim believability, or advertisement credibility. [17]

**FIGURE 14.19 General types of comparative advertising techniques**

*Intensity of Comparison*

| | Low | Moderate | High |
|---|---|---|---|
| *Direction of Comparison*<br><br>Associative | The advertisement does not identify the competing brand(s) by name, but it casually refers to it in other ways such as "the leading brand." The comparisons stress the similarities between the sponsored brand and the competing brand(s). | The name of the competing brand(s) is identified but is mentioned infrequently. The comparison does not occur on a point-by-point basis. The similarities between the sponsored brand and the competing brand(s) are emphasized. | The competing brand name(s) is identified and is mentioned frequently in a point-by-point comparison. The comparisons emphasize the similarities between the sponsored brand and the competing brand(s). |
| Differentiative | The advertisement does not identify the competing brand(s) by name, but it casually refers to it in other ways such as "the leading brand." The comparisons stress the differences between the sponsored brand and the competing brand(s). | The name of the competing brand(s) is identified but is mentioned infrequently. The comparison does not occur on a point-by-point basis. The differences between the sponsored brand and the competing brand(s) are emphasized. | The competing brand name(s) is identified and is mentioned frequently in a point-by-point comparison. The comparisons emphasize the differences between the sponsored brand and the competing brand(s). |

*Source:* Charles Lamb, William M. Pride, and Barbara A. Pletcher, "A Taxonomy for Comparative Advertising Research," *Journal of Advertising*, no. 1 (1978), p. 45.

In summary, comparative advertising is one category of creative presentation technique open to you. Within this category you have choices concerning the exact nature of comparative approaches you wish to use. As to opinions on the effectiveness of the technique, you will find wide disagreement among the experts. Quite probably, a great deal depends on the type of product you are selling, the type of market you are facing, and the current strength of your competitive position.

*Proof-through-a-Test*

Advertisements in this category either put a brand through some type of trial situation or report on the results of such a trial. This may be a test in actual consumer use, a professionally conducted test, or a test especially conducted for its dramatic effect. In any case, the presentation centers around the idea that the brand has "proved itself." Very often, there is also brand comparison in such ads, but it is usually indirect comparison with the major emphasis placed on the test itself. Figure 14.20 shows examples of the technique.

*Brand Personification*

Some advertising is dominated by a character that has been created to define the brand in terms of a living or at least lifelike personality. The advertising character is used to "stand for" or personify the brand or its qualities, to

**FIGURE 14.20 The proof-through-a-test technique**

*Master Lock puts its product through a severe, high-powered rifle test to demonstrate its strength—a specific brand feature appeal.*

*Windsor bases its appeal on the feature of taste and uses a report on an informal taste test as its presentation technique.*

Courtesy of Master Lock Company

Used with permission of National Distillers Products Company—© Copyright National Distillers Products Company

endow it with special meaning, and to bring it to life. Because the character is typically used in a long series of advertisements, this technique can also add strength to your campaign by generating a more powerful repetitive impact effect. Figure 14.21 shows how brand personification can be used. Other examples include the "Lone Bull" of Merrill-Lynch and the "Marlboro Man."

*Slice-of-Life Dramatization*

"Slice-of-life" is a term that is used to describe a short dramatization in which the brand is shown to play an important role in the everyday lives of ordinary people with whom your target audience can identify. Sometimes the people in the dramatization have their lives changed or influenced by the use of the brand or possibly, in the negative version, by failure to use it. Ads built on the basis of reinforcement theory, as described in Chapter 9, are a special class of slice-of-life dramatizations. Figure 14.22 illustrates the slice-of-life approach.

**FIGURE 14.21 Brand personification as a creative presentation technique**

*The basic appeal in Maytag's advertising is the brand's dependability and reputation for a minimum of repair problems. The "lonely Maytag repairman" has very effectively "personified" this overall brand quality appeal for a number of years.*

Courtesy of The Maytag Company, Newton, Iowa

*Spokesperson-Centered Advertising*

In this technique, an identified person speaks for the brand and says either directly or by implication that he or she uses or endorses it. The spokesperson may range from a well-known celebrity to the "average person on the street." The character and audience acceptance of the spokesperson become extremely critical because so much of the advertising strategy is built around her or him. Figure 14.23 shows two such advertisements.

You encountered some basic ideas about spokespersons in Chapter 9 when the issue of source effects was discussed. As indicated then, the basic principle is that you should seek a spokesperson who is perceived as believable, attractive, and (possibly) possessing power to punish or reward the message receiver. Our previous discussion concerning the desirability of these three qualities related to communication in general. At this point, we will examine additional and more specific findings regarding these qualities as they relate to advertising in particular. With respect to the qualities of attractiveness and credibility, you will see that questions have been raised regarding the universality of their importance and, in some cases, even their desirability as factors to consider in choosing an advertising spokesperson.

*Negative Findings Concerning Source Attractiveness and Credibility.* As far as attractiveness is concerned, one team of investigators found that although a physically attractive spokesperson did seem to help bring attention to and increase the liking of an advertisement, she did so at the expense of generating a less positive purchase probability. Their conclusions included the observation that, "in trying to sell a non-romantically oriented product to males, an

**FIGURE 14.22 Slice–of–life presentation techniques**

*In this toothpaste commercial, the appeal is built on a combination of specific brand features, solution to a problem and enhancement of the consumer's lifestyle. The creative presentation technique is "slice-of-life."*

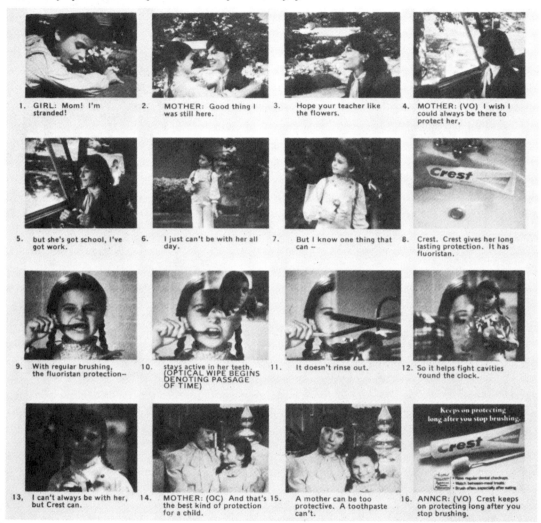

1. GIRL: Mom! I'm stranded!
2. MOTHER: Good thing I was still here.
3. Hope your teacher like the flowers.
4. MOTHER: (VO) I wish I could always be there to protect her,
5. but she's got school, I've got work.
6. I just can't be with her all day.
7. But I know one thing that can –
8. Crest. Crest gives her long lasting protection. It has fluoristan.
9. With regular brushing, the fluoristan protection–
10. stays active in her teeth. (OPTICAL WIPE BEGINS DENOTING PASSAGE OF TIME)
11. It doesn't rinse out.
12. So it helps fight cavities 'round the clock.
13. I can't always be with her, but Crest can.
14. MOTHER: (OC) And that's
15. the best kind of protection for a child.
16. A mother can be too protective. A toothpaste can't.
16. ANNCR: (VO) Crest keeps on protecting long after you stop brushing.

Courtesy of The Procter & Gamble Company

unattractive female model may be more persuasive in creating eventual product purchase than an attractive model."[18]

As for credibility, one research team found that under certain circumstances, "A highly credible source may [actually] undermine the acquisition of positive attitudes."[19] The findings of still another study suggest that a high credibility source is more effective if the audience is initially opposed to the

**FIGURE 14.22 (continued)**

*Hunt's Manwich portrays its features of hearty taste and wholesome ingredients, combining brand features and enjoyment appeals, in the setting of a "slice-of-family life."*

Courtesy of Hunt-Wesson Foods, Inc.

topic. However, if the audience starts out with a favorable point of view, a source who is only moderately credible may be more effective.[20]

***Special Considerations in Choosing a Celebrity Spokesperson.*** The relevance of credibility and attractiveness as factors to consider in choosing a spokesperson has been even more seriously challenged when studied in terms of celebrity testimonials and endorsements. One such study involved a nationwide survey conducted among 2,500 men who were asked how well they knew, respected, liked, and trusted a list of famous sports personalities. The survey was sponsored by a group of national advertisers and was intended to help improve their choices of athlete-spokespersons for advertising campaigns. A portion of the findings provided a major surprise for the sponsors. "Joe Namath—who showed up in the survey as one of the least admired, least liked and least trusted of all top athletes—has, in fact, been one of the most effective spokesmen in actual advertising situations."[21]

In other words, the findings intimate that if you gave unqualified acceptance to the general principle concerning attractiveness and credibility, you might place yourself in the position of precluding a celebrity who would make a very successful advertising spokesperson. This does not prove that attractiveness and credibility should be totally discounted in your selection process. It does, however, suggest that at the very least there may be exceptions to the general

THIS IS THE WRONG TIME TO FIND OUT YOU DON'T HAVE THE RIGHT INSURANCE.

Independent Insurance Agents of America, Inc.
Hicks-Greist Advertising

**FIGURE 14.23 Spokesperson-centered presentation techniques**

*A recognizable personality helps the Independent Insurance Agents of America present a "problem-plus-solution" appeal.*

principle or, perhaps more importantly, that there are additional factors which should be considered.

***Source Congruity.*** Many advertising people feel that one such additional and very vital factor is something known as the "hook." The idea of the hook is that there must be a logical connection between the product being advertised and the celebrity who is endorsing it. In more behaviorally oriented terms, the hook can be described as "source congruity." Historic examples of successful celebrity endorsements that illustrate the principle of the hook—or source congruity—include Dorothy Hammill speaking for Short and Sassy shampoo, "Mean Joe" Green speaking for Ideal toy trucks, Bruce Jenner speaking for Wheaties, and O. J. Simpson speaking for Hertz Rental Cars. In each of these cases, the celebrity spokesperson was chosen because her or his reputation or appearance relates to the basic appeal being made in the advertisement. The personality and the appeal are congruent and reinforcing.

In the Dorothy Hammill/Short and Sassy relationship, it has been noted that, "during her brief Olympic career, she became known as much for her hair style as for her skating style. . . . 'When she spins, her hair goes out and falls right back in place. She is able to demonstrate how the product works.' "[22]

In the "Mean Joe" Green/Ideal toy truck example, the hook is described as "ruggedness." In that commercial, Green tried to crush the toy truck and failed. His reputation for power was transferred to the brand's reputation for strength and sturdiness. In the Bruce Jenner/Wheaties example, the tie-in was "wholesomeness." This is part of the basic appeal advertised for the brand and a quality also widely associated with Jenner.

**FIGURE 14.23 (continued)**

*This television campaign featuring O. J. Simpson for Hertz Rental Cars has been described as one of the most effective celebrity campaigns ever run.*

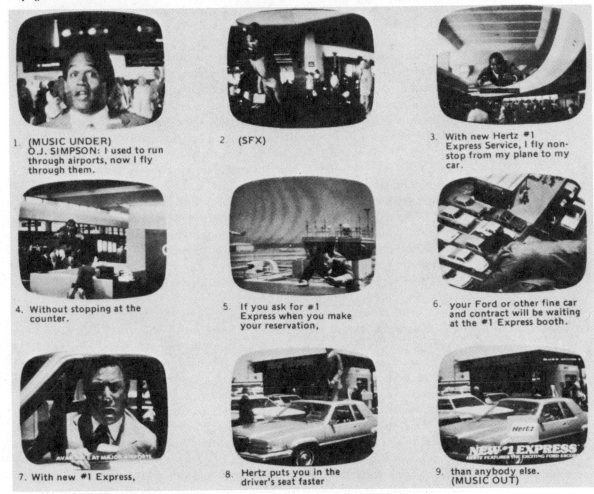

1. (MUSIC UNDER)
   O.J. SIMPSON: I used to run through airports, now I fly through them.

2. (SFX)

3. With new Hertz #1 Express Service, I fly non-stop from my plane to my car.

4. Without stopping at the counter.

5. If you ask for #1 Express when you make your reservation,

6. your Ford or other fine car and contract will be waiting at the #1 Express booth.

7. With new #1 Express,

8. Hertz puts you in the driver's seat faster

9. than anybody else.
   (MUSIC OUT)

Courtesy of the Hertz Corporation

The O. J. Simpson/Hertz Rental Cars relationship has been rated one of the most successful in the history of celebrity testimonials. The hook is speed, and it was developed as follows:

> [Research] revealed that businessmen, who are the heaviest users of rental cars, see little difference between Hertz and its scrappy competitor, Avis. Other research indicated that what businessmen looked for most in a car rental company was speed in service. Hertz instructed the Bates agency to produce a commercial that would appeal to the businessmen and emphasize speed. Bates came up with the slogan, "Superstar and rent-a-car" and then went out looking for a superstar. [23]

Notice that they were not looking for just any superstar. They sought one whose perceived public image centered around a quality that was congruent with the basic appeal to be emphasized in the advertising—speed. The superstar they found was Simpson. The campaign reportedly raised public awareness of Hertz by forty percent and enabled the company to increase its market share lead to fourteen percent above Avis.

***General Guidelines Regarding Attractiveness and Credibility.*** We considered basic concepts concerning the source effect in Chapter 9. Now you have seen some extensions and modifications concerning those initial concepts, at least as they apply in advertisements using testimonials or implied endorsements as a creative presentation technique. Two generalizations can be made that seem reasonable guides to choosing a spokesperson in such situations. First, the credibility and attractiveness of the spokesperson should be considered. However, possible exceptions to the importance or desirability of these factors should also be considered. At least in terms of advertising endorsements, credibility and attractiveness do not always seem to have exactly the simple, straightforward, and positively correlated effects that are commonly mentioned in communication theory. Second, when you are choosing a celebrity as a spokesperson, you should start by considering the basic advertising appeal you plan to use. The ideal celebrity is likely to be one whose reputation and character have some clear and logical relationship to the essential point you are trying to make in your campaign.

***Co-orientation Versus Expertise as a Basis for Credibility.*** Of course, not every spokesperson used in advertising is a celebrity. Many are represented as rather anonymous and ordinary people. When this is the case, there is evidence that suggests you should seek to employ a spokesperson with whom your target consumer can easily identify. A technical term sometimes used to describe such ease of identification is "co-orientation." In reporting his findings regarding its importance when selecting an advertising spokesperson, one researcher stated, "A communicator's credibility often is assumed to be only a function of his expertise. On the basis of this assumption, many television commercials feature experts delivering the message. However, the findings of this and other studies, suggest that source credibility is also a function of co-orientation which can be more effective than expertise persuasion."[24]

***Humor***

Humorous creative presentations attempt to attract audience members by amusing them. The idea is to be funny while still delivering a persuasive message. Figure 14.24 shows you an illustration of advertising in which humor is involved as a technique. Humorous creative techniques are used in a fair proportion of advertisements, especially those appearing on radio or television. The E'Suberante campaign, described in the last chapter, is an example of a very successful use of humor in radio commercials. One study indicated that roughly fifteen percent of the television commercials monitored included humor in their presentation.[25] However, despite the relative frequency of its use, there are those who feel that humorous advertising can be a hazardous

**FIGURE 14.24 Humor as a creative presentation technique**

*The appeal of this ad is a light-hearted approach to lifestyle enhancement. It also includes a special offer. The presentation technique relies on humor.*

Courtesy of the California Avocado Commission

technique. One leading advertising executive has been quoted as saying that advertising planners who rely on humor are "a group of dreaming, frustrated literary people who want to have fun with words regardless of what it does to their sponsor's sales."[26]

A review article on the subject summarized its findings by listing the positive and negative aspects of humor as a creative presentation technique.[27] The positive findings were that humorous presentations offer you several potential advantages. First, they often seem to help attract greater attention to the advertisement. Second, they may actually increase the persuasive power of the advertisement by partially distracting the audience. Presumably such distraction might lower audience resistance to persuasion and reduce "counter-argumentation." Third, in many cases they tend to increase both the credibility and attractiveness of the source. To the extent that this increases acceptance of the source it should strengthen the possibility of achieving a positive response. Finally, a humorous approach can sometimes produce a reinforcement effect because humorous messages may be more easily recalled than non-humorous messages.

On the negative side, the writers concluded humor can have some serious disadvantages. One possible disadvantage arises from the fact that humor may take away from or overwhelm the basic message that the advertiser wants to transmit. When this happens it interferes with proper decoding and interpretation of the message. Your prospect gets the joke but misses the basic appeal. A second disadvantage can occur because appreciation and acceptance of specific types of humor may vary among different portions of the audience. What is funny to some people may be anything but funny to others. Therefore, when using humor you may risk offending a portion of your target market group.

*Fantasy or Playful Exaggeration*

Some advertising presents its message by picturing situations that range from being clear and obvious overstatements of reality to being totally and recognizably unreal. For an example see Figure 14.25. The key words are "clear," "obvious," and "recognizably unreal." Because the situations presented in these ads are such manifest fantasies and exaggerations, it is usually assumed

Courtesy of Maidenform, Inc.

**FIGURE 14.25 Fantasy as a presentation technique**

*Maidenform has very successfully used a fantasy technique for many years.*

that the people in your audience will recognize them for what they are. Therefore, one of the advantages of this presentation technique is that it permits you to make some extremely strong and compelling statements without much chance of drawing criticism for possibly misleading your audience. (A potential exception can occur in the case of advertising directed to children. In this instance, an advertiser must be careful not to overdo fantasy so as to build totally false expectations about the product.) Although there is little or no published data regarding the effectiveness of this technique, it might be reasonable to speculate that fantasy may often offer an advertising strategist a means of building extra power into an advertisement with a touch of light-hearted escapism that dramatizes the basic appeal.

## FINAL COMMENTS ABOUT ADVERTISING CREATIVITY

Now that we have considered both a list of basic appeals and a list of presentation techniques which, taken together, help demonstrate the diversity of creative approaches available to you, it is appropriate to consider a question concerning the basis for choosing among the alternatives. Given a specific product, a defined target audience, and a designated set of competitive circumstances, is there likely to be any particular combination of appeal and presentation technique that is optimum? At least in theory, there probably is. However, in practice, no one has devised a method of determining in advance just what that combination might be. The evidence suggests that no particular appeal, presentation technique, or combination of the two is universally or unquestionably the best in every case. In one study, a variety of magazine ads using different mixtures of appeals and presentation techniques were compared to see if one or another of the strategies was dominant in attaining high readership. The investigators failed to find that any one of them stood out as superior and concluded, "When the present findings are placed alongside previous studies of magazine advertising copy and design, one finds that the creative function remains resistant to attempts at quantification. It has survived yet another form of analysis and seems to remain largely an artistic—if disciplined—function."[28]

When building creative strategy, therefore, there are no absolute rules to guide you in choosing among the available options. Even after you have made your decision concerning your appeal and presentation technique, you face still further decisions regarding the details of your creative execution. Your choices among such detailed communication symbols as words, music, and visual treatments are virtually unlimited. The communication models and theories discussed in Chapter 9 can help you chart your course but they provide no clear or undisputed routing plan. One advertising person has observed, "Rules lead to dull stereotyped advertising, and they stifle creativity, inspiration, experimentation, initiative and progress. The only hard and fast rule I know of in advertising is that there are no rules. No formulas. No one right way. Given the same problem, a dozen creative talents will solve it in a dozen different ways."[29]

This does not mean that great creative strategies spring full-blown out of thin air. It does mean that after you have studied your audience, your product, and your competition and after you have considered all of the options open to you, there is a subtle factor that has to be added. That factor is "creative ability," which somehow puts things into place and brings the advertising to life. Based on an extensive review of writings on the subject, one observer concluded that, in the end, outstanding creative accomplishments in advertising are mainly a function of fortuitous events rather than formula.[30] As an active advertising practitioner has stated, "You do your homework. You visit the market place. Read the research. You talk to the marketers. And then, very occasionally, the writer inside you produces something so astonishing that you are in awe because you have no idea where a terrific commercial, where a great headline, where a new product idea came from."[31]

## SUMMARY

As a creative advertising strategist you must work under certain handicaps not faced by your colleagues who deal with personal selling. The two major handicaps are the need to communicate with an unseen and diversely structured audience and the lack of immediate feedback. Both of these factors suggest that you must find some way to visualize your audience in advance and then attempt to anticipate the kind of reaction your advertisements will receive from audience members. There are three commonly discussed approaches to doing this. In the first approach, you begin with your product and then reason outward to determine what its features and benefits will mean to people in your target market. In the second approach, you begin by studying small samples of target consumers on an informal, first-hand basis. You then make the inference that the persons in your small sample accurately represent the full audience you seek to reach. In the third approach, you work from statistical profiles to derive a description of typical consumers, which is then interpreted in terms of its implications concerning the role your product would logically play in the lives of your designated audience members. Of course, you can also combine any or all of these three approaches. In any event, you will usually want to build a message that is particularly appealing to an especially important portion of your target consumer group. However, that message should also carry a positive appeal to as many of the remaining prospects as possible.

Individual advertisements can be thought of in terms of two major dimensions. The first of these involves the basic appeal, which is concerned with what the advertisement is trying to say. The second involves the creative presentation technique, which is concerned with the general style chosen to deliver the basic appeal. There are no standard lists of basic appeals or creative presentation techniques. However, to illustrate the variety of creative approaches available to you, we considered thirteen appeals and eight creative presentation techniques. In practice, one advertisement can blend a combination of appeals with a combination of presentation techniques. When the potential combinations are considered in terms of the further refinements and variations they can take, there are an almost unlimited number of creative strategies open to you.

After you have decided on the general pattern you wish to use, you still face the task of choosing the specific words and visual effects that will bring your creative strategy to life. Advertising people tend to share the view that there are no absolute rules to guide you. There are, of course, ways to test audience reactions to an advertisement once it has been produced. However, the original production of a successful advertisement demands careful study of the total situation coupled with creative talent; and creative talent remains an art rather than a science.

## DISCUSSION QUESTIONS

1. A mid-sized retailer of women's fashions has decided to expand its chain of stores into a new region of the country. In the words of the company's president, "This venture cannot fail. Women in this region are ready for our unique line of haute-couture look alikes." As the advertising executive for the account, outline three possible methods for testing the president's opinion and for developing advertising strategies to introduce the stores to prospects in this region. Which method do you think would be most effective and why?

2. Construct a tentative consumer profile of the "typical" coffee drinker based on the demographic data given below. What are some of the advantages and limitations in using such a statistically derived profile as a starting point for your ad campaign?

| Demographic Categories | Percentage of Total Heavy Coffee Drinkers in Category |
| --- | --- |
| By: Age/years | |
| 18–25 | 14% |
| 26–35 | 20% |
| 36–45 | 34% |
| 46–55 | 18% |
| Over 55 | 14% |
| By: Sex | |
| Male | 62% |
| Female | 38% |
| By: Education | |
| High School | 41% |
| 2 years or less of college | 28% |
| College graduate | 31% |
| By: Income/annual | |
| Under $10,000 | 17% |
| $10,000–15,000 | 23% |
| $15,000–20,000 | 23% |
| $20,000–35,000 | 30% |
| Over $35,000 | 7% |

3. In your own words, explain why the lists of basic appeals and creative presentation techniques may be thought of as an "inventory of advertising types." What significance does this have for planning a creative advertising strategy?

4. Comment on the following statement: "Comparative advertising may benefit the competition named in the advertisement. Therefore, it should be rejected as an effective means to sell a product."

5. Are there any situations in which comparative advertisements may be particularly effective? Find several specific instances where comparative advertising is currently being used and discuss the probable reasons for its use in each case.

6. What are the major advantages and disadvantages of humor as a presentation technique?

7. As discussed in the text, humor was a creative presentation technique used in the E'Suberante campaign. In light of the demographic and psy-

chographic characteristics of the E'Suberante target segment, select another creative presentation technique that you think might be appropriate for this campaign. Be specific in describing the special characteristics of this technique and be specific in your reasoning as to why it might be especially appropriate for E'Suberante.

8. Select three current advertising campaigns that rely heavily on a spokesperson-centered presentation technique and that use a celebrity as the spokesperson. Discuss the probable strengths and weaknesses of that spokesperson in terms of the characteristics outlined in the text. Suggest alternative spokespersons who might have a stronger impact and explain your reasoning.

9. Why does corporate image advertising pose special challenges? Can you think of any general approaches beyond those mentioned in the text that might serve to improve its effectiveness?

10. Comment on the following statement: "Advertising is simply salesmanship in print."

## REFERENCES

1. John E. Matthews, "A Two Course Survey of 'Creative Country,'" *Journal of Advertising,* vol. 4, no. 2 (1975), p. 15.

2. Robert M. Reeves, "Why Creativity is Suspect in a Creative Industry," *Advertising New York,* 5 May 1978, p. 24.

3. Christopher Gilson and Harold W. Berkman, *Advertising: Concepts and Strategies* (New York: Random House, Inc., 1980), p. 384.

4. Louis Kaufman, *Essentials of Advertising* (New York: Harcourt Brace Jovanovich, Inc., 1980), p. 313.

5. William M. Weilbacher, *Advertising* (New York: Macmillan Publishing Co., Inc., 1979), p. 154.

6. James E. Nelson, *The Practice of Marketing Research* (Boston: Kent Publishing Company, 1982), p. 209.

7. For an excellent, managerially oriented discussion of this topic, see Chester R. Wasson and Richard R. Shreve, *Interpreting and Using Quantitative Aids to Business Decisions* (Austin, TX: Austin Press, 1976).

8. John M. Keil, "Can You Become a Creative Judge?" *Journal of Advertising,* vol. 4, no. 1 (1975), p. 30.

9. Charles O. Bettinger, Lyndon E. Dawson, Jr., and Hugh Wales, "The Impact of Free-sample Advertising," *Journal of Advertising Research,* June 1979, p. 39.

10. John J. Burnett and Richard L. Oliver, "Fear Appeal Effects in the Field: A Segmentation Approach," *Journal of Marketing Research,* May 1979, pp. 181–190.

11. Brian Sternthal and C. Samuel Craig, "Fear Appeals: Revisited and Revised," *Journal of Consumer Research,* December 1974, p. 31.

12. "Ogilvy tells why most corporate ads are flops," *Advertising Age,* 14 November 1977, p. 10.

13. Lewis J. Haugh, "Once-tarnished ITT cleans up its image," *Advertising Age,* 6 March 1978, p. 78.

14. Philip Levine, "Commercials that Named Competing Brands," *Journal of Advertising Research,* December 1976, p. 14.

15. V. Kanti Prasad, "Communications Effectiveness of Comparative Advertising: An Elaboratory Analysis," *Journal of Marketing Research,* May 1976, p. 135.

16. Anthony C. Chevins, "A Case for Comparative Advertising," *Journal of Advertising,* vol. 4, no. 2 (1975), p. 36.

17. Linda L. Golden, "Consumer Reaction to Explicit Brand Comparisons in Advertisements," *Journal of Marketing Research,* November 1979, p. 531.

18. Michael J. Baker and Gilbert A. Churchill, Jr., "The Impact of Physically Attractive Models on Advertising Evaluations," *Journal of Marketing Research,* November 1977, p. 553.

19. Ruby Roy Dholakia and Brian Sternthal, "Highly Credible Sources: Persuasive Facilitators or Persuasive Liabilities?" *Journal of Consumer Research,* March 1977, pp. 223–232.

20. Brian Sternthal, Ruby Roy Dholakia, and Clark Leavitt, "The Persuasive Effect of Source Credibility: Tests of Cognitive Response," *Journal of Consumer Research,* March 1978, pp. 252–260.

21. "Playing the endorsement game," *Dun's Review,* August 1977, pp. 43–46.

22. *Ibid.*

23. *Ibid.*

24. George P. Mochis, "Social Comparison and In-

formal Group Influence," *Journal of Marketing Research*, August 1976, p. 241.

25. J. Patrick Kelly and Paul J. Solomon, "Humor in Television Advertising," *Journal of Advertising,* vol. 4, no. 3 (1975), pp. 31–35.

26. Donald Herold, *Humor in Advertising and How to Make it Pay* (New York: McGraw-Hill Book Company, 1963), p. 13.

27. Brian Sternthal and C. Samuel Craig, "Humor in Advertising," *Journal of Marketing*, October 1973, pp. 12–17.

28. Alan D. Fletcher and Sherilyn K. Zeigler, "Cre-

ative Strategy and Magazine Ad Readership," *Journal of Advertising Research*, February 1978, pp. 32–33.

29. Hank Seiden, *Advertising Pure and Simple* (New York: AMACOM, 1977), p. 44.

30. Timothy A. Bengston, "Creativity's Paradoxical Character," *Journal of Advertising,* vol. 11, no. 1 (1982), pp. 3–9.

31. James V. O'Gara, "Personality Cult and Ad Luck, Van Slyke says," *Advertising Age*, 7 November 1977, p. 27.

# CHAPTER FIFTEEN

# Appraising Advertising Media

## FOCUS OF THE CHAPTER

The bulk of your advertising budget will be spent purchasing time and space in media vehicles. For this reason, the choices you make in formulating your media plan comprise some of the most important advertising decisions you will face. Because you have so many media options open to you, they can also represent some of the most complex decisions you will face. Following the outline introduced in Chapter 13 (see p. 415), the process of building a media strategy centers around six primary decision areas. The first and most elementary of these involves determination of the general media categories to be used. In a sense, this is the most critical area because it sets the foundation for your media plan and impinges directly or indirectly on most of the subsequent media decisions that follow. Our coverage of media planning will begin in this chapter with descriptions of the media categories open to you and assessments of their relative strengths and weaknesses; we will continue in Chapter 16 which details steps in developing media strategy.

# PROFILING THE MAJOR CATEGORIES OF ADVERTISING MEDIA

As pointed out earlier, a *media vehicle* is a specific carrier of advertising messages such as *Time*, *Glamour*, "Sixty Minutes," "Good Morning America," the *Cincinnati Post*, or the *New Orleans Times-Picayune*. A *media category* is a general grouping of vehicles, all of which have the same general physical characteristics and capabilities. Examples of media categories are magazines, television, and newspapers.

In line with these definitions, any mechanism that can carry an advertising message is a potential advertising vehicle. This includes a variety of miscellaneous media such as trade directories, handbills, telephone directories, match book covers, and skywriting. Although any one of these miscellaneous types could form a part of your total media plan, it would usually be a relatively small part. In most cases, you will be investing the great majority of your advertising effort and dollars in one or more of the major media categories—television, radio, consumer magazines, farm publications, business publications, newspapers, outdoor advertising, and direct mail. With this in mind, we will concentrate our attention on these eight major media categories. To equip you with a general basis for making comparisons among categories, and among vehicles within any given category, each will be profiled in terms of the following four dimensions: (1) General Nature and Transmission Capability of the Media Category, (2) Reception Environment, (3) Audience Measurement Techniques and (4) Bases for Comparing Vehicles within the Category.

## General Nature and Transmission Capability

This dimension deals with some of the broad characteristics that describe, define, and distinguish each media category. The essential function of any medium is to transmit messages. Because every message has to be encoded into a set of symbols before it can be transmitted, the medium's basic transmission capability depends on the kinds of symbols it can carry, for example, printed words, spoken words, motion pictures, or still pictures. Under this heading then, we will be asking, "What is this media category all about and how suitable is it for sending the type of symbols required to fulfill our creative strategy goals?"

## Reception Environment

This involves the situation, setting, or atmosphere in which your audience is likely to receive your message and the resulting degree to which audience members are likely to involve themselves in the message. Quite commonly, the reception environment is thought to vary depending on the particular media category in which your message appears. For instance, people may receive advertisements in newspapers differently from the way they receive advertisements on television. For that matter, there can also be differences in reception environment among different media vehicles within the same media category. Under this heading, we will be asking the question, "What is the general mood and attitude of the audience when they are exposed to advertisements in the vehicles within this category, and how might that influence the effectiveness of your advertising?"

| | |
|---|---|
| **Audience Measurements** | The chief thing for which you are paying when you buy time or space is delivery of an audience. Therefore, you want to know how the size of the audience is being measured. In addition to total size, you will probably also want to know something about the kinds of people who make up that audience, especially in terms of demographics and psychographics. Our question under this heading is, "How can you obtain data to tell you how many and what types of prospects you are likely to reach through vehicles in this media category?" |
| **Comparing Media Vehicles Within the Media Category** | Different vehicles within the same category will vary in terms of the number of prospects they will deliver per dollar. They can also differ in terms of the amount of favorable impact they add to your advertising message because of the audience's attitudes toward the vehicle itself. The question under this heading is, "What methods are commonly used to rate various media vehicles in terms of relative effectiveness?" A much-used reference source for media planning is *Standard Rate and Data Service*. It provides media strategists with basic facts and figures on vehicles in all of the major categories. In particular, it details current space and time rates, base circulations for print media, transmission power for electronic media, plus a variety of other technical and ordering information. |

# TELEVISION

| | |
|---|---|
| **General Nature and Transmission Capability** | Television is the newest of the major advertising media categories. Since 1941, when commercial television was first authorized in the United States, it has grown to be one of the most dominant forces in American life. An estimated 81.5 million American homes now have at least one television set.[1] That represents over ninety-eight percent of the total households in the country. Furthermore, the typical home which has a television set uses it heavily. One report placed the average total usage rate at over six hours and fifty minutes per day.[2] |

**Extensive Symbol Capacity.** In terms of its power to transmit symbols in a variety of different forms, television is the strongest of the media. It enables you to encode your message via printed words, spoken words, still pictures, motion pictures, and music. Because eighty-eight percent of television homes are equipped with color sets you can also achieve excellent color reproduction of your advertising. Given this versatility in transmission capability, television offers you exceptional creative opportunities.

**Lack of Durability.** A principal deficiency of television with respect to its transmission capability is the fact that the message you send is not durable. Message reception occurs at one point in time and then it vanishes. Further, your audience cannot slow the message down, look at it again, or store it for future study and reference. Of course, you can repeat the message at a later point in time. However, each time you do so you are again creating only an ephemeral impression.

*Reception Environment*

***The Issue of Inattention.***  It is rather common to hear television audiences described as being "glued to their sets." A frequently voiced impression is one of people having their total attention completely captured by the fascination of television. This point of view is being increasingly challenged. As one report has put it, television viewing "may be a training course in the art of inattention."[3] This comment, incidentally, was applied not merely to the commercials that appear on television but to the programs themselves. In the experiment that led to this observation, electrodes were attached to the heads of persons watching "exciting" television shows, to measure brain wave patterns. The experimenter anticipated patterns associated with high attention. Instead, he found an increase in the output of alpha waves which suggested the viewer was in a passive state. Remember, this occurred when the subjects were watching the programs themselves, not the commercials. Presumably commercials would be even less likely to generate high attention.

***The Problem of Clutter.***  The effectiveness of television commercials is also thought to be lowered by increasing amounts of "clutter." Clutter refers to all nonprogram material such as commercials, schedule announcements, and public-service messages. Because television has become such a popular advertising medium, your commercial may often be surrounded by a string of such messages. In other words, it is competing in a crowded or cluttered environment. One study found that, "in general, as the amount of nonprogram material is increased, there is a consistent decrease in T.V.-commercial effectiveness scores."[4] In a survey of viewers, only twelve percent of those who had seen a television program during the evening could recall the commercials on that program the next day.[5]

***The More Positive Side.***  Commercial clutter and the passive nature of the typical television audience are points to take into consideration when planning your advertising program. However, they should not necessarily deter your use of television. For one thing, some types of commercials can break through a passive and cluttered environment and gain strong viewer attention. This applies, in particular, to commercials for "high involvement" products in which the audience has a genuine interest and desire to secure more information.

Surprisingly, when you face an opposite type of promotional situation and are advertising low-involvement products, in which the audience is not intensely interested, it is possible that the rather cluttered and passive nature of television may provide a highly suitable reception environment for a somewhat unusual reason. The logic and evidence behind this opinion is that because the television audience tends to be partially inattentive and distracted its resistance to persuasion may be lowered. However, because the inattentiveness is only partial, not total, significant points of the message can still be received and processed by your audience. On this basis, some analysts see the clutter and audience passivity of television as providing an ideal low-involvement atmosphere.[6] The message is received even though it is not carefully studied. It meets reduced resistance because it is not fully analyzed by the audience, yet it retains power to persuade prospects that your brand offers desirable features and benefits.

*Audience Measurements*

To understand how television audiences are measured and how charges for television time are determined, it is helpful to become familiar with the following four basic terms:

1. *Coverage,* which refers to the total number of television households that are in the signal range of any given television station. The coverage for a television network would be the total number of television homes in the combined signal ranges of all stations included in the network.
2. *Homes Using Television* (HUT), which refers to the percentage of television homes that have their sets turned on during a given time period. (This is also referred to as "sets-in-use.")
3. *Ratings,* which are the percentages of *all television homes* that are tuned to particular stations or programs.
4. *Audience Shares,* which are the percentages of *homes using television* (HUT) that are tuned to particular stations or programs.

The data on these four factors provide you with a base reading on the number of households you are reaching and the way in which your audience is being formed. We will now consider an example of how the terms are employed and how they relate to each other.

***Relationships Between Coverage, HUT, Audience Shares, and Ratings.*** If you were sponsoring a commercial on a major national network, your coverage should be approximately all of the television households in the country. In 1981, that would have placed your coverage at about 81.5 million. Suppose that over the course of the program during which your commercial appeared the average HUT was sixty and the average audience share for the program was thirty. The rating of that program would then be eighteen. The arithmetic works out as follows:

- *Coverage* = Total television households in area = 81,500,000
- *HUT* = 60 = 48,900,000 Households or 60% of Coverage
- *Audience Share* = 30 = 14,670,000 Households (30% of HUT)
- *Rating* = 18 = 14,670,000 Households or 18% of Coverage

Of course, you do not require all four data items to calculate the size of your audience. Merely knowing the coverage and the rating figures would be sufficient. For example, in this case your rating of eighteen times the coverage of 81.5 million produces your 14,670,000 households. If you had been airing your commercial on a local station that had a coverage of 2 million homes, that same rating of eighteen would have delivered your advertisement to 360,000

**FIGURE 15.1 HUT patterns over the course of a day, November, 1970 and 1981**

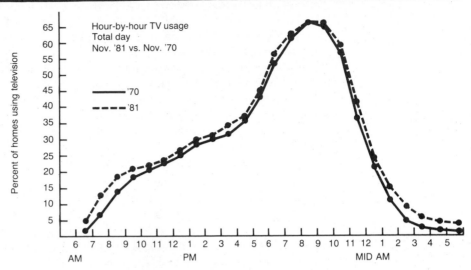

*Source:* William S. Hamill, "The Pragmatic World of Media Research," *Nielsen Newscast*, no. 1 (1982), p. 8. Copyright 1982 by A. C. Nielsen Company. Reproduced with permission.

households. The value of considering all four data items lies in the fact that knowledge of the way in which they interact can help you understand some basic points about the way television audiences are formed and the way television time charges are determined.

***HUT Patterns by Dayparts as They Affect Time Charges.*** Figure 15.1 portrays hourly HUT percentages over an average day in November based on audience figures for 1970 and 1981. As shown there, although television use in general was higher in 1981, the overall hour-by-hour configuration changed very little over the decade. The total size of the potential television audience available to any program tends to be small in the early morning hours. It increases throughout the day and reaches a peak in the middle of the evening. Then it drops sharply. Not surprisingly, rates for television advertising tend to follow this same general pattern. The most expensive commercials are usually those scheduled in "prime time." This is usually the time between 7:30 PM and 11:00 PM on the east and west coasts. In the central and mountain time zones it runs between 6:30 PM and 10:00 PM. The hour or so immediately preceding prime time is called "early fringe." The time immediately following prime time is termed "late fringe." Rates for "fringe times" are normally lower than the prime rate but higher than those for daytime television. For instance, the following were the ranges estimated for the cost of an average thirty-second network television commercial for different time periods during the spring of 1982:[7]

| | |
|---|---|
| Prime time | $71,500 to $84,500 |
| Early evening news (fringe) | $31,850 to $36,400 |
| Daytime | $9,600 to $12,000 |

*Ratings and Audience Shares as They Affect Time Charges.* Of course, time of day and the resulting HUT is only one consideration in determining a program's rating. The other major determinant is audience share. Notice that the time charges listed above are averages and are described within rather broad ranges, not as precise amounts. When it is anticipated that a program will draw an exceptionally large audience share during a heavy usage period, you may have to pay a good deal more than $84,500 to purchase a thirty-second commercial. As an illustration, the estimated charge for a thirty-second spot during Super Bowl XVII was placed at $400,000.[8]

*Sources of Data on Television Audience Size.* Data on HUT, audience shares, and program ratings are collected and reported by several independent research firms. Their reports are based on telephone surveys, viewing diaries kept by a sample of consumers, and mechanical recording meters attached to television sets in participating homes. Two major suppliers of such information are A. C. Nielsen and Arbitron. Table 15.1 summarizes some of the major features of the network analysis provided by A. C. Nielsen and the local station analyses provided by Arbitron. These television audience reports have drawn their share of criticism. Some observers have raised questions concerning the accuracy of the reports. Still others object on the theory that the rating systems encourage networks to seek high audience shares by following questionable television programming practices, in particular by often scheduling programs that appeal to the lowest common denominator of public taste. Although not everyone will agree with it, a reasonable assessment of the rating system has been offered by a network executive who stated, "In sum, the television ratings system is an undertaking with many strengths and some deficiencies. On balance, one has to feel that the ratings serve the purpose for which they are intended—measuring the broadcasting audience for the mutual use of the buyer and seller, as well as the public interest needs of the viewer."[9]

*Comparing Media Vehicles Within the Media Category*

*The Basic CPM Formula.* To compare the relative efficiency of placing your commercial on one station, network, or program versus another, a cost-per-thousand (CPM) figure is commonly used and is calculated as follows:

$$CPM = \frac{\text{Cost of One Unit of Time} \times 1000}{\text{Number of Households Reached}}$$

The number of households reached is determined by applying the rating against the coverage. The following is an example of how the calculation works: Suppose you buy a thirty-second commercial during prime time on one of the major networks. It costs you $72,000 and the program achieves a rating of 19.7. Because the network should cover just about all of the television households in the country, the coverage totals 81,500,000. Your commercial, then, will have been delivered to 19.7% of these homes or a total of 16,055,500 households. Your CPM formula produces this result:

$$CPM = \frac{\$72,000 \times 1000}{16,055,500} = \$4.48$$

**TABLE 15.1  Audience studies available for television**

| Supplying organization | *Nielsen Television Index (NTI), A. C. Nielsen Co. (New York and Northbrook, IL) | Arbitron Co. (New York) |
|---|---|---|
| Scope of coverage | National Network Television (ABC, NBC, CBS, PBS, and WTBS); "ad hoc networks" available on special order | 210 local television markets (all stations within each market covered) |
| Audience studied | Households and individuals by program viewing | Households and individual viewing by station and program |
| Sample size and source | 1,250 households with TV meter attached to set and 2,400 households recording viewing by diary method; participants randomly chosen from all U.S. housing units | Size varies by market from 200 to 2,300 for households maintaining diaries and (in four metered markets) from 350 to 500 households with meter on set; participants randomly chosen from telephone listings |
| Data collection method | Either by viewing diaries maintained by participants or by meters attached to sets | Either by viewing diaries maintained by participants or by meters attached to sets |
| Main audience breakdowns supplied | Average quarter-hour viewing on household and individual basis with breaks by age and sex; also by five Nielsen region geographic breakdowns | Average quarter-hour viewing on household and individual basis with breaks by age, sex, and working women; other breaks available on custom basis |
| Audience duplication data | Available for vehicles within medium by computer tape analysis | Available for vehicles within medium by computer tape analysis |
| Report frequency | Basic reports every two weeks; supplemental reports for detail of demographics throughout the year | Four reports per year for most markets; weekly reports for metered markets (New York, Chicago, Los Angeles, San Francisco) |
| Forms of reports available to purchasers or subscribers | Printed copy; computer tape; special tabulations available | Printed copy; computer tape; special tabulations available |

*Other Nielsen surveys provide data on local television, cable, and non-broadcast video such as games and computers.
*Note:* Information in this table is based on various published data available at the time of this writing. Some details may vary over time.

Among other things, the CPM formula dramatizes something very important about television. The initial cost of television time, especially on a network basis, tends to be quite high. However, in terms of the number of households reached, it is quite inexpensive. In this case, it costs you less than half a penny to deliver your message to each household.

*Refinements of the CPM Formula.* Although cost-per-thousand households is a commonly used figure, you will probably want to refine it to consider costs on other bases. Because the rating services also provide data on the numbers and types of viewers per household it is quite possible to do this. For instance, suppose that in the above situation you are really interested in the total number of *people* exposed to your commercial instead of merely the total number of households. The rating service data might tell you that there are 1.9 viewers on average per viewing household. Multiplying the households reached by 1.9 yields 30,505,450 viewers. On a per-viewer basis, rather than a per-household basis, your CPM formula can be stated as follows:

$$CPM = \frac{\text{Cost of 1 Unit of Time} \times 1000}{\text{Number of Viewers Reached}}$$

Using the figures above, it produces the following result:

$$CPM = \frac{\$72,000 \times 1000}{30,505,450} = \$2.36$$

Because there is usually more than one person watching an average television set when it is on, your cost-per-viewer will generally be extremely low because audience size is often so large. In this case the cost is slightly over two-tenths of a cent per person. However, there is another and less desirable aspect to be considered in relation to the comparatively large audience sizes and consequent low cost per viewer reached. Because they tend to be so large, television audiences also tend to be made up of all kinds of people. In other words, television in general is a relatively nonselective medium.

*Comparing Costs on a Target Prospect Basis.* Although television audiences are less selective than those you may find in some of the other media categories—notably magazines and radio—this does not mean television vehicles are totally nonselective. To an extent, you can match audiences with your primary prospect group, especially on certain demographic characteristics. For example, daytime television tends to deliver a high proportion of married female viewers, Saturday morning television attracts a large child audience, and Monday night football has a heavy percentage of male viewers.

Recalling that we have emphasized the desirability of defining your target market as carefully as possible, you may prefer to measure CPM in terms of the cost-per-thousand *target prospects*. Again, it is possible to do this at least on a demographic basis by using the detailed audience data available from the rating services. Your CPM is almost certain to increase because you are now eliminating the count of waste circulation going to people who are not logical prospects for your brand. Suppose, for instance, that you defined your primary target market as being made up of married women between the ages of 18 and 49. Suppose also that the supplementary rating data told you that only twenty percent of the audience fit in this category. In that case, the program we have been using for these examples actually exposed your message to only 6,101,090 prime prospects. All other viewers comprised waste circulation. On this basis you will be working with the following formula:

$$CPM = \frac{Cost\ of\ 1\ Unit\ of\ Time\ \times\ 1000}{Number\ of\ Prospects\ Reached}$$

$$CPM = \frac{\$72,000\ \times\ 1000}{6,101,090} = \$11.80$$

If you are seeking to choose television programs or times that fit the psychographic profile of your primary market, you may have more difficulty. In one study on this subject, a researcher drew the following conclusion:

> [T]elevision program type audiences are relatively heterogeneous in terms of the personality and lifestyle characteristics examined. Therefore, if advertisers define their target markets using [psychographic] characteristics, it appears that it will be difficult, if not impossible, to identify television audiences where people with such characteristics are concentrated. ]10]

***Comparing Television Vehicles on a Program Mood Basis.*** There is still another question that you must consider in choosing between different television programs. This deals with the particular "mood" that the program type may have on the audience and the result of that mood on the way individual audience members process your message. As one network executive has stated, "Television ratings are strictly a behavioral measure. They are not attitudinal. . . . [and a rating] reveals nothing about why [or how] the program was viewed. Judgements on that question are essentially conjecture, not research."[11]

In at least one reported study, the ability of viewers to recall advertised products varied significantly depending on the program during which they had seen the brand advertised. Some programming types appeared to be much more effective in achieving brand recall than others.[12] Ratings data will not provide assistance in gauging the impact of program type on commercial effectiveness. In choosing between programs, you must use your judgment or customized research to supplement the usual facts and figures.

***Postscript on Television, Videotech, and the Future***

Competitive pressures and technical advances have altered the natures of most media in the past and will almost certainly cause further changes in years to come. Although speculative forecasts might be offered for all of the media categories at which we are looking, we shall confine our attention to television because a variety of clearly apparent and ongoing developments could affect the use of that medium as a carrier of advertising messages in the very near future.

The appraisal of television just presented pictured it as attracting large but rather nonselective audiences and as being especially well-suited to delivering short advertising messages at a low-cost per viewer. Television is also often portrayed as being dominated by three major networks—ABC, NBC, and CBS—along with their local affiliated stations plus independent stations whose programming formats are very similar to those of the networks. Recently, the word "videotech" has been coined as an umbrella term to describe both conventional television transmission and a cluster of electronic innovations that also make use of standard television receivers. The innovations seen as potential disrupters of the established television scene can be classed as *innovations that may reduce* total commercial audiences and *innovations that may fractionize* total commercial audiences.

***Innovations That May Reduce Total Audiences.*** The three principal items under this heading are video games, home computers, and video recorder/ player devices. All are possible contenders for the same picture tube that now delivers advertising messages. As of 1982, six video game systems were on the market, and the users of these systems could choose from about 400 different game cartridges.[13] The immediate effect of video games on television networks was an infusion of added revenues as game marketers spent an estimated $100 million purchasing time for television commercials during the 1982–1983 season.[14] However, such games have the capacity to induce a less desirable effect from the networks' standpoint by taking television sets out of normal viewing usage and decreasing the size of commercially available audiences. Although network ratings do not seem to have been greatly damaged to this point, video games are still a force to be considered as potential threats.

Home computers are sophisticated first cousins to video games. Some units feature a combination of game and computational capabilities. Initial consumer reaction to home computers was somewhat slower than that to video games, but computers present television networks with a roughly similar threat in terms of providing an alternative use for television screens.

Video cassette and disc players began growing in popularity in the early 1980s. As of 1982, approximately 3.4 million such units were estimated to be in American homes, with their sales curve moving sharply upward.[15] All provide their users with the ability to play prerecorded materials including full-length motion pictures. Cassette machines also permit off-the-air recording so that a user can save television programs for future viewing. Conceivably, well-liked programs could be taped and viewed repeatedly. The exact effect of such recording possibilities on program ratings is likely to be somewhat mixed. If playbacks are taken into consideration, popular shows could rise in total viewership. However, because cassette and disc machines also enable their owners to replace standard telecast programming with a different type of video entertainment, ratings for television in general could drop.

***Innovations That May Fractionize Total Audiences.*** The two main entries under this heading are cable systems and satellite transmission. Our commentary will be confined to the first of these because it is currently the more active force. However, the second entry may eventually become the more dominant as transmission from station-to-satellite-to-home might create a multitude of television stations all bypassing local cable systems to reach viewers directly on a nationwide basis.

As for cable systems, there are now approximately 4,600 such enterprises operating on a local basis throughout the United States. About fifty percent of the television homes in the country are in areas served by such systems and about fifty percent of those homes are actually connected to a cable service. That means that well over 20 million households are now on cable and the number is growing.[16] Originally, cable systems were attractive to set owners simply because they provided better picture quality coupled with access to distant stations. As they grew in size and popularity they began adding supplementary services. One such supplementary service is pay television, presently subscribed to by about half of the cable-linked homes.[17] Among other things, this service allows viewers to enjoy first-run movies and other entertainment completely devoid of advertising. Cable systems also carry the programming of stations and networks specially developed to serve the cable market. A notable example is WTBS and its Cable News Network originating from Atlanta, which operates twenty-four hours a day and concentrates on an all-news format that is beamed to local cable systems throughout the country. Other cable-related networks concentrate on such specialized topics as sports, health, music, weather, movies, black-oriented entertainment, ethnic programs, cultural offerings, and women's interests. Since each local cable system has the theoretical potential of simultaneously filling one hundred or more channels, the amount and variation of programming that could be presented is enormous. Even with cable channel usage held far below its maximum, if any large share of cable households decided to desert the mass-appeal networks in favor of the much more specialized cable presentations, the result could be a highly fragmented television audience.

Because cable networks with their specialized programming reach much smaller audiences, they offer advertisers far lower time charges than do the standard networks. If the selective appeal of a cable network attracts a selective audience that forms a good match with an advertiser's target prospect group, the result is a significantly reduced cost-per-prospect contacted. The lower time charges also make longer commercials more economically feasible. In consequence, a number of national advertisers have experimented with a new form of commercial type dubbed the "infomercial," which basically is a lengthy television advertisement measured in minutes rather than in seconds. In a sense, infomercials can become miniature television shows in their own right. In fact, one cable channel, the Modern Satellite Network, has run programs consisting of nothing but infomercials. On average, a typical infomercial might last about nine minutes, which poses a new challenge to creative advertising strategists. What do you do with that much time? It is apparent that when a television advertisement jumps from thirty or sixty seconds to a period several times that long, the entire format must change. No longer are you merely attempting to achieve a quick impression and deliver a brief, simple message. Instead you must aim at holding viewers' attention for several minutes by providing useful and interesting information. A Revlon infomercial for its home permanent line provides an example of how this can affect advertisement structure. In contrast to the typical glamour appeal that might form the basis for a thirty-second ad, Revlon's extended time approach goes into great detail in instructing people on how to give permanents at home. Agency executives have mixed opinions regarding the feasibility of infomercials as a durable advertising phenomenon.[18] Some point to fast audience wearout as a severe limitation. Audiences now accept many repeat exposures to short commercials, but will they be willing to sit through the same five-minute or ten-minute advertising story over and over again? If not, advertisers will be forced to produce a greater variety of lengthier commercials and this may prove financially unworkable without a sacrifice in commercial quality. Other observers question the need for creating special presentations for cable audiences under any circumstances. They reason that viewers have little or no interest in the technology by which television reaches them. Therefore, a commercial transmitted to the audience by a cable is no different than one delivered via conventional telecasting and, by the logic of these observers, should not be handled differently by the sponsoring firm.

***Predictions Concerning the Effects of Videotech on Advertising Practice.***
There is always risk attached to speculation about the future. Forecasts in print can survive long after their inaccuracy has become apparent. Nonetheless, we will begin by quoting and endorsing the prediction of a long-time media observer who believes that "even in 1990 when at least half the homes are on the cable . . . and a fifth have disc or cassette players [VCRs], network television will continue to have the lion's share of prime-time viewing, though less than the present 85%."[19] The reasoning underlying this forecast is that the bulk of the television audience seeks entertainment of a type and quality that only network television can afford to deliver at a price viewers will pay on a consistent basis. VCRs and specialized cable attractions draw off portions of the total audience as does public television, but on average they draw only rather small and selective portions. An industry analyst estimates that cable subscribers were allocating about five percent of their viewing time to cable in the early 1980s and the proportion would top out at fifteen percent by the early 1990s.[20] As currently seen then, innovations tending to fractionize the total television audience are likely to do so only to a limited degree.

With respect to innovations that could reduce the total audience for telecast programming, the evidence suggests their appearance is causing little or no such reduction. As you saw in Figure 15.1, television usage in November 1981 actually increased over the comparable month in 1970 despite the fact that such devices as video games, video players, and home computers were beginning to gain in popularity. One explanation for their ability to coexist stems from the upsurge in multiset television homes. By 1981, almost one-half of the total television households had more than one set[21] and survey data suggest the percentage is probably much higher among homes purchasing auxiliary video equipment. For example, a study of early purchasers of video cassette devices found that eighty-seven percent of them were in multiset homes.[22] The presence of a second or third television set in a household allows the viewing of network shows and the use of video equipment to occur simultaneously. Recalling that primary television ratings are based on households using television and not individuals watching it, such simultaneous use could leave ratings untouched even if it drew some family members out of the audience. To the advertiser, the question of importance is, "Which family members, if any, are drawn away?" Again, the cost figure of real meaning is cost-per-thousand-prospects, which might or might not be affected. Thus, the increased presence of videotech equipment in American homes reinforces the need for more detailed analysis of the make-up of the viewing audience.

Our earlier description of television as an advertising medium will probably remain applicable in the near future, at least in its general outline. Standard network or network-type programming is likely to hold its dominant role even if reduced somewhat in its total share of the audience. More topically specialized channels that reach homes either by cable or satellite seem destined to expand in importance, and they form what amounts to a subcategory of the television medium. The appeal of this subcategory to advertisers will be its ability to deliver smaller but more selective audiences. When such an audience matches a firm's target audience needs, cable or satellite channels may be used to supplement or in some cases supplant standard, network-type television. However, for most widely used and frequently purchased consumer goods standard television will almost certainly remain a powerful route of commercial message transmission.

Of course, because electronic technology is a volatile and fast-developing field, it is always possible that some currently nonexistent or embryonic innovation could upset everything we have been discussing. For example, two-way television communication is now operating on a test basis.[23] One of the many possibilities of this development is in-home shopping. Potentially, this could mean that television becomes an instant-purchase medium through which a prospect sees your commercial, pushes a button or two, and buys the product. Although two-way television could bring about an entirely different style of advertising, it also goes beyond the mere issue of promotional techniques. Shopping by television would amount to the creation of a new channel of distribution and affect every aspect of marketing.

# RADIO

*General Nature and Transmission Capability*

Radio is limited to the transmission of sound. It is impossible to use the medium for visual impact. This does not mean that radio is a weak medium. On the contrary, radio has been used very successfully by many advertisers. The E'Suberante example in Chapter 13 is just one illustration of successful results attained through radio advertising. Like television, radio is also "time oriented." Once a radio commercial has been run it is gone. There is no way the message receiver can turn back to study it more carefully or show it to someone else.

| Reception Environment | Radio is generally considered to induce even less undivided attention than does television. It is often used as a sort of "companion" while the listener is doing something else such as reading, cleaning house, or driving an automobile. Again, this could be both a disadvantage and advantage for the same reasons that were cited in the case of television. To the extent that your message is not receiving close attention, it may be somewhat more difficult to ensure that your entire message is clearly understood. On the other hand, distraction may work to your benefit by arousing less counter-argumentation from the audience. |
|---|---|

| Audience Measurements | One thing that is certain about radio is its widespread popularity. The Radio Advertising Bureau has estimated that there are something on the order of 470 million radio sets in the United States, approximately two sets for every man, woman, and child in the country.[24] Because a large percentage of these sets are either portable or installed in automobiles, radio is a very flexible medium. People listen to it both in and out of their homes. By dayparts, the pattern of radio listenership is much different from the television pattern we looked at earlier. As you can see from Figure 15.2, among persons 18 years of age and older, radio listenership is high in the morning and then falls off to a low in the evening. Peak listenership for teenagers is in the afternoon and early evening. Not surprisingly, the time charges for radio commercials tend to be established on the basis of the listenership pattern shown in Figure 15.2. |
|---|---|

The size and nature of radio audiences are measured by several research firms. Table 15.2 summarizes features of surveys conducted by two such firms—RADAR on a national basis and Arbitron on a local basis for major market areas. Notice that unlike television, radio surveys use individual listeners rather than households as their basic unit of measurement. This is because radio usage tends to be more of an individual activity rather than a group or family situation.

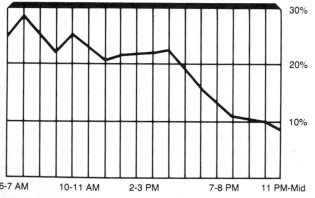

Average percentage of adults* listening per quarter hour, Monday through Friday

*(18 years of age or older)

6-7 AM    10-11 AM    2-3 PM    7-8 PM    11 PM-Mid

30%    20%    10%

**FIGURE 15.2 Weekday radio audience patterns by dayparts**

Source: *Radio Facts* (New York: Radio Advertising Bureau, Inc., 1983), p. 25.

**TABLE 15.2 Representative audience studies available for radio**

| Supplying organization | RADAR (Statistical Research) (Westfield, N.J.) | Arbitron Co. (New York) |
|---|---|---|
| Scope of coverage | Radio on a *national* basis including eleven wired networks | Radio on a local basis for 256 market areas |
| Audience studied | Persons 12 years of age and older | Persons 12 years of age and older |
| Sample size and source | 6,000 individuals chosen on a probability basis by random digit telephone dialing | Varies by market from 250 to 13,000; individuals randomly selected by possession of telephone |
| Data collection method | Telephone interviews | A listening diary maintained by participants and returned by mail |
| Main audience breakdowns supplied | AM/FM listening by station for dayparts or quarter hours, audience for all commercials within programs; standard demographic and a variety of geographic breaks | Listening by station for dayparts and/or quarter hours; age and sex breakdowns; reports on AM/FM in-home versus out-of-home; share trends and geographic breaks within areas |
| Audience duplication | Available among various radio networks by computer tape analysis | Available among vehicles within radio medium by computer tape analysis |
| Report frequency | Semiannual | One to four times per year |
| Forms of reports available to purchasers or subscribers | Printed copy; access to computer data base and special tabulations available | Printed copy; computer tape and special tabulations available |

*Note:* Information in this table is based on various published data available at the time of this writing. Some details may vary over time.

**Comparing Media Vehicles Within the Media Category**

Cost comparisons between various radio times, stations, and programs can be made using the same sort of CPM formulas described for television. On a per-commercial basis, radio is a relatively inexpensive medium. For instance, in 1982 the cost of a one-minute commercial on the ABC Entertainment Network was estimated to be between $2,500 and $3,500. Of course, radio also draws audiences that are much smaller than the usual television audience. The average rating for network radio was calculated as being between 1.0 and 1.5—far below the typical ratings for television network shows.

*Matching Audiences with Target Market Profiles.* One of the reasons that any given radio station or program is likely to have a low rating is the fact that radio is highly fragmented. The national radio audience is divided among about 9,100 radio stations throughout the country. Although this produces comparatively low ratings for most individual stations, it also has a very beneficial side effect from the standpoint of advertisers. Because there are so many stations, each tends to specialize in its programming and to aim at very well-defined audiences. In other words, radio is strongly segmented. To the extent that you can find a radio station that has audience characteristics which match those of your target market group, you can improve your media efficiency by cutting down drastically on waste circulation.

## CONSUMER MAGAZINES AND FARM PUBLICATIONS

*General Nature and Transmission Capability*

***The Diversity of Available Vehicles.*** Consumer magazines and farm publications are customarily grouped together even though, in one sense, farm publications are somewhat more like business publications because they are oriented toward a particular type of occupation. Among both consumer magazines and farm publications, you can choose between those which appeal to *general interest* groups and those which appeal to more *specialized interest* groups. General interest consumer magazines include such vehicles as *Reader's Digest, TV Guide,* and *People.* General interest farm publications include such vehicles as *Successful Farming* and *Farm Journal.* A general interest publication will usually give you quite a large but rather diverse audience. Normally, the higher the publication's circulation is the less selective is the audience that that vehicle will deliver. Specialized consumer magazines include such titles as *Model Railroader, Ceramics Monthly,* and *Camping Journal.* In the field of farm publications, specialized vehicles include such titles as *Sugarbeet Grower, Rice Farming,* and *Soybean Digest.* Apart from strictly general interest and strictly highly specialized vehicles, there are also many journals that appeal to something less than a totally general audience but something more than a highly specialized audience. Examples include *Sports Illustrated* for sports enthusiasts, *Glamour* for young women, and *Retirement Living* for senior citizens.

The diversity of the audiences you can reach by choosing among these vehicles explains one of the reasons for their continued heavy use by advertisers. Even more than radio, consumer magazines and farm publications can sometimes offer you exceptional possibilities in terms of reaching your specific target consumer group with a minimum of waste circulation.

***Tangibility of the Print Media.*** A major distinguishing characteristic of all print vehicles—as contrasted to radio and television—is that they are tangible. Audience members can hold them, touch them, and retain them for future use. For instance, an interested prospect can clip out your coupon or save your ad for later reference. Furthermore, print vehicles are temporally durable. This is especially true of consumer magazines and farm publications. The typical radio or television commercial has a lifespan measured in seconds. A monthly magazine, however, should have a lifespan of at least four weeks and quite possibly more. This provides you with opportunities for repeat exposures of the same ad to the same prospect over an extended period. A weekly magazine, by the same token, should provide you with the potential for repeat exposures of your advertisement for at least seven days. Again, this gives readers ample opportunity to study your message, to show it to and discuss it with other people, or to clip it out for future action.

*Graphic Reproduction Qualities.*   Most magazines and farm publications also provide you a potential for building strong visual appeal into your advertising. Generally, you can use high fidelity color reproduction to inject compelling graphic interest into your advertising presentation.

*Reception Environment*

There is a fairly widespread belief that the audiences of print media are much more actively involved in what they are doing than are the audiences of television and radio. For instance, to read a magazine or farm publication an audience member must make something of a special effort and concentrate on what he or she is doing. As a result, that reader is not likely to be as passive or open to distraction as might be the case when the same person is watching television or listening to the radio. For this reason, advertising in print vehicles may generate closer scrutiny and perhaps achieve fuller understanding on the part of audience members. Is this good or bad? From the standpoint of delivering an advertising message that effectively persuades your audience, it could be either. One communication analyst has observed:

> The reader is thought to be . . . more involved in the message since he is forced to participate creatively in this more impersonal type of communication. Such creative participation is supposed by some observers to be persuasively advantageous, but the hypothesis has never been tested. It may be added that creative participation, if it exists, seems not unlikely to produce at least occasional critical reactions and, at least at such times, to hinder persuasion. [25]

*Audience Measurements*

The basis for measuring the audience size for a magazine or farm publication begins with circulation data that are generally audited by the Audit Bureau of Circulations (ABC). The ABC report provides figures on the number of copies circulated and information concerning the manner in which circulation was obtained as well as its geographic dispersion. Because any one issue of a consumer magazine or farm publication could be read by several people, an additional statistic of interest to advertisers is the number of readers per copy. At least for the large-circulation publications, this information is often available from independent syndicated research services such as Simmons Market Research Bureau. For small-circulation publications you may have to rely on readers-per-copy estimates made available by the individual vehicles themselves.

Organizations such as the Simmons Market Research Bureau and Mendelsohn Media Research can also provide you with a variety of supplemental data concerning readers of various magazines. Table 15.3 summarizes some major details of these two syndicated survey services. The Simmons report includes breakdowns on percentages of readers who are light users, medium users,

**TABLE 15.3 Audience studies available for magazines**

| Supplying organization | Simmons Market Research Bureau (New York) | Mendelsohn Media Research (New York) |
|---|---|---|
| Vehicles studied | 103 consumer magazines | Seventy-seven consumer magazines |
| Sample size and source | 19,000 persons, nationwide; selected on a clustered, probability basis from census data | 15,000 persons, nationwide; drawn from computer file data and census data |
| Data collection method | Personal interviews | Mailed questionnaires via repeated mailings |
| Main audience breakdowns supplied | By major demographic categories and various geographic areas; also by lifestyle characteristics using VALS format. (Plus others) | By major demographic categories and various geographic areas (Plus others) |
| Audience duplication data | Data available on duplication of audiences both among vehicles in this category and with vehicles in other media categories from computer tape | Data available on audience duplication among vehicles within this category |
| Report frequency | Annual | Annual |
| Forms of reports available to purchasers or subscribers | Printed copy; computer tape for on-line access; special tabulations available | Printed copy; computer tape; special tabulations available |

*Note:* Information in this table is based on various published data available at the time of this writing. Some details may vary over time.

heavy users, or nonusers of your product category or even of the various brands within that category. Again, such detailed supplemental data are usually available only for the major, large-circulation vehicles.

*Comparing Media Vehicles Within the Media Category*

By combining circulation data with readers-per-copy data and then taking relative costs into consideration, you can compare the various magazine and farm publication vehicles on the same type of CPM bases described for television and radio. To illustrate how this might be done, we will use rough and partly hypothetical figures involving two popular publications, *Time* and *Psychology Today*. Assume you have decided you want to run a one-page, four-color advertisement. You have defined your target market group as being men and women between the ages of 18 and 34. Now you want to compare costs between the two magazines. The basic figures with which you are working are the following:

*Time*

| | |
|---|---|
| Circulation Base | 4,250,000 |
| Cost of a 4-color Page | $63,895 |
| Estimated Adult Readers per Copy | 4.97 |
| Percentage of Readers age 18 to 34 years | 49% |

*Psychology Today*

| | |
|---|---|
| Circulation Base | 1,175,000 |
| Cost of a 4-color Page | $22,990 |
| Estimated Adult Readers per Copy | 3.52 |
| Percentage of Readers age 18 to 34 years | 71.3% |

The three CPM formulas you can use to make your comparisons are

**1.** For comparison of costs using base circulation figures:

$$CPM = \frac{\text{Cost of One Unit of Space} \times 1000}{\text{Circulation Base}}$$

**2.** For comparison of costs per thousand potential readers:

$$CPM = \frac{\text{Cost of One Unit of Space} \times 1000}{\text{Circulation Base} \times \text{Number of Readers per Copy}}$$

**3.** For comparison of costs per thousand readers in your defined target audience group:

$$CPM = \frac{\text{Cost of One Unit of Space} \times 1000}{\begin{array}{c}\text{Circulation Base} \\ \times \text{ Number of Readers per Copy} \\ \times \text{ Percentage of Readers in Target Market as Defined}\end{array}}$$

If you compute by these formulas using the figures above you will find that on the basis of circulation alone, *Time* would cost you $15.03 per thousand and *Psychology Today* would cost you $19.56 per thousand. When you take the number of readers per copy into consideration, *Time* would cost $3.02 per thousand and *Psychology Today* would cost $5.56 per thousand. Finally, when you figure CPM on the basis of your defined target market, *Time* would cost you $6.17 per thousand and *Psychology Today* would cost you $7.80 per thousand.

These are useful figures because they put all publications on a common denominator basis. In other words, despite the fact that *Time* magazine would cost almost three times as much per page and deliver a lower percentage of prospects, the CPM comparisons tell you that it would still be somewhat less expensive than *Psychology Today* on a prospects-per-dollar basis. However, while such cost comparisons are useful on a preliminary basis, most media analysts want to take other factors into consideration as well. Each consumer magazine and farm publication tends to have a "personality." The type of editorial material it contains and perhaps even the other advertising it carries set a certain tone that can affect the way in which your message may be received by readers. For this reason, many media planners go beyond the CPM comparisons and also use a supplementary rating format to compare publications on relevant qualitative characteristics.

However, there appears to be rather little agreement as to precisely what type of format should be used or as to exactly how specific magazines rate in relation to each other on qualitative bases. For example, in one study sixty media experts from ten different advertising agencies were asked to compare a group of magazines on the basis of advertising quality.[26] All were given the same briefing regarding the product, the marketing strategy, and the target market. However, their ratings of vehicle quality varied widely. Even among media planners within the same agency, there were often sharp disagreements.

# BUSINESS PUBLICATIONS

*General Nature and Transmission Capability*

A business publication is a print vehicle with a format very much like that of a consumer magazine or, occasionally, like that of a newspaper. Its distinction lies in the nature of the audience it reaches as well as in the purpose for which it is read. Business publications circulate to persons in various types of industries, trades, and professions. These people read them mainly to improve their abilities at performing their jobs. The proportion of advertising material in such publications is frequently very high relative to editorial material. Furthermore, the advertising in the publication is often a major attraction to the reader because it informs her or him about products and services which relate to important job activities.

The same characteristics of tangibility and durability of messages that apply to consumer magazines and farm publications are equally applicable to business publications. Just as in any other print medium, advertisements in business publications can be analyzed, studied, and saved by readers.

***Types of Business Publications.*** The majority of business publications can be classified into one of the following five basic categories:

1. *General business publications* aim at a broad scale business audience that cuts across many types of industries and many types of jobs within those industries. Examples include *The Wall Street Journal, Business Week,* and *Forbes.*
2. *Vertical industrial publications* reach an audience that is involved in some particular type of manufacturing or service industry. However, the readers may be employed in a wide variety of different job types and levels within that industry. Examples include *Iron Age, Advertising Age,* and *Women's Wear Daily.*
3. *Horizontal industrial publications* are aimed at people who are specialists in various types of occupations. However, the occupations themselves may be applicable to several different types of industries. Some examples are *Traffic Management, Industrial Maintenance and Plant Operation,* and *Purchasing World.*
4. *Trade publications* are edited for persons involved in wholesaling and/or retailing. They often concentrate on resellers who deal with specific types of merchandise lines. Examples include *Drug Topics, Music Retailing,* and *Supermarketing.*

**5.** *Professional publications* are edited to appeal to persons in one or another of the professions. Examples include *The American Bar Association Journal, Journal of the American Medical Association,* and *Architectural Digest.*

As you can sense from the above listings, advertising in business publications can be used to fulfill a variety of promotional functions. It is used to reach consumers in the industrial market, generally to prepare for calls by sales force members. It is employed to reach resellers in an attempt to solicit their further support in your promotional program. Finally, it is sometimes used as a means of reaching professionals in attempting to convince them either to buy your product or to recommend or prescribe it for others.

*Reception Environment*

As previously noted, print advertising is generally thought to call for more audience involvement than is usually associated with television or radio advertising. The degree of such involvement is likely to be much higher for messages in business publications than for those in any other print media category. Their readers have both the expertise and motivation to examine your advertising more carefully and perhaps with more critical eyes.

Many of these vehicles are read on the job. In fact, they may virtually be required reading as a part of an employee's job responsibilities. For this reason, business publications may often provide you with the most positive reception environment you can find and may give you an opportunity to reach important decision makers at the very time they are in the process of reaching their decisions.

*Audience Measurements*

Some business publications are sold. Others are provided free of charge to persons who qualify by virtue of their occupation or membership in a trade or professional association. In the case of those that are sold, data on base circulation are often provided by the Audit Bureau of Circulations mentioned in connection with consumer magazines. When the business publication is provided free of charge, it is described as having "controlled circulation." The base circulation of a publication distributed by a controlled circulation method may be reported by either of two organizations, Business Publication Audit (BPA) or Verified Audit Circulation (VAC). As in the case of consumer magazines, these basic data are often supplemented by additional readership data which may be either gathered by an independent research organization or sponsored by the vehicle itself. It is generally the case that the larger the circulation of the business publication, the more likely it is that you will be able to secure a substantial amount of independently-gathered, detailed information on its readership.

*Comparing Media Vehicles Within the Media Category*

As with the other media categories discussed, cost comparisons between various business publications can be made by calculating cost-per-thousand figures. The appropriate CPM formulas are the same as those presented for consumer magazines and farm publications. Again, the most meaningful comparisons will be those based on cost-per-thousand readers in your defined target market.

Of course, in this case your target market will be defined differently than it is when you are promoting to ultimate consumers. Instead of the customary demographic and psychographic measures, you will be turning to such considerations as types of industries, job titles, and sizes of firms in which the publication circulates.

Just as in the case of consumer magazines, qualitative differences between business publications are often considered when choosing among the different vehicles. Such issues as "editorial climate," surrounding advertising, and prestige of the vehicle can be estimated and considered. Again, you will find disagreement among the experts as to how specific business publications rate in these respects. Two additional factors often taken into account when comparing business publications are the basis of the circulation (paid versus controlled) and the "inquiry" rate.

**Basis of Circulation.**   Some advertisers believe that publications with a paid circulation are preferable to those which are distributed on a controlled or "free-of-extra-charge" basis. The reasoning behind this thinking is that direct payment for the privilege of a subscription is a good indicator of the reader's genuine interest in the publication. This may or may not be true. There are probably many controlled circulation vehicles which receive little or no attention from most readers, whereas others may be read more intensely than publications for which a subscription price must be paid each year. In the end, each situation has to be thought through as an individual case.

**Inquiry Rates.**   The "inquiry" rate may give you an additional useful indicator of relative vehicle value. It is common for many business publications to invite readers to fill out a postcard or other printed form to obtain further information on products and services advertised in that issue. The number of such information requests mailed back produces the inquiry rate. Because this can provide one fairly good and immediate measure of response to advertising, it is frequently used to rank one aspect of the "pulling power" of the vehicle.

# NEWSPAPERS

*General Nature and Transmission Capability*

**Tangibility.**   Like any print medium, newspapers have a degree of tangibility and durability. They can carry coupons and their advertising can be kept, studied, and shown to others. Of course, the durability aspect is somewhat limited; you would normally expect a newspaper to last for about one day.

**Reproduction Quality.**   In general, the quality of mechanical reproduction in newspapers is far below that which you can typically achieve in magazines. Especially in terms of reproducing photographs and color artwork, most newspapers have some distinct limitations. For this reason, much of the artwork consists of line drawings. Four-color advertising is comparatively rare although there are numerous exceptions. Included among the exceptions is the growing use of preprinted "spectacolor" pages. These are produced elsewhere on superior quality paper and then delivered to newspapers by the advertiser for insertion.

***Expense and Geographic Flexibility.*** Newspaper advertising can be expensive compared to other media categories if you are thinking in terms of a national campaign. Recall that the estimated average cost of a prime-time, network television commercial might be approximately $80,000. A four-color page in a major magazine with high circulation might cost you around $65,000. What do you think it would cost you to run a full page, black and white ad in the newspapers covering the top one hundred markets in the United States? The answer is about $800,000, which is many times the costs for network television or national magazines.

Of course, it is also true that you need not buy space as large as a full page and you may not want to buy space in all of the newspapers in all of the top market areas. Most newspaper space purchases by national advertisers are made on a much more selective market basis. They frequently are also run in cooperation with a local retailer, which qualifies them for a lower rate. This last point brings up two important issues about newspapers as advertising vehicles. The first involves the "two-tiered" rate structure system. The second involves the use of newspaper advertising to assist in gaining reseller support.

***The "Two-Tiered" Rate Structure.*** There is a price distinction that most newspapers make between national and local advertisers. Local advertisers receive a much lower rate that can differ from that charged national advertisers by as much as fifty percent or seventy-five percent. Naturally, this does not always please national advertisers. One way to circumvent paying the national rate is to have your advertising placed by a local retailer, which qualifies it for the lower local rates. Then you can reimburse that retailer for the cost.

***Reseller Support and Cooperative Advertising.*** Because retailers make such heavy use of newspaper advertising for their own businesses they tend to place a great deal of importance on this media category. By running advertising for national brands in the same papers that carry ads for retailers who sell those brands, it is thought that you can often encourage more reseller support and enthusiasm. You can also take things one step further by "cooperating" in the reseller's advertising, which means that you pay all or a portion of the cost of featuring your product in an advertisement run by a retailer. Any media category can be used for cooperative advertising. However, newspapers are the most frequently used vehicles. More will be said about this in Chapter 19.

**Reception Environment**

***Reader Involvement.*** With very few notable exceptions such as the *Christian Science Monitor,* newspapers are local media vehicles. This is an important factor in terms of their appeal. They provide in-depth coverage of local news, as well as reporting on national and international events. As a result, their readers are generally thought to be very much involved with their newspapers because the newspaper is an important source of current and interesting reports on what is happening in the immediate area. Presumably, this puts the audience in a mood that is especially receptive to up-to-the-minute information, including that which appears in newspaper advertisements. In fact, some observers feel that the typical American prefers newspaper advertising over the advertising which is run in any other media category. Of course, like the editorial content, much newspaper advertising is also local in nature. It tells people what they can buy, where they can buy it, and at what price. In this sense, it is "newsworthy" advertising.

Newspapers, then, are usually credited with having the same reader involvement atmosphere of other print media *plus* a feel of excitement and immediacy that can create an excellent communication climate for both local and national advertisers.

*Audience Measurement*

Circulation figures for large daily newspapers are audited by the Audit Bureau of Circulations. In major metropolitan markets, very useful supplementary data can be purchased from syndicated research services. Information on two such services is summarized in Table 15.4. For most weekly newspapers and

**TABLE 15.4 Audience studies available for newspapers**

| | | |
|---|---|---|
| Supplying organization | Simmons Market Research Bureau (New York) | Scarborough Research (New York) |
| Scope of coverage | Daily and Sunday newspapers in seventy-nine markets | Daily and Sunday newspapers in top fifty markets (one hundred markets beginning in 1984) |
| Audience studied | Adult readers | Readers 18 years of age and older |
| Sample size and source | 58,000 individuals chosen on a probability basis by random digit telephone dialing | 60,000 individuals chosen on a probability basis by random digit telephone dialing |
| Data collection method | Telephone interviews requesting information on newspaper usage "yesterday" and "last Sunday" | Telephone interviews |
| Main audience breakdowns supplied | Variety of demographic breaks | Major demographics plus product usage data |
| Audience duplication | Available among vehicles within newspaper medium | Available both for vehicles within newspaper medium and among other media categories |
| Report frequency | Biannually for each market | Annually for each market |
| Forms of reports available to purchasers or subscribers | Printed copy; computer tape for on-line access and special computer tabulations available | Printed copy; computer tape; on-line access to computer data base and special tabulations available |

*Note:* Information in this table is based on various published data available at the time of this writing. Some details may vary over time.

some daily newspapers, you may have to depend on a sworn "publisher's statement" or "post office statement" to obtain base circulation data.

Newspaper audiences are highly selective on a geographic basis. However, they are not normally very selective on a demographic or psychographic basis. Although newspaper readership tends to correlate slightly with education, income, and age, it is still true that all kinds of people read the average newspaper. This means that, for many advertisers, a newspaper will generate a fairly high amount of waste circulation.

*Comparing Media Vehicles Within the General Media Category*

As just mentioned, newspapers are usually rather nonselective in terms of demographic or psychographic characteristics of their audiences. When you have a choice between two or more newspapers in a given market, you may still want to compare them on the basis of the type of readers they attract. You may also want to consider the reputation of the newspaper and whether it is a morning or afternoon publication. In general, however, comparisons between specific newspapers tend to emphasize differences in relative cost per base circulation and in readership rather than qualitative factors.

Many newspapers sell space by the column inch. However, by tradition, others state advertising rates on the basis of the "agate line." An agate line is one column wide and 1/14 of an inch deep. Nobody would buy that small amount of space even if one could. The agate line is simply a starting point for determining newspaper space charges. If you were buying newspaper space that was three columns wide by three inches deep you would be buying 126 agate lines. To calculate the cost of your space you would multiply the line rate by 126.

The standard approach to measuring cost variations among newspapers is slightly different from the CPM formulas we looked at in connection with the other media. This time, the comparison is made on the basis of a standard termed the "milline rate." The formula can be stated as follows:

$$\text{Milline rate} = \frac{\text{Agate line rate} \times 1,000,000}{\text{Base Circulation}}$$

For instance, if you were considering buying space in a paper that had a circulation of 300,000 and an agate line rate of $1.25, the milline rate calculation would be as follows:

$$\text{Milline rate} = \frac{\$1.25 \times 1,000,000}{300,000} = \$4.17$$

As with the CPM formulas, the idea behind the milline rate is to allow you to compare advertising costs between vehicles in such a way that circulation differences are taken into consideration.

# OUTDOOR ADVERTISING

*General Nature and Transmission Capability*

*Forms of Outdoor Advertising.* The standard forms of outdoor advertising are posters, painted bulletins, and spectaculars. Posters are advertisements printed on several large sheets of paper. These sheets are then assembled and mounted on a structure that has been specially constructed to hold them. In common parlance, this is usually called a "billboard." A grouping of posters in a given market area is generally sold to an advertiser for a minimum period of one month. They are available in several different sizes, the most popular of which is the thirty-sheet poster that measures 115 inches high and 259 inches across.

Painted bulletins are made by painting the advertisement onto movable steel panels and then mounting those panels onto the sign structure. Painted bulletins are both more expensive and more durable than posters. For this reason, they are usually used for longer than a one-month period. However, the panels may be moved from time to time to different locations in order to reach a more diversified audience. Although there is no standard size for painted bulletins, they tend to be larger than normal outdoor posters.

Spectaculars are custom designed. They are usually large and expensive, and are sometimes complex. They may include exciting lighting effects, moving parts, simulated smoke, or most anything else a designer can conjure up and an advertiser can afford. Because of their high costs you will usually find spectaculars only in extremely heavy traffic locations.

*Nature of Audience.* Like the audience for newspapers, the audience for outdoor advertising is very selective on a geographic basis, but is nonselective in terms of demographics or psychographics. It consists of anyone who is likely to ride or walk by your sign. Of course, to some extent, you can control audience selection by choosing neighborhoods or locations that are most likely to attract people with the demographic characteristics in which you are interested. For example, you could concentrate signs in high income areas or selected ethnic areas which contain an especially high proportion of good prospects for your brand.

*Reception Environment*

The other media discussed to this point provide the audience with some kind of editorial or entertainment material designed to attract and hold prospects' attention. That editorial or entertainment material also serves as something of a backdrop for your advertising. Presumably, it induces a certain type of mood among the people who will see or hear your ad. Outdoor advertising is quite different. When people are exposed to an outdoor sign they are not usually "media oriented." They are in the process of doing something entirely different, and your advertising must therefore draw their attention away from that activity. Furthermore, because your audience is generally on the move, the amount of copy you can include in an outdoor advertisement is very short.

This does not imply that outdoor advertising is not a powerful medium. It simply means that it has to be used somewhat differently than the other media. Your selling message must be stated very quickly. Ideally, your artwork should be so highly imaginative that it seizes the attention of those passing by despite all the distractions. The fact that its audience is "going somewhere" also gives outdoor advertising something of a unique advantage in that it often means outdoor viewers are on the way to spend money. For instance, restaurants and motels often use outdoor advertising because it can reach people who will shortly be looking for a place to eat or to stay for the night.

| | |
|---|---|
| Audience<br>Measurements | **Impression Opportunities.**   In outdoor advertising, circulation is measured as the estimated number of people who will pass a given outdoor sign and be likely to see it. The gathering of this information starts with a traffic count, which may be taken routinely by a governmental agency such as the highway department or which may be done especially for the purpose of measuring the outdoor advertising potential. This latter type of count may be audited by, or sometimes taken by, the Traffic Audit Bureau, Inc. (TAB). Because not everyone who passes a sign is going to see it, the base count is reduced to include only half of the pedestrians, half of the automobile passengers, and one-fourth of the passengers in mass transit vehicles. The resulting figure is termed the number of "impression opportunities." |

**GRP Packages.**   The outdoor industry has attempted to standardize its basis of selling posters by developing a measure designated as the GRP package. Again, GRP stands for Gross Rating Points and is a subject you will be reading more about in the following chapter. In the case of outdoor advertising, gross rating points are estimated by first determining the number of impression opportunities that a certain number of posters in a given locality would produce on an average weekday. This figure is then divided by the number of people living in the market area. The resulting percentage figure becomes the GRP level. To see how this would work, we will use a simple example.

Suppose you are buying posters in a market area that has a population of 1 million people. You buy enough posters so that on an average weekday you attain 750,000 impression opportunities. When you divide the number of impression opportunities by the number of people in the market, the result is seventy-five percent. Your GRP level is then seventy-five and this is the number designated as the size of your GRP package. Importantly, you should realize that this does not mean you reach 750,000 different people. It is quite probable that your impression opportunities are developed by exposure to a lesser number of persons who pass the signs on average more than once a day. For example, you may reach only 250,000 different people, each of whom passes one of the posters three times during a typical day.

*Comparing Media*
*Vehicles Within the*
*General Media*
*Category*

Outdoor advertising is bought on a geographic or market-by-market basis. In a sense, then, the outdoor signs in each market area can be thought of as a separate outdoor vehicle. In comparing such vehicles to each other, there is little in the way of qualitative differences to be considered. Outdoor advertising has no editorial or entertainment environment and, at least on a market-wide basis, tends to be nonselective in demographic or psychographic terms. For this reason, comparisons are made mainly on a CPM basis between market areas using the estimated GRP figures.

You can purchase various sized GRP packages, which are usually sold in multiples of twenty-five; for example, there is a twenty-five GRP package, a fifty GRP package, a one hundred GRP package, and so on. The number of posters that will be required to make up such a package depends on the size of the market area. The more populated the market, the more posters you will need and the more it will cost you to buy them to obtain an equivalent GRP package. For example, using a recent year for purposes of this illustration, a one hundred GRP package in Des Moines, Iowa would require sixty outdoor units and cost you $6,460 for a month. A one hundred GRP package in the Los Angeles area would require 594 posters and cost you $121,106 for a month. You can calculate the cost-per-thousand impression opportunities by using the following CPM formula:

$$CPM = \frac{Cost\ of\ GRP\ Package \times 1000}{Population\ in\ Market\ Area \times (No.\ of\ GRPs/100) \times No.\ of\ Days}$$

In the case of Des Moines, using a population base of 389,400, a 100 GRP package, and figuring thirty days for a monthly showing, this works out to

$$CPM = \frac{\$6,460 \times 1000}{389,400 \times 1 \times 30} = 55¢$$

As this illustration suggests, outdoor advertising is generally low priced when figured on a cost-per-impression basis. Of course, it must be borne in mind that the amount of information and persuasive power you achieve per impression may also be relatively low compared to that in a television commercial or magazine advertisement.

# DIRECT MAIL

*General Character and Transmission Capability*

Direct mail is much different than any of the other media categories we have been discussing. It is more or less a print medium, but really has no standard form. It might be a letter, a catalogue, a circular, a folder, a brochure, an envelope stuffer, or even a sample of the product. In short, in terms of transmission capability, it is anything you are able to send through the mail. Furthermore, it is really a medium that you create yourself. You not only choose the format but you also decide on the circulation and the timing. These features suggest that direct mail is in some ways the most flexible of all media categories. This is part of its appeal. It can often be tailored very precisely to fit your specific goals.

*Reception Environment*

Direct mail offers its audience no editorial or entertainment appeal; it is advertising pure and simple. For this reason there is something of a popular impression that the audience has little incentive to pay attention to it. You will frequently hear jokes and complaints about "junk mail." These suggest that many direct mail pieces are resented and discarded as soon as they arrive. According to figures from the United States Postal Service, however, this does not seem to be true. A survey by that organization showed that sixty-three percent of direct mail is opened and read.[27] Another survey indicated that about sixty-three percent of the people in the United States had purchased something as a result of seeing direct mail advertising.[28] In other words, direct mail advertising seems to be rather well received compared to other forms of advertising and on the whole it can be highly effective. Much of its effectiveness is explained by the very imaginative techniques often employed in creating it. In addition to the work done by regular advertising agencies, there are copywriters and artists who specialize entirely in the development of direct mail pieces.

**Audience Measurement**

Direct mail audiences are formed by using mailing lists, which can be set up by several methods. The simplest and most frequently used method is to work from your own customer or prospect list. You can also build mailing lists using such sources as trade directories or even telephone directories. It is also possible to rent lists from other advertisers or from firms that specialize in building and selling them. If you wish to rent a mailing list, Standard Rate and Data Service will assist you with a volume that includes information on about 52,000 different lists available for a fee. The description of each is thorough and includes facts on how it was formed and what types of prospects it includes. You will also find information on the source from which you can obtain the list along with the costs and any restrictions that might apply to its use.

**Comparing Media Vehicles Within the General Media Category**

Because a direct mail vehicle is one you build yourself, the cost and quality comparisons we have been discussing in connection with other media categories are not quite applicable. However, there are still cost decisions to make. You must decide on the value of preparing an elaborate versus a simple mailing piece and on how large a mailing campaign you want to undertake. Both of these factors will affect your cost. There are also some important points concerning the cost of direct mail that deserve special discussion.

*High Cost per Contact.*   On a cost-per-contact basis, this tends to be an expensive medium. At current rates, third class postage alone will cost you a minimum of 8.4¢ per unit. Merely allowing for this postage cost starts you off with a base price of 84 dollars per thousand circulation. When you compare that figure with some of the CPM figures you saw earlier, you can begin to acquire a sense of the size of budget necessary to reach as many people by direct mail as are commonly reached by a prime time television commercial. Apart from the postage cost, you also have to think of the expenses of preparing the mailing piece, having it stuffed in the envelopes, and the charge for renting a suitable mailing list.

*Highly Tailored Circulation Potential.*   There is another and more positive aspect of the expense picture. Because you control the circulation you can limit its size to make it fit your budget. In other words, although per-unit expense may be relatively high, you can adjust the extent of the mailing so that your total cost remains rather low. In fact, this is an advantage that frequently makes direct mail an appealing alternative to relatively small advertisers. Furthermore, by selecting your mailing list carefully you can minimize waste circulation and concentrate closely on an audience that fits your specific prospect description.

# SUMMARY

Any mechanism that can carry an advertising message can be considered as a media vehicle. In this sense, a wide variety of media categories are available to you. As a practical matter, the great bulk of advertising dollars are spent among vehicles in the following eight major media categories: television, radio, consumer magazines, farm publications, business publications, newspapers, outdoor advertising, and direct mail. Each of these can be considered in terms of four principal aspects, which are general nature and transmission capability, reception environment, audience measurements, and methods of comparing media vehicles within the category.

Every category has its own general strengths and weaknesses. In choosing among the individual vehicles within each category you will be examining a variety of factors. One critical factor is the ability of the vehicle to deliver your message to target prospects on a cost-effective basis. A standard method of comparing vehicles on this factor is the CPM or cost-per-thousand formula. An equally critical factor is the vehicle's ability to deliver effectively the kinds of symbols called for in your creative strategy. These are mainly spoken or printed words, still or motion pictures in color or black and white, and perhaps auxiliary symbol forms such as music. Additionally you will want to consider the durability, tangibility, and reproduction quality with which each vehicle can deliver those symbols relative to your total promotional goals plus the effect of the vehicle's image or environment on message acceptance.

Television is the most versatile medium with respect to the symbol forms it can transmit. It is also powerful in terms of ability to reach a very large audience. Coincident with this large audience size is the fact that audience makeup is comparatively nonselective with respect to demographic or psychographic characteristics. Although the initial cost of television time tends to be high, especially on a network basis, the cost-per-viewer reached is extremely low. Because it is an electronic medium, television advertisements lack durability and tangibility. Additionally, they are likely to be received in an atmosphere of inattention, distraction, and clutter that may inhibit careful study of your message by audience members. This last feature has both negative and positive implications. On the negative side it may retard comprehension, but on the positive side it may reduce counter-argumentation and resistance on the part of the receiver.

Like television, radio is an electronic medium and shares the limitations of nondurability and intangibility of messages. It also shares the same general character of a distracting reception environment with the same potential consequences in terms of positive and negative effects on message reception. Unlike television, radio permits advertisers to reach highly selective audiences because individual stations tend to be specialized in their programming. It is also a low-cost medium and one that can reach listeners in a variety of situations both in and out of the home.

Consumer magazines, farm publications, and business publications are all similar in terms of essential format and share the same central qualities. The distinction among them lies in the nature of their target audiences and their editorial thrusts. Within all three categories you can find individual vehicles tailored to appeal to extremely selective audiences. Coupled with audience selectivity, these media enjoy the advantages of tangibility and durability. Most have a lifespan of at least one week and all permit readers to save, study, or clip out advertising materials. Although messages are limited to symbolic transmission via printed words and pictures, most of these publications provide excellent graphic reproduction that facilitates the use of strong and compelling artwork. Furthermore, many enjoy a great deal of reader loyalty and surround your advertising with an editorial climate that acts to enhance consumer participation in the communication process.

Newspapers, though less durable and less sophisticated in terms of reproduction possibilities, provide advertisers with many of the same advantages of the magazine-type media. In particular, because much of their news coverage is local in nature, readers are thought to identify especially closely with particular newspapers. Newspapers also have an action-oriented and up-to-the-minute personality that is associated with immediate decision making, including decision making connected with consumer purchases. For this reason, retailers are heavy users of newspaper advertising space, which in turn upgrades the medium's communication value for many national advertisers.

The two remaining major media categories, outdoor advertising and direct mail, differ from all those discussed to this point because they are advertising carriers with no editorial or entertainment backdrop. Outdoor advertising competes in the hectic world of traffic and is limited to short copy messages. While nonselective on a demographic basis, it does offer good audience selectivity in geographic terms. It enjoys the advantage of an extremely low cost per impression opportunity along with the power to reach people who are on the move and, in many cases, may shortly find themselves in a purchase decision situation.

In the case of direct mail, the entire advertising format is left to the discretion of the advertiser. This makes direct mail extremely versatile in terms of creative techniques that can be employed, though it is essentially limited to symbol transmission associated with the print media. Despite its frequent derogation as "junk mail," the evidence demonstrates that direct mail can be a potent selling tool. Although it is relatively expensive on a cost-per-contact measure, it remains a viable media route for many small firms because circulation size is completely controlled by the advertisers and can be held to a level which fits budget constraints. The ability to tailor the mailing list to serve each unique promotional situation also makes direct mail an unexcelled media category in terms of concentrating messages on carefully chosen target prospects with a minimum of waste circulation.

As these descriptions demonstrate, there is no single media category that stands out as possessing ultimate superiority. The first task in constructing a media strategy is to consider communication needs and audience requirements and then to attempt to choose media categories which will serve most effectively in reaching your firm's total promotional objectives. In some cases, the decision may result in concentrating all of your efforts within one type of medium. However, in many instances your decision may be to choose vehicles among a variety of media categories, each of which is chosen because it has singular qualities that complement those of the other categories in your full media mix.

## DISCUSSION QUESTIONS

1. Each major media category was profiled on the basis of four dimensions. For each dimension describe the relevant considerations for each media category.
2. Discuss the special problems and opportunities presented by the reception environment of television. Contrast this environment to that of radio.
3. Draw up a list of specific situations in which it would be more advantageous to use radio over television, and vice versa.
4. Define the four basic terms involved in measuring television audiences and outline the relationships between them.
5. Determine the basic CPM for a commercial on the following television program: "The Wild World of People" is a national network TV show. The average HUT during its time period is fifty and its average audience share is thirty. Commercials on this popular program cost $68,000.
6. Compare the average ratings for network radio with those of typical television network situations. What causes this phenomenon and what does this imply about the situations in which radio would be preferred over television, and vice versa?
7. Suppose consumer magazine A costs $5.00 per thousand (on the basis of your defined target market) whereas magazine B costs $5.50 per thousand. As an account executive for a consumer product describe the importance these figures would play in your decision to select a media vehicle and what other special characteristics would affect your final decision.
8. Explain what is meant by the "two-tiered rate structure" of newspapers.
9. If newspapers do not have mechanical reproduction capabilities comparable to those of magazines, and if their cost on a national basis is relatively high, why do many national advertisers still want to advertise in this media category?
10. Contrast the reception environment of outdoor advertising with that of radio and newspapers. What implications might these comparisons have for a manufacturer of athletic footwear who wishes to select one of these media categories?

## REFERENCES

1. *Media Costs and Coverage* (Chicago: Leo Burnett U.S.A., 1982), p. 5.
2. *Ibid.,* p. 9.
3. "Learning to Live with T.V.," *Time,* 28 May 1979, p. 50.
4. Peter H. Webb and Michael L. Ray, "Effects of T.V. Clutter," *Journal of Advertising Research,* June 1979, p. 9.
5. Herbert E. Krugman, "What Makes Advertising Effective?" *Harvard Business Review,* March/April 1975, p. 97.
6. Herbert E. Krugman, "The Impact of Television Advertising: Learning Without Involvement," *Public Opinion Quarterly,* Fall 1965, pp. 49–56.
7. *Media Costs and Coverage,* p. 6.
8. Anita Seelig, "The Network TV Connection," *Advertising Age,* 6 September 1982, p. M-7.
9. William S. Rubens, "A Guide to T.V. Ratings," *Journal of Advertising Research,* February 1978, p. 18.
10. Kathryn E. A. Villani, "Personality/Lifestyle and Television Viewing Behavior," *Journal of Marketing Research,* November 1975, pp. 436–437.
11. Rubens, "A Guide to T.V. Ratings," p. 14.
12. Gordon L. Wyse, Herbert E. Brown, and Myron K. Cox, "The Effect of Program Type and Other Variables in Reaching the Daytime Television Viewer with Advertising Messages," *Journal of Advertising,* volume 4, no. 3 (1975), pp. 41–46.
13. "Video Wars," *New York Times News Service,* 12 December 1982.
14. *Ibid.*
15. Leo Bogart, "Media and a Changing America," *Advertising Age,* 29 March 1982, p. M-52.
16. *Ibid.*
17. *Ibid.*
18. B. G. Yovovich, "Videotech—Wired for Change," *Advertising Age,* 15 November 1982, p. M-11.

19. Bogart, "Media and a Changing America," p. M-53.
20. Susan Spillman, "Measurement Still Major Cable Woe," *Advertising Age,* 15 February 1982, p. 86.
21. *Media Costs and Coverage,* p. 5.
22. "First Look at Cassette Audience," *Media Decisions,* March 1979, pp. 146–150.
23. "QUBE—A marketing tool puzzles its owners," *Media Decisions,* May 1979, pp. 72–104.
24. *Radio Facts* (New York: Radio Advertising Bureau, Inc.., 1983), p. 4.
25. Joseph T. Klapper, *The Effects of Mass Communications* (New York: The Free Press, 1960), pp. 110–111.
26. Russell I. Haley, "Do We Really Know What We Are Doing?" *Combined Proceedings 1971* (Chicago: American Marketing Association, 1971), pp. 217–219.
27. "The Direct Mail Stream," *Advertising Age,* 21 November 1973, p. 119.
28. "USPS studies ad mail, finds 63 % have bought," *Advertising Age,* 7 May 1973, p. 2.

# CHAPTER SIXTEEN

# Developing Media Strategy

## FOCUS OF THE CHAPTER

Having considered some basic facts and features associated with major media categories, we are prepared to resume discussion of the primary decision areas involved in devising your total media strategy. This chapter will examine essential issues pertaining to each of the six planning steps outlined in Figure 16.1. As will be illustrated, professional advertising experts are not always in full agreement concerning the most appropriate way to handle some of the decisions involved. Where disagreements exist, our coverage will attempt to suggest factors that you will want to evaluate in formulating your own opinions and reaching your own conclusions.

## DETERMINING MEDIA CATEGORIES TO BE USED

**The Wide Variety of Media Options**

Brief appraisals of the major categories of advertising media were outlined in Chapter 15 along with descriptions of the strengths and weaknesses associated with each. Any media category can offer you a wide assortment of individual vehicles from which to choose. The approximate number of choices open to you within the United States is as follows:[1]

**FIGURE 16.1 Primary media decision steps in the advertising planning process**

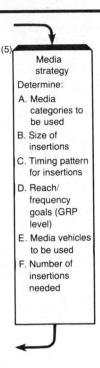

(5) Media strategy

Determine:

A. Media categories to be used

B. Size of insertions

C. Timing pattern for insertions

D. Reach/ frequency goals (GRP level)

E. Media vehicles to be used

F. Number of insertions needed

- Television stations—766
- Radio stations—7,971
- Consumer Magazines and Farm Publications—1,700
- Business Publications—3,600
- Newspapers—1,505

Add to these the variety of outdoor advertising and direct mail alternatives available and you can begin to see why the development of a media plan can become extremely intricate.

*Variables to Consider in Initiating a Media Plan*

The first issue you must resolve is whether to concentrate entirely on vehicles in one media category or to divide your budget among vehicles in two or more different media categories. This latter choice is referred to as "media mix." There are no immutable precepts to guide you in determining which of these routes to pursue or which media categories to choose. A sampling of the complex of variables which can affect your strategy has been summarized by one observer who stated, "Some of the variables influencing the solution are the availability of effective advertising copy for use in alternative media, the competition's choice of media, the size of the firm's total appropriation, the exposure of prospective customers to the media, the environment provided by the media for the advertising message, and the cost schedules of the media."[2]

*To Mix or Not to Mix?*

*Media Concentration.* A strong argument for placing all or most of your media budget into one media category runs as follows. Given your transmission capability needs (based on your creative plan) and given your target

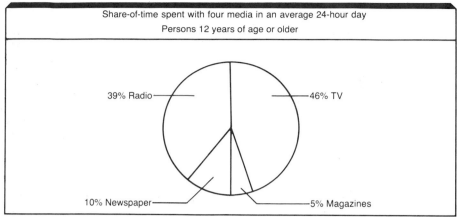

FIGURE 16.2 How consumers divide their media day among four major media

Share-of-time spent with four media in an average 24-hour day
Persons 12 years of age or older

39% Radio

46% TV

10% Newspaper

5% Magazines

Source: *Target Marketing and the Media* (New York: Radio Advertising Bureau, 1982), p. 7.

market audience, one media category will often stand out as being clearly the best. Therefore, by concentrating your dollars on vehicles in that category you maximize your effectiveness and also achieve the most intense cumulative impact for your ads. For instance, Figure 16.2 shows how consumers divide their media day among four of the major media. Assuming you are aiming at a very broad target market and that the transmission capability of television fits your creative plan, the extremely heavy usage of television by the general public might suggest it as the best and only media category you should use. Television stations often promote this view with the slogan, "Spend your advertising dollars where your customers spend their time."

*Media Mix.* A viable argument for diversifying and using a variety of media categories is premised on the belief that this route may allow you to reach a greater diversity of prospects. The idea is that, to some extent, the degree of usage of different media categories varies among audience segments. For instance, whereas the data in Figure 16.2 apply to all persons aged twelve years or older, Figure 16.3 focuses on a more specific demographic segment—adult males in professional and managerial occupations. Among this group, television viewing is still important but the time spent listening to radio is greater. Additionally, both newspapers and magazines show sizable gains. One interpretation of these data might be that if your overall media stress is on television but your total target market includes professional-managerial males as one of its important component parts, thought should be given to supplementing television with another medium.

There are other reasons to consider a division of advertising effort among several media categories. For instance, you might feel that your basic creative approach demands the use of television to generate high awareness and interest for your brand. At the same time, you may want to capitalize on that awareness and interest by stimulating trial of your product. If you decide that a coupon technique is the best way to stimulate trial, you will be unable to

**FIGURE 16.3 How one demographic segment divides its media day**

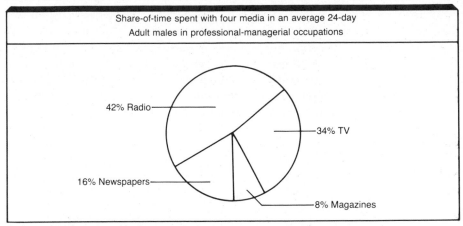

Source: *Target Marketing and the Media* (New York: Radio Advertising Bureau, 1982), p. 7.

achieve that objective through television. To achieve it, you need to include some sort of print medium in your mix—such as newspapers or magazines. In another situation, you might feel that your advertising is of a type which people will want to study and consider carefully. Consumer magazines might be your choice as the appropriate medium to serve this purpose. Simultaneously, you may wish to assure frequent exposure of your brand name to reinforce your print messages. Television and/or outdoor advertising might be the auxiliary media categories you choose to achieve this aim.

The media mix is a much-debated topic. Decisions regarding it must be reached on a case-by-case basis and must be tailored to fit your particular situation.

## DETERMINING THE SIZE OF INDIVIDUAL ADVERTISING INSERTIONS

***Size of Insertions Versus Quantity of Insertions***

In most media vehicles you have choices to make regarding the size of your advertisements. For instance, if you are buying television time you can choose among twenty-second, thirty-second, and sixty-second commercials. In consumer magazines you can buy full-page ads, half-page ads, or smaller units. The larger the size of the advertising units you purchase, the more each one will cost and the smaller the total number of units you will be able to run for the same dollar amount. In short, you are faced with a trade-off situation. The essential question becomes, "Should I opt for a larger number of smaller ads or a smaller number of larger ads?"

***The Case for Choosing Smaller Insertions.*** The bulk of the available pertinent evidence deals with the amount of attention and readership that an advertisement draws in relation to its size. There is little or no research available to tell you much about the effectiveness of different sized ads in causing people to change their attitudes about brands. Readership studies of print advertising have generally shown that increasing the size of an advertisement increases the readership, but it does not increase readership in direct proportion to insertion size. If you double the size of an advertisement, you will attain more readership but you will not attain twice as much.[3] This means that on a readers-per-dollar basis smaller ads will tend to be more effective. At least some media analysts have argued this fact is often overlooked and that larger ads are preferred for illogical reasons. Here is how one advertising executive has expressed this point of view:

> It seems that the people who control the purse-strings are infatuated with big ads. "Big Company, Big Ads!" . . . Limited ad dollar investments would invariably work much harder if split up among smaller ad units. Then there would be more insertions, there would be more coverage of markets and there would be more total readers and more readers delivered per dollar. [4]

***The Case for Choosing Larger Insertions.***   Other advertising people see things differently, as the following statement demonstrates:

> If advertisers bought on a straight cost-per-thousand noters basis, there would be no ads higher than an inch. This is one area, obviously, where we've learned that the numbers disguise the reality of communication. . . . When television commercials went from a length of 60-seconds to the much more profitable 30-seconds in the late 1960's, research was done that purported to show that the half-length unit had virtually the equivalent communication effect. (A recent study shows that immediate recall among viewers is down by 1/3.) [5]

***Creative Needs and Insertion Size***

What all of this suggests is that determining the size of insertions is both a media problem and a creative problem. Viewed strictly from the standpoint of media efficiency—readers- or viewers-per-dollar—you are likely to be better off with small advertisements. However, your creative strategy objectives will demand some minimum amount of time or space per insertion. Furthermore, copywriters and artists are likely to prefer larger or longer units because these afford them more opportunity to develop a strong and complete selling story. One sensible approach to resolving this issue is to consider creative strategy first, but to consider it critically in terms of the size of advertisements it demands. Are larger ads a genuine need or would a more imaginative approach make it possible to do an equally effective job with less time or space per insertion? As one group of writers has suggested, "In fact, 30 seconds can be *too much* time for some messages, and the shorter 10-second commercial can be more effective."[6]

# DETERMINING THE GENERAL TIMING OF INSERTIONS

***Three General Approaches to Scheduling Strategies***

Most advertising programs are planned to run over some stated time range. Among large national advertisers the most common planning range is one year. In developing your media program, you must determine the general timing schedule for your advertising over the course of the planning range; and to do this you have three broad approaches open to you. They are (1) a

**FIGURE 16.4
Approaches to the timing of advertising insertions**

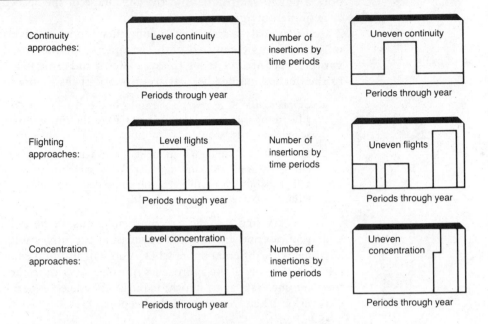

continuity approach, (2) a flighting approach, and (3) a massed, concentration approach. In a *continuity approach* advertisements are spread out over the full planning time span. This is also called a "sustaining" or "spaced-out approach." In a *flighting approach* your ads run throughout the full time span but you follow a "stop-and-go" cluster pattern. In a typical flighting pattern you might alternate between weeks or months when you run a rather heavy schedule of advertising insertions and weeks or months when you run no advertising. This is also called a "pulsed approach" or a "wave approach." In a *massed or concentration approach* you bunch all of your advertising into part of the full time span with no advertising running during the remainder of the time. As shown in Figure 16.4, variations are possible within each of these approaches.

**Choosing Among the Approaches**

How do you choose the best timing approach for your advertising program? In many cases, a seasonal sales pattern will dictate your decision. As noted in Chapter 5, sales of products such as barbecue sauce and cold remedies have well-delineated sales peaks and valleys during the year. Logically, in cases such as these, your advertising timing will be related to the seasonal buying patterns. However, in many instances, you will be dealing with a product which has reasonably steady sales throughout the year. Then which approach should you choose? In comparing the effectiveness of various timing patterns, the experts are not in agreement. After reanalyzing the data from a classic study, one writer concluded that a continuity approach is likely to be your most effective choice. He summarized his report by noting "The most important finding is that, for a given advertising budget and a given campaign time period, a campaign that spreads the exposures as widely as possible over the period produces much more sales impact (as measured in recall-weeks) than does a pulsed campaign. And the advantage of the spaced campaign is very large in percentage terms."[7]

Another analyst developed a computer model of advertising effects based on experiments conducted with consumers. He then used the model to test various types of advertising timing patterns and came to a conclusion opposite to the one just quoted. A partial summary of his report follows:

1. *Schedule ads close together.* The results of the program make it clear that single advertising exposures alone do not have the impact of the same exposure scheduled close to another exposure.

2. *Use flights.* Grouping ads in flights has a synergistic effect resulting in more effectiveness per ad than single ads. At the same time, putting too many ads in a flight is also wasteful, creating unneeded awareness when sales are low, falling, or simply not changing. [8]

The inconsistency of these recommendations is reflected in advertising practice. You can find examples of advertising executives who strongly advocate any one of the different approaches. You will also find examples of advertisers who feel that one of the approaches must be superior to the others but, because they are uncertain as to which one it is, they keep experimenting. Here is an illustration taken from a published report:

During the remainder of the fourth quarter . . . VW will be employing a pulsing technique in its network TV schedule. "For two-week periods, [the schedule] will be extremely heavy, then extremely light for the following two weeks," [according to a company executive.] "Up 'til now, we've tended to have a smooth schedule." . . . The move to pulsing, he said, came as a result of testing different TV weights in six areas of the country earlier this year. [He] was unable to say that the technique will become permanent in VW's future TV buys. "All I can say about it now is that it is something we're looking at, just as we are looking at increasing our involvement in tennis and getting into soccer." [9]

Timing is, therefore, another aspect of your advertising planning that you will have to determine without the benefit of absolute guidelines. Such factors as the size of your budget, the seasonality of your product, and your own philosophy on timing will influence your decision. However, there is no clear answer as to exactly what constitutes the best timing approach. If possible, you would be well advised to experiment with different schedules in test market areas in an attempt to ascertain whether one or another of the approaches is clearly most effective for your particular advertising situation.

# DETERMINING REACH, FREQUENCY, AND GROSS RATING POINT GOALS

To measure one facet of the power and size of a media schedule it is common to speak in terms of Gross Rating Points (GRPs). The GRP level is a highly valuable and much used measurement in national advertising. Among other things, it serves as a consistent yardstick for comparing one aspect of the

*Developing Media Strategy*

relative weights of different advertising campaign plans; its meaning is appreciated by a variety of marketing practitioners. Advertising agencies can speak to their clients in terms of GRP levels. The sales force can refer to the GRP level as a selling point when calling on resellers. Suppose, for example, that you are attempting to persuade a supermarket chain to stock and promote a new brand your company is about to introduce. If you can inform supermarket management personnel that your new brand will be supported by a weekly GRP level of 200 during its introductory period, they will understand what you mean. A level of one hundred GRPs per week is widely considered to be a fairly intense schedule. A level of 200 GRPs per week would be an extremely heavy schedule and should help produce some strong initial demand from their customers. Therefore, it should stimulate reseller interest in cooperative efforts.

But, what exactly are gross rating points?

## Defining Some Basic Terms

To explain the meaning of gross rating points we must first define its two companion terms, "reach" and "frequency." These are the basic measurements from which GRPs are calculated.

*Reach* is the *percentage of total prospects* in your target market who are exposed to advertisements for your brand one or more times during some stated time period. For example, if your market includes 20 million prospects and if, during a one month period, 16 million of those prospects have been exposed to one or more of your advertisements, your reach for that month is eighty, because your advertising reached eighty percent of your target prospects.

*Frequency* is the *average number of exposures* to advertisements for your brand that were received by those prospects who were reached during the given time period. To illustrate how frequency is figured we will continue with the example begun above. You reached 16 million prospects. Suppose that 8 million of those prospects were exposed to six of your advertisements and another 8 million were exposed to four of your advertisements. Your frequency is the average of those exposure figures. In this case, your frequency for that month is five, because the 16 million prospects you reached were exposed to your advertising an average of five times.

*Gross Rating Points* are calculated by *multiplying the reach times the frequency*. In the illustration we are using, your GRP level would be 400 for that month, because your reach of eighty times your frequency of five totals 400.

## Some Cautions About the Meaning of GRP Levels

The GRP level conveys important information concerning one ingredient contributing to the power of an advertising program. However, there are other critical ingredients it does not take into account. Two of the most vital aspects *not* considered in GRP calculations are (1) the size of the advertisements that are generating the exposures and (2) the relative creative effectiveness of each advertising exposure. Each point deserves a brief comment before we pursue the topic of GRP levels at greater length.

***Size of Individual Advertisements in the Schedule.*** As for the size of insertion, we will use television as an example. Assume you build a schedule that calls for twenty prime-time, network commercials during a one month period and delivers a GRP level of 450 for that month. Would it make any difference whether those were sixty-second commercials, thirty-second commercials, twenty-second commercials, or even ten-second commercials? The answer is that it would not make any difference in terms of your GRP level.

Of course, it would make a very substantial difference in terms of the resultant advertising budget. Furthermore, you might anticipate that it would make at least some difference in terms of the selling power of the schedule. We previously noted the suggestion that some thirty-second commercials might be more effective if they were reduced to ten seconds (see p. 520), but this suggestion refers to *some* commercials, not all of them or even most of them. In general, advertising people would be likely to feel that longer commercials would have more consumer impact than shorter commercials, assuming both categories were equally well handled. At the very least, the lengthier commercials would provide you more time to present your selling points. The same basic assumption would hold true if you were planning a magazine or newspaper schedule and considering full-page ads versus half-page ads.

*Creative Effectiveness.*  The GRP level says nothing about the creative effectiveness of the advertising. It simply summarizes data concerning the portion of prospects who have been exposed to your advertising and how often exposures have occurred. As we noted in our earlier treatment of communication principles, simple attainment of exposure does not assure attainment of attention to your advertising and falls far short of guaranteeing a favorable prospect response. One advertising schedule with a GRP level of 500 per month could be rejected by the people to whom the advertising was exposed. Another campaign with a lower GRP level could arouse intense interest and excitement about your product. The GRP levels by themselves will not reveal the difference. These limitations do not detract from the meaningfulness of gross rating points as one dimension of the strength of an advertising campaign. However, they do demonstrate that there are other dimensions you must simultaneously examine before you can form any opinion about the total potential strength of the campaign.

*A More In-depth Look at Reach, Frequency, and Gross Rating Points*

The definitions of reach, frequency, and gross rating points along with a cursory illustration of each has been given. However, to appreciate their full implications, you also require a grasp of the way in which reach, frequency, and gross rating points are developed through a particular media schedule. That calls for more complex illustrations.

*The Mechanics of Reach and Frequency.*  Suppose you are introducing a new brand of low-calorie cake mix. You define your target market as comprising all female homemakers between nineteen and forty years of age. Your research data show there are 25 million prospects in this category. You schedule twenty television commercials to run during a particular month to reach this primary market and attempt to schedule them to be shown when they will be

**TABLE 16.1 Distribution of Advertising Exposures Among Prospects in a Primary Target Market**

*An Illustration of How a Media Schedule
Might Produce 440 GRPs in a One-Month Period*

| Groups of prospects in target market based on number of times each individual has seen ads for the brand during the month | (A) Number of times that each individual in this group was exposed to your advertisements | (B) Number of individuals in this group | (A × B) Total exposures registered among all individuals in this group |
|---|---|---|---|
| Group 1 | 20 times | 1 million | 20 million |
| Group 2 | 18 times | 1 million | 18 million |
| Group 3 | 16 times | 1 million | 16 million |
| Group 4 | 14 times | 1 million | 14 million |
| Group 5 | 12 times | 1 million | 12 million |
| Group 6 | 10 times | 1 million | 10 million |
| Group 7 | 8 times | 1 million | 8 million |
| Group 8 | 6 times | 1 million | 6 million |
| Group 9 | 4 times | 1 million | 4 million |
| Group 10 | 2 times | 1 million | 2 million |
| **Net Audience** (Total number of individual prospects exposed to your advertising at least once.) | | 10 million | |
| **Total Gross Impressions** (Total number of times that the total number of prospects has been exposed to your ads.) | | | 110 million |

seen by as many of your target prospects as possible with a minimum of waste circulation. It is a virtual certainty that not every prospect will be exposed to your commercials the same number of times. Some might see all twenty, others might see some but not all. Still others will see none of them. For purposes of our illustration, assume the pattern of exposure you achieve among your 25 million target prospects is as described in Table 16.1.

The "Total Exposures," shown in the far right-hand column of the table, are simply the number of exposures per individual (A) times the number of individuals in each group (B). Notice that two new terms appear at the bottom of the table. The first is "Net Audience." The second is "Total Gross Impressions." These terms are directly related to reach and frequency in the following ways: Reach is equal to net audience divided by your total number of target market prospects. In this case the reach is 10 million divided by 25 million, which yields a reach of forty. (By inference, there were 15 million prospects, or sixty percent, who did not see a single one of your advertisements.) Frequency is equal to total gross impressions divided by net audience. In this case the frequency is 110 million divided by 10 million, which produces a frequency of eleven. The gross rating point level is forty times eleven or 440 GRPs.

***The Purpose of Analyzing Underlying Mechanics of Reach, Frequency, and GRP Levels.*** Understanding how reach, frequency, and gross rating points are achieved is important because it can guide determination of your media plan. At the outset, there are three basic facts to consider:

1. You can attain exactly the same number of gross rating points with many different combinations of reach and frequency.
2. You can attain exactly the same reach, frequency, and gross rating point level with many different distributions of gross impressions among prospects in your target market.
3. In practice, the patterns of reach/frequency combination and gross impressions distribution can have a significant impact on the effectiveness of your advertising campaign, beyond that implied by your GRP level.

*Variations in Reach and Frequency Patterns That Produce the Same GRP Level*

In the example just cited, your media schedule generated 440 GRPs in a month, with a reach of forty and a frequency of eleven. You could have secured the same level of 440 GRPs from *any* alternative combination of reach and frequency that multiplies to 440. Figure 16.5 illustrates a few such alternatives.

Assuming that you could obtain any one of these reach and frequency combinations for approximately the same amount of money, which one would you choose?

> A reach of 22 with a frequency of 20?
>
> A reach of 40 with a frequency of 11?
>
> A reach of 55 with a frequency of 8?
>
> A reach of 88 with a frequency of 5?

There is no simple answer. In fact there are sharply divergent opinions regarding the optimum handling of your reach/frequency combination.

***The Case for Emphasizing Reach.*** One respected and often-quoted advertising person has argued that the first objective to seek is maximization of reach. He has observed, "Is it better to reach a smaller audience, yet reach it more times? Or is it better to reach a bigger audience—yet reach it less often? . . . The answer, of course, is buy dispersion [maximize reach]."[10]

If forced to choose between the four alternatives shown in Figure 16.5, this practitioner would presumably have opted for the reach of eighty-eight with the frequency of five. In fact, if his words are taken literally, he would logically prefer a reach of one hundred with a frequency of 4.4, if that combination were attainable. His view is thought to be a fairly common one among many advertising professionals. "[It has been] observed that national advertisers usually seek first a maximum *unduplicated* audience per dollar invested [reach], before concerning themselves with repetition [frequency]. This suggests that advertisers and their agencies do not really believe in increasing effects of repetition." (Italics added.)[11]

FIGURE 16.5 Four different reach/frequency patterns that produce the same GRP level

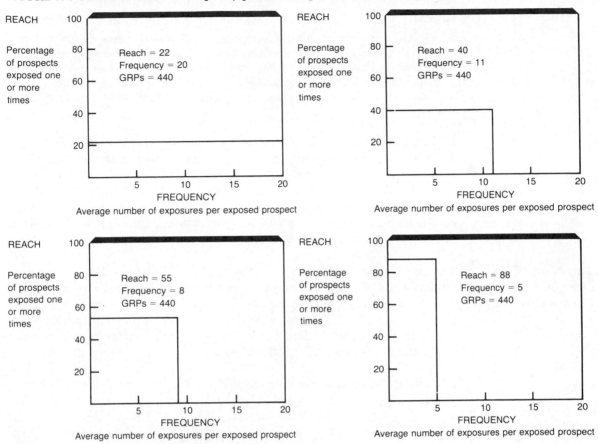

The Case for Emphasizing Frequency.   The opposite point of view is voiced by other professionals and is supported by at least some field research. For example, one researcher has reported, "In a study on the effects of repetitive advertising in newspapers, [it was found] that substantial repetition was required to achieve efficient purchase results. . . . The lowest advertising costs per 'extra' purchaser did not appear until the 15th consecutive advertisement had appeared. A short campaign of only 4 repeat insertions was quite inefficient."[12]

This second opinion holds that you will probably need at least a minimum amount of frequency to induce a response from your prospects. Recall that one of the advantages of advertising as a promotional element is its power of repetition. Advertising allows you to remind your prospect of your message over and over again more effectively and less expensively than any other type of explicit promotion. With this in mind, and assuming that you are convinced of the importance of repetition, you will start by selecting some minimum frequency level and then build your GRP package with that frequency level in mind. Reach will be treated only as a secondary goal. For instance, if you were selecting from among the four choices on p. 526, your reasoning might be as follows:

My advertisements are not going to have much impact unless my prospects receive repeated exposures to them. An average of about eleven exposures during the month should be adequate. My budget precludes the purchase of anything more than 440 GRPs in the media vehicles I want to use. Therefore, I am going to build a media schedule which generates a reach of forty and a frequency of eleven.

*Choosing Between the Two Points of View.*   As you can see, the experts differ once again. Therefore, on this as on many other issues in advertising, you must exercise your own judgment. There is no one and absolutely unchallenged solution. However, there are some further considerations that can assist you in forming guidelines for your own decision making. Before presenting them, we need to consider different distributions of gross impressions that can produce the same reach, frequency, and GRP levels.

## Variations in Distributions of Gross Impressions

Not only is it possible to derive exactly the same GRP level through different combinations of reach and frequency patterns, but, as noted earlier it is also possible to generate exactly the same reach and frequency patterns—and therefore the same GRP levels—through different gross impression distributions. Furthermore, the distribution of gross impressions can also make a substantive difference in your advertising effectiveness.

*A Basic Example Using a Level Distribution.*   Returning to the data presented in Table 16.1, you will recall that target prospects who saw your advertising were arranged in ten different groupings. The group into which an individual fell was determined by the number of your ads she had seen during the month. There were an equal number of people—one million—in each group. Because there were 25 million people in your total target market, each group accounted for four percent of the people in your total target market. The one million prospects in Group 1 had seen all twenty of your ads during the month; the one million in Group 2 had seen eighteen, and so on down the line until the last group of people had seen only two of the ads.

This distribution of gross impressions is shown graphically in Figure 16.6. Like Table 16.1, this diagram can be examined to reveal a reach of forty and a frequency of eleven for a GRP level of 440. It displays ten groups with four percent of your target market in each. Ten groups times four percent each equals forty and that is your reach. It also displays an equal number of people receiving twenty exposures, eighteen exposures, sixteen exposures, and so on. By summing the exposure levels along the bottom and then dividing by ten (the number of groups) you will once more arrive at eleven as your frequency, or average number of exposures per prospect exposed. In actuality a distribution pattern as level as this would be highly improbable. Our reason for introducing such an unlikely and noncomplex distribution is merely to provide a backdrop against which more uneven distributions can be evaluated.

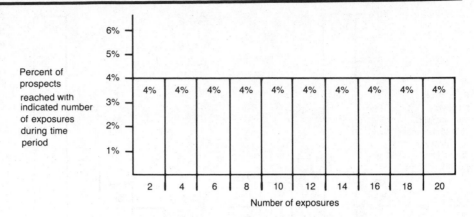

**FIGURE 16.6 One possible distribution of gross impressions producing a reach of 40, a frequency of 11 and a GRP level of 440**

*Alternative Distributions Producing Identical Reach, Frequency, and GRP Levels.* Figure 16.7 pictures two of the many other distributions of gross impressions that would also deliver a reach of forty with a frequency of eleven and a consequent GRP level of 440. At the top of the figure you see a concave distribution in which most prospects reached are exposed at either the high-end or the low-end of the exposure range with relatively few prospects exposed at the mid-points of ten or twelve times. The lower portion of the figure exhibits the opposite, center-peaked possibility with half the prospects reached exposed at the mid-points of ten or twelve and rather few exposed either very lightly or very heavily.

*Choosing the Most Efficient Distribution of Gross Impressions*

Suppose your media strategy calls for a GRP level of 440 with a reach of forty and a frequency of eleven, and suppose that you can control the distribution of gross impressions by manipulating your media scheduling to obtain any one of the three distribution patterns just displayed. What general rule should you follow to direct your choice? In this case, there is wide agreement among advertising experts. The basic recommendation has been stated in these words: "A good general rule is that the preferred plan is one that tends to concentrate message deliveries at the middle of the frequency range rather than at the extremes."[13]

The reasoning on which this recommendation is based has been expressed by one expert as follows, "Good advertising gets attention, and its message lasts long enough through a few exposures to make one or two points. Optimally, these exposures should reach the target audience with an effective balance of a few exposures to most persons in the audience, rather than one exposure to many and many exposures to a few."[14]

On the basis of this rule, the center-peaked pattern would be the preferred choice among the three examined. In reviewing the three options, we find that in the level-distribution pattern, thirty percent of the prospects reached were exposed six times or less. That may be too few exposures to make an impression sufficiently potent to raise their preference levels for your brand. On the other hand, another thirty percent of the prospects who saw your ads were

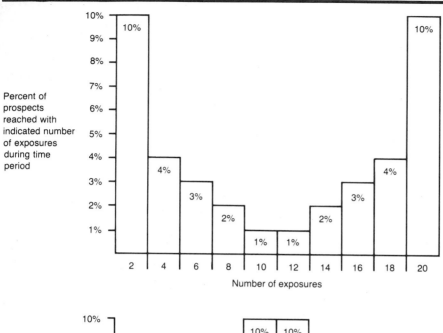

FIGURE 16.7 Varia-
tions in distributions
of gross impressions
that produce the same
reach, frequency, and
GRP level

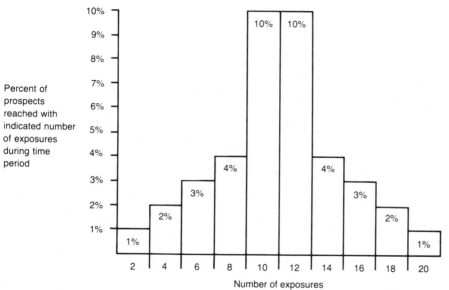

exposed sixteen times or more. That may be far more exposures than necessary to accomplish the task. In consequence, with the level-distribution pattern
you may be either underexposing or overexposing the majority of the prospects who were reached. The second, concave distribution pattern concentrated even more of the exposures at the extremes and thus could produce even
greater degrees of underexposure or overexposure.

Admittedly, both of the above judgments rest on the premise that there is some optimum exposure level or range and that straying too far from that optimum results in either underexposure or overexposure. In this instance we are assuming that you would attain maximum effectiveness at, or very close to, ten or twelve exposures per prospect reached during the month. The immediate rationale underlying this assumption is based on the fact that your target frequency was initially set at eleven. In setting a frequency goal you are implying that the most effective number of exposures per prospect will be at, or very close to, that average frequency figure. In the present illustration, when you first decided you wanted a frequency of eleven, you also implied that exposing a prospect to your advertising approximately eleven times during the month would be most productive in terms of your advertising objectives. Although none of our three hypothetical examples delivered exactly eleven exposures to any group of prospects, the center-peaked distribution clearly approximated that goal most closely with half of the prospects reached receiving either ten or twelve exposures.

Of course, stating that there is some theoretically optimum exposure level raises another problem. How do you decide on an ideal frequency? To deal with this question, we will begin by reviewing a relevant and underlying concept that has been designated as the "three-hit" theory.

*The "Three-Hit" Theory*

Based on analysis of both previous research plus studies of his own, one advertising expert has set forth a proposition that has come to be known as the "three-hit" theory.[15] This proposition states that to successfully influence any given prospect with any given advertisement you must reach that prospect with at least three *effective* exposures. According to this view, a person's first effective exposure to the advertisement generates initial attention and arouses curiosity, but it is not sufficient to build any meaningful level of brand preference or purchase intentions. The second exposure begins to arouse the consumer's interest in your brand, assuming that the message deals with evaluative criteria and/or lifestyle goals of importance to the prospect. It is at this juncture that the receiver really becomes actively involved in decoding and interpreting your communication. The third exposure reminds the prospect of what he or she has previously learned about the brand. At this point, your prospect makes a tentative decision either to consider trying your brand or to forget it for the time being.

It should be emphasized that most of what has been written about the three-hit theory seems to be speaking in terms of advertising for national brands. Much local retail advertising, for instance a newspaper ad by your local supermarket, is built on the premise that one hit will achieve some fairly quick consumer response. It should also be pointed out that acceptance of the three-hit theory is far from unanimous among advertising practitioners. It is certainly not the only available guide for determining an optimum frequency goal.[16] However, because it has been received with a sizable amount of interest, we shall use it as a basis for discussing procedures for working toward an efficient distribution of gross impressions. At the end of that discussion, suggestions will be offered for applying the same general procedures in situations in which you may wish to work from some basis other than the three-hit theory.

**Translating Total Exposures into Effective Exposures**

Does the "three-hit" theory mean that in building your media schedule you should aim at a frequency of three? No! That oversimplification is not applicable because the proposition is based on the measure of effective exposures rather than total exposures. As a practical matter, to attain three effective exposures you will probably need more than three total exposures because most advertising exposures are not "effective." The theory's originator has commented on this point as follows:

> Most people filter or screen out TV commercials, for example, by stopping at the "What is it?" response. Then these same people, suddenly in the market months later for the product in question, may see and experience the twenty-third exposure to the commercial as if it were the second—that is, the twenty-third exposure will be only the second time it really commands their attention. [17]

This seems to return us to our starting point in terms of trying to ascertain an optimum frequency level. If you accept the three-hit theory you want three effective exposures, but the standard frequency measure is expressed in terms of total exposures, not effective exposures.

**The Proposal of an Effective Rating Points Approach.** One management consultant has proposed that a logical starting point for building schedules that maximize effective exposures might be founded on the frame of logic pictured in Figure 16.8. As the top diagram suggests, if three exposures represent the absolute minimum threshold of effectiveness, any exposure level below that number should be discounted in calculating the power of an advertising schedule. Furthermore, if one posits a hypothetical upper boundary of effectiveness existing at the level of ten exposures, all exposures above that level should also be discounted. On this basis, he advocates a new measure—Effective Rating Points (ERPs)—as more meaningful than GRPs. ERPs would be determined by deducting all ineffective exposures from total gross impressions. In essence, his ERP measure would substitute effective exposures for total exposures as a basic component measurement. As shown in this example, this would reduce the estimate of power for schedules with an imbalance of exposures at the extremes and lead to a target schedule centered around a modal point of six to seven exposures.

**A Proposed Format for Translating Effective Exposures Desired into Total Exposures Required.** A media professional has come up with an interesting alternative for handling the same task. Although we cannot go into full detail concerning his approach, we will explore his general concept and consider one example of the type of answer it can produce.

He begins with two assumptions. The first is that the proper time period to envision when considering effective exposures is the repurchase cycle. For

**FIGURE 16.8 An effective exposures measurement approach**

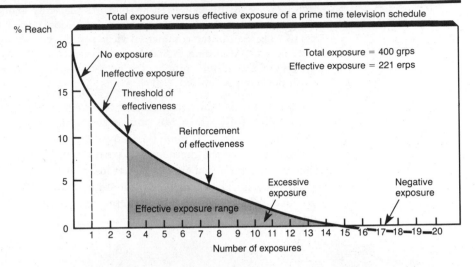

Total exposure versus effective exposure of a prime time television schedule

% Reach

Total exposure = 400 grps
Effective exposure = 221 erps

No exposure
Ineffective exposure
Threshold of effectiveness
Reinforcement of effectiveness
Excessive exposure
Negative exposure
Effective exposure range

Number of exposures

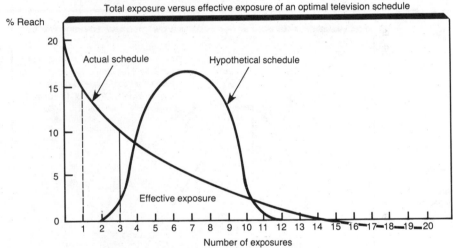

Total exposure versus effective exposure of an optimal television schedule

% Reach

Actual schedule
Hypothetical schedule
Effective exposure

Number of exposures

*Source:* Alvin A. Achenbaum (Canter/Achenbaum/Heekin Associates–New York) as cited in B. G. Yovovich, "Media's New Exposures," *Advertising Age,* 13 April 1981, pp. 5–8.

example, if yours is a product which the typical consumer buys about once each month, you would want to think of effective exposures within a four-week period. If, on the other hand, yours is a product which the typical consumer buys about once every two months, then you should plan in terms of effective exposures over an eight-week period.

The second assumption is that you have access to data through which you can estimate the percentage of your total advertising exposures per prospect that are or are not making an effective impact on your audience. From this percentage you can derive the frequency needed to produce three effective exposures during your appropriate time period. For instance, he has pointed out that:

We know from Burke related recall scores that only about 70 percent of the program audience is available to view the [television] commercial and only about 20 to 25 percent of the commercial viewers can recall anything about the commercial. . . . According to Starch measurements, on an average only about 25 percent of a magazine's primary readers can associate a black-and-white page ad with the brand advertised. [18]

In other words, though audience members vary in their susceptibility to being meaningfully affected by any single exposure to an advertising message, the overall percentage is low. Based on such audience survey data, this author offers examples of the mathematics with which you can calculate the average frequency at which you should aim at in order to maximize the three effective exposure levels called for by the three-hit theory. Illustrative results for one particular advertising situation are depicted in Figure 16.9. In this instance, it is estimated that an average of only nine percent of prospects exposed to an

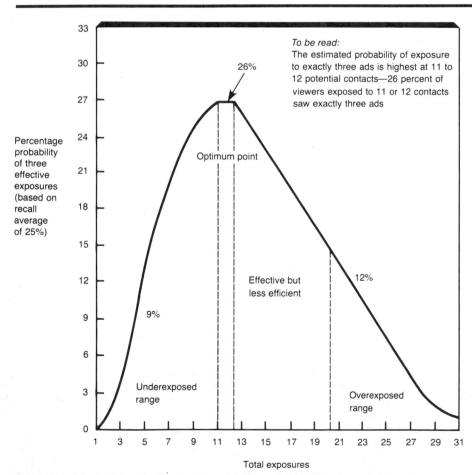

**FIGURE 16.9** Estimated probability of actual or effective exposure to exactly three ads at potential frequency levels

*Source:* Howard Kamin, "Advertising Reach and Frequency," *Journal of Advertising Research,* February 1978, p. 24.

advertisement a total of ten times or less will be *effectively* exposed *exactly* three times. Most of the remainder of this group will be underexposed. Similarly, only twelve percent of those exposed a total of twenty times or more will be *effectively* exposed *exactly* three times. Most of the remainder of this latter group will be overexposed. However, twenty-six percent of the prospects exposed eleven to twelve times will be effectively exposed exactly three times. The conclusion in this specific case is to aim at a frequency of eleven to twelve exposures during the period. This is not intended to suggest that such a frequency is right in each and every situation but merely to demonstrate a procedure through which you can utilize readership, viewership, and listenership data to estimate the average frequency level needed to maximize a previously determined number of effective exposures.

*A Recap—And Some Alternatives*

The purpose in surveying the three-hit theory is to help you think through your own media scheduling decisions; it is not claimed that this approach should be accepted as an undisputed fact. Remember that the experts still disagree on what your goal should be in terms of reach and frequency. Therefore, if you do decide to work with the three-hit theory, there are at least three different ways in which you can employ it. (1) You may choose to use it as is and in its entirety. (2) You may choose to use it—or something akin to it—with modifications to suit your own needs or information. (3) You may choose to use it merely as a basis of comparison to help you develop alternative ways of planning reach and frequency targets. We will look at the role the three-hit theory might play in each of these usage modes.

**Using the Three-Hit Theory "As-Is."**   If you decide to use an unamended version, your logical route of application would trace a sequence of six major steps. First, you would determine the usual repurchase cycle for your product (e.g., two weeks, four weeks, eight weeks, one year). This time period would serve as the temporal basis for all of your strategic planning of reach, frequency, and GRP goals. Second, you would aim at achieving three *effective* exposures among as many of the prospects you reach as possible within the previously specified time period. Third, through research or judgment you would attempt to determine how many *total* exposures are needed to deliver three effective exposures to the largest single share of prospects. In the fourth step, you would set that total exposure level as your desired frequency. At step five, you would determine the reach you want or can afford given the frequency level set in step four. Finally, with your reach and frequency goals in mind, you would build a media schedule that delivers frequency in a "bunched up" fashion through a center-peaked distribution similar to that shown in the lower portion of Figure 16.7, and with your chosen frequency level at or near the mid-point.

**Using the Theory with Modifications.**   If you decide to modify the three-hit theory, you can make a variety of alterations to suit your situational needs or strategic philosophy. One possible modification to consider is raising the number of effective exposures that you seek—for example going to five or six.

You might consider doing this if you feel your product is one with very low consumer involvement, for instance, hot chocolate mix or motor oil. You might also want to do this if you think that the "distinctively different" benefits of your brand are not very strong or exciting, and therefore they will require more exposures to gain attention.

An opposite potential variation is to lower the number of effective exposures you want in the time period to two or even one. You might consider doing this if you think your product has very high consumer involvement or if your brand has very distinctive benefits. For example, suppose that you were advertising an automobile that delivered one hundred miles to a gallon of gas. Perhaps one effective exposure per relevant period would be adequate.

Still another revised version that is possible is to choose something other than the average repurchase cycle as the time period with which you want to work. This could be advisable if your product is infrequently purchased and is one that consumers tend to study and evaluate over an extended time span before reaching a buying decision. If this were the case, you might wish to consider time in the context of a decision cycle rather than a repurchase cycle.

***Using the Theory Merely as a Basis of Comparison.*** As noted earlier, the three-hit theory represents only one view regarding optimization of frequency. You may decide to work from some other perspective and utilize the concept merely as a basis of comparison. For instance, you may choose to aim at maximizing reach first with frequency treated only as a secondary consideration. Even in this event, the three-hit theory or some alternative to it might still help you decide how much frequency you want after you have achieved your first goal of maximizing reach.

## DETERMINING SPECIFIC VEHICLES TO BE USED AND NUMBER OF INSERTIONS NEEDED

You have selected the media categories most compatible with your promotional objectives, creative needs, and audience definition. You have determined the sizes of insertions needed to accomplish your communication requirements and have chosen an appropriate timing pattern. Your planning concerning reach, frequency, and gross rating point goals has been completed. It is at this point that the actual media buying strategy must be finalized. This requires the detailed specification of the media vehicles to be used and the number of space or time units to be scheduled in each vehicle. We will consider these two steps together because, at least in large-scale and sophisticated media buying programs, they are somewhat interwoven.

*General Guidelines* The prime considerations influencing selection of specific vehicles were outlined in our discussion of media appraisal criteria. Essentially, you are seeking vehicles that will deliver messages to your target prospects on the most cost-efficient basis while at the same time conveying a general reception atmosphere, reputation, and image that reinforce the strategic objectives of your messages. The prime considerations affecting the number of insertions to be used stem from the reach, frequency, and GRP levels previously set along with the frequency distribution of gross impressions that you desire. Viewed in relation to the specific vehicles to be used, these virtually demand some *minimum* number of insertions. Since each insertion purchased increases the total advertising expenditure required, there is always a budgetary constraint that places a ceiling on the *maximum* number of insertions feasible.

# DETERMINING VEHICLES AND INSERTION QUANTITY IN NONCOMPLEX ADVERTISING PROGRAMS

In relatively small and simple media schedules, your approach to accomplishing these steps can be fairly straightforward and uncomplicated. For instance, if you are constructing a media schedule for a local retail advertiser you most probably will not concern yourself with a formal gross rating point analysis. Instead, you may rely almost entirely on qualitative and cost-per-thousand-prospects comparisons between media vehicles. Much the same thing might be true if you are working with a small-scale national advertising campaign.

*Audience Duplication in Large-Scale Advertising Programs*

When you encounter national campaigns in the multimillion dollar category, however, your decisions about media vehicles and insertion levels become more complex. In a qualitative sense, you can still evaluate media vehicles independently of each other. However, when you are making quantitative evaluations concerning the efficiency of vehicles in terms of prospects exposed per advertising dollar expended, the individual-vehicle CPM figures described in the preceding chapter serve mainly as initial screening devices for making intervehicle comparisons. In the more advanced phase of your scheduling process, you will need to compare combinations of vehicles in terms of audience delivery patterns and relative cost effectiveness.

The issue that underlies the need for group comparisons of media vehicles is the existence of audience duplication between those vehicles. You may recall that the summaries of media audience data available from syndicated research services included an entry line labeled "Audience Duplication Data" (see Tables 15.1, 15.2, 15.3, and 15.4). Audience duplication refers to the fact that many of the same prospects who read, view, or listen to any given vehicle in your schedule may also read, view, or listen to one or more of the other vehicles in that same schedule. To the extent that the vehicles carrying your advertising duplicate each other, you will experience an increase in frequency with a decrease in reach. To the extent that they deliver unduplicated audiences, you will experience an increase in reach with a decrease in frequency. Hence, the survey data collected by these and similar services provide a basis for improved estimates of reach and frequency delivered by any stated assortment of vehicles, taking the presence of audience duplication into account.

***The Mechanics of Audience Duplication.*** To illustrate the manner in which audience duplication can be examined, we shall work with a hypothetical example. Suppose you are comparing three national consumer magazines—*Women's Digest, Career Woman,* and *Distaff.* You are considering running ads in two of these vehicles and wish to determine which pair to select. On a qualitative basis, you rate them as equal. On a prospect and CPM basis, they compare as follows:

| | Cost Per Four-Color Page | Total Readers | Percent of Readers in Your Target Market | Total Prospects in Audience | CPM Prospects |
|---|---|---|---|---|---|
| Women's Digest | $10,000 | 1,800,000 | 50% | 900,000 | $11.11 |
| Career Woman | $10,000 | 1,500,000 | 60% | 900,000 | $11.11 |
| Distaff | $10,000 | 1,000,000 | 90% | 900,000 | $11.11 |

If your analysis ended at this stage you could choose any two of these vehicles on the basis of whim or random chance. However, your analysis would fail to take the resulting patterns of reach and frequency into account. To evaluate individual vehicles in a schedule using several different vehicles, you must also look at the audience duplication among them. Suppose that study of such duplication revealed the situation illustrated in Figure 16.10.

In terms of net audience and gross impression patterns, your three possible magazine combinations would produce the following results:

| Magazine Combination | Prospects Exposed Once | Prospects Exposed Twice | Net Audience (Prospects) | Gross Impressions |
|---|---|---|---|---|
| Women's Digest/Career Woman | 200,000 | 800,000 | 1,000,000 | 1,800,000 |
| Women's Digest/Distaff | 800,000 | 500,000 | 1,300,000 | 1,800,000 |
| Distaff/Career Woman | 600,000 | 600,000 | 1,200,000 | 1,800,000 |

If there are 2.5 million individuals in your target market, your reach, frequency, and GRP levels would be as follows:

| Magazine Combination | Reach | Frequency | GRPs |
|---|---|---|---|
| Women's Digest/Distaff | 52 | 1.385 | 72 |
| Distaff/Career Woman | 48 | 1.5 | 72 |
| Women's Digest/Career Woman | 40 | 1.8 | 72 |

As noted above, the more duplication between combination vehicle audiences, the higher your frequency but the smaller your reach. The less duplication between combination vehicle audiences, the lower your frequency but the larger your reach. The magazine combination that would represent your most appropriate choice in this illustration would depend on an assessment of your advertising needs. If you determine you need at least two exposures to convince most prospects to consider your brand, you should pick the *Women's Digest/Career Woman* combination. It delivers only 1 million total prospects. However, 800,000 of those prospects will be exposed twice, which is far more double exposures than either of the other combinations produces. If you decide that one exposure per prospect would be adequate, you should schedule the *Women's Digest/Distaff* combination. It delivers your message to 1.3

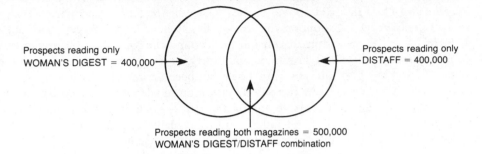

Prospects reading only
WOMAN'S DIGEST = 400,000

Prospects reading only
DISTAFF = 400,000

Prospects reading both magazines = 500,000
WOMAN'S DIGEST/DISTAFF combination

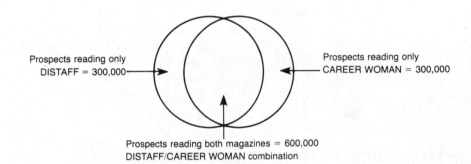

Prospects reading only
DISTAFF = 300,000

Prospects reading only
CAREER WOMAN = 300,000

Prospects reading both magazines = 600,000
DISTAFF/CAREER WOMAN combination

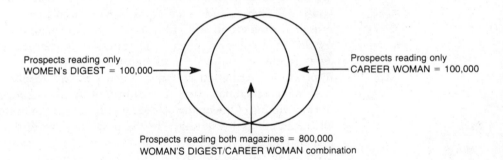

Prospects reading only
WOMEN's DIGEST = 100,000

Prospects reading only
CAREER WOMAN = 100,000

Prospects reading both magazines = 800,000
WOMAN'S DIGEST/CAREER WOMAN combination

million different prospects. This gives you better reach than either of the other combinations, although it does so with a lower frequency as only 500,000 prospects will be exposed more than once. The *Distaff/Career Woman* combination is a compromise that fails to maximize either reach or frequency.

This example illustrates why media vehicles bought in combination must be analyzed in combination to assess their audience duplication effect. In this case, assuming you began with a preference regarding optimum reach and frequency but relied only on a separate vehicle-by-vehicle breakdown, and left the ultimate selection to whim or chance, the odds are two to one *against* your arriving at the vehicle combination that would best fit your advertising objective.

**Audience Duplication Data in More Extensive Vehicle Combinations**

If you are considering only two insertions and three potential vehicles, as we did above, analysis of audience duplication poses few problems. However, suppose you are dealing with a high-budget, national campaign aimed at ultimate consumers. You may be considering fifteen or twenty or more potential insertions and thirty or forty or more potential media vehicles. Your analysis in this case can become intensely complex.

At the outset, you require adequate data on listenership, viewership, and readership of media vehicles—including figures on audience duplication. Such data are rather readily available for most of the large-audience vehicles in television, radio, consumer magazines, newspapers, and farm publications. It may not always be perfect, but the majority of media experts agree that it is sufficiently accurate to be useful and usable. A variety of such information may be purchased from commercial research firms including A.C. Nielsen, Arbitron, Simmons Market Research Bureau, and others.

In addition to the data, you must have a method of analyzing it to reveal the reach, frequency, and duplication patterns that would result from the many possible combinations of media vehicles. Because of the mathematical enormity of the analytical task, sophisticated media planning is likely to require computer assistance at this point.

## THE USE OF COMPUTERS IN MEDIA PLANNING

We have considered a diversity of data types that a media strategist must confront. They include such items as base circulation figures, coverage data, ratings for television and radio shows, various breakdowns of audience sizes by demographic groupings, space rates, time charges, audience duplication data, frequency figures, reach figures, gross rating point levels, and gross impression distribution patterns. When you seek to plan, compare, and analyze media schedules, the potential mix of number combinations can become overwhelming. One media planner has described the difficulty of coping with all the numbers by stating, "In the past we have worked at it with stubby pencils and people, many people. However, no matter how much time and how many people, we have had too many factors to contend with."[19]

Given a situation such as this, it is not hard to appreciate why media strategists have turned for assistance from a machine which is unsurpassed at processing large batches of numbers with speed and accuracy. Of course, the machine with this capability is the computer. The introduction of the computer has brought about the development of a variety of mathematically based media planning programs. For our purposes, it will be helpful to classify these as falling into the two general categories of: (1) optimization programs and (2) simulation programs.

**Optimization Programs**

An optimization program is one in which the computer compares stated media schedule objectives against stated vehicle costs and audience characteristics and outputs a recommended "optimum" media schedule to achieve the objectives. Figure 16.11 shows a very general overview of how an optimization program

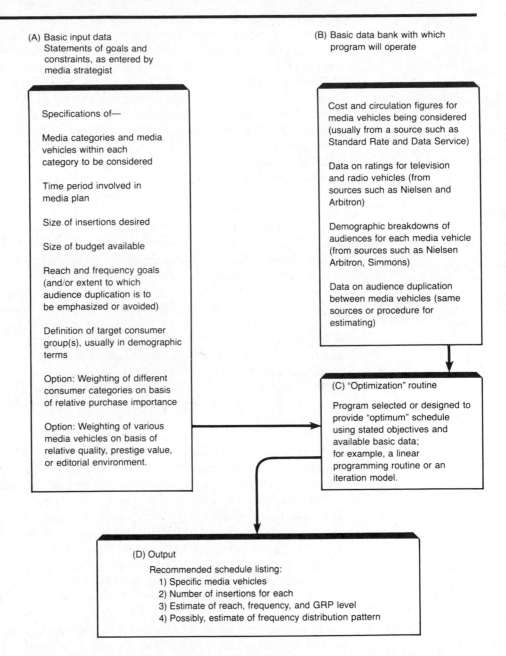

**FIGURE 16.11 A general overview of media optimization programs**

(A) Basic input data
Statements of goals and constraints, as entered by media strategist

Specifications of—

Media categories and media vehicles within each category to be considered

Time period involved in media plan

Size of insertions desired

Size of budget available

Reach and frequency goals (and/or extent to which audience duplication is to be emphasized or avoided)

Definition of target consumer group(s), usually in demographic terms

Option: Weighting of different consumer categories on basis of relative purchase importance

Option: Weighting of various media vehicles on basis of relative quality, prestige value, or editorial environment.

(B) Basic data bank with which program will operate

Cost and circulation figures for media vehicles being considered (usually from a source such as Standard Rate and Data Service)

Data on ratings for television and radio vehicles (from sources such as Nielsen and Arbitron)

Demographic breakdowns of audiences for each media vehicle (from sources such as Nielsen Arbitron, Simmons)

Data on audience duplication between media vehicles (same sources or procedure for estimating)

(C) "Optimization" routine

Program selected or designed to provide "optimum" schedule using stated objectives and available basic data; for example, a linear programming routine or an iteration model.

(D) Output

Recommended schedule listing:
1) Specific media vehicles
2) Number of insertions for each
3) Estimate of reach, frequency, and GRP level
4) Possibly, estimate of frequency distribution pattern

might operate. It does not represent any particular program. It merely outlines the overall nature of steps and data requirements involved in such a program. Notice that there are four essential segments: (1) basic input data, (2) a data bank of information concerning media vehicles, (3) an optimization routine, and (4) the output. Through the *basic input data,* the media planner specifies the aims of the schedule relative to audience coverage. These inputs impose certain

*The Use of Computers in Media Planning*

limits on the schedule in terms of such dimensions as media vehicles to be considered, insertion sizes, and maximum amount of budget available. The *data bank of information about media vehicles* includes a variety of details concerning such things as circulation, audience analyses, time and space costs, ratings, and so forth. The *optimization routine* centers around a mathematical format or program by which the computer is given the set of rules it must follow to process the data and arrive at a solution. The *output* is the recommended media schedule that presumably tells you the best way to divide your budget dollars among the various media vehicles in order to achieve maximum effectiveness under the constraints you have previously stated.

Although all parts of such a model are important, the choice of a proper optimization routine is both especially critical and controversial.

### The Background of Optimization Model Development.

Some of the earliest attempts at applying computer technology to media scheduling involved optimization programs and some of the earliest proponents of such programs may have exaggerated claims concerning program capabilities. To the extent that excessive enthusiasm encouraged the view that the computer could replace human judgment and produce unquestionably perfect schedules, it soon led to disappointment.[20] In some cases, critical examination of the models resulted in severe challenges to the basic tenets on which they had been constructed. For instance, a number of programs utilized a linear programming technique. Assessment of this category of optimization routines led one pair of observers to the decision that "[linear] models are crude devices to attempt to apply to the media selection problem. The linearity assumption itself is the source of much difficulty."[21]

### Current Uses of Optimization Programs in Practical Applications.

Although optimization programs will always be characterized by some degree of limitation owing to their necessarily mechanistic nature, many media planners find substantial value in using such routines for assistance in buying space and time. The newer and more advanced optimization models overcome many of the objections raised concerning their predecessors. For example, Figure 16.12 presents a brief summary and partial illustration of an advanced iteration model called "Benchmark." This is one of an assortment of programs offered by Telmar Group Inc., a leading supplier of media planning and analysis systems to the advertising industry. Notice that among other features this program allows injection of a weighting factor to recognize differences in qualitative values among vehicles under consideration, as those differences are judged by the media analysts. The weights used in this case appear in the "Impact" column of section A.

As shown in section B, the program output begins with preselection rankings of the individual vehicles under consideration based on cost-per-thousand target prospects. In this illustration, target prospects are defined as men from twenty-five to forty-nine years of age and living in the Pacific region. The applicable cost figures are printed in the column headed "CPM Delivery." These preselection rankings are followed by a presentation of the order in

FIGURE 16.12 A partial illustration of the Benchmark optimization program

Planning Process:  Plan Development and Analysis
Function:  Reach and Frequency via Optimization Models
Telmar System:  Benchmark
BENCHMARK:  Used to determine the optimal magazine schedule against a single target audience or a weighted target audience. This program accommodates reach/frequency goals, target weights, media weights and maximum/minimum insertion levels.

EXAMPLE:  We have looked at three alternative desirable schedules for Fogged-in Airways. As a new airline, Fogged-in Airways' strategy last year was to maximize reach. For a basic comparative analysis of last year's strategy versus this year's 5+ effective reach strategy, we will let Benchmark optimize on maximum reach. Last year Fogged-in Airways had $350,000 to spend on magazines. They considered the following magazines with a few special requirements:

| Mag | Minimums/Maximums | Impact |
|---|---|---|
| Business Week (BW) | * Minimum 3×, Maximum 6× | .85 |
| Newsweek (NSW) | | .90 |
| Time (TI) | | .90 |
| Fortune (FOR) | | .80 |
| Wall Street Journal (WSJ) | Maximum 7× | .65 |
| TV Guide (TVG) | | .50 |
| New Yorker (NY) | | .75 |
| Forbes (FRB) | | .80 |
| Reader's Digest (RD) | * Minimum 2× | .70 |
| Sports Illustrated (SI) | | .65 |
| People (PEO) | | .65 |
| National Geographic (NG) | | 1.0 |

For each magazine, page rates were based on a four-color page (Wall Street Journal was based on $43,000/page). Which magazines should have been bought, and how many insertions in each to optimize reach?

* Minimum insertions that must be purchased if magazine is bought at all.

*Source: User's Guide to Telmar Media Analysis and Planning Systems* (New York: Telmar Group, Inc., 1982). Copyright 1982 by Telmar Group, Inc.; used by special permission of copyright holders.

*Section A:* Statement of Basic Objectives and Constraints

which Benchmark "bought" space in the individual vehicles to fulfill the designated reach and frequency goals. As used here, the program was instructed to buy a schedule that would maximize reach. In section C, you find a print-out of the full schedule selected by the program and then data detailing anticipated results of this schedule in terms of such factors as reach (86.62), frequency (3.74), and GRP level (323).

It should be emphasized that an optimization program such as this is best employed as a supplement to rather than as a replacement for human judgment. There are many aspects of media decision making that the program makes no attempt to handle. It presumes the media planner has settled prior questions concerning media categories to be used, size of insertions most appropriate, general timing patterns for the insertions, and correct reach and frequency patterns. It then searches among a group of individual vehicles that have also been chosen by the strategist to find a purchase pattern that best fulfills prespecified exposure goals. In short, the program introduces neither

**Figure 16.12 (continued)**

TELMAR BENCHMARK SYSTEM II 9-NOV-81 14:51

VERS. 2.2

MEN AGE 25–49 IN THE PACIFIC REGION

*MEDIA OBJECTIVES*

REQUIRED BUDGET: $350,000

OPTIMIZATION
BASED ON: REACH

MEDIA WITH
MINIMUMS: 2

*PRE-SELECTION RANKING*

(Showing individual ranking based on cost efficiencies.)

| *Rank* | *Use* | *Media* | *Audience* | *CPM* | *Delivery* | *CPM Delivery* |
|---|---|---|---|---|---|---|
| 1 | 1 | PEO | 858 | 11.12 | 557 | 17.10 |
| 2 | 1 | NSW | 933 | 16.39 | 839 | 18.21 |
| 3 | 1 | NG | 1406 | 18.27 | 1406 | 18.27 |
| 4 | 1 | TVG | 2070 | 10.82 | 1035 | 21.64 |
| 5 | 1 | TI | 1140 | 23.46 | 1026 | 26.06 |
| 6 | 1 | SI | 861 | 29.60 | 559 | 45.53 |
| 7 | 2 | RD | 2600 | 28.16 | 1165 | 62.79 |
| 8 | 1 | WSJ | 339 | 54.72 | 220 | 84.08 |
| 9 | 1 | FOR | 119 | 75.21 | 95 | 93.93 |
| 10 | 3 | BW | 462 | 58.60 | 249 | 108.72 |
| 11 | 1 | FRB | 57 | 153.51 | 45 | 191.32 |
| 12 | 1 | NY | 48 | 163.54 | 36 | 216.99 |

*SELECTION PROCESS VIA MEDIAC MODEL*

This shows the order in which Benchmark bought.

| | CUME | | | |
|---|---|---|---|---|
| *Media* | *Cost* | *% Reach* | *Avg. Freq.* | *GRP* |
| 1 PEO | 9540 | 14.41 | 1.00 | 14 |
| 1 NG | 35230 | 33.52 | 1.13 | 38 |
| 1 NSW | 50525 | 41.67 | 1.29 | 53 |
| 1 TVG | 72925 | 60.13 | 1.47 | 88 |
| 1 TI | 99675 | 64.81 | 1.66 | 107 |
| 1 NG | 125365 | 68.36 | 1.92 | 131 |
| 1 TVG | 147765 | 74.45 | 2.23 | 165 |
| 1 TI | 174515 | 76.47 | 2.42 | 185 |
| 1 TVG | 196915 | 79.15 | 2.78 | 219 |
| 1 NG | 222605 | 80.72 | 3.02 | 243 |
| 1 NSW | 237900 | 81.61 | 3.18 | 259 |
| 2 RD | 311108 | 85.47 | 3.54 | 302 |
| 1 TI | 337858 | 86.33 | 3.73 | 321 |
| 1 FOR | 346808 | 86.62 | 3.74 | 323 |

*** Budget goal reached

*Section B:* Media Schedule Selected by Optimization Program

FIGURE 16.12 (continued)

### BENCHMARK II SUMMARY AND ANALYSIS

| Uses | Media | Cost | Impact | Prob |
|------|-------|------|--------|------|
| 2 | NSW | 30590 | 0.90 | 1.00 |
| 3 | TI | 80250 | 0.90 | 1.00 |
| 1 | FOR | 8950 | 0.80 | 1.00 |
| 3 | TVG | 67200 | 0.50 | 1.00 |
| 2 | RD | 73208 | 0.70 | 1.00 |
| 1 | PEO | 9540 | 0.65 | 1.00 |
| 3 | NG | 77070 | 1.00 | 1.00 |
| 15 | | 346808 | | |

### MARKET SEGMENT SUMMARY

| Demo Name | Foggy |
|-----------|-------|
| Population | 5955 |
| Gross Impressions | 19291 |
| CPM Gross impressions | 17.98 |
| Gross rating points | 323 |
| Net reach | 5158 |
| Percent net reach | 86.62 |
| CPM net reach | 67.24 |
| Average frequency | 3.74 |
| Demo weight | 1.00 |

This schedule reached 5,158,000 or 86.62% of the demo. It should be noted that this is a weighted figure based on our specified impact weights.

*Source* : SMO

*Section C:* Analysis of Selected Schedule in Terms of Reach, Frequency, and GRPs

magic nor imagination into the scheduling process. However, it does enable you to examine and compare many different vehicle combinations and/or reach and frequency alternatives so that you can improve formation of your own conclusion regarding a potentially optimum schedule.

***Simulation Programs***

The term "simulation program" is used with somewhat divergent meanings by different writers. We will use a very broad definition that can be phrased as follows: A simulation program is one in which a proposed media schedule is analyzed by the computer to estimate the results of that schedule. Those results can be measured in various ways, depending on the number of assumptions made in the program. In some cases very extended results are estimated. For instance, the program might attempt to measure actual communication effects—the extent to which the advertising schedule will influence prospects' attitudes toward your brand. Other extended simulation programs go even further and attempt to predict effects on sales or profits.

There is a second type of simulation program which is somewhat less ambitious in what it attempts to do. In this second type, the simulation is limited to measuring the reach, frequency, gross rating point level, and possibly the frequency distribution pattern that your proposed media plan will produce. We will refer to this second type of simulation program as an "exposure evaluation program." Now we will consider each type.

*The Use of Computers in Media Planning*

***Extended Simulation Programs.*** Extended simulation programs tend to be quite complex and seek to predict a great deal about the results of any given media schedule. For example, one program called ADMOD begins by generating and testing a number of alternative insertion schedules on a sample of consumers. This is all done within the computer using an assortment of estimates and assumptions. The program then traces through a sequence of results as follows:

> In evaluating an insertion schedule, ADMOD examines its likely impact upon every individual in the sample. The impact will depend upon the net value of the decision or cognition change involved (the segment effect), the number and source of exposures to the individual created by the schedule (advertisement exposures), and the impact of the exposures upon the probability of obtaining desired cognition changes or decisions (the repetition function). Using appropriate scaling factors, the result is projected to the real population, providing the total expected profit generated by that media schedule. [22].

Other extended simulation programs have been devised that attempt to delve rather deeply into the communication effects or sales effects of a media schedule. Two examples of such models that you might want to examine are CAM[23] and MEDIAC.[24] Extended simulation programs tend to be viewed with a high degree of caution and reservation by many experts. As one writer has pointed out, "Computers, alas, merely process data, and much media analysis is qualitative rather than quantitative. Computer technology can certainly be used to analyze quantitative data but the qualitative aspects are subject to many widely differing interpretations."[25]

***Exposure Evaluation Programs.*** The second and more direct type of media simulation program is the exposure evaluation program. Its objective is to evaluate proposed media schedules in terms of reach, frequency, and gross rating points. Although the output is much less ambitious than that of the extended models just described, it also is dependent on far fewer intricacies and assumptions. As a practical matter, this is the kind of computer simulation program you are likely to find most frequently applied in actual advertising decision making. Figure 16.13 shows in abbreviated form the essentials of the process that is involved. To work with this kind of simulation program, the media planner first develops several alternative schedules aimed at reaching a designated target market. The program then evaluates each media schedule, drawing on a variety of statistical information concerning the audiences of the media vehicles included. In effect, the program is attempting to simulate what would happen if that schedule were actually to be bought and run. In this sense, an exposure evaluation program is similar to the extended simulation models described above. However, predictions are restricted to the pattern of message dispersion you would attain among members of your target audience. In other words, the output is limited to such results as reach, frequency, gross rating points, and distribution of gross impressions. Like any of the other programs, an exposure evaluation program must also rely on sample data and on certain estimating procedures. However, its assumptions are rather simple and straightforward.

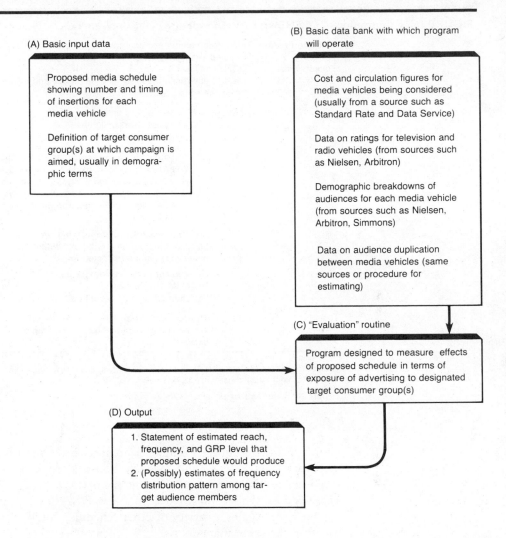

**FIGURE 16.13 A general overview of exposure evaluation programs**

(A) Basic input data

Proposed media schedule showing number and timing of insertions for each media vehicle

Definition of target consumer group(s) at which campaign is aimed, usually in demographic terms

(B) Basic data bank with which program will operate

Cost and circulation figures for media vehicles being considered (usually from a source such as Standard Rate and Data Service)

Data on ratings for television and radio vehicles (from sources such as Nielsen, Arbitron)

Demographic breakdowns of audiences for each media vehicle (from sources such as Nielsen, Arbitron, Simmons)

Data on audience duplication between media vehicles (same sources or procedure for estimating)

(C) "Evaluation" routine

Program designed to measure effects of proposed schedule in terms of exposure of advertising to designated target consumer group(s)

(D) Output

1. Statement of estimated reach, frequency, and GRP level that proposed schedule would produce
2. (Possibly) estimates of frequency distribution pattern among target audience members

Figure 16.14 illustrates some major features and data outputs associated with an exposure evaluation program available from Telmar, Inc. In this case, the media planners again defined their audience as consisting of men in the Pacific region between the ages of twenty-five and forty-nine. Several alternative schedules, using magazines considered appropriate for the campaign and the intended audience, were given to the computer for comparison. The program does not actually attempt to tell the media planner which schedule is best. Its function is to provide assistance that will allow the planner to reach her or his own conclusions.

In the two examples shown, the second schedule (Report 2) requires a budget fifteen percent higher than the first schedule. However, it raises the GRP level by 19.5% (from 221 to 264). An even more critical comparison is between the percentages of target prospects who are exposed five or more times during the schedule period. This is important because the advertising planners have deter-

**FIGURE 16.14 Illustration of QRFNEW/OLD: An exposure evaluation program**

Planning Process: Plan development and analysis
Function: Reach & Frequency
Telmar System: QRFNEW/OLD
QRFNEW/OLD: Used to determine the reach and frequency and cost efficiency of user entered magazine schedules

DIMENSIONS: Twenty-five bases
Twenty-five schedules
One hundred reports

EXAMPLE: You are considering three magazine plans for Fogged-in Airways. You need to run QRF to determine the schedule that best meets your R/F goals. Additionally, you have determined the effective-reach for prospects of Fogged-in Airways is at the "5+" exposure level. A frequency distribution must also be included to show your effective reach.

NOTE: QRFNEW implies you are working with new bases. These bases are entered in the program and tabbed within the program. When tabbing bases the computer is determining:

A) Audiences for each magazine
B) CUME audiences
C) Duplication between all pairs of magazines

This tabbing can also be done in UNITAB, and all tabbed information can be stored in demo files, which then can be used in QRFOLD (old bases).

*Source: User's Guide to Telmar Media Analysis and Planning Systems* (New York: Telmar Group, Inc., 1982). Copyright 1982 by Telmar Group, Inc., used by special permission of copyright holder.

*Section A:* Statement of Program Objectives

mined that this frequency range per prospect is required for the most effective exposure level. The second schedule boosts the reach attained at the "5+" exposure level by forty-one percent (from 14.97 to 21.12). On the basis of these figures, the second schedule might well be chosen as preferable despite its higher cost. Again, a variety of other schedules could be evaluated and compared in the same manner.

# SUMMARY

You can choose either to concentrate your advertising in a particular media category or to use a media mix involving two or more categories. There are arguments favoring both approaches. In either case your decision regarding the category or categories you will use must be based on an analysis of the complete set of precise objectives and needs of your own advertising strategy. Apart from the audiences they deliver, each category possesses specific characteristics especially well suited to particular communication needs.

In determining the size of individual advertising insertions, you face a trade-off situation. With a fixed budget size you can opt for either a larger quantity

**FIGURE 16.14 (continued)**

REPORT 1

TELMAR REACH & FREQUENCY: METREX RF

MEN AGE 25–49 IN THE PACIFIC REGION

POPULATION: 5,955

| Media Name | Number of Uses | Unit Cost | Average Audience | CPM | Percent Coverage |
|---|---|---|---|---|---|
| Newsweek | 3 | 15,295 | 933 | 16.39 | 15.67 |
| TV Guide | 2 | 26,750 | 2,070 | 12.92 | 34.76 |
| Reader's Digest | 3 | 36,604 | 1,300 | 28.16 | 21.83 |
| Business Week | 4 | 9,025 | 154 | 58.60 | 2.59 |
| Sports Illustrated | 2 | 25,485 | 861 | 29.60 | 14.46 |

| | | |
|---|---|---|
| TOTAL COST | $ 296,267 | |
| TOTAL USES | 14 | |
| NET REACH | 4,314 | This schedule reaches 4,314,000 men 25–49 in the Pacific region, representing 72.45% of the target population. |
| PERCENT NET REACH | 72.45 | |
| CPM NET REACH | 68.67 | |
| GROSS IMPRESSIONS | 13,177 | |
| CPM GROSS IMPRESSIONS | 22.48 | |
| AVERAGE FREQUENCY | 3.05 | |

| Frequency Level | Exposed % | Exposed (000) | Exposed at Least % | Exposed at Least (000) |
|---|---|---|---|---|
| 0 | 27.55 | 1641 | 100.00 | 5955 |
| 1 | 15.71 | 936 | 72.45 | 4314 |
| 2 | 18.47 | 1100 | 56.74 | 3379 |
| 3 | 14.12 | 841 | 38.26 | 2279 |
| 4 | 9.17 | 546 | 24.14 | 1438 |
| 5–14 | 14.97 | 892 | 14.97 | 892 |

841,000, or 14.12% of men 25–49 in the Pacific region were exposed to this schedule exactly 3 times.

According to our criteria for effective reach, 892,000, or 14.97% of men 25–49 in the Pacific region were exposed to this schedule at the desired frequency level (5+ times).

*Source:* 1980 SMRB study.

*Section B:* Analysis of Proposed Media Schedule 1

of smaller insertions or a lesser number of larger insertions. Presumably, there is some minimum size of insertion required, which is based on your creative needs. However, selecting the most effective size remains to some extent a matter of individual judgment. It is wise to consider your needs carefully, and to field test if necessary to discover whether insertion sizes could be safely reduced to allow you to run more separate ads.

Major advertising campaigns are typically planned to run over some stated time period. The most common planning period is one year. You must decide how insertions are to be spaced out over the course of your full planning

**FIGURE 16.14 (continued)**

REPORT 2

TELMAR REACH & FREQUENCY: METREX RF

MEN AGED 25–49 YEARS IN THE PACIFIC REGION

POPULATION: 5,955

| Media Name | Number of Uses | Unit Cost | Average Audience | CPM | Percent Coverage |
|---|---|---|---|---|---|
| Newsweek | 2 | 15,295 | 933 | 16.39 | 15.67 |
| TV Guide | 3 | 26,750 | 2,070 | 12.92 | 34.76 |
| Reader's Digest | 3 | 36,604 | 1,300 | 28.16 | 21.83 |
| Business Week | 2 | 9,025 | 154 | 58.60 | 2.59 |
| Sports Illustrated | 4 | 25,485 | 861 | 29.60 | 14.46 |

|  |  |
|---|---|
| TOTAL COST | $  340,642 |
| TOTAL USES | 14 |
| NET REACH | 4,445 |
| PERCENT NET REACH | 74.64 |
| CPM NET REACH | 76.64 |
| GROSS IMPRESSIONS | 15,728 |
| CPM GROSS IMPRESSIONS | 21.66 |
| AVERAGE FREQUENCY | 3.54 |

| Frequency Level | Exposed % | Exposed (000) | Exposed at Least % | Exposed at Least (000) |
|---|---|---|---|---|
| 0 | 25.36 | 1510 | 100.00 | 5955 |
| 1 | 14.53 | 865 | 74.64 | 4445 |
| 2 | 13.76 | 820 | 60.11 | 3580 |
| 3 | 16.68 | 994 | 46.35 | 2760 |
| 4 | 8.54 | 509 | 29.66 | 1766 |
| 5–14 | 21.12 | 1258 | 21.12 | 1258 |

*Source:* 1980 SMRB study.

*Section C:* Analysis of Proposed Media Schedule 2

period. The three general alternatives open to you are (1) a *continuity approach,* with insertions spaced out more or less evenly, (2) a *flighted approach,* with alternating periods in which the advertising is either running very heavily or not running at all, and (3) a *concentrated approach,* with advertisements running only during one period in the year. Neither advertising practice nor published research suggests any absolutely clear answer as to which approach is the best. Your decision will be influenced by the size of your budget, the seasonality of your product, and your own philosophy or field research.

The gross rating point level is a very useful measure used to express the power or weight of an advertising program. However, factors such as size of insertions and creative impact should also be considered along with GRPs to assess the total power potential of a campaign. The gross rating point level for some specified time period is found by multiplying reach times frequency. "Reach" refers to the percentage of your prospects who have been exposed to your advertising. "Frequency" refers to the average number of times they have been exposed.

It is important to recognize that you can achieve exactly the same GRP level with many different combinations of reach and frequency and also that you can achieve exactly the same reach and frequency with many different patterns of gross impression distributions among the people who see and/or hear your advertisements.

As to the second point, there is strong agreement as to what you want. That is a distribution of gross impressions such that everyone reached by your advertising is exposed approximately the same "ideal" number of times (or as close to that ideal as you can achieve). In coping with the problem of determining an ideal number of exposures, we again face an area of disagreement among advertising experts. Some seem to be saying, "One exposure should be enough. Therefore, stress 'unduplicated audience.' Aim at maximum reach and let frequency take care of itself." Others espouse the view that repetition is needed for an advertising message to take hold and thus you should first aim at some minimum level of frequency.

A widely discussed method of determining an appropriate minimum frequency level is the "three-hit" theory. This suggests you need a minimum of three *effective exposures*. However you may require a much larger number of total exposures to attain three exposures that are *effective*. Brief examples were presented to outline procedures for applying the three-hit theory to determine a frequency objective. Alternative ways of determining frequency objectives were also outlined.

Your reach and frequency targets will ultimately form bases for deciding on the number of insertions you will require and the vehicles you choose to carry them. When two or more vehicles are used concurrently, your pattern of audience delivery will be a result of the combination of audiences reached by all the vehicles used. To the extent that separate vehicles duplicate audiences, the combination will increase your frequency. To the extent they do not duplicate audiences, the combination will increase reach. Therefore, considering vehicles in combination requires something more complex than straight CPM analysis for each vehicle. In the case of large-scale national advertising campaigns, the paperwork required to analyze this aspect of a media schedule thoroughly can become impracticably cumbersome. One way to resolve the problem is through the use of a computer program. Basically, there are two types of programs which can be used, optimization programs and simulation programs. Both require substantial input data on such matters as costs, size and nature of audiences, and extent of audience overlap. An optimization program processes these data to produce a recommended media schedule. A simulation program uses the same types of data to analyze a proposed media schedule.

There are a number of different sorts of programs available within each type. In current advertising practice, one of the most widely applied approaches is a variety of the simulation program that might best be termed an "exposure evaluation program." Its purpose is to examine a proposed schedule and output the estimated reach, frequency, GRP level, and distribution pattern of gross impressions. In a sense, a program of this variety is rather modest in terms of what it is trying to do. However, it provides a media planner with a great deal of useful information regarding important aspects of the media planning process and it facilitates comparison of potential alternatives in scheduling strategies in terms of their likely audience impact and relative cost effectiveness.

## DISCUSSION QUESTIONS

1. Discuss the advantages and disadvantages of concentrating your entire budget on one media category as opposed to spreading your budget across several media categories.
2. Does it follow that increasing the size of an advertisement increases your communication power? Comment on the two opposing viewpoints on this issue. How can this controversy best be resolved?
3. Three approaches for determining the general timing schedule for your advertising were discussed. Briefly outline each method, and based on the discussion in the text, propose timing schedules for athletic equipment, home insulation, and personal computers; explain your reasoning.
4. Define "reach," "frequency," and "gross rating points," and demonstrate how these three terms are related.
5. Many combinations of reach and frequency can produce the same GRP level. In general, is it better to maximize reach or frequency?
6. What are gross impressions? What general rule applies to optimizing their distribution and why?
7. If you are following the "three-hit theory," what is the ideal number of advertising exposures per prospect at which you should aim at any given time period?
8. Is it good or bad to have heavy audience duplication among vehicles in your advertising schedule? Explain your answer.
9. What is the difference between optimization programs and simulation programs in media planning? Are the two types mutually exclusive?
10. What limitations exist in terms of applying extended simulation programs in practical marketing situations?

## REFERENCES

1. *Media Costs and Coverage* (Chicago: Leo Burnett U.S.A., 1982), p. 5.
2. Alfred A. Kuehn, "Models for the Budgeting of Advertising," in Peter Langhoff, ed., *Models, Measurements in Marketing* (Englewood Cliffs, NJ: Prentice-Hall, Inc., 1965), pp. 132–133.
3. David A. Aaker and John G. Meyers, *Advertising Management,* 2nd ed. (Englewood Cliffs, NJ: Prentice-Hall, Inc., 1982), pp. 452–453.
4. H. H. Platek, "Space-Unit-Size Dilemma," *Marketing and Media Decisions,* April 1980, p. 92.
5. Leo Bogart, "Mass Advertising: The Message, Not the Measure," *Harvard Business Review,* September/October 1976, p. 114.
6. James F. Engel, Martin R. Warshaw, and Thomas C. Kinnear, *Promotional Strategy: Managing the Marketing Communications Mix,* 5th ed.
(Homewood, IL: Richard D. Irwin, Inc., 1983), p. 299.
7. Julian L. Simon, "What Do Zielske's Real Data Really Show About Pulsing?" *Journal of Marketing Research,* August 1979, p. 419.
8. Edward C. Strong, "The Spacing and Timing of Advertising," *Journal of Advertising Research,* December 1977, p. 30.
9. John J. O'Connor, "VW Ad Plan: A Soft, Thrifty Sell," *Advertising Age,* 17 October 1977, p. 2.
10. Rosser Reeves, *Reality in Advertising* (New York: Alfred A. Knopf, Inc., 1963), p. 124.
11. Barton, *Media in Advertising,* p. 58.
12. Dick Warren Twedt, "How Can the Advertising Dollar Work Harder?" *Journal of Marketing,* April 1965, p. 42.
13. William M. Weilbacher, *Advertising* (New York: Macmillan Publishing Co., Inc., 1979), p. 297.
14. Herbert E. Krugman, "What Makes Advertising

Effective?'' *Harvard Business Review,* March/April 1975, p. 103.

15. Krugman, ''What Makes Advertising Effective?,'' pp. 96–103.

16. For an excellent, extended discussion of different approaches see Michael L. Ray, *Advertising and Communication Management* (Englewood Cliffs, NJ: Prentice-Hall, Inc., 1982), Chapters 7 and 16.

17. Krugman, ''What Makes Advertising Effective?,'' pp. 96–103.

18. Howard Kamin, ''Advertising Reach, and Frequency,'' *Journal of Advertising Research,* February 1978, pp. 21–25.

19. Herbert Maneloveg, ''Linear Programming,'' *1962 Regional Conventions* (New York: American Association of Advertising Agencies, 1962), p. 36.

20. William T. Moran, ''Practical Media Decisions and the Computer,'' *Journal of Marketing,* July 1963, pp. 26–30.

21. Frank M. Bass and Ronald T. Lonsdale, ''An Exploration of Linear Programming in Media Selection,'' *Journal of Marketing Research,* May 1966, p. 179.

22. David A. Aaker, ''ADMOD: An Advertising Decision Model,'' *Journal of Marketing Research,* February 1975, p. 38.

23. Simon R. Broadbent, ''A Year's Experience of the LPE Media Model,'' *Proceedings, 8th Annual Conference* (New York: Advertising Research Foundation, 1962).

24. John D. C. Little and Leonard M. Lodish, ''A Media Planning Calculus,'' *Operations Research* January-February 1969, pp. 1–35.

25. Lewis Kaufman, *Essentials of Advertising* (New York: Harcourt Brace Jovanovich, Inc., 1980), p. 152.

# PART FIVE

# *Sales Promotion and Publicity*

# CHAPTER SEVENTEEN

# Sales Promotion

## FOCUS OF THE CHAPTER

"Sales promotion involves marketing activities, other than personal selling, advertising, and publicity, that stimulate consumer purchasing and dealer effectiveness."[1] Because it encompasses diverse methods and can be used for so many different purposes, the precise positioning of sales promotion in terms of marketing strategy and organizational responsibility is often vague. The confusion regarding its status has led observers of the field to urge that it be given more study and executive attention than it currently receives in many firms.

One writer has pointed out, "The increase in sales promotion spending in the consumer goods field is greater than that of advertising promotion.

However, it is important to know that a substantial part of this money is being misspent, some of it through poor planning."[2] Another published review noted, "Sales promotion is an orphan child of marketing. Both sales promotion budgets and sales promotion objectives are virtually ignored by senior management."[3] After an extensive study of the field, a researcher concluded that, "We need a more sophisticated approach to [sales] promotion management not only because it is a financially and strategically important area, but also because it has been virtually ignored."[4] With commentaries such as these in mind, this chapter will seek to equip you with a perspective for both appraising sales promotional opportunities and more effectively integrating them into your total persuasive communications mix.

# THE UNIQUE CHARACTER OF SALES PROMOTION

Like other promotional elements, sales promotion can be aimed to reach any of three general audience types. However, as also suggested in Figure 17.1, it often serves as an adjunct promotional component, in which case it may be so thoroughly merged with another element that it virtually loses identity as a separate entity. This is especially true when it is assigned a subsidiary role in a mix dominated by advertising or personal selling. Its frequent use as a distinctly auxiliary or subordinate avenue of promotion is the first of three issues that make it unique and, in a sense, more complex than other promotional elements. A second such issue derives from the fact that at least some sales promotion techniques must be used with special care owing to their potential for producing unwanted repercussions. The third issue involves the heterogeneous nature of the field. The assortment of techniques included under this heading often bear little surface resemblance to each other.

In covering the topic, this chapter will deal with the three issues listed above

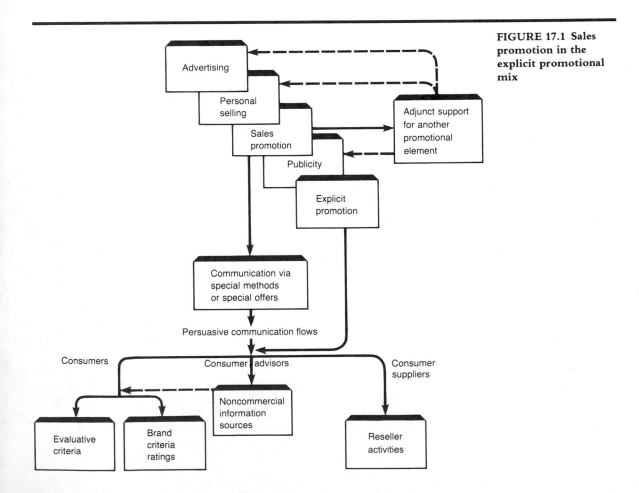

FIGURE 17.1 Sales promotion in the explicit promotional mix

in reverse order. We will begin by reviewing fourteen major techniques available to you as sales promotion tools. Seven of these can be classified as *special communication methods*. The other seven can be classified as *special offers*. Included in this review will be illustrations of how specific techniques have been used with success in actual practice. As each technique is discussed, we will propose general guidelines to consider when working with it. Following that, discussion will turn to cautions that should be kept in mind when working with methods whose misuse can be dangerous. The chapter will also present a format to assist you in surveying your full promotional mix to consider points at which particular sales promotion alternatives might be most effectively injected to augment its total force.

## SPECIAL COMMUNICATION METHODS

Advertising and publicity reach your audiences mainly through conventional mass media channels. Personal selling uses an individualized, face-to-face channel. Seven sales promotion techniques offer you additional or supplementary message routing variations. They are as follows:

1. Advertising specialties
2. Point-of-purchase promotional materials
3. Point-of-purchase demonstrations
4. Sampling
5. Visual aid materials for salespeople
6. Exhibits at trade and professional shows
7. Training programs for resellers and industrial users.

*Advertising Specialties*

An advertising specialty is an item of useful or interesting merchandise given away at no cost or obligation to the receiver and often carrying an imprinted or implied promotional message. Most advertising specialties are relatively low in cost although some may be fairly expensive. Almost any product can serve in this role. Examples of frequently used specialties are thermometers, ash trays, letter openers, balloons, and pocket knives. This list barely begins to outline the possibilities. In practice, observers of the advertising specialty field estimate that there are more than fifteen thousand different products currently employed for this purpose.[5]

In its simplest application, an advertising specialty can be used merely as an alternative advertising vehicle. As an illustration, you have probably seen book matches that promote local retail outlets or even national brands, but that are not directly linked to any other promotional mechanism. However, advertising specialties can also be employed to communicate in combination with another explicit promotional element and it is in this latter type of use that they are more accurately considered as sales promotion devices. This type of application opens up a multitude of imaginative possibilities for reinforcing your mix, very often at surprisingly low cost. To demonstrate how an advertising specialty can be treated as a creative piece of sales promotion rather than merely as a simple advertising vehicle, we will consider three examples.

*Source:* George L. Herpel and Richard A. Collins, *Specialty Advertising in Marketing* (Homewood, IL: Dow Jones-Irwin, Inc., 1972), p. 142.

**FIGURE 17.2 Using specialty advertising to secure sales leads and demonstrate a unique feature**

*Demonstrating a Unique Product Feature and Securing New Sales Leads.* Figure 17.2 illustrates a matchbook which was used very successfully by the Phifer Wire Products Company of Tuscaloosa, Alabama to meet a particular marketing objective.[6] The target audience consisted of window screen fabricating firms, none of whom had any previous contact with the company. Phifer was introducing a new aluminum solar screen which blocked the glare of the sun without obstructing the view. The company sought an inexpensive yet distinctive means of reaching its target prospects with two objectives in mind. The first was to dramatize the main selling feature of their product. The second objective was to stimulate interest and response from a new customer group. The matchbook itself was oversized and had a specific product feature printed on each large match. Included in back of the matches was a swatch of the screening material. Along with the advertising specialty itself, each prospect received a personalized letter introducing the company and its product. Recipients were invited to conduct a self-demonstration by lighting a match and holding it behind the screening material to prove that the product actually lived up to the claim being made for it. Almost one-third of the target group who received the mailing requested further information and samples. Over one-fourth of the total group originally contacted placed orders with Phifer, resulting in sales of more than $100,000 directly attributable to this comparatively simple specialty advertising approach.

**FIGURE 17.3** Using specialty advertising to recruit new distributors at a trade show

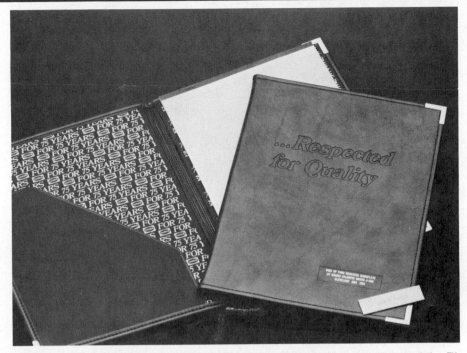

Source: George L. Herpel and Steve Slack: *Specialty Advertising: New Dimensions in Creative Marketing* (Irving, TX: Specialty Advertising Association International, 1983), p. 120.

***Attracting Potential New Distributors to a Trade Show Exhibit.*** The executive desk folder shown in Figure 17.3 was used by the Harris Calorific Company as part of a campaign to expand its distributor network.[7] Harris manufactures welding equipment and the target audience consisted of 240 firms engaged in the business of selling such equipment to industry. Firms were selected to receive the folder on the basis of their reputation as successful dealers for similar competitive products. Although these firms were spread out all over the United States, most would be sending representatives to the American Welding Society's trade show. The objective of this specialty advertising effort was to encourage as many of those representatives as possible to visit the Harris booth while at the show. This would give Harris salespeople an opportunity to spend time talking with prospective new dealers and initiating contacts that could lead to their recruitment into the Harris distributor network.

The desk folder itself was a high quality item and was embossed with Harris' Corporate slogan, "Respected for Quality." A key aspect of the design of this specialty advertising piece was the small recessed area at the lower right portion of the folder cover. Informational copy in this area invited each recipient to visit the Harris booth at the show and obtain a nameplate bearing his or her name. That plate would fit into the recess and turn the folder into a personalized item.

The Harris executives estimated that a show of this kind would normally

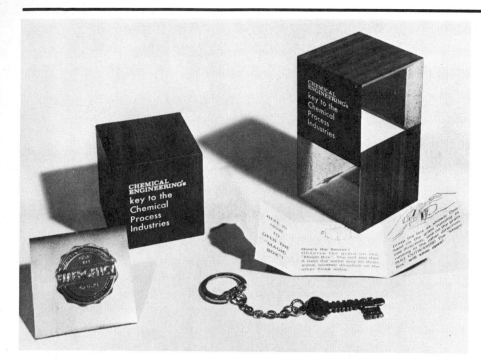

**FIGURE 17.4 Using specialty advertising to assist in a sales presentation**

*Source:* George L. Herpel and Richard A. Collins, *Specialty Advertising in Marketing* (Homewood, IL: Dow Jones-Irwin, Inc., 1972), p. 168.

produce an average of five to seven leads toward finding desirable new distributor firms. In this case, sixty-three targeted distributors visited the Harris booth and twenty-five concrete leads were developed. In other words, the use of specialty advertising material improved the results of this trade show objective by roughly 400 percent.

***Reinforcing a Sales Presentation.*** In this illustration the target prospect group was made up of advertising space buyers.[8] The sponsoring organization was *Chemical Engineering,* a business publication. Sales executives of *Chemical Engineering* sought a means of providing their field representatives with a physical focal point to hold prospects' attention during a presentation. The tool chosen for this task was the "magic box" shown in Figure 17.4, which is a puzzle that requires some skill to open and, when the puzzle is solved, reveals a large key and key chain. After presenting the box to the customer, the salesperson used it as a centerpiece for a presentation built around the idea that the publication was a key to unlocking markets for the advertiser. During the period this specialty item was used, *Chemical Engineering* increased its advertising by 519 pages, even though the competitive magazine industry as a whole was suffering a drop in its revenues.

***Guidelines for the Use of Advertising Specialties.*** These three brief examples suggest that advertising specialties can serve a variety of promotional objectives. However, advertising specialties which are used successfully generally have four qualities in common. First, they are aimed at a clearly defined target audience and selected to be both attractive and useful to the targeted group. Second, they are used with some definite promotional goal in mind. In the examples just presented, the goals ranged from demonstrating a unique product feature to building excitement for a trade show demonstration to fortifying the power of a personal presentation. However, all represented clear and definite goals, and not merely random giveaways of trinkets. Third, ideal specialty advertising items are designed in such a way that they bear a clear and unmistakable relationship to the full promotional program in which they are used. They blend with the central promotional appeal. Fourth, the best specialties are those that are designed and applied with imagination and the capacity for provoking active participation on the part of their recipients. Many specialty applications are originated by advertising agencies or the advertising departments of the sponsoring firms. Additionally, there are approximately 3,500 distributors of advertising specialties in the United States, most of whom represent a large number of specialty manufacturers. An important function of these distributors consists of studying their clients' promotional needs and then creating a complete advertising specialty plan that fulfills those needs.

*Point-of-Purchase Promotional Materials*

As their name implies, these are devices used to communicate to consumers who are in the process of shopping. Such materials are normally associated with the display of merchandise in a retail outlet. They may be originated by the retail outlet itself. However, most point-of-purchase materials originate with manufacturers of national brands who either sell or give them to the retailer. They can take any number of forms. For example, some are relatively small devices such as "shelf strips" and "shelf talkers" which are attached to the shelf where the product is regularly displayed and are designed to call special attention to your brand. Others are large devices such as "dump bins" and "island floor stands," which are free-standing fixtures that display your brand in its own separate location. Although their history traces back to antiquity, the growth and importance of self-service retailing has brought point-of-purchase materials to their current intense marketing importance. One observer has said, "as any veteran of the food and grocery business knows, the so-called 'self-service' revolution owes much of its success to the selling power of displays. For the display almost singlehandedly has assumed the function of countless sales clerks."[9]

Retail outlets abound with rival brands all competing for shoppers' attention. Developing point-of-purchase materials that make your product stand out from the crowd presents you with a creative challenge. Achieving prominent placement of such materials at the retail level presents you with a personal selling challenge. Especially when your aim is placement of something as big as a dump bin or island floor stand, you can encounter severe resistance. As one report has stated, "The problem for marketers is that in the scramble to make the most of in-store promotions, a kind of promotional clutter sets in. Every week there are about 200 products vying for perhaps 16 display areas in the average supermarket."[10]

**FIGURE 17.5 An in-store display to promote light bulbs in supermarkets**

*Source:* Photo courtesy of North American Philips Lighting Corporation, Bloomfield, NJ.

*A Case Example.*   Chapter 19 will survey methods used to solve the problem of securing display space. As a preview, we will consider a short example at this point. Figure 17.5 shows island floor stands developed by the North American Philips Lighting Corporation to promote the sale of light bulbs in supermarkets. To persuade retail management to allocate space for such a display in stores which also carried another competing and well-accepted brand of bulbs required well-planned and energetic efforts by salespeople. The presentation used by the sales force was structured around three selling points. First, the cost of the Norelco bulbs to the retailer was as much as twenty percent below that of competitors' brands, which gave the store higher gross profit per sale. Second, the stand was offered free of charge to the retailer and could serve as a valuable store fixture. Finally, and very critically, previous studies had shown that the addition of a second brand can increase total bulb sales by up to twenty-five percent; thus the Norelco promotion could boost the retailer's volume rather than simply lead to brand switching.

Reportedly, the initial response to the offer was so successful that the company had to increase its original order for the promotional piece.[11] As illustrated by this brief case history, your planning of point-of-purchase materials must include careful preconsideration of their effect on matters of interest to retail management. The display piece most likely to get placement is one that clearly is a profit builder for the store as well as the manufacturer.

*Point-of-Purchase Demonstrations*

In a full-scale demonstration approach, a manufacturer hires a demonstrator to contact customers directly in a retail outlet. The demonstrator usually either provides customers with a sample of the product, shows them how it can be used, or dramatizes some of its features. A demonstration technique can be used in almost any product category, but it is most common in fields such as grocery items and cosmetics. On a cost-per-contact basis it is a relatively expensive sales promotion tool, and requires fairly high customer traffic if it is to be economically feasible. Demonstrations can be particularly useful in helping to introduce a new brand.

A less expensive alternative to the full-scale demonstration is a self-demonstration arrangement. In this variation, display materials are set up to allow the customer to conduct his or her own demonstration without the assistance of a paid demonstrator. Like any promotional tool, a demonstration is most successful when it is conceived and executed so as to work smoothly with other elements in the full communication mix. To illustrate how imaginative demonstration approaches can be successfully tied into a total promotional program, the "Pepsi Challenge" campaign provides an excellent example.

*The Pepsi Challenge.* Based on prior in-home research in which over 3,000 interviewees compared unidentified samples of Pepsi-Cola against arch-rival Coca-Cola, with Pepsi emerging as the winner, Pepsi-Cola management decided on a "Challenge" theme as a national advertising campaign and promotion. A major component in the campaign was the use of local Pepsi Challenge booths in stores and shopping malls through which consumers were invited to compare the two brands without being aware of their identification and then to indicate which one they preferred. As shown in Figure 17.6 each booth included a scoreboard for tallying the results as they occurred at each location. According to one account, the power of the overall Pepsi Challenge campaign was strong enough to propel Pepsi-Cola ahead of Coca-Cola in terms of market share in supermarkets and to induce Coca-Cola to attempt a variety of counterattack procedures.[12]

Two important items should be stressed with respect to the success of the Pepsi Challenge booth approach. First, the booths were skillfully synchronized with other promotional elements; they prominently displayed the nationwide preference claim that formed the theme for national and local advertising efforts. The coordinated promotional thrust also included sales force efforts to secure secondary displays in Challenge booth stores along with newspaper advertising scheduled to run concurrently with the booths and

**FIGURE 17.6  The Pepsi Challenge**

*The centerpiece of the challenge*

*One example of the coordinated advertising*

Source: Pepsi-Co, Inc.; materials used with special permission.

*The core of the personal sales presentation used in the full promotional mix*

In 1981, the Pepsi Challenge will create excitement for your dealers.

Here's how:

Your dealer is always looking for different, unusual things to bring people into his store.

You can offer him that excitement through locally produced Challenge radio and television commercials tagged with his store's name and the dates the Challenge booth will be there.

He can use Challenge retail ad slicks to tell his customers about the Challenge.

You can offer to give his workers Challenge hats, T-shirts, or visors to wear during the Challenge.

And, of course, your good, courteous service, excellent merchandising and your commitment toward helping him make money with Pepsi.

In exchange for your commitment to his business, you should ask him to give you a firm date as to when to schedule a booth. A secondary display of Pepsi and Diet Pepsi is a *must*. And he'll make full mark-up at regular price.

We are committed to making Challenge work for you. T-stuffers, shelf talkers, pole signs and window banners all urge consumers to "Let Their Taste Decide," "Take the Pepsi Challenge!"

All we ask is that you get involved and "Take the Pepsi Challenge."

carrying price-off coupons. Second, because the program required retailer cooperation, the company planned it with retailer interests in mind. A summary of points suggested for use by company representatives in promoting the idea to store management is shown in the bottom portion of Figure 17.6. A primary advantage to the retailer is the Pepsi Challenge booth's ability to add excitement and increased traffic potential to the store. Moreover, the Pepsi Challenge provided an opportunity to publicize the store's name through radio, television, and print advertising and, very importantly, to increase soft drink sales at full markup.

*Sampling*

A sample is some quantity of the brand given to a prospect free of charge to induce trial. It is an explicit promotional technique that allows the implicit promotional content of your product to speak directly for itself. Sampling is likely to be most effective when some or all of the following three conditions exist. First, you are introducing a new brand or attempting to acquaint prospects with an improved version of an existing brand. Second, your brand has a clear differential advantage in one or more evaluative criteria weighted highly by your target consumer group, and the features that fulfill those criteria are self-demonstrating in usage situations. Third, the features involved are hard to describe adequately through some other explicit promotional technique such as advertising. For instance, the taste of a new snack food might be difficult to convey merely through words or pictures. The user would need personal experience to fully appreciate its nature and sampling might best serve to prompt such experience.

This does not mean that sampling is used only when all three of these circumstances exist; merely that it is especially useful in this climate. In practice, sampling is utilized for many types of products—old as well as new, nondistinctive as well as distinctive, and with features easy-to-describe as well as hard-to-describe. It is frequently employed simply as a supplementary mechanism to draw heightened attention to a brand. As a general rule, the feasibility of sampling tends to be restricted to products which are frequently repurchased and comparatively low in unit value. Above all, the brand must be readily divisible because a fairly small amount must be adequate to demonstrate its value and special features.

***Particularized Decision Areas Associated with Sampling Programs.*** The execution of a sampling campaign is relatively expensive on a cost-per-contact basis. You incur not only the expense of the product itself but also the costs of special packaging, distribution, and, very often, preparation of inserts or other materials to accompany the sample. Two issues require careful planning if you are to ensure cost efficiency. These center around the manner in which samples will be distributed and the size of each unit.

Much sampling is done on a "selective" basis. That is, the company defines its target market as carefully as possible and then attempts to distribute samples mainly to persons predetermined as extremely good prospects for the brand. For example, a firm might decide to limit sample distribution to areas within a city or other geographic subdivision that has demographic character-

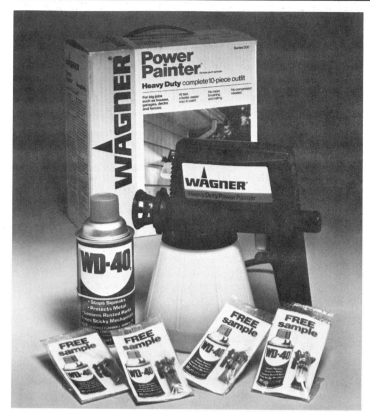

**FIGURE 17.7 A sampling campaign targeted to a specific prospect group**

*Source:* Louis E. Repaci, "Sampling Program Meets Marketing Objectives of Two Different Companies," *Marketing News,* 16 April 1982, p. 5.

istics that closely match those of predefined target prospects. Another route sometimes chosen to ensure that samples reach the best possible prospects is the packaging of the free sample with another compatible product being purchased by your prospect. For instance, the manufacturers of laundry detergents frequently distribute samples in new home laundry equipment.

Figure 17.7 illustrates an interesting and successful sampling program that makes use of this compatible product approach. WD-40 is a lubricant/cleaner that can be used for a variety of purposes. One such purpose is the protection and maintenance of electrically powered equipment. The WD-40 company entered into an agreement with Wagner Spray Tech to include samples of WD-40 with the Wagner Power Painter Outfit. Along with the sample, each purchaser received an instructional brochure explaining how WD-40 can be used to help maintain the paint spray unit properly and keep it in top working order. Because proper maintenance creates better customer satisfaction, the inclusion of the sample and brochure was beneficial to Wagner. At the same time, it enabled WD-40 to reach an especially good target consumer group with its sampling program. The manager of marketing services for WD-40 commented, "What is especially appealing is that both companies share equally in the program's costs and benefits. The national sampling program answers Wagner's product performance concern, and affords us the opportunity of placing samples with new customers or suggesting additional uses to already satisfied customers."[13]

The choice of a correct unit size to use for your sample can be critical. As the unit size increases, the cost of your promotional effort rises, and this fact argues for holding to a small size. However, it is essential that the amount of product your prospect receives is adequate to present your brand to its best advantage. For instance, the makers of Gainesburgers Dog Food reportedly tested a sampling program before using it on a market-wide basis and found that the sample originally planned actually induced a negative customer response because it was undersized.[14] They had intended to distribute samples consisting of one patty of the dog food. When this was done in a test market, the proportion of recipients who later purchased a full-sized package was disappointingly low. Follow-up research revealed the problem was not in the product but in the quantity sampled. After eating one Gainesburger, dogs were still hungry because the amount consumed was not enough to satisfy their appetites. This caused prospective purchasers to identify the brand as a snack item rather than a full meal for their pets. When the sample size was increased to two patties, the product was better able to demonstrate its merits, the rate of purchase increased substantially, and the brand went on to a successful introduction as the "Canned Dog Food Without the Can."

*Visual Aid Materials for Salespeople*

These are designed for and used by sales personnel to assist them in making presentations. A wide diversity of aids exists, ranging from relatively simple articles such as flip charts or product bulletins to more formal items such as slide presentations and motion pictures. You will recall from Chapter 10 that salespeople work with visual aid materials in a variety of ways and that they often tailor the choice and use of aids to fit the needs of each sales call. This customization process should begin with appraisal of the specific selling situation including the basic aim of the call, the personality and needs of the prospect, the style of the sales representative, and the setting in which the presentation will take place. As an example, we shall repeat a portion of the comments made by Ms. Durek in that earlier chapter. "For instance, if the presentation is to a business and the people are stuffy, an overhead projector or flip chart might be used along with formal typewritten handout material. In another presentation, I might just use a table easel and a felt-tip pen."

In preparing visual aid materials for your sales force, the needs of your sales representatives should be carefully studied at the outset. You will want to know what they feel has helped them in the past. You will also want to know what sorts of aids are considered comfortable to work with by your salespeople. If at all possible, you should consider offering alternative types of materials so that sales representatives can choose among them to fit varied selling situations. To ensure that visual aid materials are used to their full potential, it is often necessary that their introduction to the sales force be accompanied by a program that builds enthusiasm for and expertise in their use.

*A Case Example of a Successful Visual Aid Package.* An illustration of a well-conceived visual aid program that was set up to cope with a unique promotional problem is provided by the Bradley Corporation, a Wisconsin-based plumbing fixtures manufacturer.[15] In line with building code revisions mandating improved public access facilities for handicapped persons, Bradley engineered new lines of washroom equipment designed to meet "barrier-free" architectural needs. The company then found that it faced a serious promotional challenge in reaching architects and other influential decision makers to establish the company's desired position as a leading resource for barrier-free plumbing fixtures.

To attack the problem, the firm set up an integrated promotional program centering around a thirty-six-minute motion picture in which a panel of experts discussed the need for and nature of the products in question. This was supplemented by an eight-minute film that demonstrated applications of specific Bradley products in solving related design problems. A sales kit was also produced that contained detailed instructions and materials for promoting and presenting the films to prospects. The kit included a list of potential prospect groups in each sales area, sample invitation forms, and illustrated brochures. The entire program was unveiled for sales representatives in a national meeting during which a substantial amount of time was devoted to training the sales force in techniques of working with the materials. This initial effort was followed up with weekly newsletters plus special two-day professional seminars.

The results of the campaign were reported to be excellent, with the firm achieving its goal of establishing a leadership position in the field. During the first three months the films were presented to more than five thousand decision makers or decision influencers. In the words of the company's marketing vice-president, "For the complete professional staffs of architectural firms to spend anywhere from one to two and one-half hours in a presentation and discussion, the attraction must be virtually unprecedented."[16] Again, a key ingredient in the success of this visual aid program was the method through which it was presold to the sales force and coordinated with other promotional forms in a systematic communications plan.

*Exhibits at Trade and Professional Shows*

Most trade, professional, and industrial associations stage periodic conventions or shows where booths may be rented to promote various products and services. When you rent such a booth you are, in a sense, establishing a miniature, temporary field sales office. Because these events are usually aimed at specialized occupational groups, they allow you to target narrowly defined types of prospects. For instance, in our earlier discussion of advertising specialties, reference was made to Harris Calorific Company exhibiting at the American Welding Society's trade show. Harris was aiming at 240 very clearly designated prospects. The exhibit gave them an opportunity to reach these people in a manner that would have been impossible through normal sales calls. In short, meetings of this sort can generate a very valuable customer traffic situation. They offer your sales force an opportunity to demonstrate products, acquire new prospect leads, and refresh relationships with existing customers. Social events such as luncheons or cocktail parties are often sponsored in conjunction with the trade show exhibit. In general, exhibits at such shows are considered more important as a background for future selling efforts rather than for the direct writing of orders at the show. One expert has observed, "One of the purposes of [exhibits at trade and professional shows] is to write orders, but this is just one of the objectives. . . . Interested parties usually leave their names with the corporate representative. These names are given to company sales representatives or distributors' sales reps [for follow up.]"[17] It is important to remember that exhibits should be viewed in terms of your overall, long-term strategy.

The traffic generated at many of these shows can give them an atmosphere somewhat resembling a supermarket. There are a large number of potential customers walking the aisles and "shopping." However, you must vie with numerous competitors in order to obtain prospects' attention and interest. Furthermore, you are dealing with a sophisticated and sometimes hard-to-attract group of shoppers. An observer of the field has noted, "The trade show audience is one presumably well-versed in the product displayed . . . [B]ecause of the sophistication of the audience in the particular industry, they also have a tendency to ignore certain exhibits because they think they are fully familiar with all aspects of these lines, particularly those of prominent companies."[18]

Another authority in the field has pointed out that a successful trade show exhibit is really a mixture of several different communication forms, each of which demands careful planning as to objectives and execution. In speaking of exhibits, she has said, "They communicate to the prospective buyers by the exhibit structure, graphic images, sales personnel, and collateral sales support materials. Because one exhibit is dependent on the integration of as many as five or six media, the problems accompanying the development of the exhibit plan are more complex as well."[19]

Like any promotional mechanism, trade show exhibits cost money. In fact, they are usually rather expensive when outlays for travel, hospitality suites, and the time of sales personnel on duty are taken into consideration. For this reason, the objectives of the exhibition should not only be clearly specified in advance but clearly analyzed after the fact.

The [post-] show audit should verify the projected target audience. Sales personnel should have maintained accurate records of sales leads, if that was an objective, by name, title, etc., to verify what percent of the projected target markets and actual target audience were contacted at the exhibit. . . . Follow-up of contacts should be emphasized to sales personnel even if sales were not an objective. Otherwise, show attendees may feel that their expressed interest was of no concern to the company. . . . For complete evaluation of the show, the company needs qualitative information such as show attendees' reaction to meetings and exhibits, average time spent on the company's booth by target audience members, and competition's activity at the show. This is subjective information and can best be obtained by surveying a sample of the target audience, the show attendees and the company's sales personnel. [20]

These are special workshops that are sponsored and usually paid for by a firm to provide training for persons outside its own organization. They are meant to assist outside personnel in learning either how to sell or use the manufacturer's product. Although this may be the core objective, some programs are more extensive and also provide more general training in selling techniques, retail management procedures, or current technical developments in an industrial field. You have seen reference to this type of sales promotion technique at earlier points in the book. For example, in Chapter 10 we discussed the importance placed on such training programs in marketing certain industrial products. Tad Collins, the manufacturers' representative who sells packings and seals, said "The big thing we are finding you can really sell is *knowledge*—sophisticated solutions and training programs for your customers." To emphasize the broad spread of applications in which this sales promotion approach can prove valuable, we will look at one more example.

*The Homelite Traveling Clinic.*  The Homelite division of Textron has been reported to allocate one quarter of a million dollars per year in promotional expenditures to a continuous, nationwide training program for the sales and service staffs of its dealer organizations.[21] This program has four trainers on the road who present sessions in a clinic format. During one year, the Homelite trainers covered 100,000 miles delivering short courses to 7,000 employees of outlets handling Homelite chain saws. Their presentations were offered in four different lengths and topic areas, and ranged from a two-hour presentation centering around product and selling information to an all-day class designed to turn newly hired service people into chain saw mechanics. The clinics are free of charge to dealers and coordinated with the efforts of the company's own district sales managers who determine the type of training most needed in their areas. As with most training programs, measurement of results in terms of direct sales response is difficult to calculate with precision. However, in one report on the Homelite program it was noted that not only did it produce evidence of improved goodwill among dealers, but also that "Homelite salesmen are happy, too. [The training director] has a growing file of reports on sales they've made to dealers who are still basking in the glow of a trainer's visit."[22]

# SPECIAL OFFERS

Special offers are temporary inducements made available to consumers, resellers, or company sales personnel. They all require some type of action on the part of the recipient in order to enjoy the benefits of the offer. The seven types of special offers we shall review are as follows:

1. Coupons
2. Price-off deals and combination offers (also referred to as "Price packs" and "Bonus packs"
3. Money-refund offers and factory rebates

4. Trade inducements and performance allowances
5. Premiums
6. Contests and sweepstakes
7. Recognition programs

Estimates of the frequency of usage during 1981 for the first five of these special offer types are depicted in Figure 17.8.

Coupons

A coupon is a certificate that entitles the holder to a reduced price on the purchase of merchandise and is the most commonly employed form of special offers to consumers. In the extreme case, a coupon may entitle the holder to obtain the product at no charge. As shown in Figure 17.9, the number of coupons distributed has grown steadily with over 100 billion issued by manufacturers during 1981. One estimate places the average coupon as offering the user a saving of about eighteen cents on the purchase price of the product.[23] On this basis, if all of the 1981 coupons had been redeemed they would have been worth close to 18.5 billion dollars. In practice, only about four percent of the coupons issued actually are redeemed,[24] but even this low redemption rate establishes their worth at approximately 740 million dollars to the consumers who use them.

Figure 17.9 also analyzes coupon dissemination modes in terms of the six most common forms of distribution. In 1981, over fifty percent of the coupons appeared on the regular pages of daily or Sunday newspapers. About six percent were attached to packages of the brand itself or packages of other brands, although this mode was dropping in popularity. Roughly twelve percent were run in magazines and slightly over three percent were mailed directly to prospects. The fastest rising form of coupon distribution is the free-standing insert, a preprinted page on heavy-stock paper that is separately placed within a newspaper. Introduced during the 1970s, free-standing inserts have gained rapidly in popularity among national advertisers because they offer the promoting firm far greater control over the timing and selectivity of coverage than does the standard newspaper coupon. By 1981 they accounted for over one-fourth of the national couponing effort.

**FIGURE 17.8**
**Estimates of relative usage for five major categories of special offers in 1981**

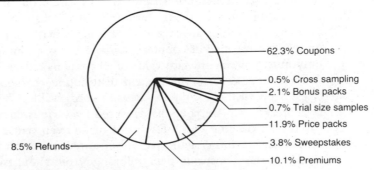

62.3% Coupons
0.5% Cross sampling
2.1% Bonus packs
0.7% Trial size samples
11.9% Price packs
3.8% Sweepstakes
10.1% Premiums
8.5% Refunds

*Source:* Dancer Fitzgerald Sample, Consumer Promotion Report (New York: Dancer Fitzgerald Sample, Inc., 1981).

*Special Offers*

573

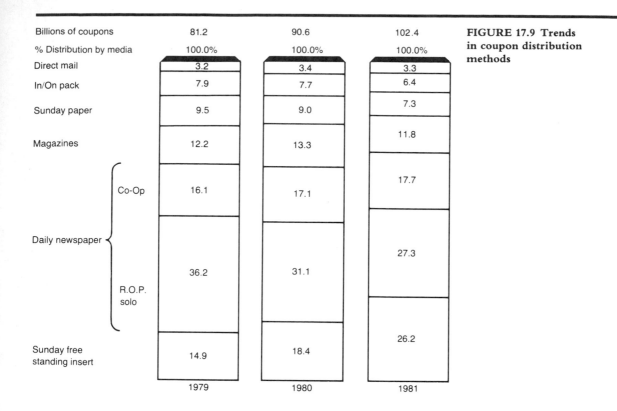

| Billions of coupons | 81.2 | 90.6 | 102.4 |
| % Distribution by media | 100.0% | 100.0% | 100.0% |
| Direct mail | 3.2 | 3.4 | 3.3 |
| In/On pack | 7.9 | 7.7 | 6.4 |
| Sunday paper | 9.5 | 9.0 | 7.3 |
| Magazines | 12.2 | 13.3 | 11.8 |
| Co-Op | 16.1 | 17.1 | 17.7 |
| Daily newspaper R.O.P. solo | 36.2 | 31.1 | 27.3 |
| Sunday free standing insert | 14.9 | 18.4 | 26.2 |
| | 1979 | 1980 | 1981 |

**FIGURE 17.9 Trends in coupon distribution methods**

*Source:* "Analyzing Promotions: The Free-Standing Insert Coupon," *The Nielsen Researcher*, no. 4 (1982), p. 17.

***Comparative Redemption Rates and Costs by Distribution Modes.*** Figure 17.10 compares ratios of redemptions for coupons mailed directly to consumers as opposed to those distributed by magazines, newspapers, and on-package techniques. As shown there, although newspapers are the heaviest carrier of coupons their redemption rate can be relatively low. Figure 17.10 reveals something else about coupon redemption. The higher the value of the coupon, the higher the redemption ratio. In this case, coupons worth fifteen cents consistently outpaced those worth ten cents. This is hardly surprising. However, it is an important factor to consider when planning a couponing program. The issuance of coupons can be a costly promotional technique. Not only must you pay the face value of all coupons redeemed, but you also incur further expenses for printing and distributing the coupons plus processing charges on all those coupons actually used. Table 17.1 illustrates estimated cost breakdowns on coupons delivered by various circulation methods. It is based on a coupon with a face value of fourteen cents. As you can see, even though the customer will save only fourteen cents on the purchase, the full charge to the sponsoring firm will range from about twenty-five cents up to seventy-five cents per coupon redeemed.

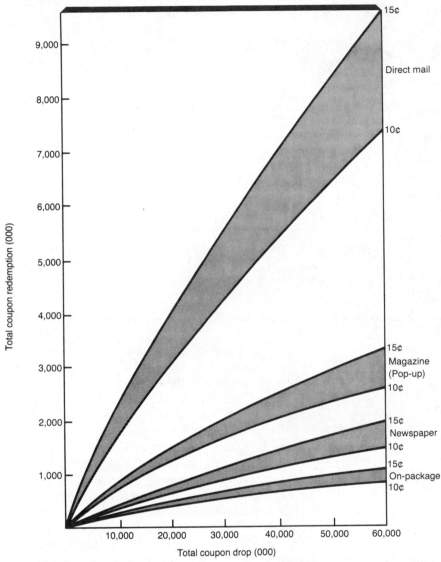

**FIGURE 17.10** Coupon redemption rates by distribution modes and coupon value

*Source:* Adapted from Ronald W. Ward and James E. Davis, "Coupon Redemption," *Journal of Advertising Research,* vol. 18, no. 4 (1978), pp. 55–57.

***Purposes of Couponing Programs.*** Although couponing is relatively expensive on a cost-per-response basis, it remains a heavily used promotional instrument because it can contribute very effectively toward achieving a variety of specific promotional objectives. The most common of these objectives are (1) adding excitement and appeal to advertisements, (2) generating a temporary lift in sales for an established brand, (3) stimulating trial of a new brand, and (4) encouraging retailers to stock and display a brand. As for the first objective, one trade publication report noted "there is evidence to suggest that coupons

**TABLE 17.1 Cost per coupon redeemed based on redemption rates**

| Circulation Method | Cost per Thousand Printing/Delivery | Average Redemption | Distribution Cost[a] | Total Number of Redemptions[b] | Redemption Costs[c] | Total Program Cost | Cost per Coupon Redeemed |
|---|---|---|---|---|---|---|---|
| **DIRECT MAIL** | | | | | | | |
| SOLO[e] | $90 | 16.2%[d] | $2,250,000 | 4,050,000 | $810,000 | $3,060,000 | 75.5¢ |
| **MAGAZINE** | | | | | | | |
| SOLO[e] | $ 6 | 3.5% | $ 150,000 | 875,000 | $175,000 | $ 325,000 | 37.0¢ |
| **NEWSPAPER** | | | | | | | |
| 600-line ad | $ 3.75 | 2.4% | $ 93,750 | 600,000 | $120,000 | $ 213,750 | 35.6¢ |
| Supplements SOLO[e] | $ 6 | 3.1% | $ 150,000 | 775,000 | $155,000 | $ 305,000 | 39.3¢ |
| Free-standing inserts Coupon only | $ 2.25 | 5.4% | $ 56,250 | 1,350,000 | $270,000 | $ 326,250 | 24.1¢ |

[a]Distribution cost based on circulation of 25,000,000; some programs have more, others less distribution.
[b]No allowance made for misredemption, estimated by some industry sources at 20%.
[c]Average cost based on 14¢ face value plus 5¢ handling charge, and 1¢ internal handling charge. Redemption rates based on A. C. Nielsen Co. figures when available or industry sources; distribution costs based on published rates and industry estimates.
[d]Estimated.
[e]Single coupon not distributed on cooperative basis.

*Source:* "Coupon use up 15%, Nielsen Says; face value average now tops 14¢," *Advertising Age,* 25 October 1976, p. 112.

boost ad readership, although it is difficult to estimate the degree of readership improvement the coupon will induce."[25] With respect to generating a temporary lift in sales for an established brand, the same report suggested that "couponing provides massive short-term movement potential." This aspect of couponing power relates in part to the discussion in previous chapters regarding the fact that purchase intentions are a matter of probability rather than certainty. If your brand enjoys an initially positive purchase intentions level, its likelihood of purchase may be greatly enhanced if the consumer is carrying your coupon while shopping. However, there is a caution to consider in this connection. Coupons are essentially a supplemental stimulus. Their effectiveness is directly proportionate to the basic strength of your brand. In and of themselves they are not likely to revive a weakening brand. This point is illustrated by the data in Table 17.2. If coupons are used merely to stimulate sales for a product with a declining trend caused by other problems, any gains

**TABLE 17.2 The effect of coupons and in-store "specials" on brand sales[a]**

| Brands With: | Before Promotion | During Promotion | After Promotion |
|---|---|---|---|
| Declining Trends | 100 | 98 | 93 |
| Stable Sales | 100 | 105 | 100 |
| Increasing Trend | 100 | 110 | 107 |

[a]Using sales index figures with prepromotion indices set at 100.

*Source:* James O. Peckham, Sr., *The Wheel of Marketing* (Chicago: A. C. Nielsen, 1973).

**FIGURE 17.11 Couponing to introduce a new brand**

Courtesy of the Nestlé Company, Inc.

achieved are likely to be short-lived. A preferable strategy in such situations is to examine other elements in the mix to locate and resolve the underlying core of the marketing problem.

*A Case Example of Successful Couponing.* Coupons are probably at their best when you are attempting to stimulate trial of a new brand or an improved version of an existing brand. In these cases, they can also help your sales force assure good retail availability of the brand. If the coupon offer is strong and placed in a soundly conceived setting of other promotional techniques, resellers are likely to be much easier to convince. Figure 17.11 illustrates an advertisement used to successfully introduce a new brand via a couponing effort.

The details behind the full marketing strategy, of which this coupon effort formed one part, were outlined in an article citing it as an example of a strongly conceived promotional effort.[26] Nestlé management had three major goals in mind: to encourage retailers to include the new line of cookie mixes in their inventories, to secure as many in-store displays as possible for the new product entry, and to stimulate trial of the item by consumers. Because Nestlé sought an exceptionally strong incentive as a means of reaching these goals, the coupon offer required no cash outlay at all on the part of the consumer. The coupon alone entitled its holder to receive a box of Nestlé Cookie Mix, which would normally retail for ninety-five cents, absolutely free of charge.

The coupon itself was part of a full page newspaper ad run on a national basis except for the far western portions of the country. It was preceded by an intensive network television advertising campaign that began one month before the appearance of the coupon. Prior to the advertising, retailers were contacted through personal selling effort and offered a display allowance along with delayed billing for merchandise. In total, the budget for the introductory campaign was estimated as costing $5 million, including charges for advertising media, trade allowances, and coupon redemption expenses. As a result of this coordinated campaign, Nestlé achieved over eighty percent distribution in its targeted retail outlets with displays in over seventy percent of the stores contacted by the sales force. Within one month following the coupon's appearance, thirteen percent of the targeted consumer group had tried the product. Importantly, it should be noted that though a coupon played a central role in this promotion, the role it played was only part of a total, well-structured and integrated strategy.

***The Problem of Misredemption.*** A final word is in order concerning a special problem associated with couponing. This derives from fraudulent practices used to collect a coupon's value without the actual purchase of the merchandise. One aspect of misredemption involves retailers who allow customers to misuse coupons on a small scale. Usually this means permitting the consumer to cash the coupon on some other brand. A second aspect of misredemption can be even more serious. This involves mass cheating by persons running illegal coupon "clip-houses." In a clip-house operation large quantities of coupons are systematically cut from newspapers and then illegally redeemed, either through existing or fictitious retailers. When police raided one such clip-house in Brooklyn, New York, they reportedly found coupons worth over $250,000 neatly stacked and awaiting improper redemption.[27] Some estimates place total fraudulent use of coupons at ten to twenty percent of total redemptions. Although there are organized efforts to fight this type of fraud, it remains a very real problem at present.

***Price-Off Deals and Combination Offers***

In a price-off deal the manufacturer offers its brand to be sold to the consumer below the regular price. The amount of the price reduction usually is prominently displayed on the package. In a combination offer the customer can purchase two or more products together for less than their total normal price if purchased separately. In some cases a combination offer may involve two units of the same brand, in others it involves two different brands and, in the extreme situation, the customer may obtain the second product free on purchasing the first. Both price-off deals and combination offers are used to achieve the same objectives as coupons and their use should be considered with similar cautions in mind.

One extensive analysis of these techniques concluded they are most effective in an atmosphere in which one or all of three conditions exist.[28] The first condition is the recognition that they are best used only periodically and at widely spaced points in time. The second condition is the coupling of the price offer with the introduction of a new brand or promotion of an improvement in an existing brand. In these situations, combination offers can often prove especially advantageous. For example, if you can package your new or improved brand with a popular existing brand on a combination-offer basis you can frequently achieve rapid trial for the new entry among an important portion of your target prospect group. The final condition is use of the price-off deal or combination offer only as one part of a well-conceived promotion mix. This means that it should both support and be supported by concurrent advertising, personal selling, and/or other sales promotion efforts. In brief, price-off deals and combination offers should be treated as supplements to other promotional efforts rather than as substitutes for them.

***Money-Refund Offers and Factory Rebates***

Like the coupon, price-off deal, and combination offer, the money refund or factory rebate uses a straightforward economic appeal to attract consumer interest. It requires that purchase at the regular price be made first. Some portion of that price will then be refunded to customers who apply directly to the manufacturer and submit "proof-of-purchase" such as a certificate enclosed with the product or some portion of the package. Figure 17.12 shows an example of an advertisement featuring such a promotion. As mentioned in Chapter 2, one beneficial aspect of this approach is that it tends to capitalize on both the informational and transactional dimensions of price. The basic informational aspect is maintained because the purchaser pays the regular price. The transactional aspect is enhanced because the refund offer allows the customer to save money on the purchase.

***A Case Example—Kleenex and Contac.*** The offer illustrated in Figure 17.13 features two products marketed by different firms but related to each other in

**FIGURE 17.12 A refund offer used in the price promotion of a small appliance**

| Sale Price | **17.87** |
| Less Factory Rebate | **-4.00** |
| Cost After Rebate | **13.87** |

**PRICE AFTER REBATE** **13.87**

**1400-W Pro Pistol Dryer**
2 speeds, 4 heat settings.
With attachments, stand.

Rebate limited to manufacturer's stipulation.

Courtesy of General Electric Company, U.S.A.

*Special Offers* 579

*Source:* Courtesy of SmithKline Beckman Corporation.

terms of consumer use. Because each is a strong brand in its own right, the pairing of Contac and Kleenex tends to provide cross-reinforcement for the users of one brand to become users of the other. As in the case of the previous sales promotion offers cited, this refund was only part of a total communication package. However, it was an important part. The objectives, basic idea, strategy, budget, and results were described as follows in a trade publication article.[29]

The major goal behind the refund offer was to stimulate retailers to increase their inventories of the two brands and to allocate space for secondary, off-shelf displays of the products in their stores. The program was timed so that the inventory increases and supplementary displays would coincide with the beginning of the cold and flu season. Resellers were offered prepackaged displays of the Contac and Kleenex combination featuring the one dollar refund offer. Cooperating stores received special display promotional allowances. During the display period, the offer was backed with advertising in *Family Circle* and *Woman's Day* magazines, both of which circulate primarily to supermarket customers. Reportedly, this offer and the converging promotional efforts that accompanied it resulted in more trade displays used than ever before with approximately 540,000 refund responses. Contac prepack sales were described as being at their highest point in fifteen years with the ten-capsule pack running 130 percent over the original goal.

## Trade Inducements and Performance Allowances

The special offers described thus far have all been directed at motivating *consumers* by some form of economic attraction. Those to be described under the present heading involve economic attractions directed toward resellers. They are special discounts, payments, or rewards offered to wholesalers or retailers for their cooperation in a manufacturer's promotional program. Trade inducements are special offers aimed at convincing resellers to order and stock larger quantities of a brand so that it will be more readily available to consumers. Performance allowances are special offers designed to encourage retailers to promote a brand more actively through advertising, in-store displays or personal selling efforts.

***Trade Inducements.*** The basic and on-going consideration that motivates a reseller to carry your product is the markup earned on each unit sold. For instance, if yours is a brand that the retailer buys for seventy-five cents per unit and sells for one dollar per unit, the continuous twenty-five percent markup percentage realized on sales is the store's essential reason for carrying it. This assumes that the brand enjoys sufficiently high demand among the retailer's customers to produce an adequate volume of sales. Trade inducements offer resellers an additional attraction by essentially increasing the reseller's markup potential, usually for a short-run period. Some of the major trade inducements frequently used are the buying allowance, the buy-back allowance, the count-and-recount arrangement, and the free goods deal.

The *buying allowance,* sometimes called an "off-invoice allowance," is simply a temporary reduction in the cost of the merchandise to the reseller. It usually requires that the reseller purchase some minimum quantity of your brand and its major purpose is to attempt to increase the size of the reseller's current order. The *buy-back allowance* is a variation of the buying allowance and it generally works in the following manner. Upon placing one order with your firm, the reseller acquires the option to place another order, at a later date, at a reduced price. However, the amount of product that will qualify for that reduced price on the second order can be no greater than the amount purchased on the first order. The intention of the buy-back allowance is, again, to induce the merchant to place an extra-large order. In a *count-and-recount* arrangement, a wholesaler or retailer is rewarded for transferring merchandise out of the warehouse and into the store. The objective is to move as much of your brand as possible onto the retail shelves and displays where the ultimate consumer will be shopping. The count-and-recount technique usually starts with your sales representative taking an inventory of your brand in the reseller's warehouse. At the end of the count-and-recount offer period, the sales representative takes a second warehouse inventory. The reseller is then given an incentive payment based on the amount of product that has moved through and out of the warehouse.

In all of the three above arrangements, the trade inducement involves either a reduction in price or the payment of money. In a *free-goods deal* the inducement is merchandise rather than money, although the effect is approximately the same. In the most common variety of free-goods deal, the reseller firm is informed that, if it will purchase a certain quantity of one of your brands, you will agree to ship an additional quantity of the same brand—or perhaps another one of your brands—at no additional charge.

*Performance Allowances.*   As the name suggests, these require that the reseller agrees to engage in or perform some additional cooperative activity beyond merely placing an order or moving goods out of the warehouse and into the store. The three most commonly used classes of performance allowances are the display allowance, the advertising allowance, and cooperative advertising support. A *display allowance* is some amount of money or product given to a retailer for featuring your brand in a predetermined and agreed-on in-store display arrangement. An *advertising allowance* is paid to the reseller in return for the inclusion of your product in his or her local advertising efforts—again on the basis of some prearranged and agreed-on amount and type of advertising. A typical advertising allowance is a temporary offer that is usually geared to a special purpose. *Cooperative advertising* is similar in nature to the advertising allowance; however, it is often based on a relatively continuous agreement and the amount paid is related to the quantity of your brand that a retailer buys.

The general topic of promoting your brand to resellers will be given lengthier attention in the chapter devoted to reseller activities (Chapter 19). However, trade inducements and promotional allowances have been introduced, defined, and briefly discussed at this point for a very important reason. They form a part of your total inventory of sales promotion techniques. Therefore, they should be thought of in conjunction with all of the other sales promotion tools available to you. As you have seen from the examples introduced earlier in this chapter, the successful use of many other sales promotion techniques—such as point-of-purchase displays, premiums, and price-off deals—often depends on developing a coordinated sales promotion campaign that includes trade inducements and promotional allowances.

**Economic Offers Versus Psychic Offers**

Each of the special offers covered thus far has been purely economic in nature. Coupons, price-off deals, combination offers, money refund or factory rebate offers, trade inducements, and performance allowances all seek to prompt action on the basis of strictly monetary or money-equivalent attractiveness. The three special offers that will be covered next—premiums, contests and sweepstakes, and recognition programs—also have an economic aspect. However, they are generally designed and presented in a manner that stresses their desirability from more than merely a money-value perspective. One writer has dubbed such efforts as "psychic promotions" and offered the following commentary regarding their distinction from offers which are purely economic:

[The economic promotion] is a discount, it is rational, quantitative and emphasizes "less." The ["noneconomic" or] psychic promotion is emotional, qualitative and emphasizes "more," in addition to economic value. The consumer's *needs* are met by the economic promotions; the consumer's *wants* are met by the [noneconomic or psychic promotion]. . . . If we segment the consumer world into the pragmatists and the dreamers, the pragmatic camp tends to favor the economic "pay less" promotions, while the dreamer group tends to see fantasy fulfillment and "get more" in the psychic type promotion. Since each real consumer has some of each element, a change of promotional pace is healthy to fit their varying moods. [30]

On the basis of this reasoning, you may wish to consider long-term planning of special offer programs with a view toward interspersing offers of one type with those of the other, both for the sake of achieving variety and for the purpose of building a broader base of consumer appeal. When moving to a psychic offer approach, you will encounter an additional decision problem not faced in the instance of purely economic offers. Apart from determining *how much* should be offered you must also decide on the qualitative nature of your offer. Ideally, a premium, contest prize, or recognition award should be chosen in such a way that it not only holds a powerful attraction for the particular target audience at whom you are aiming but also provides a reinforcing relationship to your product and the general theme of your related promotional efforts.

## Premiums

A premium is an item of additional merchandise that a customer receives for purchasing a particular brand of product or purchasing at a particular retail outlet. The premium may be made available either at no added charge or at an extra but lower-than-usual price. Premiums are generally used on a temporary or intermittent basis as are the other special offers we have been examining. The purposes to which premiums are put are similar to those cited for coupons, refunds, combination offers, and price-off deals, and so are the cautions. In these respects, they can be thought of in much the same way as those other sales promotional devices. For a short period of time they can inject added power to your total promotional mix. They can draw attention to your product and stimulate immediate consumer action. However, their ability to make a contribution to the long-term success of your brand will again depend on how well they interact with your implicit promotion and the rest of your explicit mix.

Because premiums fall into the psychic offer category, the choice of a premium item should also take into consideration the relationship between the nature of the item on the one hand and the interests of your target customer group plus the overall theme of your promotional efforts on the other. The most effective premium is one whose intrinsic character conveys an image that is consistent with that projected by your advertising and other communication efforts.

### A Premium Case Example—The Marlboro Country Store.
The makers of Marlboro cigarettes developed a premium program centered around a catalogue featuring a western "country store" theme. One expert has cited it as an example of an exceptionally well-conceived and successful sales promotion

effort.[31] Marlboro has won an extremely large market share in a highly competitive field through an advertising campaign that associates the brand with the glamour, excitement, and adventurous tradition of the American west and the American cowboy. The objectives of this premium offer were to contribute to a strengthening of that image as well as to build increased awareness for the brand. The advertising program and the premium program can be considered cross-supportive in terms of theme and audience appeal. Logically, a sizable portion of prospects attracted to the advertising and the brand might also have an interest in acquiring related items of merchandise featuring an authentic western motif.

A broad assortment of such merchandise appeared within the pages of Marlboro's premium catalogue. Ranging in price from five-dollar cigarette lighters to one-hundred-dollar signed western prints, all were displayed within a unifying, pictorial setting billed as the "Marlboro Country Store." The catalogue itself was advertised in a two-page spread running in major consumer magazines and featured in store display pieces. The premiums were all "self-liquidating," that is, the price paid for each premium was sufficient to cover the cost to the sponsoring firm, even though it was below the normal retail price for the same piece of merchandise. The results of this effort were measured mainly in terms of consumer response to the premium offer itself. On this basis, the promotion was considered to be highly successful, with consumers purchasing over 30,000 items valued at more than $500,000.

| | |
|---|---|
| *Contests and Sweepstakes* | Contests and sweepstakes are both promotions in which you offer entrants an opportunity to win a prize or prizes. A contest is a promotional event in which participants compete on the basis of skill. A sweepstakes is a promotional event in which participants simply submit their names, with winners chosen by a lottery. Because a sweepstakes is clearly a game of chance rather than skill, it must be handled carefully to avoid possible legal complications. The sponsor of a sweepstakes does not usually require entrants to make a purchase because such a requirement could lead to potential prosecution under anti-gambling laws. |

Contests and sweepstakes can be used as promotional devices directed at either consumers, resellers, or members of your own sales force. Typically, though not always, promotions directed to resellers or sales force members tend to be contests, rather than sweepstakes, and the prizes are awarded as recognitions for achievement. For this reason, we will defer coverage of reseller and sales force contests until we reach the topic of recognition programs later in the chapter. At this point, we shall concentrate on contests and sweepstakes aimed at consumers.

Like premiums, contests and sweepstakes have an important psychic character in their appeal. They do not offer the consumer a direct or assured economic benefit. Instead, they promise excitement and the *possibility* of a sizable reward. One pair of experts has suggested that contests and sweepstakes have the potential of being as strong as the strongest premium offer with the advantage of usually being more powerful than the weakest premium offer.[32] The size of the prize is a meaningful factor in determining the appeal of

**FIGURE 17.14 A sweepstakes based on a theme aimed at reaching an important market segment**

*Source:* Courtesy of the Archives, the Coca-Cola Company.

a contest or sweepstakes. However, the full success of such a promotion stems from more than merely the prize value alone. Because prizes are often awarded in the form of merchandise or travel, the *nature* of the prize can be a significant factor in the success of the total promotion. When a contest is involved, the nature of the skills required of entrants can also play a major role.

Both the nature of the prize chosen and the nature of the required skills contribute most effectively when they are creatively aligned with the nature of the target audience you seek to reach. In addition, the more closely you can coordinate the contest or sweepstakes theme with the general theme of your advertising and product image, the more impact you are likely to produce. To illustrate how these principles can be activated in a promotional campaign, we will consider an example of each. The sweepstakes promotion was sponsored by Coca-Cola, and is illustrated by the advertisement shown in Figure 17.14. The contest is the long-running Pillsbury Bake-Off ©, advertised as pictured in Figure 17.15.

*The Coca-Cola "Denimachine Sweepstakes."*  In terms of demographics, the heavy-user group in the soft drink market is dominated by young consumers. In particular, the fifteen-year-old through twenty-nine-year-old age category is considered highly critical to the sales success of most soft drink brands. As reported in one article, the "Denimachine Sweepstakes" was introduced by Coca-Cola to create a special appeal to this consumer segment.[33] Another important objective of the promotion was to equip local Coca-Cola bottlers with a selling platform for securing additional off-shelf display space in supermarkets. To appeal to its target audience group, the company chose to as-

Source: Courtesy of the Pillsbury Company.

**FIGURE 17.15 An annual contest designed to reinforce a strong brand reputation**

sociate itself with a pair of merchandise items, both of which enjoyed tremendous popularity among young consumers at the time the sweepstakes was run. The two items were Levi's jeans and customized vans. The vans, plus 7,500 Levi's jean outfits, were offered as sweepstakes prizes.

Although no purchase was required to enter, the relationship between the sweepstakes theme and the Coca-Cola brand was emphasized through a variety of coordinated promotional efforts. These included heavy advertising on television and radio, insertions in Sunday supplements and youth-oriented publications such as *Hot Rod* and *Motor Trend,* and powerful, sweepstakes-related display pieces for point-of-purchase communication. Seventy-seven customized "Denimachine" vans were created and used by local bottlers for regional promotional activities. Coca-Cola received a total of 3,563,769 entries, the most it had received in any contest or sweepstakes it had sponsored for fifteen years. Moreover, Coca-Cola realized a measurable increase in sales and market share that analysts felt could be associated with the sweepstakes effort.

*The Pillsbury Contest—"America's Bake-Off ©."*   The Pillsbury Company has sponsored this highly successful promotional event for well over a quarter of a century. Entrants compete by submitting recipes and, ultimately, the finalists compete by actually baking their recipes in a group competition. In addition to its basic goal of extending and enhancing the Pillsbury image among a relevant target prospect group, the contest is a device for obtaining publicity in the trade press and for equipping the sales force with a means of encouraging greater reseller promotional participation. Entries are solicited both through advertisements and through in-store display pieces. The yearly version of the contest featured in Figure 17.15 was associated with specific product promotions for seven different Pillsbury items. It offered over $81,000 in prizes to the winners and culminated in a network-televised bake-off session held at the Statler-Hilton Hotel in Boston. Coordinated promotional efforts included coupon and refund offers run in conjunction with the contest itself. According to one published report the total promotional effort, of which this contest served as the centerpiece, helped to increase market shares of the brands advertised by from five to ten percent during the life of the promotion.[34]

**Recognition Programs**

A recognition program centers around a special award intended to motivate either a reseller or a member of your sales force. The award may or may not involve cash. Even when it is a cash award, it will usually be treated in a manner that makes it distinctly different from a normal commission, discount, bonus, allowance, or other routine type of cash payment. The more that a cash award can be dramatized as something special and out of the ordinary—in other words, endowed with psychic as well as economic appeal—the more effective it is likely to be. In many instances, an award in some form other than cash may be a more powerful motivator. It has been pointed out that, "The potency of cash as an incentive weakens as an individual's unfulfilled needs are pushed further up in the need hierarchy. Once basic physiological needs and safety and security needs are satisfied, whatever potency money retains as an incentive relates to unfulfilled esteem and achievement needs. Non-cash prizes are capable of filling these needs better than cash."[35] A primarily psychic approach, then, can take the form of anything from a certificate or trophy to an all-expenses-paid trip to an exotic overseas resort.

Like the other sales promotion techniques that have been discussed, recognition programs serve best as periodic or intermittent complements to your basic promotional mix. They are not substitutes for a soundly conceived sales compensation plan, a strong advertising program, or any other essential aspect of your overall promotional strategy. Ideally, a recognition program will meet at least three basic tests. First and most vitally, the award involved will be well worth the winning. Its worth may often be largely a function of its economic value, but the total worth will be greatly enhanced if the award presentation is well publicized within the sales organization or among other people in the same line of business. Second, the recognition program should be designed so that all sales force members or resellers both have a reasonable prospect of winning and recognize that they do. The criteria for choosing winners should be as clear, objective, and reasonably achievable as possible. Furthermore, the criteria should be fully explained to everyone who is eligible. Third, the recognition program should be focused on achievement of some specific promotional objective for the company. The SAM Award, a special-purpose recognition event sponsored by the Paper Mate Division of Gillette, serves as a good example of how a successful program can be designed by following these guidelines.

***The Paper Mate SAM Award.*** The SAM Award has been described as "the highest honor that any member of Paper Mate's sales force can achieve." The award was originated as a means of motivating sales force members to develop innovative approaches in their selling strategies and to provide a vehicle for disseminating information about such approaches throughout the sales organization. When a Paper Mate representative discovers a creative solution to handling a common problem, such as acquiring a new account or generating additional sales volume among a certain category of customers, he or she is urged to write it up in a detailed report. Based on these reports the company's district sales managers nominate candidates for the SAM Award.

The nomination itself carries a degree of recognition because a full description of the achievement that earned it appears in a booklet prepared by the sales promotion department and distributed to the entire sales staff. This booklet also carries a picture of the nominee.

At the end of the year, the top sales executives of Paper Mate choose ten finalists for the SAM Award from among all the nominees of that year. These finalists are then ranked by the same executives. The first place winner receives both a trophy and a five-day trip for two to any location of his or her choosing. Runners-up each receive $500. Of equal or greater importance than the prizes themselves is the manner in which winners are recognized and the setting in which the prizes are presented. According to the sales promotion manager, "We build up the presentation just like the Academy Awards, announcing the finalists first, then the runners up, and finally the winner."[36] Paper Mate executives have been reported to believe that the contest has served as a very effective promotional stimulant and that a large measure of its success can be attributed to its psychic reward component.

# CAUTIONS TO CONSIDER IN PLANNING SALES PROMOTION PROGRAMS

As noted in the opening section of this chapter, one aspect of sales promotion that makes it somewhat unique and more complex than other promotional elements is its degree of potential for misuse. This description is primarily applicable to those sales promotion techniques labeled as "special offers." You saw statements regarding cautions to consider in using these techniques at several points during the review of special offer categories. The issue is important enough to merit reemphasis at this juncture.

Some degree of risk is encountered whenever you use any promotional element. At the very least, all require an investment of funds that may be lost if the communication effort fails to achieve its purpose. At the worst, misjudgments in the use of elements such as advertising or personal selling could prove offensive to the audiences they are intended to persuade and produce negative results rather than positive accomplishments. Apart from these considerations, however, there are three added factors inherent in special offers that require you to analyze the propriety of their use with extra care.

The first factor stems from their frequent ability to achieve a positive sales response more rapidly than other promotional elements. Because they can often produce rather quick results, it can be tempting to use them hurriedly without a clear consideration of their full impact on your total promotional mix.

The second factor relates to their ability to serve as palliatives. On a short-term basis they can often compensate for a critical defect in some essential area of your strategy. For example, attractive refund or coupon offers may *temporarily* raise sales despite an anemic advertising strategy or weak personal selling efforts. To the extent that a special offer deceives you into overlooking the real problem in such cases, it can cause long-range trouble.

Third, special offers that are based on couponing, rebates, refund offers, combination offers, price-off deals, premiums, trade inducements, or performance allowances are essentially variations in forms of price competition. There are two serious flaws in any marketing program that relies too heavily on price as a competitive weapon. First of all, it is a strategy that can be easily and quickly copied by competitors. Second, even if it does not generate competitive retaliation, such a program tends to lose its effectiveness over time. Consumers eventually think of your "special, low price" as actually being your regular price. In consequence, if they use price in the context of its informational dimension as discussed in Chapter 2, consumers may downgrade your brand criteria ratings and lower their purchase intention levels for your brand.

*A Case Example of Special Offer Misuse*

The three-brand profit trend disaster as shown in Figure 17.16 is an illustration of how the overuse or misuse of special offers can lead to ruinous results. According to the published report,[37] Brand W and two major competitors shared over half the market in a product category in which sales were increasing at twice the rate of population growth. Brand W held the smallest market share of the three leading competitors. Its brand manager opted to seek a gain in share by switching emphasis from advertising to sales promotion—principally in the form of higher trade inducements. The far left portion of Figure 17.16 traces the consequences. The pattern of promotional decisions and effects can be described as follows, with the letters beside each line in the graph keying them to their representation in the figure.

(A) Over a three-year period, Brand W greatly increased its total expendi-

FIGURE 17.16
Negative results that
ensue from over-
reliance on special-
offer promotions

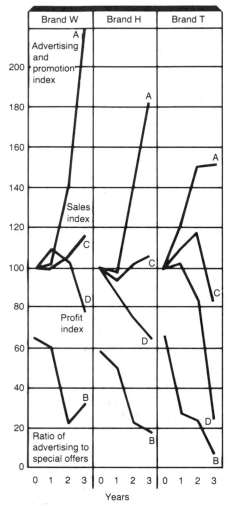

*Source:* Roger A. Strang, "Sales Promotion—Fast Growth, Faulty Management," *Harvard Business Review*, July/
August 1976, p. 123.

tures for advertising and sales promotion combined. (B) The increased promotional dollars invested by Brand W went to sales promotion whereas the advertising budget was actually reduced. (C) Sales did increase for Brand W, but not nearly in proportion to the increased promotional expense. (D) Profits rose briefly and then turned sharply downward. The middle and right portions of the figure picture the competitive responses undertaken by the two major rival brands in terms of the same four variables and over the same time span. Briefly stated, Brand W's two major competitors quickly followed the essentially price-oriented special offer strategy that Brand W had initiated. The only real consolation for Brand W might be that Brands H and T suffered even more serious profit setbacks.

*Implications
Regarding the
Climate in Which
Special Offers
Should Be Used*

Having enthusiastically discussed seven different categories of special offer promotion techniques, it may seem inconsistent to place so much emphasis on the potentially negative side-effects of some of these same techniques. The issue to be stressed is that special offers are ideally used to further strengthen an already sound promotional program rather than to cosmetically disguise flaws in a weak one.

It is true that their ability to serve as temporary palliatives or first aid measures may also prove useful when applied with discretion. For instance, it is often suggested that firms maintain a budget reserve for special offers to facilitate rapid response to a sudden and unforeseen competitive threat. As an illustration, if a rival brand introduces a new product feature or an intensified advertising program which threatens to erode your market share, quick action to fend off the immediate effects may be in order. In such a situation, a firm with a contingency-oriented sales promotion plan is well equipped to offset competitive inroads on a short-term basis while the company reformulates its basic promotional strategy. In these instances, being able to move swiftly by initiating a technique such as a combination offer, a trade inducement, or a refund can provide you with a means of *temporarily* blunting the force of your competitor's assault while you devise a longer-range and more complete program to hold your market position. However, a technique used in such a first-aid capacity should be treated only as a transitional measure that gives you time to regroup your entire array of promotional forces.

The general fact remains that a sound special offer strategy must exist as part of a sound and well-balanced promotional mix. Importantly, you should recall the positive examples of sales promotion that were set forth, including positive examples involving price-oriented special offers. The cautions refer to possible overuse or misuse of these techniques, and are not meant to imply an indictment of special offers per se as being universally dangerous.

## POSITIONING SALES PROMOTION IN THE FULL PROMOTIONAL MIX

In one sense, the fourteen sales promotion techniques we have reviewed are quite diverse. At first glance, such alternatives as product samples, recognition programs, and consumer sweepstakes seem to have little in common. However, viewed together they form an inventory of tools you can use to supplement and strengthen your overall promotional mix. Their essential commonality lies in the fact that each is normally employed as an adjunct device to help achieve some specific but relatively limited goal within a total strategy that relies on advertising or personal selling as its lead element. In addition, each tends to be useful mainly on a temporary, periodic, or intermittent basis whereas advertising and personal selling are relatively continuous in nature.

The need for skillful alignment with collateral elements has been repeatedly emphasized in our coverage of each individual promotional element. In the case of sales promotion, this need is especially pronounced. This is true partly because of the just-discussed perils that can underlie misuse of special offers. In addition, and more importantly, it is true because sales promotion is so often employed in a distinctly supportive capacity, with its success almost totally dependent on its close interaction with and contribution to your advertising or personal selling efforts. With this in mind, it can be helpful to picture the assortment of sales promotion techniques at your disposal as existing within a comprehensive strategy structure. Normally, that structure will rely most heavily on advertising and personal selling. Individual sales promotion options will tend to be located at various points along the path of the communication flow traced by the structure. The actual location of each technique and the feasibility of its use will vary with each unique promotional situation. Nonetheless, to illustrate how such a pictorial interpretation might look, we will work with two generalized possibilities. The first assumes that you are dealing with an ultimate consumer good and the second assumes that you are promoting an industrial market item.

*Positioning Sales Promotion in an Ultimate Consumer Market*

In Figure 17.17, a variety of sales promotion techniques have been tentatively placed into position as they might logically fit at specific points in a total promotional strategy structure. It is true of course that there is no absolute rule which restricts the use of any specific sales promotion technique to a particular role. However, the arrangement shown in Figure 17.17 represents widely used and typical positionings for sales promotion in the marketing of products aimed at ultimate consumers. For instance, if you were promoting a new brand of laundry detergent, the structural flow shown in this illustration provides a reasonably complete picture of the main sales promotion options you would want to consider and the points at which they would most logically apply.

It is important to notice two critical features of this illustration. First, all sales promotion techniques have been placed in the context of the total marketing program. In terms of explicit promotion, it is assumed that you have two major target audiences to whom your efforts must be channeled. The route on the left is concerned with promotion aimed directly at ultimate consumers. Your explicit promotional thrust in following this route is likely to begin with and center around advertising. The route on the right is concerned with influencing the resellers who make your brand available to ultimate consumers. In following this route, it is quite likely that your principal promotional activities will be centered around personal selling. Various types of sales promotion approaches can be injected along both routes. In every case, however, the sales promotion device is merely part of a total integrated strategic plan. It has an assigned role to play, usually on a temporary basis.

Second, the structure as pictured stresses the importance of defining specific objectives for sales promotion. A communication goal is indicated in the box superimposed above each potential sales promotion technique to emphasize that the technique is subordinate to the objective. You must determine that objective first and consider its probable value in helping you achieve your end goal. *After* you have done that you can turn to your sales promotion inventory to determine which tool might achieve that objective most efficiently. It is unlikely that you would decide to use all of the illustrated techniques simulta-

**FIGURE 17.17 Potential positionings for sales promotion techniques in the marketing of a new ultimate consumer good**

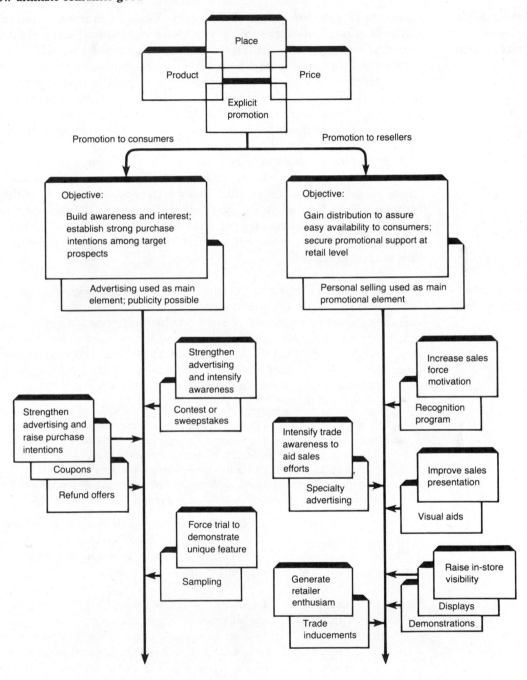

neously, although this is remotely possible. It is more probable that you would use various techniques over time as your needs and objectives change.

## Positioning Sales Promotion in an Industrial Market

Figure 17.18 illustrates some of the ways that sales promotion techniques might fit into the marketing of an item aimed at industrial users. Again, the notion of an integrated, total promotional mix is emphasized. This time the underlying assumption is that personal selling is your primary lead element. When this is true the route on the left serves principally as a preparatory phase of your strategy. In earlier chapters you have seen examples of how advertising can be used as one arm of an industrial selling program and can be assigned the function of obtaining leads for the sales force or of preparing the ground for sales representatives' direct contact efforts.

The route on the right centers around personal selling, which must act as the main line of communication. Again, sales promotion can be employed to achieve some very definite objectives along each of these routes. As in the case of the previous illustration, decisions concerning the use of sales promotion should begin by considering the objective that you seek to achieve. The choice of a particular sales promotional technique can then be appraised in relationship to that objective.

## Choosing Among Objectives of Sales Promotion

There is no undisputed set of guidelines to tell you precisely what objectives can be best served by any particular sales promotion technique. The general examples shown in Figures 17.17 and 17.18 are fairly representative of rather commonly discussed relationships between objectives and techniques. However, there are many different points of view as to what tasks sales promotion should be called on to perform in the total mix. For instance, a survey of the field led one writer to make the following observation:

> One bank, for example, broadly defines the role of [sales] promotion as increasing the use of its services by present customers, while advertising is aimed at attracting new customers. However, a manufacturer of consumer non-durable goods uses advertising to attract new customers and to maintain loyalty, and uses [sales] promotion primarily as a defensive tactic. One advertising agency sees [sales] promotion as a short-term incentive to attract new customers who will be retained through the long-term benefits expressed in the advertising. [38]

Because sales promotional objectives can be so different, the structural diagrams we have reviewed are useful mainly as broad concepts. The details of implementation must be tailored to fit the market setting and management philosophy accompanying each individual strategy situation.

## A Format to Guide Sales Promotion Strategy

Figure 17.19 compresses the recommendations which have been presented in connection with the preceding discussion of positioning possibilities for sales promotion, as well as cautions to be considered in using some of the techniques. The suggested decision sequence follows the same type of flowchart pattern previously introduced for personal selling and advertising. Because the full recommendations have just been covered, additional commentary on the flowchart will be brief.

**FIGURE 17.18 Potential positionings for sales promotion techniques in the marketing of an industrial product**

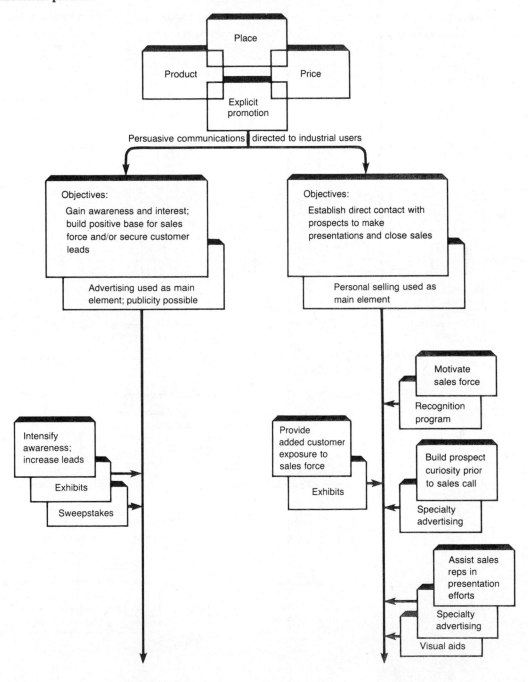

**FIGURE 17.19 Sales promotion in the promotional strategy process viewed as a sequence of decision fields**

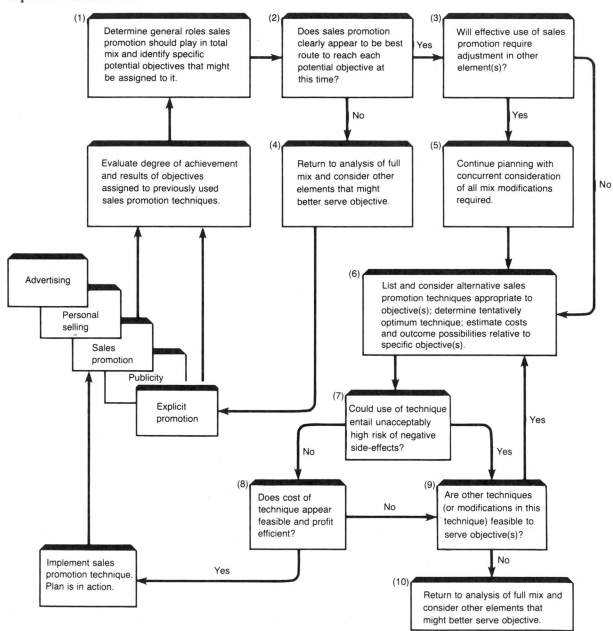

The procedure suggested in Box 1 is only a slight variation from the opening procedures suggested for personal selling and advertising. One change is that the word "roles" is deliberately put in the plural because sales promotion consists of a variety of techniques and can be adapted to several different objectives simultaneously. Following Box 1, you see an unusually high proportion of cautionary decision boxes calling for Yes or No answers that produce different decision paths. Their general purpose is to ensure that strategy formulation takes adequate account of two points emphasized in our previous discussion. First, sales promotion is generally used to inject a temporary infusion of power into your promotional structure; it is not a long-term substitute for an inherent weakness in some other element of your mix. Second, it normally operates in such close conjunction with one or more other elements that the need for cross-coordination is especially critical. These issues are reflected in the boxes numbered 2, 4, and 7.

Box 8 poses the question of budget feasibility. As with advertising, a sales promotion budget may be either predetermined or strategy-determined. In either event, the ideal procedure begins with the development of a total sales promotion planning proposal, covering all techniques envisioned for use over a suitable planning time frame, such as a one year period. In the case of a predetermined budget, cost feasibility must then be evaluated relative to pre-imposed constraints. In the case of a strategy-determined budget, feasibility must still be tested in terms of available funds. Because of the variety of sales promotion techniques available, the flowchart suggests that when a given technique does not appear to be economically possible or desirable, you explore alternative sales promotion techniques which might serve the same objective. If no such alternatives are appropriate, your decision path moves back to a reconsideration of the full explicit promotional mix.

As in the case of any promotional element, achievement should be measured after the fact based on the originally designated objectives. If at all possible, post-evaluation of a sales promotion technique should include assessment of communication effects. It should also attempt to isolate the role that sales promotion played in fulfilling the objective.

However, because sales promotion is frequently so intertwined with one or more other promotional activities, measurement on an absolutely pure and isolated basis may not always be possible. For this reason, somewhat oblique measurements and subjective interpretations often are employed. Examples of these were presented through the chapter. For instance, in the case of the Homelite Traveling Clinic, results were evaluated largely in terms of sales force reports on customer reactions. Because the clinic itself is so intimately associated with sales force activities, such an appraisal procedure is both practical and logical. A similar appraisal procedure prevailed in the illustration dealing with visual aid materials developed by the Bradley Corporation.

In other situations, the results of the sales promotion may be tested by some quantitative standard which is regarded as an indirect indicator of success. For example, the number of entries received in the Coca-Cola "Denimachine Sweepstakes" was used as a primary indicator of the achievements of the event. Regardless of the exact standards used to measure sales promotion results, it is important that those standards be decided upon in advance and agreed upon as providing meaningful measures. Your post-evaluation of results should then be used to provide a backlog of information for the guidance of future sales promotional planning.

# SUMMARY

Sales promotion embraces a diversity of techniques that can be classed under the two general headings of special communication methods and special offers. Special communication methods provide you with additional channels beyond the conventional mass media or direct personal contact through which you can deliver messages to your target audience. Special offers are added inducements intended to prompt action on the part of consumers, resellers, or company sales personnel. Both special communication methods and special offers are commonly employed as adjuncts to other promotional elements and are aimed at achieving some specific but relatively limited goal within a total strategy mix.

*Special Communication Methods*

Special communication methods include advertising specialties, point-of-purchase display materials, point-of-purchase demonstrations, sampling, visual aid materials for salespeople, trade or professional show exhibits, and training programs for resellers and industrial users.

An advertising specialty is an item of useful or interesting merchandise given away at no cost or obligation to the receiver. It can take almost any form and be put to a wide variety of uses. Basic guidelines for use of advertising specialties center around selection of an item that relates well to the audience, the particular objective sought, and the total promotional mix. Additionally, it should be designed and utilized with imagination and originality. Point-of-purchase display materials are normally associated with the promotion of merchandise at a retail outlet. The growth of self-service retailing has magnified their importance and made them especially powerful and critical marketing tools for many brands. Point-of-purchase demonstrations involve in-store display techniques that directly dramatize or demonstrate product features. Because the successful use of both point-of-purchase displays and point-of-purchase demonstrations requires cooperation from an independent merchant, their planning should be undertaken with consideration of both the consumer and the reseller in mind. To assure favorable placement in retail outlets, their value as profit builders for the store must be carefully studied and effectively communicated to store management.

A sample is a small quantity of a brand given to a prospect to induce trial. In practice, sampling is used in a wide variety of market situations. However, it generally tends to be most effective when you are introducing a new or improved brand that has clear, self-demonstrating advantages that are difficult to describe adequately through words or pictures. To control costs, a sensible sampling plan often involves limiting distribution to categories of individuals who have been previously identified as especially good target prospects. Careful consideration of the sample size can also be critical.

Visual aids for salespeople range from comparatively simple devices such as flip charts to rather complex and formal media items such as slide presentations or motion pictures. Because their proper use requires the understanding and cooperation of sales force personnel, they should be conceived and designed in light of sales representatives' particular needs. Further, the visual aids should be introduced to the sales force through a program that both generates enthusiasm and develops expertise in using them properly.

Exhibits at trade and professional shows offer firms a means of reaching prospects in a climate much different than that which accompanies normal sales calls. In a sense, such an exhibit represents a temporary branch sales headquarters placed in a heavy traffic location. Not only should the objectives of the exhibit be carefully thought out and specified in advance but the achievement of those objectives should be measured through a postshow audit.

Training programs for resellers and industrial users center around the objective of assisting participants in learning how to sell or use the manufacturer's product. They tend to be conducted in close association with a personal selling program. For this reason, their development should be coordinated with personal selling efforts and should include a high degree of sales force involvement.

*Special Offers*

Special offers can be classed into the two main categories of economic offers and psychic offers. Economic offers are primarily cash-oriented in their appeal. They attract recipients on the basis of money saved or received. Four types of special offers that fall into the economic category are coupons, price-off deals and combination offers, money-refund offers and factory rebates, and trade inducements and performance allowances.

Psychic offers emphasize some reward that has an emotional or qualitative dimension beyond any economic value it possesses. The three major types of special offers that fall into the psychic grouping are premiums, contests and sweepstakes, and recognition programs.

Coupons are the most widely used type of special offers to consumers. They entitle the holder to a reduced price on the purchase of merchandise. Price-off deals and combination offers are forms of price reductions sponsored by manufacturers and usually featured on the packaging of the brand. Money refund offers and factory rebates are variations of price-off offers in which the purchaser first pays the regular price of the item in question and then has a portion of that price returned to him or her upon proof of purchase. In general, all three of these techniques can serve any of four primary objectives. They can add excitement and appeal to advertisements, create a temporary sales lift for an established brand, help stimulate trial of a new item, and help convince retailers to stock or display a brand. The evidence suggests that they are most beneficial when the brand itself is strong and the offer is woven into a network of related promotional efforts. When utilized by themselves in an attempt to revive a faltering brand, they are much less likely to prove successful.

Trade inducements and performance allowances are special offers directed to resellers. Their intent is to help persuade retailers to stock or promote particular brands. As with the special offers directed to consumers, their success is likely to be directly proportionate to the initial strength of the brand with which they are used and their incorporation as one component in a broader promotional mix. A premium is an item of additional merchandise that a customer receives with a purchase. A contest is a promotional event in which participants compete on the basis of demonstrating skill, whereas a sweepstakes is an event in which they participate merely by submitting their names, and winners are chosen by a lottery. Premiums, contests, and sweepstakes can add short-term power to a promotional mix. Because this power is related to the psychic aspect of the offering, the qualitative character of these techniques should be planned with care and creativity. Ideally, that character will have particular appeal to the designated target audience and will be related in theme to the rest of your promotional program.

Recognition programs aim at influencing either resellers or company salespeople. The award involved is something that stands out over and above ordinary compensation. For this reason, its form and manner of presentation can be more important than its sheer monetary value. In an ideal recognition program, the focus is on the achievement of some clear objective of importance to the company, and all potential participants have an opportunity to compete on a reasonably equal and understandable basis.

Sales promotion techniques which fall into the special offer category can carry risks in terms of their potential for misuse. Although they can prove extremely helpful as part of a larger and well-conceived promotional program, they should not be used on a long-term basis to offset deficiencies in other segments of your strategy. Furthermore, special offers that center around price appeals can both invite competitive retaliation and if pursued for a prolonged period may cause degeneration of your product image via the workings of the price-quality effect.

With these cautions in mind, special offers can provide strong impetus toward fulfillment of promotional objectives when correctly positioned within a sound strategy framework. Although the precise objectives assigned to a particular technique can vary, based on market conditions and managerial philosophies, certain generalities regarding their use can be followed as guidelines for relating them to promotional goals. With that in mind, a procedure for ascertaining and evaluating the role of sales promotion within the full strategy framework was suggested.

## DISCUSSION QUESTIONS

1. Why is it useful to treat advertising specialties as sales promotion devices rather than merely as special advertising media categories?

2. Recalling the role assigned to sales promotion in the E'Suberante promotional mix (Chapter 13),

suggest four additional types of sales promotion techniques that could have been employed and assess the value of each in terms of strengthening the total E'Suberante campaign.

3. What is a "postshow audit"? What are the essential points to be covered in such an audit?

4. Talcott Enterprises has a sales force of approxi-

mately ninety people. Its members call on a variety of industrial firms, ranging from very small businesses to corporate giants. The company hired an outside agency to produce visual aid materials for its sales team. Agency personnel worked closely with Talcott's headquarters marketing staff to develop a colorful visual aid package centered around a slide presentation. The package, including a slide projector, was mailed to each sales representative with complete instructions for its use. In reviewing the results one year after the mailing, Talcott's marketing vice-president said, "I have serious doubts about the amount of good we got out of all that effort." Comment on this situation.

5. What is the difference between psychic offers and economic offers? Why might the same firm wish to use both in formulating its sales promotion program?

6. The vice-president of marketing for a division of a major automobile company was disappointed with the results of a consumer sweepstakes promotion conducted the preceding year. It seemed to have produced no results in terms of market share increase. He attributed this to the value of the prizes involved. (The grand prize had been

an all-expense two-week vacation for two in England.) He recommended that the value of all prizes be doubled in a similar sweepstakes promotion planned for the coming year. What do you think of this recommendation?

7. Discuss the basic difference between a trade inducement and a performance allowance and describe situations in which each could be especially useful.

8. The president of a major food company has hired you to advise her on marketing strategy. During one discussion she makes the following statement: "Some years back, our company became involved in a whole series of special offers. After some very bad experiences we have now given them up completely." How would you reply?

9. What general principles should be used in designing a recognition program for your sales force or resellers and why are these principles important?

10. What special aspects of sales promotion call for a decision flow process somewhat different than those suggested for advertising and personal selling?

## REFERENCES

1. Committee on Definitions, *Marketing Definitions, A Glossary of Marketing Terms* (Chicago: American Marketing Association, 1960).

2. Benson P. Shapiro, "Improved Distribution with Your Promotional Mix," *Harvard Business Review*, March/April 1977, p. 116.

3. "Building the Brand Versus Merely Moving the Product," *Marketing & Sales Promotion* (A Special Report in *Sales and Marketing Management*, 1979), p. 4.

4. Roger A. Strang, "Sales Promotion—Fast Growth, Faulty Management," *Harvard Business Review*, July/August 1976, p. 119.

5. George L. Herpel and Steve Slack, *Specialty Advertising: New Dimensions in Creative Marketing* (Irving, TX: Specialty Advertising Association, International, 1983), p. 3.

6. George L. Herpel and Richard A. Collins, *Specialty Advertising in Marketing* (Homewood, IL: Dow Jones-Irwin Inc., 1972), pp. 142–143.

7. This example is based on Herpel and Slack, *Specialty Advertising: New Dimensions in Creative Marketing*, pp. 120–121.

8. This example is based on Herpel and Collins, "Specialty Advertising in Marketing," pp. 168–169.

9. *Display Ideas for Supermarkets* (New York: Progressive Grocer, 1958), p. 2.

10. "Building the Brand vs. Merely Moving the Product," p. 5.

11. *Ibid.*, p. 14.

12. John Kotten, "Coca-Cola executives believe 1980 is critical in battle with Pepsi," *The Wall Street Journal*, 6 March 1980, p. 1.

13. Louis E. Repaci, "Sampling Program Meets Marketing Objectives of Two Different Companies," *Marketing News*, 16 April 1982, p. 3.

14. Milton P. Brown, et al., *Problems in Marketing*, 4th ed. (New York: McGraw-Hill Book Company, 1968), p. 776.

15. "Bradley Sells to Architects, Designers by a Film Program," *Industrial Marketing*, September 1978, p. 48.

16. *Ibid.*

17. William G. Nickels, *Marketing Communications and Promotion* 3rd ed. (Columbus, OH: Grid, Inc., 1984), p. 242.

18. Rudolph Lang, *Win, Place and Show: Effective Business Exhibiting* (New York: Oceana Publications, Inc., 1959), p. 19.

19. Suzette Cavanaugh, "Setting Objectives and Evaluating the Effectiveness of Trade Show Exhibits," *Journal of Marketing,* October 1976, p. 101.

20. *Ibid.,* p. 103.

21. "Homelite's Traveling Clinics," *Sales Management,* 12 December 1977, p. 14.

22. *Ibid.*

23. Ronald W. Ward and James E. Davis, "Coupon Redemption," *Journal of Advertising Research,* vol. 18, no. 4 (1978), p. 55.

24. *Ibid.*

25. Louis J. Haugh, "Massive Couponing Efforts Support New, Mature Brands," *Advertising Age,* 12 September 1977, p. 73.

26. William A. Robinson, "Top Promos of '76 Show Logic, Pertinence and Thoroughness," *Advertising Age,* 11 April 1977, p. 72.

27. Sam Cremin, "Coupons for non-existent detergent help police, postal service catch misredeemers," *Marketing News,* 4 May 1979, p. 14.

28. C. L. Hinkle, "The Strategy of Price Deals," *Harvard Business Review,* July/August 1965, pp. 75–85.

29. William A. Robinson, "76 top promos: Little goes long way—if you know way," *Advertising Age,* 9 May 1977, p. 58.

30. Louis J. Haugh, "Promotion Hotline," *Advertising Age,* 19 June 1978, p. 52.

31. Robinson, "Top Promos of '76 Show Logic, Pertinence and Thoroughness," p. 57.

32. John F. Luick and William Lee Ziegler, *Sales Promotion in Modern Merchandising* (New York: McGraw-Hill Book Co., 1968), p. 76.

33. Robinson, "Top Promos of '76 Show Logic, Pertinence and Thoroughness," p. 57.

34. *Ibid.,* p. 72.

35. Richard R. Still, Edward W. Cundiff, and Norman A. P. Govoni, *Sales Management: Decisions, Policies, and Cases,* 4th ed. (Englewood Cliffs, NJ: Prentice-Hall, Inc., 1981), p. 462.

36. Sally Scanlon, "Moving It," *Sales and Marketing Management,* 11 April 1977, pp. 33–36.

37. Roger A. Strang, "Sales Promotion—Fast Growth, Faulty Management," *Harvard Business Review,* July/August 1976, p. 123.

38. *Ibid.,* p. 123.

# CHAPTER EIGHTEEN

# *Publicity*

## FOCUS OF THE CHAPTER

Some writers use the terms "public relations" and "publicity" interchangeably. Others treat them as having somewhat different meanings. When a distinction is made between them, public relations is usually regarded as being the larger field of which publicity forms one part. For instance, the following is a typical definition. "Public relations comprises the actions of a corporation, a small business, a government, or an individual in promoting goodwill between itself or himself and the public."[1]

As viewed in this manner, public relations deals with a variety of "publics," including stockholders, employees, and legislators as well as consumers, resellers, and noncommercial information sources. Its activities include but are not confined to fulfillment of marketing objectives. For this reason, public relations specialists will find that their work overlaps that of specialists in

several other units of the firm. For example, that portion of the public relations effort that is aimed at employees is likely to be of concern to the personnel department as well as to the public relations department.

In this book, our preeminent interest is in the application of public relations as a promotional tool. Therefore, we will concentrate on those public relations activities that are intended to help promote products in a direct manner. In this limited sense, public relations is virtually synonymous with product-oriented publicity that will be the topic of concern in this chapter. However, the fact that publicity activities often are implemented by specialists who are part of a public relations rather than a marketing department and who are charged with responsibility for areas other than market-oriented publicity hints that promotional coordination of publicity may pose some special organizational problems. We will consider the nature of those problems later in the chapter.

# THE GENERAL NATURE OF PUBLICITY AS A PROMOTIONAL ELEMENT

*Promoting Candy through Motion Picture Publicity*

In the summer of 1982, theaters throughout the United States attracted extremely long lines of patrons waiting to see a film commonly known by an extremely short title. The film was *E.T.* and before the year was out it was on its way toward establishing box office records. Publicity was one factor that contributed to the success of the motion picture. However, an even more emphatic illustration of the power of publicity is the effect that *E.T.* had on the sale of Reese's Pieces, a candy produced by Hershey Foods. Reese's Pieces were not mentioned by name in the film but did appear very briefly when Elliot, the young hero, used them to help establish a friendship with E.T. himself. That brief appearance of the candy was enough to cause sales of the brand to increase by seventy percent in a one-month period.[2]

The relationship between *E.T.* and Reese's Pieces stands as a notable illustration of how even a very subtle publicity association can sometimes produce profound promotional effects. Reportedly, the producers of the picture contacted Hershey Foods only after the brand had been included in the filming, to suggest that Hershey might wish to participate in tie-in promotions. Hershey agreed and that decision was followed by the development of "E.T." point-of-sale materials, "E.T." premiums offered in conjunction with purchases of Reese's Pieces, and extensive distribution of the product in motion picture theaters, a retail outlet type not used for the brand prior to the film. In short, a publicity occurrence both raised sales and initiated a set of related revisions in the full marketing program.

*Promoting a Financial Service through Newspaper Publicity*

An even stronger testimonial to the power of publicity as a promotional mechanism is that connected with the sudden growth of Reserve Fund, the pioneer money-market mutual fund.[3] The originators of Reserve Fund sensed a marketing opportunity when they observed that savers could earn almost twice as much interest on money-market instruments as they were currently earning from passbook savings accounts. The obstacle that prevented the average person from taking advantage of the higher rate was the fact that money-market instruments required an investment of approximately $100,000, a sum that put them beyond the reach of the typical depositor. Reserve's solution was a mutual fund in which many small savers could pool their accounts to make possible the purchase of the higher-yielding investment. Promoting this innovative approach proved to be a formidable task. For the first two years, Reserve's main promotional efforts concentrated on personal selling activities, which met with little success. Then, the *New York Times* ran an article on the Reserve Fund and the resultant publicity suddenly changed a struggling business into a major financial force. The assets of the fund surged from under one-half million dollars to almost $2 million in less than one month following the story, and then kept growing. By 1982, the Reserve Fund had assets of $3 billion and its success had caused widespread changes in banking and related financial practices.

Admittedly, the two examples sketched above are exceptional illustrations of customer reaction to publicity. Not only were the market responses unusually pronounced and rapid but the immediate sales increases appeared to be due almost entirely to the effect of publicity; the other explicit elements played minor roles at most. It is more commonly the case that publicity makes its contribution in a less dramatic fashion and forms only one portion of a mix dominated by some other element. Nonetheless, because these two examples tend to isolate publicity as a promotional element they can serve as worthwhile models to use as backdrops for our discussion. As well as illustrating publicity's potential power, they provide points of reference regarding some critical features of its singular nature.

*Working with an Independent Transmission Vehicle.* As noted in the definition presented in an earlier chapter, "Publicity is nonpersonal stimulation of demand for a product, service or idea by means of commercially significant news planted in the mass media and not paid for directly by a sponsor."[4] Both this definition and the two examples emphasize the feature that makes publicity unique. This is the fact that it always works through a mass communication vehicle that is acting independently of the sponsoring company. That mass communication vehicle may be one which normally carries no standard commercial messages such as a motion picture. Alternatively, it may be a vehicle such as a magazine, newspaper, or television program that carries paid advertising and may *also* serve as a carrier of publicity items. In either event, final control over transmission of the message rests in the hands of the vehicle rather than in the hands of the sponsoring company. This circumstance makes publicity distinctly different from advertising not merely in terms of its audience appeal but also in terms of the planning and strategy that you must undertake in order to use it as a promotional element.

The outside decision makers who control the vehicle possess complete freedom to pick, choose, and alter the persuasive message you wish to send to your target audience. For this reason, when you seek to use a mass media vehicle as a channel to reach prospects through publicity, it is useful to think of the persuasive communication flows that are required as occurring in two stages. The first stage is concerned with efforts to persuade the vehicle to cooperate in your strategy plan. The second stage involves persuasive communication reaching consumers, consumer advisors, or consumer suppliers via the mass media.

As presented in Figure 18.1, the first stage begins with development of a company publicity effort that usually takes one of three main forms: an information release, a special event, or a "participation." Descriptions of each of these forms and examples of how you can work with them will be presented in greater detail later in the chapter. Following such development, your next task is communication with each vehicle sought as the message carrier. At this point, you should consider that vehicle as being a special class of prospect that must be "sold" on the idea of working with you and serving as a noncommercial information source that will deliver your message to consumers, resellers,

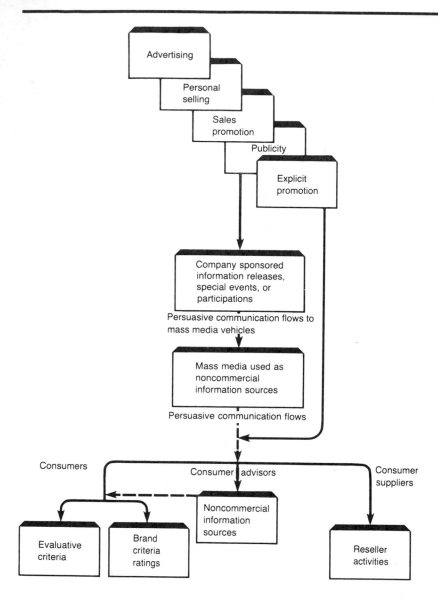

FIGURE 18.1
Publicity in the
explicit promotional
mix

or other noncommercial information sources in the second stage of communication flows.

The fact that the vehicle is acting independently has two important implications. On the positive side, when you obtain favorable publicity, the independent status of the message carrier can make the communication especially powerful in terms of persuading target audience members. On the negative side, the freedom of media vehicles to reject or alter your publicity material presents an obstacle that must be overcome. Both of these implications merit some further comment.

***The Positive Side—Unusually Strong Persuasive Potential.*** In comparing the value of publicity to the value of advertising, one writer stated "We are dealing with two factors in relating editorial [publicity] to paid advertising. Editorial [publicity] has far greater credibility. Editorial exposure is often assumed to be worth from three to five times that of comparable advertising space or time."[5]

A leading marketing authority has drawn an even sharper and more colorful comparison as follows:

> The very fact of advertising's enormous ubiquity, and the consequent difficult and costly struggle for the consumer's attention, makes it especially surprising that public relations is so marginally employed in the communication mix of heavy advertisers. . . . If advertising's very abundance creates a high coefficient of agnosticism, then public relations has a special claim to merit. Its distinction is the greater credibility of its message. [6]

As these commentaries indicate, promotion through publicity benefits from the source effect that was discussed in Chapter 9. Over time, many of the individuals who make up your target market have become familiar with certain media vehicles and have come to trust them as reliable information outlets. A vehicle may thus acquire attractiveness and credibility, which make it a more influential information source. Some of that influence may be transferred to your message when the vehicle carries your advertising. However, in an advertising context you will probably acquire only a portion of it at best because sponsorship of the message is still clearly identified with your brand rather than with the vehicle itself. On the other hand, when you receive favorable publicity, you should benefit much more fully from the vehicle's inherent influence because that vehicle is now acting as *both* message sponsor and message presenter. In the case of *E. T.* and Reese's Pieces, it would appear reasonable to surmise that the aura of whimsical attractiveness that attached to the motion picture influenced audience perceptions of the product and enhanced its desirability. In the case of the Reserve Fund and the *New York Times,* it is equally reasonable to hypothesize that the long-established credibility and prestige of the newspaper conveyed almost instant stature to an organization that was new and unorthodox in its approach.


***The Negative Side—Obstacles to Obtaining Publicity.*** If you could secure all the publicity you wanted it would probably be one of your most heavily used promotional elements. In practice you can usually not achieve nearly as much publicity coverage as you would like. Because it involves no direct charge and because it can prove so effective as a persuasive impetus, you will find yourself competing with many other firms that are also seeking valuable time and space in publicity vehicles. Most such vehicles accept only a small fraction of the materials and proposals offered to them. For instance, one report indicated that the business and financial editors of newspapers reject about ninety percent out of the one hundred or so publicity releases which reach their desks each day.[7] This does not mean that editors and other media people are antagonistic to publicity. On the contrary, the indication is that they are highly receptive to publicity possibilities *which serve their editorial or entertainment needs*. For instance, the producer of a popular network television program has said, "I keep urging public relations people to contact us with ideas for guests, but we still usually have to seek out our own guests. I have seen relatively low interest from PR people. We like to hear from people with ideas, and we need help from publicists."[8]

When writers, editors, producers, and other media personnel say they are always looking for more publicity items, they mean more items that will appeal to their readers, viewers, or listeners and will fit the formats of their shows or publications. Building your planning from this perspective is a key feature in putting publicity to work as part of your promotional mix. For instance, in preparing news releases you must understand the personalities and interests of the vehicles to whom you are sending your messages and prepare those messages accordingly. Above all, you should not make the mistake of treating publicity releases as simply another type of advertisement. One practitioner draws the following distinctions between the preparation of good publicity as opposed to the preparation of good advertising:

> The advertising writer . . . does not concern himself so much with news value but concentrates on creating a message that will produce maximum interest and will compete successfully with other print ads or commercials. . . . The public relations specialist looks for an element in the product, its application, or its users that has legitimate news value. [9]

Another expert, using newspapers as his example, offers this advice:

> *"Thinking like the editor"* is the key to success in writing news and feature stories for American newspapers. . . . [The] way to start is to forget the kind of stories *you* want to run and, instead, consider what the editor might want to run. . . . Good public relations people make a habit of reading and understanding the newspapers to which they send releases. . . . [The] kind of stories that a newspaper wants in every department is plain for anyone to see in every day's issue. Editors are naturally flattered when those who offer them a news story give evidence of having read and appreciated their paper. Stories should be written, for example, for readers with the special interests of people in the editor's own town or area. [10]

With a few appropriate modifications this counsel is applicable not merely to newspapers but to any publicity vehicle at which you may be aiming. Apart from thinking in terms of news or entertainment value rather than merely advertising value and apart from gearing your presentation to the focus of the vehicle, you will need to prepare your publicity material in a manner that expedites its use. This means devoting attention to small details. It also means making it as easy as possible for editors, program planners, or other media personnel to evaluate your material. In essence, you are designing a special sort of product that must please a special group of consumers. The critical details and the precise format will vary as the vehicle varies. Therefore, you must be alert to special needs on a case-by-case basis.

# MAJOR FORMS OF PUBLICITY EFFORTS

As suggested in Figure 18.1, when you seek to use publicity as a promotional element your efforts to initiate the process will normally take one or more of three major forms. These can be classified as *information releases, special events* sponsored by your firm, and *participations* in newsworthy or entertainment-oriented activities which are essentially extraneous to your firm and your product.

An information release is a story or background material for a story that is submitted to a mass-media vehicle such as a newspaper, trade journal, or radio station. The story itself may revolve around new developments or improvements in the benefits and features of your product, or around innovative applications in which your product is or could be used. In any case, its merits rest on its ability to provide fresh information of particular interest to the viewers, listeners, or readers of the vehicle. A special event is a newsworthy situation created by a sponsoring firm in an attempt to generate press, radio, or television coverage. A participation involves placement of your product into the context of a public occurrence or creative production originated independently of your own firm but possessing a potential for drawing favorable attention to your brand. We will now consider each of these forms in greater detail.

*Information Releases*

Information releases are referred to by an assortment of designations such as "press releases," "publicity releases," and "news releases." Regardless of the designation, when used as a promotional device their common format is built around provision of information. Because that information is drawn from a situation that already exists rather than one that must be newly created for publicity purposes, information releases are usually the least expensive and most widely used form of publicity effort. The task is one of searching for interesting story possibilities, determining the vehicles for which the stories would be of most value, and then preparing releases especially designed to appeal to those vehicles and their audiences. The most expeditious search route for story possibilities will vary by product category but generally includes a survey of one or more of the following topical areas:

- New products
- Significant improvements in existing products
- Favorable product test results, especially when reported by outside testing agencies
- Significant contract awards
- Innovative potential usage applications
- Case histories of successful usage situations

**Publicity Based on Stories Concerning New or Improved Products.** Product developments can often make interesting news. The Reserve Fund case described earlier is a notable example of how an innovative market offering can evoke positive and valuable editorial coverage. To achieve extended and enthusiastic media response for a new or improved product, your brand must usually show promise of possessing a truly meaningful or at least intriguing difference over competition. In short, when seeking to obtain publicity based on product news, you are looking for something "out of the ordinary" or something which can be portrayed in a newsworthy manner. If you are simply introducing a new brand of toothpaste with a difference in flavor, your probability for obtaining publicity based on this fact alone is negligible. However, if you are introducing a new brand of toothpaste with demonstrated superiority in reducing cavities you have a solid base for a publicity campaign. The original introduction of Crest toothpaste is an illustration of just such a circumstance. Other examples have been cited by an expert who has written, "Take the classic automotive introduction of the original Ford Mustang. Everyone first learned about it via editorial exposure. . . . Many years ago, an editorial mention of Vicks [medicated ointment] and [later] one for Kent Cigarettes, detonated an avalanche of sales."[11]

When you have a reasonable probability of garnering publicity based on new product development, you will need to be prepared to exploit your advantage as fully as possible. Product publicity of this sort may be somewhat easier to obtain in the industrial market than in the ultimate consumer market. Because there are so many business publications aimed at specialized and relatively narrow industrial segments, you can often frame your product development information in several different publicity releases, each of which appeals to a distinct audience. For instance, when the P. R. Mallory Corporation developed a new type of silicon rectifier, the firm prepared an assortment of information releases each targeted to specific audience categories.[12] The material that Mallory sent to the general press emphasized how the new rectifier could improve television and radio sets. This story was used on major news services and received coverage in over seventy newspapers. The financial press was sent a release emphasizing potential contributions the innovation could make to the electronics industry in general and to Mallory's sales in particular. It resulted in stories in such business publications as the *Wall Street Journal* and *Business Week*. A third publicity package went to publications circulated to the electronics manufacturing industry. The fourth went to business publications edited for service and repair segments of the electronics field. In each case, the information release was tailored to fit the needs and interests of both the media vehicles to which it was sent and the final audiences for which it was intended.

***Test Reports, Contract Awards, Innovative Usage Proposals and Case Histories.*** When an independent agency tests your product and gives it a favorable report, you have a valuable publicity opportunity. For instance, *Road and Track* magazine conducts periodic tests on various types of automobiles and then publishes the results. When a make of automobile is evaluated favorably, the published report provides an excellent base for publicity efforts and merits exploitation through information releases to other vehicles. In similar fashion, if your company is awarded a substantial or important contract, you again have a logical setting for an information release. The award is likely to be of interest to other potential customers and the publications that serve them. In a sense, the award represents not only an opportunity to call attention to your firm but also a type of endorsement that can help fortify your image and prepare the way for personal selling efforts.

Articles about an innovative use for your product can be an excellent path to opening up new markets. Developing such stories can require some effort. However, that effort can pay handsome rewards. For example, one team of communications consultants has described the publicity program that they developed for a manufacturer of sophisticated, automated materials-handling systems. Competition in the field was intense and rival companies were especially anxious to secure the business of large-scale users such as postal systems and major mail-order distribution firms. In the rush to sell to such accounts, prices were being slashed. Meanwhile, another part of the potential market was being almost entirely overlooked. This segment was made up of smaller firms that could save substantial amounts of money by automating their order-picking process. However, these firms were largely unaware of the basic equipment that was available and, for that matter, equally unaware of their need for such a product. The decision was made to attempt to reach this latter group of customers using publicity as an opening wedge. The rest of the story has been recounted as follows:

> They [the smaller firms] wouldn't be reading the broad-based materials-handling magazines, looking at ads for a system to meet their needs, because they didn't know they had such needs. The answer was to contact editors of magazines serving the specific industries our client had pin-pointed. With each, we talked about the exciting possibilities for substantial cost savings to their readers by converting to automated handling. We offered to prepare an in-depth article analyzing the benefits of such a conversion in terms of the needs of that industry. And we found the editors were as excited about the idea as we were. . . . The results: A number of six to eight magazine page articles in a variety of publications, bylined by the president of our client's company, including several cover treatments. Note well: The topic was *not* our client's specific systems; it was the whole *concept* of introducing automation in order handling. But, of course, in illustrating the concepts, we were able to use his specific systems as examples. And his company was clearly established as a place to call if you wanted to work with the leaders of the field. Reprints of these articles became important sales-support material for use in direct mail to target industries, for trade show hand-outs, inquiry response, sales door-openers, and the like. [13]

Publicity based on innovative concepts talks about *what can be accomplished*. In contrast, publicity based on case histories talks about *what has been accomplished* through use of the product. The same team of communications consultants just quoted offered the following commentary on the use of case histories:

> When one of your customers uses your product or service to achieve top results, that's the real world! It's the ultimate endorsement. . . . The case history is particularly effective when it shows your firm providing extraordinary or innovative techniques in contributing to the end result. In fact, this factor can make

the case history an exception to the rule that your product or service has to be new and newsworthy to rate feature treatment. If the way you've helped a customer to make use of it is new and interesting, that may be all you need. . . . One of our more successful case history articles involved another client, which offers computerized design of printed circuits to the electronics industry on a service bureau basis. This client worked with a customer firm to develop a computer program that could design the very difficult boards which use high-speed logic. Not only did the story spread the word that our client was now able to design this particular kind of board, but it also showed them to be willing and eager to explore problem areas of whatever kind with customers and help them find solutions. [14]

*Special Events Sponsored for Publicity Purposes*

In all of the information release examples cited above, the ingredients for publicity existed before the publicity materials were created. The promotional task was mainly one of putting things into the proper form and aiming at the proper vehicles. When you lack existing events to publicize, or perhaps when you lack enough of them, you may wish to create the event that is needed for your publicity base. The three most commonly used types of special events employed for this purpose are (1) press tours, (2) newsworthy company projects, and (3) commercially sponsored news "happenings."

*Press Tours.*    The press tour is a special event in which reporters or editors are guests of the sponsoring company on a promotionally oriented trip. For instance, press tours are a common practice in the travel industry. Resorts, state tourist bureaus, and airlines invite members of the press to participate in expense-paid tours so that they can experience first hand the attractions being promoted by the sponsoring organization. With some creative imagination, press tours can be adapted to serve the goals of many other industries. As an illustration, the North Atlantic Seafood Association has sponsored a series of tours for food editors. On these trips, the media personnel have visited such places as Norway, Iceland, and the Maritime Provinces of Canada. An industry publication reported the following reasoning behind the planning of one of these tours. "[The] purpose of the trip was to validate promotional claims made as to the quality of North Atlantic fish, as well as to demonstrate to food editors of consumer magazines the many ways frozen fish can be prepared and served. The tour included processing centers far above the Arctic circle."[15]

*Newsworthy Company Projects.*    Another way to work at developing a situation which can generate publicity is to initiate a "newsworthy company project." Such projects are commonly more useful as a means of promoting a firm's overall public image rather than promoting specific products. However, the publicity produced may serve as a worthwhile base that can assist other promotional efforts. In describing and commenting on such projects, one public relations professional has advised, "Set up a museum of your types of products. Build a fanciful, futuristic display to show the on-going results of your [research and development program], start a scholarship fund."[16]

He also tempered this advice by suggesting that these projects be employed with restraint unless they can be clearly handled in a manner that promises delivery of promotional results. "While such activities are definitely good-will builders, note that they play a limited, indirect role in increasing your chances of increasing your sales, and remember—that is the real purpose of a market-oriented program. If they are attached to your market-oriented effort, they can drain the budget very easily and dilute the effectiveness of everything else."[17]

***Commercially Sponsored News "Happenings."***   This can often be the most expensive way to acquire publicity. On the other hand, it can also yield extremely powerful and profitable media coverage. For instance, in Chapter 3, you were asked to try to think of how you might get good press coverage to publicize a breakfast cereal or a chain saw—or to introduce a new chemical that retards the wetting of paper to make it stronger and less likely to break. Each of these situations was actually the subject of a commercially sponsored news happening. The approaches involved are fairly straightforward, yet they display creativity and a flair for injecting drama into rather ordinary product situations.

The breakfast cereal was Quaker's "100% Natural" and, to build a publicity base for it, the company sponsored Jim Fixx, author of *The Complete Book of Running*. Fixx made 10,000-meter runs in cities representing seven of Quaker's top market territories. While the campaign was in progress, the publicity value of these appearances was artfully integrated into a well-coordinated total promotional mix. The campaign was reported as follows:

> In each of the seven cities, Fixx appears at a press breakfast and goes on a "test run" with local sports writers and prominent runners. He also appears on TV and radio talk shows, discussing proper diet for runners (he unsurprisingly advocates low-fat carbohydrate-rich foods), his book and the nutritional benefits of 100% Quaker Natural cereals. . . . In the 3 weeks preceding each run, run-oriented TV spots appear up to 200 times a week and ads featuring Fixx appear in leading dailies in the city. . . . A tie-in promotion on packages of 100% Natural offers a copy of the first paperback edition of Fixx's running book. Posters and place cards with entry forms are displayed in sporting goods and athletic shoe stores and some supermarket breakfast food sections. [18]

The chain saw was the Homelite brand. The publicity event was "The Tournament of Kings," a competition in which professional loggers could compete on the basis of their prowess in felling large trees with chain saws. Not only did the tournament generate press coverage that helped boost Homelite's reputation, but it also helped create a higher level of reseller support. Homelite's director of advertising was quoted as saying, "On top of marketing success with the pro's there has been tremendous secondary excitement at the retail level. Dealers who are carrying pro and consumer models are gaining benefits for both."[19]

As for the chemical for treating paper, the happening created to intensify its newsworthiness displayed remarkable creativity as illustrated by the following account:

> The product had many important potential uses, such as in making shopping bags which would not burst and other protective packaging; but simply to tell

about it was very dull. The solution was a *demonstration.* . . . A press conference was set up at the Waldorf-Astoria Hotel in New York City. The main feature, besides the usual press kits of releases, fact sheets, pictures, and statements by company officers, was a large and very wet bath shower spraying into a temporary pool in the middle of the room. At the proper moment, a beautiful woman arrived, dressed in a paper bathing suit, and skipped into the shower. Needless to say, nothing happened to the bathing suit. Thanks to the new chemical, it *was* water-resistant. . . . Other paper objects were also dunked, but the bathing suit made the biggest impression and the best pictures. [20]

## Participations

A participation operates on much the same principle as the borrowed reward technique discussed in Chapter 9. It makes use of a promotional opportunity residing in a preestablished event or setting not created by your firm and not having any inherent relationship to your brand but generally possessing high audience attraction and appeal. The successful publicizing of Reese's Pieces via that brand's appearance in *E.T.* is one example of a participation. The Goodyear blimp is another. By means of its blimp, Goodyear participates in an assortment of events, such as the telecasting of NFL football games. The blimp also was featured as a major point of interest in a motion picture, *Black Sunday.* As a platform for publicity, Goodyear's blimp creates a type of communication that may convey a more powerful and authoritative perception of the company's products than could be achieved through an equal amount of advertising. Goodyear astutely uses the blimp in its advertising as well as its publicity efforts, thus interweaving two elements of its promotional mix in a manner that strengthens both.

In seeking participation opportunities you need not confine yourself to television or motion picture settings. With ingenuity and a capacity for improvisation it is sometimes possible to inject your product into unusual public events and realize significant publicity from a seemingly unlikely relationship between the event and your brand. As a case in point, consider the possibility of reaping publicity benefits for a household textile dye by associating it with a rock music festival. This is what skillful public relations experts managed to do for Rit brand dyes.

The festival was held in Woodstock, New York. Its attendance and eventual fame surprised even the people who originally conceived it. Over the course of ten days, it attracted over 50,000 people, most of whom were in their teens and early twenties. Woodstock provoked national and even international attention. Pictures and stories of the festival crowded the pages of newspapers and magazines, and television gave it heavy coverage. At its outset the staff of a public relations agency sensed a potential for using Woodstock as a means of promoting a seemingly unrelated product. One of the participants in the publicity planning process reported, "At the legendary Woodstock Rock Festival, we arranged to give away hundreds of tie-dyed T-shirts. Media coverage of the participants wearing these shirts helped create the now-storied 'tie-dyed generation' boosting the sales curve of our client, Rit Dye."[21]

Granted, the "Rit-at-Woodstock" example may represent a relatively uncommon opportunity. Nonetheless, the promotional inventiveness embodied in its conception can be a useful model to keep in mind when exploring participation possibilities.

Much more frequent opportunities exist in connection with motion picture and television programs. Based on a study conducted by a major advertising agency, the appearance of a brand in such settings can be a low-cost but highly effective means of reinforcing an advertising campaign and strengthening consumer awareness of your brand name.[22] To expedite your search for such opportunities you can hire the services of firms that specialize in placing products in movies and on television shows. Working on either a yearly retainer basis or on a fee-per-placement, these organizations review scripts in advance, suggest appropriate brand-appearance possibilities to the producers, and then arrange to have the products available on the set during the filming. As one article on the subject has pointed out, "It is . . . no accident that Clark Kent had a breakfast of Cheerios in *Superman*, that a bottle of Kikkoman soy sauce was part of the backdrop in the Alan Alda film *The Four Seasons* or that American Express T.V. commercials were part of the story line in *Oh God, Book II.* And how many times does the hero or heroine depart on a TWA flight?"[23]

Because such an appearance by your product does not afford you an opportunity to make straightforward statements about its benefits and features, it should not be regarded as a replacement for advertising. Its value centers around its power to augment your standard advertising program through a positive and seemingly noncommercial public exposure.

## POSITIONING PUBLICITY IN THE FULL PROMOTIONAL MIX

*Organizational
Considerations*

As pointed out at the opening of this chapter, publicity exists in the context of general public relations. Often this implies that its execution may be in the hands of persons who are not in the advertising or marketing departments. In fact, based on some of the commentaries noted earlier, it could be argued that publicity belongs in a special unit because it requires types of expertise different from those possessed by specialists in personal selling, sales promotion, or even advertising. If publicity is to be integrated with the rest of your mix, however, coordination with other explicit elements is vital. The sort of organizational cooperation required to achieve good coordination may not come easily, a fact recognized in the following analysis:

> The educational backgrounds of marketing and public relations practitioners differ considerably, producing almost two separate "cultures." . . . No wonder the two groups carry around denigrating stereotypes of each other. Marketing people often view public relations people as press agents, flacks, sponsors of pseudo-events [e.g., Miss "Pickle Queen of 1985"]. Public relations people view marketers as hucksters, "numbercrunchers" and deodorant salesmen. Often each views the other's function in its narrowest perspective. [24]

Because of this sometimes uneasy relationship, the first matter of concern in positioning publicity in your mix centers around improving communications between marketing and public relations specialists. Marketing decision makers should recognize that the person with special skills in publicity can be a most valuable contributor to the strategy team, even though he or she must also be concerned with broader, nonmarketing concerns of the firm. A group of writers who examined this issue drew the following conclusion:

> [P]ublic relations is a powerful but often underused sales tool in marketing management. Public relations and marketing departments in the same organization need to collaborate and synchronize their marketing planning. Without this cooperation, valuable resources are wasted. Organizations that do not have public relations departments but occasionally use consultants also should emphasize more integrative or collaborative efforts. [25]

**A Format to Guide Publicity Strategy**

*Setting Objectives.* Figure 18.2 proposes a very general strategy guidance procedure for publicity that is similar to those presented for the other explicit elements. Once more, your strategy planning process should begin with consideration of the general role that publicity is intended to play in your total mix and with delineation of objectives that might be assigned to it. Because publicity is ostensibly "free," or at least does not have a direct charge associated with it, there can be a temptation simply to seek as much publicity as possible without clear assessment of the purposes it might serve. Under one line of reasoning, "All publicity is good publicity." This view is characterized by the sometimes-voiced statement, "I don't care what they say about me as long as they spell my name correctly."

Especially when viewed in the context of a product promotion effort, the prudence of this statement is highly suspect. For example, whereas the marketing executives involved were highly pleased to see motion pictures in which Superman ate Cheerios and in which E.T. was attracted to Reese's Pieces, there have been other brand name references in motion pictures that have been viewed with less gratitude. Two notable illustrations in which the product's makers were reportedly chagrined have been described by an observer who wrote, "In the movie *Chinatown*, Jack Nicholson slogged along in a drainage ditch complaining about his 'god-damn Florsheim shoes,' and John Travolta carried a bottle of J&B Scotch with him to the men's room in *Blowout*."[26]

Although it is remotely possible that even such negative references could somehow have a salutary effect on consumer attitudes, the general conclusion of promotional strategists is that publicity of this sort should be prevented if at all possible. Stated in a very general manner, the overall objective of publicity is to achieve *favorable* representation in the mass media and, ideally, to place your brand in situations that fortify the image built for it through other explicit promotional activities. One public relations specialist with a long involvement in product publicity efforts has offered a list of much more specific objectives that publicity can serve in relationship to other elements. Some of the alternative goals he suggests are the following:

> [Paving] the way for sales calls to the trade. Familiarity [through publicity] breeds interest and receptivity.

**FIGURE 18.2 Publicity in the promotional strategy process viewed as a sequence of decision fields**

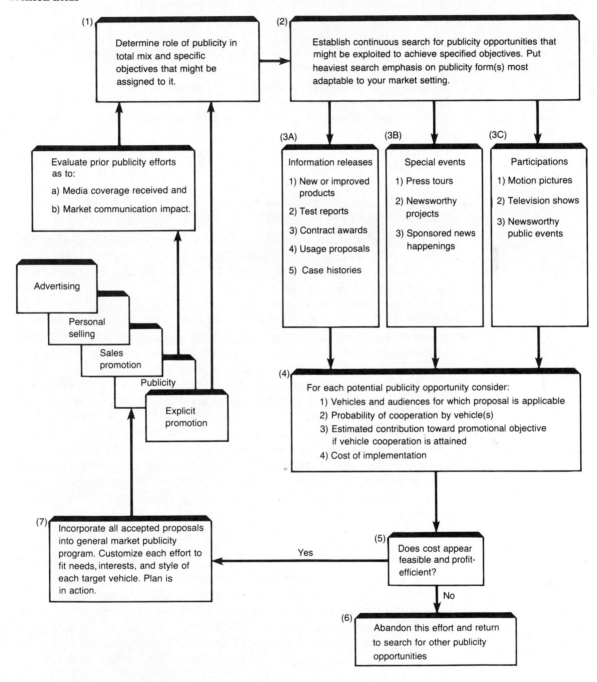

[Obtaining] new sales leads. Trade publications are primary sources of information in many industries.

[Offering opportunities] for article reprints to merchandise to purchasing agents, company executives, and thought leaders.

[Merchandising] sales and promotional literature. Trade publication "new literature" sections often pull requests surprisingly, [and by implication can aid further in securing leads for your sales force].

[Helping the sales force merchandise point-of-purchase display materials.] When chain store executives know there is a large publicity push behind a brand, they are more likely to allow display materials [and] allot increased shelf space [to your brand].

[Gaining] mass exposure for sensitive products or specialized markets—like the youth market—where advertising might be especially mistrusted or indelicate. Fads can be started or accelerated.

[Providing] consumer education on the product and its use. How-to articles and recipes are examples of the educational function of publicity. [27]

These examples hardly exhaust the objectives you may wish to consider, but they do outline some major possibilities and provide a starting point to aid you in sharpening your appraisal of functions that publicity might fulfill as a component in your promotional scheme.

***Searching for Publicity Opportunities.*** Once the objectives have been identified, your active publicity efforts begin with a search for possible opportunities to achieve those objectives. Because the acquisition of publicity is always dependent on securing voluntary cooperation from some independent media organization, it is important to stress at the outset that you are dealing with *possibilities* rather than certainties. Success depends on locating news or entertainment situations that will serve the interests of the communication vehicle as well as furthering your own purposes. With this in mind, Box 2 in Figure 18.2 proposes that a continuous search procedure be maintained to uncover and explore opportunities for publicity efforts consistent with your objectives and showing promise of having appeal to the media.

In line with our previous coverage of publicity efforts, exploitation of publicity opportunities will usually follow the route of either information releases, special events, or participations. The relative degree of emphasis you place on seeking publicity through each of these forms will vary depending on the industry in which you are operating. Some industry categories lend themselves especially well to information releases because they are inherently newsworthy. Others do not. For example, one survey of editors indicated that certain product and service fields automatically tend to be treated as "high news value" whereas others are considered "low news value."[28] High news value fields include airlines, automotive firms, and aerospace companies. In contrast, product areas such as appliances, office equipment, and tobacco products are widely thought to have low news value. If yours is a product that has a natural news value appeal to potential publicity vehicles, the bulk of your publicity thrust might be focused on searching for opportunities relating to information releases. On the other hand, if you are working in a category with low media interest, your search may lean toward seeking opportunities for special events or participations.

*Preevaluating Potential Publicity Efforts.* Compared to the other explicit promotional elements, publicity is likely to represent a rather small portion of your budget. When it works properly for you, its payout potential can be relatively high. Still, generating publicity does involve expenses. Your basic cost is in the time of the personnel employed in a continuous search and review of publicity opportunities. Beyond this, the actual execution of specific publicity efforts will require investments in time, effort, and money. Box 4 of Figure 18.2 suggests that you estimate both the cost and potential results of each proposed effort. Especially in the case of special events which must be created to build publicity, a careful appraisal is in order. If you are not convinced that the potential cost-benefit ratio of the effort is favorable, the proposal should be abandoned. When that ratio does appear to be favorable you can move on to the task of implementing the project.

*Postevaluating Results.* Evaluation of results after a publicity effort has been undertaken entails two separate measurements. The first is fairly direct and straightforward, and involves appraisal of the results in terms of actual media coverage. At this stage, you are really asking, "How successful was this program in attracting the target vehicle or vehicles?" It is often tempting to evaluate time or space secured via publicity on the basis of the cost you would have incurred through actual purchase of that time or space at standard advertising rates. One criticism that has been cited for this approach is the fact that publicity space or time can be much more valuable than comparable advertising space or time. As pointed out earlier in our discussion, material appearing in a noncommercial setting is widely thought to be more believable and attractive than advertising. On this basis, you are underestimating the value of the publicity if you measure it only in terms of what it would have cost you to buy the same time or space for the placement of advertisements.

The second postevaluation measurement that you should consider involves the publicity effort's effect on the final audience you are trying to reach. At this stage you are asking, "How successful was this effort in influencing consumers, resellers, or professional advisors?" Attaining the correct answer to this question can pose some serious problems. For one thing, the effects of publicity may be so thoroughly intermingled with those of other promotional elements, principally advertising, that they are virtually impossible to identify on a separate basis. Second, even if you wished to set up a formal experimental situation to isolate the impact of a publicity effort, it would probably be impossible to do so because the final timing and placement of publicity is not under your direct control. In most instances, the best that can be done amounts to largely subjective evaluations based on general feedback. One executive expressed himself on this subject by stating, "As many times as we've tried, we have yet to specifically measure the value of a dozen or more stories resulting from a single news release, but we do know publicity is working.

Customers and prospects are aware of our products and advantages. They know who we are and what we can do for them."[29]

Postevaluation procedures may be less than perfect, but they are nonetheless worthwhile. To the extent that you can quantify results, you should. When this is impractical, informed subjective interpretations may have to suffice. In either case, as with any other promotional effort, your evaluation of past efforts can provide input for your planning of future strategy.

## SUMMARY

Publicity is nonpersonal stimulation of the demand for a product, service, or idea by means of commercially significant news or entertainment material that is carried in some mass media vehicle, such as a magazine, newspaper, television program, or motion picture. There is no *direct* charge for the time or space used to carry the message, and the vehicle operates independently of the sponsoring company. This vehicle independence has both positive and negative aspects from the standpoint of the firm seeking to benefit from publicity.

On the positive side, the fact that the newspaper, magazine, or other publicity vehicle is acting independently may add a significant amount of attractiveness and credibility to the communication. Powerful illustrations of how this can occur were offered by examples dealing with publicity for Reese's Pieces and the Reserve Fund. The negative aspect of vehicle independence stems from the fact that the sponsoring company must undertake special efforts to obtain media cooperation and that the company never exercises the same degree of control over the message as it does in working with the other promotional elements.

There are two persuasive stages involved in securing the delivery of publicity communications. The first stage centers around convincing some appropriate vehicle to cooperate in presenting your publicity material to its readers, viewers, or listeners. If you are successful, the second stage consists of the actual flow of persuasive communication about your brand via the vehicle to your final audience of consumers, resellers, or noncommercial information sources. In implementing the first step, you should think of each vehicle as a special type of prospect. This implies that you should study its particular nature, needs, and interests and then carefully tailor your publicity efforts to make them especially appealing to that vehicle.

Three headings under which the major forms of publicity efforts can be classified are: (1) information releases, (2) special events, and (3) participations. Information releases provide stories or background material about a product or the company that produces it. They may focus on a new product, an improved product, test reports about product performance, new contract awards, innovative usage proposals, or case histories concerning product applications. Special events are newsworthy situations created by a firm for the express purpose of generating publicity coverage. Participations involve the association of your brand with a preestablished and essentially nonrelated event that is likely to possess high audience attraction and appeal.

All three of the above forms of publicity effort require that you first locate a suitable opportunity to exploit. The amount of emphasis you choose to place on one or another of these forms in designing your overall strategy is likely to vary depending on the type of industry in which you are operating. When you are in a field that tends to be considered as having "high news value," your primary emphasis may be on information releases. However, if yours is a product category generally treated as having "low news value," you may place more stress on finding opportunities for special events or participations.

Publicity is usually treated as part of a larger public relations function. Because the public relations specialists who handle product publicity are often housed outside of the marketing department and charged with many nonmarketing responsibilities, the implementation of product publicity can easily be impeded by problems associated with faulty interdepartmental communication. To overcome this potential hurdle, it is important to work at establishing and maintaining an atmosphere of cooperation and understanding between marketing and public relations specialists.

As with any promotional element, the inception of your publicity strategy should begin with determination of the objectives you wish to achieve through this element and the role it should play in your total mix. Because the attainment of publicity depends on first locating appropriate news and entertainment opportunities, a sound strategy also requires an active and continuous search for such opportunities.

Postevaluation of the results of a publicity effort has two phases. The first phase involves measurement of effects in terms of achieving the media exposure sought. The second phase involves an attempt to assess the actual results of publicity in terms of the degree to which it served as a positive persuasive force in influencing the consumers, resellers, or professional advisors who form the final target audience. The first phase of measurement is relatively easy to undertake. In the second, you may have to rely largely or entirely on general feedback coupled with subjective judgments. Despite the fact that these second phase measurements may be less than perfect, they are worth pursuing in as formal and systematic a fashion as possible to provide inputs to guide your future publicity strategy planning.

## DISCUSSION QUESTIONS

1. Discuss the differences between publicity and public relations.
2. In what respects is publicity a stronger promotional element than advertising? In what respects is it weaker?
3. Your company has developed a new treatment for upholstery fabric that makes it burn-proof and stain-proof. The treatment must be applied to new fabric before the furniture is manufactured. Describe the types of media vehicles at which you might aim information releases and outline the different points you might wish to stress for each type of vehicle.
4. Your company produces a candy bar that is spe-

cially fortified with vitamins and minerals. It has only been sold regionally on the west coast. The brand is about to be introduced to major markets in the midwest. You are in charge of the promotional program. What form or forms of publicity efforts might be applicable in that program? Describe your ideas and the reasoning behind them as fully as possible.

5. An insurance company that specializes in coverage of business risks for industrial firms (e.g., fire, theft, and workmen's compensation), is interested in gaining more visibility via publicity. What suggestions would you offer for this company's consideration?

6. Why do publicity and advertising sometimes coexist uneasily within the same organization? What can be done to integrate these two elements more fully?

7. How can the results of publicity efforts be evaluated?

8. The Amalgamated Lock Company developed a new and improved lock for sliding glass doors. A press release was written by the company's advertising staff and sent to over two hundred publications. Only two of them used the story. Discuss the possible reasons for this poor acceptance rate.

9. In an earlier chapter, it was mentioned that the import firm distributing E'Suberante wine was interested in obtaining participations in suitable motion pictures. Considering the details sketched out in the *E.T.*/Reese's Pieces example, do you think they should aim for a particular type of motion picture involvement, or would the exact nature of the picture and E'Suberante's role in it be of little or no consequence?

10. Crawfish is a popular food in some parts of the country, especially in Louisiana, but reportedly it has an undeservedly poor image among millions of prospective customers who have never actually tasted it. You have been assigned to promote crawfish to a broader market. How might publicity be used as part of a total promotional program for crawfish?

## REFERENCES

1. R. P. Lovell, *Inside Public Relations* (Boston: Allyn & Bacon, Inc., 1982), p. 13.

2. Joseph M. Winski, "Hershey Befriends Extra-Terrestrial," *Advertising Age*, 19 July 1982, p. 1.

3. "Two Guys and an Idea Worth Millions," *Time*, 17 January 1983, p. 35.

4. Committee on Definitions, *Marketing Definitions, A Glossary of Marketing Terms* (Chicago: American Marketing Association, 1960).

5. Donald G. Softness, "What Product PR Can Do for You in Today's Advertising World," *Advertising Age*, 2 August 1976, p. 19.

6. Theodore Levitt, *The Marketing Mode* (New York: McGraw-Hill Book Company, 1969), p. 200.

7. John S. Schafer, "What the Editor Thinks about Publicity," *Public Relations Journal*, January 1969, p. 22.

8. Kathy Rand, "How to Work with TV Talk Shows," *Public Relations Journal*, March 1977, p. 20.

9. Philip Musgrave, "Eleven Steps for Planning and Evaluating Your Public Relations Campaign," *Management Review*, August 1976, p. 44.

10. J. E. Marston, *Modern Public Relations* (New York: McGraw-Hill Book Company, 1979), p. 142.

11. Softness, "What Product PR Can Do for You in Today's Advertising World," p. 20.

12. Robert V. Cummins, "Blasting a New Product into Orbit," *Industrial Marketing*, August 1959, pp. 46–67.

13. Caroline Pohl and David Apker, "How to Use In-Depth Trade Press Articles to Expand Your Markets," *Marketing News*, 23 March 1979, p. 7.

14. *Ibid.*

15. "North Atlantic Seafood Association Takes Editors to Norway's Frozen Fish Centers," *Quick Frozen Foods*, August 1978, pp. 179–184.

16. John Peters, "Good PR Strategy Can Reinforce All Efforts in Communication," *Industrial Marketing,* February 1976, p. 55.

17. *Ibid.*

18. "Quaker Push Uses Runner Fixx, a "Natural" for 100% Natural Brand," *Marketing News*, 3 November 1978, p. 4.

19. "Marketing Briefs," *Marketing News*, 9 August 1978, p. 2.

20. Marston, *Modern Public Relations*, pp. 288–289.

21. Softness, "What Product PR Can Do for You in Today's Advertising World," p. 20.

22. L. J. Haugh, "Promotion Trends," *Advertising Age*, 29 November 1982, p. M-28.

23. *Ibid.*
24. Philip Kotler and William Mindak, "Marketing and Public Relations," *Journal of Marketing*, October 1978, p. 17.
25. Jonathan N. Goodrich, Robert L. Gildea, and Kevin Cavanaugh, "A Place for Public Relations in the Marketing Mix," *MSU Business Topics*, Autumn 1979, p. 57.
26. Haugh, "Promotion Trends," p. M-28.
27. Softness, "What Product PR Can Do for You in Today's Advertising World," p. 20.
28. Schafer, "What the Editor Thinks about Publicity," p. 23.
29. Gerald S. Schwartz, "Planning Product Publicity Pays Off," *Nation's Business*, September 1978, p. 35.

# PART SIX

# *Promoting Through Distribution Channels*

# CHAPTER NINETEEN

# *Promoting Through Resellers*

## FOCUS OF THE CHAPTER

As pointed out in Chapter 1, the place component of your marketing mix can have two distinct promotional aspects (Figure 19.1). The first can be thought of as an *image transfer aspect.* This implies that at least in some cases the reputation or image that prospective purchasers attribute to a particular reseller can affect their perceptions of the brands carried by that reseller. The second is the *reseller participation aspect.* This deals with the degree of support and cooperation you obtain from resellers toward fulfilling your promotional objectives. Such support and cooperation can range from the reseller's merely having your product in stock and available for customers to giving it prominent display space to promoting it very actively through energetic explicit promotional efforts. Although the bulk of this chapter will focus on the reseller participation aspect, we will begin by considering a brief case in which a firm's exceptionally successful promotional program includes careful handling of both aspects.

*An Example of Place/Promotion Strategy*

There are approximately four hundred companies in the United States that produce greeting cards. If you were to ask someone to name as many of those companies as she or he could remember, it is likely that the first and possibly the only response you would receive is "Hallmark." Hallmark's dominance of the greeting card industry is the result of a combination of sound business

**FIGURE 19.1 Two aspects of reseller influences that can affect purchase decisions**

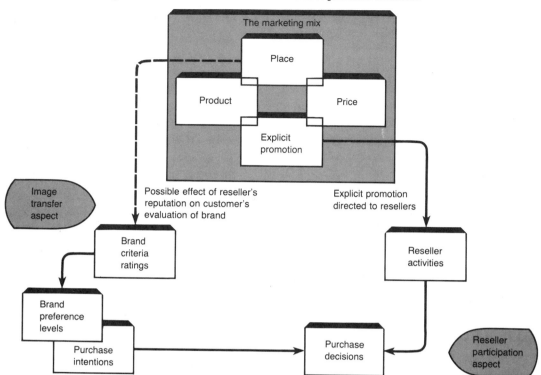

practices encompassing all areas of the firm's operations.[1] One such area involves Hallmark's approach to reseller relationships, which is based on consideration of both the image transfer aspect and the reseller participation aspect.

*A Distribution Strategy Designed with Consideration of Image Transfer.*
Because of the impact of image transfer, Hallmark limits distribution of its brand to retail outlets whose character conforms to the reputation the firm has carefully cultivated through the nature of its products and the advertising it uses to communicate about them. For example, you will not find Hallmark cards in supermarkets or discount stores. You will find them in such outlets as stationery stores, gift shops, and drugstores whose environment and perceived status is compatible with the brand personality Hallmark seeks to project. (To exploit the volume potential available through supermarkets and discount stores, the company produces a subsidiary line under the name "Ambassador Cards.")

*Strengthening the Reseller Participation Aspect.* With respect to the impact of reseller participation, Hallmark concentrates on achieving prominent instore display of its merchandise. This is accomplished by providing retailers with special display fixtures that are designer-fashioned, color-coordinated, and "mood-lighted" to show off the Hallmark line in the best possible setting. Hallmark was a pioneer in concentrating special attention on retail display efforts and much of the company's success rests on the imaginative innovations it introduced in display techniques.

***Generalizing from the Hallmark Example.*** It should be stressed again that Hallmark's approach to promoting through resellers is only one part of a total business strategy that begins with a study of consumer needs and desires and then proceeds through careful product development plus a coordinated blend of effective explicit promotion. However, the company's recognition of the importance of a well-conceived reseller promotional policy is a further important ingredient in its total strategy plan. Of course, the exact policies followed by Hallmark are not universally applicable. For many products, such as popular brands of razor blades or laundry detergents, the image transfer aspect may be negligible or nonexistent. Consumers expect to find such brands in a wide variety of outlet types and probably think of the brand independently of the store at which it was purchased.

In terms of the reseller participation aspect, most manufacturers might find it difficult if not impossible to obtain the extensive amount of display space that Hallmark has achieved. Alternatively, many manufacturers might find it more profitable to focus on stimulating some other form of reseller support such as personal selling efforts by resellers' sales personnel. Nonetheless, though the specifics of the Hallmark example may not be universally applicable, the general approach it illustrates can be very useful to bear in mind as you formulate your own program. Briefly stated, this approach involves giving careful study to all effects that resellers can have on sales of your brand and then engineering a specially tailored strategy plan that will maximize those effects in the most positive manner.

## SOME BASIC ISSUES AND TERMS

To lay the groundwork for discussing methods of promoting through resellers, it will be helpful to start with a quick review of two topics relating to reseller policies. The first deals with the general nature of distribution channels and strategies. The second deals with the basic outlook and focus of the independent business firms through whom you distribute your products.

*The General Nature of Distribution Channels and Strategies*

Comprehensive and extended discussions of the intricacies involved in the relationships between producing firms and reseller firms can be found in a variety of excellent published materials that concentrate on that subject.[2] The coverage in this book will be abbreviated and confined mainly to those portions of such relationships that center around methods of generating promotional support from three major types of resellers—manufacturers' representatives, merchant wholesalers, and retailers. However, to place that coverage in proper perspective we will begin with a short overview of the essential nature and role of resellers in marketing.

***Reseller Types and Channel Length.*** Resellers may be either retailers who sell to ultimate consumers or wholesalers who sell to industrial users or to other resellers. Both types of resellers are also referred to as "middlemen" or "marketing intermediaries." They form links in a channel of distribution through which producers can make their goods and services available to target prospects. In some distribution schemes, conventional resellers may be eliminated entirely. For instance, IBM and Xerox have customarily marketed major equipment items directly to industrial users without the assistance of middlemen. Similarly, firms such as Mary Kay Cosmetics and Shaklee have been successful in selling products to ultimate consumers without the use of traditional classes of middlemen. However, most producers work through a distribution channel that includes at least one level of reseller organizations. For instance, a company may sell its products to retailers who in turn sell to ultimate consumers. Frequently, the distribution channel may include several levels of resellers. As an illustration, a consumer goods firm may sell through one type of wholesaling organization that then resells the product to another wholesaling firm that markets it to the retailers who serve the ultimate consumers for whom the product is intended.

The decisions concerning the number of reseller levels you should employ are affected by an assortment of factors outside the realm of promotion. For example, such matters as efficiency and economy in performing transportation and storage functions can be important considerations in determining the proper length of your distribution channel. At the same time, however, there is also a promotional issue involved in decisions about channel length, which arises because the addition of any reseller level to your channel causes you to lose some degree of control over the flow of persuasive communication about your market offering. In consequence, an increase in the length of your distribution channel tends to produce a coincident increase in the complexity of developing a clear plan for working with resellers to encourage their participation in your promotional efforts.

***Intensity of Distribution.*** In addition to decisions concerning the appropriate length of its distribution channel, a firm has to make decisions concerning the appropriate "intensity" of its channel plan. This refers to the number of reseller firms through which it will distribute its products at any given level in the channel. For example, will you make your brand available to all retailers who will agree to carry it or will you restrict its availability in some manner? The three broad choices open to you are (1) intensive distribution, (2) selective distribution, and (3) exclusive distribution.

Under an *intensive distribution* policy, you do not restrict availability but seek broad reseller coverage. Your brand will be open for sale by any middleman organization that wishes to handle it. Under a *selective distribution* plan your product is made available only through some limited number of resellers in each market area. The Hallmark case illustrates a selective distribution policy at the retail level. Under an *exclusive distribution* arrangement only one reseller firm is given the right to carry your product in any given region. While selective and exclusive distribution tend to reduce your market visibility and customer access, they also usually strengthen the relationships you enjoy with those reseller firms through whom you market your offerings. For this reason, when a selective or exclusive distribution policy is feasible and desirable, it will normally upgrade the amount of influence you can exert in seeking active reseller promotional support.

*The Basic Nature and Outlook of Resellers*

Your plan to achieve active promotional participation from your resellers should begin with clear recognition of two vital points regarding the character and business outlook of the middlemen you seek to influence. First, each reseller firm is an independent business unit with goals and interests of its own. These may sometimes be different from your goals and interests. Second, resellers are usually more concerned about their relationships with the customers they serve than their relationships with the firms whose products they carry. One pair of observers has commented on this matter by stating, "Despite efforts on the part of managers to organize an efficient and effective channel system, such efforts are sometimes futile, because they do not fully account for the differences in perspective and orientation of independent middlemen. The latter are in business to satisfy their customers and are not in business to satisfy the desires of other channel members."[3]

Your programs to induce reseller support will be most effective when they can be clearly seen as furthering the resellers' independent interests and strengthening some aspect of the resellers' customer contact activities. Chapter 17 presented several examples of how such programs can be successfully undertaken. For instance, the Pepsi Challenge promotion was designed in such a way that it not only helped stores sell more Pepsi-Cola but also created a sense of in-store excitement and attracted customers who would buy many items other than Pepsi-Cola. The Homelite Traveling Clinic aimed not merely at assisting dealers to sell Homelite products but also at improving their power in attracting and retaining customers through better repair and service capabilities. To inject a note of contrast, it may be useful at this juncture to demonstrate what can happen when a manufacturer thinks only of its own goals and fails to take the independent status and customer orientation of the reseller into account. Consider the following brief illustration:

> [A] well-known tire manufacturing company, which prided itself on its dealer point-of-purchase promotional pieces, learned, after conducting a research study on the subject, that its promotional programs were largely wasted; dealers did not want the promotional materials and discarded them almost immediately upon receipt. The tire company found that dealers were primarily concerned with getting customers into their stores and not with selling the consumers once they entered the stores. [4]

Working with your resellers, then, demands that you first take pains to acquaint yourself with their point of view and design strategies compatible with that point of view. Sometimes your understanding of resellers may evolve as an outgrowth of formal market research studies. More often, it is likely to be a result of feedback supplied by members of your own personal selling organization who are in constant contact with your resellers. The provision of such feedback data can be one important function of your sales staff. For this reason, it can make good sense to devise a plan to train and motivate your sales force to gather and report such information as one part of their regular duties.

## PROMOTING THROUGH WHOLESALERS

**Working with Manufacturers' Representatives**

The terms used to designate manufacturers' representatives varies by industry. They are also referred to as "manufacturers' agents" and, in the grocery field, as "food brokers." Their major function is to sell the products of several different producers in some designated sales territory. They do not buy or take title to the goods they sell; they rarely maintain inventories or become involved in transportation of merchandise. Typically, they forward orders to the producer for direct delivery to the customer. Normally, they represent brands that are in related product lines but not direct, head-on competitors. Manufacturers' representatives essentially are independent salespersons. Promotion, mainly in the form of personal selling, is their specialty. They may be used in place of a company sales force or they may be used to supplement a company sales force.

For many purposes you can think of a manufacturers' representative in the same way that you think of your own full-time sales representatives. To this extent, much of what you read in Chapters 10, 11, and 12 is applicable. However, like all resellers, they are *independent* business people rather than persons in your direct employ. Therefore, you have less control over them. Furthermore, other manufacturers' brands will generally be competing for their time and attention. For these reasons, you may want to make special efforts and offer special incentives to gain extra support from them. The typical manufacturers' representative receives a percentage commission rate; the sheer size of the commission is one factor that can influence the amount of promotional emphasis your brand receives. However, building an optimum relationship with your manufacturers' representative goes beyond merely setting an attractive commission rate.

***Establishing a Sound Base of Communication and Sense of Partnership.*** It has been pointed out that producers often fail to secure proper promotional coverage from a manufacturers' representative because they pass up the opportunity to work as closely with the representative as they could and should. The solution advocated by a variety of observers is both to think in terms of the needs and goals of the representative firm and to make that firm aware of your own needs and goals; in other words, the solution is to work toward establishing a sense of partnership. An illustration of how failure to do this can lead to trouble is dramatized by the following short case history.

A well-known publishing firm secured a manufacturers' representative to perform a part of the firm's distribution tasks—personal selling and promotion. After about eighteen months, the publisher experienced cash flow and sales revenue problems. Upon study, it was found that the manufacturers' representative was not placing the necessary effort behind the line, largely because the publisher had not really understood the needs of the manufacturers' representative. In order to do the job, the manufacturers' representative needed much more information about the marketing plans of the publisher, which the latter had failed to supply. Without being privy to this information, the manufacturers' representative could not possibly develop a coordinated selling effort. The result was serious financial problems for both parties. [5]

One expert has pointed to compatibility as being the key to a successful relationship between the producer and the representative. Furthermore, he sees the route to compatibility as being closely tied to understanding the self-esteem needs of the representative. He argues that, while the typical representative is clearly interested in the commissions earned, she or he is also highly motivated by the desire to be thought of and treated as a professional. In his words, "They seldom think of themselves as just salesmen." In order to secure effective promotion of your brands through representatives he urges that you "make your successes and your failures theirs. . . . [Put] their egos on the line, as well as the commissions they earn."[6]

***Supplying Back-up Support.*** A description of the work of a successful manufacturers' representative was given in Chapter 10 in the words of Tad Collins who sells various lines of packings and seals. Some of the points mentioned by Collins merit repetition at this point. In particular, it is worth recalling the stress he puts on support mechanisms provided by some of the firms he represents. Product samples and copies of relevant trade journal articles were two such types of sales aids; help from factory representatives in handling certain critical account presentations was another. Although the exact mechanisms may vary by product category, you should be alert to opportunities for such cooperative support to enhance the representative's efforts on your behalf.

## Working with Merchant Wholesalers

Merchant wholesalers buy and sell either a broad assortment of related goods or a deep assortment in one rather narrow product category. Generally, they offer their customers a number of competing brands. The intensity of promotional activity varies greatly among merchant wholesale firms. Some are active promoters. Others place their primary emphasis on making goods quickly and easily available to customers and in handling routine transactions without becoming deeply involved in heavy promotion of the brands they carry. As one commentary has pointed out, "The wholesale salesperson may have a catalogue with 5,000 to 10,000 items and it is impossible to do a creative job on all these items. Thus, he or she acts more like a clerk on the road, offering suggestions, answering questions, and taking orders."[7]

The existence of such wide variations in promotional intensity among this reseller group suggests you should first estimate the maximum amount of selling effort you might obtain from any given merchant wholesaler under the best possible conditions. In large measure, the extent of your attempts at generating support will then be directly related to your estimated probability of securing active promotional participation.

***Factors Affecting Your Promotional Potential.*** One major study concluded that the amount of involvement and promotional cooperation you can expect to secure from a wholesaler is related to four primary factors. They are (1) the nature and number of products carried by that wholesaler, (2) the nature and relative importance of the various customer types served by the wholesaler, (3) the nature and amount of services required by the wholesaler's customers, and (4) the nature and intensity of competition faced by the wholesaler.[8] The strategy implications that can be drawn from the findings of this study include giving serious consideration to the following four possible types of channel management techniques.

**1.** Insofar as possible, choose and cooperate most heavily with wholesalers who limit the number of products and brands they carry. Your ability to do this will vary with your product category and the nature of your brand. If you are selling toothpicks, it may be all but impossible. If you are selling major household appliances, it is not only possible, but quite sensible.

**2.** Attempt to increase the relative status of your brand as a volume component in the wholesaler's total line. The amount of attention and emphasis your brand receives will generally be directly related to its percentage of the wholesaler's total sales. Put simply, if your line accounts for twenty or thirty percent of a wholesaler's total volume, you are likely to receive much more promotional activity than you would if your line accounted for only five or ten percent. One way to influence this situation is through the intensity level of distribution that you choose. The fewer the number of wholesalers who carry your brand in any given area, the higher the sales volume is likely to be for each wholesaler who handles it. Therefore, as you move from intensive distribution to selective distribution to exclusive distribution, the relative importance of your brand will increase for those wholesalers who carry it. On this basis, in situations in which your market and competitive structure permits a choice, a selective distribution policy may give you more promotional influence than an intensive policy, and an exclusive distribution policy may give you maximum influence.

**3.** Whenever possible, seek wholesalers whose target market emphasis is congruent with your own. As is true of many marketers, a wholesaler may serve a variety of customer types, some of whom will be much more important to that wholesaler than others. For example, if you are a manufacturer of laboratory supplies, two wholesalers who carry your line along with those of other producers may service such different customer types as medical laboratories, hospitals, science departments of schools, and research units of manufacturing plants. Based on the total dollar sales potential of all the lines they handle, hospitals might be the most important customer group to one wholesaler whereas the research departments of manufacturers might be of most importance to another. In a case such as this, the amount of promotional emphasis your line receives will probably be directly related to its appeal to the wholesaler's most important customer group. If your products are oriented primarily toward hospitals, it is likely that you will achieve much stronger promotional emphasis from the first wholesaler than the second.

**4.** Set up programs to build strong channel relationships by aiding wholesalers in solving their problems and serving their customers. Although there are many exceptions, producer firms tend to be larger and have greater resources than wholesaler firms. On this basis, it is frequently suggested that producers take the lead in providing managerial assistance to their wholesale channel associates. For instance, one authority[9] advises that the producer firm should build its reseller relationships with three basic goals in mind:

1. Finding out the needs and problems of channel members
2. Offering support to the channel members consistent with their needs and problems
3. Providing leadership through the effective use of power

The type of assistance that may be extended can go far beyond promotional aid alone. It can include help in improving virtually any aspect of the wholesaler's business procedures. The net effect, however, is generally one of making the reseller firm a more enthusiastic and capable promoter of your brands as well as a more efficient total business entity. Especially when you are working with a wholesale distributor under a close and continuing relationship and a selective or exclusive distribution agreement, the idea of assuming a partnership perspective is applicable. In commenting on the results of a field study of industrial distributors, one analyst expressed this point in the following words:

> The idea of *partnership* remains essential; when the manufacturer turns to the distributor for added help, he does not give up his own responsibility for effective marketing, nor can he expect the distributor to respond positively to all suggestions. Rather, he assumes new responsibility for making the distributor more effective—through programs of product development, careful pricing, promotional support, technical assistance, and order servicing, and through training programs for distributor salespeople and management. [10]

## PROMOTING THROUGH RETAILERS

In Chapter 6 it was stated that purchase intention levels for any given brand are normally probabilistic in nature. This implies that, especially when you are promoting a product sold to ultimate consumers through retail outlets, you usually have some chance of making a sale to some proportion of consumers. In certain cases, your probability of making the sale may be one hundred percent among a portion of the total consumer population. In other words, within part of your prospect group the sale may be an absolute certainty. In other instances it may be extremely low, giving you very little possibility of making a sale. Very often, however, the probability is somewhere in between. In all of these "in-between" cases the actual outcome can be influenced substantially by other factors that occur in the purchase setting. In particular, supportive reseller activities can often be vital if you are to capitalize fully on any positive purchase intentions levels your brand possessed at the start of the purchase decision process.

Figure 19.2 illustrates the results of a pilot study of the interactions between original purchase intentions and influences operative in retail outlets. This

**FIGURE 19.2 Purchase intentions and store influences on consumers at the retail level**

| Major Product Categories | Specifically Planned [*] | Generally Planned [**] | + Substitute [***] | + Unplanned [****] | = Store Decisions |
|---|---|---|---|---|---|
| Total Study Average | 41.0% | 22.5% | 4.0% | 33.5% | 60.0% |
| Personal Care | 35.3% | 24.7% | 9.4% | 30.6% | 64.7% |
| Magazines/News-papers/Books/Stationery | 41.6% | 28.6% | 1.3% | 28.6% | 58.4% |
| Snack Foods | 22.2% | 23.8% | 4.8% | 49.2% | 77.8% |
| Drugs/Medicine | 51.1% | 12.8% | 6.4% | 29.8% | 48.9% |
| Tobacco Products | 66.7% | 8.9% | — | 24.4% | 33.3% |
| Hardware/Housewares | 16.7% | 40.5% | 2.4% | 40.5% | 83.3% |
| Prescriptions | 100.0% | — | — | — | — |
| Cosmetics | 30.8% | 23.1% | 15.4% | 30.8% | 69.2% |
| Soft Goods/Personal Accessories | 13.0% | 39.1% | — | 47.8% | 87.0% |
| Non-Alcoholic Beverages | 33.3% | 11.1% | — | 56.6% | 66.7% |
| Alcoholic Beverages | 80.0% | — | — | 20.0% | 20.0% |
| Photographic Equipment | 70.0% | — | — | 30.0% | 30.0% |
| Garden Supplies | 50.0% | 50.0% | — | — | 50.0% |
| Jewelry | — | 20.0% | — | 80.0% | 100.0% |
| Automotive Supplies | 20.0% | 20.0% | — | 60.0% | 80.0% |

[*] *Specifically planned* purchases are cases in which the consumer intended to buy the item and brand actually purchased before entering the store.

[**] *Generally planned* purchases are cases in which the consumer intended to buy the item actually purchased before entering the store, but had no specific brand in mind.

[***] *Substitutes* are cases in which the consumer intended to purchase a particular item and brand before entering the store but actually bought a different item or brand.

[****] *Unplanned* purchases are cases in which the consumer did not plan to purchase the item before entering the store.

*Source:* "Pilot Study Finds Final Product Choice Usually Made in Store," *Marketing News*, 6 August 1982, p. 5.
*Note:* Data are based on a pilot survey of 781 consumers at twelve chain drugstores and mass merchandise outlets. They do not necessarily apply with precision on a national or wide-scale basis.

survey was conducted on a limited geographic basis. Therefore, the results should not be interpreted as absolutely precise or as applicable on a nationwide scale. Nonetheless, they do provide a glimpse of the importance that can attach to securing promotional participation from retailers. For instance, among the consumers queried, less than one-third had only one specific brand clearly in mind when they entered the store to buy cosmetics and actually bought that brand before leaving. The majority entered the store either with no specific brand in mind or not even planning to purchase the item at all. Furthermore, a fairly large percentage who did have one specific brand of cosmetic in mind when they entered switched their preference and purchased an alternate brand as the result of some in-store influence.

## Classifying Types of Goods and Types of Stores

The percentages in Figure 19.2 not only demonstrate that retail store influences can have an important impact on many purchase decisions but also that there appear to be differences between product categories in terms of the general extent of initial purchase intentions strength. As examples, strong original purchase intentions levels seem to have been much more prevalent and clearly defined in the case of photographic equipment than in the case of snack foods.

The idea that the strength and nature of consumers' purchase intentions levels may vary between product categories has been formalized in an often-cited "classification of goods" system. In its basic version, this system proposes that consumer goods can be grouped into three main types—convenience goods, shopping goods, and specialty goods. The concept of a parallel classification system for retail outlets has also been advanced. It suggests that such outlets can be grouped under three similar headings—convenience stores, shopping stores, and specialty stores. A summary of the most critical aspects of consumer attitudes and search behaviors broadly associated with each type of good and each type of outlet is presented in Figure 19.3.

## Implications for Promotional Policies

When the three types of consumer goods are cross-classified with the three types of retail outlets, they outline nine very generalized situations that you might face, depending on the type of merchandise you sell and the type of outlets through which you sell it. These nine situations are detailed in Figure 19.4 and are followed by some of the possible promotional strategy goals you might wish to consider in each.

It should be stressed that the strategy goals listed should be viewed only as tentative possibilities to be used in initiating your deliberation about policy options. In actual practice, the world can be far more complex than Figure 19.4 implies. For instance, individual consumers may differ among themselves in terms of how they view any given product category. You may find your brand is viewed as a specialty good by one part of your target prospect group, whereas other parts view it as a shopping good or even a convenience good. Furthermore, your brand may be distributed through more than one type of retail outlet. Some of the retailers handling your brand might be regarded mainly as shopping stores whereas others are seen mainly as specialty stores.

Apart from these complications, a theme that has recurred throughout the

| Types of Consumer Goods | | |
|---|---|---|
| Convenience Goods | Shopping Goods | Specialty Goods |
| **Strength of Consumers' Purchase Intentions Levels for Brand(s)** <br> Nonexistent, weak, or spread among several brands | | Very strong for or concentrated entirely on a single brand |
| **Consumers' Willingness to Expend Effort to Make Purchase** <br> Very low | High for purpose of comparing offerings | High for purpose of acquiring preferred brand |

| Types of Retail Outlets | | |
|---|---|---|
| Convenience Stores | Shopping Stores | Specialty Stores |
| **Strength of Consumers' Store Preference Levels** <br> Nonexistent, weak, or spread among several stores | | Very strong for or concentrated entirely on a single store |
| **Consumers' Willingness to Expend Effort to Reach Store(s)** <br> Very low | High in the sense of searching in several stores | High if necessary to reach preferred store |

**FIGURE 19.3**
**Classification systems for ultimate consumer goods and retail outlets**

*Sources:* The general scheme of classifying goods was first proposed in Melvin T. Copeland, "Relation of Consumers' Buying Habits to Marketing Methods," *Harvard Business Review*, April 1923, pp. 282–289; the extension of this scheme to include retail outlets was proposed in Louis P. Bucklin, "Retail Strategy and the Classification of Consumer Goods," *Journal of Marketing*, January 1963, pp. 50–55; for a more extended discussion of both see Raymond A. Marquardt, James C. Makens, and Robert G. Roe, *Retail Management: Satisfaction of Consumer Needs*, 3rd ed. (Hinsdale, IL: The Dryden Press, 1983), pp. 105–107, 161–163.

book must be kept in mind: *There is no one simple, mechanistic formula for determining any portion of your promotional policy.* However, to the extent that you can identify your brand as fitting rather predominantly into one or another of the nine general situations shown in Figure 19.4, consideration of the policy implications suggested there might be useful to you as a starting point for assessing your position.

*Evaluating Alternative Retailer Support Goals*

One primary goal of any producer of ultimate consumer goods is to convince appropriate retailers to carry its brands and have them readily available for consumers. Many strategy plans also call for occasional or frequent price-special promotions. These may be activated through such sales promotion techniques as coupons, price-off deals, combination offers, and money refund or factory rebate offers. Additionally, they may be stimulated by trade inducements and performance allowances offered to cooperating retailers. Apart from seeking availability and participation on price specials, there are four

**FIGURE 19.4 Cross-classifying types of goods and types of retail outlets in relation to tentative promotional policy implications**

| Cross-Classification Situation | General Setting for Consumer Shopping Behavior | Tentative Goals for Promotional Strategies Directed toward Retailers |
| --- | --- | --- |
| Convenience Store/ Convenience Good | Customer has little or no preference for either brands or stores. Purchases tend to be made by choosing an easily available brand at a readily accessible store. | Main goal of producer is likely to be intensive distribution to make brand easily available. Producer may also make some attempt to obtain best possible shelf location or other display positioning in store. |
| Shopping Store/ Convenience Good | Customer has low brand purchase intentions levels, or none at all, and wishes to shop at several stores. Purpose of shopping is to compare merchandise, prices, and/or attempt to secure better retail service. | Fairly wide-spread distribution may be desirable but intensive distribution is less necessary. Retail advertising and in-store promotion can be critical. In-store promotion may stress displays and price specials. |
| Specialty Store/ Convenience Good | Customer has no strong purchase intentions levels among brands, but does have a strong preference level for some particular retail outlet. Purchase will probably be made at that store from among whatever brands the store chooses to carry. | Selective or exclusive distribution may be used in an attempt to encourage heavy reseller support. All forms of support such as displays, good shelf positioning, retail advertising, and price promotion can be desirable. When clerk-service is involved, the salesperson's advice and information could be critical. |
| Convenience Store/ Shopping Good | Customer goes to the most readily accessible store, then shops and compares brands carried by that store before making a purchase choice. | Brand probably needs intensive distribution. Producer is also likely to actively seek best possible shelf and other positioning in store plus such support as in-store displays, price specials, and cooperative advertising. |
| Shopping Store/ Shopping Good | Customer actively searches among several stores and brands before making a purchase decision. | Goods in this category tend to be relatively high in unit value. Producer often uses selective or exclusive distribution to induce better reseller support. In-store displays and retailer advertising for the brand can be especially critical. When clerk service is involved, advice from salespersons may be important. |
| Specialty Store/ Shopping Good | Customer prefers to buy at a particular outlet but is uncertain as to which brand to buy. Purchase will usually be made at first store visited but only after learning about and comparing assortment of brands offered by that outlet. | Same as indicated for specialty store/convenience good classification. |

**FIGURE 19.4** (continued)

| Cross-Classification Situation | General Setting for Consumer Shopping Behavior | Tentative Goals for Promotional Strategies Directed toward Retailers |
|---|---|---|
| Convenience Store/Specialty Good | Customer has extremely strong purchase intention level for one particular brand and wishes to purchase that brand at the most readily accessible store. | Fairly wide-spread distribution is needed. In-store promotion can be helpful. However, such promotion is not likely to be as critical as indicated in the cases above. Retailer-sponsored advertising for a brand can be very important because it informs prospects of convenient places to purchase. |
| Shopping Store/Specialty Good | Customer has strong purchase intention level for a brand but wishes to shop at several stores, probably to compare prices and retail services. | Selective or exclusive distribution may be used to ensure that customers' service requirements are met and to give producer a higher degree of influence over resellers' activities. Retailer-sponsored advertising for the brand can be helpful to spur shopping activity. In-store display may not be vital but could help maintain customer loyalty and convert intention level into rapid purchase. In clerk-service situations, favorable salesperson support is desirable to ensure that sale is closed effectively. |
| Specialty Store/Specialty Good | Customer has very strong purchase intention level for a particular brand and strong preference for a particular retail outlet. | Selective or exclusive distribution may be used. Emphasis is likely to be in choosing the "right stores" to maintain brand image, reach proper market segments, and strengthen motivation of chosen retailers to stock, advertise and effectively display the brand. |

additional retailer support goals that are listed in Figure 19.4 and that deserve special commentary. These are as follows:

1. Developing personal selling support at the retail level
2. Attaining high in-store visibility for your brand
3. Securing special in-store signs and displays
4. Generating advertising support from retailers

We will review some of the major points concerning each of these four goals. Then we will examine techniques you can employ to attain them, and finally we will consider how one sales representative promotes his firm's products to and through retailers using such techniques.

Much of today's retailing is done on a self-service basis. However, clerk-service is still widespread, especially among products with a reasonably high unit value. When the consumer actually comes into contact with a retail sales-person you may have an opportunity to develop active personal selling support for your brand. At the outset, it should be noted that many observers express a generally dim appraisal of the quality of personal selling at the retail level and, by inference, of the likelihood of your success in extending your promotional reach by this route. One commentator has noted, "Poor personal selling at the retail level has become almost legendary . . . . [C]ertainly, the poor quality of retail selling cannot be blamed to any great extent on inadequate manufacturer training programs—retailers are far more guilty in this regard."[11]

Another writer has commented on the same point by stating, "As presently managed, retail sales assistance is held in very poor regard by many consumers. There are some exceptions to the rule, but retail selling in general is not as good as it should be in this era of high sales cost, low margins, and consumer activism."[12]

Given this climate, a producer must first decide whether it is feasible from a cost-benefit standpoint to attempt to generate promotional support among retail salespeople. In a majority of instances it may not be. However, there are still a sizable number of marketing settings in which an active and creative program to win such support can be an important auxiliary component in a producer's total plan. Such programs usually take one or both of two forms, (1) providing special sales training or selling aid materials to retail salespeople and (2) offering special incentives to salespeople in the form of either contests or direct cash payments for sales of the manufacturer's brand.

***Providing Special Sales Training or Selling Aids.*** Both of these approaches aim at strengthening support for your brand by making retail sales personnel more effective at performing their jobs. They are likely to be especially valuable in settings where customers look to the sales clerk as possessing product-relevant expertise. With this in mind, their successful utilization frequently centers around actually making the sales clerk more knowledgeable about the product category and its usage—in other words, extending her or his product-related competence. For example, in reporting on trends in the retailing of higher-priced cosmetic items, one trade magazine singled out a beauty treatment line sold under the brand name "Clinique" as one of the most effectively marketed and profitable in the country. The report went on to note that retail salespeople in the stores that carry the Clinique line play a key role in the brand's success. In the words of a spokeswoman for the producing firm, "The gal behind the counter is our most important link to the consumer." Clinique refers to retail salespeople handling its line as "beauty consultants" and seeks to help them upgrade their competence as cosmetic experts. "Extensive training programs, ranging from one to three days, are offered to new consultants and, all year-round, Clinique training supervisors travel throughout the country offering established beauty consultants advanced classes. . . . [The] basic philosophy is that [beauty consultants] don't sell items, they sell a treatment concept."[13]

Working with a much less glamorous product category and a more limited program format, a supplier of latex paint bases improved sales by providing retail paint clerks with a selling aid that both demonstrated the product's quality and endowed the sales clerk with a greater aura of expertise. In the early period following the introduction of latex-base paints, many prospective purchasers had questions about the paint's ability to wear and last as long as conventional oil-base paints. Paint clerks felt uncomfortable in dealing with such questions because they themselves had no direct experience with the product. The problem was solved by providing retail sales personnel with a simple, in-store demonstration device, as described in the following report:

> [The firm's research and development department] pointed out that it was very easy to prove the toughness of latex paint in comparison with oil base paint [by using] a paint scrub tester. To test two paints . . . a small panel of each paint could be coated on a wooden shingle and placed in a machine. The machine is turned on for one minute. Then the abrasive brushes are raised, and any consumer can see that latex paint is just as tough as, if not tougher than, competitive products. [14]

***Special Incentive Payments and Contests.*** In some merchandise fields it is fairly common for manufacturers to provide direct economic rewards to retail salespeople who put extra effort into selling items in the manufacturer's line. The incentive payment amounts to a special class of performance allowance and is usually referred to as a "PM" (standing for push money). Product categories in which this practice is frequently used include such lines as furniture and carpeting, cameras, watches, household appliances, and television sets. PM plans have reportedly been employed by such major firms as Eastman Kodak, Sony, and Panasonic.[15]

These incentive payments are made directly by the manufacturer to the clerk, which means that the manufacturer is, in a sense, bypassing store management to influence its employees through a supplemental compensation system. In some cases, management may see this as creating a conflict of interest for its employees and forbid such payments. In other instances, retail management may feel the provision of added incentives by manufacturers permits the store itself to pay somewhat lower wages to its employees. One study found that almost seventy percent of the stores surveyed reported their salespeople received at least some PMs from manufacturers as a part of their compensation.[16]

As an alternative to a direct payment, a manufacturer may seek to provide special motivation to retail salespeople via a contest. For example, a British producer of fine china dinnerware spurred retail clerk enthusiasm by a contest in which the grand prize was a trip to England. The sponsoring company was the Royal Worcester Porcelain Company, which distributes its line in the United States through approximately 1,500 department and jewelry stores. Prior to establishing the contest, Royal Worcester produced a training film to acquaint retail clerks with facts and information about fine china. The film provided an initial mechanism for highlighting the company and its product line in the minds of retail sales personnel. The contest program that followed gave Royal Worcester a means of capitalizing on this familiarity with the line. To enter the contest, salespeople wrote a letter on the topic, "How I made a Royal Worcester Sale." The writer of the best letter received each month was awarded the grand prize trip to England. Reportedly, the contest was highly successful in terms of fostering retail clerk involvement and enthusiasm for the company's line.[17]

Where personal, across-the-counter support can be critical to the sale of your brand, special incentive payments and contests are worth your careful consideration. However, there are also some precautions to bear in mind when considering these techniques. Above all, before preparing an incentive or contest plan, you should ascertain the attitudes of the appropriate retail management personnel and design a program that will be compatible with their desires and philosophy. Additionally, it should be recognized that these techniques are essentially forms of sales promotion which fall into the category of special offers. As pointed out in Chapter 17, when unwisely used in an attempt to sidestep inherent weaknesses in a manufacturer's overall marketing program, special offers, including those directed to retail salespeople, are likely to provide only a very temporary solution, if they provide any solution at all. As with any other special offer, PMs and contests for retail personnel will prove most effective when they constitute merely one part of a total promotional program that is strong and well coordinated in all of its other aspects. Finally, you should be alert to the fact that their use is subject to restrictive guidelines laid down by the Federal Trade Commission.[18]

## Attaining High In-Store Visibility for Your Brand

Visual impact has always been an important element in retailing. After all, one of the attractions of shopping is that it provides the customer with an opportunity to actually see and compare an assortment of offerings. In today's climate of intensified competition and rising costs of store space, increased emphasis is being placed on "visual merchandising." As one team of writers has stated the issue, "Visual merchandising is a combination of every factor that can affect the consumer's visual perception of the store. Moreover, visual merchandising is the utilization of every square inch of the building, inside and out, to sell the company and its products."[19]

With this in mind, astute retail merchants have become highly skilled and sophisticated, not only in dealing with the appearance of their stores but also in making decisions concerning the management of store space and the allocation of that space among competing brands. In planning your efforts to influence these retailer decisions, you must begin by assessing the degree of sales impact that can result from two basic retailer strategies which affect the visibility of your brand. These are the general physical location of your brand within the store and the number of units (or "facings") displayed and their shelf positioning.

**General Location Within the Store.** All other things being equal, sales will increase if your brand is placed in a prominent, high-traffic area of the store. This is especially critical in the case of self-service outlets. As an illustration,

**FIGURE 19.5  The effect of general store location on unit sales**

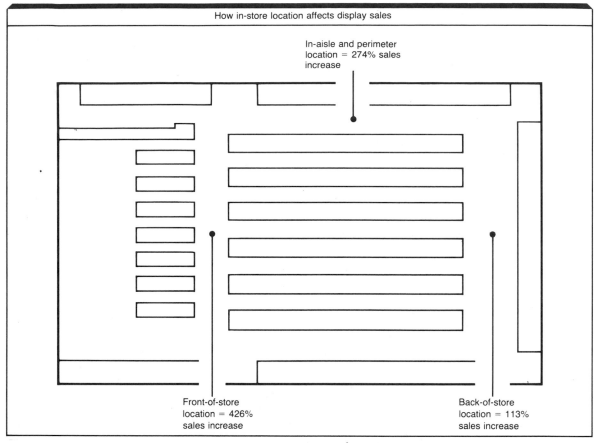

How in-store location affects display sales

In-aisle and perimeter location = 274% sales increase

Front-of-store location = 426% sales increase

Back-of-store location = 113% sales increase

*Source:* "How In-Store Merchandising Can Boost Sales," *Progressive Grocer* (January, 1981), Part 2, p. 9.

Figure 19.5 portrays some relationships between store location and unit sales found in one analysis of supermarket merchandising. Sales of merchandise tested in this study jumped by 113 percent when items were moved from a regular shelf position to a display located at the rear of the store. A perimeter display placement produced a 274 percent increase. The most dramatic sales results came from a front–of–store location.

*Number of Facings and Shelf Positioning.*   In addition to general location within the store, the number of units of the brand visible to the consumer and its shelf-level positioning can exert a significant influence on sales response. Figure 19.6 demonstrates the extent of this influence observed in one study.

The amount of space given a particular brand is commonly measured in terms of "shelf facings." A facing is essentially one unit of the product—such as a can or a box—that faces the shopper in a row along the shelf. For example, in the first instance cited in Figure 19.6 the four cans lined up on the shelf represent four shelf facings. In this study, when the number of facings was cut from four down to two, sales of the brand were reduced by almost 50 percent.

In addition to the number of facings, sales of your brand can be seriously affected by the shelf level on which it is displayed. For example, in this test, sales increased by forty-three percent when the item was moved up from the bottom shelf to the middle shelf.

**Securing Special In-Store Signs and Displays**

A brand can often benefit greatly if it is given unusual display treatment that clearly sets it apart from competitors. Figure 19.7 summarizes data discovered in one test concerning the results attributable to rather simple shelf-signing. As indicated there, the volume change associated with use of the sign varied with the type of message it conveyed. This ranged from a forty-three percent sales increase associated with a shelf sign calling attention to a new item to a 253 percent increase for a sign featuring both the price and serving suggestions. Figure 19.8 reports on results observed when point-of-purchase signing was added to a free-standing display.

**Generating Advertising Support from Retailers**

Much of the advertising time and space purchased by retailers is used to feature merchandise produced by national manufacturers and sold by the store. To the extent that you can convince retailers to include your brand in their advertising, you often stand to benefit in one or both of two distinct ways. First, and most importantly, such advertising provides prospects with information on exactly where your brand can be purchased and usually at what price. Second, such advertising not only extends your own promotional efforts but sometimes can reinforce your brand's reputation by associating it with a prestigious or locally accepted retailer by image transfer. For these reasons, it is not surprising to find that, wherever feasible, manufacturers tend to seek inclusion in retailer's advertising.

To encourage stores to feature its brand, the producer often develops a cooperative advertising program. These programs may include provision of

---

**FIGURE 19.6 Effects of number of facings and shelf location on sales volume**

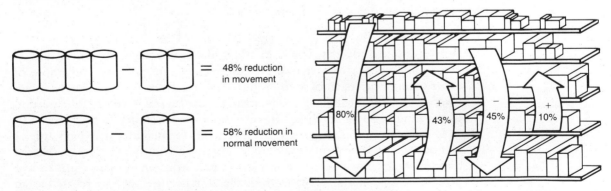

*Source:* "How In-Store Merchandising Can Boost Sales," *Progressive Grocer*, Special Report (1971).

*Promoting Through Retailers*

**FIGURE 19.7 Effects of shelf signs on sales**

How shelf signs affect sales

Price signs plus serving suggestions =
253% sales increase

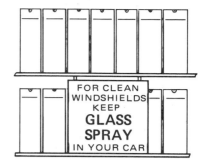

"Product use" signs
= 88% mores sales than normal

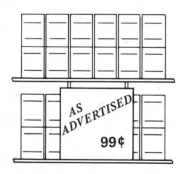

"As advertised" signs =
173% more sales than normal

Manufacturer promotion tie-in signs =
175% increase in sales

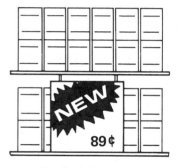

"New item" signs =
43% increase in sales

*Source:* "How In-Store Merchandising Can Boost Sales," *Progressive Grocer*, January 1981, p. 9.

either complete advertisements, to which the local retailer need only add its name and address, or materials that the retailer can combine with those of other manufacturers and use to produce a total advertisement. The manufacturer sponsoring a cooperative advertising plan also agrees to pay for a portion of the time or space purchased by the store to promote its brand.

Under a common cooperative arrangement, the manufacturer pays at least half of the cost, up to some maximum amount related to inventory purchased by the retailer. For instance, it might be agreed that an amount equal to five percent of a retailer's purchases from the manufacturer will be rebated as an advertising allowance if the retailer agrees to match that amount and use the

**FIGURE 19.8 Effects of point-of-purchase materials used with free-standing displays**

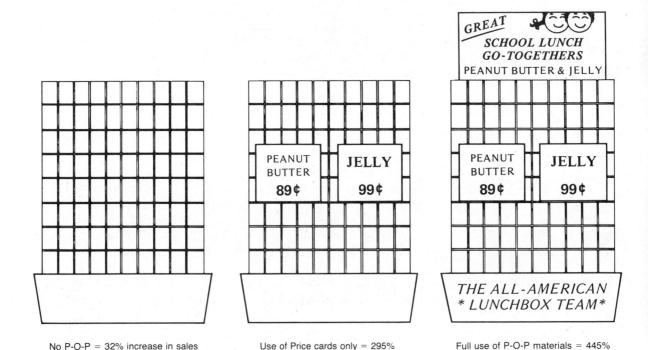

No P-O-P = 32% increase in sales

Use of Price cards only = 295% increase in sales

Full use of P-O-P materials = 445% increase in sales

*Source:* "How In-Store Merchandising Can Boost Sales," *Progressive Grocer*, January 1981, p. 9.

money to purchase local advertising. By some estimates the total value of advertising placed through such cooperative plans is between three and four billion dollars annually.[20] Furthermore, in some merchandise lines, the funds received through such plans cover the major portion of the retailers' total advertising expenditures. For example, according to one report, cooperative advertising dollars provided seventy to eighty percent of the total advertising budgets allocated by drugstores, food stores, and appliance dealers.[21]

Various observers have pointed out that despite its widespread use cooperative advertising can pose some potential disadvantages for both manufacturers and retailers. From the retailers' standpoint, the following words of caution have been suggested:

> [The] retailer must realize that such cooperative packages have varying conditions attached to them such as minimum order quantities, annual volume purchase requirements, and reporting requirements which must be observed. Additionally, adoption of a heavy reliance on cooperative advertising may cause the retail firm to lose effective control on its promotional programs which may have negative effects on the overall image of the firm. [22]

*Promoting Through Retailers*

From the perspective of the manufacturer, some of the potential dangers of cooperative advertising have been described as follows:

> The most important disadvantage of cooperative advertising to manufacturers is the relative lack of control they have over the advertising. . . . [Your brand] may become lost in a mass of products advertised by the local store. Inferior layouts, inept copy, and puerile art that would make any alert manufacturer or agency shudder are bound to crop up in some cooperative ads. . . . Also, a cooperative program may reduce needed funds for advertising in national media. If more money is needed for the [cooperative] program, the advertiser may decide that the money must come from the national budget. [23]

Another important issue is that of distributing cooperative funds equitably among retailers. Failure to do this may not only lead to strained relations with resellers who feel they have been given unfavorable treatment, but may also lead to legal difficulties. United States law requires that advertising allowances be made available on "proportionately equal" terms to all competing resellers. Failure to follow the guidelines established to carry out this regulation can result in Federal Trade Commission action against the manufacturer.[24] In summary, although cooperative advertising programs are widely utilized and have some very clear advantages as part of a manufacturer's total promotional program, they must be used with a good deal of care and with consideration of the results they deliver relative to their expense and complications.

## Techniques for Gaining Retailer Support

Whenever one or more of the above retailer support goals could play a significant role in influencing sales of your brand, your logical sequence of strategy planning involves three major steps. *First*, you should outline the most appropriate types of retailer support you might seek in your particular market setting. For example, if you are promoting stereo equipment, you may want to put major emphasis on developing personal selling support from retail salespeople and generating retail advertising support. If you are selling cake mixes, your primary retailer support goals may focus on in-store signing, shelf positioning, number of facings, and periodic, special free-standing displays. *Second*, having outlined your logical goal alternatives, you should assess the likely economic benefits of each. Obtaining retailer support can require a substantial outlay of funds for personal selling and sales promotion. Therefore, before embarking on such efforts you need to study the prospective cost-benefit relationships.

*Third*, when you are satisfied that the support goals at which you aim are viable in terms of profit potential, you are ready to develop a strategy for convincing retailers to give you their cooperation. The handling of this last stage can present some especially strong challenges. In the majority of cases, you will be only one of a number of producers vying for the promotional participation of the independent retailers who sell your brand. To convince them to give you preferential treatment, you must first attempt to understand the implications of your support goals from retail management's point of view. In other words, you must plan them in terms of benefits to the retailer as well as to your own form.

In the past, there has been a tendency to think of national manufacturing firms as being large, sophisticated, and powerful in their marketing capacities, and to think of resellers as being comparatively unsophisticated and not as powerful. Although this may have been a fairly accurate picture at one time, it is not true today. One consultant has made the following observation:

> Marketers who have an aptitude for spotting trends have noticed a dramatic marketing power shift—from manufacturer to retailer and distributor. . . . It's no secret that, today, fewer and fewer individuals are making the buying decisions for greater and greater numbers of retail outlets. For example, at one time there were at least 30,000 mom-and-pop hardware stores in the U.S., and there were also many more hardware distributors. For the most part, each was autonomous and made its own buying decisions. . . . However, now large "buying groups" are making those decisions and, in many cases, screening the purchases for the individual hardware stores. In addition, the large-volume retail chain and franchise operators are controlling hundreds and even thousands of outlets. . . . Because of this, the small manufacturer—and even the large manufacturer—can not readily dictate to these powerful retail decision makers. [25]

Another writer has offered his observations by saying, "Retailers are getting *more* information *faster* via the computer . . . so they are more sophisticated, more demanding of marketers. In the good old days, a good *gross* profit was the key to success but today they are concerned with *net* profit per item."[26]

***Coping with a Multilevel Decision-Making Structure.*** In addition to increased power, heightened profit consciousness, and more detailed knowledge, today's retailing structure tends to be characterized by more multistage and multiperson decision making. Figure 19.9 dramatizes the path a sales presentation for a new product may have to follow in a large-scale retail organization before it can actually be translated into a sale to an ultimate consumer. As depicted in this illustration, the process begins with the sales representative (pictured at lower left) presenting the case for the brand to a buyer at retail chain headquarters. If this presentation receives a positive reaction from the buyer, it initiates a series of events. However, problems can arise at any stage in that series to halt or hamper the results sought by the sales representative. Most importantly, the buyer must frequently take her or his recommendations before a buying committee. That committee is composed of representatives from various areas within the retail organization and it must be satisfied concerning the feasibility of the buyer's proposal. The process of securing approval and cooperation at this level has been termed "sell-through."[27]

In order to effectively compete in this environment, the salesperson must be aware of the internal decision-making structure and the business philosophy of the retail firm. Not only is it necessary to convince the buyer, but it is also necessary to provide her or him with a full supply of facts, figures, and persuasive information that will be required in the sell-through process.

**FIGURE 19.9  A multistage sell-through process in a large, chain-store system**

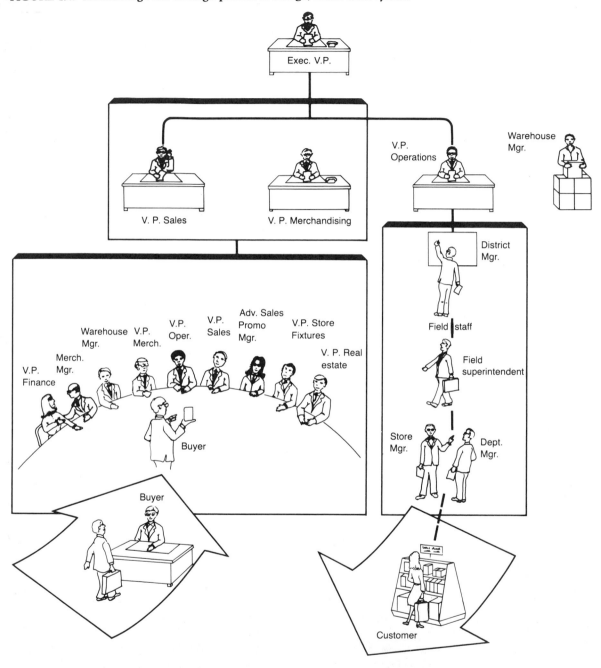

Source: Chain Store Age (General Merchandise Edition), May 1978, p. 44. © Lebhar Friedman, Inc.

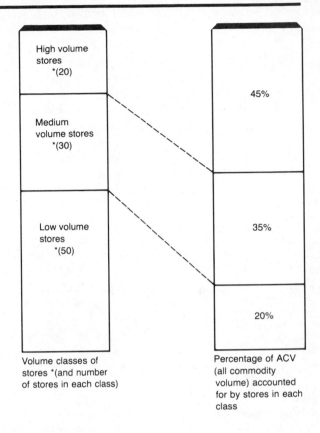

**FIGURE 19.10 Bases for determining a brand's distribution level in a trading area (total stores in area that carry commodity category equals 100)**

High volume stores *(20)

Medium volume stores *(30)

Low volume stores *(50)

45%

35%

20%

Volume classes of stores *(and number of stores in each class)

Percentage of ACV (all commodity volume) accounted for by stores in each class

***Sales Follow-up at the Field and Store Levels.*** Assuming you have been successful in obtaining a positive reaction to the sell-through at chain headquarters, you will still have promotional tasks to perform in relation to the field staff and the management personnel of the separate store units. The need for continued persuasive activities at these levels is apparent from the flow of communication and activity shown at the right-hand side of Figure 19.9. Despite the tendency toward centralized decision making for general merchandising policies, most large retailing organizations still allow their store managers a good deal of latitude in translating general policies into specific applications.

One report, based on interviews with chain store executives showed widespread agreement as to the importance of the store manager in implementing headquarter's buying decisions. A typical comment was, "The store manager's efforts to re-buy, re-stock and especially *display* a merchandise line, can make or break it."[28] Therefore, personal selling efforts aimed at chain store systems, as well as those aimed at independent, single-store merchants, usually include a plan for reinforcing retailer support by calling on individual stores.

***Determining Call Frequencies by Store Units.*** The point was made in Chapter 11 that because a salesperson's time is expensive, it can become important not only to know which customers to contact but also which customers to avoid or give much less of your attention. This is as true in dealing with retail stores as in dealing with any other class of customer. Figure 19.10 is essentially a variation of the ABC rule of account classification described in Chapter 11. However, the repetition of that concept at this juncture serves the purpose of highlighting the somewhat different form and terminology with which this concept is applied in relation to retail accounts.

One issue of importance to a manufacturer of ultimate consumer goods is the retail distribution level it enjoys in each trading area. In the past, this was commonly measured simply by the percentage of eligible stores which carried the brand. Today, it is more frequently measured in terms of All Commodity Volume (ACV). For instance, using the data in Figure 19.10, assume your brand was stocked only in the fifty high-volume and medium-volume stores. On a percentage-of-outlets basis your distribution level would be fifty percent. However, on an ACV basis it would be eighty percent because you are represented in outlets that account for eighty percent of the total volume in your general commodity category such as groceries or drugs.

In setting up a personal selling plan, a manufacturer would logically concentrate its heaviest efforts on stores that are high in terms of their ACV share and that also appear most promising in terms of response to personal selling efforts.

*Taking the Retailer's Point of View*

As pointed out earlier in this chapter, the retailers who carry your brand are business entities separate and independent from your own firm. To gain their participation you must convince them that the cooperation and support you seek is in their best interest as well as yours. Although specific managerial philosophies may differ from retailer to retailer, all share a common generalized objective, which is to increase net profit results. For this reason, most presentations to retailers revolve around demonstrations of how the manufacturer's brand or promotional program can affect one or more of four major variables that influence profits. These four variables are volume potential, gross margin or markup, traffic generation, and tie-in sales which increase the size of customers' orders.

***Volume potential*** is the most basic of the variables. Put simply, all other things being equal, retailers generally aim at carrying and promoting brands that have a strong consumer demand. For an established product, past sales results plus current promotional efforts will usually be major criteria used in estimating future volume potential. For a new product or a significantly repositioned brand, the amount of advertising support it is being given can play an especially crucial role in influencing retailers' estimates of volume potential.

***Gross margin or markup*** is the difference between what the retailer pays for the item and the price that the retailer charges the consumer. Quite naturally, again with all other things being equal, retailers will prefer to sell and give active promotion to items which offer them higher-than-average gross margins.

***Traffic generation*** revolves around attracting more customers to the store or holding them in the store longer. In general, higher store traffic translates into increased total sales. Therefore, if you can demonstrate that your brand—or a special promotional activity associated with your brand—will generate higher store traffic, you are speaking of a topic which is critically important to every retail merchant. As described in Chapter 17, this is the approach that Pepsi-Cola used in promoting its Pepsi Challenge to store managers.

***Order Size.*** The final variable of concern to retailers is *order size*. Anything that can be done to encourage customers to purchase additional items while in the store will be advantageous to the retailer. From the manufacturer's standpoint, this offers an opportunity to gain retailers' support by stressing the ability of your brand to generate tie-in sales of related products.

To illustrate a few of the ways in which these variables can be handled in developing persuasive presentations to store managers, we will close the chapter with a job description told in the words of a salesperson who calls on supermarkets. As was the case in our earlier illustrations of salespeople at work in Chapter 10, the example used here is based on an actual interview, though some specific details are disguised.

***Mr. Elsin Sells Groceries Through Supermarkets***

Dick Elsin is a sales representative who calls on retail outlets to promote the brands of a major food company. Previously, Mr. Elsin worked for a supermarket chain as a store manager. He left that position a year and a half ago to go into sales work. Here is how he describes his job.

"Our company makes a broad assortment of grocery items. To illustrate my work, I'll limit my examples to salad dressings, which are just a part of our total line.

"Our company's initial sales contacts are made with wholesalers and chain store warehouses and handled by people called 'account representatives.' Their job is to convince headquarters buyers to authorize our products and make them available to their stores. The assignment of people like myself, who are called 'sales reps,' is to follow up at the individual store level. Once the product is authorized at the headquarters office, the sales rep's most basic goal is to make sure the stores are actually carrying it. Beyond that, each sales rep aims at convincing store management to give our brands prominent shelf positioning and as many facings as possible. In addition, we're constantly on the alert for special promotional opportunities.

"I cover a territory in southwest Virginia. There are about 200 stores in the territory that carry our products. However, the great majority are too small to make routine sales calls profitable. I'll go to a small store if the manager requests it but I regard that strictly as a courtesy visit. Normally, I call on only about forty-five of the stores on a regular basis. The call frequency depends on two factors. The first is size of the store; the larger its volume, the more frequent the calls. The second factor is cooperation. The more cooperative the manager is in merchandising our products, the more often I will call on the store. If a store is large, but uncooperative I'll visit it about once a month. If it is both large and cooperative, I'll visit it weekly.

"My first stop on any call is at the manager's office. In part, that's because I want to be sure the manager knows about any special trade inducements and performance allowance plans we're offering. However, it's also because I try to establish a good personal rapport with every manager whose store I visit. After that, I'll walk each aisle in the supermarket to see whether or not our authorized items are on the shelves. If any are missing, I'll check for the source of the problem. Sometimes it's in the backroom and simply hasn't been brought out by the stockman. Sometimes the store forgot to order it. It's also possible that the merchandise is missing because the warehouse is out of stock. Once I've discovered the problem, I'll talk with the person who can correct it. For instance, if it's due to an out-of-stock at the warehouse, I call the account rep to get things taken care of at that point.

"Again, building a solid relationship with the store manager is the key to success in my job. I can hardly claim to be successful in every single case. However, in most instances, I've been able to gain the trust of the manager by seeing things from his or her point of view and by being honest. If you overstock a store or push a promotional plan that falls flat, you begin destroying your effectiveness. I don't try to sell a merchandising idea unless I've thought it through carefully and feel confident it will work.

"Getting good shelf positioning and an adequate number of facings is a constant problem. In the salad dressing field, for instance, we are up against brands like Wishbone, Seven Seas, and Good Seasons. Beyond that, each chain store system has its own private label on which they make a higher markup. Part of my job involves finding ways to show stores how they can make still more money by improving their display arrangement of our brands. To do this I start out with all of the back-up material I can get. For instance, I bring in our company's advertising schedule. Store managers know that when you have a really big advertising program about to break it will attract customers. In my presentation I try to give all the facts I can. I use market research data that's been passed along to me by the company. I also use facts and figures based on my own experience with other stores. In my presentation I'll tie all the facts and figures together to show the store manager how to improve profits by giving us the shelf space and positioning I am proposing. Let me give you an example.

"The research data show that, in my territory, our mayonnaise brand commands a market share of over forty percent. However, its markup is relatively low. Our company also produces a variety of other salad dressings that carry significantly higher markups and are well advertised and well accepted by consumers. The proposal I will make to the store manager runs this way:

Almost half of your customers will come into your store looking for our brand of mayonnaise. Most are also presold on our other salad dressings such as the bleu cheese and onion flavors. Try stocking our mayonnaise on a shelf just below eye level. Then, on the shelf just above, put in our higher-markup, flavored dressings. By doing that, you'll get your customers to search out our brand of mayonnaise and, while doing so, they'll be exposed to your display of our other flavors that are more profitable to you. The result will be that many shoppers will make additional purchases of those more profitable flavors. You'll find you both increase total sales of salad dressings and also increase your *total* gross margin.

"The fact is that this kind of a display arrangement actually works. When I can convince a supermarket to try it, I can prove the results. What I have accomplished is to increase our company's sales in that store by showing the manager a way to make more money.

"Let me just give you one more example of the kind of things you can do to improve your sales in a store. Salads are especially popular during the warmer months of the year. To take advantage of the peak salad season our company usually runs a heavy summer advertising schedule. For instance, magazine advertising will feature special salad recipes and often include price-off coupons and refund offers. They also supply us with in-store display materials that tie into the advertising theme. By developing an exciting display plan for a store, I can show the manager how to step up traffic and increase sales in several departments such as groceries, produce, meat, and dairy products. I'll plan out the entire display and even help store personnel set things up.

"Last summer I persuaded one store manager to let me put up a twenty-five-foot long display in the produce department. We brought in special tables, hung up banners and moved in salad-related items from all over the store—not just salad dressings but things such as parmesan cheese, bacon bits, and croutons. In the process, I was really helping promote the brands of companies other than my own, which is something I'm happy to do because I know we'll get our share of the increased business. We did everything possible to make that promotion a real attention-grabber and it worked. The display created a more exciting atmosphere in the store and caused a sizable jump in produce sales as well as on all the salad specialty items. The store manager was happy, I was happy, and we plan an even bigger promotion for next summer.

"To sum things up, my job is to do everything I can to make sure my company's products are receiving the best treatment possible in the major stores in my area. I do that by trying to understand the retailers' problems and objectives and then working out creative plans to show them how to solve their problems or reach their objectives. Once I've shown a store manager that I know my business and can genuinely help the store do a better merchandising job, I can usually gain that person's cooperation. The outcome has to be better results for both of us."

# SUMMARY

Reseller promotional influences involve either or both of two distinct aspects. The first is *image transfer*, which is the less common of the two and refers to situations in which customers judge the quality of your brand partly on the basis of the status and reputation of the resellers who carry it. The second is *reseller participation*, which deals with the amount of active cooperation you receive from middlemen in promoting your product.

In seeking participation from resellers it is essential that you begin by recognizing their independent status and tendency toward customer-orientation rather than supplier-orientation. Successful efforts to induce supportive reseller activities should also include a careful study of the total problems, needs, and objectives of the middlemen who form your channel of distribution. The two broad categories of such middlemen are wholesalers and retailers.

## Promoting Through Wholesalers

The major types of wholesalers singled out for discussion in this chapter were manufacturers' representatives and merchant wholesalers.

The *manufacturers' representative* is an individual or firm that specializes in handling personal selling activities on behalf of other companies. In a sense, you can think of them in much the same way you think of your own full-time sales representatives. However, because they are independent and usually represent other companies in addition to yours, you have much less control over them. Experts who have observed the situation tend to agree that you should make every reasonable attempt to give your manufacturers' representatives a sense of partnership in your strategy planning. In particular, there is a strong need to supply them with information regarding the direction of and reasons behind your marketing strategy.

*Merchant wholesalers* actually buy and take title to the goods they sell to other business units. In practice, there are a wide variety of merchant wholesaler types. The likelihood of your obtaining strong promotional support from any given merchant wholesaler tends to be inversely related to the number of products carried by that firm. Other factors that can affect wholesaler promotional support are the importance your brands represent in the wholesaler's total line and the compatibility of your target customer group with that of the wholesaler. When you sense potential opportunities to obtain substantial promotional emphasis for your brands, a widely recommended route to exploiting such opportunities calls for building an ongoing program to aid wholesalers in solving their own business problems and in serving their customers more effectively. This is especially true when you work closely with a wholesaler distributor firm under a selective or exclusive distribution agreement.

## Promoting Through Retailers

With respect to seeking retailer participation, the most basic goal of manufacturers is to convince appropriate outlets to carry their brands for ready availability to consumers. Cooperation in periodic price promotions is a second goal commonly sought by many manufacturers. Four supplementary retailer support goals that may be of importance are (1) developing personal selling support at the retail level, (2) attaining high visibility for your brand in the store, (3) securing special in-store signs and displays, and (4) generating advertising support from retailers.

The degree of relative stress placed upon any of these supplementary goals will vary depending on the type of merchandise being sold and the type of outlets through which it is distributed. For instance, if your product is a high-unit-value shopping good sold through clerk-service outlets, you may wish to emphasize techniques for fostering personal selling support. Alternatively, if you are dealing with a low–unit–value convenience good sold through self-service outlets, your promotional thrust is likely to focus on such things as shelf-positioning, number of facings, and special signs or in-store displays.

The first issue, then, in building your strategy for gaining retailer support involves defining the types of goals you will seek. Following that, you must assess their cost relative to potential payout effects. When you are satisfied that your support goals are correct, feasible, and economically viable, your next task is to develop a program for successful persuasion of the retailers involved. Your approach should begin with an understanding of the resellers' objectives and viewpoints. In general, the issues of interest to retailers center around maximization of their total net profits. Four major forces that will combine to influence such profits are volume potential, gross margin or markup, customer traffic generation, and increases in the order sizes of individual customers. As illustrated by the case example presented in the chapter, there can be some rather interesting interplays between these four forces and the merchandising practices for any given brand.

## DISCUSSION QUESTIONS

1. Because resellers and manufacturers are both in business to sell merchandise, how can there be any reason for differences in objectives between them?
2. "We sell our products through manufacturers' representatives. We pay our reps an extra high commission on the sales they make for us and let them worry about how to get the job done." Comment on this statement.
3. Discuss the following product lines in terms of the possible importance that image transfer might or might not play in selling each of them. If you believe it has possible importance, explain why and describe the nature of the reseller firms that might be most effective in exploiting it. The product lines are: skiing equipment, plumbing fixtures, imported wines, household carpeting, and industrial electronic components.
4. Some merchant wholesalers are active in their promotional efforts; others are not. What factors could account for this?
5. A producer of adhesive compounds, which are used for a variety of different industrial purposes, markets its line through wholesale distributors. Its main criterion in seeking such dis-

tributors is the wholesaler's size. Its aim is to deal through several of the largest such firms in each area. You have been called in to advise management regarding the company's total promotional strategy. What factors might you wish to investigate before making any recommendations regarding the current distribution policy and why?
6. What systems have been proposed for classifying types of goods and types of retail outlets, and what purpose can such classification systems serve in terms of considering promotional strategy alternatives?
7. Using the classification systems described in the chapter, discuss the goods and store types that would be likely to apply in selling the following products: sterling silver flatware, vitamin preparations, household furniture, hi-fi components, and tires for passenger autos.
8. With respect to the answers you gave to the preceding question, in which of the listed product categories do you think that personal selling at the retail level might be an important retailer support goal for a producing firm? What specific approaches would you suggest as possible routes to achieving this goal?
9. What is meant by the term "visual merchandis-

ing" and what specific forms of promotional goals can it suggest for a producer of ultimate consumer goods?

10. The description of Dick Elsin's work with retailers focused on personal selling activities. However, it also contained direct and implied references to other components in his company's total promotional mix. Based on the facts presented in that description, attempt to outline the roles played by each of the promotional elements in this case and discuss the interactions between them.

## REFERENCES

1. James McKinley, "If You've Got an Ounce of Feeling, Hallmark Has a Ton of Sentiment," *American Heritage*, December 1982, pp. 71–79.
2. For an especially good introductory overview see Stanley F. Stasch and James E. Gallagher, "Marketing Systems," in Steuart Henderson Britt and Norman F. Guess, eds., *Marketing Manager's Handbook*, 2nd ed. (Chicago: Dartnell Press, 1983), pp. 65–75; for more complete discussions see the texts listed under references 3, 7, and 9.
3. Louis W. Stern and Adel I. El-Ansary, *Marketing Channels*, 2nd ed. (Englewood Cliffs, NJ: Prentice-Hall, Inc., 1982), p. 251.
4. *Ibid.*, p. 448.
5. Reavis Cox, Thomas F. Schutte, and Kendrik S. Few, "Towards the Analysis of Trade Channel Perception," in Fred C. Alvine, ed., *Combined Proceedings of the 1971 Spring and Fall Conferences of the American Marketing Association* (Chicago: American Marketing Association, 1972), p. 191.
6. Edwin E. Bobrow, "Get More than Mere Time from Independent Sales Reps," *Sales and Marketing Management*, 20 August 1979, pp. 82–83.
7. C. Glenn Walters and Blaise J. Bergiel, *Marketing Channels*, 2nd ed. (Glenview, IL: Scott, Foresman and Company, 1982), p. 329.
8. Martin R. Warshaw, *Effective Selling Through Wholesalers* (Ann Arbor, MI: The University of Michigan Press, 1961).
9. Bert Rosenbloom, *Marketing Channels: A Management View* 2nd ed. (Hinsdale, IL: The Dryden Press, 1983), p. 220.
10. Frederick E. Webster, Jr., "The Role of the Industrial Distributor in Marketing Strategy," *Journal of Marketing*, July 1976, p. 13.
11. Rosenbloom, *Marketing Channels: A Management View*, p. 308.
12. William G. Nickels, *Marketing Communications and Promotion* 3rd ed. (Columbus, OH: Grid, Inc., 1984), p. 288.
13. "Cosmetics Business," *Stores*, July 1977, p. 11.
14. R. Karl VanLeer, "Industrial Marketing with a Flair," *Harvard Business Review*, November/December 1976, p. 120.
15. Roger A. Dickson, *Retail Management* (Austin, TX: The Austin Press, 1981), p. 462.
16. Dale Varble and L. E. Bergerson, "The Use and Facets of PM's—A Survey of Retailers," *Journal of Retailing*, Winter 1972–73, pp. 40–47.
17. Wayne F. Talarzyk, James F. Engel, and Carl M. Larsen, "Royal Worcester Porcelain Company, Inc.," *Cases in Promotional Strategy* (Homewood, IL: Richard D. Irwin, 1971).
18. For a more complete discussion see Stern and El-Ansary, *Marketing Channels*, pp. 382–384.
19. Raymond A. Marquardt, James C. Makens, and Robert G. Roe, *Retail Management: Satisfaction of Consumer Needs*, 3rd ed. (Hinsdale, IL: The Dryden Press, 1983), p. 220.
20. Jack Engel, *Advertising* (New York: McGraw-Hill Book Company, 1980), p. 67.
21. William Haight, *Retail Advertising* (Morristown, NJ: General Learning Press, 1976), p. 199.
22. Marquardt, Makens and Roe, *Retail Management: Satisfaction of Consumer Needs*, p. 420.
23. S. Watson Dunn and Arnold M. Barban, *Advertising: Its Role in Modern Marketing*, 4th ed. (Hinsdale, IL: The Dryden Press, 1978), p. 650.
24. For more detailed discussion see Stern and El-Ansary, *Marketing Channels*, pp. 388–389.
25. Edwin E. Bobrow, "Marketers Must Design Strategies to Cope with Power Shift to Retailers, Distributors," *Marketing News,* 16 October 1981, p. 1.
26. Gene Mahany, "Twenty Mistakes Made When Dealing with Retailers," *Advertising Age*, 2 October 1978, p. 68.
27. "Buying—No Longer a One Man Show," *Chain Store Age*, May 1978, p. 44.
28. "The Store Manager—He Is Still the Key Man," *Chain Store Age*, May 1978, p. 44.

# PART SEVEN

# *Budgeting and Control*

# CHAPTER TWENTY

# *Budgeting for Promotion*

## FOCUS OF THE CHAPTER

In theory there is a straightforward approach by which you can determine the optimum budget for each explicit promotional element. It derives from marginal analysis concepts developed in the field of microeconomics. In practice, there are severe obstacles to applying this system in any direct sense. Nonetheless, it merits review at the outset of our discussion because it portrays the ideal toward which you are trying to work. It also provides you with a basis for evaluating alternative procedures more commonly used in everyday business decision making. With this in mind, our coverage of promotional budgeting strategies will start with a short synopsis of the theoretically ideal marginal analysis approach. Following that, we will turn to discussion of five other budget-setting techniques which are more widely used in actual business practice.

## PROMOTIONAL BUDGETING IN THEORY

*Working with*
*Marginal Analysis*

*The General Approach.*  To illustrate how marginal analysis could guide you in setting promotional expenditure levels, we will introduce a very simple example. Suppose you face the problem of deciding how much to spend on personal selling in one of your sales territories during the coming year. You have several items of hard information in hand to guide your decision. You know that the price your firm will receive for each unit of product is ten dollars. You also know that the cost associated with production and sale of each unit, excluding the cost of personal selling, is eight dollars. Therefore, your gross profit on each sale before personal selling expenses will be two dollars. The expense connected with keeping each sales representative in the field for one year is $42,000. This includes her or his salary plus all other costs including those for travel and supervision. To simplify our illustration we will also assume you can assign sales personnel only on a full-time basis. You cannot vary selling-input effort on a precise hourly basis. Given this background, the only additional information you need is a schedule showing the unit sales outputs that will result from various levels of personal selling inputs. Suppose you are able to obtain or develop such a schedule. It reveals the relationships shown graphically on the left-hand side of Figure 20.1 and detailed numerically in Table 20.1. What budget level should you set for personal selling in order to maximize your profit?

***Relating Marginal Sales to Marginal Selling Efforts.*** To fully understand the nature of relationships between inputs, outputs, and profits, we must examine not only total unit sales, but also the *change* in total sales as each separate unit of selling effort is added. Each such change is referred to as "marginal unit sales." The additional input of selling activity required to achieve it is referred to as "marginal personal selling effort." The hypothetical sales productivity schedule suggested in Figure 20.1 starts with the assumption that you would enjoy a volume of 120,000 units in this territory even if you did not employ a single salesperson. The rationale behind this assumption is that a substantial number

---

**FIGURE 20.1 Functional relationships between levels of personal selling inputs and resulting sales outputs in total unit sales and marginal unit sales**

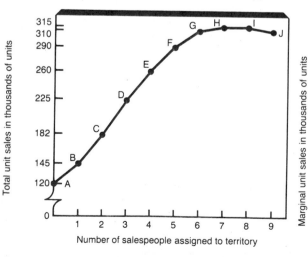
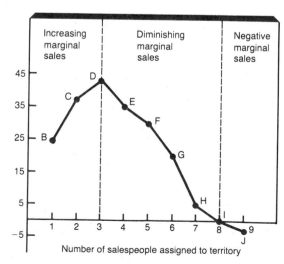

**TABLE 20.1 Functional relationship between personal selling expenditures and unit sales levels in territory X**

| Reference Point in Figure 20.1 | Number of Sales Representatives in Territory | Total Personal Selling Expense[a] | Total Unit Sales |
|---|---|---|---|
| A | 0 | 0 | 120,000 |
| B | 1 | 42 | 145,000 |
| C | 2 | 84 | 182,000 |
| D | 3 | 126 | 225,000 |
| E | 4 | 168 | 260,000 |
| F | 5 | 210 | 290,000 |
| G | 6 | 252 | 310,000 |
| H | 7 | 294 | 315,000 |
| I | 8 | 336 | 315,000 |
| J | 9 | 378 | 312,000 |

[a]In thousands of dollars.

of customers would place orders even if no salespeople were contacting them, because they would have prior experience with your product or are being influenced by some other promotional effort such as advertising. However, when you send just one sales representative into the territory, his or her activities move your total sales from point A to point B. The number of units sold rises to 145,000. In other words, the marginal unit sales associated with moving from no sales force to a one-person sales force is 25,000 units.

If a second sales representative is put into the territory, the additional or marginal sales productivity is even greater. The marginal gain is 37,000 units. Expanding from two to three sales representatives pushes demand from point C to point D, adding 43,000 marginal unit sales to your total and raising that total to 225,000. Thus, when you expand your sales force from one to two to three persons, you not only increase sales but you increase them at an increasing rate. If you will think back to our earlier coverage of personal selling, you will recall some reasons that could help explain why this might happen in certain instances. For example, it is possible that this territory is quite large geographically. With only one person in the field, he or she might have to do a great deal of traveling to reach the prime customers. However, when your first salesperson is joined by a colleague the territory can be divided between them in such a way as to reduce travel time, which permits each to devote a much higher percentage of working hours to actual customer contact. Alternatively, it is conceivable that each salesperson might decide to specialize in calling on customers in particular industries. Assuming such specialization made each of them more effective in relating your product's benefits to individual customer needs, the efforts of both sales force members could become more productive.

Although your total sales continue to grow when you expand from three representatives to four, marginal sales begin to diminish. The marginal gain associated with this expansion is only 35,000 units versus 43,000 units as a result of the prior increase. From points E through H on the curve, sales keep increasing but increasing at an even slower rate. In other words, the additional or marginal unit sales resulting from each additional or marginal unit of personal selling input is decreasing even though total sales are still on the rise.

Logically, as the sales force keeps growing larger, such a pattern would have to emerge at some point. There is an upper limit to the number of reasonably good prospects you can attempt to persuade. As the size of the sales force grows, its members must eventually begin seeking out smaller and more resistant prospects. With additional business more difficult to obtain, the costs of securing it will rise.

At least as depicted in our hypothetical selling situation, it is even possible that by placing too many people in the field you could ultimately reach a point at which total sales turn down. As shown in Figure 20.1, a move from seven salespeople to eight results in no total volume increase at all, presumably because the seven-member sales staff had extracted all of the potential volume you could possibly secure from this territory. At this point the marginal sales drop to zero. If you make the mistake of adding a ninth individual, your salespeople might become so frantic in their attempts to meet sales quotas that they begin antagonizing customers and losing sales. When this happens, your marginal sales output turns negative, and total sales decrease.

Of course, the illustration we have been following is simply one representation of a possible sales response pattern that could evolve as the size of your sales force is expanded. Although the exact response pattern will vary with each promotional situation, there are two generalizations which can be drawn from this example and applied in any similar decision-making procedure. The first is that the relationship between your personal selling budget and the resulting sales response is dependent on the interaction between the nature of the particular market involved and the nature of sales force efforts. In other words, the budgeting procedure is more than a matter of simply allocating more dollars to achieve higher volume. It is intertwined with the question of how you plan to use those extra dollars, and this decision is dependent on your analysis of the target customers on whom your sales force will be calling. It is the nature of those customers, especially in terms of their volume potential and susceptibility to persuasion, that forms the basis for making predictions about your promotional response.

Second, regardless of the exact shape of your sales response curve, it will eventually reach a point of diminishing marginal returns. In our example, this point was reached after the third sales representative was assigned and marginal unit sales responded as shown on the right-hand side of Figure 20.1. In other cases diminishing marginal returns might be reached after the first or fifth or twenty-second unit of selling effort was employed. However, in every case it will be reached at some point, and once this happens you will receive less and less return from each dollar you invest even though total sales may still be rising.

## Optimum Budget Determination Using Marginal Analysis

Given the facts and data in our illustration, your decision regarding an optimum expenditure level for personal selling would be virtually automatic. The general rule for optimizing on the basis of marginal analysis can be stated, "When the marginal revenue product of an input exceeds its [cost], it pays the producer to expand his use of that input. Similarly, when the marginal revenue product of the input is less than its [cost], it pays the producer to use less of that input."[1]

In our example, the marginal revenue product can be treated as marginal gross profit. The input costs of obtaining that marginal revenue product can be treated as the marginal costs of personal selling. Applying the relevant costs for sales personnel and unit gross profit data, the information shown in Figure 20.1 translates into the schedule of alternative budget and profit levels shown in Table 20.2. Following the rule quoted above, you should allocate $210,000 for personal selling in order to send five sales representatives into the field. At

TABLE 20.2 Schedule of alternative cost and profit levels associated with personal selling
(Costs and profits in thousands of dollars)

| Size of Sales Force | Total Cost of Personal Selling | Marginal Cost of Personal Selling | Total Gross Profit[a] | Marginal Gross Profit[a] | Total Profit[b] |
|---|---|---|---|---|---|
| 0 | 0 | | 240 | | 240 |
| | | 42 | | 50 | |
| 1 | 42 | | 290 | | 248 |
| | | 42 | | 74 | |
| 2 | 84 | | 364 | | 280 |
| | | 42 | | 86 | |
| 3 | 126 | | 450 | | 324 |
| | | 42 | | 70 | |
| 4 | 168 | | 520 | | 352 |
| | | 42 | | 60 | |
| 5 | 210 | | 580 | | 370 |
| | | 42 | | 40 | |
| 6 | 252 | | 620 | | 368 |
| | | 42 | | 10 | |
| 7 | 294 | | 630 | | 336 |
| | | 42 | | 0 | |
| 8 | 336 | | 630 | | 294 |
| | | 42 | | −6 | |
| 9 | 378 | | 624 | | 246 |

[a] Total or marginal unit sales times (price per unit less cost per unit for all expenses other than personal selling).
[b] Total gross profit less total personal selling expense.
Note: In this example we were restricted to adding personal selling inputs only on the basis of one full-time salesperson at a time. If input efforts could be controlled on a smaller unit basis, such as precise hours of selling time, we should be able to increase total profits even further by adding selling hours up to the point where the last hour of sales effort exactly recovered its cost in terms of marginal gross profit. However, the profit maximization rule remains the same: You should expand your use of an input up to the point where its marginal revenue product exceeds its cost.

that point marginal gross profit exceeds marginal costs. However, if you add one more person to the staff, your marginal gross profit will be only $40,000 whereas your marginal cost will be $42,000. In consequence, the total profit figure shown in the right-hand column of Table 20.2 reaches its maximum when the personal selling budget is set at $210,000 as the rule dictates.

## Extending Marginal Analysis to Other Promotional Elements

Although our example has been framed in terms of personal selling, exactly parallel demonstrations could be set up for each of the other explicit promotional elements. In the case of advertising, the major expense inputs would be units of space and time purchased in mass media vehicles. In the case of sales promotion, the applicable units would relate to levels of couponing, sampling, specialty advertising, or any of the other sales promotion mechanisms being used. In the case of publicity the units of input would be information releases, special events, and participations. In all cases, these unit inputs would result in required expenditure levels and would be associated with the production of marginal unit sales levels. By calculating the marginal unit sales that would result from any given increase in advertising, sales promotion, or publicity effort and comparing it with the applicable marginal cost of that increased effort you could construct a schedule similar to the one shown in Table 20.2. Then, by applying the rule cited above you could easily determine and choose the optimum amount of money to allocate for the promotional element being considered.

## Obstacles to Implementation of the Marginal Analysis Approach

Budget determination by marginal analysis is most feasible when three conditions prevail. The first of these conditions involves the existence of a rather direct relationship between units of output and the units of input required to produce them. The second requires that the output response of the input variable you are considering is either independent of the levels of all other input factors or that you can measure any interaction effects which might exist between input variables. The third condition calls for an environment which is relatively stable and not subject to sudden or continuous shifts in external forces that you cannot control or foresee.

### Indirect Input-Output Relationships.

When you consider these three conditions in the context of promotional decision making, you discover that none of them is applicable in any clear sense. The output in which you are ultimately interested is sales volume and the profit stemming from that sales volume. However, as previous chapters have stressed, the exact link between individual promotional inputs and sales volume outputs is often indirect and sometimes vague. For example, in our coverage of advertising it was suggested that the proper goals for that promotional element should be treated as communication goals rather than sales goals. In the end, you seek to use those communication goals as a step toward achieving sales, but the exact degree to which a given level of advertising will produce a given level of sales normally tends to defy precise measurement. It is true that some promotional efforts may be more closely associated with rather immediate sales response. Activities in the personal selling area are often thought of in this way. However, even in personal selling the immediate effect is very often a communication effect that enhances the likelihood of future sales rather than obtaining them immediately and directly.

*Interaction Effects.*   Our previous discussion also stressed the idea that promotional elements interact with each other and, of course, this produces complications in connection with the second of the conditions laid out above. For instance, the personal selling productivity curve in Figure 20.1 assumes that any expenditures being made for advertising, sales promotion, and publicity are being held constant. If expenditures for these other elements were to be increased or decreased, that curve could shift up or down or its entire shape might change. In short, there is almost certain to be some type of interrelationship between the amount of money expended on one promotional element and the productivity function of the other elements. Uncovering the nature of some of these interactions can sometimes be attempted through market experimentation. However, even when such testing is possible it can become both costly and complex. Furthermore, because the test must be conducted in an open market situation it is quite possible that uncontrollable, extraneous influences will intrude on the test situation and corrupt the findings. Thus, the amount of reliable information you are likely to obtain about interaction effects will usually be both scanty and imprecise.

*A Volatile and Changing Environment.*   As for the third required condition, which called for a stable environment, it is apparent that the competitive arena in which promotion operates forces it to function in a diametrically opposite type of climate. Consumer tastes and needs can change rapidly. Rival firms are likely to modify their own promotional strategies by altering their budget levels, developing new campaign appeals, and introducing new or improved brands. In short, your promotional efforts are operating in a field of turmoil rather than stability. Estimates of the marginal productivity of promotional inputs that are based on last year's results may prove highly inaccurate if applied to next year's planning.

## PROMOTIONAL BUDGETING IN PRACTICE

Given the problems that inhibit implementation of marginal analysis, the survey findings shown in Table 20.3 are not surprising. When executives of firms with large advertising expenditures were asked how they set their budgets, the great majority reported reliance on techniques other than marginal analysis. The three most widely employed approaches were arbitrary allocation, affordability, and ratio-to-sales. These, plus a frequently discussed competitive comparison approach which was not separately listed in this report, all fall into the category of predetermined budgets. As pointed out in an earlier chapter, a predetermined budget is set before the actual promotional plan has been con-

**TABLE 20.3 Budget allocation methods reported by firms with large advertising expenditures (Percentages of firms using each method)**

| Allocation Method | Consumer Goods Producers | Industrial Goods Producers |
|---|---|---|
| 1. Quantitative Models | 4 | 0 |
| 2. Arbitrary Allocation | 16 | 24 |
| 3. Affordability | 28 | 28 |
| 4. Ratio to Sales | | |
|   a) Percentage of Anticipated Sales | 52 | 32 |
|   b) Percentage of Last Year's Sales | 16 | 28 |
|   c) Per Unit of Anticipated Sales | 12 | 12 |
|   d) Per Unit of Last Year's Sales | 12 | 4 |
| 5. Objective-Task Approach | 12 | 20 |
| 6. All Others | 20 | 12 |

*Source:* Based on Andre J. San Augustine and William F. Foley, "How Large Advertisers Set Budgets," *Journal of Advertising Research,* October 1975, pp. 11–16.

structed. In effect, all ensuing strategy decisions are constrained by the dollar level specified in advance of considering the detailed objectives of the promotional design.

The objective-task approach, which was reported as being somewhat less popular among these firms than were the three budgeting techniques cited above, falls into the strategy-determined category. Under an objective-task method, you begin by developing the details of your promotional program. Your budget is determined at the end of the process by calculating the amount of money required to operationalize those details.

If you sum the percentages listed in Table 20.3 you will find that the total for methods used among consumer goods firms is 172 percent and that for industrial goods firms is 160 percent. Since both totals are far in excess of 100 percent, they are telling you something very interesting about the way in which promotional budgets are often handled in practice. Many firms do not confine themselves to one and only one budget-setting approach. Instead, they use some combination of approaches. This finding is consistent with two points that will be raised in the following discussion of alternative budgeting approaches. The first point concerns the fact that some of these budgeting alternatives overlap with each other. The second involves a recommendation that will be made later and which proposes that you may be well-advised to analyze your budget by several different approaches before reaching a final conclusion as to the amount of money you wish to allocate.

**Arbitrary Allocation.** As its name implies, this approach relies very heavily upon raw managerial judgment rather than detailed analysis. Its procedure is simple. The executive or group of executives charged with responsibility for fixing an expenditure level do so on the basis of their personal experience, business philosophy, and marketing intuition. Although it is quite possible that facts and figures enter into the budgeting process, these are presumably not treated in any highly systematic fashion. Neither objective formulas nor rigorously patterned reasoning is given much weight.

There is very little that can be said in support of a *purely* arbitrary budgeting procedure. Admittedly, some amount of subjective judgment will play a role in most promotional strategy planning because the information available to you is almost always incomplete and you must cope with uncertainties about the future environment. However, this should not force you to abandon organized analysis. Although it is hard to find grounds for endorsing an arbitrary approach, data such as that shown in Table 20.3 imply that arbitrary methods are not uncommon in setting some promotional budgets, even among large firms.

**Affordability.** Available company resources will impose an upper limit on all proposed business expenditures. Although economic constraints may be most apparent in smaller firms, even corporate giants do not have an infinite reservoir of funds with which to undertake every activity that might show promise. For this reason, affordability will play some role in all promotional budget decisions. However, in certain instances, affordability may play the dominant role. The extreme case of such dominance is referred to as the "all-you-can-afford" budgeting technique.

A simple budgeting decision path, which uses the affordability approach is traced in Figure 20.2. The key to determining whether the test of affordability will dominate your strategy or merely lead you to an alternative approach is contained in the second, centered, decision box in the figure. If you answer "No" to the question posed there, your decision route is switched to another method. On the other hand, a positive answer implies that affordability should serve as your main consideration and that you should allocate "all-you-can-afford" to the promotional element under study.

At first glance, opting for an "all-you-can-afford" approach might seem to represent a highly unscientific route which flagrantly violates the logic suggested by marginal analysis. However, on closer scrutiny you will find that this technique could be viewed as not only compatible with marginal analysis but actually serving as a simplified modification of that method *in certain situations*. The decision to spend all you can afford could be reasonable when both of the following conditions exist. First, the total funds available to the firm are severely limited relative to marketing objectives and opportunities. Second, one of the explicit promotional elements stands out as a prime mover in terms of sales response. Given these circumstances, you may conclude that even by committing all possible financial resources to that one element you will still fall short of the point at which its marginal cost exceeds the marginal gross profit it generates. If your conclusion is derived from careful study of past sales

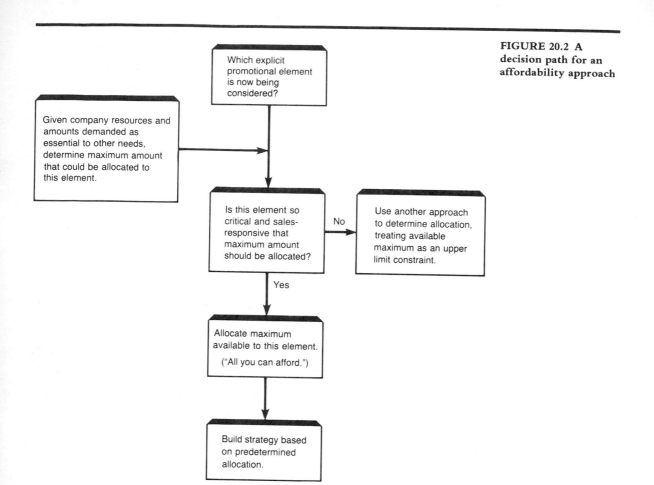

FIGURE 20.2 A decision path for an affordability approach

Which explicit promotional element is now being considered?

Given company resources and amounts demanded as essential to other needs, determine maximum amount that could be allocated to this element.

Is this element so critical and sales-responsive that maximum amount should be allocated?

No → Use another approach to determine allocation, treating available maximum as an upper limit constraint.

Yes

Allocate maximum available to this element. ("All you can afford.")

Build strategy based on predetermined allocation.

results, perhaps including some market testing, you are operating within the precepts of marginal analysis even though you may not be applying the technique formally.

As an illustration, recall the description of the E'Suberante promotional strategy that was presented in Chapter 13. There was at least a hint that E'Suberante's marketing management team was applying something akin to an "all-you-can-afford" approach when it dealt with advertising. Although an absolute upper limit on expenditures was never openly mentioned, some of the facts reported concerning the E'Suberante case suggest that financial constraints may have played a role in policy formulation. One point that gives weight to this view is the statement regarding the treatment of personal selling effort. Despite the fact that the sales force size was recognized as being comparatively limited, the planning for the year in question included no provision for upgrading the amount of personal selling. Available funds were channeled instead to advertising. As noted when the case was presented, the wisdom of concentrating effort on one element of promotion at the expense of the others can always be questioned. However, assuming that E'Suberante executives had good reason to believe that marginal sales sensitivity was much more pronounced for advertising than for personal selling, an affordability approach would be consistent with the optimum decision rule laid out in our discussion of marginal analysis.

In summary, affordability will play some role in any budgeting routine. There may be certain instances where it is appropriately used as the main criterion. However, these instances should be scrutinized very carefully and related to marginal analysis principles insofar as is possible. A commitment of funds on the basis of affordability alone seems impossible to recommend on any logical basis.

***Ratio-to-Sales.*** As presented in Table 20.3, this appears to be a method heavily relied on by many large firms in setting their advertising budgets. It is also a method that is heavily assaulted by many writers.[2] The presumption underlying its use is that profits will be maximized if promotional expenditures are held at some "ideal" proportion of total sales revenues. That proportion may be stated either as a percentage of dollar sales or as a certain amount of money per unit sold.

If you decide to initiate your promotional budgeting procedure on a ratio-to-sales basis, you will be left with a variety of subsidiary questions to investigate. A possible sequence of such questions is listed in Figure 20.3. In practice, it is quite possible that many firms using this approach simplify matters by answering "Yes" at Boxes 2 and 3. However, if the approach is to be used at all, the other questions would also seem to merit review on at least a periodic basis. If the sequence laid out in Figure 20.3 is followed judiciously, it is also possible that your answers would lead you to adopt another budgeting technique as the primary basis for your planning.

Most criticisms of a ratio-to-sales approach center around two main shortcomings. First, using sales as the basis for determining your budget reverses the logical order of the cause-and-effect relationship involved. It seems to imply that promotional expenditure levels are caused by past or anticipated sales levels. In reality, of course, the whole purpose of spending money on promotion rests on the belief that your sales levels are caused at least in part by the levels of your promotional expenditures. Second, and perhaps more importantly, the ratio-to-sales approach begins without any consideration of your specific promotional needs or objectives. It dictates that you determine how much you are going to spend before you have considered how the budget is to be spent or even if the expenditure is necessary.

Despite these criticisms, the ratio-to-sales approach also has some authorities who have come to its defense. A marketing executive who prepared a rather careful review of budgeting techniques for a leading research journal described it as being both "straightforward" and "one of the safest . . . bases for setting advertising expenditures."[3] A team of marketing academicians has proposed that, *if properly used,* it is not only more sophisticated than its surface appearance suggests but it can produce results equivalent to those achievable via marginal analysis.[4] The reasoning that leads them to this conclusion is both

**FIGURE 20.3  A decision path for a ratio-to-sales approach**

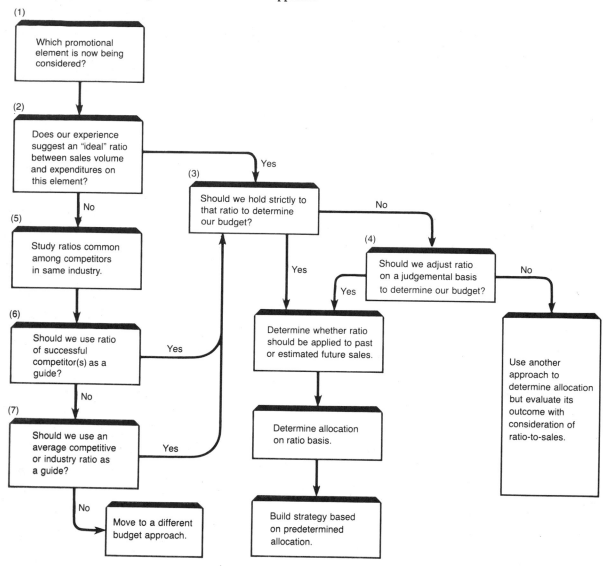

intriguing and somewhat complex, and our available space does not permit its full presentation here. However, in summary form that reasoning is based on the idea that it is theoretically possible to determine a ratio in a way which will lead to the same result described in our opening review of marginal analysis. It should be pointed out that in order to make the necessary calculations you would need virtually the same type of data required for the basic marginal approach, and that data would still be just as difficult to obtain.

Some adherents of the ratio-to-sales approach might argue that, over time, promotional experience within any given industry causes a more or less stan-

**TABLE 20.4 Advertising as a ratio-of-sales for selected product categories 1980 and 1981**

| Product Category | Advertising Dollars as a Percentage of Sales Dollars | |
| --- | --- | --- |
| | 1980 | 1981 |
| Office Furniture | 1.0 | .9 |
| Greeting Cards | 1.9 | 2.2 |
| Food and Kindred Products | 3.3 | 3.5 |
| Candy | 6.1 | 5.9 |
| Perfumes and Cosmetics | 8.8 | 9.8 |

Source: Advertising Age, 17 August 1981, p. 38; and Advertising Age, 2 August 1982, p. 41.

dard ratio allocation to evolve that comes close to approximating the theoretically optimum ratio you would discover if you could obtain all of the necessary data. For instance, the figures shown in Table 20.4 suggest that the percentage of sales spent on advertising varies greatly between industries but remains rather constant within each given industry, at least on a year-to-year basis. A strategist who chose to act on the assumption that historical industry experience causes an optimum ratio to emerge would have good reason to give thought to the queries raised in Boxes 6 and 7 of Figure 20.3. Before accepting this assumption, however, you should be forewarned that at least to this writer's knowledge there is no published research evidence that supports it.

In summary, despite the weaknesses that have been ascribed to it, the ratio-to-sales approach is widely used as at least one stage in many promotional budgeting procedures. Some authorities have also viewed it as having a degree of theoretical support. The position of this book will be that it may well deserve to be included as one aspect of your total budgeting deliberations but that, like the affordability approach, it should not be the only issue you consider. Furthermore, its rather mechanistic nature can inhibit identification of special marketing needs and circumstances that could call for an unusual variation from your past allocation patterns. Because of this last factor, it probably is not the best technique to use in the initial phase of your search for an optimum budget level.

*Competitive Comparison.* In a narrow sense, a competitive comparison budget approach can mean that you set your budget to equal or come close to equaling that of a competitor. This is generally referred to as a "competitive parity strategy." In a somewhat broader sense, the competitive comparison approach can be interpreted to mean that you give heavy emphasis to consideration of competitive budgets when planning your own budget, even though you may not decide to match any of them. Figure 20.4 lists a series of questions that might be considered in working from a competitive comparison

**FIGURE 20.4  A decision path for a competitive comparison approach**

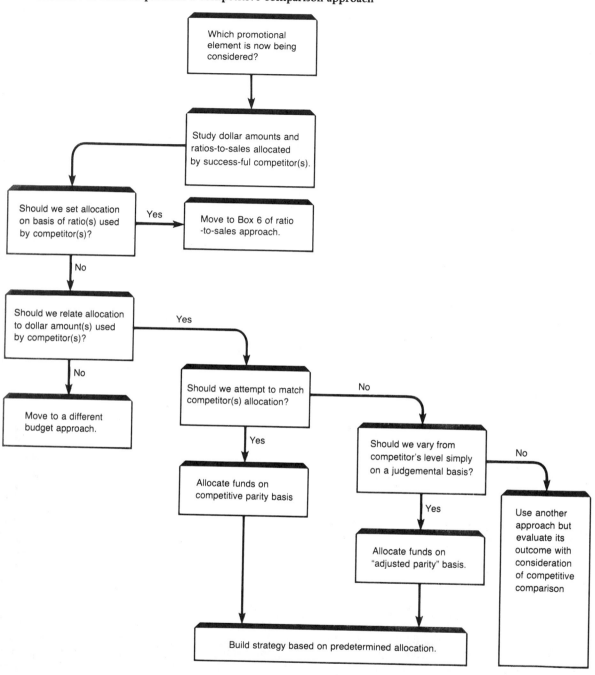

*Budgeting for Promotion*

**TABLE 20.5** An illustrative comparison of competitive sales and promotional expenditures data

| | | Last Year's Sales and Promotional Budgets Expenditures for: | | | |
| | | Advertising | | Personal Selling | |
| | Sales | Dollars | Percent of Sales | Dollars | Percent of Sales |
|---|---|---|---|---|---|
| Brand X | $100,000,000 | $4,000,000 | 4% | $2,750,000 | 2.75% |
| Brand Y | $ 75,000,000 | $2,625,000 | 3.5% | $3,000,000 | 4% |

standpoint. As noted there, one line of reasoning could induce you to stress your relationship to competitors in terms of the ratio-to-sales allotted to each promotional element. Following this course moves you back to a particular form of the ratio-to-sales approach. Alternatively, your basis of comparison might be the actual dollar amount that a successful competitor spends on advertising, personal selling, sales promotion, or publicity. The logic of following this latter type of comparison would be that it is the total dollar amount, not the percentage relationship, which really determines that degree of promotional force your competitor exerts in the marketplace.

Table 20.5 illustrates the type of basic data you might investigate in the opening phase of a competitive comparison procedure. Assume you are responsible for the marketing of Brand Y. This is a low unit-value product sold to ultimate consumers through thousands of retail outlets across the country. Your chief competitor is Brand X, the top-selling entry which controls a thirty-five percent market share. You are in second place. It makes good sense for you to pay close attention to the promotional budgeting practices of Brand X. However, if you automatically adjust your own allocations to reflect your competitor's behavior, it might make very little sense at all. For instance, the data in Table 20.5 might be interpreted as suggesting that you give careful thought to the possibility of placing less emphasis on personal selling and more on advertising. This is what your more successful rival is doing and, at least on superficial inspection, it seems to yield superior results. Nonetheless, before moving to an imitative budget strategy you would be well advised to assess a number of collateral factors.

Brand X might be able to spend both a lower percentage of sales and a lower total dollar amount on personal selling because it enjoys a very strong relationship with retailers. Your heavier expenditure in this area might be required at this time to maintain and improve your distribution levels and reseller support activities. The much heavier commitment of funds for advertising by Brand X merits close attention but not necessarily duplication. Before you conclude that your own advertising budget should be moved to or toward your competitor's dollar level, there are a variety of key questions to be asked. How would the additional funds be spent? What specific communication objectives would you seek to achieve? What is the feasibility of attaining those objectives? For example, it is possible that the evaluative criteria stressed in your advertising and on which your brand actually enjoys a competitive advantage might appeal to a different and smaller consumer segment than those possessed and advertised by Brand X. If so, merely upgrading your advertising expenditures may accomplish little unless preceded by appropriate modifications in the rest of your marketing mix.

In summary, the same generalizations proposed for the affordability and the ratio-to-sales approaches are applicable to the competitive comparison approach. Although comparisons with competitors' budgets may be useful, they must be viewed in the context of the total market setting. Otherwise, they may prove to be misleading guides. On this basis, a competitive comparison approach most probably does not represent your best starting point for budget planning.

*Strategy-Determined Budgets*

***The Objective-Task Approach.***   All of the budgeting procedures discussed to this point assume that funds should first be allocated to each promotional element with the manner of spending those funds to be determined later. The objective-task approach works in reverse fashion. The flow of decision making it embodies is summarized in Figure 20.5. As indicated there, the procedure is consistent with the decision field sequences suggested for personal selling, advertising, sales promotion, and publicity, as those were laid out in Chapters 10 through 18. Objectives are designated for each individual element, and the tasks required to reach those objectives are spelled out on the basis of past experience and strategic judgment.

For example, if the promotional element involved were advertising, the objectives might be specified in terms of percentage of prospects to be reached and the type of influence the advertising message aims at having on those prospects. These objectives would then be interpreted in terms of required creative and media tasks needed to achieve them. The advertising budget is then calculated as the cost of creating the advertising and purchasing the media space and time needed to carry out those tasks.

***Fitting the Objective-Task Approach into a Broader Strategy Frame.***   Because it initiates promotional budgeting by relating cost inputs to anticipated sales-producing outputs, the objective-task approach has been described as a very close approximation to the theoretically ideal marginal analysis.[5] Beyond this, it could be argued that the innate logic of the situation would lead firms to adopt an objective-task approach. After all, the very purpose of spending dollars for promotion is to achieve some desired result. On that basis, common sense argues that you begin by determining the result you seek and then determine the route you must follow to reach that result and the cost of pursuing that route.

A flaw sometimes suggested in this scheme of logic is that the objective-task approach "does not indicate how the objectives themselves should be chosen and whether they are worth the cost of attaining them."[6] However, the answer to surmounting this obstacle lies in first recognizing that promotional planning should not be handled as an isolated decision-making process. On the contrary, it should be viewed as part of a network of marketing mix considera-

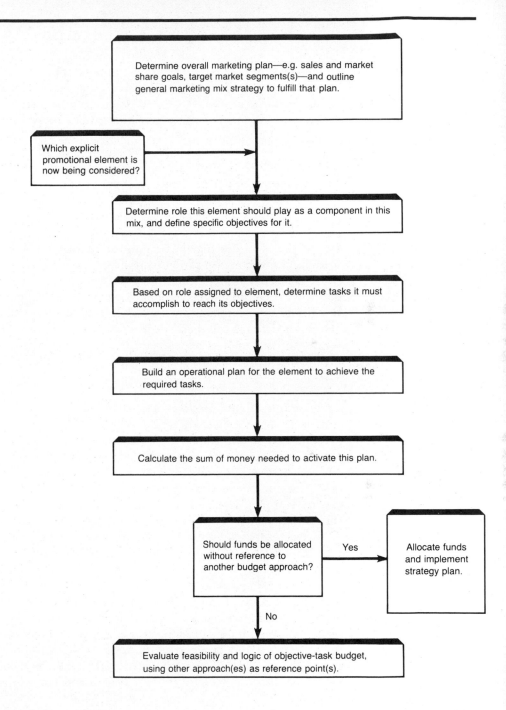

**FIGURE 20.5 A decision path for an objective-task approach**

Determine overall marketing plan—e.g. sales and market share goals, target market segments(s)—and outline general marketing mix strategy to fulfill that plan.

Which explicit promotional element is now being considered?

Determine role this element should play as a component in this mix, and define specific objectives for it.

Based on role assigned to element, determine tasks it must accomplish to reach its objectives.

Build an operational plan for the element to achieve the required tasks.

Calculate the sum of money needed to activate this plan.

Should funds be allocated without reference to another budget approach?

Yes → Allocate funds and implement strategy plan.

No

Evaluate feasibility and logic of objective-task budget, using other approach(es) as reference point(s).

tions which, in turn, are derived from basic organizational goals. A top marketing executive of a leading consumer goods firm has dubbed this view as "the total business approach." In applying the concept to setting advertising budgets, he has stated, "The total business approach looks at advertising budgets as part of the advertising strategy that has derived from a marketing strategy which, in turn, is derived from a business strategy. Using this approach, the business manager can strategically coordinate advertising funds with [other] promotion and pricing strategy and can thereby provide objectives with which to evaluate the consequences of those strategies."[7]

Figure 20.6 pictures one manner of viewing the objective-task approach as an outgrowth of prior determinations concerning overall corporate and marketing policy. As shown there, in a total business approach the objectives set for each promotional element are derived from requirements imposed by higher level decisions. In placing the objective-task method in this setting, Figure 20.6 also ties together a number of major points covered in earlier sections of this book. In particular, the figure reintroduces some of the earliest issues raised in Chapter 1 concerning the derivation of marketing objectives as outgrowths of the interplay between corporate goals, environmental forces, and company strengths and weaknesses. The decision-making sequences suggested for defining the specific role of each explicit promotional element call for use of materials presented in Chapters 10 through 18. An abbreviated illustration of the full flow of decision making is offered in Figure 20.7.

***An Example of an Objective-Task Plan.*** Skin care products, the category chosen for this example, are regarded by some industry analysts as possessing exceptionally strong market growth potential. The chief environmental force behind this anticipation of growth is the aging of the population described in our earlier coverage of demographics. The adult contingent which is gaining rapidly in numbers is a heavy user group of this category. Moreover, industry experts feel that demand can be further stimulated by educating consumers concerning proper skin treatment. On this basis, the skin care field has been predicted to "remain a focus for the industry's new product offerings in the years ahead."[8]

The corporation chosen for this example has been given the fictitious name, J. K. Ivensen, Incorporated. It markets a successful line of ethical drugs as well as a variety of proprietary drug and cosmetic items including shaving cream, deodorants, and toothpaste. Although it does not currently manufacture or sell a skin care item, it does produce a top-selling brand of suntan lotion. The firm is financially strong and expansion oriented. Its consumer brands are represented by a powerful sales organization that calls on drugstores, supermarkets, and discount outlets. From a new brand entry standpoint, the most pressing negative factor is the existence of well-entrenched competitive brands including such names as Ponds, Oil of Olay, Noxzema, Raintree, and Revlon.

A summary listing of corporate goals, environmental forces, and company strengths and weaknesses is shown in the top portion of Figure 20.7. As also indicated there, a decision has been made by the upper echelon of corporate

**FIGURE 20.6 An extended view of objective-task planning**

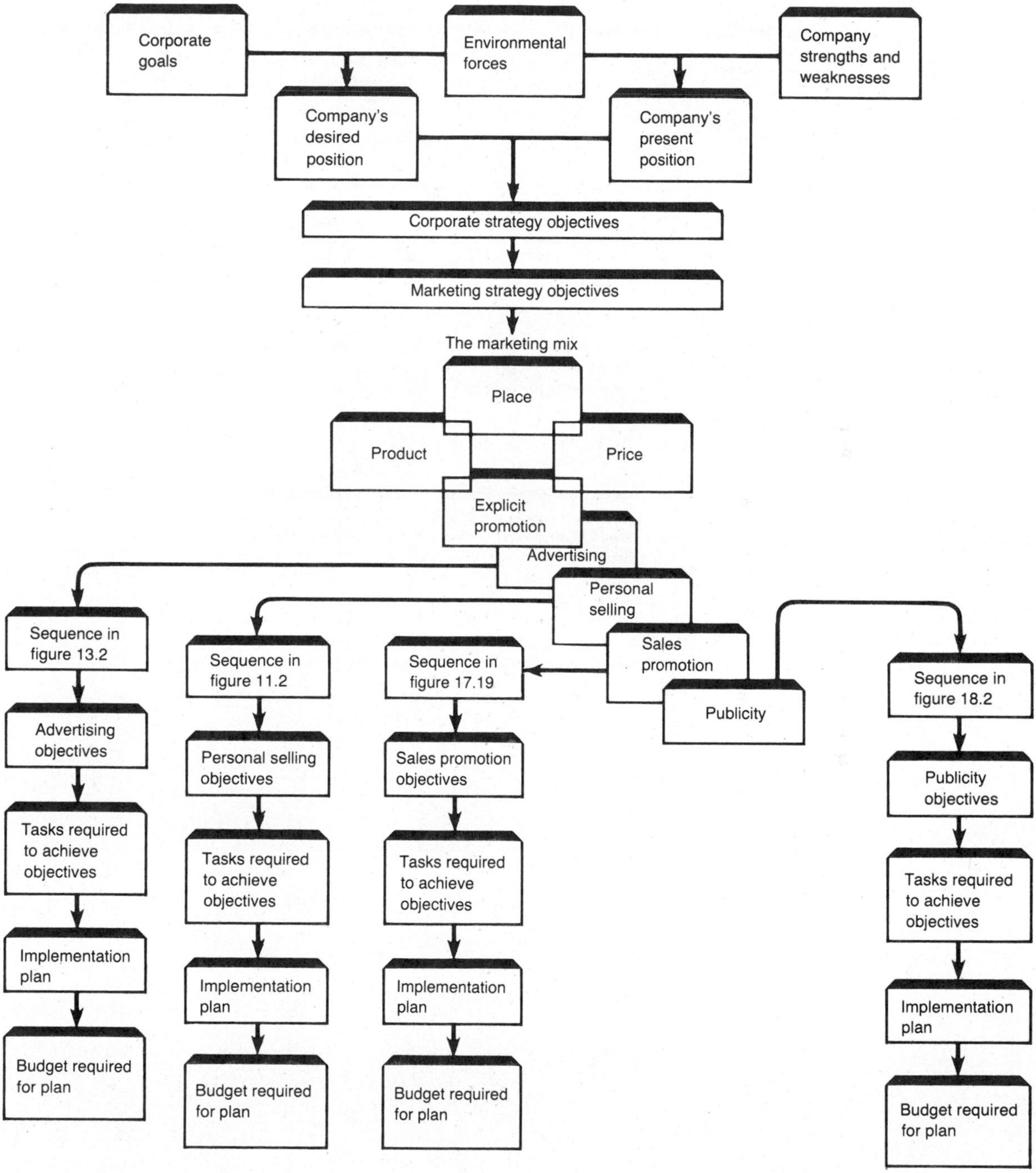

**FIGURE 20.7 Outline of the flow of an objective–task plan**

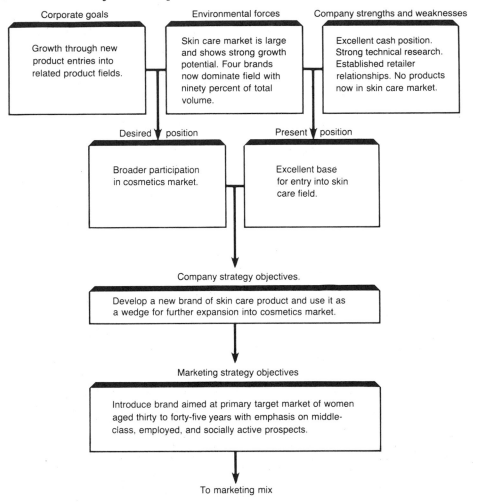

Corporate goals

> Growth through new product entries into related product fields.

Environmental forces

> Skin care market is large and shows strong growth potential. Four brands now dominate field with ninety percent of total volume.

Company strengths and weaknesses

> Excellent cash position. Strong technical research. Established retailer relationships. No products now in skin care market.

Desired position

> Broader participation in cosmetics market.

Present position

> Excellent base for entry into skin care field.

Company strategy objectives.

> Develop a new brand of skin care product and use it as a wedge for further expansion into cosmetics market.

Marketing strategy objectives

> Introduce brand aimed at primary target market of women aged thirty to forty-five years with emphasis on middle-class, employed, and socially active prospects.

To marketing mix

management to enter and achieve a prominent position in the skin care product category. Although high-level marketing personnel would be involved in the decisions to this point, the basic strategy concerns much more than merely marketing policy. It can be more accurately thought of as a broad-scale company plan.

However, as that plan is set in motion it calls for implementation through decisions that are essentially the concern of marketing strategists. These embrace not merely questions about explicit promotion per se, but also questions about the other components of the full marketing mix. In this case, we will assume that a product has been specially formulated which not only moisturizes the skin but is also especially effective in helping remove surface blemishes and dead skin particles. Its superior performance has been tested through laboratory experiments. Marketing research, conducted prior to the

**FIGURE 20.7 (continued)**

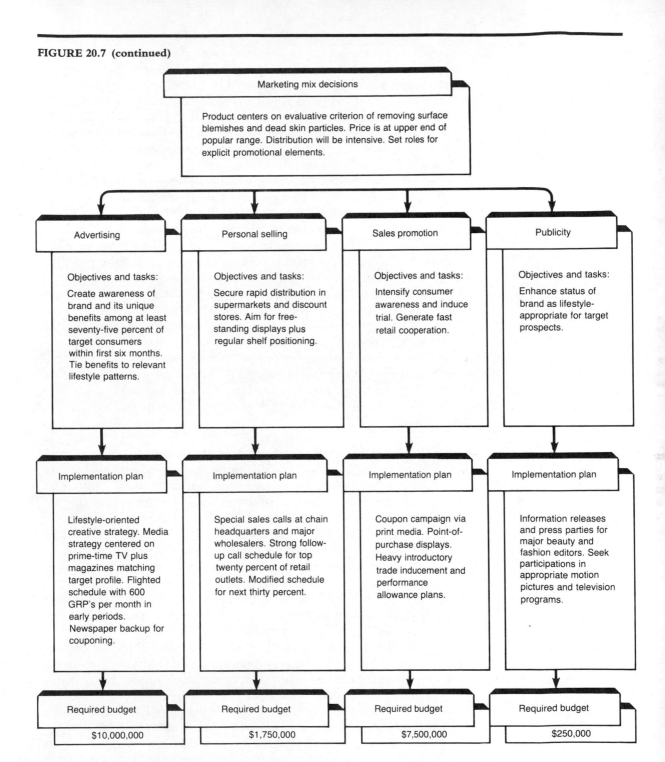

**Marketing mix decisions**

Product centers on evaluative criterion of removing surface blemishes and dead skin particles. Price is at upper end of popular range. Distribution will be intensive. Set roles for explicit promotional elements.

**Advertising**

Objectives and tasks:

Create awareness of brand and its unique benefits among at least seventy-five percent of target consumers within first six months. Tie benefits to relevant lifestyle patterns.

**Personal selling**

Objectives and tasks:

Secure rapid distribution in supermarkets and discount stores. Aim for free-standing displays plus regular shelf positioning.

**Sales promotion**

Objectives and tasks:

Intensify consumer awareness and induce trial. Generate fast retail cooperation.

**Publicity**

Objectives and tasks:

Enhance status of brand as lifestyle-appropriate for target prospects.

**Implementation plan**

Lifestyle-oriented creative strategy. Media strategy centered on prime-time TV plus magazines matching target profile. Flighted schedule with 600 GRP's per month in early periods. Newspaper backup for couponing.

**Implementation plan**

Special sales calls at chain headquarters and major wholesalers. Strong follow-up call schedule for top twenty percent of retail outlets. Modified schedule for next thirty percent.

**Implementation plan**

Coupon campaign via print media. Point-of-purchase displays. Heavy introductory trade inducement and performance allowance plans.

**Implementation plan**

Information releases and press parties for major beauty and fashion editors. Seek participations in appropriate motion pictures and television programs.

**Required budget**

$10,000,000

**Required budget**

$1,750,000

**Required budget**

$7,500,000

**Required budget**

$250,000

planning of detailed marketing strategy, has indicated that its qualities have special appeal to women in the thirty- to forty-five-year age group. In particular, the preintroduction survey suggests that women who are employed, socially active, and middle class in outlook tend to be the best prospects for the brand. The product will be price-positioned to make it competitive with the popular best sellers currently on the market. However, it will be at the upper edge of the popular price range. Distribution will be intensive. All types of retail stores currently carrying Ivensen's other cosmetic products will be sought as outlets for the new brand.

In drawing up an objective-task budget proposal, the promotional staff for Ivensen works from the above background. The objectives sketched out for advertising, personal selling, sales promotion, and publicity have been determined by careful consideration of the role each element must play in a coordinated mix that fulfills the demands imposed by the marketing master plan. Having specified what each element is intended to accomplish, it becomes the job of the various promotional specialists to ascertain the tasks required to reach the promotional objectives. At this stage, the details of activating the promotional campaign begin to emerge. In other words, the objective-task procedure now enters its task-delineation phase. For example, a media plan must be developed that will reach target prospects in a manner that generates the awareness level previously determined as being necessary. A sales call scheduling plan must be considered to fulfill the tasks imposed by distribution and reseller support objectives. The costs projected for the tasks required to achieve the promotional objectives result in the budget estimates shown at the bottom of Figure 20.7.

*Limitations of the Objective-Task Approach*

Although the objective-task approach resolves the problems connected with promotional budgeting in a logical fashion, it is also evident that adherence to the systematic line of reasoning it proposes will not automatically guarantee infallible results. Both the setting of objectives for each promotional element and the spelling-out of tasks required to achieve those objectives involve heavy degrees of managerial skill. However, when the decision process is assisted by as much information input as possible, the results are based on much more than mere arbitrary executive opinion. As noted in earlier chapters, the decision strategy sequence for each promotional element should begin with evaluation of results achieved by past efforts in that field. To supplement those evaluations, an alert promotional staff will also pay heed to pertinent research data concerning results achieved by other marketers.

Even with such data, it must be acknowledged that the set of communication flows set into motion by your promotional program must enter an uncertain and ever-changing consumer and competitive environment. For this reason, all of the assumptions that were made in developing the program should be subjected to continual review as the plan is put into action and market feedback is obtained. In this sense, an ideal objective-task approach does not terminate after the required budget has been calculated and approved. Its assumptions and accomplishments are constantly monitored by market feedback. Especially in the case of new product introductions or plans for significant revisions of ongoing promotional programs, limited-scale experimentation by test marketing is often undertaken to secure preliminary feedback before the program and its attendant budget are finalized on a full-scale basis. The process of extending the planning procedure via market feedback has been termed "adaptive control" and will be the subject of the next chapter.

*Choosing Among the Budgeting Approaches*

Given the tone of the commentaries that accompanied our descriptions of budgeting approaches, it will come as no surprise that this book supports the objective-task approach as the preferred procedure. At the same time, it must be recalled that other approaches, notably affordability and ratio-to-sales, seem to predominate in actual practice. Furthermore, our review has implied that both of these other approaches plus the competitive comparison technique have points of value that suggest they should be given at least some consideration when you are formulating your budget. With this in mind, Figure 20.8 proposes a routine for incorporating the four budgeting methods into a comprehensive process.

*A Multistage Budgeting Procedure*

If you are following a combination process such as the one in Figure 20.8 to formulate and then to screen budgeting decisions, your choice of a starting point might not be a critical issue. Regardless of the approach selected to initiate the procedure, the logic and implications surrounding each of the other methods would automatically be brought into consideration before the budget was finalized. However, because of our endorsement of the objective-task approach, we will use it to illustrate how the routine can be started. Suppose J. K. Ivensen, Incorporated has followed the objective-task approach to originate tentative budgets and arrived at the cost estimates shown at the bottom of Figure 20.7. Before allocating those amounts, Ivensen's marketing executives might want to evaluate them against each of the other approaches used as check points in the manner suggested by Figure 20.8. Affordability, as a case in point, is a test that must be considered relative to any budget proposal. If it were found that the tentative objective-task budget proposal placed a severe strain on resources being considered for allocation to other corporate activities, judgments would have to be made concerning the probability of success and profit potential of the proposed skin care promotional plan versus alternative opportunities open to the company. It is possible that the tentative objective-task proposal would stand up against this test. However, if that were not the case, the decision routine called for in Figure 20.8 routes the planning back to a revision of the original objective-task approach.

It would also be prudent for Ivensen's promotional management team to evaluate their budget proposals in comparison to expenditures made by competitors in the introduction of similar products. This does not imply that an objective-task budget should be either enlarged or reduced simply because it is out of line with competitive expenditure levels. It does suggest, however, that an allocation that represents a sharp departure from industry practices deserves careful review to make certain its underlying rationale is sound. If the tentative budget proposal varies significantly from the firm's customary ratio-to-sales level, a similar type of careful scrutiny is in order.

**FIGURE 20.8 A multistage, synthesized budgeting approach**

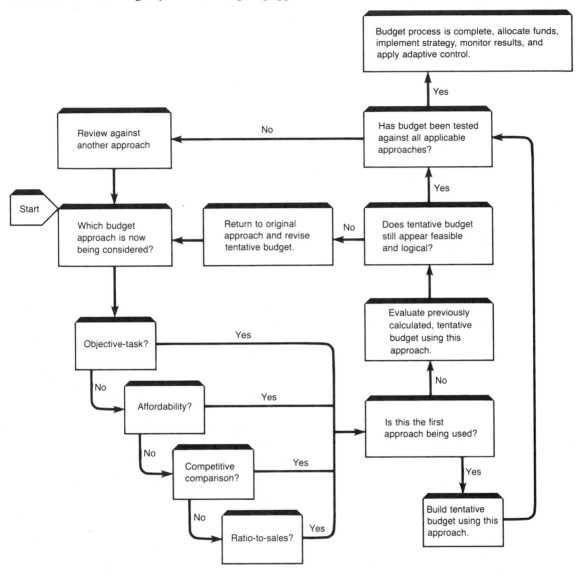

A combination-of-methods approach simply uses each approach as a standard against which the logic behind the others can be measured. The result should be a budget plan that makes sense in terms of the firm's objectives and the promotional tasks needed to obtain those objectives, as well as being defensible in terms of financial resource capabilities, competitive considerations, and past experience as to profitable relationships between promotional expense and market achievements.

# SUPPLEMENTARY ISSUES IN PROMOTIONAL BUDGETING

*Additional*
*Budgeting*
*Approaches*

The budgeting approaches discussed above represent those most commonly used or most frequently recommended by experts. However, several more imaginative and usually more complex possibilities have been proposed. For the most part, these tend to require information inputs that are difficult and sometimes impossible to obtain. Furthermore, they are usually based on theoretical concepts that remain largely untested.[9] For these reasons, these alternative budgeting approaches will not be described in detail. Nevertheless, some of them merit brief mention as proposals that you may wish to investigate further to enrich your understanding of budgeting possibilities.

***Game Theory Models.*** One family of proposed alternative budgeting methods is based on "game theory."[10] Essentially, the techniques included within this group are very specialized variations of the competitive comparison approach, though they require much more complex assumptions and calculations than the rather simple competitive comparison methods we considered earlier. Game theory techniques are based on the proposition that your sales results derive from an interplay between the size of your budget and the sizes of competitive budgets. They use various methods to find an optimum expenditure level for your firm by considering both the range of interactive effects which could occur, given varying budget relationships, and the probability that each of them might occur.

***Brand Switching Models.*** Another class of budget approaches centers around models of brand switching and brand loyalty behavior.[11] Again, these and other models that have been advanced as more sophisticated approaches to overcoming the uncertainty surrounding promotional budgeting tend to introduce problems and uncertainties of their own. For this reason, there is little evidence that they have had much impact on the way in which practitioners actually go about the business of budget setting.

*Over-Budgeting*
*Versus*
*Under-Budgeting*

No matter what method or combination of methods you ultimately choose to set your promotional expenditure levels, it is unlikely that you will arrive at a final decision which precisely coincides with the theoretically optimum expenditure level proposed by marginal analysis. It is more likely that you will conclude that the optimum amount to spend for any one of the promotional elements *probably* lies somewhere within a range of dollar possibilities. For instance, if a group of executives were seeking to arrive at a consensus regarding the correct dollar figure to allot for advertising, they might not agree on an exact amount. However, it is much more likely they could agree that the most profitable expenditure level would *probably* lie within some range of figures, such as "somewhere between $4,000,000 and $5,000,000."

Given that your marketing management team may be more confident about the range within which the optimum amount lies than it is about the precise location of the optimum amount within that range, you could be left with the question, "Because we face a high degree of uncertainty in making our deci-

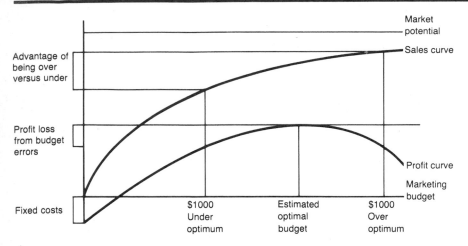

**FIGURE 20.9 A hypothetical comparison between results of underspending versus overspending on promotion**

*Source:* Adapted from Eugene Schonfeld, "Common Sense Rules in Setting Ad Budgets," *Industrial Marketing,* December 1979, p. 56.

sion, would it be better to err on the high side or on the low side?" In other words, if your actual expenditure level is almost certainly going to be at variance with the theoretically optimum expenditure level, would it be better to take the risk of overspending or underspending? Although there may not be unanimous agreement on the appropriate answer to this question, a good argument has been raised in favor of leaning toward overspending. This position has been presented based on the assumptions involved in the graphic model diagrammed in Figure 20.9.

As shown there, a promotional allocation that falls below the theoretically optimum amount will produce profits below the theoretical maximum because it results in a lower sales volume and—in consequence—a lower share of the total market. On the other hand, a budget that is higher than optimum produces a suboptimum profit result for a different reason. The additional sales it generates are not sufficient to offset the additional expense incurred. However, notice that at least in this example, the higher budget did generate additional sales and—by implication—a higher market share. Thus, within the bounds of the assumptions made in this illustration, overspending produces profit results equivalent to those resulting from an equal degree of underspending. Incidentally, this is completely in line with the data presented earlier in our discussion of marginal analysis.

On this basis, a sound argument can be put forth for leaning toward the risk of overspending as opposed to underspending. The thrust of the argument derives from the fact that, from the standpoint of immediate profit outcomes, an error in one direction may be neither better nor worse than an equivalent error in the other. However, and importantly, overspending *within reason* can carry with it some desirable side effects which will not be realized by underspending. Specifically, one management consultant argues that "the overspending error results in a stronger competitive position. It deprives competitors of sales revenues and profits that could be used against [your firm in future competitive efforts]. Moreover, entry into the industry or product category by new competitors will be made more difficult and expensive."[12]

The point raised in this argument is interesting and deserves careful consideration. To say that it is better to overspend than to underspend does not mean you should automatically revert to an "all-you-can-afford" approach. Rather, it implies that if you have a range of potential budget levels under consideration and several options in the range appear logical and defensible on other grounds, it might make sense to help resolve your uncertainty by recognizing that the higher level budgets could hold some supplementary long-term competitive benefits beyond immediate profit returns.

*Viewing Promotional Budgets as Investments*

Promotional budget proposals may originate in the marketing division of a firm. However, before a budget is authorized it will very likely traverse a course which finds it being reviewed by executives outside of the marketing division. In particular, it will almost certainly come under the close scrutiny of the organization's financial and accounting executives as well as top management, because its determination and implementation will affect all units in the business in either a direct or an indirect sense. Furthermore, from the standpoint of financial planning, a promotional budget must compete with proposals to devote dollars to alternative possibilities such as technical research and development, the building of new production facilities, or the possible acquisition of other existing firms.

For these reasons, a promotional planner must frame her or his budget within the environment set by overall corporate strategy and evaluate it on the basis of the anticipated profits it will return. It then becomes the task of corporate management to compare the potential returns expected from promotional expenditures with those that might be expected from alternative expenditure opportunities.

*Considering Promotion's Longer-Range Effects.* For accounting purposes, the promotional budget is normally treated as an expense item. That is, the amount spent on a function such as advertising or personal selling is written off in the year in which the activities take place. By implication, there is an assumption that any benefits which the firm derives from promotional activities are rather immediate. For instance, at least from an accounting standpoint, the amount spent on advertising in any given year is assumed to be related only to the enhancement of sales volume produced within that same year. However, in some situations management may wish to give open recognition to the fact that promotional dollars spent in one year can help build a base of customer acceptance and support that contributes to a stream of sales and profits which will be realized in subsequent years. In essence, this means that promotional expenditures are being treated, at least partly, as an investment for the future rather than merely as an expense of the present. For purposes of the yearly profit and loss statement, conventional accounting procedures will still be followed, but from the standpoint of corporate strategy the evaluation of the promotional budget will be viewed in longer-range terms.

**TABLE 20.6 An illustration of proposed promotional expenditures viewed in a payout planning context**
**(Dollar figures stated in thousands of dollars)**

|  | Year 0 | Year 1 | Year 2 | Year 3 | Year 4 |
|---|---|---|---|---|---|
| A. Forecasted Sales for Total Product Category | $450,000 | $495,000 | $545,000 | $600,000 | $650,000 |
| B. Percentage Market Share Goal Anticipated for Brand I | 0 | 10% | 15% | 20% | 20% |
| C. Dollar Sales Forecast for Brand I | 0 | $ 49,500 | $ 81,750 | $120,000 | $130,000 |
| D. Less Cost of Sales[a] | 0 | $ 34,650 | $ 57,225 | $ 84,000 | $ 91,000 |
| E. Gross Margin (Entry C minus Entry D) | 0 | $ 14,850 | $ 24,525 | $ 36,000 | $ 39,000 |
| F. Product R and D Budget | $ 1,000 | 0 | $ 0 | 0 | 0 |
| G. Marketing Planning and Research Budget | $ 625 | $ 250 | $ 250 | $ 250 | $ 250 |
| H. Explicit Promotion Budgets: | | | | | |
| • Advertising | 0 | $ 10,000 | $ 7,500 | $ 6,000 | $ 6,000 |
| • Personal Selling | 0 | $ 1,750 | $ 1,000 | $ 1,000 | $ 1,000 |
| • Sales Promotion | 0 | $ 7,500 | $ 5,000 | $ 4,500 | $ 4,500 |
| • Publicity | 0 | $ 250 | $ 125 | $ 125 | $ 125 |
| Total Promotional Budget (Sum of Budgets for Individual Elements) | 0 | $ 19,500 | $ 13,625 | $ 11,625 | $ 11,625 |
| I. Yearly Net Profit (or Loss) (Gross Margin Minus Total of Amount in Entries F, G, and H) | ($ 1,625) | ($ 4,900) | $ 10,650 | $ 24,125 | $ 27,125 |
| J. Yearly Net Profit (or Loss) Discounted to Present Value Basis[b] | ($ 1,625) | ($ 4,261) | $ 8,053 | $ 15,863 | $ 15,509 |
| K. Cumulative Net Profit (or Loss) Discounted to Present Value Basis | ($ 1,625) | ($ 5,886) | $ 2,167 | $ 18,030 | $ 33,539 |

[a] Cost of sales includes expenses for production, physical distribution, overhead allocation, and all other factors not separately listed. These are estimated as being 70% of sales.

[b] Formula for discounting to present value is $V = I_t/(1 + r)^t$, where V = present value of funds to be received in any given period, I = amount of funds to be received, t = number of years between present period and period funds will be received, and r = applicable rate of interest.

The idea of treating promotional expenditures as an investment rather than strictly as an expense is sometimes referred to as "payout planning." The adoption of a payout planning perspective is especially applicable in the case of new product introductions. Quite commonly, a new brand entry will require above average promotional efforts in order to gain a foothold in the marketplace. During the first year or more of its life it may diminish total company profits. When confronting such a situation, the company naturally wants to have some estimate of the length of time during which promotional dollars must be invested ahead of sales and also of the expected profit flow that will occur once the brand has become established. Table 20.6 depicts the general format that a payout planning statement might take in such a situation. The product under consideration is the same hypothetical new brand of skin care product used earlier for our illustration of an objective-task budgeting approach.

***Building a Payout Plan.*** The development of a payout plan involves a large amount of estimation and forecasting. The first issue that must be taken into consideration is the sales potential of the generic category in which the brand is competing. A variety of methods are available to estimate future product category sales. Most of these revolve around either judgments made by executives and others in close touch with the market or formalized statistical procedures which work with historical sales data and possibly with the underlying market forces that can affect category sales.[13] The firm must then estimate the share of the total market which the new brand could logically be expected to obtain at various points in time. Most commonly, it would be anticipated that the market share for a successful brand would grow in its early years and then tend to level off. In the case illustrated, the estimate is that the *average* share over the first year will account for ten percent of the total market. That average will grow to fifteen percent in year two and then settle at a twenty percent share from that point forward. When the market share percentages are cast against total product category sales they yield forecasted dollar sales expected in each year. Anticipated expenses are then deducted from total sales revenues, with the resulting profit predictions shown by years in line I of Table 20.6.

In our example, a sizable investment expenditure in planning and research is envisioned for year zero, the year before the brand is introduced to the market. During year one, while the product is being introduced to the market and gradually attaining its market position, the plan predicts that costs will exceed revenues by close to 5 million dollars largely because of the extensive introductory promotional program. It is only at the end of the second year that this brand is expected to move from a deficit position to become an actual profit producer. Since management must assess the predicted results in terms of a future flow of dollars, lines J and K take present value into consideration. Profits that will accrue in the future are discounted at the rate of fifteen percent per year because any contribution they make to the company's cash flow will be realized only at some later date. For this reason, their value must be deflated to reflect the fact that the business entity will forgo the opportunity of earning money on those dollars until they are actually received.

***Evaluating the Payout Plan.*** Given a payout plan such as this, management has two primary issues to investigate. The first concerns the comparison of anticipated profits from this venture with other options that may be under simultaneous consideration. As noted earlier, when funds are channeled into promotion for a particular brand they cannot be channeled into some other business effort. The Ivensen company might be looking not only at the possible introduction of a new skin care product but also at potential expansion of current plant facilities, increased promotional funding for an established brand, or any of an assortment of other alternatives. If the profit flow suggested by the indicated payout plan falls below estimated profits attainable from other projects, the introduction might either be aborted, delayed, or reduced in scale.

The second issue of concern is the accuracy of the predictions outlined in the payout plan. After all, the plan is built on a collection of attempts to foresee the future. Although there is no way to do that with absolute certainty, there are techniques that can be used to test portions of the plan on a small scale before a full commitment of funds is made. Futhermore, there are also techniques that can be used to monitor the promotional program as it moves forward, enabling the strategy team to make adjustments to improve its efficiency and effectiveness. A general overview of the types of techniques available to accomplish these purposes will be the topic of discussion in the next chapter.

# SUMMARY

The correct theoretical procedure for fixing an optimum promotional budget level uses a marginal analysis approach. In practice, direct application of marginal analysis is virtually impossible because you lack sufficient information and because your promotional program moves into a highly competitive and volatile market. In consequence, firms use a variety of alternative techniques to arrive at promotional budget figures. The most popular of these include an arbitrary approach, an affordability approach, a ratio–to–sales approach, and an objective–task approach. In addition, an approach frequently mentioned in marketing literature is one based on competitive comparison.

All of the approaches just listed, except for the objective–task method, can be described as *predetermined budgets*. That is, a decision is made concerning the amount of money to be spent on any given promotional element prior to development of an actual strategy plan. In an arbitrary procedure, the expenditure level is arrived at by managerial judgment and intuition with little or no systematic analysis of the underlying facts and figures. In an affordability approach the determination is made on the basis of the amount the firm has available to devote to promotion. The ratio–to–sales method ties the budget to some proportion of either past or anticipated sales volume. A competitive comparison technique relates the firm's budget plan to the budget levels commonly used by one or more directly competitive firms.

All predetermined budgeting approaches have some severe defects. In particular, none takes clear account of the exact purposes and objectives for which the money is being allocated. When any of the predetermined budgeting approaches is used by itself, objectives are dealt with only after the funding level has been finalized. However, although each of the predetermined budgeting approaches has defects, it is also true that with one notable exception each also raises some points of value for consideration in the total budgeting procedure. The one exception is the arbitrary approach, for which little support can be advanced beyond its extreme simplicity.

In contrast to predetermined budgeting methods, the *strategy-determined* objective–task approach begins with evaluation of what your firm is attempting to achieve through its promotional efforts. It then moves to specification of the tasks needed to reach the designated levels of achievement. The budget is calculated on the basis of costs required to carry out those tasks. This approach has a strong basis in logic in that it proceeds from the purposes for which funds are being allocated. In this respect, it can be described as approximating the reasoning underlying the theoretically ideal marginal analysis method.

One criticism sometimes directed at the objective–task approach is that it fails to specify how objectives are to be initially set and evaluated as to their worth. However, by tying your promotional objectives to your total marketing strategy, which derives from overall corporate strategy, it is possible to initiate the objective-task approach from a sound planning base. This does not mean that its use will automatically lead you to an optimum budget. However, it can start you on a sensible route toward introducing clearer judgment patterns and profit orientation into your allocation strategy.

A proposal for a synthesis of four different approaches was offered. The four approaches include affordability, ratio-to-sales, competitive comparison, and objective-task. Employment of such a multistage, combination process can bring into play the strong points of each approach and sharpen your effectiveness in evaluating the budget from several different perspectives. Importantly, it was also stressed that a sound budgeting system extends beyond merely finalizing and implementing the budget plan. It includes analyzing the effects of prior budget decisions by constant monitoring of market feedback. On the basis of such monitoring, you can then apply adaptive control, through which both the budget and other aspects of your promotional program are modified on the basis of market response measures.

While customary accounting practice treats promotional costs as an expense item rather than as an investment, management should also be aware of the longer range effects of promotional allocations. This is particularly true in the case of new product entries. Generally, these will entail heavy promotional expenditures at the outset and, quite often, the money spent for advertising and the other promotional elements will not be recouped during the first year or two of the product's market existence. This means that such expenditures must be viewed as investments even though they may be treated as current expense items for purposes of profit and loss reporting.

The payout plan is a formalized way of anticipating the time schedule for investing funds in promotion and then reaping the subsequent benefits over a period of years. Corporate management has an interest in closely examining the anticipated payout format for two reasons. First, it serves as a standard of comparison with other investment opportunities the firm may be simultaneously considering. Second, the payout plan represents a promise of future returns based on present activities. By formalizing that promise and spelling it out in detail, the plan facilitates attempts to investigate the likelihood that the promise will actually be fulfilled. In short, the payout plan presents management with a platform from which to initiate inquiries concerning the data, logic, and available evidence offered to support the forecasts of the plan.

## DISCUSSION QUESTIONS

1. What is the essential principle involved in a marginal analysis approach to budgeting and to what extent is that approach useful in actual business practice?

2. Which is preferable, a predetermined budgeting approach or a strategy-determined budgeting approach? Explain your reasoning.

3. Sarah Saunders is the president and principal stockholder of a medium-sized firm which she started in 1963. Last year the company's adver-

tising budget was $1,500,000. Ms. Saunders has allocated $2,000,000 for advertising in the coming year. In her words, "Last year's increase in sales and profits put us in a position to be more aggressive in our promotional strategy." What approach to budgeting is she using and how would you critique her approach?

4. As shown in Table 20.4, the average percentage of sales dollars allocated for advertising by makers of perfumes and cosmetics tends to be roughly nine times as high as that allocated by makers of office furniture. What factors do you think might account for that great a difference?

5. The marketing vice-president for Heikal Potato Chips has been studying reports which show that the company's leading rival in the potato chip business is spending an estimated $3,000,000 per year on personal selling, $4,000,000 on advertising and $2,000,000 on sales promotion. Heikal has been allocating $2,000,000 to personal selling, $3,500,000 to advertising and $3,500,000 to sales promotion. Since Heikal has been losing market share to this competitor for the past two years, the vice-president is thinking of reallocating Heikal's budget to match the competitor's pattern more closely. He has asked for your advice. How would you frame your answer?

6. "An objective-task budgeting approach is not workable because it does not provide me with a means of setting objectives in the first place." How would you respond to this statement?

7. "Promotion is aimed at achieving objectives through fulfilling specified tasks. Therefore an objective-task approach is the only budget-allocation method which should ever be used." How would you respond to this statement?

8. What is the logic behind the argument that you are better off leaning toward the risk of overspending for promotion as opposed to underspending?

9. Since promotional expenditures are clearly expenses incurred in a given year, how can it possibly make any sense to regard them as "investments"?

10. What is a "payout plan" and what purposes does it serve?

## REFERENCES

1. William J. Baumol and Alan S. Blinder, *Economics*, 2nd ed. (New York: Harcourt Brace Jovanovich, Inc., 1982), p. 374.

2. For examples see William M. Kincaid, Jr., *Promotion: Products, Services, and Ideas* (Columbus, OH: Charles E. Merrill Publishing Company, 1981), pp. 170–172; and Philip Kotler, *Marketing Management: Analysis, Planning, and Control*, 4th ed. (Englewood Cliffs, NJ: Prentice-Hall, Inc., 1980), p. 499.

3. T. Kirk Parrish, "How Much to Spend for Advertising," *Journal of Advertising Research*, February 1974, p. 9.

4. Donald S. Tull, James H. Barnes, and Daniel T. Seymour, "In Defense of Setting Budgets for Advertising as a Percent of Sales," *Journal of Advertising Research*, December 1978, pp. 48–51.

5. A. J. San Augustine and W. F. Foley, "How Large Advertisers Set Budgets," *Journal of Advertising Research*, October 1975, p. 13.

6. Kotler, *Marketing Management: Analysis, Planning, and Control*, p. 500.

7. Malcolm A. McNiven, "Plan for More Productive Advertising," *Harvard Business Review*, March/April 1980, p. 131.

8. *The Value Line Investment Survey*, 28 January 1983, p. 801.

9. James F. Engel, Martin R. Warshaw, and Thomas C. Kinnear, *Promotional Strategy*, 5th ed. (Homewood, IL: Richard D. Irwin, Inc., 1983), pp. 218–219.

10. For a good introduction to such methods see Robert L. Anderson and Thomas E. Barry, *Advertising Management* (Columbus, OH: Charles E. Merrill Publishing Company, 1979), pp. 179–182.

11. For more complete descriptions see Engel, Warshaw, and Kinnear, *Promotion Strategy*, pp. 213–217; and Kotler, *Marketing Management: Analysis, Planning, and Control*, pp. 500–502.

12. Eugene Schonfeld, "Common Sense Rules in Setting Ad Budgets," *Industrial Marketing*, December 1979, pp. 50ff.

13. For a good discussion see James E. Nelson, *The Practice of Marketing Research* (Boston: Kent Publishing Company, 1982), pp. 480–492.

# CHAPTER TWENTY-ONE

# *Market Feedback and Adaptive Control*

## FOCUS OF THE CHAPTER

From what you have read in the preceding chapter, it is apparent that the atmosphere in which budget allocation decisions must be made is characterized by uncertainty. Uncertainty is inherent in more than just the question of how much money you should spend. It also pervades decisions concerning the precise way in which promotional dollars will be used. For example, the effectiveness of your total advertising budget will be influenced not merely by its size but also by the creative and media strategies pursued in putting the allocated funds to use. It may be impossible to draw up your program with absolute assurance that your budgets and their mode of employment will produce the profit results you anticipated when planning them. However, it is quite possible to improve planning and reduce risk by paying careful attention to market feedback. The purpose of this chapter is to provide you with an outline of procedures available to obtain such feedback.

## THE CONCEPT OF ADAPTIVE CONTROL

As was indicated in the decision field flowcharts presented for each of the explicit promotional elements, well-constructed programs start from a careful evaluation of past results. (See Figures 11.2, 13.2, 17.19, and 18.2.) One of the major advantages of incorporating an objective-task perspective into your budgeting process is that it provides you with a clear set of criteria against which the results of past efforts can be evaluated. In consequence, your ability to adjust present strategies and inaugurate future planning is greatly strengthened. However, even if you do not use a formal objective-task approach, you must still have some method of assessing past results to gain guidance for future actions. One analyst has coined the term "adaptive control" to describe the continuing cycle of analyzing past promotional outcomes to guide future strategies. As he has put the matter: "A company must assemble marketing information, use it to modify its conception of the market, use the revised conception to make marketing decisions, and then arrange for the collection of new information. In short, a company needs a control system for its marketing variables."[1]

## A General Representation of Market Reaction Patterns

In an extended sense, the principle of adaptive control can be treated as the collection and analysis of feedback data on all of the effects that are produced by each aspect of your promotional strategy. This can include not only the ultimate effect you seek in terms of sales revenue dollars but also the network of intermediate communications effects discussed in past chapters. Figure 21.1 depicts one way of visualizing some of the market reaction characteristics you might wish to monitor in following an adaptive control plan.

At the outset, it should be pointed out that, while the representation shown in this figure might seem to treat the chain of events triggered by a promotional program in an overly intricate fashion, in actuality it deliberately simplifies much of the total process to prevent the representation from becoming unworkably extensive and complex. For instance, in dealing with the media strategy component of advertising, Figure 21.1 considers only gross rating point levels. It avoids direct confrontation of such other variables as media categories to be emphasized, specific vehicles to be chosen, timing patterns for insertions, and the sizes of insertions to be used. In short, it presents you with a very basic, skeletal design for considering major feedback measurement points.

***Modifying the Representation to Fit Specific Situations.*** As with any general scheme, the representation shown here is likely to need some tailoring and modification to improve its capacity to serve in your particular promotional setting. For instance, in some market settings you might wish to concern yourself with unpictured variables such as those mentioned in connection with additional media program alternatives. In other instances you might wish to simplify matters and take readings only at points that you believe are extremely critical and sensitive.

The version of the representation shown in Figure 21.1 is most directly applicable to new products being marketed to ultimate consumers. If you are dealing with an established brand or aiming at the industrial market you would probably wish to make certain alterations in its format in order to bring it into line with the realities of your particular selling climate. In the case of an ongoing consumer goods brand, for example, you might be less concerned with the objectives of establishing awareness and fostering trial among new

**FIGURE 21.1 A representation of the network of market responses to promotional efforts**

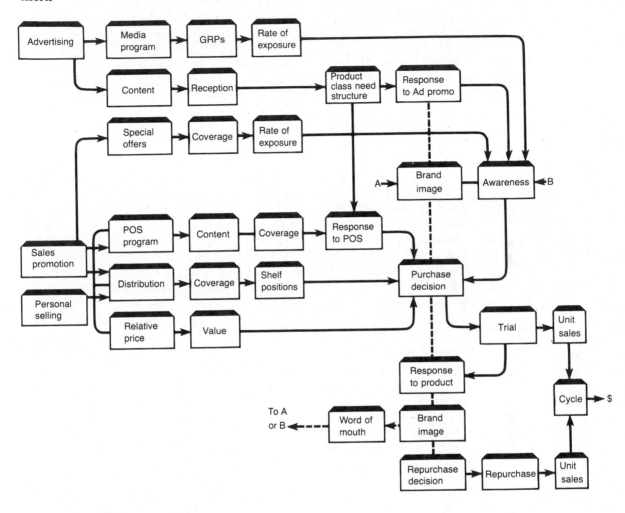

Source: Adapted from Arnold E. Amstutz and August P. Hess, "Simulated Market Response," in Steuart Henderson Britt and Norman F. Guess, *Marketing Manager's Handbook* (Chicago: Dartnell Press, 1983), p. 521.

users and more concerned with the objectives of increasing the degree of usage and strengthening brand loyalty. In an industrial marketing situation, your objectives for personal selling would likely focus on customer response to sales call efforts rather than distribution levels and retail visibility. Nonetheless, with these potentials for modification in mind, the representation can serve as a very useful prototype for relating the variety of feedback measurements that can be taken.

*The Concept of Adaptive Control*                                                                                              695

# METHODS OF GATHERING FEEDBACK DATA

A full and detailed discussion of the methods used to acquire information about the performance of your promotional program lies within the province of a marketing research text rather than a book concerned mainly with promotional strategy.[2] For this reason our discussion will be limited to a brief sampling of some of the principal measures employed, and it is meant to serve as an introduction to the subject rather than as a comprehensive review. Most feedback studies can be classified under one of three headings. These are (1) pretests, (2) market experiments, and (3) analysis of the results of ongoing programs. We will consider examples of how studies in each of these three categories can be used.

## Pretests

As the name implies, a pretest seeks to obtain advance feedback on likely customer reaction before your promotional program is implemented under actual market conditions.

## Pretests of Advertising

Pretests are especially common in the evaluation of advertising creative strategies. Most such pretests revolve around showing proposed advertisements to a sample of consumers and then assessing the reactions of sample participants.[3] However, there are diverse procedures used for presenting the advertisements to consumers as well as for obtaining responses. Under one line of approach respondents are asked to examine each advertisement and then reply to questions concerning such matters as the meaning of the message, the credibility of promotional claims, and the general effect of the ad on the individual's image of the product. In the case of print advertising, sample members are sometimes asked to look at several different advertisements and then rank them against each other.

A somewhat more subtle system for preevaluating advertising involves a technique known as "portfolio testing." In a portfolio test, one group of consumers is asked to look through a portfolio containing a number of advertisements including those being tested. A second group looks through the same type of portfolio, but one that does not contain the test advertisements. Then, both groups of respondents are asked to remember as many of the ads in the portfolio as they can. The results of the consumer recall reports are next interpreted in terms of what they imply about the visibility and communication power of the test ads.

Similar methods can be utilized to pretest radio and television commercials. Additionally, television commercials are often subjected to somewhat more elaborate trials. For example, many television commercials are first screened before samples of consumers who have been especially invited to a theater to view a pilot program for a proposed television series plus a number of commercials including those chosen for the specific test. Audience reactions may then be measured in any of several different ways. In some instances a simulated purchasing atmosphere is induced by means of a contest that requires respondents to indicate brand choices before the commercials are shown. After the commercial showings are completed the same respondents are given an opportunity to change their brand choices. Presumably, any change in choices provides a rough measure of the tested commercial's ability to influence purchase behavior. In still other theater tests the audience indicates likes and dislikes for various portions of the commercials and other materials by manipulating dials or buttons that produce an electronic record of audience reactions.

*Limitations of Advertising Pretests.*   This outline of pretests for advertising material hardly exhausts the full range of possibilities that exist in the field, though it should give you at least an introductory sense of the pattern of more commonly used techniques. It also serves as a backdrop for explaining why advertising practitioners often express reservations concerning the amount of guidance that can be gained from such pretest measures. One of the basic limitations of such procedures is that they all have a degree of artificiality about them. They require that the data be collected under circumstances that do not really duplicate a realistic market environment. One pair of analysts has addressed this point in the following way:

> [T]here are many limitations to pretesting, and the advertiser should be aware of them. Besides the fact that the test itself is an artificial situation, the test respondents are not typical prospects since most of them tend to assume the role of experts or critics and to give answers that may not reflect their real buying behavior. Consumers who do not have strong opinions about the advertisement shown are likely to invent opinions on the spur of the moment to satisfy the interviewer. Some do not want to admit that they could be influenced by the advertisement. Others may try to please the interviewer by voting for the advertisements they feel *they should* like rather than those they do like. [4]

With the limitations kept in mind, it may be best to think of advertising pretests as providing a workable means of distinguishing between extremely strong advertisements on the one hand and extremely weak or objectionable advertisements on the other. The results regarding the many "in-between" types of situations that could occur may be somewhat less clear. In any event, the findings may provide rough indicators to help you clarify certain items of uncertainty in the development of your advertising strategy. Nonetheless, they should be taken as suggestive rather than as definitive and should be judged in conjunction with other information and experience at your disposal.

*Pretesting Product Concepts*

Especially when a new brand is being considered for introduction or when a significant change or improvement is contemplated for an existing brand, the sponsoring firm may wish to test the full concept of the product—including its functional features, surrogate cues, price positioning, and potential advertising appeals—before any attempt is made to introduce it to the market or even to prepare preliminary estimates of its likely market appeal. This is especially true in the highly volatile and intensely competitive food, drug, and cosmetic package goods fields.

According to estimates by the A. C. Nielsen Company, something on the order of 6,100 new items were introduced for sale through supermarkets during the year 1981.[5] The great majority of these were variations in sizes, flavors, or other characteristics among existing brands. However, approximately 1,050 of the items were completely new brands, all seeking shelf space from store managers and patronage from the consuming public. Given this high number of new entries, it is not surprising that the odds of success for any one of them are not extremely encouraging. In fact, according to the estimate of another leading research firm, the record shows that about eighty percent will fail.[6]

Recalling the proposed introduction of a new skin care product by the Ivensen Corporation, and viewing it in the context of this brand mortality rate, you can understand why a company such as Ivensen would want to have as much pre-introduction data as possible. While the collection of such data may not guarantee that you will never introduce a product that fails, it can certainly reduce the likelihood of failure. Furthermore, supplementary questions that are asked in pretest interviews can yield valuable insights regarding such things as the types of evaluative criteria that should be stressed and the characteristics of the target consumers who form your most promising market segment.

*An Example of Preliminary Concept Test Procedures.* Figure 21.2 shows a "concept board" used as the centerpiece for the primary stage of concept

**FIGURE 21.2  A concept board used for pretesting**

Source: BASES, a Division of Burke Marketing Services, Inc.

testing by one firm active in this area. The firm involved is BASES, a division of Burke Marketing Services, and the technique involved is termed "BASES I." (In its full form, BASES is actually a four-phase system that moves from preliminary concept testing to monitoring of test markets, providing clients with computer-simulated estimates of full-scale market response as each phase is completed.)

A test for a brand such as that pictured in the illustration is begun by showing the concept board to a sample of consumers contacted in shopping malls. Based on its description of product features, benefits, and price, sample participants are queried regarding the strength of brand preference levels and purchase intentions that they believe they might have for such a brand. At the same time, information is collected regarding their current consumption behavior with respect to the product category as well as their feelings regarding relevant evaluative criteria and their interpretations of how this brand rates on such criteria. When blended with information such as anticipated distribution and awareness levels planned for the brand in its first year of market existence, the BASES system provides a preliminary estimate of the consumer trial rate likely to be achieved.

***Extending the Concept Test to Its Second Phase.*** The results of the first stage of the testing process are used not only to make decisions regarding the feasibility of the new product introduction but also to provide assistance in refining the product and its accompanying promotional plan. After this has been accomplished, a second phase of the total concept-product test is conducted as part of the BASES testing sequence. At this step, a new sample of potential consumers is shown proposed advertising materials, the package design, the product description, and key selling messages for the brand. Persons in the sample who indicate that their purchase intention level for the brand would be high are then given a sample to try in their own homes. Later, they are contacted in follow-up interviews to determine their reactions to the product based on their experience with it. Reactions measured in these interviews include such details as revised brand preference levels, purchase intentions, and likely frequency of purchase. The BASES system incorporates these data, along with information regarding the strength of the marketing program planned by the company, in a revised forecast covering not only the probable trial rate during the first year but also the repeat purchase rate, average length of time between purchases, and sales volume level that can be anticipated at the end of the first year.

## MARKET TESTS

In contrast to pretests, which obtain feedback under conditions that always have some degree of artificiality about them, a market test attempts to obtain feedback under relatively normal and realistic selling conditions. It is essentially experimental in nature. That is, marketing variables under your control are deliberately manipulated to see what market effects will be produced by the manipulation. The variable that is manipulated might be the budget level for one or more of the explicit promotional elements, the nature of the advertising media used to carry your messages, the techniques used by your sales force members, your price level, the nature of your advertising appeal, some aspect of the product itself, or any of the other components of your strategy that you can alter. The effects can be measured either in terms of final sales level variations or in terms of intermediate market responses such as changes in brand image, preference levels, or awareness of your advertising messages.

*Market Testing of Alternative Promotional Budget Levels*

As discussed in the last chapter, determination of the optimum amount to spend on promotion confronts management with problems to which there are no clear-cut solutions. None of the budgeting methods we reviewed enjoys universal or unquestioned acceptance. Even following a combination-of-methods approach, as has been suggested in this text, will provide you with no absolute assurance that your expenditure level is reasonably close to the theoretical optimum. Given the abundance of conflicting opinions and uncertainties that surround the topic, it is not surprising that a number of mathematical models have been proposed to improve the precision of promotional budget planning. The most interesting of such proposals are built around the idea of maintaining ongoing market testing of sales response as a function of promotional expenditures. Feedback from test results is then used to update the underlying mathematical model in order to set the budget for the next period. Figure 21.3 diagrams the general type of decision and feedback system around which such models center.

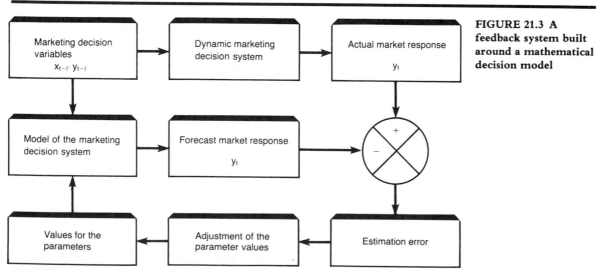

**FIGURE 21.3 A feedback system built around a mathematical decision model**

*Source:* Vijay Mahajan, Stuart I. Breitschneider, and John W. Bradford, "Feedback Approaches to Modeling Structural Shifts in Market Response," *Journal of Marketing,* Winter 1980, p. 73.

It should be noted that most such models take little direct account of the strategies, outcomes, and effects shown in the middle portion of the simulated market representation we considered in Figure 21.1. They usually tend to concentrate on the level of expenditures associated with each of the explicit promotional elements shown at the left-hand side of that representation and the sales outcomes shown at the far right-hand side. By implication, they take the position that the intervening events and effects are being investigated by some other means.

In the light of such data as you saw earlier concerning the way in which large advertisers set their budgets, there is little evidence that feedback models of this sort currently have much influence on promotional decision making. Nonetheless, they should be of interest to alert marketing managers for two reasons. First, as developmental work in this area continues, more sensitive models are likely to emerge that are more directly useful in practical situations. Second, consideration of the logic which underlies such models can assist you in clarifying your own thinking about the budget-setting process. Although detailed consideration of the mathematical techniques proposed in the modeling process falls outside the scope of this book, there are a number of good references available to aid you in pursuing investigation of the subject at greater length.[7]

## Traditional Test Marketing

A test market is a geographic area selected by the sponsoring firm for the purpose of conducting an experiment involving one or more aspects of its marketing program. The results observed in the test market area are expected to serve as a valid prediction of what would happen if the same marketing techniques were to be applied in other territories served by the firm. This usually means that the company selects certain city trading areas in which to try out a new product or a revised promotional technique and assumes those trading areas will be reasonably representative of the nation as a whole.

This approach is widely used in the marketing of consumer package goods such as foods, drugs, and cosmetics, especially when a new product entry is under consideration. For example, the hypothetical new brand of skin care product we discussed earlier would almost certainly be test-marketed by a firm such as Ivensen before it committed anything like the funding proposed in our theoretical budget payout plan. Given the size of investment and degree of risk, it is easy to see why a firm would desire as much advance market assurance as possible before plunging into a full-scale, nation-wide endeavor.

Because the results observed in test market areas will be used to estimate what would happen if the same marketing policies were introduced over the entire territory served by the company, the first consideration involved in test marketing is selection of cities that are reasonably representative of the total market. Quite commonly, the cities favored for test purposes are medium-sized—large enough to have their own radio, television, and newspaper outlets but small enough to hold marketing costs and the attendant research costs at a fairly reasonable level. Examples of market areas frequently mentioned as especially good for testing are such places as Binghamton, New York; Evansville, Indiana; Davenport, Iowa; Charleston, South Carolina; Baton Rouge, Louisiana; and Bakersfield, California.[8]

***Major Issues in Traditional Test Marketing.***   Figure 21.4 demonstrates some of the central issues involved in test market procedures. The test market under consideration is the Denver, Colorado trading district. The figures on the top show you the costs estimated by the A. C. Nielsen Company for conducting a particular, full-scale test in this area. The product involved is a mythical brand

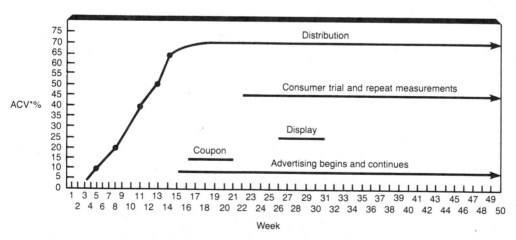

**FIGURE 21.4 Illustrative summaries of some central issues in traditional test marketing**

Dollar costs

|  | "Denver district" |
|---|---|
| Product manufacturing costs | $ 64,500 |
| Media costs: Production | 60,000 |
| Spot TV | 90,000 |
| Newspaper (FSI coupon) (includes redemption) | 17,700 |
| Store promotion | 6,000 |
| Research: Tracking | 20,740 |
| Other | 33,000 |
| Sales costs | 77,000 |
| Warehousing | — |
| Miscellaneous | 10,000 |
|  | $378,940 |
| Less value of product sold | 45,517 |
| Net costs | $333,423 |

"Denver district" timetable

ACV*%

Distribution

Consumer trial and repeat measurements

Display

Coupon

Advertising begins and continues

Week

*All commodity volume

*Source:* "Managing a Product's Future," *The Nielsen Researcher* (1982), pp. 9–10, © A. C. Nielsen Company.

called "Centaur," a new laundry additive item being considered for possible nation-wide introduction. Because the product is new and must be manufactured on a pilot production basis, manufacturing costs are abnormally high during the test period. Incidentally, this would tend to be true in most cases in which an entirely new brand is involved. Apart from manufacturing costs there are, of course, the costs associated with promotional efforts as well as special research activities to track results as they occur during the test period.

At the bottom of Figure 21.4 is a typical timetable for a test market operation. The full test is scheduled to run for approximately one year. The first several months are devoted mainly to personal selling efforts, along with suitable sales promotion efforts, directed at the retail trade. Their intention is to secure a reasonably high distribution level coupled with reseller support in the form of displays, cooperative advertising, or other program units that are planned. During this period, the sponsoring firm has an opportunity to evaluate trade acceptance and estimate the type of personal sales activities, promotional allowances, and so forth that will be required when the product is introduced on a national scale. Couponing and advertising efforts begin in the fourth month. Field research, measuring trial and repeat purchase rates, begins in the fifth month and is continued throughout the year.

A firm considering a new product introduction such as this will often conduct simultaneous tests in several market areas. By varying such inputs as sales force call levels, advertising budget rates, coupon values, and other controllable promotional variables, the firm can make comparisons between alternative promotional strategies. On the basis of those comparisons, it should be in a much improved position to determine the best course to pursue on a national basis.

***Problems and Limitations in Traditional Test Marketing.***   A variety of problems can be encountered in test market situations. The initial problem concerns the degree to which test market results can accurately indicate what will happen when the product is marketed nationally. A major research firm that has had a long involvement in the test market field has pointed out that "*all* test markets must be viewed as distortions of the national experience since no market in the United States fully replicates national or large regional exposure, and the time interval is always different from test to roll-out which alters the basic circumstances."[9]

In addition to the question of how well the test area and the test period represent the national market and the future, exposure of the product and promotional plan during the test presents certain hazards. For one thing, especially when the test period is lengthy, your competitors have an opportunity to observe your results and sometimes reap the benefits that you had intended for your own organization.

As an example, Helene Curtis Industries spent a number of months testing a new deodorant named Arm-In-Arm in three markets.[10] The brand's appeal was built largely around its natural ingredients featuring a baking soda base. The market tests showed not only a high rate of initial purchase but also heavy repeat purchasing behavior. Helene Curtis executives were reported as being jubilant and readying plans for national distribution when the makers of Arm&Hammer baking soda stepped into the picture and deflated the bright prospects for the product. Presumably relying on observation of the Helene Curtis test, the Arm&Hammer people launched a similar deodorant under their own label and moved it directly into national distribution. In consequence, when Arm-In-Arm was rolled out nationally, it was seen as merely a copy of the Arm&Hammer entry that had reached the market first. As if that weren't bad enough, the Arm&Hammer people then took Helene Curtis to court charging trademark infringement on the argument that the name, Arm-In-Arm, was too similar to their own preestablished trade name. Helene Curtis had to withdraw its product from sale.

Apart from observing your results and profiting from them, a competitor who feels threatened may attempt to disrupt your test and confuse the results. For instance, it has been alleged that the Ralston Purina Company, which markets some of the nation's top selling brands of dog food, makes a point of obtaining advance information regarding the proposed test marketing of possible rival brands.[11] Upon learning of any such plan, Ralston Purina has been described as saturating the market with coupons offering free, large-sized bags of Purina Dog Chow. Because this leaves owners well supplied with food for their pets, it takes most of them out of the market temporarily and corrupts the test efforts.

**Controlled Test Marketing**

Given the high cost of traditional test marketing, the length of time usually required and the attendant threats from competitors, alternatives to traditional test markets have been developed in recent years. In particular, a form of testing based on distribution in only a selected group of stores in the test area has gained popularity. It is known by a variety of names including "controlled test marketing" and "simulated test marketing." The stores involved have entered into prior agreements with a major research firm such as the A. C. Nielsen Company, Market Facts, or the BASES division of Burke Marketing Services.

Under these agreements the selected retailers accept immediate placement of the brand on their shelves. Such placement is generally made directly by the research firm, frequently using unmarked trucks to delay competitors' awareness of the test for as long as possible.

***Major Issues in Controlled Test Marketing.*** Figure 21.5 demonstrates the central issues surrounding a controlled test market plan for the same product used to illustrate the basic facts concerning a traditional test market operation in Figure 21.4. This information again comes from the A. C. Nielsen Company which uses the term "Data Market" to describe its approach to testing on a limited distribution basis. Notice first of all the sizable reduction in the cost of the test. This is due in part to the fact that much less product is involved, which reduces the high manufacturing expense associated with pilot production. Second, because the Data Market itself is smaller, expenditures required for advertising media are lower. Third, because distribution buildup is immediate and requires no personal selling effort, expenses for this promotional

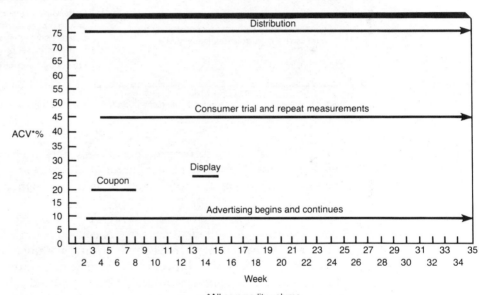

FIGURE 21.5 Illustrative summaries of some central issues in controlled test marketing

| Dollar cost | Boise data market |
|---|---|
| Product manufacturing costs | $ 6,550 |
| Media costs: Production | 60,000 |
| Spot TV | 15,500 |
| Newspaper (FSI coupon) (includes redemption) | 2,020 |
| Store promotion | 700 |
| Research: Tracking | 50,000 |
| Other | 28,000 |
| Sales costs | * |
| Warehousing | 7,000 |
| Miscellaneous | 5,000 |
| | $174,770 |
| Less value of product sold | 5,437 |
| Net costs | $169,333 |

*Included as part of data market costs.

Boise data market timeable

*All commodity volume

*Source:* "Managing a Product's Future," *The Nielsen Researcher,* no. 2 (1982), pp. 9–10, © A. C. Nielsen Company.

element are eliminated. Since fewer retail outlets are being served, sales promotion expense is also cut significantly. Research costs are higher owing to special distribution and other activities undertaken by the research organization. However, the overall cost comparison clearly favors the Data Market approach.

Of equal or perhaps greater importance is the timetable comparison. In this illustration, completion of the Data Market test takes only thirty-five weeks. It accomplishes this by eliminating the fifteen-week distribution buildup needed

*Market Tests*

**TABLE 21.1 Comparative advantages of traditional test markets and controlled test markets**

| Traditional Test Market Features: | Data Market Features: |
|---|---|
| 1. Generally larger sample size. | 1. Lower manufacturing, distribution, and advertising costs. |
| 2. Test panels represent broader, more diversified geographic areas. | 2. Less sales force efforts, disruption, and expense. |
| 3. Relatively uncontrolled retail environment likely to better reflect "real world" in which product will ultimately compete. | 3. Better management of test execution. |
| 4. Because of broader availability of competing brands, more realistic share levels, even at equilibrium shares. | 4. Greatly reduced time frame for achieving distribution and reading consumer sales behavior. |
| 5. The ability to test extent of retailer support, distribution levels, actual shelf location and facings, and other retailer-dependent variables that affect market shares. Data Market tests, by their nature, control these factors. | 5. More exact chronological reporting intervals improving ability to read retail cause and effect. |
| | 6. Better insight into repeat purchase cycle. |
| 6. Better opportunity to gauge competitive response even though this response may be excessively high or unrealistically low. | 7. More precise measurement of promotional influences at retail level. |
| | 8. Better measurement of each Data Market universe because of:<br>a. less between-store variance<br>b. higher panel coverage of universe |
| | 9. Suitability for controlled store test experiments. |

Source: "Managing a Product's Future," The Nielsen Researcher, no. 2 (1982), pp. 3–4, © A. C. Nielsen Company.

in a traditional test market approach. Not only does your firm obtain response measurements much sooner but it minimizes the dangers associated with competitors' observation of results and/or activities to contaminate the test.

*Comparing Traditional and Controlled Test Marketing*

Both traditional test markets and controlled test markets possess their own unique advantages and disadvantages. A comparison of the strong points of each, as seen by the A. C. Nielsen Company, is shown in Table 21.1. That research firm, along with others in the same field, recommends that manufacturers consider the simultaneous use of traditional and controlled test markets to obtain the dual sets of advantages.

*The Scope and Uses for Market Testing*

It should be reemphasized that, while our illustrations have dealt with the issues of traditional test marketing and controlled test marketing in terms of new product entries, these same general procedures can also be employed to experiment with variations in promotional tactics for existing brands. For instance, such things as advertising appeals, shelf locations, couponing, or intensity of personal selling effort can be evaluated by one or both of these techniques. In summary, then, traditional and controlled test marketing experiments can be used to investigate relationships between virtually any of the inputs and outputs shown in the market representation introduced in Figure 21.1.

# ANALYSIS OF RESULTS OF ONGOING PROGRAMS

Beyond formal market tests and pretests, a great deal of the feedback data used for adaptive control is derived from reports and studies that diagnose market results being generated by promotional activities undertaken in the normal course of business. Figure 21.6 pictures examples of input sources for such data along with examples of output data which can be tabulated.

**Information Input Sources**

The most basic and universally used input source is the company's own internally generated sales, market, and cost data. This will logically be broken down by such classifications as dollar and unit sales by territory, by month or season, by outlet type, and so forth. As shown at the top right portion of the figure, it is also common to make use of a variety of supplementary data supplied by syndicated research organizations which keep your firm informed of its relative competitive position. Major suppliers of such supplementary data are the A. C. Nielsen Company, SAMI (Selling Areas Marketing Inc.), Simmons Market Research Bureau, and Market Research Corporation of America. As discussed in Chapter 5, these and other organizations offer an assortment of continuing report services on a subscription basis. The facts and figures they provide broaden your feedback intelligence capability regarding such things as competitive market shares, total category sales by outlet types, and strength of distribution and reseller support being given various brands.

Your full feedback inventory can derive from numerous other information sources. Some of these may be internally originated such as the sales call and activity reports prepared by your personal selling team. Others may be obtained from research agencies that measure results attributable to particular components of a particular program. For example, the intermediate communication impact of much national advertising (as measured by consumer recall, understanding, and general attitude) is regularly surveyed by such research firms as Starch Readership Service, Gallup and Robinson, and Burke Marketing Research.[12] When a firm senses that it may be facing a special market problem or opportunity, it will often go beyond any of these more or less routine mechanisms and call for a custom survey to probe its position in greater detail.

**The Marketing Information System and Its Outputs**

As suggested in Figure 21.6 the task of fitting the fragments together and concentrating attention on those parts of the feedback mass that are most critical is best handled by establishing a well-organized marketing information system. Some examples of typical information outputs routinely derived from a system are shown in the bottom portion of the figure. Again, it is not within the purview of this book to deal with research methods or reporting systems in anything more than a cursory manner.[13] Nonetheless, because the use of such research data can be so critical to the success of your promotional program, it is appropriate to stress the importance that information systems can play in the development and monitoring of your strategy plan.

**FIGURE 21.6 Selected input–output data from a marketing information system for adaptive control of ongoing promotional programs**

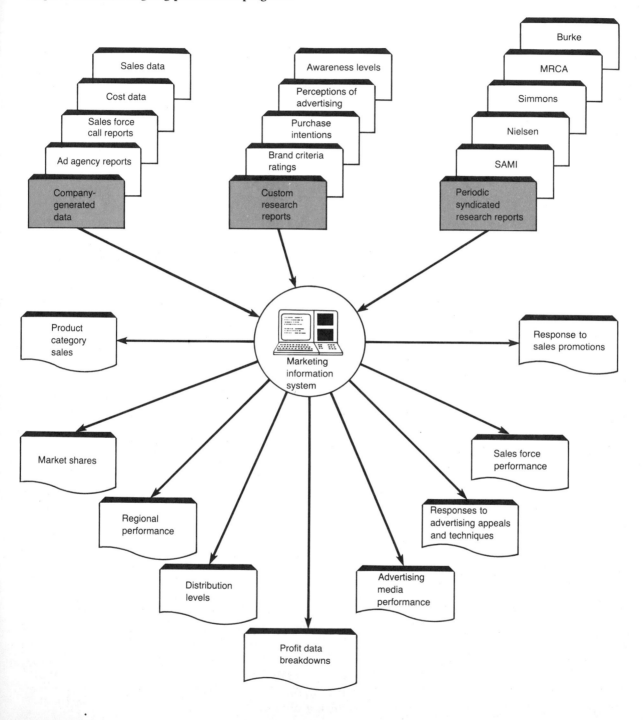

**An Illustration of Adaptive Control Based on Ongoing Analysis**

As an illustration, consider the case of Campbell's "Soup-for-One."[14] This brand offers consumers a single-serving can of soup. It was introduced in the late 1970s in response to some of the demographic trends we looked at in an earlier chapter. In particular, its development was spurred by the trend toward larger proportions of Americans living alone and eating alone. After the brand had been on the market for three years the company found its market share growth pattern had become sluggish. In a situation such as this, a well-organized marketing information system can provide you with rapid access to data that allow you to isolate the problem. Among the factors which could be retarding your volume are such things as poor product performance, inadequate distribution levels, weak reseller support, or ineffectiveness in some aspect of your advertising program. It becomes essential that you track the core problem to its source as quickly as possible. It is equally essential that your information system enables you to screen out nonproblem areas, because you wish to avoid mistakenly tampering with program components that are actually performing effectively.

In the Soup-for-One case, the problem was rapidly traced to product perceptions as they were influenced by advertising. Feedback analysis revealed that, although the advertising created high levels of awareness among prospects, it left many with a perception of the brand as merely a smaller-sized version of the standard Campbell soup line. In actuality, it is a specially developed and extra-high-quality product that retails at a higher per-ounce price. Armed with this information, the company knew which part of its promotional program needed revision. The advertising creative approach was revamped to portray Soup-for-One with more emphasis on its gourmet quality. The reported result was a prompt jump in sales.

# SUMMARY

Given the uncertainties that surround promotional strategy planning, a well-constructed program not only begins with careful evaluation of past results but is built with a view to continually gathering information inputs to guide and if necessary redirect its implementation. The process of cycling market feedback data into the decision-making structure on a systematic basis has been termed "adaptive control." Interpreted broadly, adaptive control calls for the acquisition of information, not only on sales and profit outcomes, but also on all of the intermediate communication effects generated by your promotional mix.

In general, feedback studies fall into one of three broad categories—pretests, market experiments, and analysis of the results of ongoing programs.

*Pretests* aim at securing information on either your total plan or some aspect of it before it is actually tried out in the marketplace. For instance, an assortment of pretest techniques exists to evaluate diverse aspects of advertising creativity before the advertisements are run in the mass media. Pretests are also commonly used to judge the likely market acceptance of new product ideas. A variety of methods exists for pretesting product concepts. Some are sophisticated procedures that seek to give marketing strategists feedback data on many aspects of the total plan for the new product. These aspects include general acceptance of the product idea and its related benefits, packaging, brand name, pricing, and advertising appeals.

Through extensions of such tests it is also possible to secure preliminary estimates of the degree of purchase-repurchase behavior which can be anticipated. By means of such feedback data, you can not only assess the feasibility of a new product introduction but also refine the product itself or any of the other components in the promotional mix. All pretests have a degree of artificiality about them because the brand is not presented under totally realistic market conditions. They are essentially initial screening devices that make up only one part of a much larger information gathering system.

In a *market test,* your brand or some aspect of your promotional program is tried out under relatively normal and realistic selling conditions. A true market test is basically an experiment in which you deliberately manipulate one or more variables under your control to see what effects will be produced. For example, given the uncertainty which accompanies promotional budget level determination, you might choose to obtain guidance for your budgeting procedure by varying expenditure levels between different market territories. By comparing the sales and profit results in those territories, you are in a much improved position to fine-tune your allocation strategy.

A common form of market experimentation centers around the traditional test market. This is a geographic area that is chosen to represent a much larger regional or national territory; one or more of the components of your marketing program can be examined on a limited basis in the chosen area. Test marketing is especially prevalent as a prelude to full scale introduction of a new brand. However, it can be used to acquire feedback on a proposed change in any portion of your marketing strategy.

Traditional test markets pose a variety of problems. The costs and the amount of time required are two major problems. Additionally, when an entirely new brand is being tested you face certain risks relating both to competitive observation of your results and to competitive attempts to corrupt your findings. Because of these problems, controlled test marketing has gained in popularity. The controlled test market uses only a selected group of stores that have agreed to participate in advance of the test. The overall time period for the test is shortened because no personal selling is required. Moreover, costs are reduced because of the absence of personal selling efforts and because the scale of the study is smaller. Both traditional and controlled test markets have their own advantages and disadvantages; as a consequence, they are frequently used together or in sequence.

Apart from pretests and market tests, a great pool of feedback information can be gathered through analysis of ongoing marketing activities. To have this information available for orderly and rapid use, alert firms are putting increased emphasis on marketing information systems, many of which are computer based. A well-organized system can warn you of the existence of problem areas and also aid you in pinpointing the causes behind the problems. With such a system in place, you are in a position to exercise continuous adaptive control over your promotional efforts.

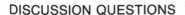

## DISCUSSION QUESTIONS

1. As noted in the chapter, the market network representation shown in Figure 21.1 actually simplifies some of the variables involved. Demonstrate this by discussing sub-topics that might be examined in studying the effects of sales promotion and personal selling on distribution.
2. "Once your marketing plan is in operation there really isn't much you can do to change it very quickly. Therefore, the only kind of feedback in which I'm interested is sales results. If sales are poor, we'll see where we go from there." Comment on this statement.
3. What are some of the principal limitations that must be kept in mind when you are attempting to pretest advertising materials?
4. What is a concept test and what types of data can you derive from such a test to guide your promotional planning?
5. Given that mathematical decision models don't seem to play a significant role in the budget planning processes followed by most large cor-

porations, why should promotional decision makers give them any attention at all?
6. Discuss the relative strengths and weaknesses of traditional test marketing versus controlled test marketing.
7. Why might a firm want to undertake test market efforts in several market areas at the same time?
8. If you were in charge of the introduction of the new skin care product being planned by J. K. Ivensen, Incorporated (as described in Chapter 20) and had to choose between *either* a traditional test market approach *or* a controlled test market approach to assess the feasibility of the proposed plan, which approach would you choose and why?
9. What purposes can a continuing marketing information system serve in guiding promotional strategy?
10. Figure 21.6 illustrates *selected examples* of input and output data that might be included in an ongoing marketing information system. List and discuss at least five other examples of such data that might be included.

## REFERENCES

1. John D. C. Little, "A Model of Adaptive Control of Promotional Spending," *Operations Research,* November 1966, p. 1075.
2. For a much more extended discussion see Thomas C. Kinnear and James R. Taylor, *Marketing Research: An Applied Approach* (New York: McGraw-Hill, Inc., 1983), Chapters 23 and 24.
3. For a very good discussion of advertising pretesting see Courtland L. Bovee and William F. Arens, *Contemporary Advertising* (Homewood, IL: Richard D. Irwin, Inc., 1982), pp. 766–778.
4. *Ibid.,* p. 778.
5. "Managing a Product's Future," *The Nielsen Researcher*, no. 2 (1982), p. 2.
6. BASES (Cincinnati: Burke Marketing Services, Inc., 1981), p. 2.
7. Some excellent sources to consult for more detailed information include the following: Vijay Mahajan, Stuart I. Breitschneider, and John W. Bradford, "Feedback Approaches to Modeling

Structural Shifts in Market Response," *Journal of Marketing*, Winter 1980, pp. 71–80; Chakravarthi Narasimhan and Subrata K. Sen, "New Product Models for Test Data," *Journal of Marketing,* Winter 1983, pp. 11–24; Julian L. Simon, "A Simple Model for Determining Advertising Appropriations," *Journal of Marketing Research,* August 1965, pp. 285–292; Russell S. Winer, "Analysis of Advertising Experiments," *Journal of Advertising Research,* June 1980, pp. 25–31; David B. Montgomery and Alvin J. Silk, "Estimating Dynamic Effects of Market Communication Expenditures," *Management Science,* June 1972, pp. B485–B501; John D. C. Little, "A Model of Adaptive Control of Promotional Spending," *Operations Research,* November-December 1966, pp. 1075–1097.
8. "Recommended Test Markets," *Advertising Age,* 22 February 1982, p. M-14.
9. *The Nielsen Researcher,* p. 8.
10. Figure 21.6 illustrates *selected* examples of in-view, June 1979, p. 69.

11. *Ibid.*, p. 70.
12. For a more extended discussion see Bovee and Arens, *Contemporary Advertising*, pp. 771–780.
13. For a more detailed discussion see Charles D. Schewe, ed., *Marketing Information Systems: Selected Readings* (Chicago: American Marketing Association, 1976); Archie B. Carroll, "Behavioral Aspects of Developing Computer Based Information Systems," *Business Horizons*, January/February 1982), pp. 42–51; Edward M. Tauber, "How to Get Advertising Strategy From Research," *Journal of Advertising Research*, October 1980, pp. 67–72; Rory C. Robicheaux, "The Database Approach," *Journal of Systems Management*, November 1980, pp. 6–14.
14. Theodore J. Gage, "New Tastes Spark Food for Thought," *Advertising Age,* 22 February 1982, pp. M-16–M-18.

PART EIGHT

# *Societal Aspects of Promotion*

# CHAPTER TWENTY-TWO

# *Legal and Social Issues*

## FOCUS OF THE CHAPTER

The past twenty-one chapters presented you with descriptions of methods to persuade consumers, compete with other business firms, and aim at maximizing your profits. The tenor of those descriptions assumed your goals and tactics were not only acceptable but beneficial to your customers as well as to your own firm. Although there were occasional hints that promotional tech-niques could be abused, little was said about the legal, ethical, or societal issues that must be taken into consideration when appraising either an individual promotional program or the field of promotion in general. It is now time to recognize those issues. This chapter will discuss them in terms of: 1. major laws that affect promotional practices, 2. the regulatory agencies that enforce such laws, 3. efforts at self-regulation, and 4. overall social concerns which transcend legal constraints.

## A GENERAL POINT OF VIEW

It should be stressed at the outset that our discussion begins with the premise that attempts to persuade, to compete, or to increase profits are neither in-nately good nor innately evil in terms of their effects on society. However, the manner in which you pursue those attempts can lead to results that may be either desirable or undesirable from a social standpoint. Commercial persuasion in its most positive role discovers consumers' legitimate needs and wants and then demonstrates how a product can fulfill those needs and wants. Competition impels a search for ways to conduct business activities in a more effective and efficient manner. Profits are rewards which accrue to those successful in providing goods and services that improve the economic and material well-being of society. On the other hand, if we look at these same activities from the most negative perspective, a totally opposite picture emerges. Commercial persuasion can be built on a base of trickery and deception. The spirit of competition can give rise to the use of vicious and unscrupulous methods to damage competitors. The pursuit of profit can assume an intensity that makes it blind to any potential harm that might be inflicted on others in the process of achieving it.

## THE BACKGROUND OF LAWS AFFECTING PROMOTION

During the nineteenth century and into the early part of the twentieth, United States law generally took the position that the free enterprise system worked best with as little regulation as possible. Presumably, the system itself provided its own checks and balances that would force businesses to act in a socially positive manner. Additionally, the buying and selling of merchandise customarily took place under the rule of *Caveat emptor* ("Let the buyer beware"). This rule assumes that the purchaser is capable of inspecting and correctly appraising the quality of the goods being sold, *regardless of the claims made by the seller.*

Perhaps both the power of inherent, self-correcting mechanisms in the free enterprise system and the logic underlying the caveat emptor principle had been overestimated from the beginning. However, with the appearance of mass production, large-scale business units and more diverse and complex products, certain serious defects in business practices became apparent. For example, a large firm could destroy a small competitor by underpricing it. The large firm could sell merchandise below cost, if necessary, until its weaker rival was eliminated. Then, the large firm could recoup its losses in a market devoid of competition. Extravagant and false advertising claims could be made for products such as patent medicines. Consumers, unable to examine the product in a way that would reveal the facts, could be misled by the advertising and waste their money on worthless or even harmful merchandise.[1]

Given this state of affairs, the need for some form of regulation became apparent. The first significant efforts at correcting such abuses began near the end of the nineteenth century. From that point on, the scope of regulatory activity in the United States has expanded greatly. Not infrequently, such expansion has occurred in the face of protests by some if not many members of the business community. It is true that regulations can make the operation of a business more complex. It is also true that not every regulation turns out to be as effective or sensible as its authors originally intended. Furthermore, the methods of administering such regulations can be controversial. Nonetheless, it should be recognized and emphasized that the aim of most regulatory legislation has been to preserve competition and to create a better climate for promotion rather than to destroy either of them. One analyst of the field has phrased the matter in this way:

> Government regulation thus serves two groups: the consumers and the business competitors. The consumer is served by the efforts of the law to prevent monopoly and, consequently, the higher prices and lower quality that may accompany monopoly. The consumer benefits too by the elimination of market practices which deceive him in his buying. Business firms are also served in two ways: Market conduct by powerful business rivals which might deprive firms of free access to the marketplace is subject to regulatory control, and business competitors are protected from rivals who choose to resort to practices which may deceive consumers. [2]

## FEDERAL REGULATIONS AFFECTING PROMOTION

Laws relating to marketing practices exist at both the state and federal levels. Some of them apply mainly to rather narrowly defined product categories or promotional methods. For example, legislation restricting the manner in which alcoholic beverages can be promoted varies from state to state. Some states also restrict or prohibit the use of certain promotional techniques such as consumer contests and lotteries. At the federal level, the agencies whose authority may influence your planning can vary depending on the particular type of commodity you are selling. One writer has pointed out, "[Today's marketing manager must operate within a] vast, highly-complex set of rules telling you what you must, can, might, can't, and mustn't do. If you work a lifetime as a marketing manager in one industry you might not even then understand all the prescriptive and proscriptive regulations which impact upon you and on your probability of success."[3]

In consequence, today's marketing managers require assistance and counsel from legal professionals. Recognizing this fact, our purpose is not to delve deeply into the full range of legal restrictions on marketing practices.[4] Rather, it is to give you a sense of the background and general direction of regulations affecting promotion. To do this, we will consider three federal agencies whose actions have an especially widespread impact on promotional practices. These are the Food and Drug Administration, the Federal Communications Commission, and the Federal Trade Commission.

*The Food and Drug Administration*

In 1906, the United States Congress passed the original Pure Food and Drug Act, which was a law concerned mainly with ensuring accurate listings of ingredients on the packaging of food and drug products. In 1938, a much stronger piece of legislation was passed in the form of the Federal Food, Drug and Cosmetic Act. This legislation gave the Food and Drug Administration (FDA) broad authority for ensuring that drugs and medical devices are safe and effective and for monitoring the safety and purity of foods and cosmetic products. For the most part, the FDA is concerned with the essential nature of the products themselves, their packaging, and their labeling. Its only direct area of authority with respect to explicit promotion applies to the advertising of prescription drugs. In 1962, the agency was given responsibility for regulating such advertising to ensure that it contains adequate information concerning side effects and complications that might arise from the use of such drugs. With respect to the remaining products with which it deals, the only advertising claims under the direct jurisdiction of the FDA are those appearing on package labels. However, the FDA works closely with the Federal Trade Commission to provide the latter agency with any evidence it obtains regarding possible violations in other forms of advertising for foods, drugs, therapeutic devices, and cosmetics.

The FDA has a staff of some seven thousand persons and is one of the most potent of the regulatory units.[5] Its inspectors are located throughout the United States and the agency can take legal action against violators through suits filed in federal district courts. It can also secure a court order to seize merchandise which is illegally mislabeled or the contents of which might endanger the health of consumers. Additionally, it conducts programs to educate the public and to provide consumers with informational publications.

The FDA is sometimes described as being notoriously cautious and at least a few business-oriented observers have leveled criticisms at the delays involved in introducing new products because of the time required to obtain FDA approval.[6] This criticism applies primarily in the case of prescription drug items. At the same time, the FDA has many supporters who interpret its caution as being appropriate, given the serious nature of some of the products with which it deals. Above all, the FDA is recognized as an exceptionally powerful agency whose effects on marketing practices in the United States have been characterized as "formidable."[7]

## The Federal Communications Commission

The Communications Act of 1934 created the Federal Communications Commission (FCC) to oversee broadcasting activities and to ensure that they are operated in the "public interest, convenience, and necessity." The agency is also assigned responsibility for interstate telephone and telegraph rates and service. With the advent of television, that medium was placed under FCC supervision as well. The performances of all radio and television stations are reviewed periodically by the FCC before their licenses are renewed. Because of its mandate to grant or refuse to grant station licenses, the FCC can exercise a great deal of influence over the general nature of everything that is presented via the electronic media. This of course includes not only the programming material but also the advertising material. The FCC's policy with respect to advertising is specified through standards of practice to which all commercial stations and networks are expected to conform. Those standards are aimed not only at the elimination of advertising that may be deceptive or in bad taste but also at controlling the length of commercials and the total amount of commercial time permitted per hour.

Although somewhat smaller than that of the FDA, the FCC staff is still ample in size with over two thousand employees serving in the Washington headquarters and twenty-four field offices.[8] A portion of the work of that staff includes spot-checking programs being broadcast or telecast to determine whether they are in compliance with commission standards. Additionally, staff members follow up on any complaints received from the public concerning programming content or commercials. A station found in persistent violation of FCC standards can become the subject of a hearing by the agency and could face a fine or, in the ultimate situation, revocation of its license. Like the FDA, the FCC cooperates closely with the Federal Trade Commission in cases dealing with improper advertising claims or techniques. Thus, in a sense, advertising transmitted by the electronic media can come under the scrutiny of at least two federal agencies.

## The Federal Trade Commission

The Federal Trade Commission (FTC) has been accurately described as "the major federal agency dealing with most aspects of business, competition and consumer protection."[9] Figure 22.1 outlines only a portion of the laws that have been passed to define the authority and responsibilities of the FTC. The congressional acts listed represent those most pertinent to broad-scale promotional activities. Some of the other statutes which fall under FTC jurisdiction include the Wool Products Labeling Act, the Fur Products Labeling Act, the Textile Fiber Products Identification Act, the Lanham Trademark Act, the Export Trade Act, the Fair Packaging and Labeling Act, and the Consumer Credit Protection Act.[10]

The original impetus giving rise to the creation of the FTC came not from consumers or consumer activists but from business firms seeking protection from the predatory practices of competitors. In essence, the initial objective was primarily one of protecting business rather than protecting consumers in any direct sense. The atmosphere surrounding the passage of the Federal Trade Commission Act in 1914 has been described as follows:

> After considerable disagreement and debate between the Congressmen, it became evident that specific definition of illegal business activities was futile; numerous exceptions to any definition and new, unidentified illicit activities would undoubtedly appear after passage of such a law. Congress, therefore, agreed on a flexible law which (1) declared unfair methods of competition to be illegal (Section 5) and (2) established the Federal Trade Commission (FTC) as an investigative and regulatory agency. [11]

In the same year, 1914, Congress passed a second law that was also aimed at preserving and strengthening the competitive, free-enterprise system. This was the Clayton Act, which outlawed price discrimination, corporate mergers, and certain forms of contractual agreements between business firms where the effect of the practice may be to substantially lessen competition or tend to create a monopoly in any line of commerce.

In its early years, the FTC took action against advertisers whose promotional claims were regarded as false and misleading. The original logic behind these actions derived from the concept that deceptive promotion constituted an unfair method of competition. In 1931, a decision by the United States Supreme Court temporarily limited the agency's efforts to prevent deceptive advertising by holding that it could not act unless there was proof that such

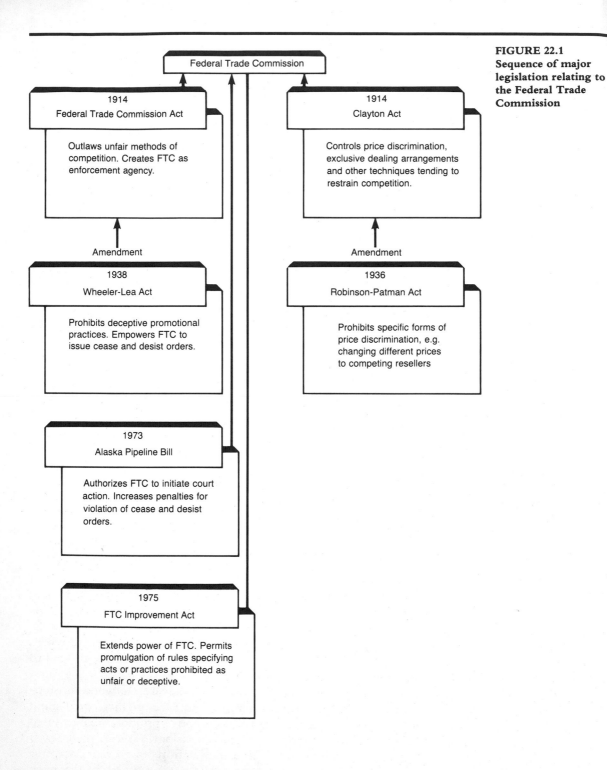

FIGURE 22.1
Sequence of major
legislation relating to
the Federal Trade
Commission

**Federal Trade Commission**

1914
Federal Trade Commission Act

Outlaws unfair methods of
competition. Creates FTC as
enforcement agency.

1914
Clayton Act

Controls price discrimination,
exclusive dealing arrangements
and other techniques tending to
restrain competition.

Amendment

1938
Wheeler-Lea Act

Prohibits deceptive promotional
practices. Empowers FTC to
issue cease and desist orders.

Amendment

1936
Robinson-Patman Act

Prohibits specific forms of
price discrimination, e.g.
changing different prices
to competing resellers

1973
Alaska Pipeline Bill

Authorizes FTC to initiate court
action. Increases penalties for
violation of cease and desist
orders.

1975
FTC Improvement Act

Extends power of FTC. Permits
promulgation of rules specifying
acts or practices prohibited as
unfair or deceptive.

advertising was actually causing substantial harm to competitors. As suggested in Figure 22.1, a significant expansion in the power and realm of the FTC occurred in the mid-1930s with the passage of the Robinson-Patman Amendment to the Clayton Act and the passage of the Wheeler-Lea Amendment to the Federal Trade Commission Act.

***The Robinson-Patman Act.***   The growth in importance of large-scale retail firms during the 1920s and 1930s enabled them to wield a great deal of influence in the marketplace. This influence could be used to pressure suppliers to grant them substantial price concessions. Those concessions might take the form of quantity discounts or special brokerage allowances. Alternatively, they might take the form of disproportionate trade inducements, and performance allowances made available to the large firms but not to their smaller rivals. The Clayton Act did not forbid such practices. Therefore, partly at the behest of small business interests, the Robinson-Patman Act was passed to preserve competition by eliminating any price advantage a large firm might be able to secure merely because of its greater bargaining power.

The act forbids discrimination in price or terms of sale unless it can "be justified by reason of a seller's diminished costs due to quantity manufacture, delivery, or sale, or by reason of the seller's good-faith effort to meet a competitor's equally low price."[12] It also prohibits the payment of brokerage fees or allowances if the brokerage firm is affiliated with either the buyer or the seller. Additionally, the act requires that a seller who makes promotional allowances or services available to one middleman must make those same allowances or services available to all other middlemen in its distribution channel on proportionately equal terms. This last provision explains the reason for the references to legal cautions in earlier chapters dealing with your handling of trade inducements and performance allowances. Responsibility for enforcement was placed in the hands of the Federal Trade Commission.

***The Wheeler-Lea Act.***   With the passage of the Wheeler-Lea Act in 1938, the FTC was, in essence, expanded into a consumer protection agency as well as a guardian of the competitive system. Furthermore, the commission was greatly strengthened in its power to act. In particular, under this law the agency was "(1) [g]iven power to initiate investigation against companies without waiting for formal complaints; (2) given the right to regulate acts and practices which deceive consumers (and not just businesses); (3) given authority to issue cease and desist orders; and (4) given power to fine companies for not complying with cease and desist orders."[13]

***Subsequent Legislation Affecting the FTC.***   In 1973, when Congress passed the Alaska Pipeline Bill, it appended certain provisions upgrading the strength of the FTC. This included a doubling of the fine for violating a final cease-and-desist order from $5,000 to $10,000 per day, and authorization to initiate lawsuits and to seek preliminary court injunctions to halt trade practices or acts that are unfair or deceptive.

The FTC Improvement Act of 1975 further broadened the scope of the agency's activities in a number of areas. One of the most significant sections of this law provided for the setting up of trade regulation rules which would define in advance specific practices prohibited as unfair or deceptive. It also permitted the agency to allot funds for including consumer groups as participants in proceedings designed to set up trade regulations. Furthermore, under the provisions of this act, the FTC could move to assist consumers in recovering certain losses they might suffer because of deceptive practices by sellers. Some of the expanded powers embodied in the 1975 law were temporarily set aside by a second FTC Improvements Act passed in 1980. Specifically, this latter law stated that the agency must defer publication of any trade rule concerning unfairness in commercial advertising for a three-year period.

*FTC Procedures.*[14]   Upon either observing or being notified of a possible violation, the FTC staff first gathers and evaluates the evidence. If the staff decides that there is evidence of an actual violation, the company involved can settle the matter through a "consent order," in which it agrees to cease the activity identified as a violation. In the absence of such a settlement, the FTC may issue a formal complaint leading to a hearing before an FTC examiner. The hearing itself is conducted much like a court trial with both the FTC staff and the firm or party charged as a violator presenting evidence to support their positions. At the close of the hearing, the examiner issues an order—ruling for one side or the other—which may be appealed to the full commission by either side. If not appealed, the order becomes final within thirty days. If the order is appealed, and if the full commission still determines a violation has occurred, a cease-and-desist order is issued. This becomes final within sixty days unless it is further appealed through the federal judicial system.

*Examples of FTC Enforcement Actions.*   In some cases, the fact that a promotional claim is false and deceitful may be readily apparent and virtually indisputable. For example, suppose a firm selling a household insecticide advertises the brand as "absolutely safe for use around food and pets," when in fact the company knows the product can be quite dangerous in this regard. Such advertising would be clearly and seriously false and deceptive. On the other hand, advertising that merely speaks of the product in a manner which may be overly enthusiastic or effusive is often treated as acceptable "puffery." Literally, "puffery" means "undue or exaggerated praise." Such statements as "the toothpaste that beautifies your smile" or "the candy bar with a flavor that's out of this world" would most likely be regarded as examples of "puffing." In general, the logic is that consumers can easily detect puffery and evaluate it accordingly. However, at some point exaggerated praise can become so strong that it ceases to be puffery and turns into deception. The problem is that *the exact point* at which this occurs is not always completely clear. Furthermore, it is possible that, whereas most consumers will recognize an effusive claim or imaginative creative presentation as puffery, some will take it to be the literal truth and, in consequence, will be deceived.

This last issue raises questions concerning the exact percentage of the audience which must be misled by an advertisement before it is branded as deceptive. In at least one instance, a federal court seemed to be saying that an advertisement could be treated as deceptive even if only a minority of the audience might interpret it in a manner that resulted in their being misled. In its ruling, the court suggested that the FTC should have the discretion to insist, if it chooses, "upon a form of advertising clear enough so that wayfaring men, though fools, shall not err therein."[15]

At times, the policy of attempting to ensure that very few persons, if any, could possibly be deceived by an advertising presentation has led to the stoppage of advertisements which might seem to pose little risk of seriously misleading the vast majority of consumers. For example, one television commercial for a laundry detergent featured a man with a stained shirt standing in a tank of rising water. He poured some of the detergent into the water. When the water level dropped back down, the audience could see that his shirt was now perfectly clean. Of course, in practice the shirt had really been washed by a standard laundry procedure rather than by the gently rising water in the tank. Was this deception or merely puffery in the form of playful exaggeration? The FTC regarded it as deception and the company discontinued the commercial.[16]

In the 1970s the FTC stepped up the intensity of its regulatory efforts and initiated two new forms of enforcement techniques—corrective advertising and an advertising substantiation program.

*Corrective advertising* was required in a number of cases in which advertisers' past claims were judged to have misled or deceived the audience.[17] Under the corrective approach, a stated amount of future advertising for the product must include a statement designed to remove any false impressions left by the prior misleading claims. For example, the FTC complained that advertisements for Ocean Spray Cranberry Juice created misleading impressions concerning the amount of food energy the brand contained relative to other breakfast drinks. As a result, Ocean Spray agreed to include the following wording in its corrective advertisements, "If you've wondered what some of our earlier advertising meant when we said Ocean Spray Cranberry Juice Cocktail has more food energy than orange juice or tomato juice, let us make it clear: we didn't mean vitamins or minerals. Food energy means calories. Nothing more."[18]

The *FTC's advertising substantiation program* was built around a procedure requiring that "advertisers submit on FTC demand tests, studies, or other data that purport to substantiate advertised claims regarding a product's safety, performance, efficacy, quality, or comparative price."[19]

Substantiation was not required for statements considered to be puffery, but it could be called for in situations where the commission questioned specific claims such as "the stopping-and-holding performance of a tire, the germ-killing effectiveness of a cleansing agent, and the reduction of annoying noises in a hearing aid."[20] Initially, the indication was that documentation called for from manufacturers was being gathered mainly for informational purposes and possible examination by consumers rather than as an implication that false or misleading claims actually were being used. However, one review of the program noted the following:

> After receiving documentation from numerous companies . . . the FTC issued a number of consent order decrees requiring various companies to discontinue making inadequately substantiated claims. Whirlpool was ordered to discontinue referring to its "panic button" as unique (only the name used to indicate fast cooling was unique) and Fedders was told to stop calling its "reserve cooling system" unique. General Motors was told to discontinue declaring that "Vega handles better" and Firestone was ordered to stop advertising that its tires "stop 25% faster." [21]

**The Current Regulatory Climate**

At the beginning of the 1980s, observers of the relationship between business and government began to comment on a changing national mood. The new mood they sensed was one that favored less government intervention and that reacted against some of the more vigorous activities pursued by the FTC and other federal agencies during the 1970s. Referring specifically to the intensified efforts of the FTC during that period, one observer concluded,

> [I]nstead of praise, it [the FTC] found itself the subject of unexpected criticism. Suddenly it seemed to be reaching down to Main Street, trifling with practices better left to state and local authority. Some of the procedures it developed for processing rules were successfully challenged in court as unfair. In [an] editorial on its proposed rule regulating TV ads to children, the Washington Post suggested the FTC seemed intent on making itself the "national nanny." [22]

In a 1982 speech before a group of advertising professionals, an industry leader was reported as expressing his view of the new regulatory atmosphere by stating, "Threats continue, but for the most part we've enjoyed some major victories in Washington this past year. . . . In part, these victories can be attributed to the antiregulatory sentiment in this country. But to a large degree, the successes came from businesses forcing the regulators and legislators to face up to their errors in judgment at a time when the public was listening to our side of the story."[23]

In describing the newly appointed chairman of the Federal Trade Commission, a speaker addressing a 1982 conference of the American Marketing Association offered the opinion that, "If Chairman Miller could swing it, the pendulum would swing all the way back to where the less-educated, the less-intelligent are not to be the concern, the mild misrepresentations are not to be bothered with, and only the most flagrant of deliberate and careless misrepresentations would be pursued. Even then, the emphasis would be on high-ticket items rather than small-ticket, repeat-purchase items."[24]

At least at the time this book is written, the immediate outlook for government regulation of promotion appears to involve a much less stringent approach than suggested by our earlier illustrations of FTC activities in the 1970s. However, before concluding that you are free to pursue your promotional goals with very little restraint, you should keep three points in mind. First, the essential laws that established restrictions on marketing practices are still very much in place and so are the agencies to enforce them. Given evidence of an increase in business abuses or a reverse swing of the political mood, those agencies could become even more forceful than they have been in the past. Second, although we have been speaking only in terms of federal agencies, it should be recalled that promotion in the United States can also be regulated on a state-by-state basis. As one authority has noted, "We now have in the vast majority of states 'little FTC acts' which are modeled after the current FTC statute. . . . I assure you most of those will remain firmly in place, so rather than being bothered by one lawsuit, which would establish the advertising standard nationwide, you may be harassed with lawsuits in Kansas, California, New Mexico, and who knows where else."[25]

Finally, and perhaps most importantly, it should be reemphasized that beyond protection of consumers, a major purpose of much regulatory legislation is the preservation and enhancement of the free-enterprise system. On this basis, it might be sensible from the standpoint of self-interest for business to view diminished levels of federal regulation as a signal for more self-restraint and for attempts at stronger self-regulation.

## MOVEMENTS TOWARD SELF-REGULATION

As indicated above, the history of government regulation of promotional activities suggests that at least a reasonable amount of sensible regulation is in the best interest of business itself. To the extent that it is feasible and workable, self-regulation would appear to provide an ideal means of lessening the need for government intervention. Many business people have accepted this point of view and advocated specific routes toward achieving it.

*The Printers' Ink Model Statute*

As long ago as 1911, leaders in the advertising industry proposed that a model law be drafted to stem the flow of false and misleading advertisements. The result was the *Printers' Ink* Statute, which states that anyone who originates or disseminates an advertisement that "contains assertions, representation, or statement of fact which is untrue, deceptive or misleading shall be guilty of a misdemeanor." Over the course of time, the *Printers' Ink* Statute, in either its original or modified form, was adopted by forty-five states. There appears to be little evidence that it has led to anything resembling vigorous prosecution by state authorities. However, the statute has been thought to be an aid to organizations such as Better Business Bureaus, which attempt to halt unethical business practices. By pointing to the fact that the law makes such practices clearly criminal in nature, the bureaus may be able to exert greater force on recalcitrant offenders.[26]

*Self-Regulation Efforts by Individual Firms*

Partly in reaction to heightened government intervention and consumer activism in the 1970s, many major business firms have initiated special efforts to improve their awareness of and responsiveness to consumer needs and problems. For example, a supermarket chain based in Washington, DC, Giant

Foods, instituted unit pricing and open-dating programs in advance of any legal need to do so.[27] The Whirlpool Corporation set up a "hot-line" system to handle consumer complaints.[28] Extensive consumer education programs were organized by a number of corporations including J. C. Penney, Montgomery Ward, and Procter and Gamble.[29] In short, there is evidence that responsible members of the business community clearly recognize the need for sound practices in promotional strategies and all other areas of their operations to ensure their own long-term market positions.

## The NAD/NARB Advertising Review Program

An extensive and highly promising form of self-regulation for advertising at the national level was begun in 1971 under the joint auspices of the Council of Better Business Bureaus and the advertising industry.[30] The two primary agencies involved in conducting this program are the National Advertising Division (NAD) of the National Council of Better Business Bureaus and the National Advertising Review Board (NARB). The latter organization consists of fifty persons drawn from the business community and the public at large. The procedures by which the NAD/NARB program seeks to curtail abuses in advertising is diagrammed in Figure 22.2. It should be noted that the goal is not only to ensure that advertising claims are truthful and accurate but also to cope with issues involving good taste and social responsibility in advertising presentations. On receiving a complaint or a query regarding advertising, the NAD first evaluates the matter. If that group finds sufficient reason to believe that a violation has occurred, the advertiser is contacted. If the response received from the advertiser does not resolve the matter satisfactorily, the offending firm is requested to change or discontinue use of the materials in question. At this point the advertiser may agree or disagree with the NAD finding. If the advertiser agrees, the issue is settled; if the advertiser disagrees, the matter can be referred to the NARB where it undergoes a similar investigative process.

Because it is not a government agency, the NAD/NARB is unable to impose any direct penalty on firms refusing to comply. However, beyond the fact that it can refer the matter to a government agency, the NAD/NARB publishes decisions concerning its investigations. The prospect of unfavorable publicity could dissuade many firms that might otherwise be tempted to continue producing advertising that was deceptive, misleading, or otherwise socially irresponsible. The program has generally been praised by those observing it. For example, an FTC official has been quoted as saying, "After about seven or eight years of vigorous operation I think we have enough evidence to conclude that the NARB is as successful an effort at self-regulation as any we have witnessed in this country."[31]

Another observer, while noting the limitations imposed by its relatively small budget, praised its general accomplishments by commenting, "NAD/NARB has a remarkable record of moving faster, more decisively and with less acrimony than the FTC, but it seldom goes beyond hard core deception. It operates on a starvation budget barely in excess of $600,000."[32]

**FIGURE 22.2 The NAD/NARB investigation procedure**

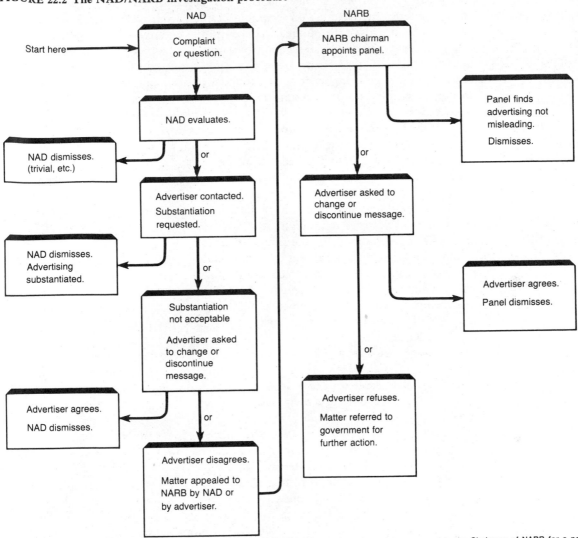

NAD

NARB

Start here→ Complaint or question.

NARB chairman appoints panel.

NAD evaluates.

Panel finds advertising not misleading. Dismisses.

NAD dismisses. (trivial, etc.) ← or

Advertiser contacted. Substantiation requested.

or

Advertiser asked to change or discontinue message.

NAD dismisses. Advertising substantiated. ← or

Substantiation not acceptable

Advertiser asked to change or discontinue message.

or

Advertiser agrees. Panel dismisses.

Advertiser agrees. NAD dismisses. ← or

Advertiser disagrees. Matter appealed to NARB by NAD or by advertiser.

Advertiser refuses. Matter referred to government for further action.

*Note:* If the original complaint originated outside the system, the outside complainant at this point can appeal to the Chairman of NARB for a panel adjudication. Granting of such appeal is at the Chairman's discretion.
*Source: A Review and Perspective on Advertising Industry Self-Regulation* (New York: National Advertising Review Board, 1978), p. 12.

# SOME FURTHER SOCIAL CONCERNS

We have been considering promotion's potential for producing undesirable social consequences mainly in terms of deceptive claims or illegal attempts to restrain trade. By no means do the charges leveled by critics end there. A variety of other questions continue to be raised concerning the responsibilities of business in relation to social needs.[33]

*Some Further Social Concerns*

Some critics charge that many business firms emphasize explicit promotion to the detriment of product quality and use tools such as advertising and publicity to force inferior merchandise on the public. Others see it as degrading the taste and social standards of the public by concentrating on unworthy lifestyle goals and glorifying senseless materialism. It has been accused of being too shrill, blatant, and annoying. Some argue that promotion raises prices because it allows a few large firms to dominate the market in many product categories through the power of their extremely large promotional budgets, which in a sense creates a form of promotionally based oligopoly. To acquire an appreciation for the tone of these accusations, we will consider some of the words with which they have been expressed.

With respect to the socially degrading effects of promotion, one critic has asked, "Have you ever taken a national magazine and computed the percentage of total pages of advertising that is devoted to liquor, nicotine, fast foods and all of the things that come under the category of indulgences? Americans are constantly exhorted to indulge and those who can't afford to do so then feel cheated and lash out against the rest of society."[34]

Another critic has argued that the work ethic is being undermined by promotion and has stated, "'If it feels good, do it!' 'Work is something to be endured until the *fun* part of the day arrives!' So goes the litany of the scripts and the lyrics and the advertisements. Let's register on that 'and the advertisements.' All those ads which urge the live-it-up lifestyle as opposed to the work ethic are in the long run self-defeating for the economic system."[35]

The results of oligopolistic market practices have been described in these terms, "The handful of companies that dominate a particular market face similar problems and tend to solve them by taking similar measures. Just as such companies tend to raise their prices at the same time, so too, they tend to lower quality at the same time."[36]

An internationally known author has observed, "After the suffering of decades of violence and oppression, the human soul longs for things higher, warmer and purer than those offered by today's mass living habits, introduced as by a calling card by the revolting invasion of commercial advertising, by TV stupor and by intolerable music."[37]

An academician has advanced the proposition that promotion helps destroy an emphasis on product quality. "Many corporations, when confronted with a product that isn't as good as it should be, rather than correct the product and improve it, simply double the advertising budget. 'Forcing a market' is the process by which a product not otherwise attractive to people can be sold in large quantity."[38]

Although there are many observers and theorists who find serious fault with promotion, there are also many who come to its defense. Most defenders are willing to admit there may be some abuses. However, they argue that promotion reflects social values rather than creating them. They further suggest, as we assumed in an earlier chapter of this book, that it is generally impossible to continue forcing the same poor product on consumers because product quality is so often a self-demonstrating factor which most buyers can judge reasonably well through actual experience. As for the matter of raising prices, advocates of promotion often counter that there is equally good evidence to suggest that advertising can intensify price competition and lead to lower prices. The following are some representative comments that view promotion from a more positive perspective.

An economic theorist, who expresses doubts that advertising can be successfully substituted for product quality, has said, "Advertising may influence tastes, it may reveal preferences and disclose to consumers the existence of goods and services that will satisfy wants, it may persuade consumers to experiment with the unknown or untested qualities of new goods and services, but it is not self-validating. . . . [C]onsumers do show loyalty to certain brands under certain conditions, but advertising seems not to be the principal agent in creating loyalty or prolonging it."[39]

Another economist has expounded the proposition that promotion has the overall effect of lowering prices rather than raising them. He holds that "because advertising provides information on many similar products, consumer demand will become more responsive to price for any given product rather than less responsive, as the critics of advertising believe. . . . [In his words], 'advertising increases information about substitutes, and this reduces monopoly power.'"[40]

A frequently expressed view is that those who attack advertising on the basis of its themes and mode of presenting them are expressing a personal point of view which contradicts that held by the majority of people in society. As one writer phrased this point, "Advertising of course is a handy instrument to blame for the ills (or perceived ills) of society, because advertising is pretty much a mirror of how we view ourselves. For the most part, I've observed [that] critics who attack advertising are really railing against our affluent way of life or a product or service they don't approve of."[41]

Another writer expressed much the same conclusion in somewhat different words when writing "I believe that one thing advertising is able to do is to widely disseminate news about the majority's value systems to a huge audience, some of whom perhaps, are not aware of them. In a sense then, advertising informs some parts of our culture what the predominant value system is, as reflected through advertising copy and layout. Whether this influences those who do not know about the masses' value, however, is indeterminate."[42]

**Establishing Your Own Point of View**

The debate between those who see promotion as producing many evils and those who see it as being primarily beneficial has raged on for many years and will almost certainly continue into the future. If either side could make a thoroughly conclusive and airtight case for its position, the debate would have ended long ago. Because it has not, it is impossible to set forth any absolutely unequivocal or unchallengeable conclusions regarding the overall effects of promotion on the welfare of society. Much depends upon one's point of view. As you might expect, anyone who writes a textbook on promotional strategy probably holds a mainly favorable view, and that is certainly true in my case. Nonetheless, even if a person tends to agree with the advocates of promotion, it can make good sense to remain alert to what the critics are saying and to refrain from dismissing their charges without giving them some careful thought.

As was noted at the very beginning of the first chapter, this book is written for promotional strategists and those planning to become promotional strategists. When you play that role, you are essentially a communicator seeking to persuade an audience to a certain point of view. In this connection, one writer has observed, "No one expects a good lawyer to present an unbiased resumé of his client's position, nor a politician to outline dispassionately the advantages and disadvantages of the course he urges, nor a clergyman to explain the possibility that some other faith may have more to commend it than the one he advocates. But a good many people seem to feel that special pleading and enthusiastic selling in advertising are somehow immoral or antisocial."[43]

The analogy is a good one. Like any other professional whose work calls for espousing a particular point of view, a promotional strategist has no reason to be ashamed of the fact that she or he urges the merits of only one particular brand. However, the analogy can also be carried somewhat further. To say that a lawyer or politician or clergyman has the right to express his or her position from its most positive standpoint is not to say that he or she can ignore ethics and good taste in order to ensure success. The same applies to a promotional strategist. In handling your professional activities, then, it is advisable that you continually and conscientiously evaluate the criticisms leveled at promotion to equip yourself to improve decisions concerning your own proper and ethical course of action.

Here's wishing you good luck as you make those decisions—and all others.

## SUMMARY

Because of abuses that have occurred in the business system, a variety of laws have been passed at the state level as well as at the federal level to curb undesirable practices. To illustrate the general nature of such legislation, this chapter concentrated on federal laws, principally those dealing with deceptive promotional practices and tactics considered to be detrimental to competition. It is important to recognize that most of the regulations that affect the conduct of promotional programs were enacted to protect business as well as to protect consumers.

The three federal agencies used to illustrate the nature of regulatory mechanisms were the Food and Drug Administration, the Federal Communications Commission, and the Federal Trade Commission. All three can play significant roles in their effects on the American marketing system. The most wide-ranging role is played by the Federal Trade Commission, which is responsible for enforcing a series of laws passed by Congress over the last seventy years.

When it was originally organized in 1914, the FTC was concerned mainly with protecting businesses from the predatory practices of rival firms. The passage of the Wheeler-Lea Act in 1938 expanded the agency into a consumer protection unit as well as a guardian of the competitive system. Since that time, its power to act against deceptive promotional practices has been strengthened by additional legislation. A major problem for the FTC, and a sometimes controversial matter, involves the question of the exact point at which an advertising claim or presentation oversteps the bounds of acceptable "puffery" and has the effect of deceiving or misleading some reasonably large portion of the audience. Especially during the 1970s the agency became more vigorous in carrying out its mandate. Among the new enforcement techniques introduced at that time were corrective advertising and an advertising substantiation program.

At the beginning of the 1980s, there appeared to be a degree of relaxation in the stringency of FTC policies. The view taken by this text is that promotional strategists would be well advised to respond to any relaxation of regulation by the FTC in a positive manner. Essentially, this implies the need for more self-restraint and self-regulation on the part of business. Beyond representing an ethical approach, self-restraint and self-regulation are in the best long-range interests of the business community itself, as well as the consumers it serves. One of the most promising moves toward industry-wide self-regulation is the NAD/NARB advertising review program.

Aside from the question of merely obeying the law or avoiding confrontation with formal self-regulatory groups such as NAD/NARB or the Better Business Bureaus, business people in general and promotional strategists in particular face a variety of ethical challenges. These involve not only matters of outright deception but also matters of good taste and consideration for the welfare of the economy and society at large. There are those who voice strong criticisms of common promotional practices and those who respond to the critics with strong counterarguments. Although this book tends to align itself with the defenders and proponents of promotion more than with its critics, it also takes the view that criticism should not be casually brushed aside. Rather, promotional strategists should attempt to pursue a course of ethical behavior that is at least equal to that expected from other professionals. To follow such a course, it makes good sense to remain alert to the criticisms launched against promotion and to evaluate them with an open mind. Even though you may not always agree with them, by giving the criticisms your careful consideration you should be able to improve your own personal and professional ethical standards.

## DISCUSSION QUESTIONS

1. Describe the historical pattern through which the present Federal Trade Commission has evolved.

2. Considering its past history, what do you see as potential future routes of development for the FTC?

3. To what extent do you think corrective advertising might prove effective in achieving its in-

tended goal? (You may wish to use the general communication model presented in Chapter 9 to help you answer this question.)

4. Choose three current advertisements that use "puffery" and discuss them in terms of the degree to which they might deceive or mislead certain groups of people.

5. If laws against deceptive promotional techniques are actually in the best interest of business as well as consumers, why do you suppose that some business people seem to oppose such regulation?

6. Discuss the effectiveness of the *Printers' Ink* model statute. How could it be made more effective?

7. If you were asked to offer recommendations for improving the NAD/NARB program, what would you suggest?

8. Do you believe the FTC's advertising substantiation program was a good or a bad idea? Explain your reasoning.

9. "If it can afford to spend enough money on promotion, a company can force consumers to accept a mediocre or even an inferior product." Comment.

10. You have read several quotes from commentaries charging that advertising debased or offended proper social values. How would you respond to them?

## REFERENCES

1. For a good discussion of the background to the rise of laws regulating these aspects of business see Fred Luthans, Richard M. Hodgetts, and Kenneth R. Thompson, *Social Issues in Business* (New York: Macmillan Publishing Co., Inc., 1980), Chapters 1 and 2.

2. Marshall C. Howard, *Legal Aspects of Marketing* (New York: McGraw-Hill Book Company, 1964), pp. 2–3.

3. H. Keith Hunt, "Government Regulation and the Marketing Manager: Developing a Perspective," in Steuart Henderson Britt and Norman F. Guess, *Marketing Manager's Handbook,* 2nd ed. (Chicago: Dartnell Press, 1983), p. 608.

4. For much more complete coverage of laws affecting marketing see Luthans, Hodgetts, and Thompson, *Social Issues in Business,* and Joe L. Welch, *Marketing Law* (Tulsa, OK: The Petroleum Publishing Company, 1980).

5. Luthans, Hodgetts, and Thompson, *Social Issues in Business,* p. 388.

6. Robert N. Corley, Robert L. Black, and O. Lee Reed, *The Legal Environment of Business* (New York: McGraw-Hill Book Company, 1977), p. 182.

7. James F. Engel, Martin R. Warshaw, and Thomas C. Kinnear, *Promotional Strategy,* 5th ed. (Homewood, IL: Richard D. Irwin, Inc., 1983), p. 149.

8. Luthans, Hodgetts, and Thompson, *Social Issues in Business,* p. 384.

9. Corley, Black, and Reed, *The Legal Environment of Business,* p. 155.

10. For a more complete discussion of these laws see Welch, *Marketing Law.*

11. *Ibid.,* p. 7.

12. Corley, Black, and Reed, *The Legal Environment of Business,* p. 288.

13. Welch, *Marketing Law,* pp. 7–8.

14. For a more detailed description of FTC procedures see: Corley, Black, and Reed, *The Legal Environment of Business,* pp. 156–158.

15. "Charles of the Ritz Distribution Corporation, v. FTC," in David Aaker and George S. Day, *Consumerism: Search for the Consumer Interest,* 2nd ed. (New York: The Free Press, 1974), p. 140.

16. "FTC Calls Campbell, Lever Ads Misleading," *Advertising Age,* 31 March 1969, p. 1.

17. For an excellent discussion of corrective advertising see John A. Miller, "Are Mandated Disclosures Deceptive Advertising? *Journal of Advertising,* Winter 1977, pp. 4–9.

18. "Legal Developments in Marketing," *Journal of Marketing,* October 1972, p. 68.

19. Dorothy Cohen, "The FTC's Advertising Substantiation Program," *Journal of Marketing,* Winter 1980, pp. 26–35.

20. *Ibid.,* p. 27.

21. *Ibid.*

22. Stanley Cohen, "Advertising Regulation: Changing, Growing Area," *Advertising Age,* 30 April 1980, p. 216.

23. "Despite antiregulatory sentiment, advertisers still must battle Washington 'policy shapers'," *Marketing News,* 30 April 1982, p. 1.

24. "Deregulation becoming two-edged sword for

business: Wallace," *Marketing News,* 9 July 1982, p. 3.

25. *Ibid.*

26. Richard E. Stanley, *Promotion: Advertising, Publicity, Personal Selling, Sales Promotion,* 2nd ed. (Englewood Cliffs, NJ: Prentice-Hall, Inc., 1982), p. 84.

27. Norman Kangun, Keith K. Cox, James Higginbotham, and John Burton, "Consumerism and Marketing Management," *Journal of Marketing,* April 1975, p. 8.

28. Gregory M. Gazda and David R. Gourley, "Attitudes of Businessmen, Consumers, and Consumerists toward Consumerism," *The Journal of Consumer Affairs,* Winter 1975, p. 185.

29. Paul N. Bloom and Mark J. Silver, "Consumer Education: Marketers Take Heed," *Harvard Business Review,* January/February 1976, pp. 33, 40.

30. For a more detailed description of this program see Cohen, "Advertising Regulation: Changing, Growing Area," pp. 217–218.

31. Richard Gordon, "AAF may revive local ad review boards," *Advertising Age,* 18 June 1979, p. 109.

32. Stanley Cohen, "What's Fair for Fairness?," *Advertising Age,* 7 April 1980, p. 22.

33. For a more extended exploration of such questions see George A. Steiner and John F. Steiner, *Business, Government and Society: A Managerial Perspective,* 3rd ed. (New York: Random House, Inc., 1981); Dalton E. McFarland, *Management and Society: An Institutional Framework* (Englewood Cliffs, NJ: Prentice-Hall, Inc., 1982); and Robert D. Hay and Edmund R. Gray, *Business and Society: Cases and Text* (Cincinnati, OH: Southwestern Publishing Co., 1981).

34. Gordon B. Carson, "Our Modern Devils," *Vital Speeches of the Day,* 1 May 1981, p. 446.

35. John A. Howard, "The Black Hole in the Businessman's Perception of His Problems," *Vital Speeches of the Day,* 1 June 1981, p. 503.

36. Marvin Harris, "Why It's Not the Same Old America," *Psychology Today,* August 1981, p. 29.

37. Alexander Solzhenitsyn, "A World Split Apart," *Vital Speeches of the Day,* 1 September 1978, p. 681.

38. Carson, "Our Modern Devils," p. 446.

39. James W. McKie, "Advertising and Social Responsibility," *Society,* March/April 1979, p. 40.

40. "A New View of Advertising's Economic Impact," *Business Week,* 22 December 1975, p. 54.

41. Rance Crain, "Advertising: The Brick and Mortar of Our Economy," *Advertising Age,* 30 April 1980, p. 1.

42. Jack Z. Sissors, "Another Look at the Question: Does Advertising Affect Values?" *Journal of Advertising,* Summer 1978, p. 30.

43. Crain, "Advertising: The Brick and Mortar of Our Economy," p. 34.

*Summary*

# SUBJECT INDEX

Id, 237–38, 239
Image transfer, 627, 628, 655
Implicit promotion, 5–7
Impulse purchases, 105–6
Incidental physical characteristics, 42–44
  use in promotional mix of, 44
Income ranges, diversity within age categories of, 224
Industrial buyers, 91, 92
Industrial publications, 502
Industrial sales representatives, 310
Information releases, 609–11
Informational dimension, 46–51
Inherent rewards, 273
In-house agency, 428
Input goals, 385
Intended promotional message, 263
Intensity, 269
Intensive distribution policy, 630
Intentional learning, 287
Interpretation, 264, 265
Interviews, focus group, 439
Intrapsychic approaches, 237–38

Jewish subculture, 188, 191–92

Lead element approach, 68–71, 84
Learning models of communications, 287–97
Legal and social issues, 12, 715–33
  background of laws affecting promotion, 716–17
  federal regulations affecting promotion, 717–25
    current regulatory climate, 724–25
    Federal Communications Commission, 718–19
    Federal Trade Commission, 719–25, 726
    Food and Drug Administration, 717–18
  movements toward self regulation, 725–27
  social concerns, 725–28
Legal constraints, 12
Lexicographic composition rule, 161–63
Lifestyle enhancement, 453
Lifestyle goals, 98–100
Lifestyle segmentation, 112
Linear-compensatory composition rule, 158–61
Local advertising, 403
Low involvement, 288–89

Manufacturers' agents, 632
Manufacturers' representatives, 629, 632–33, 655
Marginal analysis, 661–67
  obstacles to implementation of, 666–67
  optimum budget determination using, 665–66
Marginal selling efforts, marginal sales and, 662–65
Market feedback, 696–99
Market segmentation, 110–11
Market shares, 116–20
Market tests, 699–706
Marketing intermediaries, 630
Marketing mix strategy, corporate strategy and, 10
Markup, 652–53
Mass audiences, analyzing, 438
Mass media vehicles, 92
Media, 425
Media appraisal, 482–515
  business publications, 502–4
  consumer magazines, 498–502
  direct mail, 510–11
  farm publications, 498–502
  newspapers, 504–7
  outdoor advertising, 507–10
  radio, 495–98
  television, 484–95
Media category, 415, 416, 483
Media strategy, 415–17
Media strategy development, 516–53
  categories to be used, 516–19
  individual insertion size, 519–20
  insertion timing, 520–22
  in noncomplex advertising programs, 537–39
  number of insertions needed, 536–37
  reach, frequency, and gross rating point goals, 522–36
  specific vehicles to be used, 536–37
  use of computers, 540–48
Media vehicles, 415, 416, 483
MEDIAC (simulation program), 546
Merchant wholesalers, 633–35, 655
Message presenter, 266
Message sponsor, 266
Middle-aged married, 223–24
Middle-aged without children, 223–24
Middlemen, 630
Minnesota Multiphasic Personality Inventory, 243

Modular agencies, 429
Money-refund offers, 579–81
Motion, 270–71
Motivation, 381
Motivation research, 241
Multistage budgeting procedure, 683–84
Multistage interactive communications flow model, 283–87

NAD/NARB advertising review program, 726
National advertising, 403
News "happenings," 613–14
Newspapers, 504–7
Newsworthy company projects, 612–13
Noncommercial information sources, 92
Noncomplex advertising programs, determining vehicles and insertion quantity in, 537–40
Novelty, 269
Novelty drive, 295–97
Nuclear family, 222

Objective-task budget approach, 668, 676–83
Occasion segmentation, 112–13
Older married, 224
Older unmarried, 224
One-step communications flow model, 283–84
Opinion leaders, 93, 285, 286–87
Optimization programs, 540–45
Order size, 653
Organizational objectives, 8–12
Outdoor advertising, 507–10
Output goals, 385
Overall brand quality, 446–48
Over-budgeting, under-budgeting versus, 685–87

Package design, 40–42
Participations, 614–15
Partnership, 635
Perceived promotional message, 263
Perceptual mapping of market segments, 153–55
Performance allowances, 581, 582, 599–600
Personal interviews, 370–71
Personality, 233–37
  trait approaches to, 242–43
Personality-related research approaches, 245–46

# NAME INDEX